Policies for a Carbon-Neutral Industry in the Netherlands

OECD
BETTER POLICIES FOR BETTER LIVES

The publication *Policy for a Carbon-Neutral Industry in the Netherlands* was co-funded by the European Union via the Structural Reform Support Programme (REFORM/IM2020/004). This publication was produced with the financial assistance of the European Union. The views expressed herein can in no way be taken to reflect the official opinion of the European Union.

Please cite this publication as:
OECD (2021), *Policies for a Carbon-Neutral Industry in the Netherlands*, OECD Publishing, Paris, *https://doi.org/10.1787/6813bf38-en*.

ISBN 978-92-64-60836-8 (print)
ISBN 978-92-64-72238-5 (pdf)

Photo credits: Cover © iStockphoto.com/kaisorn; cover illustration: Christophe Brilhault.

Corrigenda to publications may be found on line at: *www.oecd.org/about/publishing/corrigenda.htm*.

Foreword

The report *Policies for a Carbon-Neutral Industry in the Netherlands* evaluates the consistency and cost-effectiveness of the set of policy instruments in place in the Netherlands to reach its 2050 decarbonisation objectives in the manufacturing sector and offers recommendations on adjustments of existing policy instruments and further measures. The analysis of the Dutch climate policy package illustrates the strength of combining clear commitment to raising carbon prices with ambitious technology support, uncovers the pervasiveness of provisions aimed at supporting the competitiveness of the industry, and highlights the trade-off between short-term emission cuts and longer-term technology shifts. While the Netherlands does not start from a blank page and can leverage a long experience in carbon pricing and technology support, the challenge ahead is to retrofit this extensive policy package to effectively put industry on the path to carbon neutrality. Importantly, the report offers general lessons for the low-carbon transition beyond the Netherlands, in particular European countries, which feature the same characteristics as Dutch industry.

The OECD Secretariat prepared the report for the Dutch Ministry of Economic Affairs and Climate Policy (EZK) with support from Marten Hamelink and Sander Kes. The report was funded by the Structural Reform Support Programme of the European Commission (DG REFORM) with support from Gaetano Civello. The Scientific Committee of the project comprised Herman Vollebergh, Heleen de Coninck, Ton van Dril, Carolyn Fischer, Andreas Löschel and Joëlle Noailly. Timme Lucassen and Bart Manders from the Netherlands Enterprise Agency (RVO) also provided support throughout the project.

The report was prepared by the Division on Productivity, Innovation and Entrepreneurship in the OECD Directorate for Science, Technology and Innovation, jointly with the Division on Tax Policy and Statistics in the OECD Centre for Tax Policy and Administration and the Division on Climate, Biodiversity and Water in the OECD Environment Directorate. The publication was co-ordinated by Antoine Dechezleprêtre and Guy Lalanne, under the supervision of Dirk Pilat, Deputy Director, and Chiara Criscuolo, Head of Division. Authors comprise, in alphabetical order, Brilé Anderson, Emile Cammeraat, Luisa Dressler, Nicolas Gonne, Joaquim Martins Guilhoto and Konstantinos Theodoropoulos.

Further inputs were provided by Peter Borkey and James Philp on emerging technologies; Hélène Dernis and Laurent Moussiegt on patent data; Milenko Fadic on venture capital data; and Clara Kogels on business dynamism data. Sarah Box, Florens Flues, Martijn Haring, Jasper Keuning, Natalya Rijk, Jonas Teusch, Kurt Van Dender, Rosa van der Linden and Henry van der Wiel provided valuable comments on earlier versions of the manuscript. Isabelle Desnoyer-James provided statistical support; Márcio Carvalho and Angela Gosmann provided editorial and formatting support.

External consultants also contributed to this report: Sander de Bruyn and Robert Vergeer (CE Delft); Rutger Bianchi, Max Coenen, Bert den Ouden, Joachim Schellekens, Thijs Verboon and Jan Warnaars (Berenschot); Leonidas Paroussos (E3M Modelling); Marlene Arens, Tobias Fleiter and Meta Thurid Lotz (ISI Fraunhofer); and Cornelis Zandt (Radboud University).

The OECD Committee on Industry, Innovation and Entrepreneurship declassified the report on 2 April 2021 by written procedure. The OECD Secretariat prepared it for publication.

Table of contents

Tables

Figures

Boxes

Executive summary

Countries representing more than 80% of the world economy have announced targets of carbon neutrality by mid-century. Reaching this objective requires a comprehensive set of policy instruments – a "green industrial strategy" – to trigger the necessary investments in zero-carbon energy sources and production processes across all economic sectors. As countries embark on this journey, they can benefit from learning from each other, exchanging knowledge and experience on their different roads towards carbon neutrality.

This document presents the main findings of the project "Sustainable transition of the Dutch industry", whose objective was to evaluate the consistency and cost-effectiveness of the set of policy instruments in place in the Netherlands to reach its 2050 decarbonisation objectives in the manufacturing sector, and to offer recommendations on adjustments of existing policy instruments and further measures.

The analysis of the Dutch climate policy package offers a number of lessons for countries seeking carbon neutrality. The Netherlands illustrates the strength of an approach that combines a strong commitment to raising carbon prices with ambitious technology support. These two pillars can be mutually reinforcing, as a clear trajectory of increasing carbon prices helps make the business case for investment in low-carbon technologies. At the same time, the Dutch case demonstrates the pervasiveness of provisions aimed at supporting the competitiveness of the industry and the trade-off between short-term emission cuts and longer-term technology shifts.

The first pillar of the Netherlands' approach, the carbon pricing signal, includes a carbon levy on industrial emissions that sets an ambitious price trajectory to 2030. This levy provides a strong incentive to encourage low-carbon investment in industry. It is designed so that the additional carbon price kicks in gradually, thus avoiding immediately burdening businesses with new taxes. However, the overall carbon price signal is tempered by provisions that grant extensive preferential treatment to energy-intensive users, including in the form of energy tax exemptions, lower tax rates for large energy consumers, and freely allocated carbon emission allowances. This yields a highly heterogeneous effective carbon price across sectors (e.g. on average EUR 3 per tonne in basic metals and EUR 76 per tonne for the food processing sector in 2021) and across firms, with small firms typically facing much higher energy and carbon prices than large incumbents. The economic inefficiency and horizontal equity concerns arising from this uneven price signal call for broadening tax bases and gradually removing exemptions and preferential rates.

The second pillar of the Netherlands' decarbonisation strategy aims at supporting the uptake of low carbon technologies, focusing on the cost-effective deployment of both mature (e.g. renewable electricity) and radically new technologies (e.g. hydrogen) through subsidy programmes and corporate tax incentives. The main instrument is the Sustainable Energy Transition Incentive Scheme (SDE++), which subsidises the additional costs associated with adopting a low-carbon technology. The instrument is allocated to applicants in increasing order of subsidy requirement per tonne of CO_2 reduction in a tender open to an extensive list of technologies, and is funded through a surcharge on electricity and gas use. However, the surcharge provides generous exemptions for key sectors and lower rates for energy-intensive users. These features imply that small firms may disproportionately contribute to funding the SDE++ scheme. Yet, these firms conversely have potentially little opportunity for claiming subsidies. Moreover, while the allocation design is economically efficient and ensures least-cost decarbonisation in the short run, it favours technologies that are close to the market at the expense of more radical alternatives that are still at an earlier stage of development (such as green hydrogen). Similarly, the Netherlands supports R&D mostly through broad tax credits and the Innovation Box, which are technology neutral but, by construction, benefit mostly technologies that are closest to the market.

Therefore, the analysis of the Dutch technology support policy package calls for a balanced approach that supports both emerging and mature technologies. Options include holding separate tenders across technology readiness level for deployment instruments, and combining horizontal R&D support with targeted support for emerging technologies.

Beyond the core set of climate policy instruments, regulatory instruments can play an important role to support the diffusion of particular technologies. For example, clearly defining liabilities for carbon leaks outside of storage facilities would allow investors in carbon capture and storage (CCS) to more accurately price and potentially insure this risk. Minimum content requirements and public procurement can help create markets for recycled and bio-based products to bring about a more circular and bioeconomy.

Visibility over future infrastructure plans appears key for industrial firms to undertake low-carbon investments, as many technologies rely on shared infrastructure (notably hydrogen, CCS and renewable electricity). The global nature of climate change, the significant investments that it requires and the size of typical retrofitting and demonstration projects in industry also imply that the low-carbon transition can best be tackled at the supra-national level.

Finally, the low-carbon transition requires the alignment of policy frameworks well beyond the core climate policy toolbox. This includes a fit-for-purpose proactive and responsive regulatory framework, competition and entrepreneurship policies that encourage business dynamism and the reallocation of resources toward the most energy-efficient firms, skills and science policies that ensure industry can access the right human capital and that new research into low-carbon technologies is accompanied by development of other productivity-enhancing innovations, and investment and financial policies that enable start-up businesses offering decarbonisation solutions to grow. An effective and cost-efficient shift to a low-carbon economy requires a whole-of-government approach beyond ministries and other agencies traditionally mobilised in the development of climate change policies.

The recovery from the COVID-19 pandemic and the roll-out of sizeable stimulus packages provides a unique opportunity for governments to "build back better" and to steer the economy onto a green growth trajectory. Some countries such as the Netherlands are already taking the lead, but more ambitious measures are necessary across all countries to reduce net greenhouse gas emissions to zero before mid-century. With all eyes now on COP 26 in Glasgow this year, this report provides direction and support for countries to confidently reinforce their commitments and climate policy action.

1. Main findings and policy recommendations

This chapter presents the report's main findings based on the substantive analysis in Chapters 2 to 10 and offers concrete policy recommendations in three action areas: carbon pricing, technology support, and complementary policies and framework conditions.

Note: a self-standing version of this chapter was published in the *OECD Science, Technology and Industry Policy Paper* series (Anderson et al., 2021[1]).

1.1. The global journey to carbon neutrality

1.1.1. Ambitious climate agendas in the Netherlands and beyond

The Dutch Parliament passed a new Climate Act in May 2019, which mandates the Netherlands to reduce domestic greenhouse gas emissions by 49% by 2030 compared to 1990 levels, and by 95% by 2050. **The National Climate Agreement, adopted in June 2019**, translates the national 2030 target into sectoral objectives. In particular, the Dutch industrial sector has to reduce its emissions by 14.3 Mt of CO_2 equivalent (Mt CO_2-eq) by 2030 compared to a baseline scenario, a reduction of about 59% compared to 1990.

In addition, the Netherlands has been pushing for the European Union (EU) to raise its 2030 emission reduction target from 40% to 55%. As the EU collectively adopted this more ambitious target in December 2020, the Netherlands is considering how best to adapt its reduction goal accordingly.

At the 2050 horizon, the Climate Agreement calls for a carbon-neutral industry: "By 2050, we envisage the Netherlands to be a country with a thriving, circular and globally leading manufacturing industry, where greenhouse gas emissions are almost zero."

Following the Climate Agreement, and in order to accelerate and support the decarbonisation of industry, **the Dutch government is introducing new policy instruments in 2020 and 2021**, including a carbon levy and enhanced subsidy programmes such as the Sustainable Energy Transition Incentive Scheme (SDE++) in addition to a number of existing policy instruments.

Although a frontrunner, the Netherlands is not alone in this journey to carbon neutrality. An increasing number of countries have announced, or are currently in the process of adopting or discussing climate neutrality targets, and almost all are aiming at the 2050 horizon (Figure 1.1.). The European Parliament is notably examining a European Climate Law that would enact a legally binding target of carbon-neutrality in 2050 in the context of the European Green Deal.

In this context, the objective of the project on "Sustainable transition of the Dutch industry" was to evaluate the consistency, cost-efficiency and comprehensiveness of the toolbox of instruments in place in the Netherlands to reach its long-term decarbonisation objectives *in the manufacturing sector*. The project was carried out by the OECD for the Dutch Ministry of Economic Affairs and Climate Policy and was financially supported by the European Commission's Structural Reform Support Service (SRSS). The practical aims of that report were to: 1) analyse the energy, production and technological paths consistent with industry's carbon neutrality by 2050; 2) qualitatively assess the consistency of the existing and new set of policy instruments, including European schemes; and 3) evaluate the need to adjust existing policy instruments and for further measures, in particular innovation incentives focused on some emerging technologies (Box 1.1).

This report as well as the detailed analysis focus on the manufacturing sector. For this reason, some issues, despite being of primary importance for the decarbonisation of the industry, are out of the scope of the project. For instance, dealing with intermittency is critical to ensure a reliable green electricity supply to the industry, but this concerns the energy sector. The same holds to some extent for infrastructure programs and Scope 3 emissions of the manufacturing sector. These aspects are touched upon in this report but would require further consideration.

Figure 1.1. Share of global economy that announced net-zero CO_2 or greenhouse gas emissions by mid-century

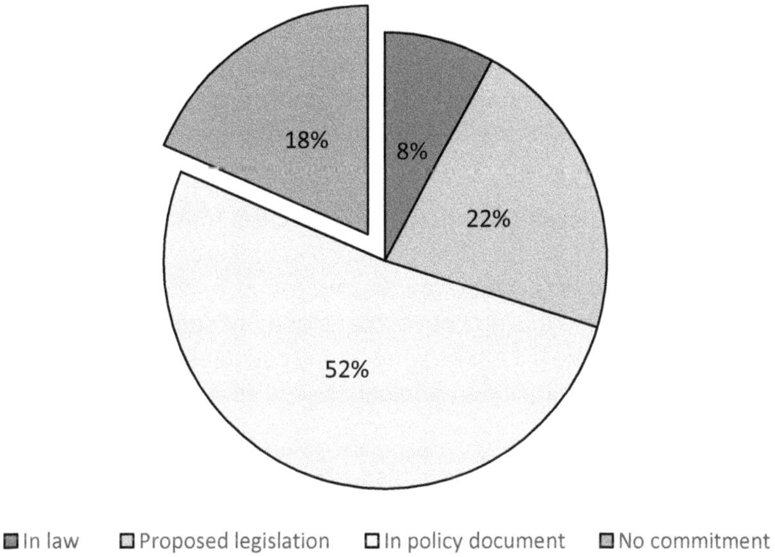

Note: In law: Sweden, United Kingdom, France, Denmark, New Zealand and Hungary. Proposed legislation: European Union (part of the EU that does not yet commit to net zero in law, including the Netherlands), Canada, South Korea, Chile and Fiji. In policy document: United States, People's Republic of China (by 2060). South Africa, Japan, Germany, Switzerland, Norway, Costa Rica, Iceland and Marshall Islands. Calculations based on the share of global gross domestic product (GDP) represented by the countries that commit according to the Net Zero Tracker (https://eciu.net/netzerotracker). Share of global GDP calculated based on GDP in 2017 taken from World Bank national accounts data and OECD National Accounts data (2021).
Source: Calculations based on Net Zero Tracker data (https://eciu.net/netzerotracker), World Bank national accounts data and OECD National Accounts data (2021).

1.1.2. General considerations about carbon neutrality policies

Reaching carbon neutrality in 2050 will require a major structural transformation towards the use of green emerging technologies, in the Netherlands as in other countries. In particular, carbon neutrality in industry entails a complete change towards zero-carbon energy sources, and more generally a shift away from fossil feedstock. Not only are large investments needed to adopt existing or close-to-the-market low carbon technologies, but emerging technologies, such as CCS, electrification, green hydrogen and bio-based materials, have to be developed and demonstrated. This requires bringing down the costs and improving the productivity of existing clean technologies, and developing new breakthrough technologies.

Public policies are needed to help trigger these investments, and are justified on the grounds of at least two well-known market failures that hinder decarbonisation. First, carbon emissions constitute an environmental externality, as the costs of the environmental damage from carbon-based production processes are borne by society as a whole rather than internalised by emitting firms. Not internalising the full cost that emissions entail for society leads business to under-invest in low-carbon products, assets and production processes. Second, technological change, which allows reducing the cost of emission abatement over time, is subject to knowledge spillovers at both local and global levels, as firms investing in or implementing a new technology create benefits for others while incurring all costs. These market failures imply that the market produces too many emissions and too little technology innovation related to decarbonisation.

Beyond these two standard externalities, other rationales can justify public action. Learning-by-doing (whereby early producers generate knowledge through the production process) can justify additional demand-pull policies. Well-known imperfections in capital markets make the financing of research and development difficult, particularly for radical or disruptive innovation, which may require public financing, for instance through direct or indirect government-sponsored venture capital. Large investments to decarbonise the industry sometimes also require co-ordination between private stakeholders, and with public stakeholders, because of the existence of network effects. For instance, some carbon-free sources of energy require large infrastructure to be deployed at scale, like hydrogen. Lock-in and path dependence, long lived capital, high upfront costs, imperfect competition in energy markets, behavioural gaps, and regulatory barriers to adoption, are all further examples of additional market failures potentially justifying public intervention.

These policies are all the more necessary as the COVID-19 crisis may jeopardise crucial investments to reduce emissions in the medium to long run. The reduction in emissions due to lockdown measures, and the economic crisis, is likely to be only temporary and will be inconsequential in slowing down climate change, while liquidity challenges, increasing debt burdens and uncertain prospects are likely to weigh on firm investments for the years to come. At a time when many countries are starting to implement recovery packages, the transition to carbon neutrality is often considered as an important dimension of these plans and an opportunity to "build back better".

Policies for the low-carbon transition in the Netherlands, and other economies, should not only focus on reducing emissions towards net-zero but also aim to achieve the transition at the least cost for society. This means reducing emissions where they are cheapest, including considering impacts on productivity, competitiveness and social outcomes. Incorporating these concerns in transition policies and communicating them well can contribute to building broad public support and make the transition politically viable.

Policies should encourage **a cost-effective transition** to carbon-neutral technologies, to preserve productivity as much as possible. Efficient policies will limit the number of losers and make the transition more acceptable.

Policies should limit the impact of the transition on the short run competitiveness of domestic firms, while not compromising on providing an incentive for decarbonisation in the longer run. On the one hand, a loss of competitiveness in the short run could not only affect economic prospects, but also, absent mechanisms to penalise carbon-intensive imports, lessen the efficiency of the low-carbon transition by partly shifting emissions abroad, rather than reducing them (a phenomenon referred to as "carbon leakage"). On the other hand, shielding carbon-intensive production from decarbonisation incentives will harm the long-run competitiveness of the Dutch economy, by slowing down the carbon-neural transition of Dutch industry, thereby leading to stranded assets and jobs.

Policies should **take into account the human side of the transition**. The journey to carbon neutrality, as a sizeable structural change, is not only about greening the existing industry. Some carbon-intensive sectors will downsize, while carbon-free sectors will flourish. Even though the Dutch transition is planned to span 30 years, some workers will be displaced and the set of skills required to thrive in the labour market is likely to evolve. Policies for the green transition need to ensure that green-related skills are accessible in initial curricula and on-the-job training and that workers can smoothly transition to other sectors. Moreover, the provision of green skills will facilitate the deployment and development of green technologies and thereby increase the efficiency of support measures.

1.1.3. The need for a "green industrial policy"

This complex set of market failures and policy objectives calls for a carefully designed strategy relying on a consistent and articulated group of policy instruments, corresponding to the definition of mission-oriented strategies.[1] The objective is not only to foster the development of a decarbonised economy, but also to "re-direct" innovation and deployment from dirty to clean technologies. Such strategy is often referred to as a green industrial policy (Tagliapietra and Veugelers, 2020[2]; Altenburg and Rodrik, 2017[3]; Rodrik, 2014[4]). Green industrial policies typically consist of a three-pronged approach:

- Transforming industry, by supporting not only the deployment of new technologies and innovation, but also affecting the direction of innovation toward green technologies. For this purpose, deployment of carbon pricing and innovation policies are an important component of green industrial policies, in order to bring down the relative cost of green technologies.
- Transforming society, by also inducing changes in producers' and consumers' behaviour, changing skills in the workforce and more generally enabling structural change. For this purpose, strong carbon pricing signals are required to drive behavioural changes, including investment in low-carbon technologies, as well as high-quality framework conditions to allow for an efficient and smooth reallocation of workers and capital.
- Transforming the world by seeking co-ordination, at the European and international level. Co-ordination is a key ingredient of green industrial policies and is needed at the local, national and regional levels (or European level in the case of European countries) to develop the technologies, the infrastructure and standards needed for the transition. This co-ordination is more generally required at the international level as climate change is inherently a global challenge and breakthroughs can benefit the whole world. The existence of integrated markets and global value chains lead to high interconnection of national economies, and result in competitiveness concerns, which require co-ordination as well.

Innovation policy and technology-support combined with strong carbon pricing signals and behavioural changes are, thus, a central feature for a green industrial policy to be successful in the long-term. **Carbon pricing, innovation policy and technology support are not substitutes but instead can be mutually reinforcing**. Technology-specific support can build the case for stronger carbon pricing in the future, by lowering the cost of future green technologies, while strong future carbon prices ensure there will be a demand for new low-carbon technologies developed thanks to technology-specific support.

But as previous waves of industrial policies attest, green industrial policy also raises a number of questions and pitfalls that need to be closely scrutinised. In particular:

- Finding the right level of support can be challenging. As for any other industrial policy, critics have pointed to potential crowding out effects of public investment that might discourage rather than complement private investment. The risk of creating windfall profits to business for activities they would have undertaken anyway is real and needs to be carefully monitored and analysed. Rebound effects (whereby improvements in energy efficiency are compensated by increases in energy consumption) also have to be considered.
- Industrial policies should refrain as much as possible from making bets on specific technologies. Indeed, the techno-neutrality of mission-oriented strategies is one of their major appeals. They are 'problem-led' pathways, rather than 'solution-led'. In fact, nobody exactly knows the exact mix of technologies that will be required to reach carbon neutrality in 2050, even if informed guesses are possible, and desirable. Yet, remaining completely technology-neutral may prove difficult in practice, in particular for green industrial policies.

Selecting which technologies should benefit from government support requires gathering a vast amount of information on the expected returns, risks, spillovers and market failures for each option. Some argue that this information is not available (be it for the government or for any other actor), while others claim that it may be easier for businesses to access than for the government. Due to this potentially asymmetric information between public and private actors, there is a risk of capture and lobbying (Romer, 1993[5]). The ability of governments to stop supporting technologies that prove inadequate (Rodrik, 2008[6]) and the risk of lock-in, have also been questioned.

Box 1.1. Context and objectives of the report

The Dutch Parliament passed a new Climate Act in May 2019, which mandates the Netherlands to reduce domestic greenhouse gas emissions by 49% in 2030 compared to 1990 levels, and by 95% in 2050. By 2050, the electricity sector as well as the industry sector should be climate-neutral. The National Climate Agreement, adopted in June 2019, translates this national target into sectoral objectives. In particular, the Dutch industrial sector has to reduce its emissions by about 59% by 2030. In addition, the Netherlands has been pushing for the European Union to raise its 2030 target for emission reductions from 40% to 55%. As the EU has just collectively adopted this more ambitious target, the Netherlands might now adapt its reduction goal accordingly.

In order to accelerate and support the decarbonisation of industry, the Dutch government is planning to introduce new policy instruments by the end of 2020, including a carbon levy and enhanced subsidy programmes such as the SDE++. The latter was initially introduced to provide subsidies to renewable energy projects but will now be broadened to emission reduction projects in all sectors. These instruments will come in addition to numerous instruments already in place and geared towards industry's decarbonisation, including, for example, existing energy taxes and surcharges, the Energy Investment Allowance (a tax allowance for investments in energy saving assets) or the Long-Term Agreements on Energy Efficiency. They will furthermore interact with other innovation support policies not targeted specifically at low-carbon technologies, such as the R&D tax credit (WBSO) and European climate policies, such as the European Union emissions trading system (EU ETS) or the ETS Innovation Fund.

The targets set by the Dutch government are ambitious and their potential impact on employment and productivity have been vastly debated in the Netherlands. Yet, the Climate Agreement is widely supported, and was designed in collaboration with the relevant sectors, in particular with industry. It is also consistent with the new objectives set out in the EU Green Deal and the EU 2030 Climate Target Plan.

In this context, there is a pressing need to evaluate the consistency, cost-efficiency and comprehensiveness of the toolbox of instruments in place in the Netherlands to reach the long-term decarbonisation objectives. The aim of this project is to: 1) analyse the energy and production paths consistent with industry's carbon neutrality by 2050; 2) qualitatively assess the consistency of the existing and proposed set of instruments, including European schemes; and 3) evaluate the need to adjust existing instruments and for further measures, in particular, innovation incentives focused on some emerging technologies. The assessment of policies is based on their cost-effectiveness in reducing emissions, but it also takes into account their impact on the competitiveness of the Dutch industry and the developments of international markets for hydrogen, electricity and carbon. The project formulates policy recommendations based on these assessments.

The project was funded by the European Commission's SRSS (DG REFORM) with reference SRSS 20NL03 "Sustainable transition of the Dutch industry".

The industrial policy literature, however, points to solutions to overcome these pitfalls. To limit the risk of capture and attenuate information asymmetries, it is necessary to **put an emphasis on the governance of green industrial policies** (Paic and Viros, 2019[7]; Romer, 1993[5]; Warwick, 2013[8]). In particular, it is necessary to:

- Favour their inclusiveness, by ensuring that all the relevant firms, including young and small, are solicited to participate.
- Plan at inception scheduled assessments and evaluations.

- Allow for failure and plan a regular refit of policies. It is even more important when risks or 'wickedness' (i.e. complexity) are high (Cantner and Vannuccini, 2018[9]; Wanzenböck et al., 2019[10]), as is the case for reaching a carbon-neutral industry.

Moreover, to avoid crowding out private investment in productivity-enhancing technologies, green industrial policies need to include instruments to ensure that workers are equipped with the adequate green skills to allow for low-carbon technology deployment and scale-up.

For these reasons, the transition to a green economy requires a systemic approach to get all the relevant institutions in motion. Policy makers should simultaneously consider economic actors, institutions and market failures, working from a clear broadly supported mission target. A transition creates complex co-ordination problems and fundamental uncertainty holds back potential investors. This requires public co-ordination, co-investing and public-private risk sharing, as well as co-operation and co-ordination at the European level (Mazzucato, 2011[11]; Schipper-Tops et al., 2021[12]).

1.2. The Dutch case in practice

1.2.1. Dutch industry: clustered, open and European

The Dutch industry structure features three main characteristics: [2]

- **Four sectors account for 90% of industry's direct (Scope 1) greenhouse gas (GHG) emissions** in 2018: chemicals, refineries, metals (iron and steel, non-ferrous metals) and food processing (Figure 1.2). The heaviest emitter is the chemical sector (notably petrochemical products and nitrogen compounds), representing 44% of industrial emissions. These four sectors also account for a significant share of industry's Scope 2 emissions (i.e. indirect emissions from electricity purchased and used), as they represent 72% of the electricity use of the manufacturing sector.[3]

Figure 1.2. Direct GHG emissions of the industry by sub-sector, 2018

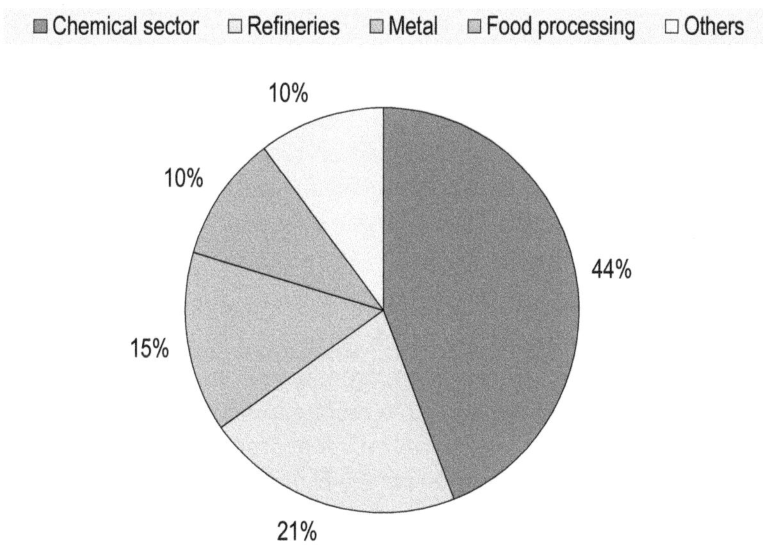

Note: This graph only includes direct emissions (Scope 1).
Source: Eurostat (Air emissions accounts by NACE Rev. 2 activity), OECD calculations.

- Dutch emission-intensive industry is very concentrated, with 12 firms accounting for more than 60% of the industrial emissions.[4]
- Five regional clusters include most of the heavy emitters (Figure 1.3): "Rotterdam-Moerdijk"; "Smart Delta Resources" (Zeeland); "Chemelot" (South-Limburg); "Noord Nederland" (Eemshaven, Delfzijl and Emmen) and "Noordzeekanaalgebied" (Amsterdam-IJmuiden).

Figure 1.3. Industry clusters in the Netherlands

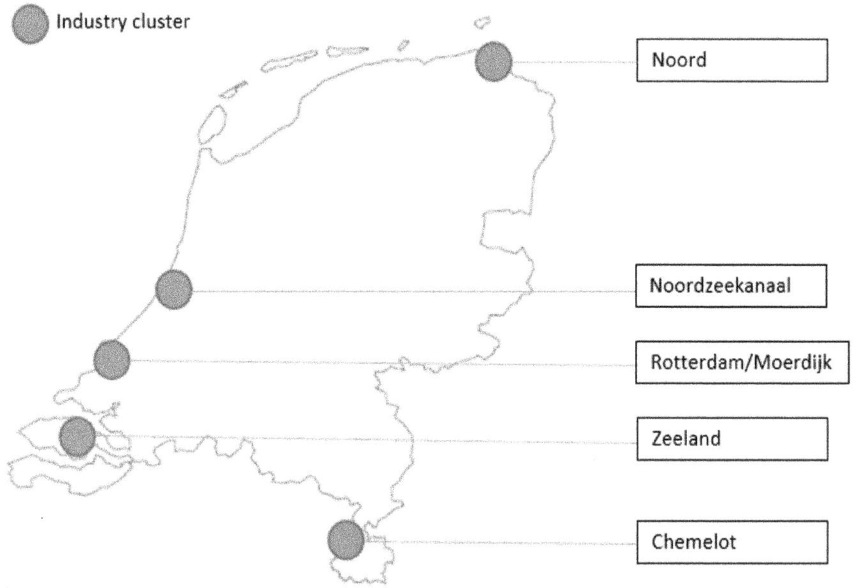

- Moreover, the Netherlands is specialised in products that are both highly traded and carbon-intensive (Figure 1.4). Together, the four main carbon-emitting sectors that this project focused on represent only 2.5% of total employment in the Dutch economy, but account for 10.9% of output and 22.9% of exports. This large export share reflects strong competitiveness in global markets: in comparison, the same four sectors represent 16.1% of exports in Germany and 14.8% in the EU-27 (respectively 8.5% and 9.1% of output).[5]

Given the export intensity of large industrial emitters, their ability to compete in international markets needs to be carefully taken into account. There are many ways to address competitiveness concerns – including subsidies to technology adoption, exemptions from carbon pricing, or adjustments at the border (OECD, 2020[13]) – but not all are compatible with decarbonisation incentives. Preference should be given to instruments that keep decarbonisation incentives in place; a qualification that exemptions from carbon pricing typically do not meet.

Finally, the Netherlands is a member state of the European Union and, as such, must articulate its national decarbonisation policy with European policies, such as EU ETS. The European policy landscape is evolving fast, with the European Green Deal being progressively unveiled. The ambition of the European Green Deal is to transform the European Union into a resource-efficient and competitive economy with no net GHG emissions by 2050. The Green Deal notably aims at proposing a revision of the EU's climate and energy legislation by June 2021, including revisions to the European Energy Tax Directive and the EU ETS Directive. In addition, several mechanisms for a potential carbon border adjustment mechanism are currently being discussed.

Figure 1.4. Carbon intensity and export intensity of manufacturing sectors in the Netherlands in 2015

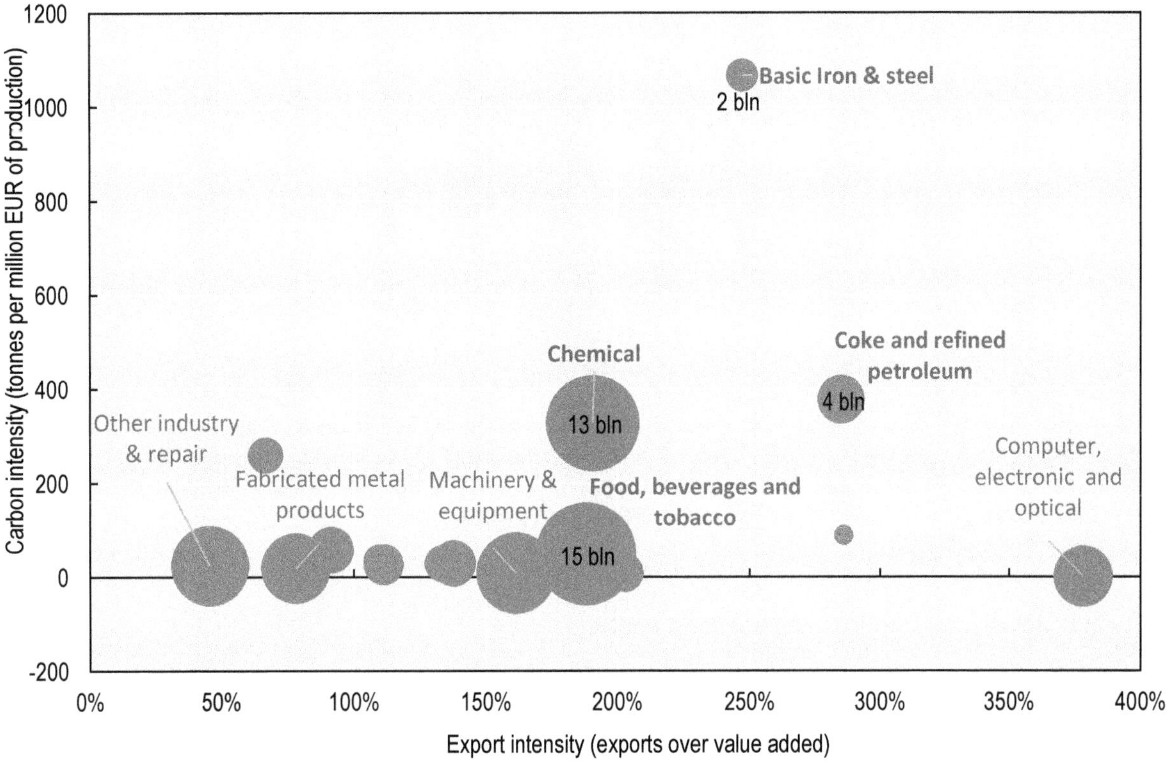

Note: The value added of the industry is presented by the size of the circles. The value added of the four main industries is as follows: 15 billion for the food industry, 13 billion for the chemical industry, 4 billion for the refineries industry and 2 billion for the basic iron and steel industry.
Source: Estimates for CO_2 emissions are based on the OECD Air Emission Accounts and the IEA CO_2 Emissions from Fuel Combustion. The estimates for value added and exports are based on the OECD's Inter-Country Input-Out (ICIO) Database (2018).

1.2.2. A diverse portfolio of low-carbon technologies

The decarbonisation of Dutch industry will rely on a diverse portfolio of technologies, as illustrated by the zero-emission 2050 scenario for the Dutch industry developed with Berenschot (Figure 1.5). At the 2050 horizon, the economic and technological uncertainty is such that this scenario can only be considered as plausible depending on certain assumptions and choices, regarding technologies, policies and the economic environment. Nevertheless, this decarbonisation scenario was designed by carefully taking into consideration the specificities of Dutch industry and its clusters, and was discussed with and validated by industry representatives and experts. Therefore, it can be considered as the most reasonable pathway given current knowledge. The scenario covers the decarbonisation of Scope 1 and 2 emissions, while Scope 3 emissions are not systematically included. Nonetheless, emissions linked to energy carriers that are used as a feedstock (e.g. crude oil in refineries, natural gas in ammonia production and coal in steel production) are considered.[6]

Figure 1.5. Contribution of different technologies in Scope 1 and 2 emission reduction, 2015-50

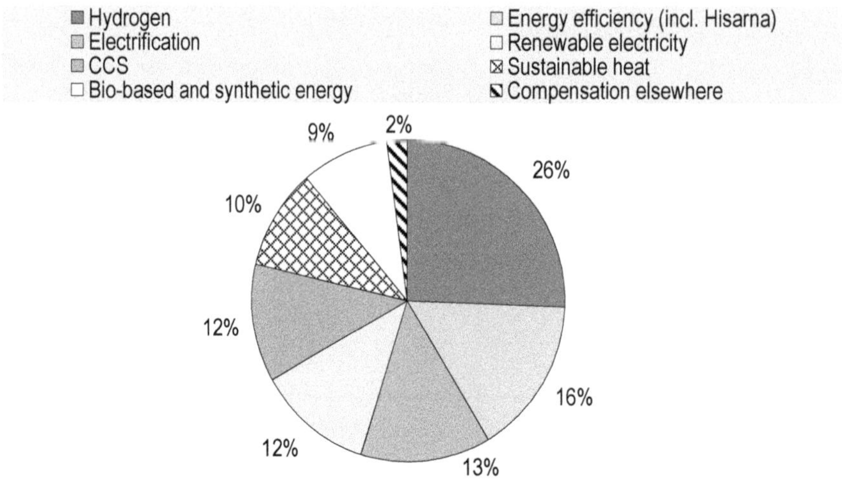

Note: The scenario covers four manufacturing sectors: chemical, metallurgy, refineries and food-processing. The contribution of "Renewable electricity" corresponds to the abatement of the 2015 Scope 2 emissions, which would be overturned by completely shifting to renewable electricity sources by 2050. The contribution of "Electrification" corresponds to additional electricity needed to reach the carbon neutrality objective in 2050, assuming that this additional electricity is also renewable and carbon-neutral.
Source: Based on Berenschot (2020[14]).

Four main conclusions come from the scenario analysis.

First, the decarbonisation of Dutch industry may significantly rely on technologies that are far from mature today, notably (green) hydrogen, which would replace natural gas in high-temperature processes.

Second, **a massive increase in renewable electricity generation is needed to support the decarbonisation of Dutch industry**. The scenario developed with Berenschot relies heavily on electricity consumption in industry, which doubles between 2015 and 2050, even without including the electricity needed to produce green hydrogen. Electricity is assumed to become fully carbon neutral in the meantime, thereby avoiding Scope 2 emissions.

Third, **CCS would still be needed in 2050**. Although this is nowadays one of the cheapest options to decarbonise industries producing flue gases with high concentration of CO_2 (such as ammonia, iron or hydrogen production from steam methane reforming), the use of CCS may slow down the development of renewable energy sources and maintain a reliance on fossil fuels. The Dutch Climate Agreement emphasises that "CCS should not impede the structural development of alternative climate-neutral technologies or activities for carbon emission reduction".

Finally, **more than half of the decarbonisation hinges on technologies that require the development or the upgrading of infrastructure**, notably to reliably provide (green) hydrogen and renewable electricity and to transport the captured CO_2 to storage locations.

1.2.3. A two-pillar strategy: carbon pricing and technology support

The Dutch government has recently introduced new policy instruments geared at achieving the targets of the Climate Agreement, most notably reducing industry emissions by 14.3 Mt CO_2-eq by 2030. These instruments come in addition to a set of existing tools at the national and European levels, resulting in a large number of instruments supporting the low-carbon transition. This set of instruments can be broken down into two main pillars.

The first pillar aims at delivering a clear carbon pricing signal over the medium term (to 2030) while cushioning the potential negative effects on competitiveness in the short to medium term. In 2021, the

Netherlands implemented a new carbon levy in industry that sets out an ambitious price trajectory until 2030, even if its survival depends on the outcome of the general elections in March 2021. The carbon levy comes on top of several other existing instruments that effectively put a price on Dutch carbon emissions: the EU ETS; energy tax on natural gas; and a sustainable energy surcharge (Opslag Duurzame Energie [ODE]) on natural gas.[7,8] Concerns over competition that domestic energy users may face from firms in countries with less ambitious carbon pricing policies have led the Dutch authorities to grant extensive preferential treatment to energy-intensive users, including generous tax exemptions, regressive energy tax and ODE rates, and freely allocated emission allowances. Providing preferential tax treatment to large energy users still constitutes widespread practice across EU countries. Importantly, beneficiaries in the Netherlands obtain tax relief on the sole criterion of energy use, with no differentiation based on the actual exposure of a sector to international competition. Moreover, proceeds from the ODE are used to finance the main subsidy scheme supporting the deployment of low-carbon technologies (SDE++), with a view to attenuating the potential costs to competitiveness.

The second pillar aims at supporting the uptake of low carbon technologies, focusing on the cost-efficient deployment of a number of emerging and radically new technologies (e.g. blue and green hydrogen, respectively, Box 1.2) through several subsidy programs and tax incentives, with the new SDE++ acting as a spearhead. At earlier stages of technology readiness (R&D and demonstration), the Netherlands mostly relies on horizontal support and EU funding.

To be successful, the two-pillar strategy requires a broader environment that is conducive to the low-carbon transition. This includes implementing complementary policies, including regulatory instruments such as standards, and rapidly deploying public infrastructure, which seems particularly pressing for Dutch industry. Framework conditions are also critical, particularly as regards innovation capabilities, training and firm dynamics. In this respect, firms in the Netherlands enjoy among the most accommodative conditions for doing business across OECD countries, which will likely facilitate the necessary reallocation of labour and capital resources.

Box 1.2. Ways of producing hydrogen: grey, blue, green

Grey hydrogen is produced via steam methane reforming or auto-thermal reforming using natural gas (or coal as in China). Grey hydrogen is the most widely used today, but its production leads to carbon emissions.

Blue hydrogen is the same process as above except the carbon emissions from burning natural gas are captured and stored, or reused. This production process drastically reduces carbon emissions compared to grey hydrogen. However, this process is not carbon neutral either, since the capture rate is usually lower than 100%.

Green hydrogen is produced from electrolysis using renewable energy. This process breaks water down into hydrogen and oxygen. Three main technologies exist today: alkaline electrolysis, proton exchange membrane (PEM), solid oxide electrolysis cells. This process is carbon-neutral.

1.2.4. A bottom-up approach: strengths and weaknesses

Policy design in the Netherlands rests on a bottom-up approach, based on detailed information provided by large firms, sectors and clusters on the availability and cost of selected decarbonisation technologies. The main support instruments, such as the abatement payment SDE++ and the corporate tax allowances, energy investment allowances (EIA) and MIA (*Milieu-InvesteringsAftrek* - environmental investment deduction), rely on lists of eligible technologies to benefit from support. These lists are regularly updated based on firms' suggestions. For SDE++, the Netherlands Environmental Assessment Agency (PBL,

Planbureau voor de Leefomgeving) provides a set of parameters for each technology (such as full-load hours, coefficient of performance, etc.), which are used to calculate the subsidy amount. The carbon levy trajectory is also based on a bottom-up approach: the 2030 carbon price was determined as the price needed to reach the 2030 emission reduction objective given an estimated abatement cost curve. This curve is regularly reassessed based on reviews of the engineering literature and on information contained in subsidy requests, in particular to the SDE++.

This strategy is very demanding in terms of information, but this information is easier to obtain than in other countries thanks to the concentrated and clustered structure of Dutch industry, which requires interacting with a smaller number of stakeholders. Clusters and their decarbonisation plans play an important role in informing national policies.

This unique bottom-up approach allows the government to fine-tune support at a granular level and ensure it corresponds to the needs of firms. However, this also makes the need for good governance more acute, and requires flexibility and reactiveness in policy-making. In particular, it is critical to try to ensure that smaller and younger firms, as well as firms outside the clusters, can also participate in the consultation processes. It is also important to maximise the "additionality" of public support, i.e. by avoiding targeting firms that would invest anyway and therefore gain a windfall profit. Regular assessments and evaluations of the policies should be provided for and their results must inform the retrofitting of the schemes in a timely manner. In a rapidly changing technological landscape, support to specific technologies must be reassessed on a regular basis and reallocations should not be considered as a failure, but as a sign of the uncertainty surrounding the maturation of these industrial processes. The trade-off between providing certainty to investors and regularly reconsidering policy targeting needs to be carefully addressed.

1.3. Carbon and electricity pricing: a clear carbon price trajectory, tempered by overlapping competitiveness provisions and uneven rates across firms and sectors

Carbon pricing is a cornerstone of the Dutch policy toolbox for industry decarbonisation. If implemented well, it is a cost-effective means of reducing carbon emissions, and a necessary but likely not sufficient condition for a cost-effective low-carbon industry transition. By raising the cost of carbon-intensive products relative to carbon-free alternatives, well-designed carbon pricing provides a technology-neutral incentive for low-carbon investment and consumption choices.

Starting in 2021, the Netherlands has implemented a new carbon levy in industry that sets out an ambitious price trajectory until 2030 (Figure 1.6), providing a clear signal to invest in long-term low-carbon assets and infrastructure. The levy adds a floating contribution on top of the EU ETS allowance price to yield a fixed price on Dutch emissions covered by the system. This price floor provides more certainty over future prices and protects investors against price volatility of the EU ETS allowances. As such, **the carbon levy sends a strong medium-term signal to encourage significant decarbonisation of industry**.

A key feature of the carbon levy is the combination of a pre-defined price trajectory with a levy base that phases-in over time. Initially generous allocation of so-called "dispensation rights" imply that the additional carbon price will effectively kick in only gradually, with the vast majority of emissions not paying the levy initially (Figure 1.6). The government's objective is to avoid immediate threats of carbon leakage. The advantage of this approach is that committing today to future price increases can **create strong incentives for low-carbon investment without immediately burdening businesses with new taxes**. The commitment device is not perfect, however, – changes in political majorities can always roll back previous policies – but the fact that the levy was developed through the widely accepted Climate Agreement has likely widened the acceptability and credibility of the instrument. The drawback of this design feature is that the allocation of dispensation rights largely erodes the carbon pricing signal in the short-run, weakening incentives for low-carbon investment for some users.[9]

Keeping the carbon levy trajectory in place (and potentially extending it to 2050) is critical for a cost-effective technology transformation, i.e. to ensure that incentives through carbon and energy pricing align with decarbonisation objectives. This applies in particular to the further development and deployment of new emerging technologies (such as carbon capture utilisation and storage, electrification of heating, recycling and bio-based materials, which all depend heavily on the relative cost of electricity compared with fossil fuel based alternatives). Providing a clear carbon price path can make these investments worthwhile. Helping these technologies to become profitable will not only stimulate their uptake, but also incentivise R&D activities, which are necessary to reduce their costs. Direct support to R&D can only partially compensate for strong carbon pricing, as investment support alone is not enough to make the business case for investing in low-carbon assets, as illustrated by the relative failure of green recovery packages adopted during the Global Financial Crisis (Agrawala, Dussaux and Monti, 2020[15]).

An important limitation of existing carbon pricing instruments in the long run is that they can in theory drive emissions down to at most zero. Yet, the modelling analyses indicate that negative emissions will likely be necessary to reach the 2050 decarbonisation goal. Questions will therefore arise on whether current policies can provide enough incentives for negative emissions and what role markets could play to stimulate negative emissions.

Figure 1.6. Total levy rate and estimated proportion of emissions paying the levy in the four key sub-sectors, 2021-30

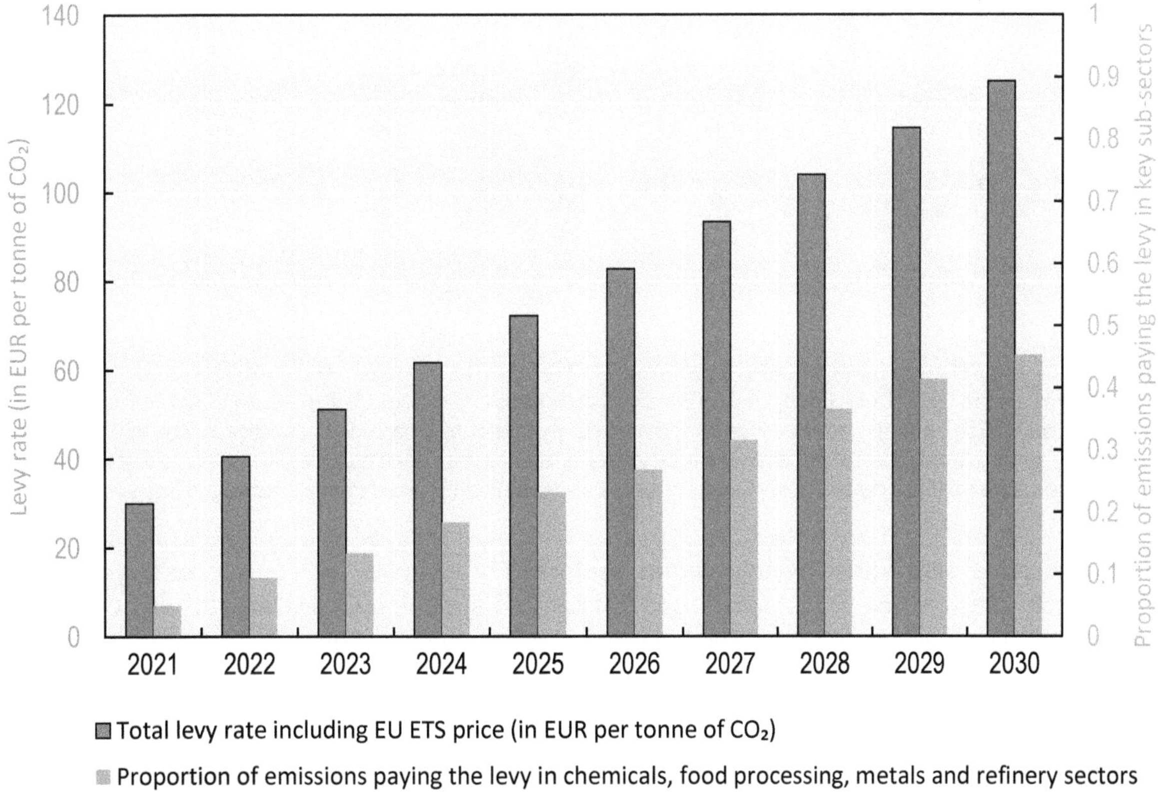

Note: The levy rate includes the floating national contribution and the EU ETS price. The estimated proportion of emissions paying the levy covers only the chemicals, food processing, metals and refinery sectors. It assumes benchmark values follow the draft revision of the EU ETS benchmarks published in December 2020. No behavioural adjustments in the emissions base, i.e. no technological shifts, no energy efficiency improvements or rebound effects compared to 2021 are assumed.
Source: CE Delft (2021[16]).

1.3.1. The Dutch Effective Carbon Rate – a synthetic indicator of carbon pricing in the Netherlands

The carbon levy comes on top of several other existing instruments that effectively put a price on Dutch carbon emissions: the EU ETS, energy taxes and ODE on natural gas.[10] However, competitiveness concerns have motivated the introduction of extensive preferential treatment to energy-intensive users – in particular the chemicals, refineries and basic metals sector – in the form of tax exemptions, regressive tax rates, and freely allocated emissions allowances. Preferential treatment for certain trade-exposed and energy-intensive industrial users are a widespread practice within Europe and the rest of the world. However, the regressive rate structure in the Netherlands provides additional relief to large energy users on the sole criteria of energy-intensity and size, with no differentiation based on the actual exposure of a sector to international competition or the carbon-intensity of energy use.

The concrete application of these instruments including the preferential treatment they entail yields a **very heterogeneous effective carbon rate across energy users within industry**.[11] Figure 1.7 indicates the variation in marginal carbon prices that apply to emissions from fossil fuel energy across the four key industry sectors in 2021. Striking differences appear. In the basic metals sector, a third of emissions are not priced at all and the rest priced at below EUR 30 per tonne. In the refinery sector, all emissions are priced below EUR 30 per tonne, whereas the food processing sector pays EUR 30 per tonne or more on 87% of its emissions. The chemicals sector stands in between and features important within-sector heterogeneity, with 63% of emissions priced below EUR 30 per tonne and 37% above EUR 30.

Figure 1.7. Proportion of CO_2 emissions from fossil fuel energy use in industry at different marginal price intervals in 2021

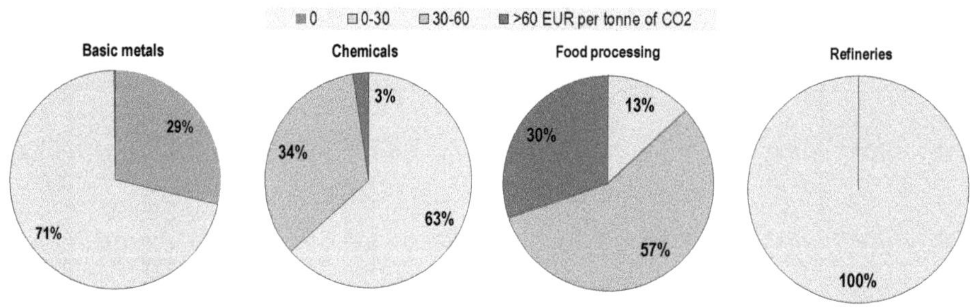

Note: Figures are based on OECD Taxing Energy Use and Effective Carbon Rates methodology (2018[17]; 2019[18]). They include price signals from energy tax and ODE on natural gas (net of exemptions) and the EU ETS permit prices (independent on whether an allowance was allocated for free or not). The national component of the carbon levy is set to zero for 2021 because of the large amount of excess dispensation rights in 2021. CO_2 emissions are calculated based on fossil fuel energy use data adapted from IEA World Energy Statistics and Balances (2020[19]).

The carbon price also varies widely within sectors. For example, in food processing given the regressive rate structure, the largest natural gas consumers pay the lowest available tax and ODE rates. Substantial taxation arises only for small and medium sized consumers of energy.

The *marginal* effective carbon rate presented in Figure 1.7 considers energy tax and ODE exemptions, but not the free allocation of EU ETS allowances. It assigns permit prices to the ETS emissions base independently on whether allowances are freely allocated or not.[12] **Accounting for freely allocated emission permits significantly narrows the base of carbon pricing in the chemicals, metals and refinery sectors as shown in** Figure 1.8.

Figure 1.8. Effective carbon rates on CO_2 emissions from fossil fuel energy use in key sectors, 2021

A. Basic Metals

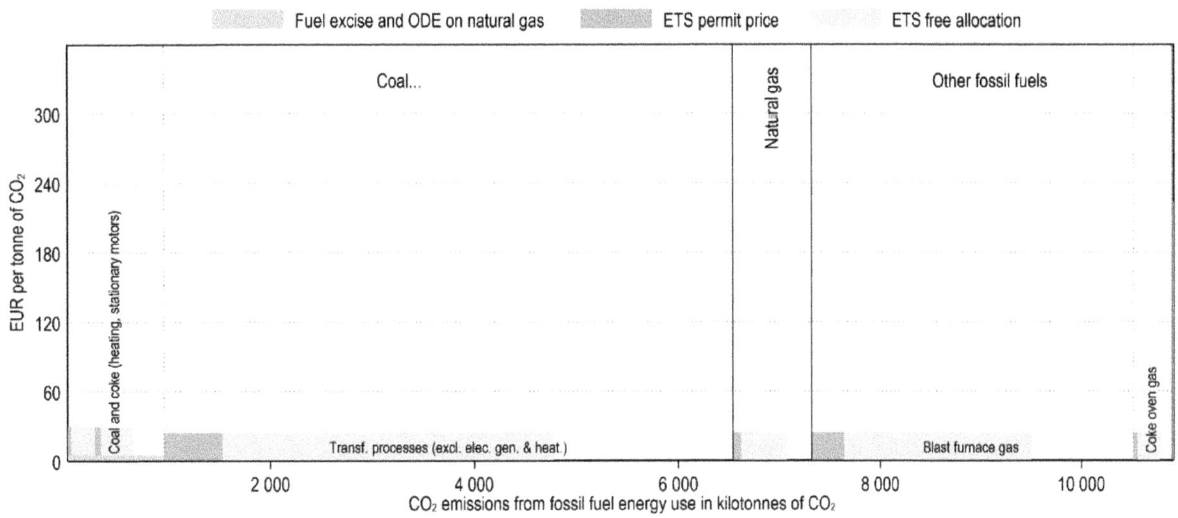

B. Chemicals

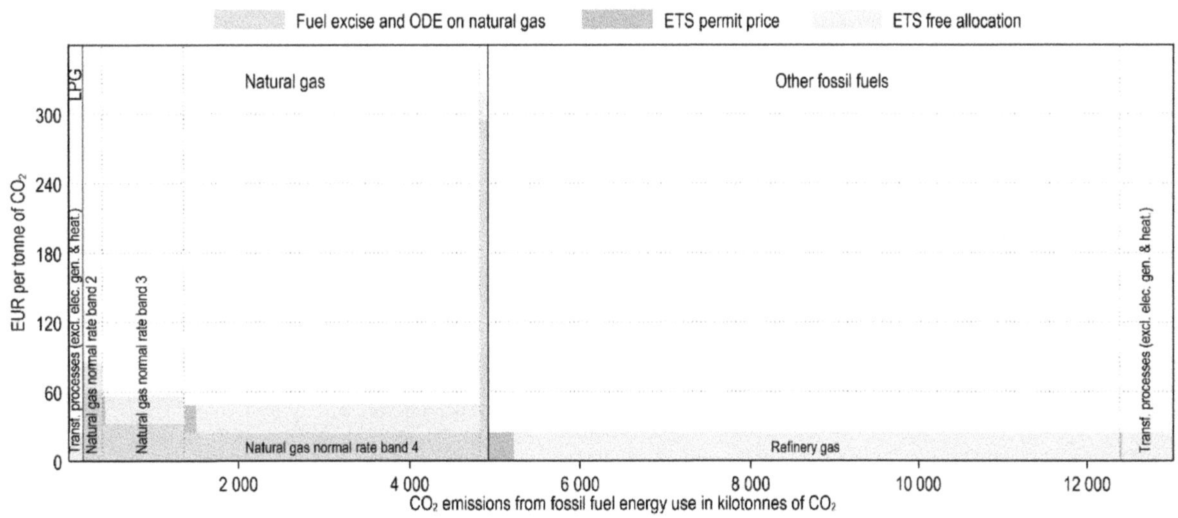

C. Food processing

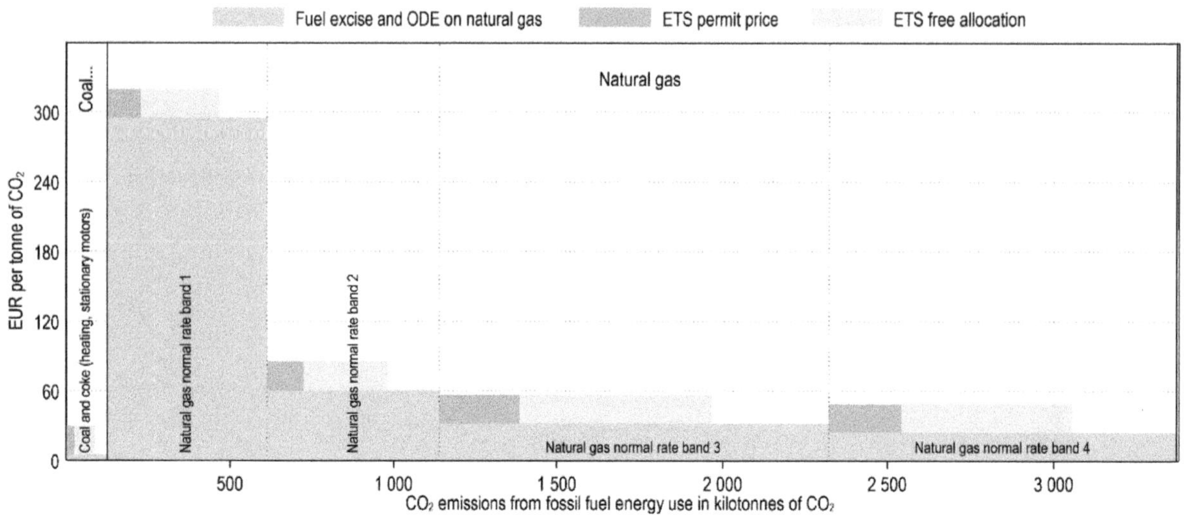

D. Refineries

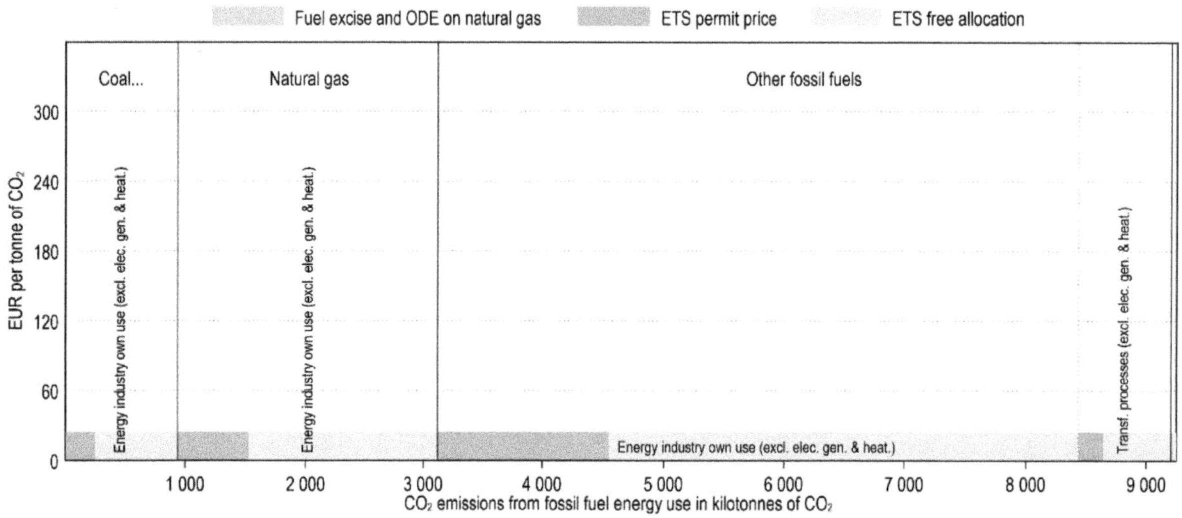

Note: Figures are based on the OECD Taxing Energy Use and Effective Carbon Rates methodology (2018[17]; 2019[18]). They include energy tax on natural gas ("fuel excise") and ODE rates on natural gas (net of exemptions) and the ETS permit price (accounting for free allocation). The national component of the carbon levy is set to zero for 2021 because of the large amount of excess dispensation rights in 2021. CO_2 emissions are calculated based on fossil fuel energy use data adapted from IEA (2020[19]), World Energy Statistics and Balance.

Taking the free allocation of emission permits in the EU ETS into consideration reveals differences that are even more notable. In 2021, the *average* effective carbon rate is estimated at EUR 76 per tonne for the food processing sector, against an average rate of EUR 13 per tonne in chemicals, EUR 3 per tonne in basic metals and EUR 7 per tonne in refineries. Importantly, applied on the current emissions base, **the carbon levy of EUR 125 per tonne would not change this unequal price signal across sectors, with average effective carbon rates estimated between EUR 24 in basic metals and EUR 92 in the food industry** under such a scenario.

From a pure decarbonisation perspective, the preferential treatment of energy-intensive users adds economic inefficiency to the overall carbon-pricing signal and entails horizontal equity concerns. Uneven prices imply that abatement efforts may not arise where they are cheapest, thereby increasing the total costs from decarbonising the Dutch industry sector. In addition, while minimal price signals reach the energy-intensive users, the less concentrated industries and small energy users pay a relatively high price per tonne of carbon.

Both observations call for **broadening tax bases and gradually removing exemptions and preferential rates**. A future review of the energy tax and the ODE on natural gas could aim to rationalise the design of the tax, establish a uniform rate across users and fuels (including coal and liquid fuels) based on their carbon content and remove exemptions. To start with, energy tax and ODE exemptions are not based on the trade exposure of industrial sectors, but rather on their energy consumption. Phasing-out inefficient and unequal tax and surcharge exemptions should be facilitated through the generous low-carbon technology-specific support for energy-intensive users introduced by the SDE++ and even more so if European trade partners simultaneously strengthen the carbon price signal. In the context of the ongoing discussions on the EU Green Deal, a revision of the Energy Tax Directive provides room for such an approach.

The recommendation to re-evaluate preferential energy tax provisions aiming at preserving the competitiveness of trade-exposed energy-intensive sectors has to be viewed in the context of recent policy developments in the Netherlands and in Europe, which questions the justification for extensive exemptions in the first place. First, **the generous technology-specific abatement payment for industrial users provided by the new SDE++ will likely reduce competitiveness concerns substantially**. Secondly, with the entire EU embarking on an ambitious journey toward carbon neutrality by 2050, competitiveness concerns with respect to other EU Member States are likely to fade away rapidly.

In the case that international competitiveness remains a concern in the future, **alternative mechanisms exist that address competitiveness concerns** of energy-intensive and trade-exposed sectors, while keeping decarbonisation incentives in place through ambitious carbon pricing. Alternative measures can be implemented at different levels of governance, e.g. nationally, at EU level, or internationally. At the European level, the implementation of a carbon border adjustment mechanism would directly reduce competitiveness concerns from firms situated outside the EU countries. Ways to implement a carbon border adjustment are currently being discussed at the European level. At the national level, carbon consumption charges could be used in addition to carbon pricing, e.g. excise taxes on domestic consumption of certain carbon-intensive basic materials, such as steel, cement or aluminium, irrespective of their production process or location.[13] Competitiveness concerns from higher prices would be reduced by passing them on in the value chain, where carbon costs are relatively less important. Carbon consumption charges could also strengthen the incentives to efficiently use, reuse and recycle such materials.

The necessity and suitability of such alternative measures in the Dutch context requires a discussion on their design features and implementation, as all measures entail advantages and have their limitations (OECD, 2020[13]).

1.3.2. Effective price signal on electricity use

An additional concern with the taxation of energy that is unrelated to the carbon pricing signal is the current design of the energy tax and ODE on electricity consumption, which does not directly encourage power producers to shift to cleaner sources of energy, and does not provide direct incentives for the decarbonisation of the power sector. The reason is that the electricity tax is not differentiated by energy source, but applies per unit of electricity used. Therefore, it increases the price on all energy sources used for electricity generation irrespective of their carbon content. Pricing the fossil fuel inputs to electricity generation, e.g. via the Dutch carbon floor price in electricity and the EU ETS, would make them more expensive relative to non-fossil energy sources.

The Dutch electricity tax and ODE also discourage the electrification of some parts of the industry sector, because taxing electricity use makes switching to electricity less profitable for end users. For example, the tax rate in gigajoule (GJ) terms is much higher for electricity than for natural gas use in all but the highest consumption bin (Table 1.1). This favours the use of natural gas over electrification of industrial processes. The total price differential between electricity and natural gas use becomes more pronounced taking pre-tax prices into account: in 2020, pre-tax prices in Dutch industry were EUR 4.7 per GJ for natural gas and EUR 17.2 per GJ for electricity for the typical industrial producer.

As with carbon pricing, the design of electricity pricing in the Netherlands raises equity concerns. Key industrial users of electricity do not pay the Dutch electricity tax and surcharge, or pay only little, either because electricity generation for own use is exempt or because large electricity consumers are subject to the lowest possible rate in the fourth consumption band. **This treatment favours concentrated, large electricity users at the expense of small industrial users as well as residential and commercial users**.

The new carbon price for Dutch power generation, which puts a floor price on emissions from electricity generation in the EU ETS, is a welcome development. Yet, the current rate of the carbon floor price falls well below the EU ETS permit price and therefore does not affect the current overall price signal. **To avoid conflicts between environmental and fiscal objectives, the phasing-down of electricity tax and ODE could be co-ordinated with the phasing-in of an effective carbon floor price in electricity and the removal of energy tax exemptions on natural gas use to generate additional revenue**. Eventually, as the energy system is approaching full decarbonisation, electricity taxes could be reintroduced if so desired (OECD, 2019[18]).

Table 1.1. Energy tax rates for natural gas and electricity in EUR per GJ in 2021

	Band 1	Band 2	Band 3	Band 4
Natural gas	13.31	2.50	0.91	0.49
Electricity	26.19	14.34	3.82	0.16

Note: Conversion follows the methodology set out in (OECD, 2019[18]) based on IEA *World Energy Statistics and Balances*. The GJ value of electricity and gas are not strictly comparable, because they are affected by conversion efficiencies, amongst others. Upstream, the electricity price depends on the fuel- and technology-specific conversion efficiency to transform primary energy into electricity. Downstream, using natural gas as an input in some industrial processes may entail larger energy losses compared to using electricity.

Policy recommendations on carbon and electricity pricing

- Maintain the carbon levy trajectory to provide a strong medium-term signal and encourage significant decarbonisation
- Gradually eliminate energy tax and ODE exemptions, as well as regressive rates, to strengthen the efficiency, effectiveness and fairness of the carbon pricing signal
- Engage in a thorough review of electricity taxation to support the country's need to electrify industrial processes, without burdening small industrial, residential and commercial consumers
- Re-evaluate provisions aiming at preserving the short run competitiveness of trade-exposed energy-intensive sectors in light of policy developments in the Netherlands and beyond

1.4. Innovation and deployment policies: the trade-off between short-term cost efficiency and long-term deep decarbonisation

By complementing carbon pricing with support for technology development and deployment, the Netherlands seeks to achieve two policy goals: the decarbonisation of the industry (which is impaired by knowledge externalities associated with the production of innovation) and the emergence of global leadership in emerging low-carbon technologies. Direct support is intended to bring down the costs of new low-carbon technologies, thereby bridging the gap between these and their carbon-intensive alternatives.

In order to provide empirical insights into Dutch industry's innovation efforts regarding emerging technologies for the low-carbon transition, an analysis of patents filed by inventors located in the Netherlands (as well as patents transferred into the Netherlands by foreign inventors, and exports of Dutch patents) was conducted in five key emerging low-carbon technologies: hydrogen, carbon capture, utilisation and storage (CCUS), electrification of heating processes, biomaterials and recycling. The analysis shows a considerable increase in innovation efforts directed at these emerging low-carbon technologies in the Netherlands between 2004 and 2010: the proportion of patents covering these five technologies in total patenting activity of the Netherlands tripled, from 0.5% to 1.5%. Interestingly, this period corresponded to a significant increase in public support for RD&D in low-carbon technologies, in particular toward CCUS and hydrogen.[14] However, this proportion has decreased since 2013 (Figure 1.9), likely driven by a global decrease in energy prices and a significant drop in domestic public R&D funding following notably the termination of the Economic Structural Strengthening Fund (Fonds Economische Structuurversterking). In 2018, the five emerging low-carbon technologies represented around 1% of total Dutch patenting activity, exactly on par with the global average, suggesting that Dutch inventors are not particularly specialised in low-carbon innovation.

Figure 1.9. Netherlands-based patents in five emerging low-carbon technologies as a share of total patents in all technologies

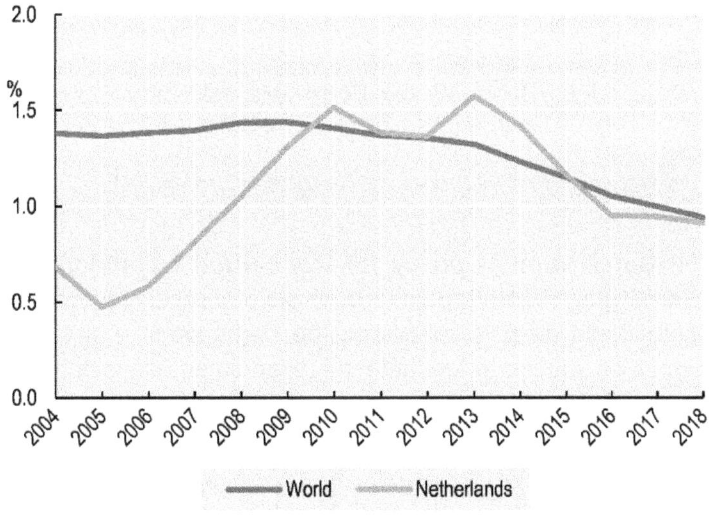

Note: Data refers to patents invented in the five selected low-carbon technologies. Statistics are based on two years moving average.
Source: OECD, STI Micro-data Lab: Intellectual Property Database, http://oe.cd/ipstats, January 2021.

As shown in Figure 1.10, Dutch inventors appear to be specialised in two technologies: CCUS and bio-based materials. These categories are also the ones that have seen the largest increases in recent patenting activity. In bio-based materials in particular, the share of Dutch innovation efforts going into this field is more than three times that of the world average in the most recent period (2014-18). In CCUS, Dutch inventors are twice as specialised as the world's average inventor. In the other three technological fields – namely hydrogen, electrification of industrial heating processes and recycling of plastics and metals – Dutch inventors appear under-specialised compared to the world average.

For a small country like the Netherlands, and given the large fixed costs associated with research into radically new technologies, it might be difficult to promote national champions in all these new technological areas. A possible strategy could be to focus on areas where Dutch inventors seem to possess some comparative advantage, which currently include CCUS and bio-based materials.[15] For other technologies, the Netherlands could rely more on imports from abroad, but adoption of technologies requires absorptive capacities, which also necessitates R&D activity – although not targeted at frontier research.

Figure 1.10. Specialisation of Dutch inventors by technology: a leadership potential in CCS and bio-based materials

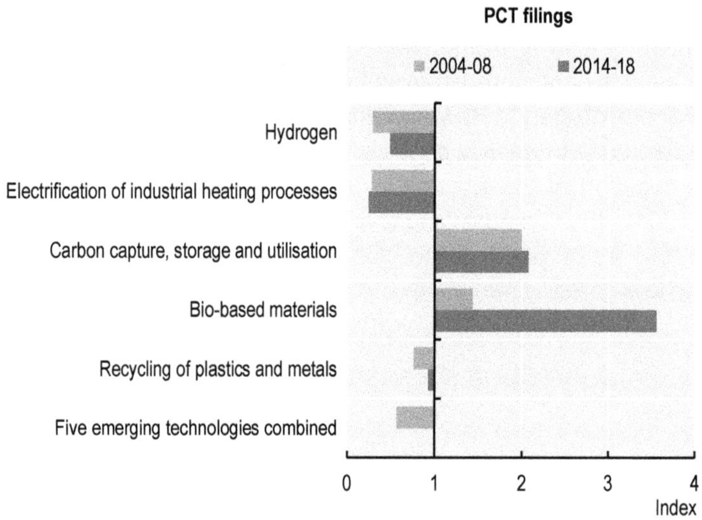

Note: The graphs shows the Relative Technological Advantage of inventors located in the Netherlands. The index is computed as the ratio of the share of patents filed for the selected technology by inventors located in the Netherlands to the share of patents in the same technology filed by inventors located in the rest of the world. Data refers to patents invented in the Netherlands for selected low-carbon technologies. Patent counts are based on the filing date.
Source: OECD, STI Micro-data Lab: Intellectual Property Database, http://oe.cd/ipstats, January 2021.

As shown in Figure 1.11, **Dutch support policy for low-carbon technology focuses on the cost-efficient deployment of emerging technologies** through several subsidy programs, spearheaded by the new SDE++. This focus on deployment is specific to the Netherlands – in comparison, Germany, for example, focuses much more on support to fundamental research and development (Chapter 6).

With a future yearly EUR 550 million budget over the long run for the industry sector (and EUR 300 million per year on average until 2030),[16] the SDE++ subsidises the additional costs associated with adopting a low-carbon technology rather than the existing carbon-intensive alternative. SDE++ is the largest support scheme, but other schemes also encourage deployment, including a tax allowance supporting energy efficiency investments (EIA) and tax allowances subsidising capital expenses for low carbon technologies (VEKI and MIA/VAMIL).

Next to deployment, most of the public funding at the national level is focused on demonstration, rather than on research and development. However, many instruments coexist, implying high administrative costs per euro of subsidy and high transaction costs, in particular for young and small firms. This is certainly alleviated by the central role of RVO in the administration of these schemes. Apart from streamlining the innovation package, possibilities to further reduce transaction costs include tailored support to promising firms to help them navigate the different types of subsidies.

In addition, the amount of funding available for demonstration support (less than EUR 300 million per year in total of which EUR 180 million comes from domestic policies, including seven policy instruments with an annual budget below EUR 10 million) is not in line with the typical scale of demonstration projects in the industry (for example, a single 100 MW electrolyser costs around EUR 50-75 million). The current package's apparent funding gap for large-scale demonstration projects contributes to tilting technology towards short-run cost-efficiency. Leveraging either the EU ETS Innovation Fund, the EU IPCEI (Important Projects of Common European Interest – one being hydrogen) or the Dutch National Growth Fund, and re-balancing the innovation policy package to close the funding gap for large-scale demonstration projects, would help breakthrough innovators escape the well-known "valley of death" of clean tech venturing (between research and commercialisation).

For earlier stages of technology readiness (e.g. at the R&D stage), the Netherlands mostly relies on horizontal support (through broad R&D tax credits – WBSO – and the Innovation Box) and on EU funding (in particular H2020). The advantage of horizontal instruments is their technological neutrality, but by construction, they benefit mostly technologies that are closest to the market. The ambitious 2050 objectives and the implied deployment of radically new technologies such as hydrogen might justify a stronger focus on targeted instruments for R&D. As for the reliance on EU funding, this enables benefiting from economies of scale by aligning research programs and co-operation at the European level and makes sense from an economic theory perspective (since knowledge externalities are much larger at the EU level than at the domestic level).

Figure 1.11. Estimated amounts of annual public funding for technology support by stage (in EUR million)

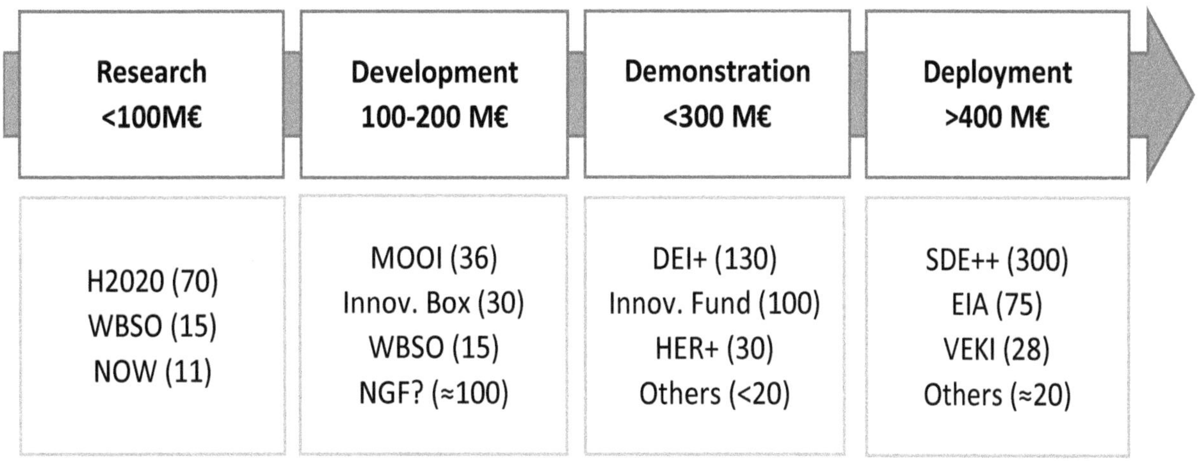

Note: On the estimated SDE++ amount and funding (endnote 16). The average of EUR 300 mln. per year over the 2022-30 period is used.

The SDE++ allocates subsidies to project applicants in increasing order of subsidy requirement per tonne of CO_2 reduction in a tender open to a large range of low-carbon technologies, such as CCS, electric boilers, heat pumps, waste heat or green hydrogen production. The abatement payment is defined per unit of avoided CO_2 emissions, i.e. the difference in operating cost (operational expenditures – OPEX) between the low-carbon and the equivalent "standard" technology, factoring in the long-term EU ETS permit price. This gives priority to least-cost options, such as CCS. Therefore, the design of the SDE++ makes the scheme less relevant to support technologies that are still at an earlier stage of development, such as hydrogen. Put differently, the SDE++ currently trades off the promotion of less mature technologies for short-term cost efficiency, thereby potentially compromising long-term cost efficiency.

In principle, SDE++ allocates abatement subsidies on a pure cost-efficiency basis as all subsidy requests are pooled in one single tender, although organised in four phases. This tends to favour close-to-the-market technologies, for which the revenue shortfall with respect to business as usual technologies is small and which can therefore bid at lower costs. Analysis of SDE++ subsidy applications in the first (2020) tender confirms this built-in characteristic: about two thirds of the total amount of requested subsidies in categories that are potentially relevant for industrial applications concern CCS, a technology with lower abatement cost and a technology readiness level (TRL) of 7, i.e. system prototype demonstration in operational environment. By contrast, a negligible share of applications concern green hydrogen, a technology with lower TRL and high operating costs (Figure 1.12).

The very high proportion of CCS applications might end up being specific to the first few tenders, but the priority given to the most mature (and hence most cost-efficient) technologies will remain. Reforming the design of the SDE++ to allow for separate tenders across technologies, production processes or TRL, could promote investment in emerging low-carbon technologies instead of solely favouring low-cost options. The design of the SDE+ (the predecessor of SDE++ aimed at the electricity sector), which provided different tenders at different subsidy levels (linked to distance to the market), could serve as a model in this regard. Such a design change would obviously lower the short-term cost-efficiency of emission reductions, but to the benefit of faster cost reductions in less mature technologies (improving long-term cost efficiency).

Figure 1.12. CCS might crowd out less mature technologies from the SDE++

SDE++ subsidy demand curve in first tender

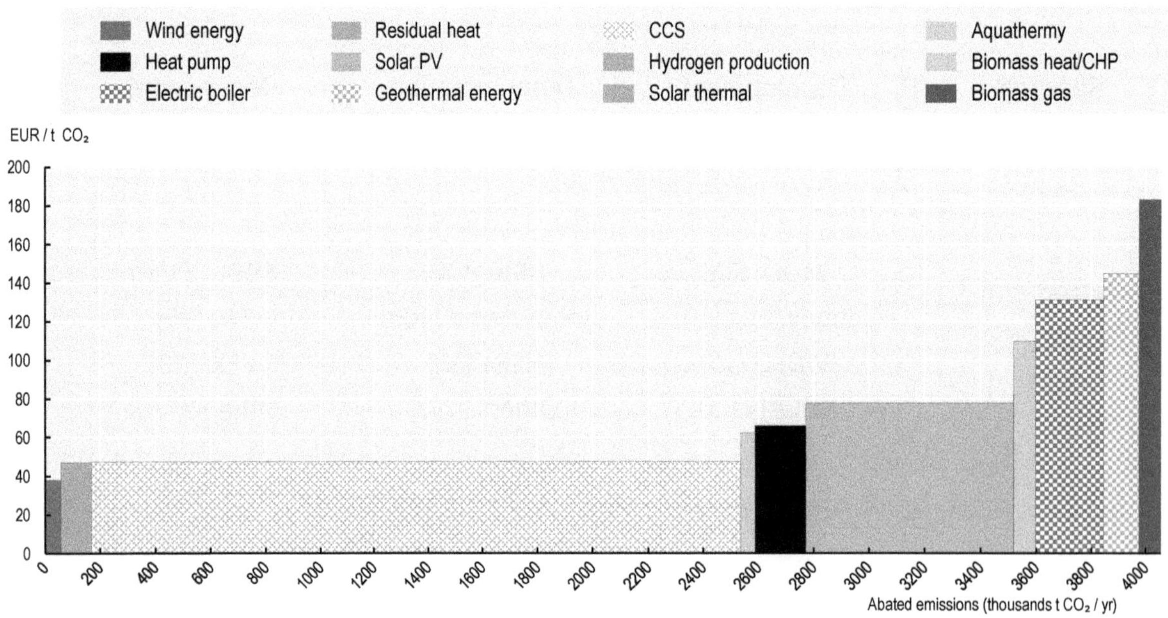

Note: areas represent the expected subsidy payment based on RVO's long-term prices; actual pay-out will depend on market prices and RVO's grant decision. Category CCS includes "blue hydrogen"; category hydrogen production is "green hydrogen". Amount tendered to categories hydrogen production and solar thermal barely visible. Average subsidy per tonne CO_2 at the technology category level and cumulated abated emissions calculated based on RVO data.
Source: Calculations based on RVO data.

Two case studies of low-carbon alternative to business-as-usual production of hydrogen illustrate the built-in bias of the SDE++ scheme in favour of high-TRL technologies. On one hand, the blue hydrogen alternative (adjunction of CCS on the standard steam-methane reforming production process) is a mature technology with the potential to bridge several chemical and refinery activities to the low-carbon economy. On the other hand, the green hydrogen technology alternative (renewable electricity-based electrolysis) lies at a lower TRL and requires further scale-up and greater cost reductions.

Figure 1.13 shows the cumulative net cash flows associated with the two projects analysed in the case studies: blue hydrogen (black lines) and green hydrogen (blue lines). The net cash flows are calculated by differencing out the business-as-usual (carbon-intensive) alternative. The solid lines correspond to a scenario where no subsidy is received, while the dashed lines show the cumulative cash flows when SDE++ support is granted. All scenarios take into account the savings from the carbon levy, with assumed dispensation rights based on EU benchmarks and counterfactual (business as usual [BAU]) projects' emission intensity.

Looking at the "no subsidy" scenarios, public support appears critical for the viability of both projects, but particularly so in the green hydrogen case. Yet, while both projects are in theory eligible to the SDE++, its design, which favours projects with the lowest abatement cost, implies that the CCS project is very likely to obtain funding while the green hydrogen project is very unlikely to receive the subsidy.

Moreover, the other key feature of the SDE++, which does not take into account savings from the carbon levy to determine the subsidy rate but only the EU ETS price, implies that the CCS project gets "overcompensated" for its emission reductions. Thus, the two case studies also illustrate the interplay of the carbon levy and the SDE++. For the blue hydrogen project, the cost savings on the carbon levy partially make up for the additional cost of CCS and the SDE++ subsidy is large enough to make the project immediately profitable. Under more favourable energy and/or carbon transportation prices, the blue hydrogen project would not even need the SDE++ subsidy to break even. By contrast, the cost savings on the carbon levy are largely insufficient to make up for the investment cost in the case of the green hydrogen project and the SDE++ subsidy – if granted, which is unlikely given the cost-efficiency allocation criterion – fails to make up for the revenue shortfall. If electricity prices remained low, the SDE++ could however make the green hydrogen project break even.

Since the carbon levy is not accounted for in the SDE++ scheme, the savings from the carbon levy therefore appear as a "free lunch" when the SDE++ is granted. It would make sense to consider ways to account for carbon levy savings when determining the SDE++ subsidy rate, just as the savings from EU ETS allowances are already accounted for. This would have the advantage of freeing up some resources for less mature technologies while maintaining the cost-effectiveness criterion.

Stronger support through demonstration-oriented instruments (DEI+ and HER+) could also help to bring about the necessary cost reductions in green hydrogen. However, further cost reductions can only be expected through scaling-up and learning-by-doing. In the absence of other available instruments to support the scaling up of green hydrogen, holding tenders by technology with dedicated budgets or accounting for carbon levy savings could help ensure that the SDE++ also supports emerging technologies in the near future.

Figure 1.13. Accounting for carbon levy savings, CCS requires less support than green hydrogen

Cumulative net cash flows for a blue hydrogen project (CCS on steam methane reformer) and a green hydrogen project, with and without SDE++ support

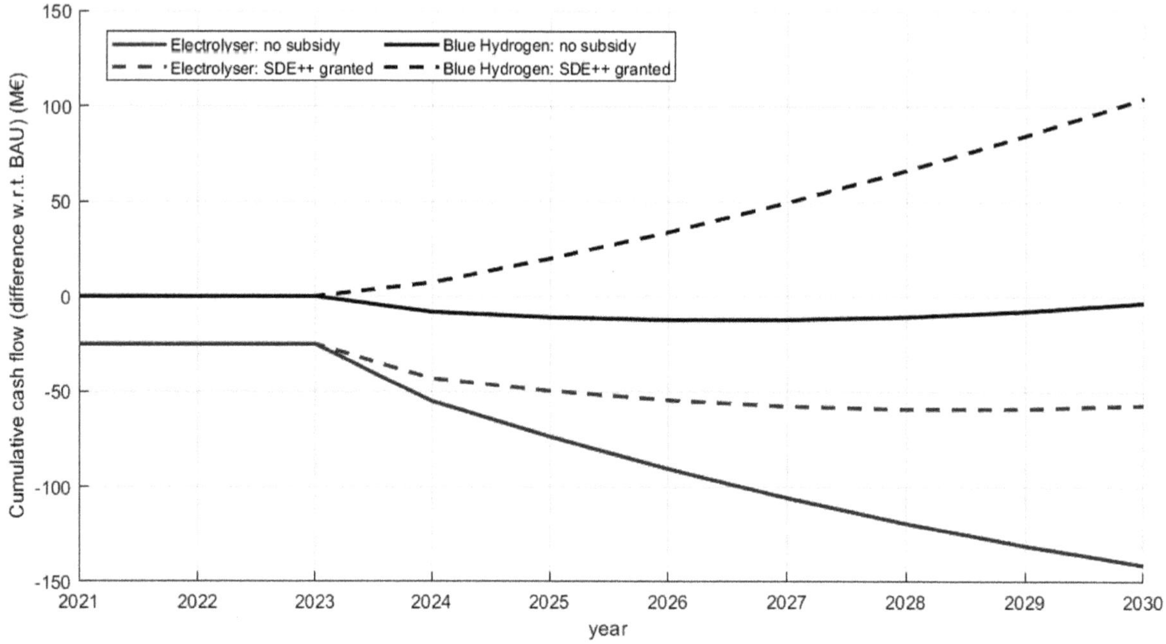

Note: high electricity prices scenario. Carbon transportation costs are taken as the mean of the PBL estimate and the Gasunie/Energie Beheer Nederland (EBN) estimate. Feasibility study cost incurred in 2021. Capital investment incurred in 2024. Savings from the carbon levy account for dispensation rights based on EU benchmarks and counterfactual (BAU) projects' emission intensity.

Policy recommendations on technology support

- Ensure greater support for technologies that are still far from the market as part of a more balanced approach to technology support across levels of technology maturity
- Consider changes in the design of the SDE++, in particular holding different tenders by technology or production process, and at least partially accounting for the savings from the carbon levy
- Ensure adequate support at all RD&D stages in areas where Dutch inventors have (or potentially have) a comparative advantage – including CCUS and biomaterials – to enable technological leadership, and boost absorptive capacity in the others
- Streamline the innovation support package, particularly at the demonstration stage, in order to improve administration cost efficiency and reduce transaction costs for young firms and SMEs

1.5. Complementary policies and framework conditions

Industry decarbonisation takes place in a broader environment, which includes regulatory frameworks, public infrastructure, competition policies, skills provision and the availability of capital. The characteristics of these framework conditions are also critical for the shift towards a low-carbon economy.

1.5.1. Standards and other regulatory instruments

An important and cost-effective way for the Dutch government to increase the necessary investments in the different green technologies can be achieved through reducing regulatory uncertainty and defining regulatory standards. Reducing uncertainty is particularly important for CCS, where project developers currently run the risk of being held liable for carbon leaks outside of storage facilities or other environmental damage. **Defining liabilities would allow investors in CCS to more accurately price and potentially insure this risk**. The industry, the financial sector and the different levels of government could work together to explore potential risk-sharing solutions should such liabilities create a barrier to market development.

Setting regulatory standards is another important complementary policy. For green hydrogen, this includes standardisation on guarantees of origin, for example if hydrogen is blue or green, but also on hydrogen purity, the design of liquefaction/conversion and regasification/reconversion facilities, for equipment specifications and for blending hydrogen into the gas grid. Standardisation would strongly promote the diffusion of technologies with network externalities. **Hydrogen-related standards would be best defined at the EU level.**

A harmonisation of standards and regulations related to the use of recycled products is necessary to promote the circular economy and, ultimately, address Scope 3 emissions. This is of particular importance in the steel industry, where **relabelling by-products of steel production at the European level (e.g. slag and fly ash) from 'waste' to 'product'** with all due care to avoid pollution hazard would reduce the administrative burden associated with purchasing scrap for companies and increase imports opportunities.

Minimum content requirements, public procurement and removal of fossil fuel subsidies are critical to help create markets for recycled products and synthetic and bio-based feedstock. While such policy efforts would be ideally implemented at the EU level, national minimum content standards and public procurement could already give a necessary boost to the recycling and bio-based industry.

1.5.2. Infrastructure

As the scenario analysis clearly shows, infrastructure needs are extremely important for the decarbonisation of Dutch industry. In particular, the transition to a low-carbon industry requires infrastructure regarding renewable electricity production and distribution, the heat network, hydrogen production and distribution, and carbon transportation (potentially using the existing gas pipeline infrastructure). These infrastructure needs were established by the Taskforce Infrastructure Climate Agreement Industry (TIKI) and the Multi-year Program Infrastructure Energy and Climate (MIEK), and the Ministry of Economic Affairs and Climate has recently announced the creation of a national Infrastructure Programme for a Sustainable Industry (PIDI).

Visibility over future infrastructure plans appear key for industrial firms to undertake investments in low-carbon technologies. **In view of the infrastructure needs implied by the modelling analysis conducted for this project, bringing more clarity and co-ordination at the national, regional and local levels seems pressing for the timely rollout of the necessary low-carbon infrastructure.** The National Growth Fund may contribute to financing infrastructure projects following PIDI's recommendations. Therefore, making PIDI operational should be a priority so that investments can take place. It is crucial that PIDI collaborates with the Exploration of Landing Wind at Sea (VAWOZ) programme, the Energy Main Structure (PEH) programme as well as with neighbouring countries, in particular Germany and Belgium. The Porthos project, which will build and operate a CO_2 transport network between the ports of Rotterdam, Antwerp and the North Sea Port is an example of such cross-country infrastructure planning, with significant financing by the Connecting Europe Facility (CEF) of the European Commission. The Athos project, which is less advanced, is planning to transport CO_2 from the Amsterdam region to the North Sea.

Infrastructure investment and management pose two key challenges, which should be carefully addressed. First, dynamic cost efficiency should be considered, particularly the risk of following too many technology routes that may prove unnecessary or even mutually exclusive, at great cost for public finance. Second, pricing the use of this monopoly infrastructure should be designed to take into account the pricing of externalities such as the integration of more renewables into the grid or demand schedule pricing allowing for intermittencies.

1.5.3. Business dynamism

The reliance on infrastructure for achieving decarbonisation is a consequence of the geographic structure of Dutch industry around highly integrated clusters. This cluster structure contributes to the cost-efficiency of decarbonisation as it promotes the internalisation of scale economies and knowledge spillovers, e.g. the efficient provision of energy carriers and the exploitation of synergies. However, it may also contribute to **locking in sectoral and geographical allocation of resources at the expense of efficiency-enhancing dynamism, therefore coming at a cost in terms of flexibility and adaptability in the longer run** – potentially a major issue at the 2050 horizon, given the uncertainty regarding the technologies that will eventually emerge in the low-carbon transition.

Figure 1.14. Relatively low business dynamism

Job reallocation rate among incumbent firms

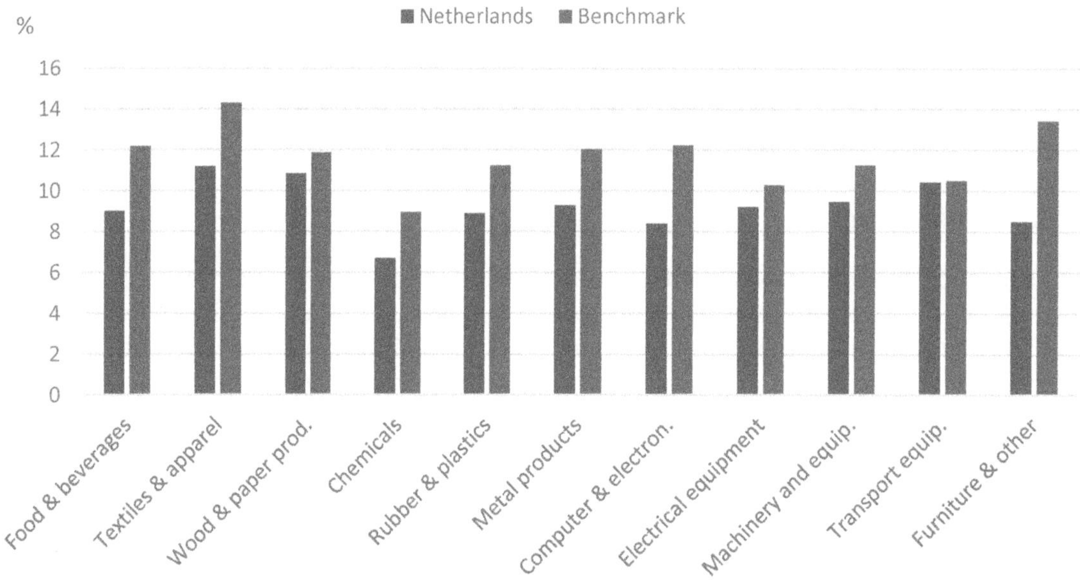

Note: churning rates of incumbents defined as the sum of the job creation rates and job destruction rates of incumbent firms, reported by SNA A38 as averages over the period of 2012-15. Benchmark countries include Austria, Belgium, Brazil, Canada, Costa Rica, Finland, France, Hungary, Italy, Japan, Portugal, the Netherlands, New Zealand, Norway, Spain, Sweden and Turkey.
Source: Calculations based on DynEmp3 Database (August 2019).

The Dutch clusters typically harbour a few large players that considerably contribute to international competitiveness. However, **young firms and start-ups are also key to foster innovation and enable the emergence of the next generation of technological leaders**. Therefore, maintaining a sufficient level of business dynamism is key to minimise the downsides of the cluster structure. First, competition should be sufficient *inside* the clusters, so that new firms can effectively enter into these structures, compete and eventually challenge large incumbents. Enabling the reallocation of production factors can have an indirect positive effect on both challengers' and incumbents' incentives to innovate. Second, resource reallocation should be enabled *between* the clusters and the rest of the country, to allow and foster the emergence of alternative decarbonisation options that do not rely on large infrastructure and can be implemented for scattered industries when relevant. This reinforces the need to **ensure that the cost of carbon emissions is the same across sectors and across small (new) and large (incumbent) firms.**

Relatively low worker churn rates across incumbent firms in Dutch manufacturing industries (including metallurgy, food processing and chemical industry) suggest a lack of business dynamism compared to other OECD countries (Figure 1.14). **Enhancing business dynamism through facilitating entry and the reallocation of outputs and inputs across firms towards their highest-valued use would contribute to enabling innovative clean tech companies to emerge**.

1.5.4. Skills for the green economy

Decarbonisation and the transition to the net-zero emission economy will affect both labour supply and demand in the industry. On one hand, skilled installation and maintenance workers are already in short supply in industry (Climate Agreement, 2019) and will be increasingly demanded in the low-carbon economy. On the other hand, decarbonisation will bring about labour reallocation of economic activity, with for example the capacity of refineries projected to decrease by (at least) 40% between 2020 and 2050.

Adequate green skills supply is particularly important for firms engaging in low-carbon technology deployment and scale-up, and likely to promote investment. More generally, it contributes to the overall absorptive capability of Dutch industry, which is a necessary condition for reaping the benefits of supra-national (mostly European) R&D and translate it into local deployment. **Re-skilling and up-skilling displaced workers with green skills through active labour market policies and adult training is immediately necessary to both address social concerns and contribute to reducing skill shortages in the future low-carbon industries.** Cross-sector training programmes can ease labour market transitions from surplus to shortage sectors. Timely and transparent information on sectoral labour markets can help workers to anticipate future labour needs and policy makers to monitor and accompany the changes. With a view to the longer run, education programmes need to incorporate new material and competences in curricula, so that the next cohort of workers can cope with the low carbon transition in the workplace.

1.5.5. Venture capital

Venture capital (VC) is instrumental in funding, supporting and scaling up young firms developing market-ready technologies. VC is a key complement to government support for technology, as it helps entrepreneurs through the "valley of death" by financing pilots and demonstrations of innovative ideas and prospective technologies, which are often the output of government-funded R&D. More generally, it allows to diversify the sources of funding for new ventures. VC is also important for small companies to move beyond an initial niche market. Moreover, it contributes to knowledge transfer across venture capitalists' portfolios. In the Netherlands, total VC investments are comparable with the OECD median. The government is very involved in providing VC funding, with half of venture capital invested in the Netherlands related to a government entity.

Importantly, a relatively large share of VC investments focuses on low-carbon technologies in the Netherlands. Data on VC deals suggest that in 2020 about 10% of total VC investments in the Netherlands concern sustainable energy technology firms, which is greater than most other European countries (Figure 1.15). This performance is remarkable given the global decrease in the share of global VC deals accounted for by clean energy since 2012 (IEA, 2020[20]).

The launch of Invest-NL is expected to further improve the Dutch VC landscape, in particular its ability to identify and fund industry decarbonisation. By launching a government-owned national investment fund with a strong focus on low-carbon technologies, the Dutch government signals that VC will be key in funding the transition to the net-zero emission economy and provides the necessary strike force for complementing its technology support policies. VC will bring capital market discipline within the bottom-up, cluster-based overall decarbonisation strategy. Against this background, both **VC investments and the needs of green tech start-ups should be monitored to ensure that Invest-NL contributes to developing a strong green VC ecosystem and promoting industry decarbonisation**.

Figure 1.15. VC investment in sustainable energy technologies across European countries

Share of total VC investment, 2016-20 or available years

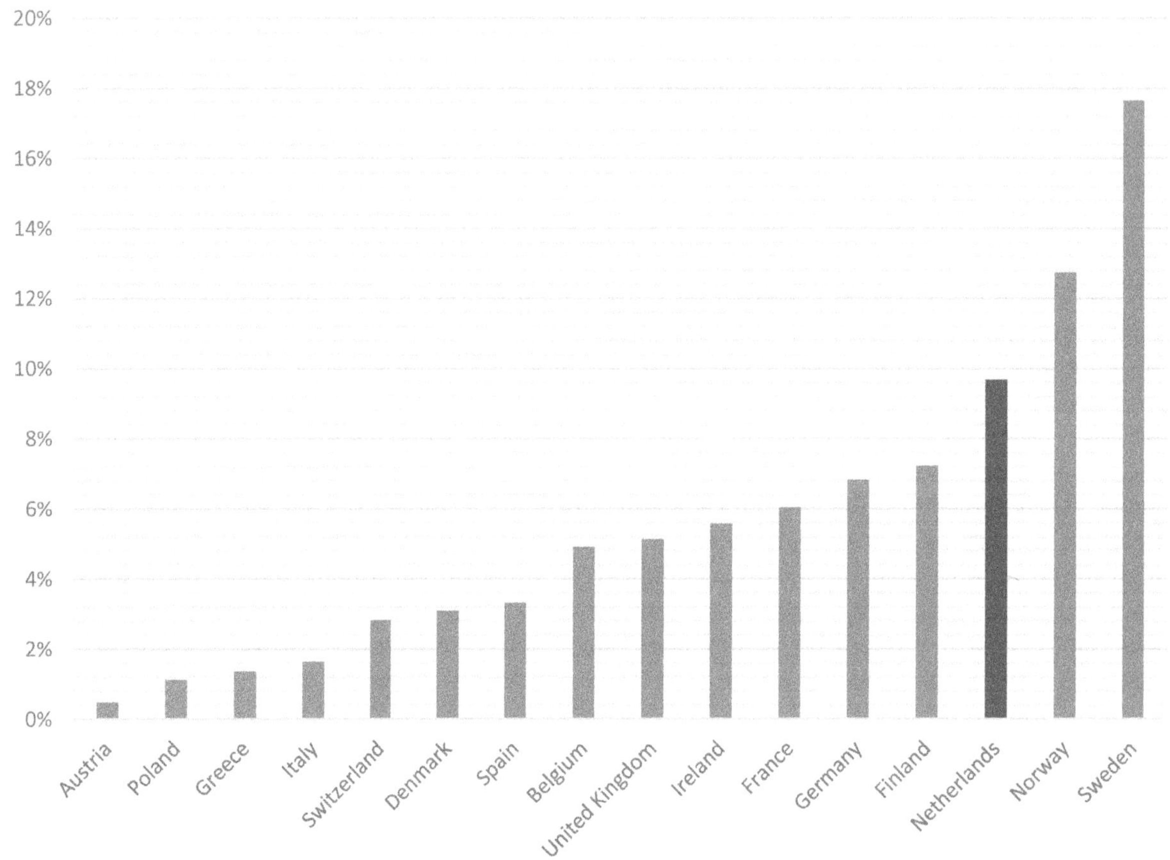

Note: share of VC investment in sustainable energy technologies as a share of total VC investment. VC investment in sustainable energy technologies in a given country is the value of all VC deals classified as "affordable and clean energy" by the data provider. Total VC investment is the total value of VC deals taking place in that country.
Source: Calculations based on DealRoom data.

Policy recommendations on complementary policies and framework conditions

- Update the regulatory framework for decarbonisation technologies (particularly CCS) and ensure standardisation (especially for hydrogen and recycling), if possible at the European level.
- Encourage the creation of markets for the circular and bio-based economy in order to address Scope 3 emissions by setting minimum content standards for recycled plastics and bio-based products, and re-labelling by-products of steel production from "waste" to "product" to ease scrap purchase.

- Provide visibility on the infrastructure programmes related to the transportation of hydrogen, electricity, heat and captured carbon, and clarify the role of the National Growth Fund in funding the low-carbon industrial infrastructure.
- Foster competition within and between clusters, ensuring a level playing field for young firms and SMEs and an adequate supply of green skills.
- Ensure sufficient funding for green start-ups, in particular through VC.

1.6. Lessons beyond the Netherlands for a green recovery

The "Sustainable transition of the Dutch industry" project provides a comprehensive evaluation of the toolbox of policy instruments in place in the Netherlands to reach its long-term decarbonisation objectives in the manufacturing sector. Many countries around the world have similarly recently committed to achieve net zero carbon emissions by 2050 as part of the global effort to slow global warming and meet the goals of the Paris Agreement on climate change, and are in the process of designing the set of policy instruments needed to reach this objective. As they embark on this journey, countries can benefit from learning from each other and exchanging knowledge and experience on their different roads towards carbon neutrality.

Dutch industry has some clear specificities – a concentration of industrial emissions in four main sectors, an industrial organisation centred around large firms and geographical clusters – and some of the policy recommendations coming out of this analysis focus on the particular design of domestic policy instruments. Yet, the four main sectors in the Netherlands share many characteristics with sectors in a large number of countries, particularly in Europe: being highly competitive, specialised in products that are highly traded internationally and responsible for significant GHG emissions, closely integrated in global value chains and in the European free trade area, relying on a highly skilled workforce, a dynamic venture capital market, etc. As such, the Netherlands faces similar challenges to many other nations around the world: achieving the low-carbon transition of industry while preserving competitiveness, avoiding carbon leakage, limiting the distributional impacts of climate policies, and promoting the emergence of future leaders in green technologies. The Netherlands, like many other countries, does not start from a blank page, but has long experience in carbon pricing and technology support. The challenge ahead is to retrofit this extensive policy package to ensure that it will effectively put industry on the path to carbon neutrality.

In this respect, what lessons can be drawn from the Dutch case for other countries? First, the Netherlands can serve as a good example of the necessity of a two-sided approach that combines ambitious technology support with a strong commitment to raising carbon pricing, developed in consultation with the relevant stakeholders. Investment support is not sufficient and needs to be accompanied by clear trajectories of gradually increasing carbon prices over the next decades, to establish a level playing field and make the business case for a low-carbon transition. The design of the Dutch carbon levy is particularly interesting in the context of the ongoing COVID-19 pandemic, with the new carbon pricing mechanism imposed in practice only well into the recovery period due to the increasing price path and a levy base that phases in gradually over time. Such a design can provide forward guidance to investors and reduce uncertainty without immediately imposing new taxes on businesses in a context of high uncertainty over short- and medium-term demand and liquidity (OECD, 2020[21]).

In this context, forthcoming post-COVID stimulus packages may orient investment towards sectors and technologies that accelerate the low-carbon transition, and improve resilience to future shocks from climate change, but they will be much more effective if accompanied by a well-designed carbon price. Carbon pricing will also direct investment towards low-carbon options resulting from stimulus packages that are conditional on green objectives, (OECD, 2020[21]).

The way in which the Climate Agreement was designed – in close co-operation with stakeholders, including industry – can also serve as a model insofar as it increases acceptability of politically difficult carbon price reform and, therefore, the credibility of the policy package. This close co-operation with stakeholders may be relatively easy in a small country like the Netherlands, with an industrial organisation centred on large firms and geographical clusters, but might also work at the regional level for larger countries.

Second, the design of the Dutch technology support policy toolbox clearly reveals the fundamental trade-off between short-run cost-efficiency and the need to switch in the longer run to radically new technologies, such as hydrogen. Technology neutrality and competitive tenders for carbon abatement projects are economically efficient and can ensure least-cost decarbonisation in the short run, but they favour technologies that are close to the market and, in the particular case of CCS, risk locking the industry into high-carbon processes rather than inducing the switch to more radical carbon-free alternatives. This calls for a balanced approach, whereby both emerging and mature technologies are supported. Mature technologies should not crowd out emerging technologies from public support, and the support to mature technologies should be regularly reassessed and removed as soon as they are competitive with fossil fuel-based alternatives. In this respect, carbon pricing helps mature technologies become cost-competitive more rapidly and enables focusing public support on technologies that are further away from market. For emerging technologies, framework conditions (such as reactive regulation, market creation, etc) are effective complements to public support.

Third, **the Dutch policy landscape perfectly illustrates the pervasiveness of competitiveness concerns related to carbon pricing**. All carbon pricing instruments (carbon levy, European carbon market, energy tax and energy surcharge) include competitiveness provisions which grant extensive preferential treatment to energy-intensive users – particularly in the chemicals, refineries and basic metals sectors. They take the form of tax exemptions, regressive tax rates, levy dispensation rights, and freely allocated emission allowances. This naturally erodes the carbon pricing signal, reduces the cost-effectiveness of the policy instrument and generates equity concerns as small firms typically face much higher energy and carbon prices than large incumbents. **Strong financial support for low-carbon technology adoption should be seen as an alternative, not a complement, to providing generous exemptions to energy-intensive industry, and allow governments to gradually remove such preferential treatments that are standing in the way of long-term decarbonisation**. The convergence of climate policy ambitions at EU level and beyond – notably among large emitters from the developed and developing world alike – is another justification for removing these exemptions. With all eyes now on COP26, the Dutch case study is a reminder of the importance of setting mutually agreed and convergent ambitious climate targets that alleviate short-run competitiveness concerns and get the industry sector ready to compete in the long run, net-zero carbon world.

Fourth, the Dutch situation underlines the value added of supra-national co-ordination and investments, in particular at the European level. This is particularly relevant for infrastructure critical to ensure transportation of hydrogen (e.g. standards are required on the origin and purity), captured carbon, and electricity across borders, notably within Europe. Beyond the cross-border issues related to carbon pricing and infrastructure, the global nature of climate change and the significant investments that it requires call for a mutualisation of the effort. For instance, the scale of investment needed and the size of typical retrofitting and demonstration projects imply that the green transition of industry can best be tackled at the European Union level, through the mobilisation of large financial resources, permitted for example by IPCEIs or the Recovery Plan for Europe (EUR 1.8 trillion, approximately one third of which is dedicated to the fight against climate change).

Finally, the Netherlands' case is a reminder that, as a structural transformation, the low-carbon transition requires the alignment of policy frameworks well beyond the core climate policy toolbox. Fit-for-purpose and reactive regulation, able to adapt swiftly to new technology developments, is a necessary pre-condition for the creation of a zero-carbon, circular and resource-efficient economy. Competition and entrepreneurship policies play a critical role to encourage business dynamism, the creation of new innovative firms and the reallocation of resources toward the most resource-efficient firms. Education, skills and science policy are necessary to make sure that industry can rely on the right set of skills and that new research into low-carbon technologies does not have to come at the expense of the development of other productivity-enhancing innovations. Investment and finance policy can support the transition by ensuring that financial resources flow to start-up businesses that can offer solutions for the decarbonisation. An efficient and cost-effective shift to a low-carbon economy thus requires the engagement of many parts of government beyond those traditionally mobilised in the development of climate change policies, possibly through a mission-oriented strategy.

References

Agrawala, S., D. Dussaux and N. Monti (2020), "What policies for greening the crisis response and economic recovery?: Lessons learned from past green stimulus measures and implications for the COVID-19 crisis", *OECD Environment Working Papers*, No. 164, OECD Publishing, Paris, https://dx.doi.org/10.1787/c50f186f-en. [15]

Anderson, B. et al. (2021), "Policies for a climate-neutral industry: Lessons from the Netherlands", *OECD Science, Technology and Industry Policy Papers*, No. 108, OECD Publishing, Paris, https://dx.doi.org/10.1787/a3a1f953-en. [1]

Berenschot (2020), *Sustainable Transition of Dutch Industry: 2050 scenario's towards a zero emission industry in the Netherlands.* [14]

Cantner, U. and S. Vannuccini (2018), "Elements of a Schumpeterian catalytic research and innovation policy", *Industrial and Corporate Change*, Vol. 27/5, pp. 833-850, http://dx.doi.org/10.1093/icc/dty028. [9]

CE Delft (2021), *Correspondance with CE Delft, February 2021.* [16]

IEA (2021), "RD&D Budget", *IEA Energy Technology RD&D Statistics* (database), https://dx.doi.org/10.1787/data-00488-en (accessed on 9 March 2021). [24]

IEA (2020), *Energy Technology Perspectives 2020 - Special Report on Clean Energy Innovation*, OECD Publishing, Paris, https://dx.doi.org/10.1787/ab43a9a5-en. [20]

IEA (2020), *Extended world energy balances*, https://doi.org/10.1787/data-00513-en (accessed on 14 December 2020). [19]

Institute, G. (ed.) (2017), *Green industrial policy: Accelerating structural change towards wealthy green economies.* [3]

Larrue, P. (2020), *New mission-oriented policy initiative as systemic policies to address societal challenges: analytical framework and types of initiatives.* [23]

Mazzucato, M. (2011), "The entrepreneurial state", *Soundings*, Vol. 49/49, pp. 131-142, http://dx.doi.org/10.3898/136266211798411183. [11]

Neuhoff, K. et al. (2016), *Inclusion of Consumption of carbon intensive materials in emissions trading*, Climate Strategies, https://climatestrategies.org/wp-content/uploads/2016/10/CS-Inclusion-of-Consumption-Report.pdf. [22]

OECD (2020), *Climate policy leadership in an interconnected world: What role for border carbon adjustments?*, OECD Publishing, Paris, https://doi.org/10.1787/8008e7f4-en. [13]

OECD (2020), *Green budgeting and tax policy tools to support a green recovery*, OECD Publishing, Paris, http://www.oecd.org/coronavirus/policy-responses/green-budgeting-and-tax-policy-tools-to-support-a-green-recovery-bd02ea23/#contactinfo-d7e2280. [21]

OECD (2019), *Taxing Energy Use 2019: Using Taxes for Climate Action*, OECD Publishing, Paris, https://doi.org/10.1787/058ca239-en. [18]

OECD (2018), *Effective Carbon Rates 2018. Pricing Carbon Emissions Through Taxes and Emissions Trading*, OECD Publishing, Paris, https://doi.org/10.1787/9789264305304-en. [17]

Paic, A. and C. Viros (2019), "Governance of science and technology policies", *OECD Science, Technology and Industry Policy Papers*, No. 84, OECD Publishing, Paris, https://dx.doi.org/10.1787/2b3bc558-en. [7]

Rodrik, D. (2014), "Green industrial policy", *Oxford Review of Economic Policy*, Vol. 30/3, pp. 469-491, http://dx.doi.org/10.1093/oxrep/gru025. [4]

Rodrik, D. (2008), *Normalizing Industrial Policy.* [6]

Romer, P. (1993), "Implementing a National Technology Strategy with Self-Organizing Industry Investment Boards", *Brookings Papers on Economic Activity. Microeconomics*, Vol. 1993/2, p. 345, http://dx.doi.org/10.2307/2534742. [5]

Schipper-Tops, R. et al. (2021), "Van overheid als marktmeester naar ondernemer en regisseur", *ESB*, Vol. 106, pp. 46-49. [12]

Tagliapietra, S. and R. Veugelers (2020), *A green industrial policy for Europe*. [2]

Wanzenböck, I. et al. (2019), *A framework for mission-oriented innovation policy: Alternative pathways through the problem-solution space*, Center for Open Science, http://dx.doi.org/10.31235/osf.io/njahp. [10]

Warwick, K. (2013), "Beyond Industrial Policy: Emerging Issues and New Trends", *OECD Science, Technology and Industry Policy Papers*, No. 2, OECD Publishing, Paris, https://dx.doi.org/10.1787/5k4869clw0xp-en. [8]

Notes

[1] Mission-oriented strategies are defined as a "co-ordinated package of [...] measures tailored specifically to address well-defined objectives related to a societal challenge, in a defined timeframe. These measures possibly span different stages of the innovation cycle from research to demonstration and market deployment, mix supply-push and demand-pull instruments, and cut across various policy fields, sectors and disciplines." (Larrue, 2020[23]).

[2] In this report, the industry corresponds to the manufacturing sectors (NACE Rev. 2 10-33).

[3] Source: Eurostat, energy supply and use by NACE Rev. 2 activity.

[4] These include Tata Steel, Shell Refinery, Shell Chemistry, BP, Zeeland Refinery, Chemelot Site Permit, Esso, Dow, Yara Sluiskil, Air Liquide, and ExxonMobil.

[5] The manufacturing sector as a whole represents 22.9% of output and 44.2% of exports in the Netherlands. In Germany, the numbers are respectively 33.0% and 69.9%. In the EU-27, 27.3% and 59.6%.

[6] Scope 3 emissions are currently not taken into account in climate policies (in the Netherlands or elsewhere), and need to be addressed internationally as part of ongoing climate negotiations.

[7] The terms ODE and surcharge are used interchangeably.

[8] Pricing instruments that are fuel specific (e.g. energy tax and surcharge on natural gas) or that target emissions directly (e.g. EU ETS) effectively put a price on carbon emissions. However, the Dutch electricity tax and the surcharge on electricity do *not* differentiate by type of fuel and their carbon content but apply on kWh electricity consumed. The latter are therefore not considered a carbon-pricing instrument and not taken into account in effective carbon rates. They are instead discussed under effective electricity pricing.

[9] Dispensation rights are allocated to carbon-efficient facilities defined on the basis of EU ETS benchmarks. Although some relatively inefficient firms will be short of dispensation rights early in the process, they can most likely acquire those rights at negligible costs due to the large amount of excess dispensation rights in early years that are not bankable, thereby losing their value for future trading periods. Eventually, only few of the most carbon-inefficient facilities will be exposed to a significant price in early years.

[10] An energy tax and ODE also applies on electricity use in the Netherlands. These are not considered a carbon price, because rates are not differentiated by energy source, but apply per unit of electricity used. Therefore, they increase the price on all energy sources used for electricity generation irrespective of their carbon content. Both are discussed below under electricity pricing.

[11] The OECD Effective Carbon Rate estimates the total price that applies to carbon emissions from fuel use as a result of market-based policy instruments: carbon taxes, specific taxes on fuel use (primarily excise taxes) and emissions trading systems (OECD, 2018[17]).

[12] The latter approach is rooted in the idea that freely allocated allowances retain CO_2 abatement incentives at the margin due to the opportunity cost (the allowance price) that they entail.

[13] For example, Neuhoff et al. (2016[22]) propose to combine an ETS and free allocation with excise taxes on carbon intensive products, where the excise taxes rate is derived from the product benchmark. The idea is that permit prices provide a marginal incentive to improve the carbon efficiency of existing products and that the excise taxes encourage the consumption of more carbon efficient goods.

[14] Average annual public RD&D support to CCUS and hydrogen was respectively EUR 15.5 million and EUR 4 million over 2004-10, against EUR 1.8 million and EUR 1.9 million over 2011-18. There was no public funding for either technology before 2004 (IEA, 2021[24]).

[15] These two technologies, however, are also those that generate the highest political resistance.

[16] The maximum budgeted expense on SDE++ subsidy for CO_2 reduction in industry increases from EUR 50 million in 2022 to EUR 550 million in 2030 for a total of EUR 2.675 billion over the 2022-30 period, or about EUR 300 million per year on average. Whether these amounts are structural remains subject to uncertainty due to current discussions regarding ODE reforms, and the need to fund more expensive abatement in other sectors in the long run.

2. Dutch industry's structure and emissions

This chapter presents a brief overview of the role of the industrial sector in the Netherlands' economy and CO_2 emissions, with a focus on four sectors which account for more than 90% of industry's direct GHG emissions: chemicals, refineries, metals and food processing.

2.1. Industry's emissions in the Netherlands

Greenhouse gas (GHG) emissions in the Netherlands have been decreasing at a constant pace since 2000 at the economy-level (as shown by the solid blue line in Figure 2.1). Industry has contributed to this, slightly more than other sectors as their share in emissions is 26.6% in 2018, compared to 28.5% in 2000. However, the downward trajectory in industry's emissions has stopped since the Great Financial Crisis, and their share in the total emissions has been rising since.

Figure 2.1. Emissions of GHG are decreasing in the Netherlands, and industry is contributing to this reduction

Emissions of GHG (Total and Industry) in the Netherlands in Mt CO_2-eq, and share of emissions from the industry

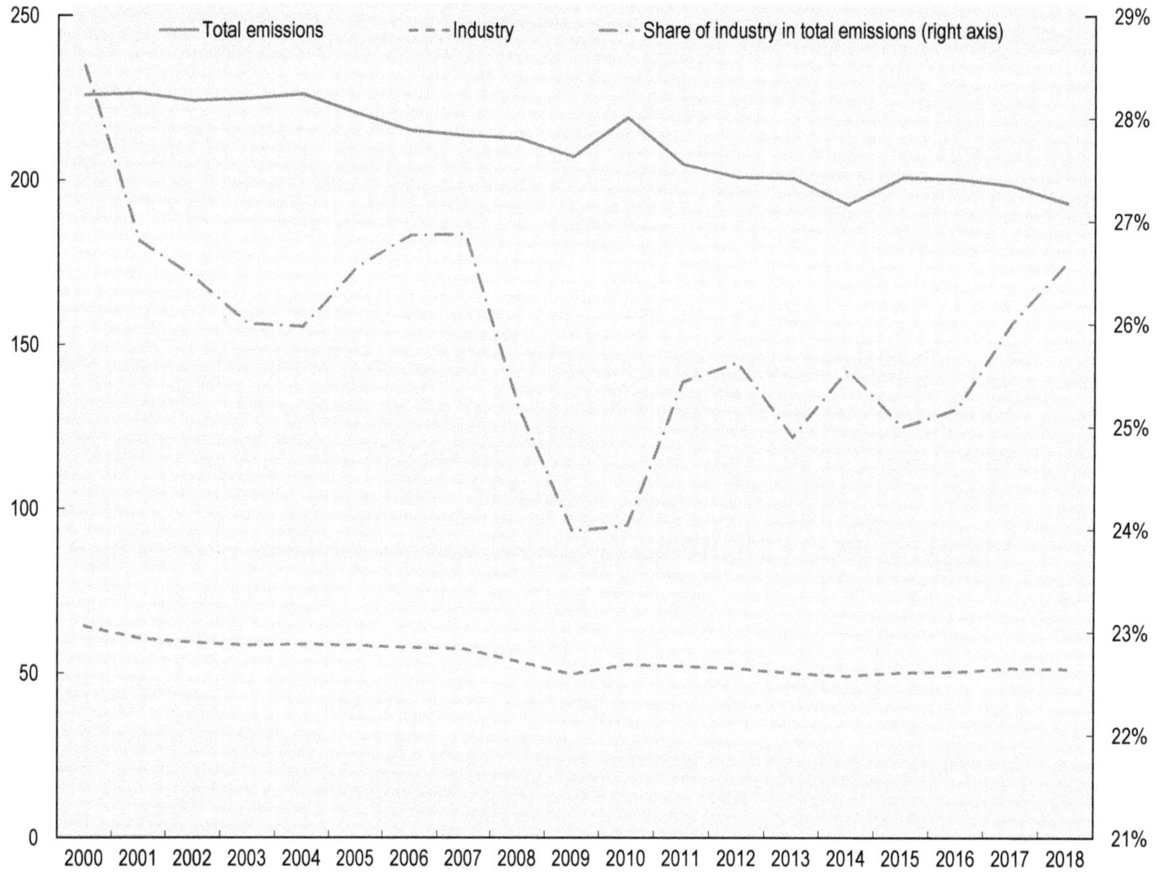

Note: Industry emissions include emissions from industrial processes and fuel combustion in refineries, manufacturing and construction.
Source: Eurostat (greenhouse gas emissions by source sector), OECD calculations.

Industry accounts for the largest proportion of direct emissions (Scope 1, Box 2.1) in the Netherlands (Figure 2.3). Other important sectors include energy production, transport and agriculture.

The rest of this chapter will focus on four industrial sectors,[1] which accounted for more than 90% of industry's direct GHG emissions in 2018: chemicals, refineries, metals and food processing. The heaviest emitter is the chemical sector, representing 44% of industrial emissions (Figure 2.4). The three other sectors included are refineries, metals and food processing. These four sectors also account for a significant share of industry's Scope 2 emissions, as they represent 72% of the electricity use of the manufacturing sector.[2] Other emitting sectors include the "manufacture of other non-metallic mineral products" (4% of industrial emissions), the "manufacture of paper and paper products" (1%) and the "manufacture of fabricated metal products, except machinery and equipment" (1%).

Box 2.1. Scope 1, Scope 2 and Scope 3 emissions

The GHG Protocol, a private sector initiative, defines emissions responsibility. IPCC summarises these definitions as follow: "*'Scope 1' indicates direct greenhouse gas (GHG) emissions that are from sources owned or controlled by the reporting entity. 'Scope 2' indicates indirect GHG emissions associated with the production of electricity, heat, or steam purchased by the reporting entity. 'Scope 3' indicates all other indirect emissions, i.e. emissions associated with the extraction and production of purchased materials, fuels, and services, including transport in vehicles not owned or controlled by the reporting entity, outsourced activities, waste disposal, etc.*"

Source: IPCC, https://www.ipcc.ch/site/assets/uploads/2018/02/ipcc_wg3_ar5_annex-i.pdf.

Figure 2.2. Overview of the definitions of scope for GHG emissions

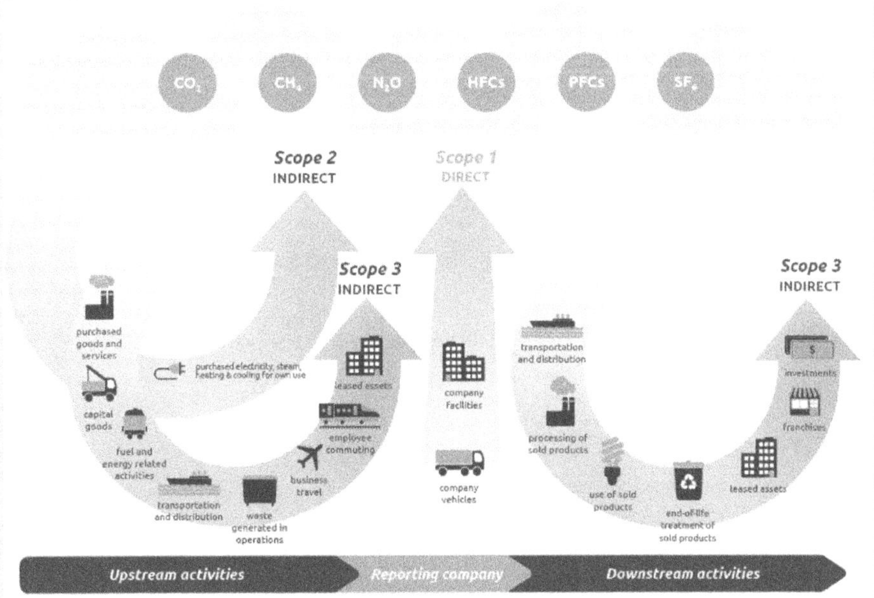

Source: GHG protocol.

Table 2.1 shows the economic importance of each industrial sector for the total economy, measured by gross output, value added, export and the number of employees. The manufacturing sector as a whole represents 12% of the total economy value-added and employs 10% of the workers in the Netherlands. However, unsurprisingly, the manufacturing sector is much more important in terms of export, with almost 45% of exports related to the industrial sector in terms of gross output and 36% in terms of domestic value-added content. When focusing on the four sectors responsible for most of the industrial emissions, they account for around a third of manufacturing value-added or employment, but half of exports (in gross output or value-added).

Figure 2.3. GHG emissions by sector, 2018

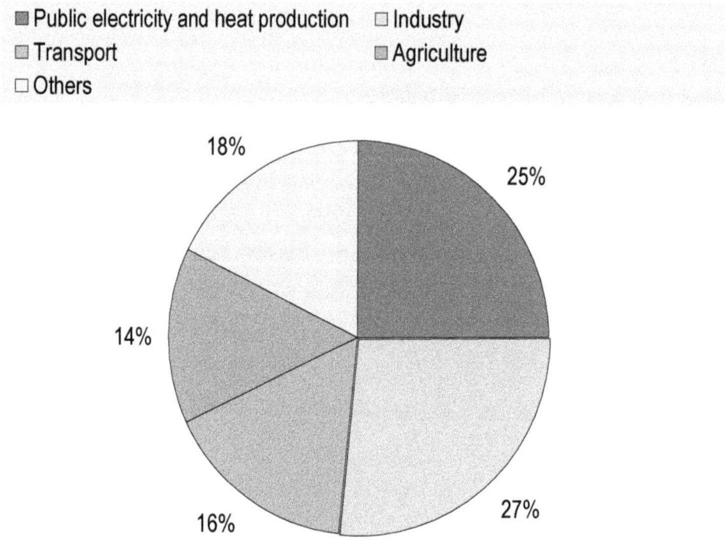

Note: Industry emissions include emissions from industrial processes and fuel combustion in refineries, manufacturing and construction. Agriculture emissions include emissions from agricultural processes and fuel combustion in agriculture, forestry and fishing.
Source: Eurostat (greenhouse gas emissions by source sector), OECD calculations.

Figure 2.4. GHG emissions of the industry by sub-sector, 2018

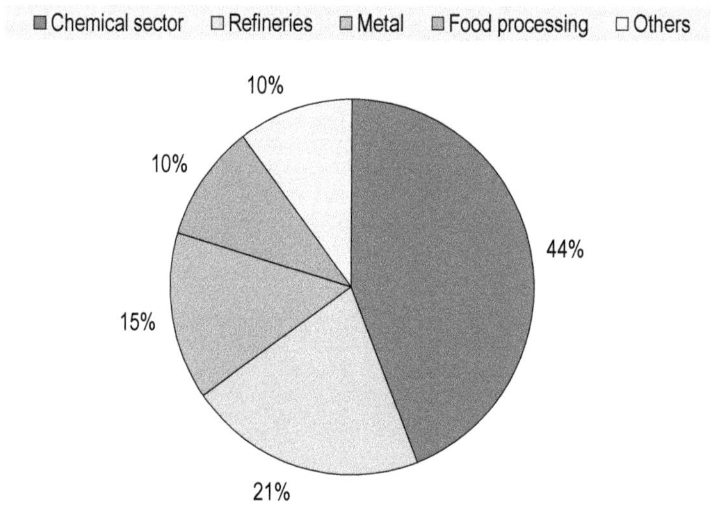

Note: This graph only includes direct emissions (Scope 1).
Source: Eurostat (Air emissions accounts by NACE Rev. 2 activity), OECD calculations.

The Netherlands is specialised in products that are both highly traded and responsible for significant GHG emissions. The challenge is therefore to decarbonise these sectors while preserving competitiveness. A loss of competitiveness could not only affect economic prospects, but also, absent mechanisms to penalise carbon-intensive imports, lessen the efficiency of the green transition globally by shifting emissions abroad rather than reducing them (referred to as "carbon leakage").

Table 2.1. Economic performance in the four sectors

	Gross output		Value added		Export GO		Export VA		Employees	
	Euro	Share	Euro	Share	Euro	Share	Euro	Share	Thsd	Share
Total Dutch economy	1 514	100.0%	693	100.0%	352	100.0%	254	100.0%	7 829	100.0%
Manufacturing (D10T33)	345	22.8%	86	12.4%	155	44.2%	92	36.4%	742	9.5%
Food, beverages and tobacco (D10T12)	72	4.8%	16	2.3%	32	9.1%	21	8.4%	127	1.6%
Coke and refined petroleum (D19)	30	2.0%	1	0.2%	11	3.2%	4	1.5%	5	0.1%
Chemicals and chemical prod. (D20)	53	3.5%	12	1.7%	31	8.8%	19	7.6%	45	0.6%
Basic metals (D24)	9	0.6%	2	0.4%	6	1.8%	4	1.5%	21	0.3%
Scope of this chapter (D10T12, D19, D20, D24)	165	10.9%	32	4.6%	80	22.9%	48	19.0%	198	2.5%

Note: Gross output and value added are measured in billion euros. Gross output, value added and the number of employees are presented for 2018 and the figures on export are presented for 2015. Estimates are based on the International Standard Industrial Classification of all economic activities, Revision 4 (ISIC Rev. 4). Export GO = export gross output (adjusted for re-exports); Export VA = Domestic value added content of gross exports. Export GO and Export VA are from the TiVA database and the latter excludes the foreign value added in exports. The figures for Export of chemicals is available at a less disaggregated level and include pharmaceutical products (D21).
Source: OECD STAN Industrial Analysis data (2020) and Trade in Value Added (TIVA) data (2018).

2.2. The five industrial clusters

Dutch industry is very concentrated with 12 firms[3] accounting for more than 60% of the industrial emissions,[4] and five regional clusters including most of the heavy emitters: "Rotterdam-Moerdijk"; "Smart Delta Resources" (Zeeland); "Chemelot" (South-Limburg); "Noord Nederland" (Eemshaven, Delfzijl and Emmen) and "Noordzeekanaalgebied" (Amsterdam-IJmuiden).

Table 2.2 shows which main sectors (chemical, refineries, metal and food) are represented in the different clusters (five geographical clusters plus the "Zesdecluster" for the rest of the country), which portrays the regional scattering of these industries. The chemical industry is represented in all six regional industry clusters, but in terms of size it is mostly concentrated in Rotterdam-Moerdijk, Chemelot and the Smart Delta Resources. Refineries are concentrated in Rotterdam-Moerdijk, with the exception of Zeeland refinery, which is located in the Smart Delta Resources. A vast majority of steel is produced by Tata Steel in IJmuiden, which is part of the Noordzeekanaalgebied cluster plan. Food processing is more spread over the geographical clusters taking place in the Smart Delta Resources, Noordzeekanaalgebied, Noord Nederland and in the sixth cluster (Zesdecluster).

Table 2.2. Correspondence between clusters and sectors

	Chemical	Refineries	Metal	Food
Rotterdam- Moerdijk	X	X		
Smart Delta Resources (Zeeland)	X	X	X	X
Chemelot (Limburg)	X			
Noordzeekanaalgebied (Amsterdam- IJmuiden)	X		X	X
Noord Nederland (Eemshaven, Delfzijl and Emmen)	X		X	X
Zesdecluster	X		X	X

Source: Based on the cluster plans (Box 2.2).

The six clusters have recently released plans for decarbonisation at the 2050 horizon, aiming for net-zero emissions in 2050. These plans are described in Box 2.2 and are consistent with the scenario presented in the following sections. Important to point out is the substantial heterogeneity in the size of the clusters, with Rotterdam-Moerwijk, alone, being responsible for 70% of the targeted emission reductions for the industrial sector for 2030. Another relevant observation is that there is substantial overlap between the different cluster plans in reported opportunities, roadmaps and conditions.

Box 2.2. Six industry cluster plans

This box describes the five geographical industry cluster plans, "Rotterdam-Moerdijk"; "Smart Delta Resources" (Zeeland); "Chemelot" (South-Limburg); "Noord Nederland" and "Noordzeekanaalgebied" (Amsterdam-IJmuiden), and a sixth cluster containing the rest of the manufacturing sector, spread over the Netherlands. Key conditions for the green transformation mentioned across plans are: sufficient supply of green electricity, infrastructure (e.g. for hydrogen and CO_2) and facilitating legislation (e.g. to allow recycling resources).

Industry cluster plan Rotterdam- Moerdijk

The goal of the industry cluster plan Rotterdam-Moerdijk is to contribute 20-25% to the national GHG reduction targets, which is 70% of the target for the total industrial sector for 2030. The size of the industry cluster Rotterdam-Moerdijk, therefore, demands a more extensive description than the other industry clusters. The main activities in this cluster relate to the harbour, the processing of raw materials, refineries, the petrochemical industry and energy.

According to the industry plan, the cluster represents 400 000 jobs and a value-added of EUR 13 billion. The cluster is known for its energy-intensive industries, using 260 PJ annually, and this energy consumption alone is responsible for 18.6 Mt of CO_2 emissions (2016).

Roadmap

Step 1 (2018-25): Efficiency measures and use of residual streams. Residual heat from industries can be used to heat houses, offices, and greenhouses and CO_2 can be captured and used in greenhouses or stored under the North Sea. The CO_2 reduction potential of step 1 is 4.9 Mt CO_2 in 2030.

Step 2 (2020 -30): Oil and gas used to heat in the production process will be replaced by renewable electricity and hydrogen (both produced and imported hydrogen, initially blue hydrogen and then green hydrogen, Box 1.2). The CO_2 reduction potential is 3.5-4 Mt CO_2 in 2030.

Step 3 (2030-50): Replace fossil fuels in the chemical sector and for transportation by biomass, recycling and re-using CO_2 in combination with hydrogen. The CO_2 reduction potential is 1 Mt CO_2 in 2030. To reach carbon-neutrality in 2050, most of these emission reductions occur between 2030 and 2050.

The industry cluster plan contains the following examples for a circular industry:

- a waste-to-chemicals factory in which plastic and mixed garbage is transferred into resources for industry
- pyrolyse scale-up projects to convert non-recyclable plastics to crackerfeed
- Biogate Europe to produce ethylene oxide and derivatives from biogenic resources
- CO_2 capture to deliver to greenhouses
- large-scale mono-manure fermentation or CO_2 fermentation factory
- extension of the bioliquefied natural gas station network
- scale-up to integrated factory/ bio refinery for cascading and
- valuation of sustainable biomass and oil in green chemistry and fuels.

According to the cluster plan, the necessary conditions for the green transformation are clear and stable multi-year legislation, financial conditions that make green investments economically rewarding, and investments in infrastructure. Conditions related to hydrogen, electrification, use of residual heat and circular use of resources are: enough supply of sustainable energy (e.g. to produce green hydrogen); infrastructure for hydrogen, residual heat and CO_2 streams; increased electrolyse capacity and changes in legislation (e.g. to change the status of waste).

Smart Delta Resources

The Smart Delta Resources (SDR) is located in Zeeland and Oost-Vlaanderen (Belgium) and includes the North Sea Port, which is a 60-kilometre-long cross-border port area that stretches from Vlissingen on the North Sea coast in the Netherlands to Ghent in Belgium. The industries in SDR claim to be responsible for an (in)direct employment of 100 000 people, and a value-added of EUR 14.5 billion, of which 33 000 jobs and EUR 5.6 billion value-added for Zeeland. The SDR region includes the production of chemicals, steel, energy and food. In addition, it is known for its current application of (grey) hydrogen (520 kt), which corresponds to 33% of total industrial consumption in the Netherlands, and has the potential to grow to more than 1 Mt annual (mostly green and blue) hydrogen production in 2050 (Box 1.2, on the processes to produce hydrogen). The Schelde-Deltaregion is the largest hydrogen producer and consumer in both the Netherlands and in Flanders with only Rotterdam having a similar scale The presence of large-scale wind parks offer an opportunity for the production of green hydrogen.

The SDR region reduction target (Zeeland and Oost-Vlaanderen) is 11 Mt in 2030 and the provisional ambition for 2050 is to reduce emissions by 18 Mt CO_2 (which is not yet enough to reach climate neutrality). Most reduction will be achieved by replacing grey hydrogen with mostly blue hydrogen in 2030 and mostly green hydrogen in 2050, and by deploying carbon capture and storage (CCS), carbon capture and utilisation (CCU) and electrification. The GHG reduction plan consists of four main programs: Hydrogen Delta, Carbon Connect Delta, Spark Delta and Heat Delta. The SDR region is considered to be the motor of green wind-energy with Windpark Borsele 1, 2, 3 and 4.

Conditions mentioned in the industry plan to make the GHG reduction a success are regional hydrogen infrastructure, infrastructure for CCUS, enough sustainable energy and favourable regulations (e.g. issue necessary permits, and resolve obstacles caused by differences in regulations between the Netherlands and Belgium).

Chemelot

Chemelot is a chemical business park consisting of leading chemical producers and a knowledge and innovation campus. It has approximately 8 000 employees.

Chemelot is responsible for 6 Mt CO_2 emissions per year. The target is to reduce GHG by 50% in 2030 (relative to the 1990 benchmark) and become climate neutral in 2050. To reduce GHG, the target is to produce 50 kt (blue) hydrogen in 2030 and 200 kt (blue and green) hydrogen in 2050. In addition, the Chemelot cluster has the ambition to be the first circular hub.

The two strategies to reach these goals are the replacement of fossil-based resources by sustainable alternatives and the electrification of production processes using sustainable electricity. There are three underlying themes related to this: process innovations, circularity and hydrogen.

Two concrete solutions for 2030 are the reduction of nitrous oxide emissions and CCS. Nitrous oxide is not yet included in the Emission Trading System (ETS) system and therefore, some low-hanging fruits still exist to reduce the annual emissions of nitrous oxide by 0.9 Mt CO_2 (equivalent) by 2030. On the Chemelot site, a substantial quantity of almost pure CO_2 is available to capture. A challenge remains to find a solution to transport this carbon to the North Sea.

Infrastructure for hydrogen and CO_2 is a crucial condition to reach the GHG reduction goals along with strengthening the electricity network. Market-based solutions for this do not yet exist.

Other conditions mentioned in the plan are a level playing field, removing legislative hurdles and increasing subsidies for required investments that are not profitable.

Regioplan Noordzeekanaalgebied

The regional industry cluster "Noordzeekanaalgebied" (Amsterdam, Zaanstreek, IJmuiden) represents almost thirty companies in the North Sea canal area. The industry plan claims that these industries generate approximately 78 000 jobs and a value added of EUR 9 billion. Important sectors are Steel (Tata Steel), food and energy (Vattenfall, AEB). GHG emissions in this area are 18.3 Mt per year (11% of CO_2-emissions in Netherlands), of which 6.3 Mt by Tata Steel.

The GHG emission reduction target for this area agreed in the Climate Agreement is 4.2 Mt in 2030, but potential projects to reduce emissions exceed this amount.

Conditions mentioned in the industry plan to reach the GHG reduction targets are a smooth collaboration between the stakeholders, a decrease in uncertainty for investors (e.g. about future subsidies and the price of CO_2), an increase in subsidies to allow for important non-profitable investments and finally improvements in the energy-infrastructure (e.g. hydrogen infrastructure).

Noord-Nederland

The Noord-Nederland cluster is one of the smallest industry clusters, generating approximately 15 000 jobs and a value added of EUR 2 billion, according to the cluster plan. Industries related to this cluster are concentrated in Eemshaven, Delfzijl and Emmen and consist of the chemical industry, food, data centres, metal and biorefinery. The industry cluster Noord Nederland is responsible for 30% of Dutch electricity production.

GHG reductions in this industry cluster are reached by process innovation (30%), changing energy sources (25%) and energy-efficiency (17%).

Het Zesdecluster

The sixth cluster is called "Zesdecluster" (literally meaning sixth cluster), which contains firms spread over the country and do not contain the twelve biggest emitters which are all represented in the five other clusters. The sixth cluster consists of the following nine sectors: food processing, paper, chemical, glass, ceramic, waste and recycling, Information and Communication Technologies (ICT), metallurgical, oil and gas.

The reduction target is 4.3 Mt CO_2 and the roadmap to reach this target consists of process efficiency, electrification, alternative resources, sustainable energy, geothermal heating, using warmth efficiently and innovative techniques.

Conditions mentioned in the cluster plan are the following: 1) access to infrastructure (strengthening of the electricity grid, infrastructure for hydrogen and networks for geothermal energy, heat supply and CCUS), 2) R&D support, 3) reliable and affordable energy, 4) facilitating legislation and 5) access to finance and subsidies.

To summarise, the main conditions for a successful transition of the different clusters are a sufficient supply of green electricity; infrastructure for hydrogen, CO_2 and (geothermal and residual) heating; steady multi-year subsidies to make investments in the green transition economically rewarding; innovation-friendly legislation (e.g. allowing the recycling of resources).

Source: This box is based on the information provided in the six (regional) industry cluster plans.

Notes

[1] In the rest of this report, the industry corresponds to the manufacturing sectors (NACE Rev. 2 10-33).

[2] Source: Eurostat, energy supply and use by NACE Rev. 2 activity.

[3] Among which Tata Steel, Shell, BP, Zeeland Refinery, Chemelot Site Permit, Esso, Dow, Yara Sluiskil, Air Liquide, ExxonMobil.

[4] Source: Climate Agreement.

3. Zero-emission scenario for Dutch industry

This chapter describes and discusses a zero-emission 2050 scenario for the Dutch industry. It is based on a detailed account of the technologies currently used in the largest firms and emitting sectors in the Netherlands, and on the technologically feasible decarbonisation options for each of them. The robustness of the results is assessed through a comparison with other available decarbonisation scenarios.

Note: the zero-emission 2050 scenario for the Dutch industry described in this chapter was originally designed by Berenschot (2020[1]).

3.1. Scope and methodology for the zero-emission 2050 scenario

3.1.1. Scope of the emissions

All Scope 1 (direct emissions) and Scope 2 (emissions from electricity use) emissions are included in the modelling. Scope 3 emissions are not systematically included as the identification of these emissions would be challenging and result in double counting with the emission reduction in other sectors that would be difficult to identify. Nevertheless, the scope of this chapter includes emissions linked to energy carriers that are not used as a source of energy, but as a non-energetic feedstock. Three prominent examples are crude oil in refineries, natural gas in ammonia production and coal use in the steel making process.

3.1.2. Methodology used for determining the zero-emission scenarios

For all four sectors, the zero-emission scenarios are the result of a desk study, which comprised a review of the technologies and their future prospects along with a modelling exercise. In a second step, this scenario was discussed with experts and industry representatives through four sectoral meetings, and amended accordingly.

In most industries, there are, in fact, different options to reach zero emissions. At the 2050 horizon, the economic and technological uncertainty is such that these scenarios can only be considered as plausible and dependent on certain assumptions and choices, regarding technologies (e.g. green hydrogen production), policies (e.g. development of CO_2 pipelines to enable carbon transport) and the economic environment (e.g. ability of the Netherlands to maintain a comparative advantage in heavy industries).

The price evolution of different technologies and energy carriers, including due to public policies, is one of the main sources of uncertainty surrounding the scenario. The scenario is not based on cost-optimisation and does not rely on a price trajectory for the energy carriers and corresponding technologies. It rather rests on an analysis of the feasibility of the different options based on the available knowledge[1], the current fuel prices and some expected developments (such as the construction of hydrogen or CO_2 infrastructure for the main clusters). The report includes an analysis of the impact of the cost of energy carriers on the Dutch economy.

Rather than using available global scenarios, a particular effort has been made to design these routes according to the specificities of the Dutch industry and its clusters. These have been validated with industry representatives and experts. This chapter also comprises a comparison of this scenario with other available scenarios.

Scenarios were modelled using the Energy Transition Model (ETM) of Quintel Intelligence. This model simulates the Dutch energy system and allows users to adjust parameters such as demand developments, efficiency improvements and new technologies. The ETM does not provide cost-optimal dynamic paths to carbon neutrality but quantifies the impact of external technological and economic assumptions on all energy carriers from supply to conversion, final demand and CO_2 emissions. The ETM is an open source model and is publicly available at www.energytransitionmodel.com.

3.2. A zero-emission chemical sector

The chemical sector in the Netherlands consists of 445 companies, representing 45 000 employees and 1.7% of gross domestic product (GDP)[2] in 2018. It is organised around five main clusters and three main economic activities: NACE 2014 - manufacture of organic basic chemicals (including petrochemicals), NACE 2015 - manufacture of fertilisers and nitrogen compounds (including ammonia and its derivatives) and NACE 2013 - manufacture of other non-organic chemicals.

The chemical sector is responsible for 44% of Scope 1 industrial emissions in the Netherlands and is the top emitter in the industry. The chemical sector is also the main user of electricity, and is responsible for a sizeable part of Scope 2 emissions. Finally, the widespread use of oil and natural gas as a non-energetic feedstock in the petrochemical industry is also a major source of indirect emissions.

In this section[3], hydrogen production is not considered to be part of the chemical sector (Box 2.1 gives further details on the different ways to produce hydrogen). In theory, hydrogen production is included in the chemical sector (NACE 2011 – Manufacture of industrial gases). Since the production of hydrogen is for the time being limited and hydrogen is considered as an energy carrier, rather than as a chemical product, the production of hydrogen is left out of the scope of this chapter. However, it is briefly discussed in the final section of this chapter and the challenges of a carbon-neutral hydrogen production is discussed in Chapter 7.

3.2.1. Description of the sector and the main processes

The majority of the Dutch chemical industry is based around the **five industry clusters**: Rotterdam, Chemelot, Smart Delta Resources, Noord-Nederland (Delfzijl and Emmen)[4], and Amsterdam/ Noordzeekanaal (Box 3.1, Box 2.2 and Figure 3.1). These clusters are integrated parks with pipeline grids for a whole range of chemical substances including acetic acid, acetylene, chlorine, ethylene, hydrogen chloride, methanol, naphtha petroleum, natural gas, nitrogen, oxygen, propylene and steam. The clusters are well connected with multiple transport options and pipelines for chemical products and industrial gases between them.

Figure 3.1. CO_2 emissions of the Dutch chemical industry by community

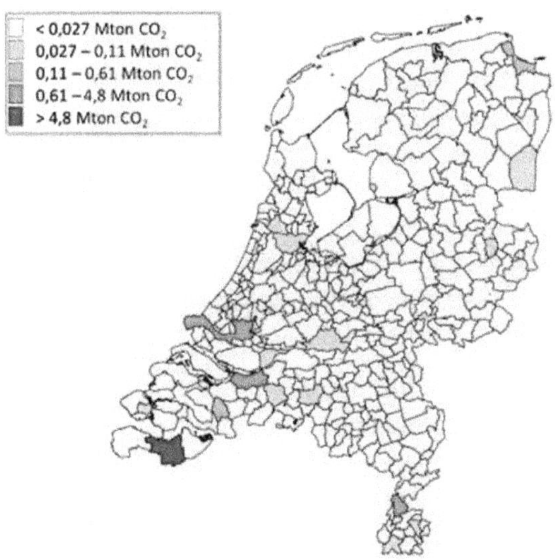

Source: www.emmissieregistratie.nl, Berenschot calculations.

Petrochemicals make up the largest part of the chemical industry with about 60% of the energy use and 75% of feedstock within the chemical industry (Figure 3.2). Ammonia and derivatives represent 10% of the energy use of the chemical industry and use about 13% of feedstock. Non-organic base chemicals take up about 10% of the total energy demand of the chemical industry, but use less feedstock compared to the other product groups, about 6% of the total. Industrial gases, rubber and plastics, colouring and paints, and other chemicals make up the rest of the energy usage (20%) and feedstock usage (6%) within the chemical industry.

Figure 3.2. Consumption of energy carriers, as energy and feedstock, in the chemical sector, 2015 (PJ)

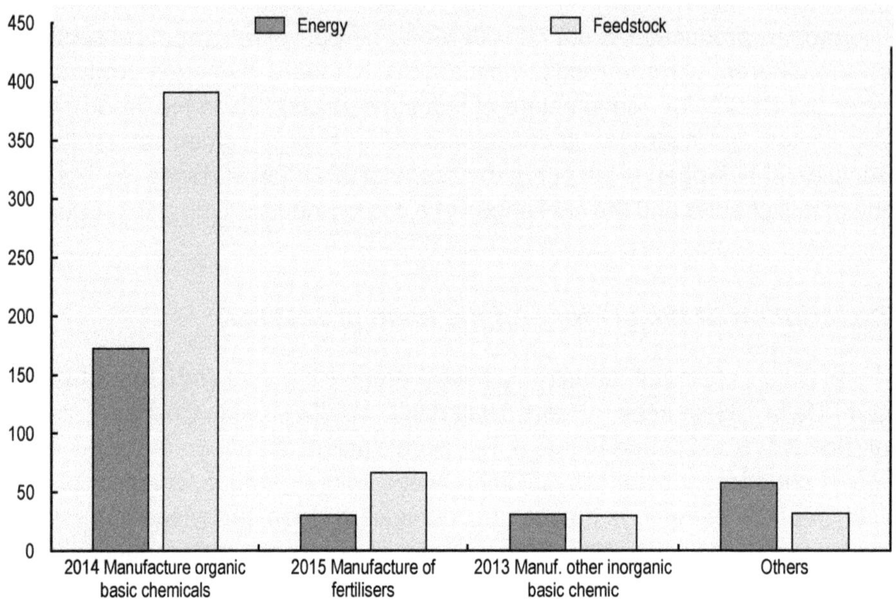

Source: CBS, Energy balance sheets by sector.

The **petrochemical industry** uses naphtha, benzene, diesel and other products from refineries as inputs. The chemical companies then produce, for example, propylene and ethylene by cracking naphtha. Six naphtha crackers produce most of the petrochemical building blocks (e.g. ethylene, propylene and BTX) and intermediates. These intermediates are used by many economic sectors, including downstream firms in other chemical industries. Many products, ranging from construction materials to paints and from car parts to mobile phone components, rely on these intermediates. This industry mainly rests on petroleum products and heat as energy sources Figure 3.3). Even if not linked to Scope 1 or 2 emissions, this sector relies heavily on petroleum products as a non-energetic feedstock (Figure 3.4), which are cracked to produce smaller molecules. In the Netherlands, the petrochemical industry is based in Chemelot, Smart Delta Resources (Zeeland) and Rotterdam-Moerdijk.

The **fertilisers and nitrogen compounds industry** produces urea, nitric acid, melamine, acrylonitrile and caprolactam. Most of these nitrogen compounds require the production of ammonia via Haber-Bosch synthesis, which consists of combining hydrogen and nitrogen. The hydrogen (in this part of the industry) is obtained through steam-methane reforming (combining methane/natural gas with steam).[5] Therefore, the main source of energy and the main feedstock in this industry is natural gas (Figure 3.3 and Figure 3.4). In the Netherlands, the fertiliser industry is located in Chemelot and Smart Delta Resources (Zeeland).

The Dutch chemical sector also produces non-organic base chemicals such as chlorine, caustic soda and vinyl chloride. These products are made with the help of an electrolysis process. In this part of the industry, the main energy carrier is natural gas, along with heat and electricity. Petroleum products are the main feedstock.

Figure 3.3. Consumption of energy carriers as energy source, by type and subsector, 2015 (PJ)

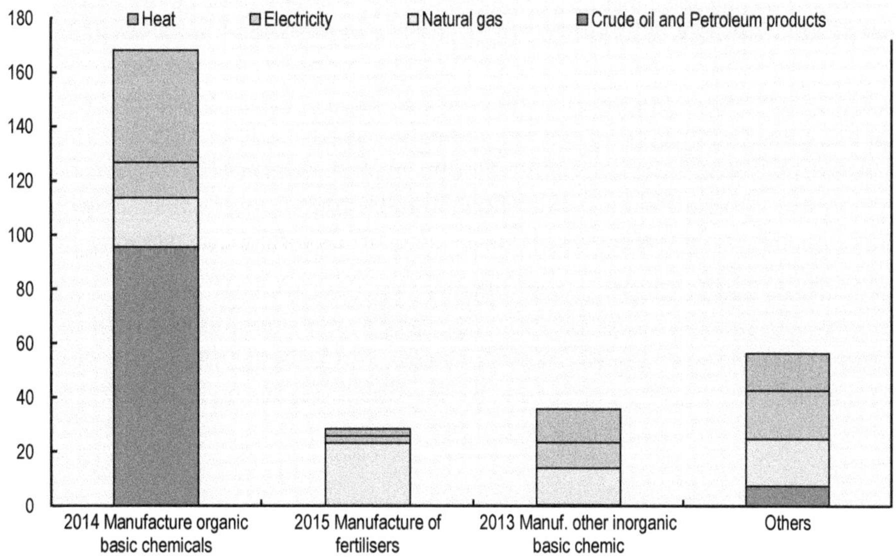

Source: CBS, Energy balance sheets by sector.

Figure 3.4. Consumption of energy carriers as feedstock, by type and subsector, 2015 (PJ)

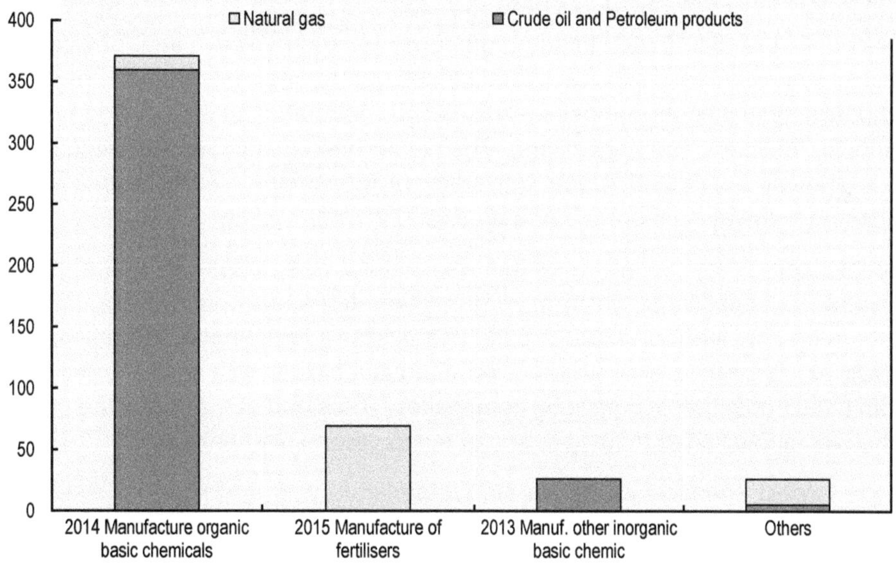

Source: CBS, Energy balance sheets by sector.

3.2.1. Main technologies to be implemented for the reduction of emissions

The sectoral professional association of the Dutch chemical industry published a roadmap towards emission reduction. It identifies six solutions that can be used in combination (Figure 3.5): closure of the material chain, alternative feedstock, energy efficiency, renewable energy, carbon capture and storage (CCS), and sustainable products. It is likely that the sector will decarbonise by deploying these technologies sequentially. For example, CCS could be a first option to reduce emissions in the near-term for certain chemicals (e.g. CCS is relatively affordable in ammonia production because of the concentration of the CO_2 stream), whilst in the intermediate future the electrification of processes may become viable (e.g. electrification of crackers), and in the long-term be followed by a shift towards circular feedstock.

Renewable energy and **energy efficiency** are promising routes for the three main products of the chemical industry. Research into electric crackers is being undertaken and could reduce direct CO_2-emissions. Electric boilers, heat pumps and mechanical vapour recompression can contribute to the electrification of the heat production within the industry. Using heat pumps and mechanical vapour recompression would also lead to energy savings due to high coefficients of performance.[6] Once the electricity from the grid is also carbon free, electrification will lead to further emission reductions. However, in the short term, depending on the electricity source, electrification might also lead to higher emissions.

Geothermal heat could be used to supply sustainable heat to the chemical industry, but the applicability is low. Not all locations are suitable, especially for high-temperature geothermal heat in the Netherlands. According to Platform Geothermie, DAGO, Warmtenetwek and EBN (2018[2]), only 25 PJ is projected to be used by the manufacturing industry and mostly by the food processing industry and the paper industry.

Box 3.1. The five clusters and the chemical sector

Amsterdam has an upcoming chemical industrial area. Currently, only chemical companies with a relatively limited energy consumption are located here. Potential connections with Tata Steel in IJmuiden to exchange hydrogen, oxygen and CO_2 are being investigated by Dow and by Nouryon. The cluster is connected to two universities: Vrije Universiteit (VU) Amsterdam and the University of Amsterdam (UvA). The Amsterdam cluster is also strongly connected to institutes of the Science Park, for example the Van't Hoff Institute for Molecular Sciences.

Chemelot, located in the South of Limburg, produces petrochemicals and nitrogen compounds. Historically built as a one company site, it is characterised by a strongly integrated energy infrastructure. The site now houses multinational companies like SABIC (petroleum chemicals and plastics) and OCI Nitrogen (ammonia, fertilisers and derivatives). The cluster also comprises the Brightlands Chemelot Campus and is strongly connected to the University of Maastricht. Chemelot has a river harbour, railway, pipeline and highway connections and an airport in close vicinity.

Delfzijl is characterised by its availability of salt and natural gas, thanks to a sea harbour, railway, pipeline and highway connections, which provide multiple transport opportunities. The focus of this chemical cluster is on chlorine (non-organic base chemicals) and methanol (organic base chemicals) and their derivatives. Emmen is a relatively small chemical cluster with a strong focus on high-tech development and the production of polymers, composites, fibres and yarns. It has the ambition of being a knowledge hub for innovation and applied research into green fibre chemistry.

Rotterdam is the largest chemical cluster in the Netherlands with its focus on base chemicals and petrochemicals. It houses 45 chemical companies and 5 oil refineries. The port of Rotterdam aims to integrate its complex with those of Antwerp (Belgium), Moerdijk (also in the Rotterdam Cluster), Terneuzen and Vlissingen (both in Zeeland/Smart Delta Resources) to create one large chemical cluster. The pipeline of Air Liquide is an example of integration of these clusters. The combination of the Rotterdam Harbour, a rail connection to Germany and pipelines to transport raw materials and products provides outstanding transport opportunities for the Rotterdam cluster.

The Zeeland (Smart Delta Resources) chemical cluster is connected to the Terneuzen mainport, which enables deep sea transport. It houses large chemical companies like Dow, Yara, and Sabic. The focus of the cluster is on petrochemicals and ammonia and derivatives. In this cluster, there is a strong aim to use each other's (waste) products, targeting industrial symbiosis. The cluster is tightly connected to the Belgian industry in East-Flanders.

For some processes that require high temperatures, electrification may be difficult or costly. In that case, the industry is expected to rely on alternative and sustainable fuels such as **hydrogen, pyrolysis oil or biomass**.

Finally, **CCS** will be required to capture CO_2 emitted by the remaining fossil fuel combustion and the industrial processes themselves.

Regarding feedstock, a combination of circular, bio-based and synthetic feedstock should replace fossil feedstock. Nowadays, the chemical industry uses mainly virgin fossil feedstock to produce chemical products. Once these products are at their end-of-life, they are typically burned in waste incinerators and emit CO_2. The only way to avoid these Scope 3 emissions (from the point of view of the chemical industry) is to capture carbon in waste incinerators or to compensate for these emissions elsewhere.

Figure 3.5. Main technological options for a carbon-neutral chemical sector

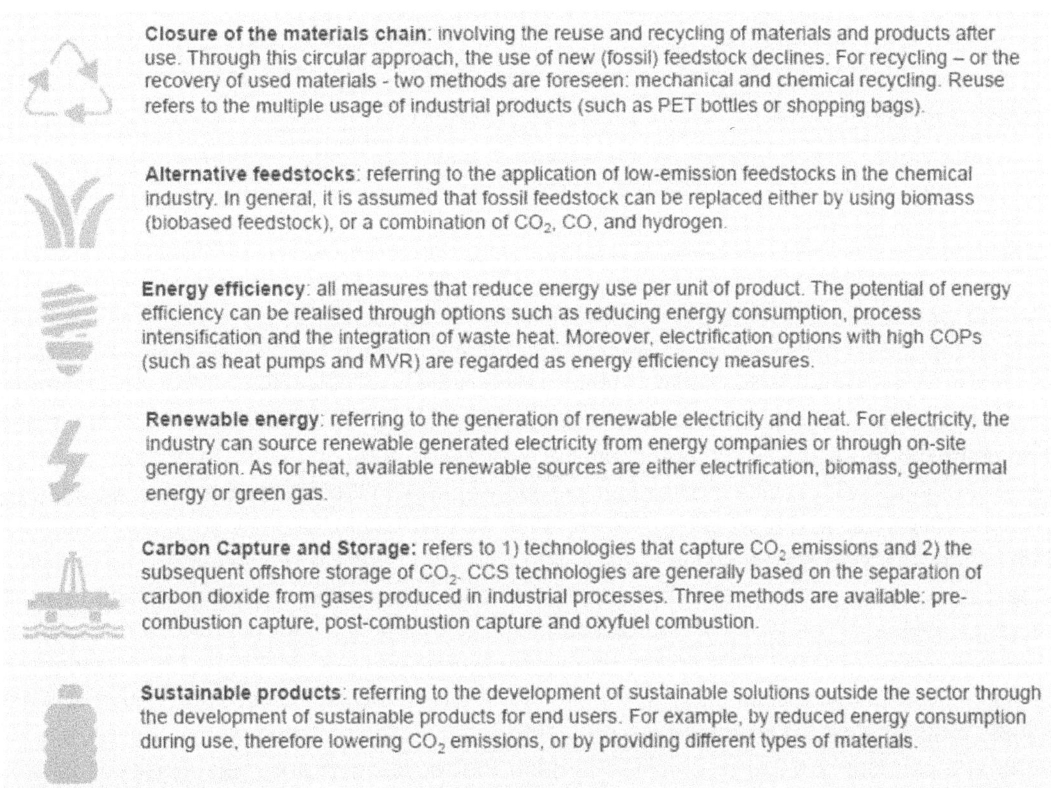

Source: Ecofys and Berenschot (2018[31]).

Mechanical or chemical recycling, in contrast, could transform these products into new feedstock, thereby **closing the materials chain**. Mechanical recycling (e.g. of plastics) does not involve any chemical reaction. In chemical recycling, the molecules are usually broken down into smaller components that can be used as feedstock. Mechanical recycling could be performed on 40-50% of the end-of-life streams. Chemical recycling could recycle potentially 30% of the streams, through the production of pyrolysis oil, which can then be used as a feedstock for crackers in the petrochemical industry.

However, this will not suffice to decarbonise the feedstock of the chemical sector. First, recycling all materials is unfeasible. Second, recycling itself is not a 100% efficient process. Third, virgin materials will be needed to meet a growing future demand. Still, a well-functioning recycling industry will be necessary to decarbonise chemical products.

In order to become to a fully carbon-neutral system, the use of alternative sustainable feedstock is necessary: bio-based feedstock and synthetic feedstock.

Bio-based feedstock can be carbon-neutral if it is harvested in a sustainable way.[7] The carbon released when burning bio-based chemical products at the end of their life corresponds to carbon that was captured in the air by the biomass. This cycle is thus neutral on the amount of carbon in the atmosphere.

Synthetic organic feedstock is produced from two types of molecules:

- Hydrogen required for ammonia production or the petrochemical industry can be blue (methane – possibly green methane – combined with CCS) or green (electrolysis from water). As reaching a 100% capture rate is technologically difficult and potentially very costly, blue hydrogen entails residual CO_2 emissions, which need to be compensated elsewhere to reach carbon-neutrality. Green hydrogen as a by-product from cracking of bio-based feedstock is a route that could be interesting for some ammonia plants that already benefit from integration with the petrochemical industry (e.g. in Smart Delta Resources). For ammonia production at sites that receive renewable electricity, green hydrogen from electrolysis might be more logical, electricity is then also required to produce the nitrogen with air separation units and to supply the compressors for the Haber-Bosch process.
- Synthetic carbon monoxide or carbon dioxide is also fully carbon neutral as long as the carbon comes from a sustainable source (e.g. waste).

Applying these technologies in the subsectors

Regarding the **petrochemical industry**, decarbonisation could occur, in particular, from electrification, and also from the use of hydrogen as an energy source, sustainable heat, CCS, closure of the material chain and the use of alternative feedstock. Electrified crackers are under development and together with heat pumps, mechanical vapour recompression (MVR) and electric boilers will lead to large electrification within the chemical industry. For some chemical processes requiring high temperatures, hydrogen, pyrolysis oil or biomass will provide the solution to supply energy to the processes. CCS would require the development of transport and storage capacities, such as the Porthos project, which would connect the Rotterdam cluster and depleted oil fields of the North Sea via a pipeline (for storage).The relative weight of naphtha-based routes is an asset to the sector in case a share of feedstock is replaced by biobased materials (e.g. bioethanol) because of the relative flexibility of crackers. An alternative route is based on the methanol-to-olefins process. This option would ensure the reduction of Scope 3 emissions, but at the expense of a higher energy consumption, since the methanol production is energy-intensive. It is assumed that synthetic methanol will be produced out of hydrogen in 2050, combined with sustainable sources of CO_2 (Wong and van Dril, 2020[4]) or obtained through the recycling of polymers (gasification process).[8] The 2050 scenario therefore assumes that the hydrogen needed for methanol can become green hydrogen produced from electrolysis. This could either be made on site or bought from suppliers from other origins:

- The plausible pathway for **fertilisers and nitrogen compounds** is based on hydrogen, CCS to capture the process emissions and renewable electricity (Batool and Wetzels, 2019[5]).
- Hydrogen could both be produced on site as well as supplied via a pipeline. If produced onsite, green hydrogen, although more costly to produce, may be chosen for landlocked-sites that cannot easily ship the CO_2 captured for the production of blue hydrogen. This is especially the case for Chemelot (about a third of the ammonia production), where the green hydrogen route via green methane from the crackers with sustainable feedstock is preferred. The site in Zeeland is capable of producing green hydrogen on site from electrolysis, because of the close proximity to offshore wind power.
- Renewable electricity is needed to supply the nitrogen through air separation units and to drive the compressors for the Haber-Bosch process.

For **other non-organic base chemicals**, the route to zero-emission focuses on electrification and, to a lesser extent on the use of biomass (Scherpbier and Eerens, 2020[6]).

3.2.2. Sectoral assumptions

For the chemical sector, a 1% annual growth from 2020 to 2050 is assumed, except for fertilisers and nitrogen compounds, for which a 0.5% annual growth is assumed, due to the implementation of a more circular agriculture and a smaller increase of fertiliser use.

The energy efficiency of the sector will increase over the same period by 0.5% annually, which is half of the historical trend. It is in the lower range of estimates available in other analyses such as Wong and van Dril (2020[4]). However, the switch to new technologies could lead to higher energy usage. For the fertilisers and nitrogen compounds industry, the energy efficiency improvements follow the historical trend of 1% growth per year, since the processes will remain similar.

3.2.3. Zero emission scenario: Impact on energy carriers and emissions

Scope 1 and 2 business as usual (BAU) emissions from the Dutch chemical sector would reach 32 $MtCO_2$, which can be reduced to net-zero by 2050 using the scenario above. Figure 3.6 shows the contributions of each technology to the reduction of emissions. The uptake of hydrogen as an energy source will contribute to around 30% of emission reductions. Electrification and the transition to renewable electricity will contribute to 27% of emission reductions. The rest of emission reductions come from the shift to sustainable heat (16%), energy efficiency (14%) and the use of biomass (7%). The latter will not only reduce Scope 3 emissions, but also reduce direct emissions when used as a source of energy in crackers.

Figure 3.6. Emission reductions in the Dutch chemical sector by technology in 2050 compared to BAU under zero-emissions scenario

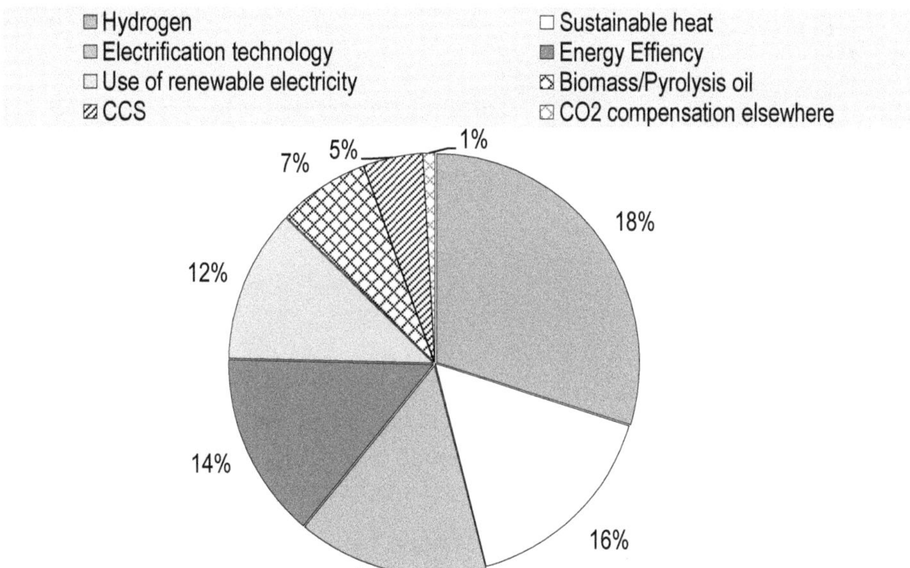

Note: The contribution of "use of renewable electricity" corresponds to the abatement of the 2015 Scope 2 emissions, which would be overturned by completely shifting to renewable electricity sources by 2050. The contribution of "electrification technology" corresponds to additional electricity needed to reach the carbon neutrality objective in 2050, assuming that this additional electricity is also renewable and carbon-neutral.
Source: Berenschot.

Regarding the energy carriers used as an **energy source** (Figure 3.7), hydrogen would provide 60 PJ by 2050. Due to electrification, electricity demand rises from 45 PJ in 2015 to 104 PJ in 2050. Finally, 36 PJ of pyrolysis oil and biomass are used in 2050. In parallel, the use of fossil fuels (petroleum products and natural gas) is reduced to 26 PJ of oil, compensated with CCS. It would correspond to crackers operated in clusters with an easy access to CO_2 transport and storage under the North Sea.

Regarding the energy carriers used as **non-energetic feedstock** (mainly in the petrochemical sector), a significant part of the petroleum products and natural gas are replaced with hydrogen, biomass and pyrolysis oil. To ensure sustainability, the 27 PJ of methane required in 2050 can be produced through green methane. In this scenario, however, 167 PJ of oil would be used as non-energetic feedstock by the chemical sector. The strong interactions between the petrochemical sector and the refineries requires a joint effort, as refineries should produce the decarbonised feedstock that is necessary for the petrochemical sector. Some of the main petrochemical plants are indeed owned by firms operating in the refinery sector, and highly integrated with the refineries (Shell Moerdijk, Shell Pernis and ExxonMobil Rotterdam plants).[9]

Figure 3.7. Energy carriers for Dutch chemical sector (energetic and non-energetic) in 2015 and 2050 (PJ)

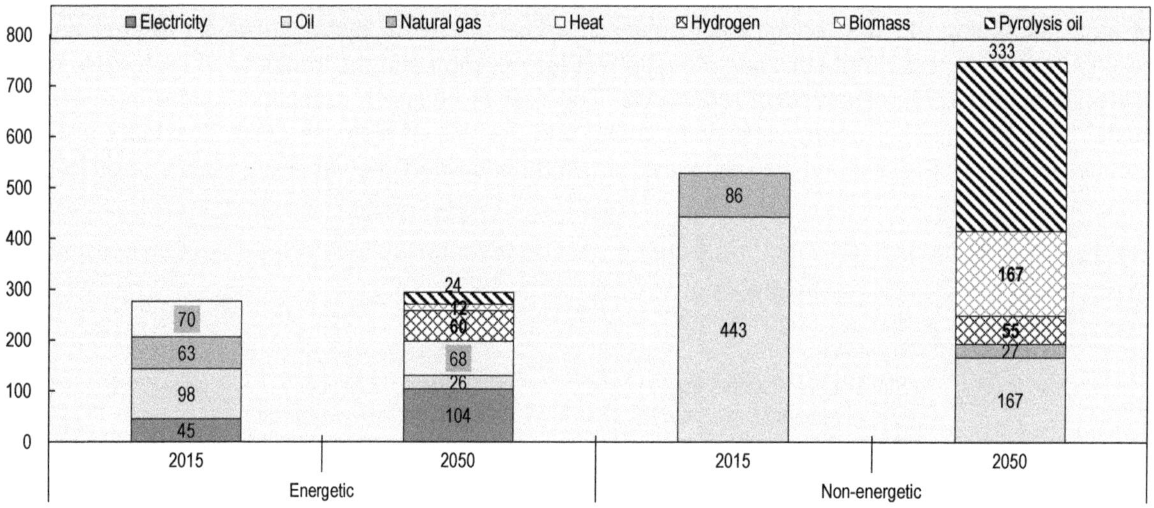

Source: Berenschot.

3.3. A zero-emission refineries sector

The refineries sector in the Netherlands consists of 20 companies, representing 5 000 employees[10] and 0.2% of GDP[11] in 2018. The refineries sector corresponds to the ISIC sector 192 "Manufacture of refined petroleum products".

The Dutch refineries sector is responsible for 21% of Scope 1 industrial emissions, and is the second main emitter in the industry. The sector heavily relies on crude oil as an energy source, but firstly, as a feedstock for the production of the petroleum products.

3.3.1. Description of the sector and the main processes

The six main refineries are located near the North Sea. Five of them are located in the port of Rotterdam: BP, Gunvor Petroleum Rotterdam, Vitol (Koch) and ExxonMobil. The five refineries are affiliated with the organisation "Port of Rotterdam", which is the authority that manages, operates and develops the port and industrial area of Rotterdam and is responsible for all shipping activities. Zeeland Refinery is located in Zeeland and is part of the Smart Delta Resources cluster (Figure 3.8). The sea ports lead to a high accessibility for supply of crude oil. Therefore, all refineries have excellent sea transport facilities.

When crude oil is refined into smaller products, it is sold and transported to other sectors, and notably to the chemical industry. Petroleum products are transported to the hinterland via pipelines, rail and inland shipping. In total, the Dutch refineries have access to an extensive pipeline network of 1 500 kilometres. These pipelines connect Rotterdam with different chemical clusters in the Netherlands, Germany and Belgium. This infrastructure for intermediates offers a safe, efficient and environmentally-friendly transport solution. Most pipelines are 'dedicated connections' that transport one particular product to one particular company. However, some pipelines are used by multiple companies.

Figure 3.8. CO_2 emissions of the Dutch refineries by community

Source: www.emmissieregistratie.nl, Berenschot calculations.

In the refining process, useable oil products are produced from crude oil. This consists of four main processes: distillation, cracking in order to process the intermediates into lighter products, increasing the quality of the intermediates, and blending.

In the **distillation** process, crude oil is separated into products as naphtha, gasoline, kerosene and gasoil. The first distillation is performed at atmospheric pressure, and the remaining parts are distilled under vacuum condition, resulting in vacuum gasoil. All six Dutch refineries are able to carry out these processes.

Some products from the distillation process, such as vacuum gasoil, need a further treatment to be converted into lighter products, using **catalytic cracking** ('hydrocracking').

Some products are then processed to increase their quality. For example, the amount of sulphur is decreased for the production of fuels (due to fuel standards). Catalytic reformers are used to increase and stabilise this product quality.

Unsurprisingly, the main energy carrier in this industry is crude oil and petroleum products. However, 13% of the energy consumed in this sector comes from natural gas and 11% from heat (Figure 3.9).

Figure 3.9. Consumption of energy carriers, as energy and feedstock, in the refineries, 2015 (PJ)

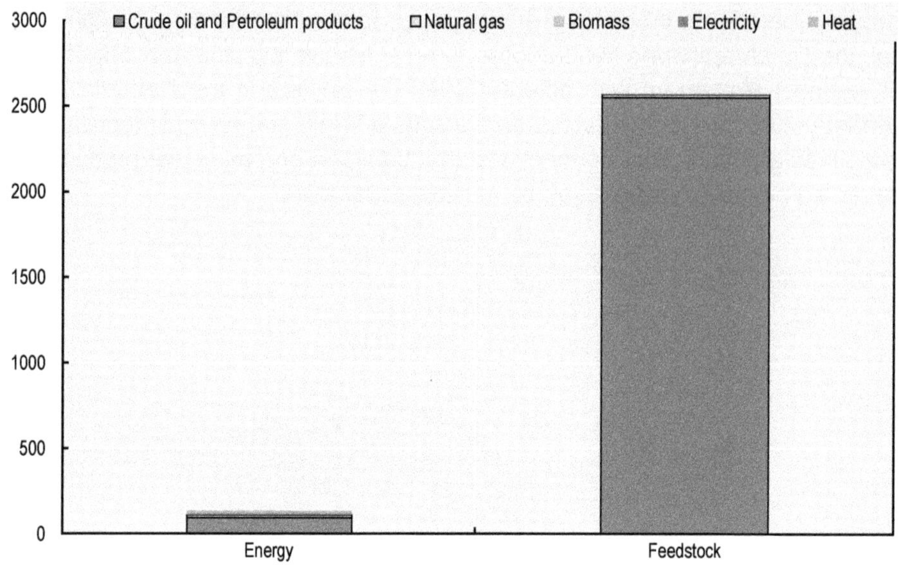

Source: CBS, Energy balance sheets by sector.

3.3.2. Main technologies to be implemented for the reduction of emissions

Oliveira and Schure (2020[7]), as part of **the MIDDEN project** (Manufacturing Industry Decarbonisation Data Exchange Network), analysed different decarbonisation options for the refinery sector. These options, shown in Table 3.1, are divided into four categories: 1) Carbon capture; 2) Fuel substitution; 3) Feedstock substitution; 4) Process design.

Table 3.1. Relevant decarbonisation options for the refinery sector

Category	Technology	Relevant process
Carbon capture	Carbon capture and storage	For the production of blue hydrogen (see below), for fluid catalytic cracking and for gasification units
Fuel substitution	Electric furnaces	Replacement for all gas-fired equipment
	Electric boilers	Steam boilers
	Electric shaft equipment	Steam Turbine replacement
	Blue/green hydrogen as fuel	Replacement for all gas-fired equipment
Feedstock substitution	Co-Processing (5-10%) pyrolysis bio oil	CO-feed for fluidised catalytic cracking
	Blue/green hydrogen as feedstock	Hydro treating and hydrocracking processes
Process design	Standalone plant for biofuels production via pyrolysis bio oil upgrading	Alternative for production of liquefied petroleum gas (LPG), gasoline, kerosene and diesel
	Biomass gasification using the Fischer-Tropsch process for fuels production	Alternative for production of LPG, gasoline, kerosene and diesel

Source: Berenschot, from Oliveira and Schure (2020[7]).

The **port of Rotterdam** (2018[8]) made a clear pathway towards zero emissions. This pathway consist of three consecutive steps, which include the four options of Oliveira and Schure (2020[7]). The three steps can roughly be described as: 1) energy efficiency & infrastructure; 2) change in processes; 3) change in feedstocks.

The first step takes place between 2020 and 2025 and focuses on energy efficiency through the optimisation of processes and the use of excess energy. In parallel, infrastructure for heat, CO_2, steam, electrification and hydrogen is further developed. For instance, excess energy can be supplied as heat towards green houses and residential housing. To prepare for future electrification, the electricity grid is upgraded. Carbon Capture and Storage is used in prototypes and test facilities. The reinforcement of the electricity grid and CCS rather apply to other sectors of this cluster, in particular the chemical sector.

In the second step (2025-30), the first changes towards a new energy system are made. In this step, electrical and hydrogen infrastructure is further reinforced. The first pilots of renewable heating processes are performed through electrification (low and middle temperature) or the use of hydrogen fuelled boilers (high temperature).

Electrification of heating process is possible in multiple ways, e.g. heat pumps for water or electric boilers for steam. The cracking in the refinery industry uses high temperatures that cannot be produced with electricity, but hydrogen (blue and green) can be a solution.

One example of the use of the production of blue hydrogen in the refinery industry is the project H-Vision. The project partners are piloting a large-scale production and utilisation of blue hydrogen. In H-vision, blue hydrogen is produced using natural gas and refinery fuel gas. CO_2 captured during production will be safely stored in depleted gas fields under the North Sea or used as a building block for basic chemicals such as methanol (Section 3.2). H-vision anticipates the development of green hydrogen, which will produced via electrolysis using power sourced from renewable sources like offshore wind farms.

The third step (2030-50) relies on the assumption that green electricity and green hydrogen are largely available. It will require an extensive infrastructure for both energy carriers and be well connected to the industrial facilities in the Rotterdam-Moerdijk cluster. Under these conditions, hydrogen and electrical heating can be implemented on a large scale.

This step also entails the development of a recycling and biomass hub in Rotterdam, through pilots. Dutch refineries would in particular use the pyrolysis process to transform polymers into naphtha.

3.3.3. Sectoral assumptions

Refineries' capacity is projected to decrease by 40% between 2020 and 2050, since the demand for fossil fuels will significantly drop.

The energy efficiency of the sector is assumed to remain constant over the period, since investments will mainly be directed towards new sustainable technologies.

3.3.4. Zero emission scenario: Impact on energy carriers and emissions

Scope 1 and 2, BAU emissions from the Dutch refineries sector would reach 4.3 $MtCO_2$, which can be reduced to net-zero by 2050 using the scenario outlined above. Figure 3.10 shows the contribution of each technology to the emission reduction. The uptake of hydrogen, in particular for the cracking process, will contribute to more than 70% of emission reductions. The rest of the emission reductions come from the use of biomass (16%), shift to sustainable heat (7%) and renewable electricity (5%).

Figure 3.10. Emission reductions in the Dutch refineries sector by technology in 2050 compared to BAU under zero-emissions scenario

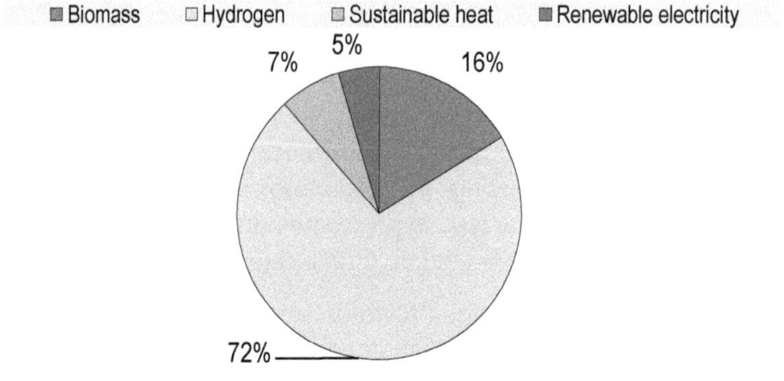

Source: Berenschot.

Regarding the energy carriers used as **energy source** (Figure 3.11), the introduction of hydrogen leads to the use of 40 PJ by 2050. In addition, 13 PJ come from biomass in 2050. The majority of the heating processes is based on hydrogen-fired boilers and, to a smaller extent biomass-fired. The heat provided by the energy sector to the refineries becomes sustainable. In parallel, the industry ceases to use fossil fuels (crude oil and natural gas) as an energy source.

Regarding the energy carriers used as **non-energetic feedstock**, a third of crude oil is replaced with biomass and pyrolysis oil. In this scenario, however, 950 PJ of oil would still be used as non-energetic feedstock by the refinery sector, and exported outside Europe. This is one of the major uncertainties of this scenario, which relies on the world demand for fossil-based refined products and the ability of the Dutch refineries to compete with foreign refineries in this market. If this would prove impossible, refineries would have to rely more on non-fossil feedstock, which raises questions on the availability of biomass and pyrolysis oil, or to downsize more than in this scenario.

Figure 3.11. Energy carriers for Dutch refineries sector (energetic and non-energetic), 2015 and 2050 (PJ)

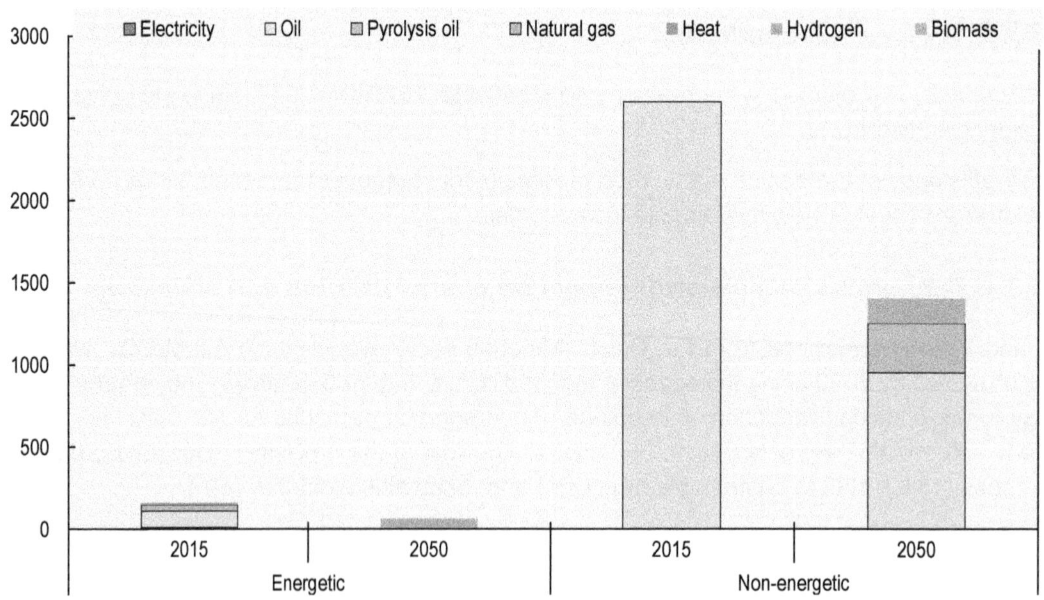

Source: Berenschot.

3.4. A zero-emission metallurgical sector

Dutch metallurgy includes primary and secondary steel, non-ferrous metals (i.e. aluminium and zinc), and foundries. According to the OECD STAN database, 175 companies work in Dutch metallurgy, employing 21 000 people and representing 0.4% of GDP in 2018. Annual turnover is approximately EUR 9 billion, whilst the export value is EUR 5.7 billion (Berenschot, 2020[11]), of which 85% goes towards the rest of the European Union (Berenschot, 2020[11]).

Dutch metallurgy is responsible for 23% of industry's total CO_2 emissions in 2015 (9.2 $MtCO_2$ direct and indirect). Figure 3.12 depicts the spatial clustering of these emissions throughout the Netherlands. The bulk of emissions comes from primary steel production (presently owned by Tata Steel) in IJmuiden, which produces high quality steel for engineering, automotive and packaging industries. This plant produces approximately 7 Mt of steel in 2015, out of a global primary steel production of 1 800 Mt. Dutch aluminium is predominately used in planes, automotive, trains, ships, packaging and construction industries (Aldel, 2020[9]). DAMCO Aluminium is the largest producer of primarily aluminium in Delfzijl, whilst anode production for primarily aluminium production is concentrated in Vlissingen (Smart Delta Resources cluster) and Rotterdam. Smaller re-melters (for secondary aluminium production) are scattered across different sites throughout the Netherlands. Zinc is located in Budel (at Nyrstar Budel B.V.) and is not part of any cluster. Foundries mainly recast steel and aluminium, with the largest facility in Zaltbommel (again, not part of any cluster). Casting is a type of metalworking that involves pouring liquid metal into a mould or form to create complex and detailed parts. For example, steel castings are used when cast iron cannot deliver enough strength or shock resistance, for instance steel castings are found in gears, railroad truck frames, hydroelectric turbines, amongst other applications.

Figure 3.12. Scope 1 CO_2 emissions of the Dutch metallurgy by community

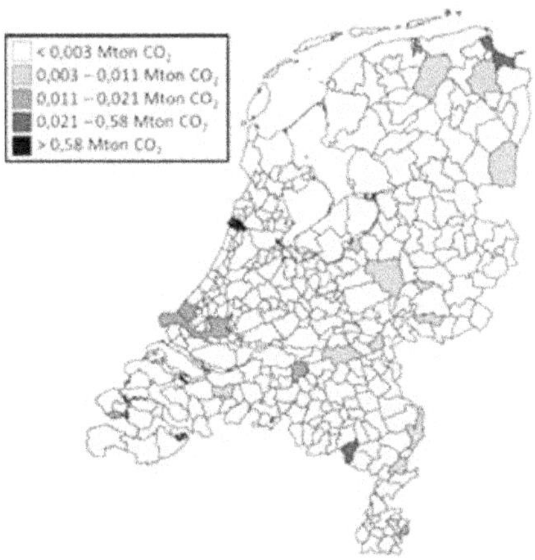

Source: www.emmissieregistratie.nl, Berenschot calculations.

3.4.1. Description of the sector and the main processes

Figure 3.13 shows that primary steel production accounted for nearly 91% of these Scope 1 CO_2 emissions from Dutch metallurgy (6.29 $MtCO_2$) in 2015. With the exception of primary steel, Scope 2 emissions (grey bars in Figure 3.13) are estimated to account for over half of the CO_2 emissions in each of the subsectors (i.e. secondary steel, non-ferrous metals and foundries) (Berenschot, 2020[11]). In other words, *indirect emissions from purchased energy* are estimated to be greater than direct emissions from facilities in these sub-sectors (blue bars in Figure 3.13), estimated by Berenschot (Berenschot, 2020[11]).

Figure 3.13. Breakdown of CO_2 emissions from Dutch metallurgical industry in 2015

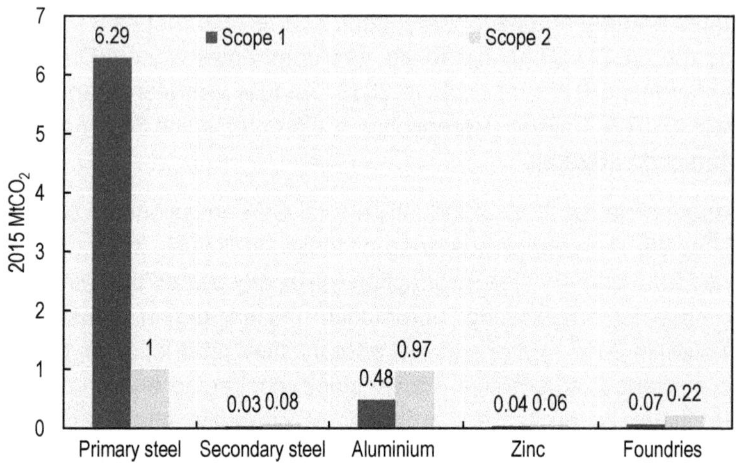

Note: Scope 1 emission estimates for primary steel includes coke production.
Source: Berenschot.

Scope 1 emissions from primary steel production partly comes from the continued use of Blast Furnaces-Blast Oxygen Furnaces (BF-BOF) at their site in IJmuiden. BF-BOF converts coal to coke, which is then mixed with iron ore (imported into the Netherlands) to produce high quality steel products.

The main energy carrier in Dutch primary steel production is, by consequence, coal (as it is a feedstock which falls under Scope 3). Approximately 80.2 PJ was consumed in primary steel production in 2015 (as shown in Figure 3.14), followed by natural gas (9.7 PJ) and electricity (6.8 PJ).

Tata Steel mill in IJmuiden already operates with very high energy performance and is one of the most efficient steel mills in the world. IJmuiden gradually reduced energy usage by 32% between 1989 and 2017 via heat insulation, innovated design, start-stop management, and hot connect – all of which reduces Scope 1 and Scope 2 emissions. Incremental energy efficiency improvements, however, have become increasingly difficult, meaning that energy efficiency improvements will be insufficient to reduce its remaining emissions (Jägers and Kiesewetter, 2018[10])).

Tata Steel used 1.4 Mt of steel scrap in 2015 (approximately 20% of its production volume). Blast furnaces, though, can only accommodate about 16% of scrap in input volume. Even with this limited amount, however, maximising scrap in BF-BOF has been shown to reduce Scope 1, 2, and 3 emissions in Sweden Germany, India, China (Rammer, Millner and Boehm, 2017[11]). This said, alternative production processes (e.g. HIsarna, see below) are likely to allow a higher share of scrap and its uptake could be constricted by its availability in addition to its quality.

In contrast to primary steel production, the majority of emissions from secondary steel production are estimated to be Scope 2 (Figure 3.13). In particular, the use of electricity, which amounted to 0.5 PJ.

The bulk of non-ferrous emissions comes from aluminium, rather than zinc, as shown in Figure 3.13. Primary and secondary aluminium production is combined in Figure 3.13, totalling 1.45 $MtCO_2$ (Scope 1 and 2). The bulk of CO_2 emissions in 2018 were indirect from electricity use (i.e. Scope 2), meaning largely depending on the Dutch electricity mix. Total Dutch aluminium production reached 180 kilotonnes (kt) in 2015 (out of a global primary aluminium production of 58 456 kt).[12] The annual production of secondary aluminium in the Netherlands is unknown. Globally, however, the share of secondary production has remained at around 32% of primary production since 2000 (IEA, 2020[12]).

Figure 3.14. Energy carriers in the production of primary and secondary steel in 2015 (PJ)

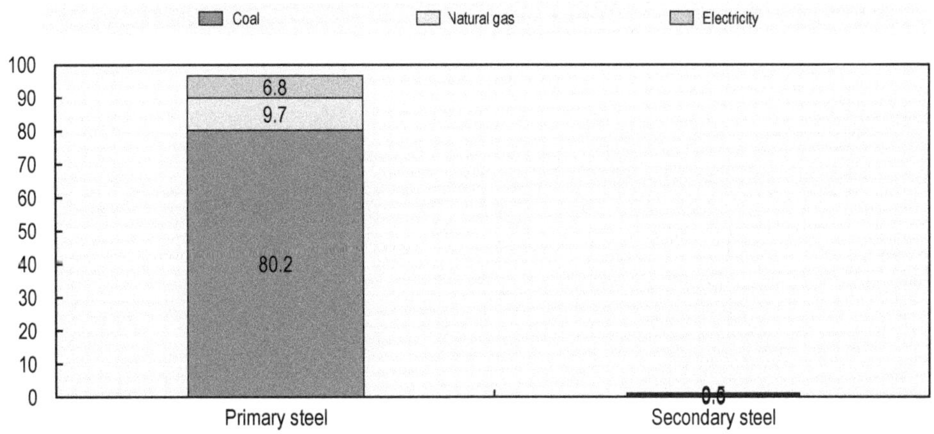

Source: Berenschot (2020[1]).

Dutch primary aluminium production uses the Hall-Héroult process for smelting, which relies on electrolysis to reduce aluminium oxide (also known as alumina) using carbon anodes. Scope 1 emissions are, therefore, a by-product of the efficiency of this process and the consumption of carbon anodes (approximately 480 kt of anodes were produced in the Netherlands in 2015, mainly for export). Scope 1 emissions additionally come from the step preceding Hall-Héroult of converting the bauxite into alumina.

Primary aluminium production is approximately ten times more energy-intensive than secondary production globally (IEA, 2020[12]) . Therefore, further reductions could be reached by greater uptake of scrap in the sector. At Aldel's aluminium production facility 33% of the inputs were scrap. Scrap-based production tends to cost less than primary production, so the key constraint is scrap availability (similar to steel). Aluminium recycling rates are relatively high, but aluminium, as many other metals, remains locked in products until their end of life, so even with better collection rates there is an upper limit on the potential for recycled production.

Dutch Zinc production led to 0.1 $MtCO_2$ in 2015 (Scope 1 and 2, as shown in Figure 3.13) (producing 283 kt of zinc in 2015). Similar to aluminium, electricity is the main energy carrier, and therefore, the bulk of emissions are indirect from electricity. Taken together (combining aluminium and zinc), non-ferrous production used 8.4 PJ of electricity and 3.1 PJ of natural gas (Figure 3.15).

Dutch Foundries produced approximately 95 kt of metal in 2015, which produced 0.2 $MtCO_2$ in 2018 (Scope 1 and Scope 2, as shown in Figure 3.13). The process for foundries is to heat metal (typically, steel and aluminium) to very high temperatures in furnaces that is then poured into moulds; these furnaces can be fuelled by coal (0.4 PJ consumed in 2015), natural gas (0.5 PJ in 2015), or electricity (1.5 PJ) (Figure 3.15). The choice of furnace depends on the alloys of the metal. Switching away from the use of coal and natural gas furnaces towards electric or hydrogen furnaces would contribute to reducing Scope 1, potentially at the expense of Scope 2 emissions, whilst decarbonising Dutch electricity would reduce Scope 2. Presently, Dutch foundries only use about 5% of scrap in production; therefore, increasing the use of scrap could further reduce emissions. Similar to aluminium, a key limitation is the availability of scrap.

Figure 3.15. Energy carriers in the production of non-ferrous metals and foundries in 2015 (PJ)

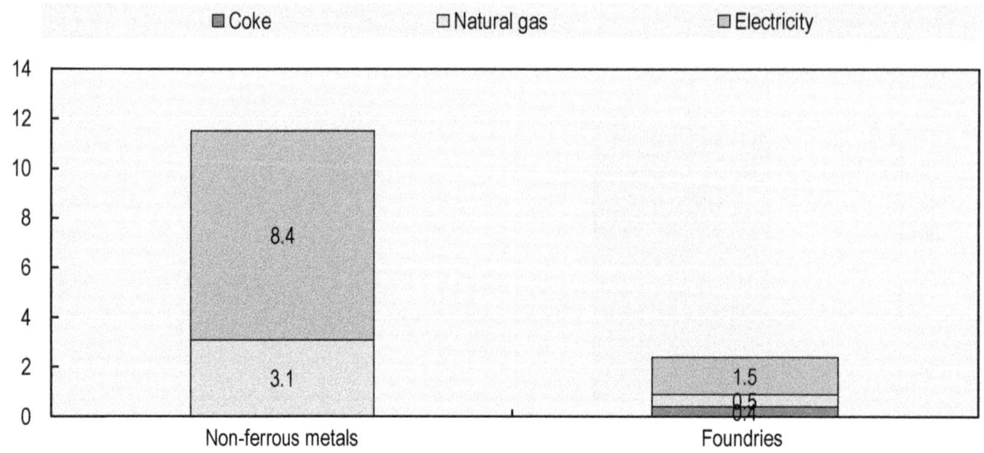

Source: Berenschot (2020[1]).

3.4.2. Main technologies to be implemented for the reduction of emissions

As shown in the previous section, the sources and processes of emissions in each of the subsectors in Dutch metallurgy are diverse.

Reducing emissions from primary steel production requires alterations to the BF-BOF production process. The options presently under consideration by Tata Steel include HIsarna, CCS and direct reduction ironmaking (DRI). If, in the future, Tata Steel sells the IJmuiden plant to SSAB, prioritisation and options under consideration could change:

- Tata Steel already has a pilot plant with HIsarna in IJmuiden and is investing in a larger scale plant in India but could see IJmuiden as another potential location for a larger-scale plant. The HIsarna process avoids the pre-processing steps that involve iron ore and coke when using BF-BOF. HIsarna is a new type of furnace in which iron ore is directly injected and liquefied in a high-temperature cyclone so that it drips to the bottom of the reactor where powder coal is injected. The two react into liquid pig iron. The pilot HIsarna plant achieves reductions of energy and CO_2 emissions of approximately 20%. In addition, the flue gas is highly concentrated CO_2, which is well suited for CCS. HIrsana can accommodate larger quantities of scrap than BF-BOF, up to 35%.
- Tata Steel is expecting to capture 4Mt of CO_2 by 2030 (from the BF-BOF). The Athos project, with the participation of Tata Steel, is exploring storage options in the North Sea. However, CCS will never capture 100% of CO_2 emissions, meaning reaching net-zero requires offsetting or negative emissions. The options for negative emissions include, for example, direct air capture and CCS at green methane sites.
- Another way to produce steel is DRI. Iron ore is reduced in a DRI reactor to Direct Reduced Iron using hydrogen, which can then be processed in an Electric Arc Furnace or BF-BOF. The Direct Reduced Iron is stable and can be transported. Therefore, iron reduction could occur in a country with abundant renewables, and then shipped to the Netherlands for steel production.

Scope 2 emissions associated with production could be reduced by investing in renewables on the Tata site or by using offshore wind farms nearby (directly or through the electricity grid).

For non-ferrous production, the biggest portion of emissions are secondary and are, therefore, dependent on the energy efficiency of processes and the decarbonisation of the electricity mix in the Netherlands. For primary aluminium production, Scope 1 emissions could be reduced by improving the Hall-Héroult process, such as prebaking carbon anodes, using liquid aluminium or further optimising electrolysis (e.g. central point feeder, magnetic compensation or slotted carbon anodes), in addition to using alternative baking methods (e.g. inert or bio based anodes).

Similar to non-ferrous metals, the Scope 2 emissions from Foundries could be tackled by improving energy efficiency and decarbonising Dutch electricity. Switching from coal and natural gas furnaces to either electricity or hydrogen would reduce Scope 1 emissions, if the electricity were from renewables.

Scope 1 and 2 emissions from Dutch metallurgy could be further reduced by greater use of scrap in production – producing greater amounts of secondary steel and aluminium, along with greater use of recycled metals in foundries. All these processes use less energy, and therefore, fewer emissions than primary production. The ability to shift towards greater use of scrap in production is restricted by its availability, in addition to technical requirements regarding the quality of the metal (e.g. steel).

3.4.3. Zero-emission scenario: Sectoral assumptions (energy efficiency, demand growth)

The plausible scenario assumes 1% annual growth for all product groups from 2020 to 2050. To reach net-zero by 2050:

- Tata Steel switches to the HIsarna production process with CCS[13]. Scrap is used to the greatest extent possible in primary production, i.e. up to 35% of inputs. As mentioned above, negative emissions will still be needed elsewhere in the Netherlands to compensate for the remaining CO_2 from primary steel production (approximately 0.9 Mt). Secondary steel companies will switch to scrap to the greatest extent possible.
- The efficiency of electrolysis in primary aluminium production improves its efficiency, whilst there is greater uptake of recycled aluminium. Both of which increase the energy efficiency of aluminium production, which means that even though the production grows by 45% by 2050, energy demand only grows by 20%.
- Foundries will largely switch to using scrap (to the greatest extent possible) and induction ovens with electric heating in 2050. In some circumstances, replacing gas-fired ovens with hydrogen will be viable. In 2050, 70% of energy consumption is assumed to be from electricity and 30% from hydrogen.

3.4.4. Zero emission scenario: Impact on energy carriers and emissions

BAU emissions from Dutch metallurgy would reach 10.3 $MtCO_2$, which can be reduced to net-zero by 2050 using the scenario above. Figure 3.16 shows the total amount of $MtCO_2$ reduced by technology in 2050 compared to the BAU and the percentage of this reduction. The uptake of CCS in primary steel production accounts for nearly half of emission reductions in Dutch metallurgy compared to BAU in 2050 (4.9 $MtCO_2$), whilst the HIsarna production process reduces 1.4 $MtCO_2$ compared to BAU, approximately 14%. It is worth noting that not all emissions from Dutch metallurgy can be reduced in 2050, and therefore, nearly 9% of emission reduction would rely on compensation. Since the capture rate of CCS is assumed to remain below 100%, HIsarna will still emit CO_2 and reaching net-zero carbon emission will need an offset via negative emissions elsewhere (green in Figure 3.16).

In 2050, Dutch metallurgy substantially decreases its usage of coal as an energy carrier for energetic use by 60%, from 25 PJ in 2015 to 10 PJ in 2050, and to a lesser extent natural gas, which decreases from 9 PJ to 7 PJ between 2015 to 2050 (Figure 3.17), but fossil fuels are still used to provide energy to the HIsarna process. Dutch metallurgy ups their usage of electricity as an energy carrier by 53% from 17 PJ in 2015 to 26 PJ in 2050 and hydrogen to 5 PJ (Figure 3.17). The **consumption of coal for non-energetic use increases from 2015 to 2050 from 55 PJ to 64 PJ**, which is due to the expected increase in production of primary steel.

Figure 3.16. Emission reductions in Dutch metallurgy by technology in 2050 compared to BAU under zero-emissions scenario

Emissions in $MtCO_2$, percentage of emission reductions achieved with a given technology

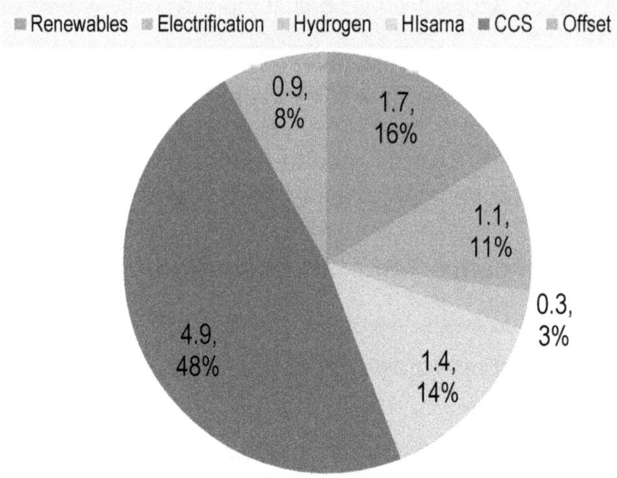

Note: Offset means that emissions are reduced elsewhere, for example, via direct air capture and CCS at green methane sites. The contribution of "Renewables" corresponds to the abatement of the 2015 Scope 2 emissions, which would be overturned by completely shifting to renewable electricity sources by 2050. The contribution of "Electrification" corresponds to additional electricity needed to reach the carbon neutrality objective in 2050, assuming that this additional electricity is also renewable and carbon-neutral.
Source: Berenschot (2020[1]).

Figure 3.17. Energy carriers for Dutch metallurgy (energetic) in 2015 and 2050 (PJ)

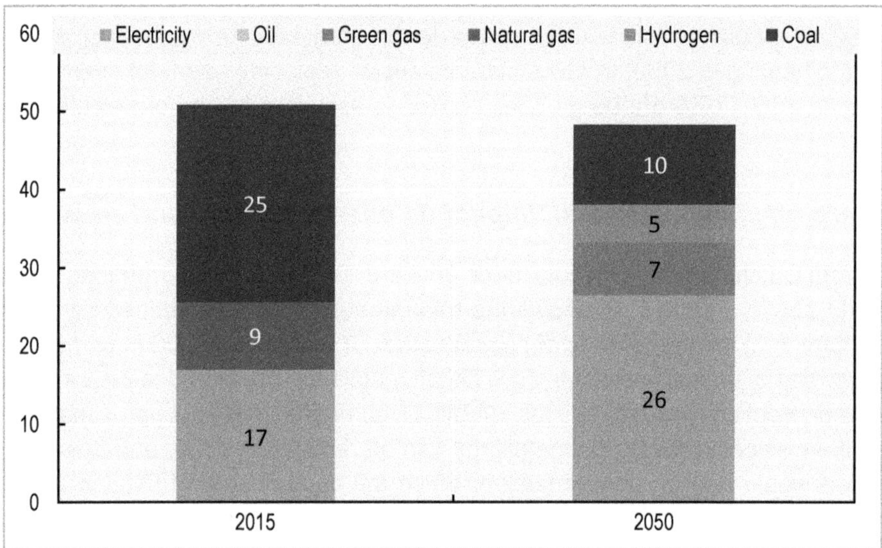

Source: Based on Berenschot (2020[1]).

3.4.5. Major uncertainties in the 2050 zero emission scenario

The uncertainty in the zero emission scenario for metallurgy stems from: 1) the availability of scrap in 2050; 2) the potential change in ownership of IJmuiden steel mill; 3) the potential for negative emissions; and 4) future demand for the products:

- The ETM assumes that all production processes use the maximum amount of scrap possible, e.g. 35% of the inputs into HIsarna would be scrap and foundries could conceivably use up 100%. Whether or not this quantity of scrap will be available in 2050 remains to be seen. First, many of these metals are locked into products with long lifetimes (e.g. automobiles, airplanes, buildings). In addition, the quality of the scrap varies substantially, which can affect the integrity and strength of the reprocessed metal. Therefore, even if scrap is available, not all of it may be usable, for the high quality steel products produced in IJmuiden. Moreover, the infrastructure needs to be in place to properly process scrap, e.g. waste processing facilities. If this cannot all be provided domestically, then there needs to be trade in scrap and waste. However, a number of hurdles remain to freely trade in scrap and waste. On the one hand, even within the European Union, scrap metal can be classified as waste, scrap, or even hazardous waste, all of which has varying regulations preventing it from being freely traded amongst member states. Other countries have import or export bans of scrap, e.g. Russian smelters and re-melters lobbied for an export ban on scrap aluminium to ensure greater supply domestically. As a result, a number of hurdles would need to be overcome in order to ensure access to scrap required in the zero emission scenario.
- Tata Steel may sell the IJmuiden plan to SSAB Steel in Sweden in 2021. The zero emission scenario for steel was heavily informed by Berenschot's consultation with Tata Steel and their desire to concentrate on HIsarna, Direct Reduction Ironmaking, and CCS. SSAB could prioritise these avenues differently for decarbonisation – e.g. HYBRIT –, which is under exploration in Sweden. SSAB is developing this in Sweden with LKAB and Vattenfall, and it is presently constructing its pilot plant. Essentially, this involves the direct reduction of iron into steel with hydrogen and renewable energy using EAF, which generates water as a by-product instead of carbon dioxide. If the preferred technologies for the decarbonisation of steel changes with the ownership of the IJmuiden plant, then the need for negative emissions could, in turn, also change.
- Lastly, Berenschot assumes a growth of 1% in demand for all metallurgical products until 2050 – with no differentiation between carbon content. However, recent policy developments suggest that greater differentiation between products may emerge over the next few decades. For example, the Border Carbon Adjustment under consideration in the EU would differentiate between the carbon content of products under the EU Emission Trading System (ETS), for example, for steel and cement. Therefore, the demand for metallurgical products may not be evenly distributed, which could, in turn, influence preferences and opportunities for technologies to decarbonise.

3.5. A zero-emission food processing sector

The Dutch food-processing industry (excluding agriculture) is diverse: vegetables; coffee, tea and cacao; fish and shellfish; potatoes; meat; livestock feed; tobacco; dairy; beverages and grain products. Despite this diversity, the processes can be *broadly* grouped into: 1) heating; and 2) mechanical processes. The former includes pasteurisation, distilling, melting, evaporating, baking and cooling, most of which require temperatures between 60 to 250°C, provided by natural gas and electricity. The latter includes mixing, filtering, packaging, or grinding, typically driven by electric motors.

Approximately 2 500 companies operate in the Dutch food processing industry, and it employs 127 000 people and represents 2.3% of GDP in 2018[14]. The total output is EUR 72 billion, and around 50% of products are consumed in the Netherlands. The industry has EUR 32 billion value in exports, mainly to Belgium, France, Germany and the United Kingdom. The sector is relatively scattered throughout the Netherlands (when compared to chemicals, metallurgy and refineries) as shown below in Figure 3.18.

Figure 3.18. CO_2 emissions of the Dutch food-processing sector by community

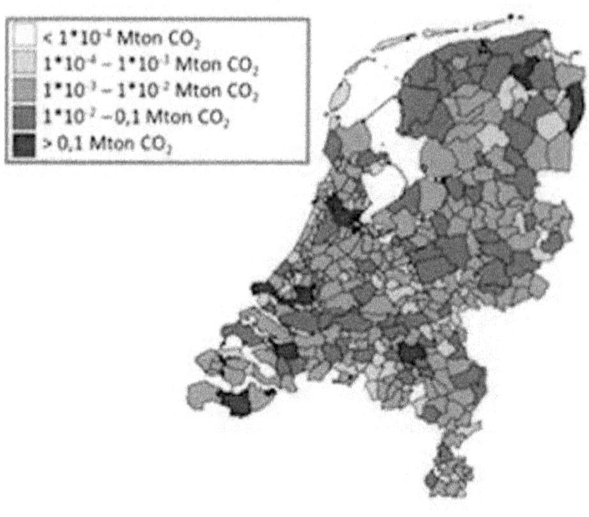

Source: www.emmissieregistratie.nl, Berenschot calculations.

Figure 3.19. Main energy carriers for food industry

As a share of total primary energy use

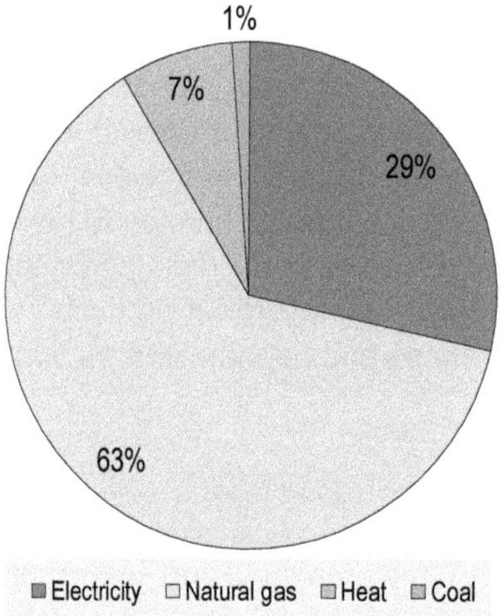

Source: Based on Berenschot (2020[1]).

3.5.1. Description of the sector and the main processes

The food processing industry is responsible for approximately 6.5 $MtCO_2$, approximately 4.0 Mt are Scope 1 and 2.5 Mt are Scope 2 in 2018. Therefore, the bulk of emissions are Scope 1, meaning from the production process itself. The main energy source used in the food industry is natural gas. Other important sources include electricity and heat, whereas coal is marginal (Figure 3.19).

The plausible scenario for the Dutch food industry to reach net-zero is based on dairy, sugar and potato, and then expanded to the rest of the food industry (since these are fairly representative of the challenges for decarbonisation and technological options in the sector). The Dairy industry accounts for about 10% of the annual turnover (around EUR 7.5 billion), potatoes approximately 2.5% of annual turnover (EUR 2 billion), and sugar approximately 1% of the annual turnover (around EUR 0.7 billion):

- The energy consuming processes in the dairy industry include heat treatments, evaporation, spray drying and membrane processing. All of which need temperatures of less than 100°C, with the exception of evaporation, where some processes exceed 250°C. Most of these processes are heated with a central steam network that uses gas boilers.
- The typical processing of potatoes is to sort, wash, peel, wash, cut, blanch, fry, cool, freeze and then package. Frying is the most energy-intensive portion of potato processing, which traditionally uses gas boilers. For peeling and blanching, pressurised steam is used, which is reached with temperatures of less than 100°C. All other steps in potato processing use electricity. The final energy consumption is approximately 3.3 gigajoule (GJ) per tonne today.
- There are two large sugar factories in Netherlands that process beets. The process includes juice production (uses water at 75°C), juice purification (90°C), juice evaporation (130°C), and crystallisation (at 80°C). Each of these steps uses steam or electricity provided by a combined heat and power installation, which uses a natural gas boiler.

3.5.2. Main technologies to be implemented for emission reductions

Since most of the processes take place at a relatively low temperature, heat pumps are a viable option to replace gas boilers in all three subsectors, which could then use available waste heat as an input. For example, in dairy processing, the waste heat from spray drying (60 to 90°C) could be reused as an input to heat pumps to provide temperatures of up to 140°C.

However, heat pumps are not the only option to replace gas boilers, other options exist in each of the subsectors:

- In the dairy industry, using a sustainable boiler in the central steam network would greatly reduce emissions – e.g. electric, green gas,[15] or hydrogen. Each of the three has its advantages and disadvantages. An electric boiler is a relatively simple device compared to a gas boiler (since they do not use complicated heat exchanges). However, electric boilers require a substantial amount of electricity; therefore, generating the power to run the electric boiler could also increase Scope 2 emissions depending on the emission intensity of the power supply. Hydrogen is still very expensive and its future distribution, transmission and storage still need to be resolved, especially for scattered production facilities as in the case of the dairy industry. The advantage of green gas is that it can already be used in current boilers, but its future availability is unsure. The central steam network used by the dairy industry could likewise switch to the use of geothermal energy, where possible.
- For the frying stage in the potato industry, green gas is a viable option. A large part of the potato is unused in processing, and this waste could be used for biogas or green gas (meaning it does not face the same hurdles as the dairy industry). Green gas has the same characteristics as natural gas, so could be used directly in the boiler, whilst biogas currently does not fit. Other substitutes include electric boiler (which is already commercially available) and hydrogen.
- Sugar processing is similar to frying. Sugar processing produces a lot of waste, which could be used to create biogas or green gas that could then replace natural gas in the combined heat power installation.

Mechanical Vapour Recompression is a viable option for higher temperatures, for example, in the evaporation stages in the dairy and sugar processing. A MVR reduces steam consumption. It makes use of the evaporator's outlet steam and increases its pressure and temperature by compressing it, thereby making it suitable for evaporation of moisture from the incoming feed. This lowers the steam consumption significantly, thereby saving energy.

3.5.3. Zero-emission scenario: Sectoral assumptions (energy efficiency, demand growth)

The plausible scenario assumes 1% annual growth for all product groups from 2020 to 2050 and energy efficiency gains of 1.2% per year. The plausible scenario applies to the entire food industry, not only dairy, potatoes and sugar.

In the plausible scenario, low-temperature processes are substituted with either electrification or heat pumps, and the high temperature processes are substituted by boilers on green gas or hydrogen. The exact choice of technology depends on local circumstance, e.g. a large supply of waste as seen in the potato and sugar industries enhances the viability of green gas. Modelling by Berenschot projects a mix of technologies in the food industry by 2050: geothermal (10%), electrification (40%), green gas/bio gas (25%) and hydrogen (25%).

3.5.4. Zero-emission scenario: Impact on emissions and energy usage

Under BAU, Scope 1 and 2 emissions would increase to 7.5 $MtCO_2$ by 2050. To reach net-zero, energy efficiency improvements account for nearly 36% of reductions (2.6 $MtCO_2$) followed by the uptake of green gas, which leads to further reductions of 27% (1.9 $MtCO_2$), as shown in Figure 3.20. The remainder of reductions are accounted for via the uptake of hydrogen, electrification, and renewables.

The uptake of these technologies eliminates the use of coal and natural gas as energy carriers by 2050, as shown in Figure 3.21, whilst substantially increasing electricity usage from 23 PJ to 42 PJ. In addition, the use of hydrogen, heat and biomass, which were not being used at all in 2015, also become key in 2050.

Figure 3.20. Emission reductions in the Dutch food industry by technology in 2050 compared to BAU under zero-emissions scenario

Emission reductions (in $MtCO_2$ and as a share of total emissions reductions) achieved with a given technology

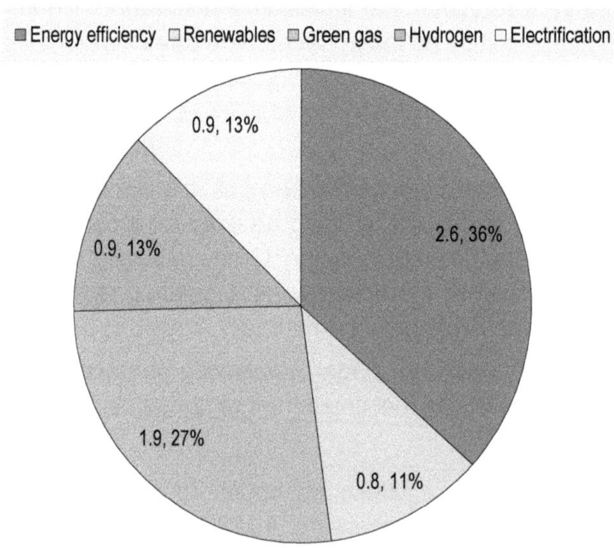

Note: The contribution of "Renewables" corresponds to the abatement of the 2015 Scope 2 emissions, which would be overturned by completely shifting to renewable electricity sources by 2050. The contribution of "Electrification" corresponds to additional electricity needed to reach the carbon neutrality objective in 2050, assuming that this additional electricity is also renewable and carbon-neutral.
Source: Based on Berenschot (2020[11]).

Figure 3.21. Energy carriers for Dutch food industry in 2015 and 2015

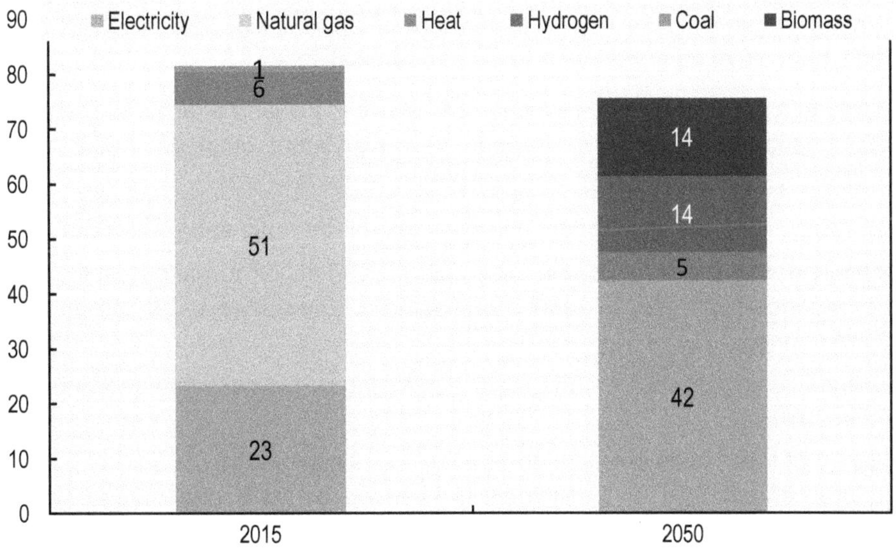

Source: Based on Berenschot (2020[1]).

3.5.5. Major uncertainties in the zero emission scenario

The food processing industry is very heterogeneous, with different processes used from product to product. Therefore, the decarbonisation pathway will vary from company to company. The zero emission scenario above provides a sketch of what could happen, but reality will likely deviate for any particular company.

3.6. The zero-emission scenario for the industry

This section presents the aggregated scenario, by combining the scenarios for the four above-mentioned subsectors. It does not correspond to the whole Dutch manufacturing sector, but accounts for more than 85% of emissions, and 37% of value-added.

3.6.1. Role of the different technologies for the zero-emission scenarios over time

Hydrogen is the technology that contributes the most to the transition, accounting for more than 25% of emission reductions (Figure 3.22). It plays a role in the four subsectors but is of major importance in the chemical sector and refineries.

Five other technologies are of prime importance for the transition of the Dutch industry, each of them accounting for 10-16% of emission reductions:

- Energy efficiency, mainly in the chemical and food processing sectors.
- Electrification of industrial processes. This is an important solution for the provision of heat, except for processes requiring a high temperature, such as in refineries.
- CCS is required in the chemical and metallurgical industry because these sectors will remain partly reliant on fossil fuels in 2050. Because reaching a capture rate of 100% would imply extreme costs, the capture rate is assumed to be 85% and the remaining emissions will need to be compensated elsewhere.

- Renewable electricity. Assuming that the energy production (out of the scope of this report) shifts to renewable sources (wind and solar for instance), the Scope 2 emissions of the industry will be abated.
- Sustainable heat plays an important role in the chemical sector.

Even though energy efficiency leads to a reduction of 15% in the use of energy, the technology analysis shows that carbon neutrality is achieved through very significant changes in the **energy sources** (Figure 3.23):

- Hydrogen, which is barely used today, becomes one of the main energy carriers (119 PJ in 2050).
- The electricity demand almost doubles to reach 177 PJ in 2050, without including the electricity needed to produce hydrogen. In 2050, this electricity is assumed to be carbon neutral, avoiding Scope 2 emissions.
- Other sustainable energy sources (pyrolysis oil, green gas, biomass and sustainable heat) amount to 148 PJ in 2050.
- Finally, 36 PJ of fossil fuels are needed in 2050, combined with CCS and carbon compensation. Although the consumption of fossil fuels is reduced by 91% and natural gas is completely eliminated, oil and coal remain necessary in the chemical and metallurgical industries respectively.

Figure 3.22. Role of different technologies in emission reductions, 2015-50

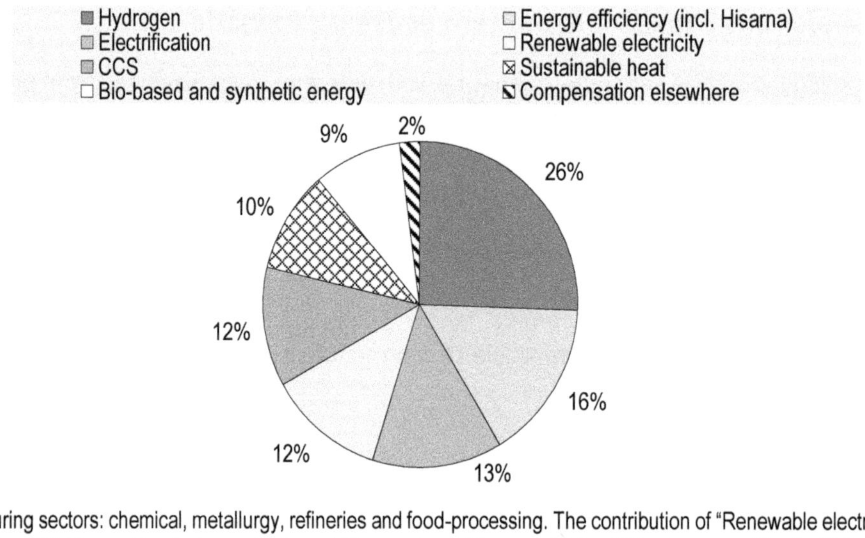

Note: Four manufacturing sectors: chemical, metallurgy, refineries and food-processing. The contribution of "Renewable electricity" corresponds to the abatement of the 2015 Scope 2 emissions, which would be overturned by completely shifting to renewable electricity sources by 2050. The contribution of "Electrification" corresponds to additional electricity needed to reach the carbon neutrality objective in 2050, assuming that this additional electricity is also renewable and carbon-neutral.
Source: Based on Berenschot (2020[1]).

The use of energy carriers as feedstock also drastically changes (Figure 3.24). Whereas the energy content of feedstock is reduced by more than 40%, fossil feedstock experiences a 60% decrease. Crude oil is still used in refineries and part of the refined products are then used as a feedstock for petrochemicals. In addition, coal is still needed as a source of carbon atoms for the production of steel. Sustainable feedstock (pyrolysis oil, hydrogen and biomass) represents close to 35% of the energy carriers used as feedstock in 2050.

Figure 3.23. Energy carriers used as an energy source in 2050 (PJ)

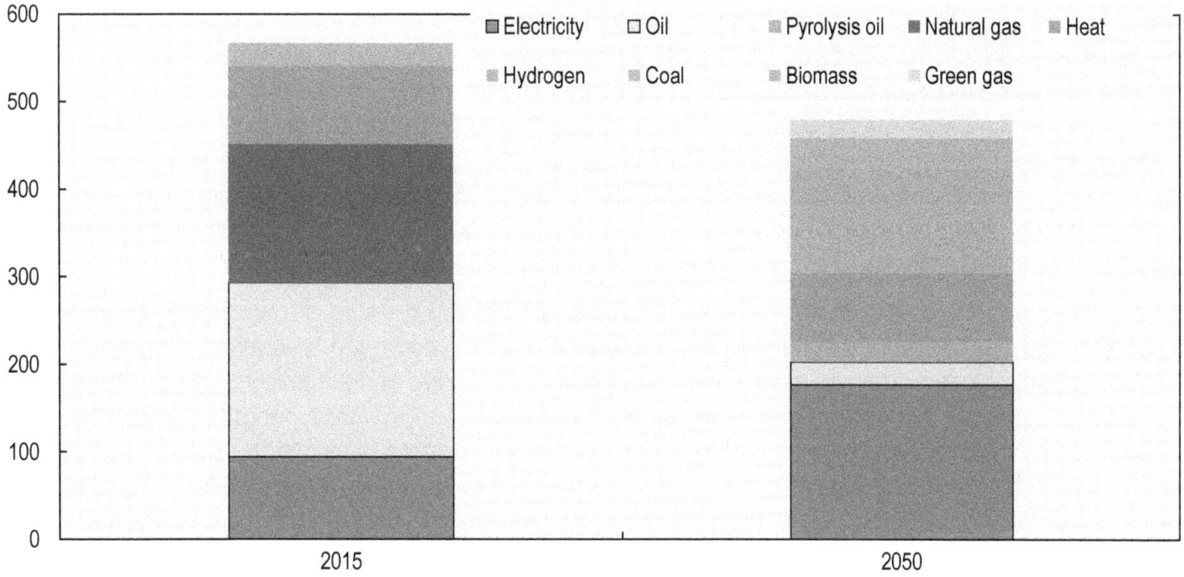

Note: Four manufacturing sectors: chemical, metallurgy, refineries and food-processing.
Source: Based on Berenschot (2020[1]).

Figure 3.24. Energy carriers used as feedstock in 2050 (PJ)

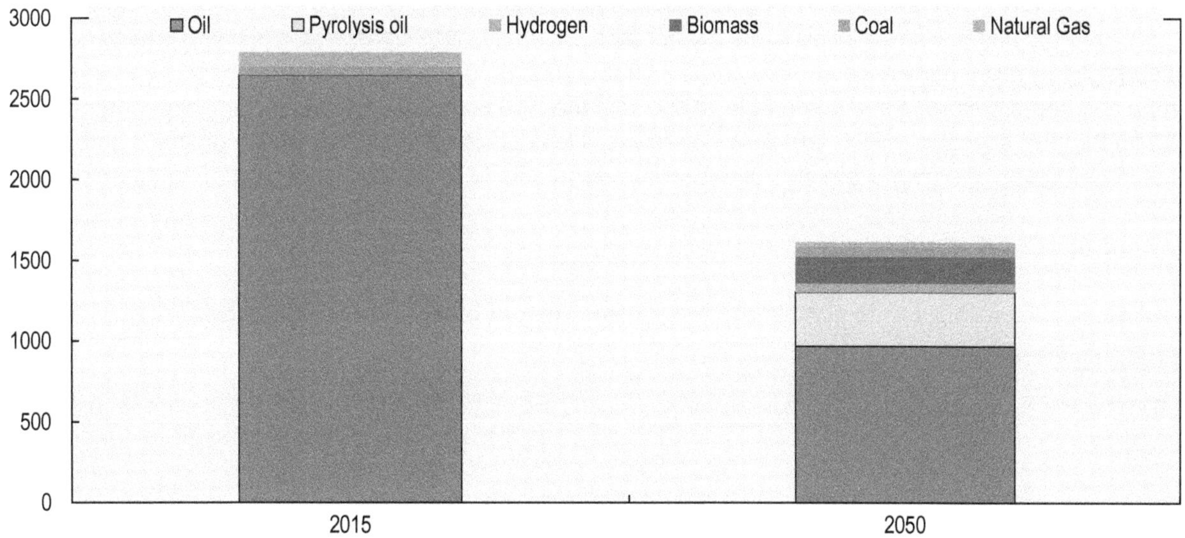

Note: Three sectors of the industry: chemical, metallurgy and refineries. The use of energy carriers as feedstock in the food-processing sector is negligible (0.3 PJ in 2015). This graph is not the sum of the graph of the three subsectors. 150 PJ of biomass used as feedstock in the chemical industry is green naphtha produced by the refineries using biomass, and should not be counted twice. The same is true for the use of oil and pyrolysis oil in the chemical sector.
Source: Based on Berenschot (2020[1]).

3.6.2. Reaching net-zero by 2050: The implications of industry's decarbonisation on the energy system

This scenario points to four main challenges facing the Dutch energy and industry sectors for the decade to come.

The first challenge is the **production and transport of carbon-neutral hydrogen**. This scenario relies on the use of 175 PJ of hydrogen (energy source and feedstock). If it were 100% domestic green hydrogen, it would require around 265 PJ of renewable electricity, more than doubling the projected requirement in the scenario, in which the direct use of electricity amounts to 177 PJ. If it were 100% domestic blue hydrogen, it would still require 45 PJ of renewable electricity and 174 PJ of natural gas. In addition, if the capture rate remain below 100%, reaching carbon neutrality in blue hydrogen production would require a significant amount of negative emissions to compensate. The last option is to rely, at least partly, on imported hydrogen. It would of course only shift the question of hydrogen availability to neighbouring countries. Finally, even if the scenario assumes the use of hydrogen for clustered sectors, it requires the construction of a large infrastructure to deliver the hydrogen, especially if it is imported.

Second, the scenario presented above relies heavily on increasing the use of **electricity** as an energy carrier (Figure 3.23, particularly if a significant production of green hydrogen is required). Increasing use of electricity could place a strain on other sectoral pathways to net-zero and the ability of the power system. In general, the greater demand for electricity (during peak hours and months) in industry and other end-use sectors, the lower flexibility given to the power system to decarbonise, since the power system may need to rely on fossil fuels to ensure the reliability of supply (if sufficient storage is absent). This, in turn, could mean greater reliance on carbon dioxide removal (CDR) technologies later in the century. Moreover, high-energy demand scenarios can be more costly, because of the need to build an electricity infrastructure to cover a few hours in the days of winter, to satisfy peak demand from end-use sectors.

Lowering the rate of growth in energy demand in the Netherlands would reduce the necessity to scale up the electricity system (generation, networks) substantially, translating into lower system costs and lower electricity prices (IEA, 2019[13]) as well as benefits to biodiversity, requiring less land, water and materials consumption (von Stechow et al., 2015[14]). Figure 3.25 illustrates this trade-off at the global level and is extracted from the IPCC Special Report on 1.5°C. The figure proposes four scenarios to achieve the goal of limiting warming to 1.5°C by 2100 under different levels of energy demand. Scenarios with higher levels of future energy demand will need to rely more heavily on the use of CDR later in the century. This is assumed to be bioenergy with carbon and capture storage in this scenario, in line with the "P4" scenario, than those with lesser demand (in line with the "P1" scenario) (IPCC, 2018[15]). Therefore, it is important not to forget that industry is embedded in the larger Dutch energy system and its decarbonisation should be evaluated in relation to other sectors.

Figure 3.25. Different illustrative global emissions pathways to 1.5°C by 2100

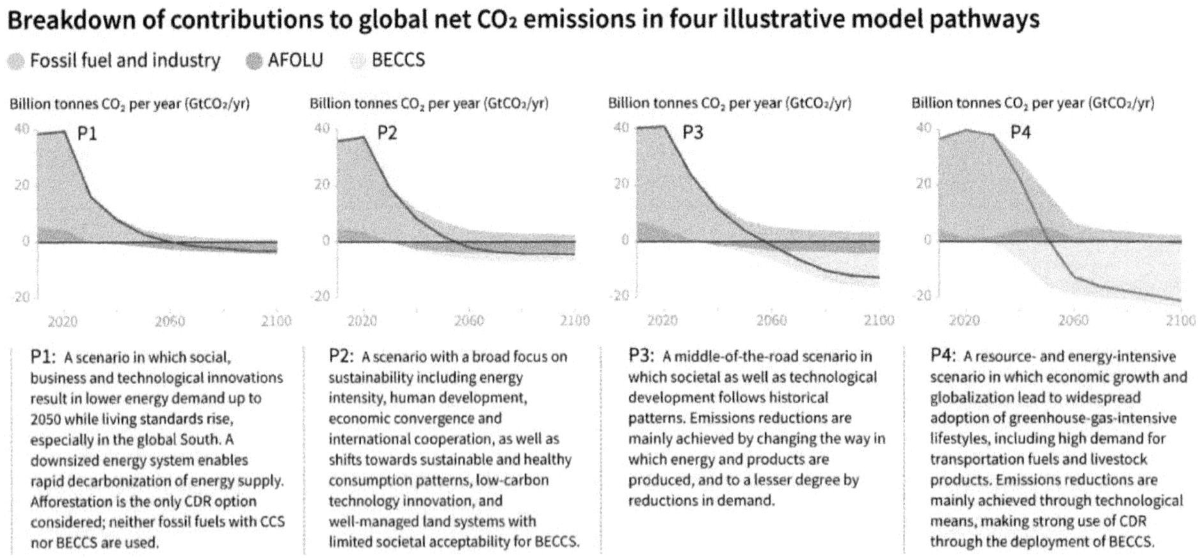

Note: AFOLU stands for Agriculture, Forestry, and other Land Use. BECSS stands for Bioenergy with Carbon Capture Storage.
Source: IPCC (2018[15]).

In addition, the potential for negative emissions in 2050 in the present scenario remains to be seen. Depending on the decarbonisation of other industrial subsectors and sectors, there could be more or less wiggle room for industry to rely on negative emissions to reach its targets. The interlinkages between sectors are not modelled in this report; therefore, whether the potential for negative emissions in 2050 is equivalent to what would be needed is unknown.

Third, the scenario also relies on a significant use of **biomass**. Some biomass will presumably be imported from abroad, to meet the total domestic demand. The biomass requirements (around 220 PJ in 2050, including green gas) is close to the domestic potential for yearly biomass production, estimated to be about 250 PJ in 2050 (Table 3.2). In 2050, there is a possibility to be able to import more biomass from abroad. In 2050 the Netherlands' import of biomass could roughly double the biomass availability to about 500 PJ (CE Delft, 2020[16]). Globally, about a third of this biomass could come from forestry and two thirds from agricultural origins. In the Netherlands, agricultural products make up a larger part of the biomass potential (75%), and an efficient use of all waste streams is foreseen. Forest sources could provide the other 25% in 2050.

Table 3.2. Maximum potential of biomass in the Netherlands

	Current yearly production (PJ)	2050 production potential (PJ)
Domestic biomass	121	230
Seaweed (North Sea)	0	18
Total	121	248

Source: PBL (2018[17]).

Finally, the net-zero scenario proposed requires **large investments**, from both the public and private sector, in low-carbon technologies and infrastructure (notably carbon and hydrogen pipelines). Unfortunately, COVID-19 could stall such investments by Dutch industry (OECD, 2020[18]). Great economic uncertainty could lead firms to reduce or postpone investment in innovative activities. In addition, the collapse of oil prices weakens incentives for low-carbon and energy efficiency investments. Moreover, young and small firms (rather than large incumbents) tend to develop radical innovations needed to decarbonise industry, but these are also the firms that have been disproportionately impacted by the crisis. Lastly, a dip in the addition of renewable energy capacity is expected globally because of supply chain disruptions from COVID-19. It is within this context that Dutch industry is making its way to net-zero. Because of this, the Dutch government will need to step up, maintain governmental support for innovation, and take risks to finance businesses working on emerging technologies further from the market.

3.7. Comparison with other decarbonisation scenarios

3.7.1. Scenarios available at the 2050 horizon

A thorough comparison of the above-mentioned scenario has been carried out by Berenschot et al. (2021[19]). Overall, the scenario is consistent with the other available scenarios (Figure 3.26), such as total energy use in industry, electricity, oil and biomass consumption. Available scenarios however differ significantly in terms of hydrogen consumption and CCS. The main results from the comparison of these scenarios are as follows.

Production volume growth and energy efficiency improvements are key scenario parameters. These parameters can have a dramatic effect on the scenario energy mix and energy demand. The reference scenario assumes relatively large production volume growth rates. In the TNO scenarios, some industrial subsectors feature declining production volumes. The assumptions in the reference scenario are more in line with the (general) assumption of the Koninklijk Instituut van Ingenieurs (KIVI) scenario.

Large differences in the size of the refinery sector. In the reference scenario, production of fuels for export is included, while other scenarios exclude this type of production. Given that the Netherlands has one of the most advanced refining industries in the world, Berenschot (2020[11]) assumes that part of the refinery industry will produce oil-based fuels for export, even if the domestic demand is significantly reduced. Therefore, the reference scenario assumes a much larger refinery sector in the Netherlands in 2050 than all other scenarios. This has major consequences for the energy consumption. To compare all scenarios, Figure 3.26 makes adjustments for this difference in assumptions.

Figure 3.26. Final energy consumption of Dutch industry in 2050 according to various scenarios (PJ)

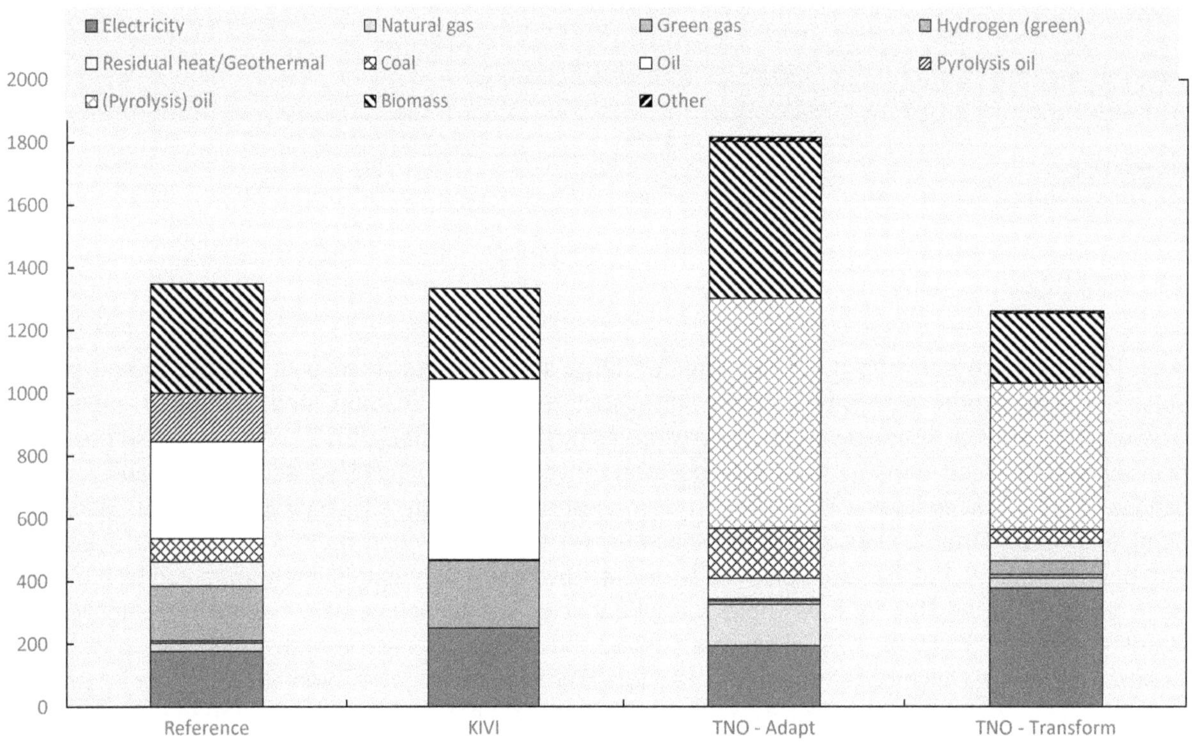

Note: The total energy demand for the 'OECD' scenario differs from the previous subsection. Indeed energy used to produce exported fuels for ships and airplanes is not included in this graph, in order to make the scope comparable with the three other scenarios. An extensive discussion of the models and assumptions underlying these projections is available in Berenschot, Kalavasta and E3M (2021[19]).
Source: Berenschot, Kalavasta and E3M (2021[19]).

No consensus on (green) hydrogen use in industry. The (green) hydrogen demand differs per scenario. Hydrogen does not appear, or seems to play only a marginal role in the energy consumption of Dutch industry at the 2050 horizon according to TNO's scenarios. In fact, TNO assumes that hydrogen is produced onsite and is not considered as an input in their simulation, but part of the industry indeed relies on hydrogen as a carbon-free energy source. The TNO Transform scenario also features a limited use of hydrogen in industry due to an extremely low demand for fertilisers. Consequently, the (green) hydrogen demand of the reference scenario, which can only be compared with one of the KIVI scenarios, seems realistic. Actual demand for (green) hydrogen in 2050 will depend on availability of required infrastructure (international), market development and technological breakthroughs (affecting competitiveness).

Biomass remains a very important energy carrier in 2050. Biomass demand increases in all 2050 scenarios. In the TNO Adapt scenario, biomass demand from industry increases to ~500 PJ and is used for energetic purposes as opposed to the reference and KIVI scenarios. This is because TNO assumes that the combination of biomass combustion and CCS, in principle leading to negative emissions, is a viable option. However, the use of biomass for energy purposes is no longer being considered in the Netherlands after the SER Advice and its assessment by the Government.

The use of CCS is heterogeneous across scenarios and linked to the underlying narrative. The reference scenario includes CCS in steel, refinery and fertiliser industries. TNO Adapt also includes CCS. In this scenario, in combination with biomass (bioenergy with carbon capture and storage [BECCS]), negative emissions can be created to compensate for emissions in other sectors this is necessary to meet the carbon reduction goal. KIVI and TNO Transform do not contain CCS, since CCS is not in line with the scenario narratives.

3.7.2. The shift to alternative sources of energy does not start before 2030

This survey of available scenarios was also the opportunity to compare the projections for the 2030 horizon (Figure 3.27). When compared to the current situation, total final energy demand, and in particular the use of fossil fuels, does not necessarily decrease in the industry. This relative stability predominantly comes from the demand for energy carriers as a feedstock.

The introduction of new technologies remains very limited at the 2030 horizon. This affects energy demand and energy mix. The usage of new technologies varies across the scenarios. KIVI assumes the use of DRI in the steel industry, while in the TNO Adapt scenario the steel sector strongly relies on CCS. The mix of technologies determines the energy mix. Considering that the technology mix in the 2050 scenarios will differ more from the current situation than the technology mix in the 2030 scenarios, the heterogeneity in energy carriers among 2050 scenarios is larger than in 2030 scenarios.

The use of green hydrogen in industry is almost non-existent in 2030. When compared to other sectors, adoption of new technologies within the industry requires some time, because adjusting continuous industrial processes requires long-term planning, result in high CAPEX investment and as such have long lead times. In case hydrogen is produced on-site by Steam Methane Reforming (SMR) or Auto-Thermal Reforming (ATR) in combination with CCS, this will still result in an increase in natural gas demand.

Most scenarios expect an increase in overall electrification in 2030. However, the PBL cost-optimal and TNO adapt scenario show none, to limited electrification growth when CCS is allowed. Electrification trends in other scenarios are in line with the reference scenario for 2050. Energy efficiency improvements are one of the reasons to introduce electric technologies, in particular heat pumps and electric boilers for the production of low-temperature heat.

Geothermal and residual heat are scarce. They are key energy carriers in an energy-efficient scenario, although only useful in specific industrial subsectors as they provide low-temperature heat rather than high-temperature heat. In 2030 the amount of geothermal heat is deemed limited.

All mid-term scenarios show a capacity increase of wind energy and solar energy in particular. Some scenarios project more renewables than others; this can mainly be explained by the underlying scenario narratives. Furthermore, the projection of the 2030 scenarios are more or less in line with the 2050 scenarios. When comparing the 2050 scenarios with the 2030 scenarios the installed capacity almost triples.

3.7.1. EU and international scenarios also underline that carbon neutrality will hinge on a diverse portfolio of technologies

Berenschot, Kalavasta and E3M (2021[19]) also show that, at the EU or international level, a diverse portfolio of technologies is needed to support emission reductions in the energy-intensive industries, both in the short term (2030) and in the longer term (2050).[16] Short-term emission reduction in industries are primarily based on accelerating progress in low-hanging fruits such as energy efficiency achieved through the implementation of best available technologies (BAT), heat recovery, horizontal energy management, electrification of industrial processes and reduced oil and coal consumption through fuel switching. However, pursuing the carbon neutrality by mid-century would imply transformative changes along with disruption in value chains and business models. This is a big challenge for European industries, considering the inertia of the sector, the high investment amounts required and the 1-3 investment cycles in most industries by 2050.

Figure 3.27. Final energy demand (energetic and non-energetic use) in the Dutch industry according to various scenarios in 2030, compared to 2019 (PJ)

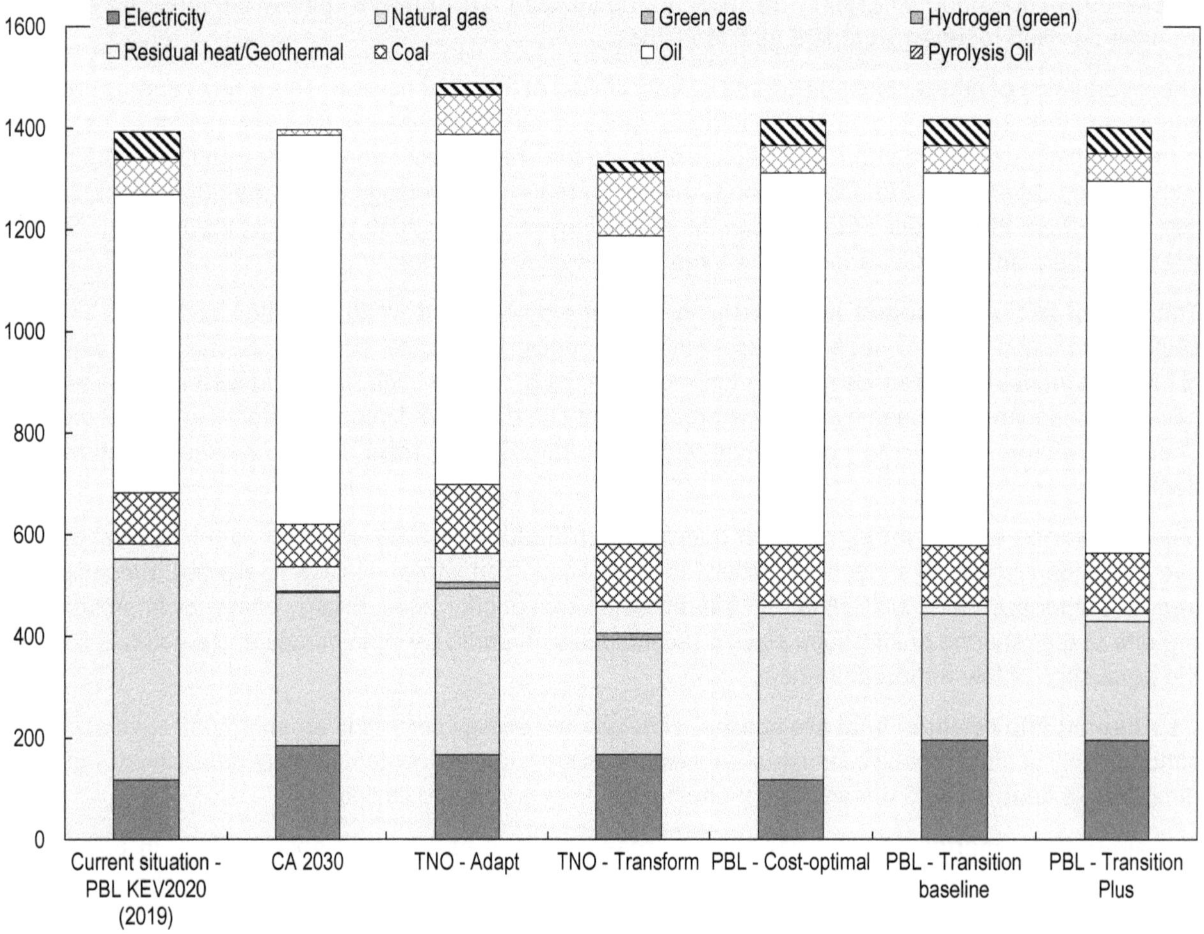

Note: An extensive discussion of the models and assumptions underlying these projections is available in Berenschot, Kalavasta and E3M (2021[19]).
Source: Berenschot, Kalavasta and E3M (2021[19]).

The emergence of breakthrough technologies is vital for achieving deep decarbonisation. The novel mitigation options include the deep electrification of industrial processes (e.g. through the uptake of high-temperature heat pumps), the switching to renewable energy carriers (e.g. green hydrogen, advanced biofuels, clean synthetic fuels), the emergence of carbon capture, utilisation and storage (CCUS) options and the accelerated improvements in energy and material efficiency embedding industrial processes in the circular economy. In order to avoid both direct and indirect emissions, the decarbonisation of European industries crucially depends on the provision of carbon free electricity and hydrogen from energy supply sectors.

The full decarbonisation of some industrial sectors may not be achievable without the implementation of CCUS technologies. The technology pathways in the European iron and steel sector are largely based on two novel options: 1) increased use of secondary steel, coming from steel scrap and electricity (assuming that power generation has been decarbonised); 2) hydrogen-based steelmaking by shifting away from blast furnace.

More generally, the road towards climate neutrality by mid-century can be achieved through: 1) the significant upscaling of current mitigation efforts (i.e. energy efficiency, fuel switch); 2) the deployment of innovative options, including: green hydrogen, e-gas, deep electrification, circular economy, CCS, embedding CO_2 in products and industrial symbiosis. Strong electrification of industrial processes should be combined with clean-gas and green hydrogen (H_2) solutions to decarbonise hard-to-abate energy intensive industries, while CCS is also required to eliminate remaining emissions in some industrial sub-sectors. Each technological mitigation option has pros and cons, but their combined development (together with the circular economy) is a cost-efficient way towards ensuring carbon neutrality of European industries by mid-century.

References

Advani, V. and T. van Dril (2020), *DECARBONISATION OPTIONS FOR EXXONMOBIL CHEMICALS ROTTERDAM*, https://www.pbl.nl/sites/default/files/downloads/pbl-2020-decarbonisation-options-for-exxonmobil-chemicals-rotterdam-4230.pdf. [21]

Aldel (2020), *Aluminium*, https://aldel.nl/product/ (accessed on 30 November 2020). [9]

Batool, M. and W. Wetzels (2019), *Decarbonisation options for the Dutch fertiliser industry*, PBL Publishers, https://www.pbl.nl/sites/default/files/downloads/pbl-2019-decarbonisation-options-for-the-dutch-fertiliser-industry_3657.pdf. [5]

Berenschot (2020), *Sustainable Transition of Dutch Industry: 2050 scenario's towards a zero emission industry in the Netherlands.* [1]

Berenschot, Kalavasta and E3M (2021), *Analysis and comparison of Dutch industry transition scenario's for 2030 and 2050.* [19]

Block, T., S. Gamboa Palacios and T. van Dril (2020), *Decarbonisation options for large volume organic chemical production,Shell Pernis*, https://www.pbl.nl/sites/default/files/downloads/pbl-2020-decarbonisation-options-for-large-volume-organic-chemical-production-shell-pernis_4274.pdf. [25]

CE Delft (2020), *Bio-Scope - Toepassingen en beschikbaarheid van duurzame biomassa*, https://www.ce.nl/publicaties/2454/bio-scope-toepassingen-en-beschikbaarheid-van-duurzame-biomassa. [16]

Ecofys and Berenschot (2018), *Chemistry for Climate: Acting on the need for speed - Roadmap for the Dutch Chemical Industry towards 2050*. [3]

IEA (2020), *Aluminum*, https://www.iea.org/reports/aluminium (accessed on 7 December 2020). [12]

IEA (2019), *World Energy Outlook 2019*, OECD Publishing, Paris, https://dx.doi.org/10.1787/caf32f3b-en. [13]

IPCC (2018), *Global warming of 1.5°C. An IPCC Special Report on the impacts of global warming of 1.5°C above pre-industrial levels and related global greenhouse gas emission pathways, in the context of strengthening the global response to the threat of climate change, sustainable development, and efforts to eradicate poverty*, IPCC, Geneva, https://www.ipcc.ch/sr15/. [15]

Jägers, G. and H. Kiesewetter (2018), *Sustainable development in Steel Industry*, Tata Steel, https://energy-now.nl/wp-content/uploads/2018/05/Breakout-Session-TATA-Steel-2-Energy-Now-2018-1.pdf (accessed on 7 December 2020). [10]

Keys, A., M. van Hout and B. Daniëls (2019), *Decarbonisation options for the Dutch steel industry*, https://www.pbl.nl/sites/default/files/downloads/pbl-2019-decarbonisation-options-for-the-dutch-steel-industry_3723.pdf. [24]

Khandelwal, M. and T. van Dril (2020), *DECARBONISATION OPTIONS FOR THE DUTCH BIOFUELS INDUSTRY*, https://www.pbl.nl/sites/default/files/downloads/pbl-2020-decarbonisation-options-for-the-dutch-biofuels-industry_3887.pdf. [20]

OECD (2020), *COVID-19 and the low-carbon transition: Impacts and possible policy responses*, http://www.oecd.org/coronavirus/policy-responses/covid-19-and-the-low-carbon-transition-impacts-and-possible-policy-responses-749738fc/. [18]

Oliveira, C. and K. Schure (2020), *Decarbonisation options for the Dutch refinery sector*. [7]

PBL (2018), *Negatieve emissies: technisch potentieel, realistisch potentieel en kosten voor Nederland*, https://www.pbl.nl/sites/default/files/downloads/pbl-2017-negatieve-emissies-technisch-potentieel-realistisch-potentieel-en-kosten-voor-nederland_2606.pdf. [17]

Platform Geothermie, DAGO, Warmtenetwek and EBN (2018), *Geothermal Energy in the Netherlands - A broad foundation for sustainable heat supply*, https://geothermie.nl/images/bestanden/Masterplan_Aardwarmte_in_Nederland_ENG.pdf. [2]

Port of Rotterdam (2018), *In drie stappen naar een duurzaam industriecluster - Rotterdam-Moerdijk in 2050*, https://www.portofrotterdam.com/sites/default/files/in-drie-stappen-naar-een-duurzaam-industriecluster-rotterdam-moerdijk-in-2050.pdf?token=nUYiyTOs. [8]

Rammer, B., R. Millner and C. Boehm (2017), "Comparing the CO2 Emissions of Different Steelmaking RoutesVergleich der CO2 Emissionen verschiedener Verfahren zur Stahlproduktion", *BHM Berg- und Hüttenmännische Monatshefte*, Vol. 162/1, pp. 7-13, http://dx.doi.org/10.1007/s00501-016-0561-8. [11]

Scherpbier, E. and H. Eerens (2020), *Decarbonisation options for the Dutch chlor-alkali industry*, https://www.pbl.nl/sites/default/files/downloads/pbl-2020-decarbonisation-options-for-the-dutch-chlor-alkali-industry_3478.pdf. [6]

Sensfuss, F. and B. Pfluger (2014), *Optimized pathways towards ambitious climate protection in the European electricity system (EU long-term scenarios 2050 II).* [22]

Tsiropoulos, I. et al. (2020), *Towards net-zero emissions in the EU energy system by 2050.* [23]

von Stechow, C. et al. (2015), "Integrating Global Climate Change Mitigation Goals with Other Sustainability Objectives: A Synthesis", *Annual Review of Environment and Resources*, Vol. 40/1, pp. 363-394, http://dx.doi.org/10.1146/annurev-environ-021113-095626. [14]

Wong, L. and T. van Dril (2020), *Decarbonisation options for large volume organic chemicals production, Shell Moerdijk*, https://www.pbl.nl/sites/default/files/downloads/pbl-2020-decarbonisation-options-for-large-volume-organic-chemicals-production-shell-moerdijk_3483.pdf. [4]

Notes

[1] In this respect, this exercise is close to the MIDDEN project (Manufacturing Industry Decarbonisation Data Exchange Network: https://www.pbl.nl/en/middenweb).

[2] STAN database, OECD.

[3] This section partly relies on previous analysis by Berenschot (Ecofys and Berenschot, 2018[3]).

[4] Although they are some distance apart, Delfzijl and Emmen co-operate closely and are regarded as one cluster in the Netherlands.

[5] This process is often referred to as grey hydrogen, or blue hydrogen if combined with carbon capture, (Box 1.2).

[6] The coefficient of performance is defined as the ratio between the heat supplied by a system and the energy provided to this system.

[7] In theory, using feed to make energy is just about accelerating the cycle of carbon, but it is hard to ensure that the process is completely carbon neutral. First, the use of fertiliser would imply (more or less, depending on the process) some release of nitrous oxide (not carbon, but still a GHG). Second, it could generate some land-use change.

[8] Biobased methanol could also be produced, but the limited availability of biomass could affect the attractiveness of this option (Khandelwal and van Dril, 2020[20]).

[9] Wong and van Dril (2020[4]), Block, Gamboa Palacios and van Dril (2020[25]) and Advani and van Dril (2020[21]).

[10] CBS Statline.

[11] STAN database, OECD. ISIC sector 19.

[12] https://www.world-aluminium.org/statistics/#map;
https://www.statista.com/statistics/748414/secondary-unwrought-aluminum-production-worldwide/.

[13] The assumed CCS capture rate is 85%, as in other sectors. However, the capture rate for HIsarna might be higher as the concentration of CO_2 is very high in the flue gas (Keys, van Hout and Daniëls, 2019[24]).

[14] Source: OECD STructural ANalysis Database (STAN), 2020.

[15] Green gas is upgraded biogas in the form of biomethane (with same quality as natural gas, which is why it can use the same infrastructure).

[16] This section is based on the analysis of the PRIMES European Commission Reference 2016 scenario, Sensfuss and Pfluger (2014[22]), the IEA World Energy Outlook 2020, the IRENA REmap Case scenario and Tsiropoulos et al. (2020[23]).

4. Optimal decarbonisation policy mix

This chapter presents theoretical insights from the literature on the "optimal" decarbonisation policy mix and links these insights to the specificities of the Netherlands. It also reviews existing research to present the current state of knowledge on the design of a decarbonisation policy portfolio. It first describes the range of decarbonisation policy instruments and underlying market failures that justify government intervention. It then presents the main takeaways from an existing state-of-the-art model developed for analysing interacting market failures and complements them with additional elements that are particularly relevant in the Dutch context (international competitiveness and carbon leakage, international knowledge spillovers, innovation path dependency, business dynamics and risk-sharing).

Achieving industry decarbonisation in the Netherlands requires a diverse set of policy instruments that account for specificities of the Dutch industry, namely small open economy with an industrial specialisation in emission-intensive trade-exposed activities, organisation around industrial clusters and strong integration in the European Union, both economically and politically. Keeping up the approach combining carbon taxation and innovation support is necessary to overcome the two-pronged barrier to industry decarbonisation, namely the lack of economic incentives both for carbon emissions minimisation and for long-term investments in low-carbon technologies. In addition, implementing policies that facilitate the provision of the necessary infrastructure and preserve business dynamism is required to enable both incumbent industrial firms' decarbonisation investments and innovative incumbents to emerge in the transition to the 2050 zero-net emission economy.

4.1. The wide range of policy instruments for decarbonisation

A myriad of policy instruments promoting a sustainable transition in the industry co-exist in the Netherlands and in other countries alike (Chapter 5, the current policy package). These instruments aim at achieving industry decarbonisation through different mechanisms addressing different intermediary objectives. Examples of such instruments include renewable energy portfolio standards, e.g. required production shares from wind and solar energy; emissions pricing, e.g. taxes or cap and trade systems; performance standards, e.g. maximum emission rates for steel production; financial incentives for R&D and subsidies for demonstration and technology deployment, e.g. tax credits or investment subsidies for green hydrogen production.

Pervasive interactions exist between decarbonisation instruments and create complex interplay between incentive mechanisms. Understanding whether "the whole is more or less than the sum of its parts" (i.e. whether these multiple policy interventions work together or at cross-purposes) is necessary for ensuring the efficiency and consistency of the portfolio of policy instruments and achieving decarbonisation (Fischer and Preonas, 2010[1]). For example, a policy portfolio including emission pricing and subsidies for low-carbon technology R&D and deployment can reduce carbon emissions at a significantly lower cost than any single policy alone (Fischer and Newell, 2008[2]). By contrast, in the presence of a binding emission cap, subsidies to renewable energy do not lead to further emission reductions but instead to a decrease in the price of emissions allowances, which often benefits the most carbon-intensive energy sources (Böhringer and Rosendahl, 2010[3]). International knowledge spillovers pose further challenges for the design of an efficient domestic decarbonisation policy mix. For example, fiscal support for photovoltaic energy production in developed countries in effect subsidised Chinese solar panel manufacturers' learning-by-doing (Peters et al., 2012[4]).

Understanding the interactions between instruments requires looking at their underlying rationale and the channels through which they operate. Recent OECD work proposes a new taxonomy allowing such an analysis based on two main dimensions (Criscuolo et al., forthcoming[5]). First, one can distinguish between supply-side instruments (e.g. innovation support policies) and demand-oriented instruments (e.g. taxes on carbon content, regulatory product standards or public procurement practices). Second, among supply-side instruments, one can distinguish those that affect efficiency within firms, e.g. R&D incentives, from those that affect the allocation of production factors between firms, e.g. framework instruments such as entrepreneurship, exit, competition and trade policies.

Critically, adequate framework conditions are a necessary complement to the policy mix for a cost-efficient decarbonisation. A dynamic business environment facilitates the green transition by enabling a reallocation of production factors from inefficient firms to more efficient firms – whether large incumbents, SMEs or start-ups. While competition is key to achieve such efficiency-enhancing reallocation, anti-carbon leakage policies can help maintain a level playing field between domestic firms and firms in environmentally laxer jurisdictions, and build a stronger and broader public support to the transition. Finally, regulation should strike the balance between credibility and adaptability in order to reduce the risk of investment in the transition.

4.2. Combined decarbonisation market failures: Technology and the environment

Two key market failures hinder decarbonisation. First, carbon emissions constitute an environmental externality, as the environmental damage from carbon-intensive production processes is borne by society as a whole – current and future generations in all countries – rather than internalised by the emitting firm. Second, technological change, which drives the cost-benefit trade-off of emission abatement over time, is subject to knowledge spillovers at both local and global levels, as firms developing or adopting a new technology create benefits for others while incurring all costs. These market failures imply that the market produces too much emissions and too little technology innovation, and their existence justifies policy intervention.

In theory, one policy instrument – namely a well-designed carbon price – would suffice to incentivise private industrial firms to internalise the external cost of CO_2 emissions *if the emission externality were the only market inefficiency*. In that case, policies that come on top of an emission tax or cap-and-trade system only distort the market allocation of emission abatement and, hence, increase overall abatement costs. However, *in the presence of additional market failures*, a carbon price alone cannot correct them all at the same time. In particular, the combination of carbon emission externalities and knowledge spillovers associated with technological innovation and adoption necessitates a portfolio of policy instruments that promotes both emission abatement and the development and diffusion of low-carbon technologies.[1]

The choice of an optimal portfolio of low-carbon and technology policy instruments in the context of pollution externality and knowledge spillovers is the object of a number of studies at the nexus between innovation and environmental economics.[2] For the purpose of this report, the general lesson from this literature is twofold. First, in an optimal scenario, carbon emissions are priced at their marginal external cost, R&D is subsidised at the spill over rate, and adoption is subsidised at the rate of learning-by-doing spill over. Second, actual policy contexts are significantly more complex than canonical models acknowledge, notably due to the existence of overlapping jurisdictions, the difficulty to identify and price all relevant market failures or even list all instruments, and the political economy of pricing externalities.

4.3. A benchmark framework for analysing decarbonisation policy mix

The economic literature on environmental and technology policy offers theoretical guidance regarding the design of a decarbonisation policy mix. For theoretical insights, this section relies on a state-of-the-art framework developed for analysing interacting market failures in the US power sector in order to gain general insights into industry decarbonisation (Fischer, Preonas and Newell, 2017[6]). The next sections discuss how the specificities of the Dutch industry affect the findings of the benchmark model.

In order to analyse the cost-efficiency of policy combinations for reducing emissions, the model under consideration includes four overlapping market imperfections: 1) an environmental externality due to carbon emissions; 2) knowledge spillovers from R&D; 3) learning-by-doing; and 4) undervaluation of the benefits of energy efficiency investments. The main conclusion is that complementing emissions pricing with technology support policies can reduce the overall cost of achieving decarbonisation in the presence of technology market failures, however, overcompensating for these failures can be welfare-decreasing.

Over-ambitious policies to support the deployment of non-fossil energy may not be cost-efficient alongside emissions pricing. Indeed, emissions pricing decreases the relative price of non-fossil energy and, thus, makes large deployment subsidies for non-fossil energy unnecessary, particularly in the case of mature technologies where learning-by-doing spillovers are relatively small. By contrast, strongly correcting market failures arising from R&D spillovers is typically a cost-efficient complement to emissions pricing to achieve significant emission reductions.[3]

In the case of the Dutch industry, a “simple” policy mix of domestic emission pricing and technology support is likely not sufficient because of the specific characteristics of the Netherlands, namely a small open economy with an industrial sector largely specialised in the production of carbon-intensive tradeable products. Therefore, the next sections discuss three key elements in the Dutch context:

- Carbon leakage and international competitiveness (OECD, 2020[7]).
- Cross-sector (Dechezleprêtre et al., 2013), cross-TRL (technology-readiness level)[4] stage (Popp, Hascic and Medhi, 2011[8])and cross-jurisdiction knowledge spillovers (Dechezleprêtre, Martin and Mohnen, 2017[9]), and path dependency (Aghion et al., 2016[10]).

In addition, the design of instruments is important for the efficiency of decarbonisation. Two further factors are discussed below:

- the role of business dynamics for innovation, including the provision of “green skills” and
- uncertainty and imperfect commitment, which call for risk-sharing and signalling.

Further factors potentially affect the decarbonisation policy mix but fall beyond the scope of this report, focused on the manufacturing sector: technical factors related to energy supply, such as intermittency of renewable or grid matters; strategic and resilience-related factors such as energy supply diversification.

Finally, the considered framework offers insights into Scope 1 and Scope 2 emissions, namely direct emissions and indirect emissions associated with the production of purchased electricity, heat and steam. It does not tackle Scope 3 emissions, namely other indirect emissions associated with the extraction and production of purchased materials, fuels, and services, including transport in vehicles not owned or controlled by the reporting entity, outsourced activities, waste disposal, etc. Reduction of Scope 3 emissions is discussed in the sections on recycling and bio-based materials in Chapter 7 on emerging technologies.

4.4. International competitiveness and carbon leakage

Unilateral environmental policies may create international cost competitiveness issues.[5] As they affect the cost structure of domestic carbon-intensive industries (and potentially all along the value chain), domestic producers can be put at a cost disadvantage relative to foreign (unconstrained) producers vis-à-vis both imports and exports, which could affect investment and production location decisions in the longer run, in particular in small open economies (Chapter 8).

Specifically, tighter environmental regulation can provide incentives for firms in emission-intensive trade-exposed (EITE) industries to shift production to laxer jurisdictions – the so-called pollution haven hypothesis.[6] Such production shifting can happen through incumbent domestic firms relocating abroad and/or increasing their holdings of foreign assets (outward foreign direct investment), as well as through new firms choosing foreign locations and foreign firms reducing domestic investment (inward foreign direct investment). While available empirical evidence supports the pollution haven hypothesis, the magnitude of the effect has been found to be small – e.g. Garsous, Kozluk and Dlugosch (2020[11]).

Overall, OECD research shows that implementing more stringent environmental policies has had little aggregate effect on economic performance over the last three decades, despite achieving significant environmental benefits (OECD, 2021[12]). Yet, small average effects across the economy hide heterogeneous impacts across industries and firms. Environmental policies create winners and losers as capital and labour are reallocated from high-emission to low-emission industries and firm (OECD, 2021[12]). On one hand, more stringent environmental policies negatively affects the performance of EITE industries, at least in the short run – e.g. steel and petrochemicals, Aldy and Pizer (2015[13]) – and of the least-productive firms. On the other hand, environmental stringency positively affects the productivity of front-runner industries and firms and the exports of low-pollution industries.

Carbon leakage is a possible consequence of unilateral carbon pricing policies and the resulting disparities in the carbon price across countries, whereby part of the emissions avoided through domestic environmental regulations are shifted to other locations. Meta-estimates of the magnitude of the leakage rate (defined as the ratio of foreign increase in emissions over domestic reductions) from *ex-ante* analyses based on computable general equilibrium models lie in the 5-25% range at the aggregate level (Branger and Quirion, 2014[14]). Yet, large disparities across industries reflect differences in carbon intensity and trade exposure, with partial equilibrium showing leakage ratios of up to 30% in aluminium industries and 50% in steel industries (Demailly and Quirion, 2008[15]). Moreover, leakage is larger the smaller the economy implementing unilateral emission pricing and the more ambitious the reduction target (Böhringer, Fischer and Rosendahl, 2014[16]).

By contrast to ex-ante analyses, *ex-post* evaluations suggest that competitiveness concerns have been overstated to date (Arlinghaus, 2015[17]; Flues and Lutz, 2015[18]). These evaluations typically find only a small effect of climate policies on carbon leakage and competitiveness, especially when compared with other determinants of trade and investment location decisions (Venmans, Ellis and Nachtigall, 2020[19]). However, the small effects observed so far may be driven by the low stringency of past climate policies, which, lacking strengthening, would fall short of achieving the net-zero emission economy by 2050. Policies that are more ambitious may have greater effects if they increase the cost handicap vis a vis trading partners, in particular if EITE industries display threshold effects and non-linearities in the relationship between environmental and economic performance.

From a theoretical perspective, disparities in carbon pricing may lead to leakage through several channels (Cosbey et al., 2019[20]):

- The competitiveness channel, due to the substitution from domestic carbon-intensive goods production, changes in FDI patterns or offshoring of carbon-intensive production ("direct leakage" or "trade channel").
- The energy market channel, due to the price effect of reduced domestic consumption of fossil fuels on the world fossil fuel market ("indirect leakage" or "international energy price channel").[7]
- The income channel, due to changes in real exchange rates triggered by the introduction of carbon pricing, which affects the terms of trade and, therefore, global income distribution.[8]
- The technology spillovers channel (negative leakage, i.e. lower foreign emissions), due to carbon policies inducing innovation which spills over and lead to emission reductions abroad (see the section below).

Concern regarding potential competitiveness issues both undermines global decarbonisation efforts and erodes industry support for climate policy, calling for policy intervention to level the playing field (OECD, 2020[7]). Two main types of instruments can partially tackle the issue by addressing direct leakage (or competitiveness channel): border carbon adjustments (BCA) and domestic taxes and subsidies.

A BCA consists of trade measures to put products from foreign producers who operate without a carbon price on an even footing with products from domestic producers who face a carbon price – see e.g. OECD (2020[7]) or Cosbey et al. (2019[20]). For example, one version of a BCA could combine a domestic carbon price with a mechanism that sets a price at the border and an export rebate, based on the carbon content of products and the domestic carbon price, effectively only taxing emissions from domestic consumption.[9] A meta-analysis of ex-ante studies based on computable general equilibrium models suggests that a BCA would significantly reduce direct leakage (Branger and Quirion, 2014[14]). Beyond addressing the direct leakage issue, a BCA has two main advantages: 1) for countries being affected by the BCA, it changes the benefit of co-operating in climate agreements (Helm, Hepburn and Ruta, 2012[21]); and 2) it is politically acceptable in the implementing jurisdiction. However, it has two major drawbacks: 1) observing carbon content of imported products is challenging;[10] and 2) implementation must be at the level of a free trade area and faces WTO legal uncertainty.

Domestic taxes and subsidies consist in the combination of a carbon consumption tax and a carbon price, potentially including output-based rebates or other types of subsidies, such as abatement payments. In theory, such a combination can achieve the same result as a BCA (Grubb et al., 2020[22]; Pollitt, Neuhoff and Lin, 2020[23]; Böhringer, Rosendahl and Storrøsten, 2017[24]; Böhringer, Rosendahl and Storrøsten, 2019[25]). While the challenge of observing carbon content remains, the advantage of such an option is that it can be implemented unilaterally by any country within a free trade area.

When overlapping with supranational emission trading schemes, unilateral carbon pricing may have another leakage effect, referred to as the "waterbed effect". For example, in the case of the EU Emission Trading System (ETS), any unilateral emission reduction is exactly offset by an emissions increase elsewhere absent in the compensation mechanism: the "waterbed effect" is 100%. Compensation mechanisms, such as the newly-implemented EU ETS Market Stability Reserve, "puncture" the waterbed by cancelling a fraction of surplus allowances so that unilateral action can achieve emission reductions overall instead of just leading to leakage within the system. While the effect of such compensation mechanisms remains debated, overlapping unilateral policies can be designed to limit the waterbed effect – e.g. Perino, Ritz and Benthem (2019[26]) or Böhringer and Fischer (2020[27]).

4.5. Cross-sector, cross-country and cross-TRL knowledge spill over and path dependency

Green and low-carbon knowledge spills over, in particular: 1) across sectors (Dechezleprêtre et al., 2013); 2) across countries (Dechezleprêtre, Martin and Mohnen, 2017[9]), as domestic technology investments decrease the global price of renewables (Fischer, Greaker and Rosendahl, 2018[28]);[11] and 3) across different stages of the innovation and adoption process or TRLs (Popp, Hascic and Medhi, 2011[8]). From an efficiency perspective, this suggests that knowledge spillovers should be tackled at the largest possible level of (supranational) government.

Technological knowledge spills over across different stages of the innovation and adoption process (i.e. across different TRLs), implying that instruments favouring innovation have an effect on adoption. However, innovation does not necessarily fully translate into adoption even though it removes technological barriers (Popp, Hascic and Medhi, 2011[8]), which raises the issue of absorptive capacity (Aghion and Jaravel, 2015[29]) and of financing and risk sharing (Section 4.7). The necessary co-ordination arising from the complexity of technological spill-over patterns is an argument for resorting to green industrial policy (Criscuolo et al., forthcoming[5]).

The stock of local knowledge affects geographical spillovers: a firm is more likely to innovate in clean technologies if its "inventors" are located in countries where other firms have been undertaking more clean innovations (Aghion et al., 2016[10]). The effect of the local knowledge stock is likely to be magnified by trade, as the exposure of domestic firms to foreign exporters' technology promotes further innovation (Aghion et al., 2019[30]).

Technological change is characterised by path dependency, i.e. persistence of technological change along well-defined pathways. Technology regimes are an assemblage of technological artefacts, institutions and regulations, so change tends to be cumulative and competing regimes rarely emerge (Berkhout, 2002[31]). Such path dependency can lead to inefficient lock-in, as learning-by-doing and increasing returns to scale lead to systematic exclusion of competing and possibly superior technologies (Arthur, 1989[32]). It can also lead to institutional entrapment, that is, embedded institutional, political and economic commitments to a particular technology (Walker, 2000[33]).

Path dependency is a key issue for decarbonisation, as dirty innovation is more likely at firms that already performed dirty innovation (Aghion et al., 2016[10]). The presence of an environmental externality implies inefficiently high innovation in dirty technologies in the decentralised equilibrium, calling for governments to "re-direct" innovation and restore the social optimum based on a mix of innovation subsidy and emission pricing (Acemoglu et al., 2012[34]).[12]

An important policy consequence is the risk involved with privileging specific technologies to achieve decarbonisation. However, promising the technologies, path dependency implies the existence of a trade-off between focusing exclusively on these technologies and maintaining a diverse range of options to preserve reversibility. While preserving reversibility is costly, especially for a small economy like the Netherlands, articulating a hybrid strategy of relying on co-ordinated supranational R&D effort, e.g. at the European Union level, while supporting the deployment of a broader range of technologies, is a potential strategy.

Moreover, if the only rationale for green innovation is emission reduction, one may wonder whether the government of a small open economy with important absorptive capability should have its own R&D and innovation programs at all, or rather promote technology diffusion (i.e. focus on end of TRL stages) and rely on international (in particular European) R&D subsidy initiatives. If another rationale is technological leadership, an option is investing a few selected technologies, if possible, in co-ordination with European countries, and absorbing the rest.

4.6. Business dynamics

Decarbonisation policy instruments aim at affecting the structure of the economy and, therefore, interact with business dynamics and the level of competition. In general, horizontal instruments intended for the green transition that affect firms across the board are not detrimental to competition; on the contrary, they can contribute to fostering business dynamics to the extent that they promote innovation. By contrast, targeted instruments – either technology-specific or location-specific – may give an advantage to specific firms over others if badly designed and create barriers to firm entry and exit; ultimately, this may slow down innovation and decarbonisation.

Encouraging the entry of new, innovative firms and the exit of less productive firms is thus key and complementary to decarbonisation incentives. Start-ups are often the vehicle through which radical innovations enter the market, while older incumbent firms often focus on incremental changes to established technologies. Lack of business dynamism may prevent low-carbon innovations from overtaking fossil fuel-based incumbents and secure market shares, even if they are more efficient.

Distinguishing instruments that affect firm performance ("within instruments") from those that affect the allocation of production factors between firms ("between instruments") is key for understanding innovation dynamics. On one hand, "within" instruments such as R&D tax credits and subsidies help to address the under-provision of investment in low-carbon technologies by internalising knowledge externalities. On the other hand, "between" instruments promoting the reallocation of production factors from old to young firms with a superior technology can be a major driver of aggregate productivity, including carbon efficiency (Aghion and Howitt, 1992[35]). By enabling entrants and small firms to compete and eventually challenge large incumbents, promoting reallocation can have an indirect positive effect on both challengers' and incumbents' incentives to innovate, in particular in low-carbon technologies.

In addition, the knowledge spill-over theory of entrepreneurship suggests that, by promoting the spin-off of existing but not commercialised environmental knowledge from incumbent firms, between instruments support growth within entrepreneurial firms in the low-carbon energy transition (Malen and Marcus, 2017[36]; Colombelli and Quatraro, 2019[37]).

Green skills –defined as those "needed by the workforce, in all sectors and at all levels, in order to help the adaptation of products, services and processes to the changes due to climate change and to environmental requirements and regulations" (OECD, 2014[38]) – are a necessary complement to green supply-push policies. Green support programs have been shown to be more effective in geographic areas where green skills are more prevalent (Chen et al., 2020[39]).

4.7. Risk sharing and signalling

Investment risks related to decarbonisation are relatively large. Financing costs are typically larger for low-carbon technologies, as these are often more capital-intensive than high-carbon ones, for which the main costs are fuels (Steckel and Jakob, 2018[40]; Schmidt, 2014[41]; Hirth and Steckel, 2016[42]). Moreover, uncertainty is significant regarding which low-carbon technologies will emerge.

Green risk sharing, or green de-risking, decreases the risk of low-carbon investments, thereby lowering the financing costs of emission abatement and promoting decarbonisation (Steckel and Jakob, 2018[40]).[13] Risk sharing transfers parts of the expenses associated with the realisation of a negative event away from the investors to other parties, typically the public sector, e.g. risk insurance, contracts for difference or guarantees provided by development banks. Government-sponsored green venture capital funds and government funds of green funds also contribute to sharing the risk of low-carbon investments.

In addition, the risk of low-carbon investments also comprises the uncertainty stemming from the regulatory environment over the run of projects, which dampen decarbonisation (Popp, Newell and Jaffe, 2010[43]). Volatile emission prices also weaken low-carbon investment (Flues and van Dender, 2020[44]). Policy instruments that stabilise the price of carbon or signal the government's long-term commitment to a pre-determined price path, possibly set by law, also improve the risk-return profile of investments in low-carbon technologies.

4.8. Value chain emissions

Focusing on direct emissions only offers a partial picture when it comes to industry decarbonisation. Indirect emissions from the generation of purchased energy (Scope 2) and those associated with the extraction and production of purchased materials, fuels, services, (outsourced activities including transport, waste disposal, etc.) and use of sold products (Scope 3) are typically large in the industry, and larger than direct (Scope 1) emissions (Hertwich and Wood, 2018[45]). Therefore, constantly addressing carbon emissions along the entire value chain is necessary.

Long-term carbon neutrality implies a quasi-fully circular economy. For the industry, neutrality raises the issue of end-of-life emissions of sold products. The combination of designing products in order to minimise end-of-life emissions and recycling industrial waste, offers a way forward for the industry, which heavily hinges on the use of synthetic and bio-based feedstock.

References

Acemoglu, D. et al. (2012), *The environment and directed technical change*, Nordhaus and Boyer, http://dx.doi.org/10.1257/aer.102.1.131. [34]

Acemoglu, D. et al. (2016), "Transition to clean technology", *Journal of Political Economy*, Vol. 124/1, pp. 52-104, http://dx.doi.org/10.1086/684511. [53]

Aghion, P. et al. (2019), *Spreading knowledge across the world: innovation spill-over through trade expension.* [30]

Aghion, P. et al. (2016), "Carbon taxes, path dependency, and directed technical change: Evidence from the auto industry", *Journal of Political Economy*, Vol. 124/1, pp. 1-51, http://dx.doi.org/10.1086/684581. [10]

Aghion, P. and P. Howitt (1992), "A model of growth through creative destruction", *Econometrica*, Vol. 60/2, pp. 323-51, https://doi.org/10.2307/2951599 (accessed on 1 March 2021). [35]

Aghion, P. and X. Jaravel (2015), "Knowledge Spillovers, Innovation and Growth", *The Economic Journal*, Vol. 125/583, pp. 533-573, http://dx.doi.org/10.1111/ecoj.12199. [29]

Albrizio, S., T. Kozluk and V. Zipperer (2017), "Environmental policies and productivity growth: Evidence across industries and firms", *Journal of Environmental Economics and Management*, Vol. 81, pp. 209-226, http://dx.doi.org/10.1016/j.jeem.2016.06.002. [49]

Aldy, J. and W. Pizer (2015), "The competitiveness impacts of climate change mitigation policies", *Journal of the Association of Environmental and Resource Economists*, Vol. 2/4, pp. 565-95, http://dx.doi.org/10.1086/683305. [13]

Arlinghaus, J. (2015), *Impacts of carbon prices on indicators of competitiveness: A review of empirical findings*, OECD Publishing, Paris, https://doi.org/10.1787/5js37p21grzq-en. [17]

Arthur, W. (1989), "Competing Technologies, Increasing Returns, and Lock-In by Historical Events", *The Economic Journal*, Vol. 99/394, p. 116, http://dx.doi.org/10.2307/2234208. [32]

Berkhout, F. (2002), *Technological regimes, path dependency and the environment*, Elsevier Ltd, http://dx.doi.org/10.1016/S0959-3780(01)00025-5. [31]

Böhringer, C. and C. Fischer (2020), "Kill Bill or Tax: An analysis of alternative CO2 price floor options for EU Member States", *CESifo Working Paper*, No. 8631, CESifo, Munich, http://www.RePEc.org (accessed on 11 February 2021). [27]

Böhringer, C., C. Fischer and K. Rosendahl (2014), "Cost-effective unilateral climate policy design: Size matters", *Journal of Environmental Economics and Management*, Vol. 67/3, pp. 318-339, http://dx.doi.org/10.1016/j.jeem.2013.12.008. [16]

Böhringer, C. and K. Rosendahl (2010), "Green promotes the dirtiest: On the interaction between black and green quotas in energy markets", *Journal of Regulatory Economics*, Vol. 37/3, pp. 316-325, http://dx.doi.org/10.1007/s11149-010-9116-1. [3]

Böhringer, C., K. Rosendahl and H. Storrøsten (2019), *Smart hedging against carbon leakage*, https://www.cesifo.org/DocDL/cesifo1_wp7915.pdf. [25]

Böhringer, C., K. Rosendahl and H. Storrøsten (2017), "Robust policies to mitigate carbon leakage", *Journal of Public Economics*, Vol. 149/1, pp. 35-46, https://doi.org/10.1016/j.jpubeco.2017.03.006. [24]

Braathen, N. (2007), "Instrument mixes for environmental policy: How many stones should be used to kill a bird?", *International Review of Environmental and Resource Economics*, Vol. 1/2, pp. 185-235, http://dx.doi.org/10.1561/101.00000005. [54]

Branger, F. and P. Quirion (2014), “Climate policy and the ‘carbon haven’ effect”, *Wiley Interdisciplinary Reviews: Climate Change*, Vol. 5, pp. 53-71. [50]

Branger, F. and P. Quirion (2014), “Would border carbon adjustments prevent carbon leakage and heavy industry competitiveness losses? Insights from a meta-analysis of recent economic studies”, *Ecological Economics*, Vol. 99, pp. 29-39, http://dx.doi.org/10.1016/j.ecolecon.2013.12.010. [14]

Chen, Z. et al. (2020), *Green stimulus in a post-pandemic recovery: The role of skills for a resilient recovery*, https://www.cesifo.org/DocDL/cesifo1_wp8419.pdf. [39]

Colombelli, A. and F. Quatraro (2019), “Green start-ups and local knowledge spillovers from clean and dirty technologies”, *Small Business Economics*, Vol. 52/4, pp. 773-792, http://dx.doi.org/10.1007/s11187-017-9934-y. [37]

Cosbey, A. et al. (2019), “Developing Guidance for Implementing Border Carbon Adjustments: Lessons, Cautions, and Research Needs from the Literature”, *Review of Environmental Economics and Policy*, Vol. 13/1, pp. 3-22, http://dx.doi.org/10.1093/reep/rey020. [20]

Criscuolo, C. et al. (forthcoming), *A fresh look at industrial policies: old challenges, new perspectives*. [5]

Dechezleprêtre, A., R. Martin and M. Mohnen (2017), *Knowledge spillovers from clean and dirty technologies*, https://www.lse.ac.uk/GranthamInstitute/wp-content/uploads/2013/10/Working-Paper-135-Dechezlepretre-et-al_updateOct2017.pdf (accessed on 1 March 2021). [9]

Demailly, D. and P. Quirion (2008), “European Emission Trading Scheme and competitiveness: A case study on the iron and steel industry”, *Energy Economics*, Vol. 30/4, pp. 2009-2027, http://dx.doi.org/10.1016/j.eneco.2007.01.020. [15]

Fischer, C. (2010), “Renewable portfolio standards: When do they lower energy prices?”, *Energy Journal*, Vol. 31/1, pp. 101-20, https://doi.org/10.5547/ISSN0195-6574-EJ-Vol31-No1-5. [48]

Fischer, C., M. Greaker and K. Rosendahl (2018), “Strategic technology policy as a supplement to renewable energy standards”, *Resource and Energy Economics*, Vol. 51, pp. 84-98, http://dx.doi.org/10.1016/j.reseneeco.2017.05.006. [28]

Fischer, C. and R. Newell (2008), “Environmental and technology policies for climate mitigation”, *Journal of Environmental Economics and Management*, Vol. 55/2, pp. 142-162, https://ideas.repec.org/a/eee/jeeman/v55y2008i2p142-162.html (accessed on 11 February 2021). [2]

Fischer, C. and L. Preonas (2010), “Combining policies for renewable energy: Is the whole less than the sum of its parts?”, *International Review of Environmental and Resource Economics*, Vol. 4/1, pp. 51-92, http://dx.doi.org/10.1561/101.00000030. [1]

Fischer, C., L. Preonas and R. Newell (2017), “Environmental and technology policy options in the electricity sector: Are we deploying too many?”, *Journal of the Association of Environmental and Resource Economists*, Vol. 4/4, pp. 959-984, http://dx.doi.org/10.1086/692507. [6]

Flues, F. and B. Lutz (2015), *Competitiveness impacts of the German electricity tax*, OECD Publishing, Paris, https://doi.org/10.1787/5js0752mkzmv-en. [18]

Flues, F. and K. van Dender (2020), *Carbon pricing design: Effectiveness, efficiency and feasibility: An investment perspective*, OECD Publishing, Paris. [44]

Garsous, G., T. Kozluk and D. Dlugosch (2020), "Do energy prices drive outwards FDI? Evidence from a sample of listed firms", *The Energy Journal*, Vol. 41/3, http://dx.doi.org/doi:10.5547/01956574.41.3.ggar. [11]

Gerlagh, R. and O. Kuik (2014), "Spill or leak? Carbon leakage with international technology spillovers: A CGE analysis", *Energy Economics*, Vol. 45, pp. 381-388, http://dx.doi.org/10.1016/j.encco.2014.07.017. [52]

Goulder, L. and W. Parry (2008), "Instrument choice in environmental policy", *Review of Environmental Economics and Policy*, Vol. 2/2, pp. 152–74. [47]

Grubb, M. et al. (2020), "Consumption-oriented policy instruments for fostering greenhouse gas mitigation", *Climate Policy*, Vol. 20/sup1, pp. S58-S73, http://dx.doi.org/10.1080/14693062.2020.1730151. [22]

Helm, D., C. Hepburn and G. Ruta (2012), "Trade, climate change, and the political game theory of border carbon adjustments", *Oxford Review of Economic Policy*, Vol. 28/2, pp. 368-394, http://dx.doi.org/10.1093/oxrep/grs013. [21]

Hertwich, E. and R. Wood (2018), "The growing importance of scope 3 greenhouse gas emissions from industry", *Environmental Research Letters*, Vol. 13/10, p. 104013, http://dx.doi.org/10.1088/1748-9326/aae19a. [45]

Hirth, L. and J. Steckel (2016), "The role of capital costs in decarbonizing the electricity sector", *Environmental Research Letters*, Vol. 11/11, p. 114010, http://dx.doi.org/10.1088/1748-9326/11/11/114010. [42]

Jaffe, A., R. Newell and R. Stavins (2005), "A tale of two market failures: Technology and environmental policy", *Ecological Economics*, Vol. 54/2-3, pp. 164-174, http://dx.doi.org/10.1016/j.ecolecon.2004.12.027. [46]

Malen, J. and A. Marcus (2017), "Promoting clean energy technology entrepreneurship: The role of external context", *Energy Policy*, Vol. 102, pp. 7-15, http://dx.doi.org/10.1016/j.enpol.2016.11.045. [36]

Mehling, M. and R. Ritz (2020), "Going beyond default intensities in an EU carbon border adjustment mechanism", *Cambridge Working Papers in Economics*, https://ideas.repec.org/p/cam/camdae/2087.html (accessed on 1 March 2021). [51]

OECD (2021), *Assessing the Economic Impacts of Environmental Policies: Evidence from a Decade of OECD Research*, OECD Publishing, Paris, https://dx.doi.org/10.1787/bf2fb156-en. [12]

OECD (2020), *Climate policy leadership in an interconnected world: What role for border carbon adjustments?*, OECD Publishing, Paris, https://doi.org/10.1787/8008e7f4-en. [7]

OECD (2014), *OECD Green Growth Studies : Greener Skills and Jobs*, OECD Publishing, Paris. [38]

PBL (2018), *Kosten energie- en klimaattransitie in 2030: Update 2018*, Planbureau voor de Leefomgeving, Den Haag, https://www.pbl.nl/sites/default/files/downloads/pbl-2018-kosten-energie-en-klimaattransitie-in-2030-update-2018_3241.pdf. [55]

Perino, G., R. Ritz and A. Benthem (2019), *Understanding overlapping policies: Internal carbon leakage and the punctured waterbed*, National Bureau of Economic Research, Cambridge MA, https://www.nber.org/papers/w25643.pdf. [26]

Peters, M. et al. (2012), "The impact of technology-push and demand-pull policies on technical change - Does the locus of policies matter?", *Research Policy*, Vol. 41/8, pp. 1296-1308, http://dx.doi.org/10.1016/j.respol.2012.02.004. [4]

Pollitt, H., K. Neuhoff and X. Lin (2020), "The impact of implementing a consumption charge on carbon-intensive materials in Europe", *Climate Policy*, Vol. 20/sup1, pp. S74-S89, http://dx.doi.org/10.1080/14693062.2019.1605969. [23]

Popp, D., I. Hascic and N. Medhi (2011), "Technology and the diffusion of renewable energy", *Energy Economics*, Vol. 33/4, pp. 648-662, https://ideas.repec.org/a/eee/eneeco/v33y2011i4p648-662.html (accessed on 1 March 2021). [8]

Popp, D., R. Newell and A. Jaffe (2010), "Energy, the environment, and technological change", in *Handbook of the Economics of Innovation*, Elsevier B.V., http://dx.doi.org/10.1016/S0169-7218(10)02005-8. [43]

Schmidt, T. (2014), "Low-carbon investment risks and de-risking", *Nature Climate Change*, Vol. 4/4, pp. 237--9, http://dx.doi.org/10.1038/nclimate2112. [41]

Steckel, J. and M. Jakob (2018), "The role of financing cost and de-risking strategies for clean energy investment", *International Economics*, Vol. 155, pp. 19-28, http://dx.doi.org/10.1016/j.inteco.2018.02.003. [40]

Venmans, F., J. Ellis and D. Nachtigall (2020), "Carbon pricing and competitiveness: are they at odds?", *Climate Policy*, Vol. 20/9, pp. 1070-1091, http://dx.doi.org/10.1080/14693062.2020.1805291. [19]

Walker, W. (2000), "Entrapment in large technology systems: Institutional commitment and power relations", *Research Policy*, Vol. 29/7-8, pp. 833-846, http://dx.doi.org/10.1016/s0048-7333(00)00108-6. [33]

Notes

[1] Jaffe et al. (2005[46]) for a discussion on the combined technology and environmental market failures and Goulder and Parry (2008[47]) for a general discussion of instrument choice in environmental policy.

[2] For example Braathen (2007[54]), Fischer and Newell (2008[2]), Fischer (2010[48]), Böhringer and Rosendahl (2010[3]), Fischer and Preonas (2010[1]) and Fischer, Preonas and Newell (2017[6]).

[3] Imperfections in demand for energy efficiency investments have important effects on the optimal policy mix, as they make policies that lower energy prices, such as deployment subsidies, less desirable. While this conclusion from the model under consideration is based on household behaviour regarding energy efficiency, and even if the industry is usually assumed to be more energy-efficient, it remains relevant for the purpose of this project as there exist negative abatement opportunities in the Dutch industry (PBL, 2018[55]).

[4] https://ec.europa.eu/research/participants/data/ref/h2020/wp/2014_2015/annexes/h2020-wp1415-annex-g-trl_en.pdf.

[5] Unilateral emission pricing also creates efficiency issues, as abating emissions in a cost-efficient way requires one and only one price for carbon globally (Chapter 8).

[6] By contrast, the Porter hypothesis suggests that stringent environmental regulations stimulate productivity growth via efficiency improvements and innovations aimed at avoiding the policy-induced cost of polluting. Empirical studies point to the validity of the Porter hypothesis for the most productive firms (Albrizio, Kozluk and Zipperer, 2017[49]).

[7] The energy market channel is both quantitatively important (Branger and Quirion, 2014[50]) and the most difficult to address without global carbon pricing. However, it is likely to be limited for the Dutch economy, as it represents only a small share of world GDP and energy consumption.

[8] The income channel also leads to domestic reallocation from energy-intensive sectors to the others: as the competitiveness of the energy-intensive sector deteriorates, the relative competitiveness of the other sectors improves.

[9] Analogue to the implementation of value added taxes for traded products.

[10] Solution to this challenge include proposals for a "voluntary individual adjustment mechanism" allowing producers to demonstrate that their actual carbon intensity lies below a given default value (Mehling and Ritz, 2020[51]).

[11] International technology spill over may mitigate the negative impact of carbon leakage on global emissions. The spill over of policy-induced energy-saving technological innovation in the home region to the foreign region may offset carbon leakage by improving the efficiency of foreign firms (Gerlagh and Kuik, 2014[52]). However, this mechanism is of a lower-order for small open economies, as their effect on the global stock of knowledge is likely to remain small.

[12] Consistent with the argument in previous sections, relying on emission pricing alone to direct technological change has a large welfare cost in the transition (Acemoglu et al., 2016[53]).

[13] As private investment decisions are made based on the risk-return profile of investment opportunities, decarbonisation policies can either increase the return on low-carbon investments through environmental and technology policy instruments or decrease the downside risk of low-carbon investments.

5. Current policy package

This chapter provides an in-depth description of the policy instruments most relevant for the decarbonisation of the Dutch industry and discusses the overall policy package with a view to its potential cost-efficiency, its coherence as well as its consistency with the carbon neutrality 2050 objective. The instruments are grouped into electricity and carbon pricing instruments (including energy taxes), support for R&D and demonstration projects (either horizontal or specifically targeted at low carbon innovation), adoption subsidies for low-carbon technologies, voluntary agreements, command and control instruments, infrastructure programmes and green procurement schemes.

The Dutch government is in the process of introducing new policy instruments geared at achieving the targets of the Climate Agreement (Box 1.1). These instruments come in addition to a set of existing tools that already provide incentives for industry to reduce emissions, resulting in a large number of instruments supporting a low-carbon transition. For example, the International Energy Agency's Policies and Measures database lists 130 policies in the Netherlands to reduce greenhouse gas emissions, improve energy efficiency and support the development and deployment of renewables and other clean energy technologies. An internal inventory by RVO lists 47 instruments that are particularly relevant for the industry sector. Based on this list, to which a few instruments (newly introduced or horizontal policies that might affect low carbon technologies indirectly) were added, and from which closed programmes were removed, around 50 relevant policies or measures were identified (Table 5.1).

5.1. Policy instruments that put a price on electricity or carbon

Carbon pricing is an effective and efficient decarbonisation policy. Depending on the exact design features, carbon pricing can provide a technology-neutral case for low-carbon investment and consumption. It raises the cost of carbon-intensive production and consumption behaviour, making low- and zero-carbon energy more competitive, and incentivises emission reduction by encouraging emitters to find and use economically efficient ways of cutting emissions (OECD, 2018[1]; OECD, 2019[2]).

Carbon pricing is one of the core building blocks for the transition towards a low-carbon economy. It encourages emitters to adopt and innovate low-carbon technologies across sectors of the economy, thereby allowing emission reductions to occur where they are cheapest and avoiding the need to identify and prioritise the most promising technologies, firms or sectors in advance. Well-designed instruments that address additional market or government failures and other barriers may usefully complement carbon pricing as part of a broader policy package.

The design of electricity taxation is also important for decarbonisation. Electricity taxes apply to an energy output (electricity) and are typically not distinguished by energy source. In that case, they make electricity more expensive even when it is produced from clean energy sources and fail to favour decarbonisation of the electricity mix. Therefore, they do not constitute a carbon price. They also may discourage deep cuts in carbon emissions through electrification when electricity generation itself is decarbonised.

The Dutch government employs several policy instruments that effectively put a price on carbon emissions or on electricity use. The industry sector is subject to fuel-specific energy taxes, electricity taxes, a sustainable energy surcharge and the EU ETS. While instruments that are fuel specific (e.g. energy tax on natural gas use, the surcharge on natural gas use) or targeting emissions directly (e.g. EU ETS) effectively put a price on carbon, other instruments (e.g. energy tax on electricity use, the surcharge on electricity use, the indirect cost compensation) effectively price electricity but do not differentiate by fuel and their carbon content. In addition, a 21% VAT rate applies on the purchase of energy products including excise taxes and EU ETS allowances.[1] On top of the existing instruments, the new climate agreement introduced a national carbon levy for industry and implemented changes to the energy surcharge on natural gas and electricity.

The objective of this section is to provide a detailed, numerical assessment of the role that electricity and carbon pricing currently plays in the Dutch industry. It describes policy instruments that effectively, and sometimes explicitly, put a price on electricity or carbon in the Netherlands and how they apply to Dutch industry. It discusses which industrial sectors are covered and which are (partially) exempt from pricing instruments. The section also highlights revenues that are associated with the different instruments. Sections 5.8.1 and 5.8.2 present and analyse two synthetic pricing indicators. First, the effective carbon rate summarising the different carbon pricing instruments and their application in a single measure. Second, an effective tax rate on electricity use. It provides a detailed overview of how the Netherlands price electricity or carbon emissions from energy use in industry, with a focus on the chemicals, metallurgical, food processing and refinery sectors.

Table 5.1. Overview of policy instruments

Instrument type	Policy instruments
Electricity and carbon pricing instruments	Taxes on energy use Energy surcharge (Opslag Duurzame Energie [ODE]) EU Emission Trading System (ETS) (including indirect cost compensation) National carbon levy
Voluntary Agreements	Multi-year agreements on energy efficiency (Meerjarenafspraken energie-efficiëntie [MJA-3/MEE]) (ended 2020) Front runner programmes/regional industry cluster programmes
R&D / demonstration support - generic	European programmes: H2020, EU SME Instrument; European Innovation Council (EIC); ERANET Domestic: National Science Agenda, TO2 Tax incentives: WBSO & Innovation box Nationaal Groeifonds SMEs: Innovation vouchers, DVI, SBIR Guarantees: SME credit guarantee scheme (BMKB); Growth facility Top Consortia for Knowledge and Innovation (TKI) Top Sectors: Topsectorenaanpak, PPS/TKI, Knowledge and Innovation Covenant (KIC), MOP; SME Innovation Support Top Sectors (MIT); Dutch Research Council (NWO)-KIC
R&D / demonstration support - specific	European: NER300/Innovation Fund; InnovFin EDP; SET Plan Top Sectors: GoChem; TSE-R Integrated Knowledge & Innovation Agenda Climate (IKIA) Mission-driven research, development and innovation (MOOI) Multi-year Mission Driven Innovation Programmes (MMIPs) Demonstration Energy and Climate Innovation (DEI, DEI+, DEI+ CE, HER+) Invest NL
Oes Deployment/ adoption subsidies	Stimulation of sustainable energy production and climate transition (SDE++) Energy investment allowance (EIA) Accelerated climate investment in industry (VEKI) MIA (*Milieu-InvesteringsAftrek* - environmental investment deduction) and Arbitrary depreciation of environmental investments (VAMIL) Investment Subsidy Sustainable Energy (ISDE) Green project scheme EU LIFE programme Small-scale investment allowance (KIA)
Command and control	Environmental Management Act: Obligation for investment in energy savings
Infrastructure programmes	European Structural and Investment Funds (ESIF): European regional development fund (ERDF) Porthos and Athos CO_2 network North Sea Wind Power Hub Taskforce Infrastructure Climate Agreement Industry (TIKI) Multi-year Program Infrastructure Energy and Climate (MIEK) National Program Regional Energy Strategy (RES)

5.1.1. Taxes on energy use

Taxes on energy use, such as taxes on fuel or electricity, set a tax rate per physical unit. Different from electricity taxes, fuel taxes translate into an effective carbon tax rate, in the sense that they can be converted into a rate on the carbon content of each form of energy. Although not explicitly linked to a carbon price, fuel taxes effectively put a price on carbon similar to carbon taxes in the sense that the tax liability increases proportionally to fossil fuel use. The authority responsible for implementing taxes on energy use (fuels and electricity) is the Ministry of Finance. Tax payments are made to the Netherlands Tax and Customs Administration by the consumers' respective energy supplier, who collects energy taxes via the energy bill.

The central policy objective of the Dutch Energy Tax is to fund the general budget of the State.

Tax rates

The Netherlands levies taxes on energy use within the framework of the EU Energy Tax Directive (2003/96/EC), which sets minimum rates for the taxation of energy products in EU member states. Effective 1 July 2020, the following rates apply within this framework. A coal tax of EUR 0.4755 per gigajoule (GJ) applies to coal and coke products used as a heating fuel (European Commission, 2020[3]). Coal used for other means than combustion and coal used in the generation of electricity are exempt from the tax. An excise duty applies to liquid fuels, such as diesel and gasoline. The rate for diesel use in the industry sector, either in stationary motors or for heating, is EUR 503.62 per 1 000 litres (European Commission, 2020[3]).

An additional energy tax applies to natural gas and electricity consumption in industry.[2] The tax rate for natural gas and electricity changes with consumption based on a four-bracket system. The system provides a schedule of rates that decrease with consumption. On average, a small energy user will pay a higher effective rate per unit of all energy consumed than a large energy user. Table 5.2 and Table 5.3 show the tax rates for natural gas and electricity in 2020 as reported in the Environmental Taxes Act. The energy tax does not apply to fuels used for other means than combustion, for instance the use of gas as a raw material for production of fertiliser, methanol or hydrogen. Additional sector specific exemptions apply, as discussed below. Table 5.5 and Table 5.6 provide context of how the main industrial subsectors distribute across these bands.

Table 5.2. Energy tax rates for natural gas in 2021, by consumption level

	0-170 000 m³	170 001-1 million m³	> 1-10 million m³	> 10 million m³
Tax rates for natural gas (in EUR per m³)	0.34856	0.06547	0.02386	0.01281

Note: Bands are defined for a 12-month consumption period. Different rates apply to the horticultural industry. The first band covers block heating.
Source: Environmental Taxes Act.

Table 5.3. Energy tax rates for electricity in 2021, by consumption level

	0-10 000 kWh	10 001-50 000 kWh	50 001-10 million kWh	> 10 million kWh
Tax rates for electricity (in EUR per kWh)	0.09428	0.05164	0.01375	0.00056

Note: Bands are defined for a 12-month consumption period.
Source: Environmental Taxes Act.

Energy-intensive users in the Netherlands benefit from relatively low energy tax rates compared to Dutch users that consume relatively less energy, thanks to the regressive rate structure for natural gas and electricity taxes. The main reasons for providing relief to large industrial users are concerns over competition, i.e. that these domestic users may face competition from firms in countries where energy taxes are lower. Higher domestic taxes could eventually lead to carbon leakage, whereby foreign emissions increase because production moves to countries with less ambitious climate policies (Fowlie and Reguant, 2018[4]). The small and open structure of the Dutch economy may explain the efforts to shield domestic industry from international tax competition.[3] However, the current structure of the energy tax provides relief on the sole criterion of energy use, with no differentiation based on the actual exposure of a sector to international competition. Alternatively, in the EU ETS, measures to address competitiveness concerns relate to the trade-exposure and energy-intensity of production, see below.

The regressive rate structure leads to average tax rates per unit of output that differ across producers. Such preferential treatment of large producers compared to small producers may conflict with the principle of horizontal equity, particularly if companies of different sizes produce substitute goods. Consider a small, local producer of goods or services, who pays the high tax rate of the first or second consumption bracket on the entirety of its consumption, and who competes with other producers of the same goods or services on the local market. Some of these competitors may be large and some part of their consumption may fall into the higher consumption brackets. The large consumer would then benefit from preferential tax treatment only because of its size and would pay proportionally less in taxes than the local producer does.[4] If such treatment were justified to encourage economies of scale, one would need to carefully assess the context and justification for providing such types of input subsidies.

The current rate structure does not take into consideration the carbon-intensity of energy use either.[5] Even if carbon reduction may not be a stated policy objective for the energy tax, providing reduced energy tax rates for natural gas to large energy users may provide incentives that are misaligned with the decarbonisation plans of the government, especially if these users currently rely on carbon-intensive energy sources. At the very least, smaller users of natural gas will face higher effective carbon rates than larger ones. As discussed in Chapter 9, alternative measures exist that provide targeted relief to firms that are exposed to international tax competition, while keeping the incentive to decarbonise in place. Internal and external evaluations of the Dutch energy tax are being conducted in this context.

Tax bases

Looking at the actual distribution of energy use across the different consumption bands shows that the majority of natural gas and electricity used in the Dutch industry sector is subject to the lowest available energy tax rate (Table 5.4). 89% of all gas use and 96% of all electricity use in industry are situated in the highest two consumption bands, i.e. those subject to the lowest tax rates.

Table 5.4. Distribution of energy use across consumption bands in industry, 2016

	Band 1	Band 2	Band 3	Band 4
Natural gas	5%	6%	16%	74%
Electricity	2%	3%	37%	59%

Source: CBS (2017[5])

Considering the most energy-intensive sectors in the Netherlands, the distribution of energy use across bands is particularly skewed towards the consumption bands with the lowest rates (Bands 3 and 4). Table 5.5 shows the distribution of natural gas consumption in industry by sector. The left-hand side panel shows the share of each sector in total industry natural gas use, while the right hand-side panel shows the distribution of natural gas use by consumption band. For example, the chemical sector consumes 34.3% of all natural gas that is used in Dutch industry, and the vast majority of this consumption (72.9%) falls in the fourth consumption band. This picture looks quite different for the food-processing sector, which is responsible for 24.4% of natural gas use in industry, and where 31% of energy use is subject to the highest tax rates (Bands 1 and 2).

Similarly, Table 5.6 shows the distribution of electricity consumption in industry by sector. The left-hand side panel shows the share of each sector in total industry electricity use, while the right hand-side panel shows the distribution of electricity use by consumption band. The table shows that the chemical sector consumes 34.2% of all electricity in the industry sector, with nearly 100% falling in Bands 3 and 4.

Table 5.5. Distribution of natural gas consumption by industry sub-sector, 2016

Industry sub-sector	Share in total industry natural gas use	Distribution of energy use within each sub-sector			
		Band 1	Band 2	Band 3	Band 4
Chemicals	34.3%	2.1%	4.7%	20.3%	72.9%
Food processing	24.3%	14.9%	16.3%	36.4%	32.4%
Building materials	9.7%	2.9%	7.2%	41.1%	48.8%
Refineries	8.7%	0.3%	0.7%	7.0%	92.0%
Basic Metals	6.8%	3.6%	8.4%	20.7%	67.3%
Metal products, machinery	6.2%	41.7%	19.3%	19.8%	19.2%
Other industry	10.0%	32.2%	21.5%	40.0%	6.3%

Note: The second column shows the relative contribution of each sub-sector to total natural gas consumption in industry. Natural gas used as a feedstock is not included. Columns 3 to 6 present the distribution of natural gas consumption within each sub-sector across the four consumption bands. *Building materials* (ISIC 23) includes manufacture of some non-metallic mineral products, such as cement, clay, glass, lime and plaster. *Basic metals* (ISIC 24) include manufacture and casting of iron and steel, basic precious and other non-ferrous metals (including, for example aluminium, copper, lead, nickel etc.). *Metal products and machinery* (ISIC 25-28) excludes transport equipment.
Source: Based on CBS (2017[5]).

Table 5.6. Distribution of electricity consumption by industry sub-sector, 2016

Industry sub-sector	Share in total industry electricity use	Distribution of energy use within each sub-sector			
		Band 1	Band 2	Band 3	Band 4
Chemicals	34.2%	0.1%	0.3%	13.5%	86.2%
Food	18.3%	0.8%	2.9%	53.2%	43.1%
Basic metals	15.1%	0.1%	0.2%	10.1%	89.6%
Metal products, machinery	9.4%	1.8%	4.3%	57.7%	36.3%
Other industry	22.9%	3.5%	4.7%	47.6%	44.2%

Note: The second column shows the relative contribution of each sub-sector to total electricity consumption in industry. Columns 3 to 6 present the distribution of electricity consumption within each sub-sector across the four consumption bands
Source: Based on CBS (2017[5]).

Exemptions and refunds

In addition to benefiting from the regressive rate of the energy tax, some energy-intensive natural gas and electricity users are exempt from energy taxes according to the Environmental Taxes Act. Sections 5.8.1 and 5.8.2 present the detailed effective tax rates on natural gas and electricity by industrial sector taking into account exemptions and refunds.

In particular, the energy tax applies to gas and electricity supplied via a connection to the energy grid, leaving electricity and natural gas production for own use ("auto-generation") untaxed (Art. 50). Electricity auto-generation from renewable energy sources is also exempt.

Natural gas and electricity used in combined heat and power (CHP) generation is also exempt from the energy tax for installations with an electrical efficiency of at least 30% and electric power of at least 60 kW (Art. 64, Environmental Taxes Act). The rationale for this exemption is to prevent double taxation of CHP-*generated* electricity as it is subject to the electricity tax. However, the current design of this exemption also leads to CHP-generated heat not being subject to a tax. Finally, this exemption also includes electricity produced for own use and gas produced for own heating consumption, which are both exempt from the energy tax and where no risk for double taxation exist.

In addition, specific industrial sectors benefit from a tax exemption, notably, natural gas used in metallurgical processes (i.e. the manufacture of metals in primary form, the forging, pressing, stamping and roll forming of metal and the surface treatment consisting of hardening or heat treatment of metals). This encompasses activities belonging to Code 24 or 25 of the Standard Industrial Classification of 21 July 2008 by the Central Bureau of Statistics. Natural gas is also exempt when used for mineralogical processes, including the manufacture of glass and glassware, ceramic products, cement, lime or gypsum, sand-lime bricks or aerated concrete and rock wool (Art. 64, Par 4). This includes companies with an activity assigned to code 23 of the Standard Industrial Classification of 21 July 2008 by the Dutch Central Bureau of Statistics. The use of electricity is also exempt for chemical reduction, electrolytic and metallurgical processes (Art. 64, Par 3). Sections 5.8.1 and 5.8.2 map tax exemptions to the effective energy base in the Netherlands and provide summary indicators for carbon and electricity pricing.

Businesses can request an additional tax refund for electricity consumption above 10 million kWh (excluding consumption that benefits from other exemptions) per year when they meet two criteria (Art. 66). First, businesses need to have undertaken a commitment to improve energy efficiency within one of the long-term agreements that industrial sectors have signed with government. Second, their activity needs to be considered energy-intensive in the sense that businesses need to participate in the voluntary Multi-year Energy Efficiency Agreement for EU ETS companies (MEE agreement) (Section 5.2.1). The refund is calculated as the difference between the actual tax liability on electricity supplied for business consumption in the calendar year and the potential tax liability on a quantity of 10 million kWh. Or, if the amount would be higher, the difference between the actual tax liability and the hypothetical tax liability on all business electricity consumption would apply a minimum tax rate as defined in the EU Energy Tax Directive (2003/96/EC).

Revenues

There is no direct earmarking of revenues from energy taxes[6] in the Netherlands, albeit there is a political commitment for a green tax shift, i.e. to use additional revenues from the energy tax to reduce taxation on labour and capital income. More precisely, revenues collected through the energy tax are generally assigned to the Dutch overall budget. When policy decisions are made to raise energy tax rates, the projected revenue is used to finance tax cuts on direct taxes, such as personal income and corporate income taxes. The Dutch government does not, however, track the amount of revenues generated from increases in energy tax rates (Marten and Van Dender, 2019[6]).

The generous exemptions for specific industries and the relatively low tax rates related to consumption Band 4 limits the energy tax liability of energy-intensive industrial users. This implies that energy-intensive users will contribute relatively little to the Dutch green tax shift efforts.

Table 5.7 provides a first overview on how the preferential tax treatment provided in the energy tax law spreads across industry subsectors in the Netherlands. It shows the total energy taxes on natural gas and electricity paid by the industry sector in 2017 and contrasts these tax payments to the industry sectors energy base in 2016. The figures for tax payment are net of exemptions and refunds and reflect the regressive rate structure, i.e. differing rates across consumption bands. By highlighting each industrial subsector's contribution to the industry totals, the table shows which sectors receive most of the preferential treatment. For example, cases where a subsector contributes less to total industry tax payments than it contributes to the total energy base imply a generous level of preferential tax treatment. This is the case in the petroleum, chemical, building material and metallurgical sectors.

Summary indicators on the effective tax rates per industry subsector are displayed and discussed in the carbon pricing profiles in Sections 5.8.1 and 5.8.2.

Table 5.7. Energy tax payments (2017) and energy base (2016) per industry sub-sector

	Natural Gas		Electricity	
	Tax payments (in EUR mln)	**Energy base** (in mln m³)	**Tax payments** (in EUR mln)	**Energy base** (in GWh)
Industry total	221.6	5 896.1	186.7	31 930.7
Contribution by subsector (in %)				
10-13 Food, drinks and tobacco	36.3%	24.3%	31.4%	18.3%
13-15 Textile and leather	4.0%	1.4%	4.4%	1.1%
16-18 Wood, paper and graphic industry	7.6%	4.0%	11.9%	6.9%
19 Petroleum industry	3.2%	8.7%	0.5%	2.3%
20, 21 Chemical and pharma industry	18.5%	34.3%	11.9%	34.2%
23 Building materials	0.5%	9.7%	3.2%	3.9%
24 Basic metals	0.0%	6.8%	0.0%	15.1%
25-30 Machinery (incl. transport means)	18.9%	7.3%	16.9%	11.2%
31-32, 22 Other industry and repair	10.9%	3.6%	19.9%	6.9%

Note: Small differences in the sectoral definitions across tax payments and the energy base may remain.
Source: CE Delft (2021[7]) and CBS (2017[5]).

5.1.2. ODE

The ODE was implemented as of 1 January 2013 to stimulate the transition from fossil fuels to sustainable energy. The ODE is a separate levy on natural gas and electricity that comes in addition to the energy tax described in the Section 5.1.1. It mirrors the structure of the energy tax in the sense that ODE rates vary across the same consumption bands, decreasing with the amount of energy used. Identical exemptions apply. The central policy objective of the ODE is to fund payments to renewable energy projects in the context of the Sustainable Energy Production Scheme (SDE+). The scope of the instrument was recently extended through the Climate Agreement as detailed below.

The authority responsible for implementing ODE is the Ministry of Finance, while ODE payments are made to the Dutch Tax and Customs Administration by the respective energy supplier, who collects ODE payments via consumers' annual energy bills.

ODE rates and exemptions

The government sets the ODE rates annually to cover the budget of the SDE scheme. Rates have been increasing over the years alongside the growing financing needs for renewable energy (Table 5.8 and Table 5.9). The same consumption bands apply as for the energy tax. For example, ODE receipts amounted to EUR 97 million in 2013 and increased yearly to reach EUR 1 632 million in 2019 (CBS, 2020[8]). Up until 2020, households and business contributed equally to the ODE-SDE budget (Government of the Netherlands, 2019[9]).

As with the energy tax, the regressive rate structure provides relief to energy users on the sole criteria of energy-intensity, with no differentiation on the sector's actual exposure to international competition or the carbon-intensity of energy use. Providing preferential treatment to large producers at the expense of small producers, who produce substitute goods, disadvantages local producers and introduces distortions. Overall, the same remarks apply as made in Section 5.1.1.

Table 5.8. ODE rates for natural gas, by consumption level (EUR/m³)

Year	0-170 000 m³	170 001- million m³	> 1-10 million m³	> 10 million m³
2020	**0.07750**	**0.02140**	**0.02120**	**0.02120**
2019	0.05240	0.01610	0.00590	0.00310
2018	0.02850	0.01060	0.00390	0.00210
2017	0.01590	0.00740	0.00270	0.00130
2016	0.01130	0.00420	0.00130	0.00090
2015	0.00740	0.00280	0.00080	0.00060
2014	0.00460	0.00170	0.00050	0.00040
2013	0.00230	0.00090	0.00030	0.00020

Note: Bands are defined for a 12-month consumption period. Different rates apply to the horticultural industry. Block heating is covered by the first band.
Source: Belastingdienst (2020[10]).

Table 5.9. ODE rates for electricity, by consumption level (EUR/kWh)

Year	0-10 000 kWh	10 001-50 000 kWh	50 001-10 million kWh	> 10 million kWh
2020	**0.0273**	**0.0375**	**0.0205**	**0.0004**
2019	0.0189	0.0278	0.0074	0.0003
2018	0.0132	0.018	0.0048	0.000194
2017	0.0074	0.0123	0.0033	0.000131
2016	0.0056	0.007	0.0019	0.000084
2015	0.0036	0.0046	0.0012	0.000055
2014	0.0023	0.0027	0.0007	0.000034
2013	0.0011	0.0014	0.0004	0.000017

Note: Bands are defined for a 12-month consumption period.
Source: Belastingdienst (2020[10]).

As of 2021, the new Climate Agreement_increases the scope of the SDE scheme. The extended SDE++ scheme covers low-carbon technologies and production processes beyond renewable energy, in particular technologies with the potential to reduce CO_2 emissions in the industry sector (e.g. hydrogen, carbon capture and storage [CCS], the use of residual heat). In this context, the Agreement also restructured ODE. As of January 2021, business will contribute a higher share to the overall ODE budget, from the current 50% to 67%. The Agreement also indicates that consumers in the two highest consumption bands will take on the additional charge from the extension of the SDE scheme. “This increase will be collected in full in the highest tax brackets (third and fourth brackets)” (Government of the Netherlands, 2019[9]).

The new structure of the combined ODE-SDE mechanism aims to restructure industry and strengthen abatement incentives via a revenue-neutral approach (within industry). Until 2030, industrial energy users would eventually contribute EUR 550 million per year to the ODE budget. The same amount would then be recycled back to industry in the form of SDE++ subsidies for CO_2 reductions.

Comparing ODE rates across consumption bands for 2021, it is not immediately evident to what extent energy-intensive industrial users actually contribute to the additional ODE effort as outlined in the Climate Agreement. Table 5.10 shows the new ODE rates for 2021 as indicated by the central government, and percentage changes related to 2019 rates. Between 2019 and 2021, tax rates in each consumption band increase, with the largest total rate changes arising in the third and the fourth bands (except for electricity Band 4) where 2019 rates are lowest. Table 5.11 shows the estimated ODE rates for 2025. However, these bands also receive generous exemptions. In particular, exemptions from ODE align exactly with the exemptions from the energy tax discussed above as defined by Article 64 of the Environmental Taxes Law.

As a consequence, it is far from straightforward to analyse the total contribution of different consumption bands to the ODE budget, as well as the contribution by industry sub-sectors.

Table 5.10. ODE rates in 2021 and changes compared to 2019, by consumption level

	Band 1		Band 2		Band 3		Band 4	
	2021 Rate	Change to 2019	2021 Rate	Change to 2019	2021 Rate	Change to 2019	2021 Rate	Change to 2019
Natural gas rate (EUR/m³)	0.0851	+62.4%	0.0235	+46.0%	0.0232	+293.2%	0.0232	+648.4%
Electricity rate (EUR/kWh)	0.03	+58.8%	0.0411	+47.8%	0.0225	+204.1%	0.0004	+33.3%

Source: Calculations based on Rijksoverheid (2020[11]).

Table 5.11. ODE rate projections for 2025 and changes compared to 2019, by consumption level

	Band 1		Band 2		Band 3		Band 4	
	Rate	Change to 2019	Rate	Change to 2019	Rate	Change to 2019	Rate	Change to 2019
Natural gas rate (EUR/m³)	0.1028	+96.2%	0.0283	+75.8%	0.0281	+376.3%	0.0281	+806.5%
Electricity rate (EUR/kWh)	0.03618	+91.4%	0.04968	+78.7%	0.02723	+277.0%	0.00054	+80.0%

Note: Nominal rates are reported. Projections assume there is no change in the levy base. If the base erodes over time, e.g. thanks to effective climate policy instruments, the projected rates would need to be adjusted.
Source: PBL from communication with CE Delft.

Revenue

Until 2020, ODE revenues have been fully earmarked to finance measures that stimulate the production of sustainable energy (SDE+). Starting at around EUR 100 million in 2014, the budget reached EUR 2411 million by 2020 (Table 5.12), as reported by Statistics Netherlands and the Ministry of Economic Affairs and Climate Policy (2021[12])

Table 5.12. Past government receipts from ODE on electricity and natural gas

	2013	2014	2015	2016	2017	2018	2019	2020
ODE receipts per year (EUR million)	97	174	279	421	635	1 033	1 733	2 411

Source: CBS (2020[8]) and Ministry of Economic Affairs and Climate Policy (2021[12])

Looking at the sectoral contributions to the ODE budget, the industrial sector contributed EUR 11 million to ODE in 2019 (Ministry of Economic Affairs and Climate Policy, 2021[12]). With the transformation of the ODE-SDE scheme in the year 2021, the industry sector is supposed to contribute (and receive) a maximum of EUR 550 million annually. Table 5.13 shows the industrial sector's ODE payments in 2017, differentiated by natural gas and electricity, and the contribution of different sub-sectors to total revenues in percentage. These figures are net of exemptions and account for the different rates across consumption bands in 2017.

The table also contrasts each sub-sector ODE contribution in 2017[7] to its energy base in 2016, shedding light on how preferential treatment distributes over sectors. As with revenues from the energy tax, both the generous exemptions and the lower tax rates in the third and fourth consumption band limits the contribution of energy-intensive industrial users to the ODE-SDE redistribution mechanism. If the framework for providing exemptions is not reformed in the future, small energy consumers risk contributing highly to the expanded SDE++ budget, while potentially having little opportunity to claim SDE++ subsidies, which are directed mainly at technologies for energy-intensive industry.

Sections 5.8.1 and 5.8.2 provide a more detailed picture on how fiscal instruments that put a price on carbon or electricity distribute over the CO_2 emissions base in the main sectors, highlighting in detail how strongly each tonne of carbon is priced and where the bulk of exemptions applies.

Table 5.13. ODE payments (2017) and energy base (2016) per industry subsector

		Natural Gas		Electricity	
		ODE payments (in mio EUR)	**Energy base** (in mio m³)	**ODE payments** (in mio EUR)	**Energy base** (in mio kWh)
Industry total		21.06	5 896.1	36.48	31 930.7
Contribution by subsector (in %)					
10-13	Food, drinks and tobacco	37.5%	24.3%	33.7%	18.3%
13-15	Textile and leather	3.5%	1.4%	3.1%	1.1%
16-18	Wood, paper and graphic industry	7.6%	4.0%	10.9%	6.9%
19	Petroleum industry	3.8%	8.7%	0.6%	2.3%
20, 21	Chemical and pharma industry	22.3%	34.3%	14.1%	34.2%
23	Building materials	0.7%	9.7%	4.1%	3.9%
24	Basic metals	0.0%	6.8%	0.0%	15.1%
25-30	Machinery (incl. transport means)	15.3%	7.3%	17.4%	11.2%
31-32, 22	Other industry and repair	9.3%	3.6%	16.0%	6.9%

Note: Small differences in the sectoral definitions across ODE payments and the energy base may remain.
Source: CE Delft (2021[7]) and CBS (2017[5]).

5.1.3. EU ETS

Emissions from Dutch industry are subject to the EU ETS. The EU ETS was set up in 2005 and follows a cap and trade principle to set a price on carbon emissions. It fixes the quantity of carbon to be emitted by all installations in the system (cap), which decreases over time. The newly established market stability reserve modifies this principle (see below). Installations in the EU ETS need to surrender tradable emission permits (allowances) for all their emissions of the previous year. The allowance price is determined by the market, either by an auction or the secondary market, at the intersection of the allowance supply and demand.

Since the beginning of Phase 3 of the EU ETS (2013-20), a single EU-wide cap replaces the previous system of national caps. From the beginning of Phase 4 (2021-30), the number of allowances that are put into circulation will decrease at a rate of 2.2% annually. Installations either receive emission allowances for free, based on product-specific benchmarks, or have to buy them via auctions or on a secondary market. A company can bank unused allowances for future use or trade it with other companies in the market.

The extent to which allowances are auctioned, as opposed to freely allocated, varies across sectors. While electricity generators have not received free allowances since 2013 in most countries,[8] the manufacturing sector received free allowances for 80% of its emissions in 2013 in those industrial sectors where the risk for carbon leakage was not considered to be significant. This share decreased to 30% in 2020 and is foreseen to phase out after 2026 to 0 at the end of phase 4 (2030) "unless a review of the Directive determines otherwise". (European Commission, 2020[13]). Free allocation to these sectors is planned to be phased out after 2026. Industrial installations considered to be "at significant risk of carbon leakage" (reflecting a sector's trade and emissions intensity) receive most of their allowances for free with the objective to preserve their competitiveness. That is, they receive free allowances for 100% of the benchmark emissions, which correspond to the average emissions of the 10% most efficient installations in the sector. European legislation (Decision 2019/708) determines the sectors and subsectors that are deemed at risk of carbon leakage. With regards to the industry sectors in the focus of this analysis, several subcategories in the basic metal, chemicals and food subsectors are deemed at risk. The entire refinery sector is also included.[9]

The Dutch Emissions Authority (NEa) implements and monitors the EU ETS in the Netherlands. Before the end of March each year, all EU ETS installations have to report the emissions of the past year via a verified emissions report. At the end of April, they have to surrender enough allowances to cover all reported emissions. The NEa monitors compliance and can take enforcement action if needed.

Permit prices

The average auction price of EU ETS emission allowances in 2020 was settled at EUR 24.35 per tonne of CO_2.[10] Over the course of the year allowance prices moved between a range of EUR 14.60, on 23 March 2020, and EUR 30.92, on 14 December 2020 (EEX, 2020[14]).

A market stability reserve (MSR) started operating at the beginning of 2019. The objective of the MSR is to address the existing surplus of allowances in the EU ETS and to adjust the future supply of allowances in the event of major economic shocks. The MSR would stabilise the EU ETS price by regulating the quantity of allowances in the market (European Commission, 2020[15]).[11] Contrary to other trading systems, e.g. the Californian Cap and Trade Program, it does not specify a price threshold for delivering stability support and therefore provides no guarantee against low permit prices (Flues and Van Dender, 2020[16]).

Sector coverage and free allocation

Approximately 430 Dutch companies participate in the EU ETS. A small proportion of installations contribute to the vast majority of Dutch emissions covered by the EU ETS. 81% of emissions came from 10% of the EU ETS installations in 2018. The main emitters are in the energy and chemical sector, refineries and manufacturing of primary metals (Rijskoverheid, 2020[17]).

In 2019, the EU ETS covers 45.2 million tonnes of Dutch industrial emissions (CO_2-equivalent)[12]. Emissions from electricity generation are also covered by the EU ETS. The industry sub-sectors contributing most to EU ETS emissions are chemicals, refineries and basic metals (Table 5.14). In 2019, these sectors received free allowances corresponding to respectively 96%, 73% and 85% of their verified emissions (CE Delft, 2021[7]).

Table 5.14. Verified emissions and free allocation, 2019

Industry sub-sector	Verified emissions (mln tonnes of CO_2-eq)	Freely allocated allowances (mln tonnes of CO_2-eq)	Proportion of free allocation
Chemicals	17.9	17.2	96%
Food	2.0	1.4	70%
Basic metals	11.6	9.9	85%
Refineries	11.0	10.3	73%
Other industry	2.7	2.0	94%
Total industry	**45.2**	**39.3**	**87%**

Source: CE Delft (2021[7]).

Box 5.1. Free allocation and decarbonisation incentives

Theory suggests that the EU ETS price provides an incentive for emissions abatement independently from how allowances are allocated. Because an emissions allowance could always be sold on the market, owning an allowance has an opportunity cost for forgoing emissions abatement, equal to the ETS price. The opportunity to sell allowances exists whether the allowance has been freely allocated or was bought on the market or during an auction. As such, the marginal abatement incentive remains intact independently of the allocation mechanism. This would incentivise all EU ETS participants to engage in emission reduction at the margin, for example, via efficiency improvements if no additional distortions exist.

However, preparing the shift towards a low- or zero-carbon economy requires thinking beyond abatement incentives at the margin towards deep decarbonisation and a technological switch. In such a setting, there is a need to re-evaluate the free allocation of emissions allowances. Investing in clean technologies as opposed to carbon-intensive technologies involves an investor's discrete choice that is driven by economic rents. Freely allocating emission allowances based on product-specific benchmarks that often differs across carbon-intensive and low-carbon substitutes will affect economic rents and can make carbon-intensive investments more attractive (Flues and Van Dender, 2017[18]). Depending on the allocation rules, free allocation can weaken incentives for firms to invest in break-through low-carbon technologies and undermines the trading system's effectiveness to drive decarbonisation.

For example, a traditional steel producer within the EU ETS, who receives a free allocation on all emissions, has an incentive to reduce emissions at the margin and sell the unused allowances on the market. The producer could do so by burning fossil fuels more efficiently for instance, which would be profitable as long as the expected price of the allowance sale outweighs the cost of the emissions abatement. However, if the same free allocation is not made available for clean producers, there may be no incentive to switch technologies towards existing (e.g. electric arc to melt iron) or entirely new and clean production processes (e.g. direct reduced iron using green hydrogen). For example, if the new technology is linked to a process-specific product-benchmark where free allocation is lower or nil, adopting the new technology confers an allocation disadvantage.

Flues and Van Dender (2020[16]) discuss recent empirical findings that are consistent with the theoretical argument that free allocation of permits in the EU ETS weakens abatement incentives or innovation efforts (Brouwers, Schoubben and Van Hulle, 2017[19]; Martin, Muûls and Wagner, 2016[20]; Martin, Muûls and Wagner, 2016[20]).

Indirect cost compensation

With the introduction of the EU ETS, Members States have the right to implement a national mechanism to compensate electricity-intensive industry sectors for the potential increase of electricity cost due to the EU ETS. The national measures need to be in line with EU state aid rules. Aid can be granted only upon approval by the European Commission.

In the Netherlands, a national compensation for higher electricity costs has been in place since 2014 (Article 4.4.1-4.4.13 of Regulation No. WJZ/13125043). A company needs to meet two criteria to be eligible for the indirect cost compensation. It needs to participate in the multi-year energy efficiency agreements MJA3 or MEE and to operate in one of the 15 industry subsectors as defined by the European Commission[13] (Appendix 4.4.1 of WJZ/13125043). The compensation payment is calculated based on: 1) the standardised product-specific electricity consumption profile per year; 2) a fixed CO_2 emission factor per MWh; 3) the average EU ETS future price in the previous year; and 4) a support intensity defined by the European Commission (set at 85% in 2014/2015, 80% in 2016/2017/2018 and 75% in 2019/2020). No compensation is granted for the first 1 000 MWh consumed.

Although the compensation mechanism aims to counteract a potential increase in electricity costs deriving from the EU ETS carbon price, the compensation payment in the Netherlands does not vary with the carbon content of the energy source used for electricity generation. This implies that facilities receive the same compensation per MWh whether they use electricity produced from carbon-intensive coal that pays the EU ETS price, or carbon-neutral renewable or nuclear energy that is not subject to the EU ETS.

Table 5.15 reports compensation payments for the Dutch industry sector over time. Payments vary between EUR 31.3 million in 2015 (compensation for 2014) and EUR 110.6 million in 2020 (compensation for 2019), which reflects changes in the EU ETS price and the support intensity. The largest recipients of compensation in recent years were the chemical sector and basic metal industry (non-ferrous metals, iron and steel), accounting for more than 56% and 32% of the total compensation respectively. Contrasting the compensation payments to the revenues generated from the auction of emissions allowances in the Netherlands shows that the indirect cost compensation paid in 2017-20 to industry represented 37.8%, 19.4%, 8.0%, 25.1% of auction revenues in 2016-19 respectively.

Table 5.15. Compensation payment for electricity input costs (in EUR million)

Industry sub-sector	2014	2015	2016	2017	2018	2019	2020
Chemicals				30.1	20.7	22.7	
Basic metals				17.1	12.0	12.9	
Other industry				6.4	4.2	4.7	
Industry total	52.7	31.3	45.0	53.5	36.9	40.3	110.6

Note: Payments reported in year *t* compensate for input costs incurred in year *t-1*. Sub-sectoral data available only for the years 2017-19.
Source: RVO (2020[21]).

Auction Revenues

In the Netherlands, revenues generated from auctioning EU ETS emissions allowances amounted to EUR 440 million in 2019, up from 25.6 million in 2012 (Table 5.16). Revenues are assigned to the overall budget. There is no legal earmarking of auction revenues (Marten and Van Dender, 2019[6]).

Table 5.16. Revenues generated from auctioning Dutch allowances per year

	2012	2013	2014	2015	2016	2017	2018	2019
Revenues (in EUR million)	25.61	134.24	125.63	183.57	141.59	189.63	500.84	440.13

Source: European Commission (2020[22]), European Environment Agency (2020[23]).

5.1.4. National carbon levy for industry

The Climate Agreement of 2020 announced a new carbon pricing instrument that takes effect in 2021. A legislative proposal "Wetsvoorstel Wet CO_2-heffing industrie" amends the Environmental Taxes Act and the Environmental Management Act to introduce a CO_2 levy for industry. The Lower House and the Senate adopted the proposal in November and December 2020, respectively. The national carbon levy for industry is framed explicitly as a supplement to the existing instruments (EU ETS, energy tax and energy surcharge) to achieve the carbon emission reduction target of 14.3 million tonnes in industry. It acts as a complement to the EU ETS and aims to set a domestic price floor per tonne of CO_2 for EU ETS emissions, following a pre-defined price trajectory until 2030.[14] The carbon levy is supposed to provide insurance against the risk that EU ETS prices drop to levels that threaten investment in low-carbon assets.

The Dutch Emissions Authority (NEa) is the body responsible to implement the carbon levy. Installations need to report emissions and the calculation of their levy-free base to NEa. It carries out its service under the authority of the Minister of Finance.

A separate instrument puts a minimum carbon price on electricity production that takes part in the EU ETS. If the ETS price falls below the minimum price level, the Dutch national levy will apply.[15]

Rates

The carbon levy adds a floating contribution on top of the EU ETS allowance price to yield a fixed price per tonne of CO_2. The total levy (i.e. sum of the floating national part and the EU ETS price) will start at EUR 30 per tonne in 2021 and rise linearly to EUR 125 per tonne in 2030 with an annual increase of EUR 10.56 per tonne (Table 5.17).

Table 5.17. Statutory price trajectory of carbon levy in 2021

	2021	2022	2023	2024	2025	2026	2027	2028	2029	2030
Levy rate (in EUR per tonne of CO_2)	30	40.56	51.12	61.68	72.24	82.8	93.36	103.92	114.48	125.04

Note: The rates include the floating national part and the EU ETS price.
Source: OECD calculation based on legislative proposal "Wetsvoorstel Wet CO_2-heffing industrie", Article 71p.

The levy rate has been calculated by estimating the rate required to reduce emissions by 14.3 million tonnes compared to a baseline scenario based on an abatement potential established ex-ante by PBL. The ex-ante analysis developed the price trajectory based on the marginal abatement costs of technologies that would need to be triggered to achieve the reduction target with some probability.[16]

A review of the rate trajectory is foreseen after five years in order to align with the planned update of EU ETS benchmarks and with the changes to the abatement cost curve through technology uptake. Another update of the rate was foreseen for 2020 to integrate the estimated impact on technology of the enlarged SDE++ scheme.

Committing now to a future path of gradual price increases can create strong incentives, particularly for investments in long-lived assets and infrastructure (Flues and Van Dender, 2020[16]). It will also reduce economic and competitiveness disruptions that may be driven by high prices in those sectors where costs to implement decarbonisation technologies are high in the short-run but relatively lower in the long run. One important success factor is a government's ability to commit to rising price paths (Van Dender and Teusch, 2020[24]). Price trajectories are an essential feature to trigger clean-technology investments, particularly in situations where resources are scarce, such as in the wake of the COVID-19 pandemic (OECD, 2020[25]).

Sector coverage and other design features

The instrument covers emissions from installations that are part of the EU ETS as well as emissions from waste incineration plants and nitrous oxide installations. The Climate Agreement indicates that the instrument accounts "for roughly 82% of all industrial greenhouse gas emissions" and that the "levy will affect some 250 plants/businesses".

The levy effectively acts as a baseline-and-credit system, where emissions above the baseline are taxed, and emissions below the baseline can be traded. In particular, installations have to pay the levy on their annual emissions that are not covered by a "dispensation right" (Article 71(l)1). Dispensation rights are the levy's analogue to free allocation and are attributed yearly following EU ETS benchmarks. Their amount will decrease by a specific annual reduction factor. In essence, dispensation rights are calculated as the product of the installation's output (ex-post), the EU ETS product-specific benchmark emission intensity and the annual reduction factor. Installations can trade their dispensation rights via bilateral contracts with other participants during a few months within a year. Dispensation rights cannot be carried forward (no banking), but can be carried back and used to claim back levy payments over a period of five years (Article 71q).

The number of dispensation rights (baseline) will decrease linearly every year based on a uniform, industry-wide reduction factor. The reduction factor starts at 1.2 in 2021 and will only drop below one in 2025 (Table 5.18). The gradual decrease of dispensation rights and high reduction factor in initial years aims to give businesses the flexibility to adapt to higher carbon prices in the future accounting for lead times of investments. In the context of the COVID-19 pandemic, the government recently announced an even more generous allocation of dispensation rights (Rijskoverheid, 2020[26]). According to CE Delft, dispensation rights would cover a large part of the CO_2 emissions base across all industry subsectors in the early years, implying that only few industrial emissions would effectively be subject to paying the levy (Table 5.19). Although some relatively inefficient firms will be short of dispensation rights early in the process, they can most likely acquire those rights at negligible costs due to the large amount of excess dispensation rights in early years that are not bankable, thereby losing their value for future trading periods.

Table 5.18. Reduction factor to determine levy-free base

	2021	2022	2023	2024	2025	2026	2027	2028	2029	2030
Reduction factor	1.2	1.14	1.09	1.03	0.97	0.92	0.86	0.8	0.74	0.69

Note: The government recently announced an even more generous allocation of dispensation rights (Rijskoverheid, 2020[26]).
Source: Calculation based on legislative proposal "Wetsvoorstel Wet CO_2-heffing industrie".

Table 5.19. Estimated proportion of emissions paying the levy in main sectors

	2021	2022	2023	2024	2025	2026	2027	2028	2029	2030
Chemical industry	5%	10%	14%	19%	24%	27%	32%	37%	42%	46%
Food	0%	2%	6%	11%	16%	21%	26%	31%	36%	40%
Metallurgical industry	1%	6%	10%	15%	20%	24%	29%	34%	39%	43%
Refineries	10%	14%	18%	23%	27%	31%	35%	40%	44%	48%

Note: The estimation assumes benchmark values follow the draft revisions to the EU ETS benchmarks published in December 2020. No behavioural adjustments in the emissions base, i.e. no technological shifts, no energy efficiency improvements compared to 2021are assumed.
Source: CE Delft (2021[27]).

The design of the carbon levy boils down to a 'tax and trade' system with an ambitious carbon price trajectory and dispensation rights being freely allocated across all sectors. Installations pay the levy on emissions that are not covered by a dispensation right (tax component), which was either granted by the Dutch authorities or acquired via trading. They can trade dispensation rights (trade component) with other participating installations.

In theory, if trade occurs, the allocation of dispensation rights determines an effective annual emissions cap, with the levy acting as a safety valve. If the effective cap is insufficiently tight to trigger the safety valve, dispensation rights would be expected to trade at a lower price than the levy. More precisely, the floating component of the carbon levy would theoretically settle in a range between the rate set out through the price trajectory in a given year and a rate of EUR 0 per tonne. The former reflects the upper bound of the opportunity costs of holding a dispensation right. Given the generous allocation of dispensation rights in the early years of the levy, combined with the lack of banking option for future compliance, there likely will be no effective carbon price incentive deriving from the levy in the early stages and little trade in dispensation rights.

Revenues

The primary objective of the levy is to encourage CO_2 emission reductions, not to raise additional revenue. Revenues from the carbon levy will result from the difference between the levy rate and the EU ETS price per tonne of CO_2 multiplied by the emissions base that is not covered by a dispensation right outlined in Table 5.19. Given the generous allocation of dispensation rights, not much revenue can be expected in the early years of the levy. In later years, industry is expected to shift towards zero-carbon technologies or put other mitigation measures in place, which reduces the revenue collected through the levy further. This aligns with the ideas set out in the Climate Agreement that sees the carbon levy as part of a carrot-and-stick program with the carrot being the SDE++ and other investment support instruments and the stick being the levy that emitters must pay if they do not engage in low-carbon technology investment. Revenue is expected to be channelled back to industry for decarbonisation purposes.

> *"The carbon levy is actually expected to generate little revenue, given that businesses will be able to put measures in place on time and given the comprehensive policy approach on strengthening the region, adequate labour market policy and innovation and SDE+ subsidies, as well as due to the exchange option provided within the levy charging methodology. Any revenue generated by the carbon levy will be channelled back into making industry greener. This will be achieved through a generic subsidy scheme, which will be linked to an already existing subsidy scheme." (Page 109, National Climate Agreement)."*

5.2. Voluntary Agreements

This section describes and evaluates the most important voluntary agreements, namely those on energy efficiency (MJA-3 and MEE), those included in the Top sector policies and finally, the ones related to research networks.

5.2.1. Energy efficiency – MJA-3 and MEE (ended in 2020)

The government has made two agreements with the private sector on long-term energy efficiency. MEE is the multi-year agreement to ensure that participating ETS companies make a significant contribution to improving energy efficiency by taking all possible cost-efficient measures. In 2019, there were 111 participants in the MEE agreement, covering roughly 570 PJ of energy. Energy use covered by the covenant can be attributed 52% to the chemical industry, 27.2% to refineries and 11.6% to the metallurgical sector. Other industries covered by MEE include paper, glass, beer, cement and textile production (RVO, 2020).[17]

MJA-3 is the multi-year energy efficiency agreement committing to 30% energy efficiency improvement between 2005-20. MEE and MJA-3 are not mutually exclusive, but MEE is for the larger ETS companies. It is not clear yet if there will be a follow-up of MJA-3 after 2020, as the voluntary commitments become somewhat redundant in the presence of the ambitious Climate Agreement.

Participation in these agreements is not mandatory; however, participants in MJA-3 and MEE can receive money back via the refund scheme of the energy tax, which is described in more detail in the section above on carbon pricing and other fuel and electricity taxes. Other eligibility conditions for this refund scheme are that the energy is supplied from a single connection to the electricity grid and that energy usage exceeds 10 million kWh per year. Apart from this refund scheme, no other government funding exists for these non-binding agreements.

Part of these agreements is that industry organisations set up a roadmap with long-term opportunities and the government (through RVO) helps the participating organisations to draft energy efficiency plans, support the introduction of energy management and monitors the agreements.

Firms need to submit a monitoring report every year about the realisation of the intended measures. For MEE, this concerns measures in chain efficiency and process, for MJA-3 it also concerns the generation and/or purchase of sustainable energy. If a planned measure is not realised, another measure with a comparable savings effect needs to be taken, or an explanation needs to be provided. If a firm does not submit the progress statement, it is excluded from the use of the Energy Tax Refund Scheme. If the firm does not submit the monitoring report twice then their participation in the agreement will be reconsidered, which would imply that it would be no longer eligible for the refund scheme. Also, RVO visit around 100 firms every year to check their monitoring data.

RVO monitors the progress made in process efficiency, chain efficiency, sustainable energy and systematic energy management, and aggregates this progress into a sector report. Regional authorities take participation in these agreements into account when they enforce the Environmental Management Act (Wet milieubeheer).

The MJA-3 and MEE agreements on energy efficiency were evaluated in 2013 by Ecorys and KPMG, respectively (Ecorys, 2013[28]; KPMG, 2013[29]). They concluded that the targets on energy savings are achieved and that the MJA-3 sectors achieved energy savings of 2.1% a year over the period 2005-11. However, the absence of a clear counterfactual makes it hard to evaluate the exact contribution of the agreements, and comparing its effect with the effects of other policy instruments is desirable. An important recommendation from the evaluations by Ecorys and KPMG is that more customisation in the level of ambition across sectors is desirable in order to take better account of heterogeneity across sectors.

5.2.2. Top Sector policies - TKI

The Top Sectors programme was created in 2011 as a response to the Global Financial Crisis, and aims to strengthen co-operation between firms, universities and the government in sectors where the Dutch economy has a global competitive advantage.

The top sectors are Agri-food; Chemistry NL; Creative industry; Energy; Life sciences and health; Logistics, High tech; Horticulture and propagation materials; Water and maritime and the Dutch digital delta. The three Top Sectors that are most relevant for the industry's decarbonisation are Agriculture & Food, Chemistry and Energy.

Within each top sector, corporations and research institutes have joined together in Top Consortia for Knowledge and Innovation (TKI). The TKIs have drawn up a research agenda and objectives for the coming years, share knowledge, risks and investments and receive extra research funding in return. TKIs can benefit from a Public Private Partnership (PPP) allowance, which is explained in more detail in the Section 3.3 on R&D.

Businesses within the top sectors can take advantages of various financial and non-financial arrangements, such as tax instruments, financing and guarantees, and advisory services. In 2019, all top sectors created a KIA (Knowledge and Innovation Agenda).

The Top sector policies were evaluated by Dialogic in 2017, who found that the programmes are suitable for the exchange of information between corporations, knowledge institutions and governments, but that the responsibilities of the different stakeholders are not always clear.

5.3. Research, Development and Demonstration

This section covers policy instruments related to research, development and demonstration of technologies relevant for the decarbonisation of the Dutch industry.

5.3.1. Public RD&D funding in the Netherlands

Before delving into the details of specific policy instruments, we provide an overview of public RD&D funding in the Netherlands relevant for the decarbonisation of the industry sector, as reported by the International Energy Agency's Energy RD&D Budget database. In 2018, the total public RD&D budget (by government and provincial authorities, but not municipalities) for energy amounted to EUR 225 million across all sectors and technologies. The breakdown by sector and technology is shown in Figure 5.1. EUR 26 million (11.6% of the total) went to energy efficiency measures in the industry sector. Other key enablers for the decarbonisation of the industry include CCS (EUR 10 million, or 4.6% of the total), hydrogen and fuel cells (EUR 11.5 million, 5% of the total) and renewable energy (EUR 96.7 million, 43% of the total).

The Netherlands' research and innovation strategy for the low-carbon transition, including its public funding dimension, is designed in collaboration with other European Union Member countries in the framework of the European Strategic Energy Technology Plan. Box 5.2 presents additional details on this co-ordination mechanism.

Figure 5.1. Public RD&D budget in energy technology in the Netherlands, 2018 (percentage of total)

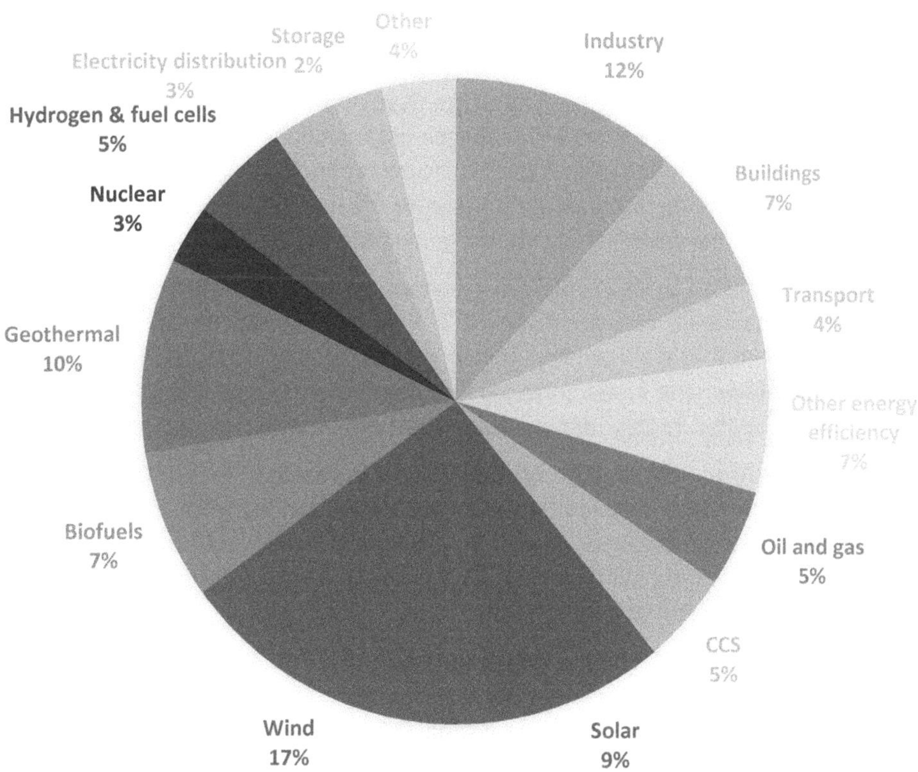

Source: IEA Energy RD&D Budget database, 2020.

The rest of this section provides details on specific policy instruments. These are organised according to the various stages of research (fundamental research, applied research and development, and demonstration).

Box 5.2. The Energy Union SET plan

The European Strategic Energy Technology Plan (SET Plan) defines the new European research and innovation (R&I) energy-related agenda for the energy system as a whole. Its objective is to boost the transition towards a climate neutral energy system through the development of low-carbon technologies in a fast and cost-competitive way. The SET Plan sets R&I targets in each of its ten priorities (including energy efficiency for industry, renewable fuels such as hydrogen, and carbon capture, utilisation and storage [CCUS]), through a collaborative process that includes national governments, industry and research actors. The SET Plan does not have its own budget; instead, it is a co-ordination mechanism. Funding for the ongoing 1203 projects within the SET Plan, mobilising a total of EUR 13.2 billion, comes mostly from national authorities (58%) and EU funds (20%). Other transnational funds and regional funds make up for the rest. The budget of these projects account for 37% of the estimated R&I needs for the execution of all implementation plans.

The SET Plan consists of the SET Plan Steering Group, the European Technology and Innovation Platforms (ETIPs), the European Energy Research Alliance (EERA), and the SET Plan Information System (SETIS).

The SET Plan Steering Group consists of representatives from all EU countries, as well as Iceland, Norway, Switzerland, and Turkey. Its role is to ensure better alignment between the different research and innovation programmes at EU and national level, as well as the SET Plan priorities. It also encourages co-operation between national programmes to avoid duplication and to heighten the impact of public investment.

The European Technology and Innovation Platforms (ETIPs) were created to support the implementation of the SET Plan by bringing together EU countries, industry, and researchers in key areas. They promote the market uptake of key energy technologies by pooling funding, skills, and research facilities. Of particular relevance for the industry sector are the ETIP on Renewable Heating and Cooling and the CCS Platform.

The EERA aims to accelerate new energy technology development by co-operation on pan-European programmes. It brings together more than 175 research organisations from 27 countries, involved in 17 joint programmes. It plays an important role in promoting co-ordination among energy researchers along the SET Plan objectives and in the technology transfer to the industry. Several Dutch universities and research centres are part of the EERA: TUDelft, Wageningen UR, Utrecht University and TNO.

The EU's SET Plan Information System (SETIS) monitors the implementation of the SET Plan across Europe. For example, the latest review of the SET Plan documents the existence of 65 projects addressing energy efficiency in the industry, totalling EUR 324 million. Importantly, however, is the massive gap reported between the funds currently mobilised and the estimated R&I needs for this plan (EUR 3.3 billion). CCUS is also largely underfunded (EUR 645 million against 2.5 billion needed).

In addition, the SETIS provides information on the state of low-carbon technologies. It also assesses the impact of energy technology policies, reviews the costs and benefits of various technological options, and estimates implementation costs. This information is useful for European industrial initiatives, private companies, trade associations, the European Energy Research Alliance, international organisations, and financial institutions.

The Netherlands actively participates in the implementation of identified actions of the various working groups of the Energy Union SET plan, such as wind at sea and CCUS. The Netherlands participates in all SET programs, with the exception of concentrated solar power, ocean energy and batteries and e-mobility. The Netherlands also participates in networks of the European Research Area Network (ERA-NET) to co-ordinate research programs in national member states and stimulate collaboration. An example is the ERA-NET for materials research and innovation, which aims to fund ambitious transnational Research and Technical Development (RTD) projects addressing materials research and innovation including materials for low carbon energy technologies and related production technologies.

5.3.2. Fundamental research funding

Basic (otherwise known as fundamental research) is defined as the experimental or theoretical work undertaken primarily to acquire new knowledge of the underlying foundation of phenomena and observable facts, without any particular application or use in view (OECD, 2015[30]).

At the European level, the main funding arm for fundamental research is the H2020 programme, whose budget is EUR 79 billion over seven years, and its replacement Horizon Europe. The Netherlands participates actively in H2020, with over 5 300 grant agreements signed (19% of EU total) and a 16% success rate (against 12% on average). The EU contribution to Dutch research through H2020 amounts to EUR 4.5 billion for the period 2014-20, including EUR 280 million for projects falling under the topic "secure, clean and efficient energy" (733 projects) and EUR 173 million for projects falling under the topic "climate action, environment, resource efficiency and raw materials" (491 projects).[18]

The EU also funds Dutch research & innovation (both at the research and development stages) toward the industry's decarbonisation through the ESIF, in particular the ERDF and, to a lesser extent (for the food industry), the European agricultural fund for rural development (EAFRD). The EU contribution amounts to EUR 372 million for the period 2014-20 (335 million for ERDF and 37 million for EAFRD). The European structural and investment funds explicitly mentions "research and innovation" and "supporting the low-carbon economy" as two of the main five focuses. For the most developed regions, 20% of ERDF resources must be channelled specifically towards low-carbon economy projects. The share is 15% and 12% in transition regions and less developed regions, respectively.

At the domestic level, research funding flows through the Dutch Research Council NWO. The National Science Agenda (NWA) sets the priorities for funding. It includes 25 'research routes', which take an interdisciplinary look at the main research priorities of the Netherlands going forward. The most important 'routes' for the industry's decarbonisation include "Energy transition" and "Circular economy and resource efficiency".

The financial contribution of NWO is laid down in the KIC 2020-23, in which knowledge institutions, the business community, governments and other public parties commit to jointly invest in innovation. The partners in the KIC have committed to invest EUR 4.9 billion annually for the period 2020-23, of which EUR 2.05 billion would come from private sources and EUR 2.85 billion from public funds. From these funds, EUR 907 million would go to "Climate and energy" (EUR 588 million private; EUR 319 million public), EUR 53 million to the "Circular economy" (EUR 41 million private; EUR 12 million public) and EUR 50 million to "future-proof mobility" (EUR 28 million private; EUR 22 million public), which together form the theme "Energy transition and sustainability". The KIC is informed by the Knowledge and Innovation Agenda (KIA) from the Top sectors, which describe the new knowledge and innovations developed to reach the missions of the different themes, from which "energy transition and sustainability" is the most important theme for this report. The KIC thus follows from the government's mission-driven top sector and innovation policy. In particular, each year, mission-driven thematic calls are developed in line with the NWA. In 2020, for example, key thematic calls related to industry decarbonisation include "Key technologies" and "Energy transition and sustainability", each with a budget of EUR 11 million.[19]

5.3.3. Research & Development instruments

This section focuses on financial support mechanisms for projects at the research and development (R&D) stage, which aim to turn new knowledge into prototypes and then products. This includes applied research, defined as "the original investigation undertaken in order to acquire new knowledge, directed primarily towards a specific practical aim or objective" and experimental development defined as "the systematic work, drawing on existing knowledge gained from research and/or practical experience, directed to producing new materials, products or devices, to installing new processes, systems and services, or to improving substantially those already produced or installed" (OECD, 2015[30]).

Horizontal instruments

A first set of instruments support R&D by firms, without any specific targeting. They are described in turn below.

H2020, EU SME Instrument and European Innovation Council (EIC)

The H2020 programme does not only fund fundamental research but also applied research and can finance private for-profit companies.

In particular, the SME instrument, funded through H2020, helps small and medium-sized enterprises to develop new innovative products, services and business models that drive economic growth and bring these onto the market. The EIC Accelerator Pilot builds on the SME Instrument Phase II and provides grant-only support as well as support in the form of blended finance (combining grant and equity). The scheme supports high-risk, high-potential small and medium-sized innovative enterprises willing to develop and commercialise new products, services and business models that could drive economic growth and shape new markets or disrupt existing ones in Europe and worldwide. The EIC Accelerator pilot has a total budget of more than EUR 1.3 billion for 2019-20.

The EIC Pathfinder offers grants of up to EUR 4 million to promote collaborative, inter-disciplinary research and innovation on science-inspired and radically new future technologies. These grants are for consortia of at least three entities from three different Members States and associated countries. The EIC Pathfinder pilot has a total budget of around EUR 660 million for 2019-20.

Overall, the net EU contribution to Dutch SMEs through H2020, including via the SME instrument and the EIC programmes, has been EUR 846 million over the period 2014-20, including EUR 163 million for the SME instrument and EUR 231 million for EIC.

For the two topics “secure, clean and efficient energy” and “climate action, environment, resource efficiency and materials”, the net EU contribution to Dutch SMEs through the H2020 programme is EUR 453 million over the period 2014-20, including EUR 5.9 million for the SME instrument (23 companies) and EUR 1.3 million for EIC (10 companies).[20] This corresponds to an annual funding for Dutch SMEs in these two topics of around 70 million per year, including around EUR 1.5 million per year for the SME instrument and the EIC combined (the EIC only exists since 2018).[21]

WBSO (tax credit for research and development)

The main R&D support instrument in the Netherlands is WBSO, which is the tax credit for research and development, with an annual budget of EUR 1.28 billion in 2020 and around 19 000 participating companies in 2019. The WBSO provides a tax credit for wage costs of employees directly involved in R&D but also for other costs of R&D projects. The WBSO R&D tax credit offers support for both development projects, covering the development of technically new physical products, physical production processes or software, and technical-scientific research, covering explanatory research of technical nature.

The tax credit rates applicable in 2021 have been increased in view of the COVID-19 crisis. They are presented in Table 5.20. The total budget has been increased to EUR 1.43 billion.

Table 5.20. WBSO rates for 2021

	Rate 2021	Rate 2020
First bracket (up to EUR 350 000 of eligible costs)	40%	32%
First brackets – innovation starters (companies less than 6 years old, and maximum 3 years of WBSO subsidy obtained)	50%	40%
Second bracket (above EUR 350 000)	16%	16%

Source: RVO

According to the WBSO evaluation conducted by Dialogic in 2019, 23% of WBSO users in 2017 were companies in the manufacturing sector. In this sector, 6.5% of firms use WBSO. We have not been able to find a breakdown of WBSO funding by sector and technology, so cannot measure the amount going to the top emitting sectors and, within those, to low-carbon technologies through WBSO.

Lokshin and Mohnen (2011[31]) perform a cost–benefit analysis of the WBSO R&D incentive programme and find evidence of additionality, which suggests that the level based programme of R&D incentives in the Netherlands is effective in stimulating firms' investment in R&D. This squares with results from the OECD microBeRD project, which provides a harmonised analysis of confidential business R&D and tax relief microdata in 20 OECD countries (OECD, 2020[32]).. Firm-level estimates of the effect of tax incentives are not provided for the Netherlands, but the cross-country micro-aggregated impact analysis shows that, on average, one extra unit of R&D tax support translates into 1.4 extra units of private business R&D.

Innovation box

The 'Innovatiebox' (with a budgetary provision of EUR 1 554 million in 2017) is the other main scheme in the Netherlands for stimulating R&D in individual firms and improving the business climate for innovation activities. It offers companies a discount rate (7% instead of 25%) on the corporate tax on the profits resulting from their innovation. The innovation box policy instrument is essentially a patent box (and started as such until 2010), but without the formal requirement of a patent, making it all the more difficult to link profits to specific immaterial assets created out of innovation activity. To be eligible, a firm must have a patent, a plant breeder's right, or formally recognised (by the tax office) R&D activities. The firm must also generate the immaterial asset itself. (Mohnen, Vankan and Verspagen, 2017[33]) show that the innovation box effectively stimulates R&D, but that the so-called 'bang-for-the-buck' (which measures the effectiveness of the policy, and which can be seen as an indicator for the degree of additionality) is smaller than 1, i.e. the extra R&D is less than the forgone tax revenue.

Nationaal Groeifonds (National Growth Fund)

The National Growth Fund is a public investment fund set up to sustainably increase the earning capacity of the Netherlands (structural gross domestic product [GDP]). The National Growth Fund follows from the Growth Strategy published in 2019. In this growth strategy, the government announced that additional investments, of an incidental and irregular nature, were necessary to increase the earning capacity of the Netherlands.

For the period 2021-26, the National Growth Fund will provide EUR 20 billion for projects in the field of knowledge development; research and development and innovation; and infrastructure. The projects must have a minimum project size of EUR 30 million. Projects will be evaluated both against their impact on the growth of the Dutch economy but also on social benefits (with climate being explicitly mentioned). Namely, any cost-benefit analyses of the proposed projects will have to factor in a price for avoided CO_2 emissions. First applications are expected to be made in 2021.

InvestNL

The recently created Invest-NL agency (launched in January 2020) provides financing to companies, particularly start-up businesses, that contribute to making the Netherlands more sustainable and more innovative. With a capital of EUR 1.7 billion, Invest-NL focuses on the energy transition and on innovative, fast growing companies (scale-ups). It provides equity funding and loans, under the conditions that at least 50% of the total funding amount is provided by other financing parties and that the total funding amount (including funding by other parties) be greater than EUR 10 million.

NWO (Dutch Research Council) and TO2

The NWO funding instruments for the KIC provide funding not only for fundamental research but also for practice-oriented research in the framework of public-private partnerships (PPP). The funding can be used for mission-driven calls, partnerships, strategic co-operation and practical instruments. As explained above, “Climate and Energy” and “Circular economy” are two eligible fields. The rate of co-financing in the case of public-private partnerships is 30%.

The Dutch government also supports public-private partnerships by directly financing institutions that engage in applied research. In particular, organisations for applied research are united in the TO2 Federation. These include the major research centres Deltares, ECN, MARIN, NLR, TNO and Wageningen Research. These institutions partner with industrial actors to come up with practical solutions to concrete industrial issues, including the low-carbon transition.

Other horizontal support instruments

There are several other innovation support mechanisms, particularly targeting SMEs, such as the Small Business Innovation Research (SBIR), the SME Action Plan, the Innovation Vouchers, the Growth facility and the SME credit guarantee scheme (BMKB) for SME loans and the Fund-of-Funds, including the Dutch Venture Initiative (DVI) of the European Investment Fund and PPM Oost. The extent to which these instruments are being used for climate neutral investments in the industry is unknown.

Targeted instruments for low-carbon technologies

Integrated Knowledge & Innovation Agenda Climate (IKIA) and Multi-year Mission Driven Innovation Programmes (MMIPs)

As part of the Climate Agreement and the coalition agreement, the policy framework for low-carbon innovation has changed towards mission-oriented innovation programmes. In the IKIA, which was set in 2019, five missions are formulated that contribute to a deep emission reduction of greenhouse gases by 2050. The missions for 2050 are a CO_2-emission free electricity generation, buildings and transport, climate neutral industry and agriculture/nature. For 2030, intermediate targets are formulated for each mission.

The knowledge and innovation needs for attaining these targets are formulated in 13 mission-driven innovations programs (MMIPs) for various sectors, of which the following three specifically concern industry:

- Closure of industrial chains (MMIP 6)
- CO_2-free industrial heat system (MMIP 7)
- Electrification and radically new processes (MMIP 8)

The MMIP 6 (closure of industrial chains) focuses on innovations in industrial chains that include residual flows. This includes the reuse of (raw) materials, waste and residual gases, the reuse of CO_2, the use of bio-based raw materials, and the use of products that facilitate circularity. The aim is to use 50% less primary raw materials by 2030 and to achieve at least 80% circular and sustainable value chains by 2050.

The MMIP 7 (a 100% CO_2-free industrial heating system) focuses on the design and (re)design of climate-neutral energy and heating systems for industrial clusters and companies and optimal process efficiency. The focus is on temperatures up to 300°C by 2030 and on higher temperature levels by 2050.

MMIP 8 (Electrification and radically new processes) focuses on cost-effective innovations for fully climate-neutral production processes by 2050, optimally electrified and fully integrated into the sustainable energy system. Green hydrogen has an important role to play in this process.

The IKIA and MMIPs are not a financial instrument. Instead, they describe the types of innovation needed to achieve cost-effective decarbonisation, which are eligible for subsidies under various programme, such as Top-Sector Energy, Demonstration Energy and Climate Innovation (DEI+), HER+ and the MOOI programme described next.

MOOI

Projects within the MOOI aim at a CO_2-free electricity system, CO_2-free built environment, climate-neutral raw materials, and circular products and processes.

Eligible projects must be carried out by a consortium of at least three companies: they should reflect an integrated, multidisciplinary approach, bringing together various stakeholders, including innovative SMEs. They can concern industrial research, experimental development or feasibility studies, but projects should lead to a first market application in one of the significant industrial sectors in the Netherlands by 2030 "or shortly thereafter". The minimum subsidy is EUR 25 000 per project participant, and the maximum amount is EUR 4 million per project. The minimum total project budget is EUR 2 million. The grant for a MOOI project is equal to 50% of eligible costs insofar as they relate to industrial research, 25% of eligible costs for experimental development, 80% of eligible costs (for "non-economic activities of research organisations consisting of industrial research and experimental development") and 50% of eligible costs for other project activities. These percentages are increased by 10 percentage points for medium-size companies and 20 percentage points for small companies.

The total budget for the MOOI scheme is EUR 95 million, including EUR 21 million specifically earmarked for renewable electricity and EUR 17 million for the industry.

In the industry, the eligible topics for 2020 were: circular plastics; carbon capture and utilisation (CCU); process efficiency for drying and dewatering; industrial heat systems; hydrogen production from electricity; electrochemical production of basic chemicals; and electrical process routes as an alternative to cracking stoves.

Top Sectors: TKI/PPP allowance (Bio-based economy, Chemistry, Energy)

The Top Consortia for Knowledge and Innovation (TKI) is a central instrument of the top sectors approach. They are responsible for developing and implementing roadmaps in line with the KIC. All Top Sectors have one or more TKIs, consisting of representatives from business, science and government. Thus, TKIs are at the centre of the co-operation between government, industry and knowledge institutions around the nine top sectors.

TKIs were set up in 2012 and 2013 to implement the research and innovation component of the Topsector approach. Each Topsector has one (or more) TKI in which representatives of the business sector (including SMEs), science community and government draw up proposals for research and innovation roadmaps to be included in the KIC. Following KIC approval, the TKIs implement the roadmaps, building networks and consortia, using all funds available. These funds include thematic funding by Ministries, NWO-calls and in-kind contributions by companies, public research organisations and higher education institutions.

Cash contributions from the private sector are topped-up by the Private-public partnerships (PPP) supplement (TKI allowance). For every euro of private R&D expenditure spent by TKIs, the Ministry of Economic Affairs and Climate adds EUR 0.30 as a "PPP bonus" to the TKI's budget. In the case of an R&D partnership, the PPP bonus reaches 40% on the first EUR 20 000 of private contributions. This PPP allowance can be used by the TKI for new collaboration projects that may consist of non-economic activities, fundamental research, industrial research and experimental development. The allowance can be used to fund 100% of the extra research if it is fundamental research, but only 50% of the additional research if it is used for industrial research and only 25% if the PPP allowance is used for experimental research.

The total amount of funds for PPP projects across all Top Sectors was EUR 1 228 million in 2019, of which EUR 581 million was invested by private companies and EUR 647 million by the government.

MIT-Scheme (SME Innovation Stimulation Region and Top Sectors)

The MIT SME Innovation Stimulation Region and Top Sectors aims to stimulate innovation in small and medium-sized enterprises across regional boundaries. The scheme can support various projects: feasibility projects; knowledge vouchers; R&D collaboration projects; innovation brokers; and network activities. MIT SME encourages SME projects to better match the innovation agendas of the top sectors, but not only firms in Top Sectors are eligible. The TKIs propose which sub-instrument of the MIT SME Innovation Support Top Sectors scheme to include in MIT-calls by RVO.

Many of these projects focus on research collaboration between SMEs and other stakeholders: for example, knowledge vouchers focus on co-operation between a "knowledge institution" and an SME on a product or process innovation; R&D collaboration projects focus on collaboration between SMEs and larger firms (with only the costs incurred by the SME being eligible).

Overall, these are small projects in terms of funding. For example, for feasibility projects, the subsidy amount can represent up to 40% of the costs, with a maximum of EUR 20 000. The maximum subsidy amount for knowledge vouchers is EUR 3 750. For innovation brokers, the maximum subsidy per SME is EUR 10 000 per year. For network activities, the maximum costs per SME participant in the network activity is EUR 1 000.

An exception is R&D collaboration projects where the subsidy can be up to EUR 200 000 per project for "small" R&D collaboration and up to EUR 350 000 per project for "large" R&D collaboration.

Total budgets are also relatively modest: for example, the total budget for the innovation broker scheme is EUR 100 000.

The MIT SME scheme was evaluated by Technopolis in 2017[22]. The evaluation shows that MIT SME Innovation Stimulation Region and Top sectors is accessible to SMEs and supports innovative processes with most of its budget spent on R&D projects. MIT SME is mostly used in the Top sectors "Creative industry"; "High tech" and "Horticulture", perhaps because these are the Top Sectors with a higher share of SMEs. The evaluation report claims that the MIT SME scheme is efficient in stimulating public knowledge and its utilisation.

TSE Industry

TSE Industry (now closed) funds R&D projects that can cost-effectively reduce CO_2 emissions, in the themes of closure of industrial chains, CO_2-free industrial heating system, or electrification and radically new processes. These projects must have a first market application in a "meaningful" industrial sector in the Netherlands by 2030 at the latest. Companies can receive up to EUR 500 000 per project. The budget for 2020 was EUR 2.8 million.

KIEM GoChem scheme

The KIEM GOChem program, an initiative from the Top Sector Chemistry in which various partners are involved (NWO, the Ministry of Economic Affairs and Climate, the TKI's Chemistry and BioBased Economy, the trade associations NRK and VNCI and knowledge institutions), supports SMEs in chemistry and chemical processing industry with green innovation projects. The scheme supports co-operative projects between SMEs and knowledge institutions. The SME partners must contribute at least 25% of the grant amount. The maximum funding is EUR 40 000. The main funding themes are: sources and raw materials; processes and technology; molecules and materials; processing and application; chain and business models; and recycling and upcycling. The total budget is EUR 2.6 million for the years 2020 and 2021.

5.3.4. Demonstration

The last RD&D phase is the demonstration phase, which corresponds to the design, construction and operation of a prototype of a technology, at or near commercial scale, with the purpose of providing technical, economic and environmental information to industrialists, financiers, regulators and policy makers (Frascati Manual).

EU Innovation Fund

The revision for the fourth phase of the EU ETS, covering the period 2021-30, has led to the introduction of the Innovation Fund as a new funding mechanism for demonstration of innovative low-carbon technologies. The fund focuses on Innovative low-carbon technologies and processes in energy intensive industries, including products substituting carbon intensive ones; CCU; Construction and operation of CCS; Innovative renewable energy generation; and energy storage.

The Innovation Fund is the successor of the NER300, which focused mostly on renewable energy. Thirty nine projects were selected at the European level, but 20 of them have since been withdrawn. None of the 19 projects that are now completed, in operation or working towards entry into operation are located in the Netherlands. All projects related to ocean energy, PV and CCS were abandoned, and 10 out of 13 biofuel projects, generally because of regulatory, technical or financing issues.

The budget for the Innovation Fund for 2020-30 is projected to be around EUR 10 billion (or EUR 1 billion per year on average), but figures are uncertain as the resources come from the auctioning of EU ETS allowances whose price fluctuates on the market. The first call for large-scale projects (above EUR 7.5 million of total capital costs) was open until the end of October 2020, while the first call for small-scale projects (below EUR 7.5 million of total capital costs) was launched on 1 December 2020. The budget for small-scale projects is EUR 100 million for the first call.

Relevant costs eligible for subsidy are defined in the Innovation Fund as the difference between the best estimate of the total capital expenditure of the innovative technology plus the net present value of operational costs and benefits during ten years of the operation, compared to the results of the same calculation for a conventional production technology with the same output. The Innovation Fund will support up to 60% of the additional capital and operational costs of large-scale projects and up to 60% of the capital costs of small-scale projects, so funding appears more generous for large-scale projects.

In response to the first call for large-scale projects of the Innovation Fund, the European Commission received 311 applications for innovative clean tech projects, including 58 for renewable energy, 204 for energy-intensive industries (out of which 56 in hydrogen), 35 for energy storage and 14 for CCUS. Thirty nine of these projects are from entities based in the Netherlands (12%). However, the proposed projects have requested a total of EUR 21.7 billion, while only around EUR 1 billion is available. Therefore, it is reasonable to expect that only a couple of projects will ultimately be funded in the Netherlands for this round.

It is interesting to note that the proposed projects promise to reduce around 1.2 billion tonnes of CO_2 during their operating period within the Innovation Fund, implying that the subsidised cost per avoided tonne of CO_2 stands at only EUR 20 on average.

InnovFin EDP

In addition to the Innovation Fund, other EU programmes support CO_2-reduction technologies at the demonstration stage. For example, the InnovFin Energy Demonstration Projects (InnovFin EDP), administered by the European Investment Bank (EIB), provides loans, loan guarantees or equity-type financing typically between EUR 7.5 million and EUR 75 million to innovative demonstration projects in the fields of energy system transformation, including (but not limited to) renewable energy technologies, smart energy systems, energy storage, and CCUS, helping them to bridge the gap from demonstration to commercialisation. EIB financing is limited to 50% of the total eligible costs of the project, which include all the costs necessary for the successful demonstration of the technology, service, manufacturing or business process. Given the high risk involved, these EIB loans are guaranteed by the European Commission in the event of default. The total budget of the scheme was EUR 30 million in 2018 and EUR 35 million in 2019 (from the H2020 programme), but it can now benefit from unused funds from the NER300.

Top Sector Energy Studies Industry

Top Sector Energy Studies (including CCUS) aims to help the industry to investigate the feasibility of an innovative pilot or demonstration project that can cost-effectively reduce CO_2 emissions, such as closure of industrial chains, CO_2-free industrial heating system, electrification, CCUS and other CO_2-reducing measures. These possibilities must have a first market application in a "meaningful" industrial sector in the Netherlands by 2030 at the latest. It is therefore similar to the TSE Industry programme, but focused specifically on pilot and demonstration projects. Companies can receive up to 50% of the total project cost as a subsidy, the maximum grant amount being EUR 500 000 per project. The budget for 2020-21 was EUR 8 million.

Demonstration Energy and Climate Innovation 2020

The DEI+ 2020 scheme focuses on: 1) pilot projects to test and improve newly developed technologies; and on 2) demonstration projects to build a new production installation that realises an environmental benefit through the duration of the project, and will remain in use after the project has ended. The duration of a project is a maximum of four years (except circular economy projects below EUR 3 million, for which the duration is one year).

The relevant themes for the industry include energy efficiency; renewable energy (including the flexibility of the electricity system, such as hydrogen and spatial integration); CCUS; and other CO_2-reducing measures in the industry or electricity sector.

The annual budget is EUR 86.1 million of grants and is allocated on a first come, first served basis (provided the project is eligible).

In addition to DEI+ 2020, the DEI+ Circular Economy (DEI+ CE) focuses on reuse, recycling and bio-based raw materials, and has a budget of EUR 44 million.

Data from RVO suggests that DEI+ has been vastly oversubscribed (EUR 159 million of grants requested) while DEI+ CE was undersubscribed (EUR 25 million requested). No breakdown of allocated grants and requests by type of project is yet available.

For reasons that are not specified, the subsidy percentage depends on the type of project (Table 5.21). However, the maximum subsidy is EUR 15 million per project. Importantly, the costs that are eligible for the subsidy are the "extra costs compared to a less environmentally friendly investment that would have been credibly made without the aid", similar in essence to the Innovation Fund.

It is important to note that there is some discretion in the evaluation of the projects' eligibility. Rejection can, for example happen if it is "unlikely that the project will be completed within the maximum allowed term", "insufficient confidence that those involved have the capabilities to complete the project", "insufficient confidence in the technical or economic feasibility" or that "the chance of success of innovation in the Dutch market and society is insufficient".

Table 5.21. DEI subsidy percentage per type of project

Type of project	Subsidy percentage
Pilot project or experimental development	25% for businesses 80% for research organisations (non-economic activities)
Other CO_2-reducing measures in the industry or electricity sector (demo)	40%
Circular economy (demo)	35%
Local infrastructure (demo)	50%
Energy-efficiency (all)	30%
Renewable energy (demo)	45% if the investments can be made as a separate investment or the investment is offset against the reference costs 30% for small installations where no comparable traditional system exists
All projects	+10 percentage points for medium-sized businesses +20 percentage points for small businesses

Source: RVO.

Hernieuwbare Energie Regeling (HER+)

The HER+ is the successor of the HER programme, which focused on renewable energy technology support. As of September 2020, the HER+ grant has been expanded to cover CO_2 reduction technologies more generally, and now includes CCS, hydrogen or residual heat utilisation. Its objective is to achieve the Netherlands' climate targets at a lower cost through innovative projects, and in particular to save on future public subsidies from the SDE++ scheme.

In practice, the objective of HER+ is to build demonstration projects that will reduce the costs of the technologies eligible to SDE++, therefore leading to savings on future subsidies under the SDE++. Project developers must demonstrate that the future savings from SDE++ (including after 2030) are greater than the grant allocated through HER+. Eligibility of a particular technology under SDE++ implies eligibility under HER+. Savings on future SDE ++ expenditure are not only related to cost savings by the project itself, but also through potential spin-off and repeated projects. The maximum CO_2 abatement cost eligible is EUR 300/tonne CO_2.

The HER+ has an annual budget for 2020 of EUR 30 million.

The HER has been assessed as an accessible instrument for SME businesses to achieve cost reduction in the transition to renewable energy and it contributes to knowledge and technology development. The evaluation report recommends to clarify the relationship between the scheme and the target groups of the HER in the Top sector energy to streamline the grant with other subsidies like SDE+

Box 5.3. Top Sector Energy : Review in figures 2012-19 (RVO, 2020)

In November 2020, RVO published a review of energy innovation projects financed with government resources within the Top Sector Energy for the period 2012 to 2019. It covers the following schemes: Top Sector Energy (TSE), Renewable Energy (HER), Demonstration Energy Innovation (DEI); Mission-driven Top Sectors and Innovation Policy; Accelerated Climate Investments for Industry (VEKI); Demonstration Energy and Climate Innovation (DEI+); MMIPs for the built environment; TNO (and predecessor ECN) financed by the Dutch Ministry of Economic Affairs and Climate Policy (EZK) and EU subsidies; NWO; Substantive assignments financed by EZK / RVO; PPP supplement; SME innovation stimulation Region and Top sectors (MIT) of the energy Top Consortia for Knowledge and Innovation (TKIs).

The analysis shows that from 2012 to 2019, more than 3 100 energy innovation projects were subsidised in the context of the Top Sector Energy (around 400 projects per year), amounting to around EUR 1.2 billion in total. The annual subsidy has grown over the years to EUR 211.9 million in 2019. These public subsidies represent around 60% of the total cost of the underlying projects across years.

Figure 5.2 shows the distribution of the annual subsidies by subsidy scheme and organisation. In percentage terms, most of the grants were awarded via the TSE, HER and DEI schemes. Together, these three schemes represent 78% of subsidies. NWO is another important source of funding (16% of total funding in 2019).

Figure 5.2. Distribution of the Top Sector Energy subsidies by scheme and organisation

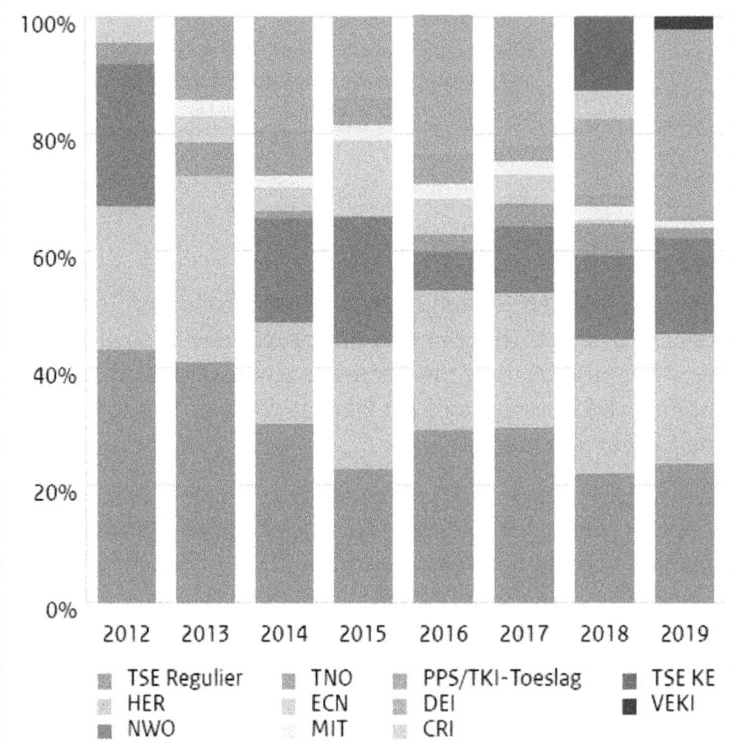

Notes: TSE KE shows the awarded subsidy for Top Sector Energy innovation financed from the Climate Envelope 2018/2019 resource.
Source: (RVO, 2020[34]).

Figure 5.3 shows the annual distribution of subsidies by innovation phase: discovery or basic research; development; demonstration; deployment and enabling ("Flanking"). The data shows an increase of the demonstration (40%) and deployment (10%) phases at the expense of development (around 35% in 2019, against more than 60% in 2013). Projects in the discovery phase are mainly subsidised via NWO and represent a tiny share of total funding. Funding for basic research is also strikingly fluctuating across years, with peaks in 2012 and 2015. The recent increase in flanking projects is attributed to the shift towards "mission-driven" innovation policy, with projects looking at the overall innovation system rather than just at particular innovations.

Figure 5.4 shows the distribution of subsidies by energy category following the International Energy Agency classification. There is a clear increase in funding for energy efficiency projects, in particular through DEI+, which now represent 40% of total funding. Subsidies toward renewable energy projects sources have been decreasing, from 60% of funding in 2012 to around 35% in 2019. Hydrogen and Fuels Cells have increased recently but remain extremely marginal, as are CCUS projects which represent most of the "Fossil fuels" category.

Figure 5.3. Distribution of the Top Sector Energy subsidies by innovation phase

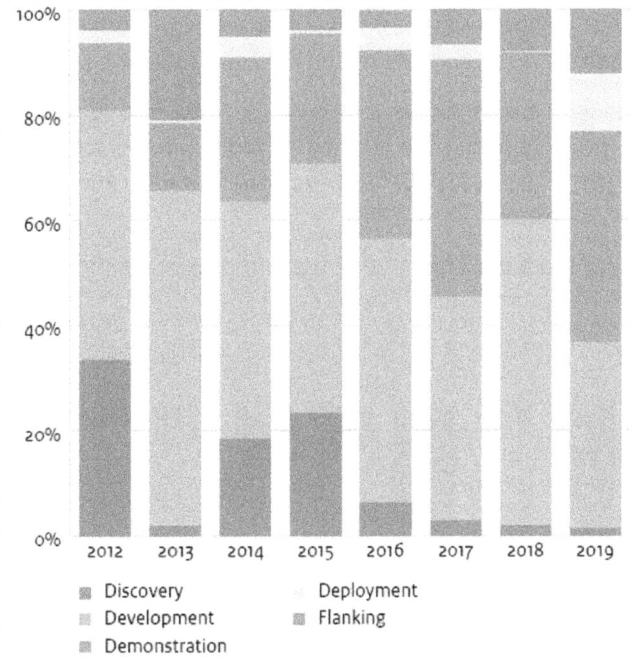

Notes: "Flanking" projects are projects to which no TRL can be linked, because they are not aimed at technological innovation, but to changes in institutions (such as regulations), behaviour and/or social acceptance with regard to technological innovations.
Source: (RVO, 2020[34]).

Figure 5.4. Distribution of Top Sector Energy subsidies by IEA category

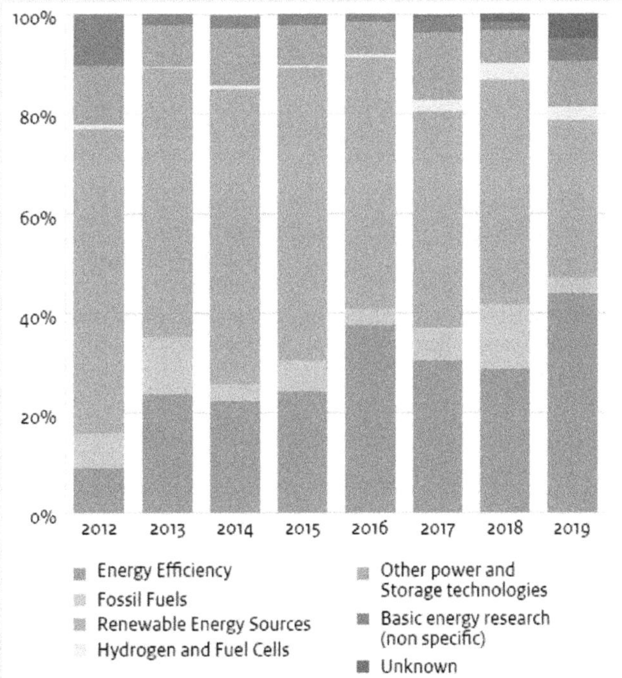

Source: (RVO, 2020[34]).

Finally, Figure 5.5 shows the Distribution of subsidies by Top Sector Energy themes and climate tables. The Top Sector Energy has five substantive themes around which the Top Consortia for Knowledge and Innovation (TKIs) has been set up. These include offshore wind, urban energy, socially responsible innovation energy (MVI energy) and system integration. Moreover, from the climate agreement, climate tables have been established: mobility, agriculture and land use, industry, built environment and electricity.

In the past eight years, 81% of subsidies have gone to projects that fit within the five TKI themes. Of these, 71% have gone to projects within the themes offshore wind, urban energy and new gas, which includes CCUS and hydrogen. The five climate tables accounted for 49% of the 2019 subsidy and 9% of the total grant from 2012 onwards.

Interestingly, around 25% of the subsidies in 2019 went to projects in the industry.

Figure 5.5. Distribution of subsidies by Top Sector Energy themes

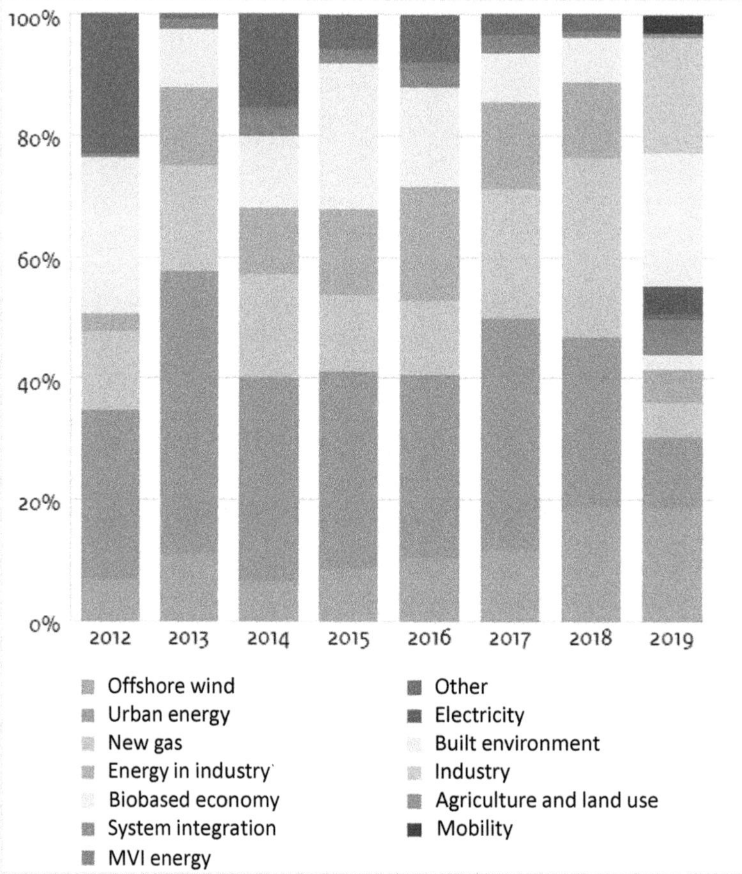

Source: (RVO, 2020[34]).

5.4. Deployment

For the same reason that the existence of knowledge spillovers implies that private firms underinvest in R&D and justifies government support to innovation activities, externalities associated with the overall scale of technology adoption, such as learning-by-doing and network effects, can justify the government's intervention in support of technology deployment.

Deployment is defined as the selection and use of a commercially available technology-based product or service in normal operations by businesses, individuals or government agencies with the aim of accelerating the diffusion and adoption of technologies or practices (IEA, 2011[35]).

This section covers policy instruments related to deployment of technologies relevant for the decarbonisation of Dutch industry.

5.4.1. Specific/targeted instruments

SDE++ (Stimulering Duurzame Energieproductie en klimaattransitie: Stimulation of sustainable energy production and climate transition)

The SDE++ is a support scheme that promotes sustainable energy and Scope 1 carbon emission reduction by subsidising firms and non-profit institutions that invest in CO_2-reducing techniques and renewable energy production. It is being implemented as an update of the 2011 SDE+ scheme.

Qualifying projects as of 2020 concern the areas of renewable electricity, heat and gas, and low-carbon heat and production, including CCUS and hydrogen. The scope of support is expected to extend in 2021 to include bio-based production, electrification on offshore oil and gas production platforms, advanced renewable fuels for transport, and the recycling of plastics. Covered areas are relevant to industrial sectors, as well as agriculture, electricity, transport and the built environment. Applications may need to come with feasibility studies and installation permits.

The SDE++ is an abatement payment per unit of avoided CO_2 emissions that subsidises the revenue shortfall of CO_2-reducing techniques, that is, the operating cost difference between the low-carbon technique and the PBL-defined benchmark technique, factoring in the market value of the achieved CO_2 reductions in terms of EU ETS allowances (*but not in terms of avoided carbon levy payments*). While the cost parameter is technology-specific and fixed over the project's lifetime, the value of both CO_2 reductions (long-term ETS price) and energy products is updated annually, so that the subsidy depends on market conditions (including the market for green certificates). Firms apply for a subsidy amount per unit of avoided CO_2 emissions in a closed envelope auction, with a maximum of EUR 300/tCO_2. The total SDE++ subsidy amount tendered is allocated to project applicants in decreasing order of subsidy requirement per tonne of CO_2 reduction. While this makes the scheme cost-effective, the priority given to least-cost options makes it less relevant to support technologies that are at an earlier stage of development, such as hydrogen. Subsidy payments can be carried back or forward when planned production and actual production differ, with a limit of 25% of annual production.

Ex-ante evaluations of the SDE++ suggest that the newest technologies (in particular hydrogen, and CCSU to a lesser extent) fit less well in the SDE scheme because of their higher reliance on shared infrastructure, their benefits beyond CO_2 reduction, higher uncertainty regarding their cost, and their lower market readiness (Trinomics, 2019[36]; PBL, 2020[37]). Evaluations of the previous SDE+ show that firms value the de-risking nature of the scheme (CE Delft, 2016[38]).

Most SDE++ projects that are relevant for the industry are expected to operate in installations participating in the EU-ETS. The PBL is working on a correction factor to feed in the calculation of the revenue shortfall, so that nonparticipants are not put at a disadvantage. Investments in CO_2-reducing technologies of which the operation is subsidised under the SDE++ are ineligible for a tax deduction under the EIA scheme, nor for a grant under the ISDE scheme (see below).

The Dutch government allocated a budget of EUR 5 billion to the SDE++ for the 2020 tender. The PBL estimates that about EUR 3 billion will go to the industry for CO_2 reduction over the period 2020-30, with the yearly expenditure expected to reach EUR 550 million in 2030.

Energy investment allowance

The energy investment allowance (EIA, *Energie-InvesteringsAftrek*) is a tax allowance available since 1997 to tax-paying firms in the Netherlands for qualifying energy-saving investment.

Qualifying investments must be in new (previously unused) assets, amount to at least EUR 2 500 and up to EUR 2.4 million per year, and be part of RVO's energy list (*Energielijst*). Assets on the list are particularly relevant for industrial processes and applications, but are also relevant for other sectors such as agriculture, electricity and retail. They cover commercial buildings, processes, means of transport, energy balancing, energy transition, energy advice and customised advice. The list is updated every year through legislation based on changes in technology availability. Renewable energy investments are excluded since 2014, as they can receive support under the SDE scheme (see above). Energy-saving asset producers can introduce requests to the RVO for inclusion of new assets on the list.

The EIA corresponds to a deduction amounting to 45% of the energy-saving investment cost from taxable income in 2020, in addition to the standard depreciation allowance. According to CE Delft's estimations, the effective EIA tax rebate lies between 10% and 15% of the investment, depending on the marginal corporate income tax rate of the firm, as well as on the EIA rate, which has varied between 41.5% and 55% over the past years (Table 5.22). Most beneficiaries are firms with an income of over EUR 200 000 (CE Delft, 2018[39]). Evaluations tend to suggest that the EIA is cost-efficient and that windfall profit is limited compared to similar instruments (PBL, 2020[40]; CE Delft, 2018[39]; Ecorys and Van Zutphen Economisch Advies, 2012[41]), even if the share of free-riders remains substantial at about 50% of users (Ruijs and Vollebergh, 2013[42]). The constantly updated technology list has also been commended in existing evaluations for reducing the information asymmetry between supply and demand for new energy-saving or sustainable technologies.

Table 5.22. EIA rate and effective tax rebate by marginal income tax rate

Year	EIA rate	Marginal income tax rate				Effective tax rebate (% of investment)				
		Corporate (firms)		Personal income tax (PIT)		Firms		Personal Income Tax payers		Weighted average
		EUR 0-200 thsd	> EUR 200 thsd	< EUR 60 thsd	> EUR 60 thsd	EUR 0-200 thsd	>EUR 200 thsd	<EUR 60 thsd	>EUR 60 thsd	
2015	41.5%	20.0%	25%	40%	50%	8.3%	10.4%	16.6%	20.8%	10.4%
2016	58.0%					11.6%	14.5%	23.2%	29.0%	14.5%
2017	55.0%					11.0%	13.8%	22.0%	27.5%	13.8%
2018	54.5%					10.9%	13.6%	21.8%	27.3%	
2019	45.0%	19.0%				8.6%	11.3%	18.0%	22.5%	
2020		16.5%				7.4%	11.3%	18.0%	22.5%	

Note: Rebates for PIT payers are approximations as PIT rates vary across years.
Source: CE Delft calculations.

Although EIA-eligible investments may also qualify for other support schemes, particularly when qualification depends on RVO's energy list, cumulating support is generally not authorised beyond standard depreciation. Specifically:

- Investment costs can be split across the EIA and the MIA (see below) schemes, but cannot be deducted under both; the effective EIA rebate is typically larger than the MIA rebate, which is discussed below;
- The EIA and the KIA deductions can be cumulated only under specific conditions (see below);

- The EIA deduction and the ISDE subsidy (*InvesteringsSubsidie Duurzame Energie* – see below) cannot be cumulated;
- Other investment subsidies, including VEKI (see below), must be subtracted from the investment costs for computing the deduction.

Note that the EIA is not compatible with the SDE++ by design (see above).

The Dutch government allocated a budget of EUR 147 million to the EIA for fiscal year 2020, in line with fiscal expenses in previous years.[23] Data on EIA take up over the period 2012-17 show a strong skew towards the retail, food, energy and chemical industries, and suggests that half of EIA investments concerns industry (CE Delft, 2018[39]) (Figure 5.6).

Figure 5.6. EIA investments by industry (EUR m.)

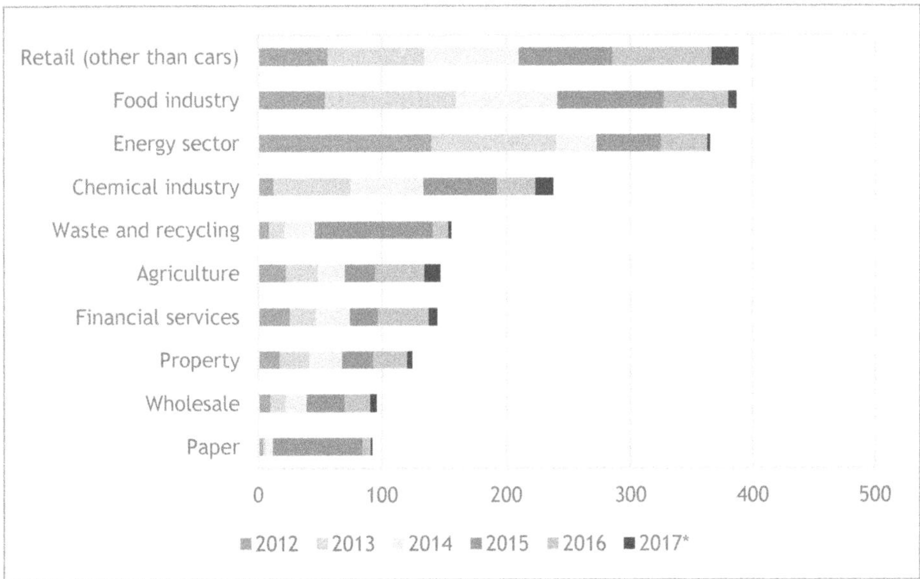

Note: 2017 as of 22 August.
Source: CE Delft (2018[43]). Beleidsevaluatie Energie-investeringsaftrek 2012-2017. CE Delft: Delft

VEKI

Since 2019, the VEKI grant (accelerated climate investment in industry, *Versnelde Klimaatinvesteringen Industrie*) supports tangible and intangible investments in the industry for the integration at a scale of commercially available carbon-reducing technologies. VEKI is a later-TRL complement to DEI+ with a similar working (Section 5.3.4).

VEKI is reserved for industrial firms. It supports the implementation of technologies that have been demonstrated at least three times in the Netherlands and of which the payback time is greater than five years. Qualifying projects must be in the area of energy efficiency, recycling and reuse of waste, local infrastructure or other CO_2-reducing measures. The main technologies are related to electrification, sustainable cold and heat demand, carbon capture, storage and utilisation, geothermal energy, and CO_2-free industrial heating according to CE Delft.

VEKI is an investment subsidy of minimum EUR 125 000 of which the rate depends on the underlying asset, with a premium of 10 points for medium-sized firms and of 20 points for small firms (Table 5.23).

Table 5.23. VEKI subsidy rate by technology (%)

Type of project	Subsidy percentage
Other CO_2-reducing measures	40%
Recycling	35%
Local infrastructure	50%
Energy-efficiency	30%

Note: medium-sized firms: +10 percentage points; small firms: +20 percentage points.
Source: RVO.

The Dutch government allocated a budget of EUR 28 million for 2020. Data on take up suggests support is skewed towards CO_2-free industrial heating technologies according to CE Delft (Figure 5.7).

Figure 5.7. VEKI support by technology (EUR mln), January to July 2019

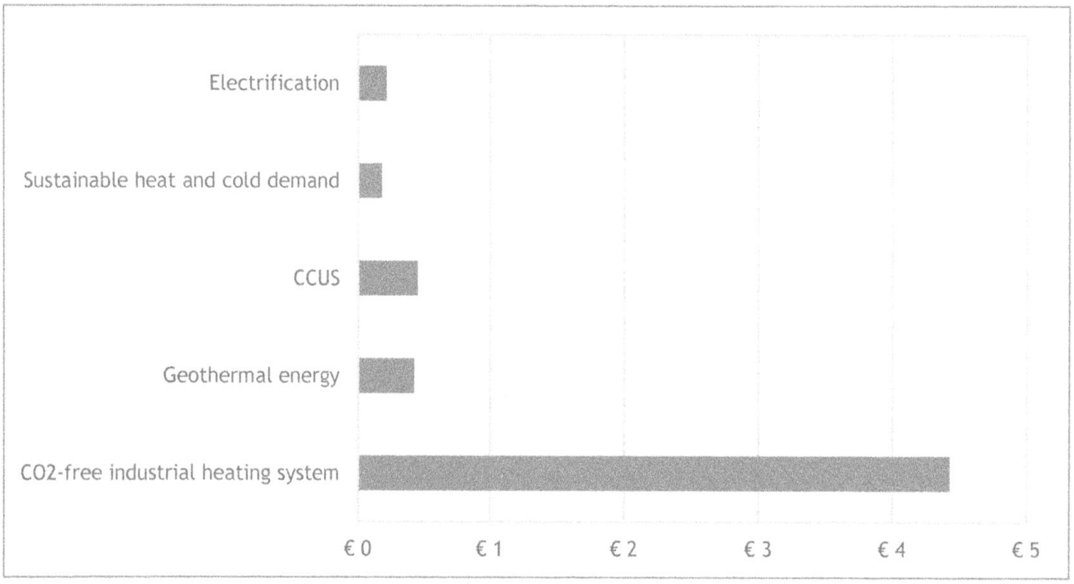

Note: Tenders open in August each year
Source: https://projecten.topsectorenergie.nl/projecten and CE Delft's calculations.

MIA and VAMIL

The MIA (environmental investment deduction, *Milieu-InvesteringsAftrek*) and the VAMIL (Arbitrary depreciation of environmental investments, *Willekeurige afschrijving milieu-investeringen*) are tax allowance schemes available to tax-paying firms in the Netherlands for eligible environment-friendly investments (excluding energy saving or renewable energy).

Qualifying investments must be in previously unused assets, amount to at least EUR 2,500 and up to EUR 25 m. per year, and be part of RVO's environment list (*Milieulijst*). Assets on the list include technologies that are relevant for industrial processes. They cover the areas of the circular economy and raw materials, carbon capture and utilisation, the bio-based economy, electrification, reduction of nitrogen and related emissions, and greenhouse gas emission reductions across all relevant sectors of the economy. The list is updated every year through legislation based on changes in technology availability. Renewable energy and energy-saving investments are excluded, as they can receive support under the SDE and EIA schemes, respectively (see above). Asset producers can introduce requests to the RVO for inclusion of new assets on the list.

MIA consists in the deduction of a fraction of the environment-friendly investment cost from taxable income in 2020, in addition to the standard depreciation allowance. Allowance rate are 13.5%, 27% or 36% depending on the type of asset. VAMIL consists in a one-off accelerated depreciation of 75% of the investment.

Firms typically combine the MIA and VAMIL schemes. Other investment subsidies must be subtracted before the MIA/VAMIL deduction is calculated. Investment costs can be split across the EIA and the MIA schemes, but cannot be deducted under both (see above). MIA/VAMIL investment may be eligible under the SDE++ scheme; in this case, the SDE++ subsidy will be adjusted to account for the MIA/VAMIL impact on the revenue shortfall parameter (see the description of SDE++ above).

The Dutch government allocated a budget of EUR 124 million for MIA and EUR 25 million for VAMIL in 2020. Data on take up over 2011-16 show that the industrial sector accounted for less than 10% of the total tax expense for MIA and VAMIL, of which virtually all went to SMEs, according to CE Delft (Figure 5.8). MIA/VAMIL investments in the area of nitrogen and greenhouse gas (GHG) emission reduction account for 2% of the total, according to CE Delft. According to an evaluation by CE Delft (2018[44]), the MIA and VAMIL schemes are cost efficient and generate relatively little windfall gains.

Figure 5.8. MIA/VAMIL investments by sector (EUR mln)

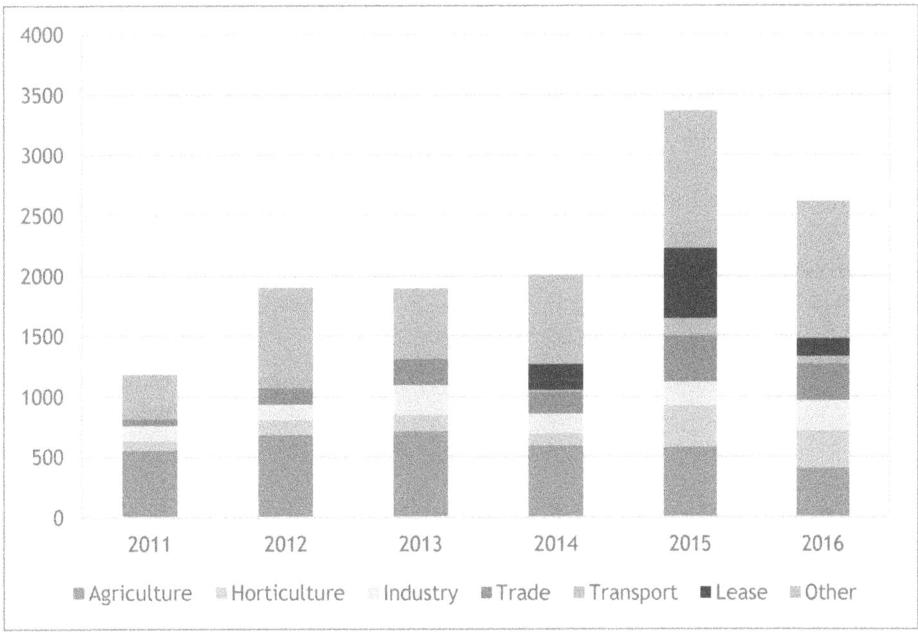

Source: CE Deflt (2018[44]). Beleidsevaluatie MIA\Vamil. CE Delft: Delft.

5.4.2. Generic and other less relevant instruments

Although not specifically targeted at the decarbonisation of the industry, other existing instruments may have a marginal impact on the deployment of low-carbon technologies.

Small-scale investment allowance

The small-scale tax allowance (KIA, *KleinschaligheidsInvesteringsAftrek*) is a generic investment tax allowance scheme available to small and medium enterprises, specifically those with yearly investment between EUR ~2 500 and EUR ~350 000, in addition to the standard depreciation allowance. The KIA deduction is available irrespective of the type of investment and may be cumulated with the EIA or the MIA under certain conditions. The budget allocation was EUR 379 million in 2019.[24]

Green project loan facility

The green project scheme (*Groenprojecten regeling*) is a subsidised bank loan facility for the financing of environment-friendly, circular economy and sustainable construction projects. The favourable tax treatment of capital gains from green funds enables participating financial institutions to charge below-market interest rates. As it only addresses the financing part of the investment, the scheme is in principle compatible with the instruments above. The tax expenditure was about EUR 62 m. in 2019.[25] In 2019, more than 50% of green project scheme investments were in construction and about 40% in energy saving and renewable energy.[26]

ISDE

The ISDE (*InvesteringsSubsidie Duurzame Energie*) is a subsidy available to firms and business owners for the purchase and installation of heat pumps or solar water heaters. The amount of the subsidy depends on the type of device to be installed. Even though ISDE-qualifying devices may be part of RVO's energy list, an EIA cannot be claimed for an ISDE-subsidised device. The Dutch government budgeted EUR 100 million for ISDE in 2020. Data on uptake shows that about 1-2% of subsidies went to the industry over the period 2016-17, mostly to small firms according to CE Delft.

LIFE

The LIFE programme is the EU's funding instrument for the environment and climate action. The aim is to support innovative projects that fit into European nature, environmental and climate policy. The LIFE programme is divided into two sub-programmes, one for environment (75% of budget) and one for climate action (25% of budget). Projects can receive co-funding of up to 60%. Any organisation in the EU can participate, from small and large firms to governments and NGOs. The current funding period 2014-20 has a budget of EUR 3.4 billion. Investments in LIFE projects in the Netherlands amount to EUR 720 million, of which EUR 223 million are from EU contributions. This budget is divided into environment and resource efficiency (EUR 466 million), nature and biodiversity (EUR 168 million), climate action (EUR 42.5 million), integrated (EUR 17.5 million) and others (EUR 26 million).

5.5. Command and control instruments

5.5.1. Environmental Management Act

The Environmental Management Act is the most important environmental act in the Netherlands and contains the general rules for environmental management. The Environmental Management Act is a framework, which means that the law mainly contains general principles, responsibilities and procedures and no detailed content. The main instruments of the Environmental Management Act are environmental plans and programs, quality requirements, permits, general rules and enforcements. The law also includes rules for financial instruments (levies, contributions and compensation). The Act also states the competent authorities for the different environmental permits and the enforcement of environmental regulation.

5.5.2. Obligation for investment in energy savings

The Environmental Management Activities Decree under the Environmental Management Act obliges companies and institutions to implement all energy-saving measures with a payback period of five years or less. This applies to companies and institutions (Environmental Management Act) that consume from 50 000 kWh or 25 000 m^3 of natural gas or an equivalent per year.

Once every four years, the company or institution reports to the competent authorities which energy-saving measures have been taken. In principle, this competent authority is the municipality in which the organisation is located, but the monitoring and enforcement tasks are sometimes delegated to an environmental agency. The authorities can start an inspection to find out if the company complied with this law, when it appears that the energy-saving measures with a payback period of five years or less are not taken. If the investigation shows that not all mandatory measures are taken, then the authorities can set a period within which the company must still comply with them. Enforcement measures may have financial consequences in the form of a non-compliance penalty.

The Environmental Management Act is enforced by the competent authority, who can decide on a penalty that needs to be high enough to prevent a rewarding violation. The penalty can vary from EUR 500 per week to 10% of the annual energy bill for each month of violation.

5.5.3. Standards

To our knowledge there are no product standards in place in the Netherlands, such as product carbon requirements.

5.6. Infrastructure programmes

At the European level, the Connecting Europe Facility (CEF) of the European Commission is planning to invest EUR 102 million in the coming years in the Porthos CO_2 transport network project, which is a project between the Netherlands and Belgium to build an open access CO_2 transport network between three of Europe's main ports (Rotterdam, Antwerp and North Sea Port). This network will lead to an offshore storage site in the North Sea. Similar to Porthos, the Athos consortium plans to use depleted offshore fields (oil, gas) or saline formations for the storage of CO_2 captured at industrial sources near the North Sea Canal, with the Tata steal plant as one of the first and largest suppliers.

Another project at the European level is the North Sea Wind Power hub which is a consortium that works on a Hub-and-Spoke system to facilitate Wind Power in the North Sea.

A third programme at the European level is the ERDF, one of the ESIF), which aims to strengthen economic and social cohesion in the European Union by correcting imbalances between its regions. It can be used for innovation, the digital agenda, SMEs support and the low carbon economy.

At the national level, the Taskforce Infrastructure Climate Agreement Industry (TIKI) advises on an effective, efficient and timely implementation of the infrastructure required for the green transition of the industrial sector as is stipulated in the Climate Agreement. In its report, TIKI first analyses the infrastructure that is already present in the Netherlands and the uncertainties and bottlenecks that exist, and then presents the infrastructure needed for the energy transition in the industrial sector, and how these networks for electricity, hydrogen and CO_2, for example, can be constructed.

The taskforce discussed the infrastructural needs with many stakeholders and came with four main recommendations: 1) An integrated main energy infrastructure should be established through agreements between industry, companies responsible for (energy) networks, and governments, in the Multi-year Program Infrastructure Energy and Climate (MIEK). MIEK gives the bottlenecks that have priority and determines how decisions to solve them are made. Examples include strengthening the electricity grid, hydrogen grid and a CO_2 pipeline network; 2) A system for the storage and re-use of CO_2 needs to be introduced, based on the projects that are already running in the Port of Rotterdam (Porthos) and Amsterdam (Athos); 3) Research on networks for hydrogen and CO_2 to Belgium and Germany should show how the Dutch economy could benefit from this; 4) Comply with a number of conditions, such as regulations, in order to be able to fully utilise the potential for CO_2 savings.

The agreements on energy infrastructure are important to get the necessary infrastructure in place for some of the most important green technologies, such as the production and processing of hydrogen, green electricity and CCS. No direct budget is linked to the TIKI and MIEK, but these reports are used as input for the infrastructure budget.

Finally, the National Program Regional Energy Strategy (RES) is a regional target which describes the strategy of the region to achieve regional energy goals. Regional choices are made on the generation of sustainable electricity, the heat transition in buildings and storage and the required storage and energy infrastructure. It is a co-operation between all regional parties, including governments and civil society organisations. The aim of the RES program is a regional strategy which describes the spatial integration of renewable energy generation, (residual) heat sources and associated infrastructure in the region. RES is related to TIKI and the Front Runner Program for the industrial sector (Box 2.2, cluster plans), which can be included in the RES. For the industrial sector, the RES can be important for delivering infrastructural aspects (e.g. heat transfers).

Box 5.4. Deployment of hydrogen technologies in the Netherlands as part of H-Vision

The Port Authority of Rotterdam and Gasunie plan to jointly construct and operate a hydrogen pipeline and will make a final decision on whether to pursue the project in the first half of 2021. This would then be connected to national hydrogen network developed by Gasunie.

Shell will construct its hydrogen plant at a dedicated site at Maasvlakte for electrolysers operated by various companies. Another project planned at this site is H_2-Fifty (the construction of a 250 MW electrolyser operated by BP and Nouryon). This facility is expected to become operational in 2025 on the coast of the North Sea. It will use offshore wind power to produce hydrogen, which will then be transported to users via a pipeline.

Source: https://www.portofrotterdam.com/en/news-and-press-releases/rotterdam-boosts-hydrogen-economy-with-new-infrastructure.

5.7. Green procurement programmes

The Dutch government has adopted a Sustainable Public Procurement system,[27] implying that the impact on the environment and social aspects should be taken into account in procurement programmes. The objective is to set the example and to boost the market for sustainable products. The government applies environmental criteria when purchasing products. Examples include computers that must be energy efficient and building materials which must be re-used for road construction projects.

The MVI (Maatschappelijk Verantwoord Inkopen) criteria tool for socially responsible public procurement gives criteria for socially responsible procurement. This tool can be used by governmental organisations, which can decide themselves how high their goals should be: basic, significant or ambitious.

The Netherlands program, which covers 45 product groups, monetises CO_2 reductions and other environmental impacts below the maximum standard. Bidders are required to use a software program called DuboCalc, which calculates the life-cycle environmental effects of materials and energy, from extraction to demolition and recycling. These effects are collapsed into an environmental cost indicator, permitting procurers to compare bids for their environmental costs. Procurers can set a maximum cut-off for this indicator, above which bidders become ineligible. Procurers can also subtract the monetised values below the standard (the environmental "benefits") from the bids in order to compare across bidders.

Green procurement is further considered in the CO_2 Performance Ladder, which is an instrument that helps public and private organisations to reduce their carbon emission through certification. The performance ladder has five rungs for procurement of construction works and materials, and monetises the appropriate rung of the latter for subtraction from the bid. A third party certifies the CO_2 performance of companies that volunteer. All this information is made available on a portal, TenderNED. Another institution, PIANOo, exists to provide advice to bidders. With a certificate on the Ladder, organisations can receive an award advantage for their registration on tenders. The instrument is used as both a CO_2 management system as well as a procurement tool.

5.8. Analysis of the policy package

This section summarises and analyses information on the policy package as described above. With regards to pricing instruments discussed in Section 5.1, two synthetic pricing indicators are presented and discussed. First, the effective carbon rate (ECR) summarising the different carbon pricing instruments and their application in a single measure. Second, an effective price signal on electricity use. The analysis of both indicators provides a synthetic view of how the Netherlands price electricity or carbon emissions from energy use in industry, with a focus on chemicals, metallurgical, food processing and refinery sectors. Finally, a summary measure on the amounts spent on technology support is presented.

5.8.1. The Dutch Effective Carbon Rate – a synthetic indicator of carbon pricing in the Netherlands

The effective carbon rate (ECR) combines prices with detailed information on the emissions base to which they apply (Box 5.5). The effective carbon rate allows for a precise appraisal of how much each tonne of CO_2 from energy used in the Netherlands pays in the context of multiple pricing policy instruments. The data builds on the OECD Taxing Energy Use (OECD, 2019[2]) and OECD Effective Carbon Rate (OECD, 2018[1]) databases and has been further refined in the context of this project.

Box 5.5. The ECR – a synthetic indicator of carbon pricing

The OECD's Effective Carbon Rate publications measures carbon pricing of CO_2-emissions from energy use in 42 OECD and G20 countries, covering 80% of world emissions. The ECR takes a comprehensive view of carbon prices, calculating the total price that applies to carbon emissions from fuel use as a result of market-based policy instruments:

- carbon taxes typically set a tax rate on energy use based on its carbon content
- specific taxes on fuel use (primarily excise taxes) typically set a tax rate per physical unit or unit of energy, but can be translated into effective carbon tax rates based on the carbon content of each form of energy
- trading systems, where the price of tradable emission permits represents the opportunity cost of emitting an extra unit of carbon regardless of the method to allocate pollution permits.

The extent to which countries choose to price carbon emissions through taxes and emissions trading systems varies substantially. Overall carbon price signals are far too weak to encourage citizens and businesses to take the climate costs of their actions into account. Recent evidence shows that taxes on polluting fuels are nowhere near the levels needed to encourage a shift towards clean energy. Adjusting taxes and subsidies and encouraging investment, will be unavoidable to curb carbon emissions.

Source: OECD (2018[1]; 2019[2]).

The ECR in Dutch industry varies widely across energy products and users, as described in detail in Section 5.1. Figure 5.9 presents the full distribution of ECR levels across the emissions base of fossil fuel use in Dutch industry at the beginning of 2021, sorting emissions according to their price level and starting at zero.[28] The horizontal axis shows the proportion of CO_2 emissions, while the vertical axis shows the ECR in EUR per tonne of CO_2. The graph identifies the share of CO_2 emissions priced at any given ECR. For example, the intersection of the blue line and the bottom dashed grey line corresponds to an ECR of EUR 50 per tonne CO_2. The ECR summarises the price signal on CO_2 emissions from energy use related to fossil fuels, thereby excluding emissions from using fossil fuels as a feedstock.

Figure 5.9 shows vast heterogeneity in the ECR of Dutch industry. According to our estimations, 14%of CO_2 emissions from fossil fuel energy use are not priced at all and only 22%are priced at or above EUR 30 per tonne. A carbon price of EUR 30 per tonne in 2025 is consistent with the slow decarbonisation scenario by 2060 according to Kaufman et al. (2020[45]). It can also be seen as a historic low-end price benchmark of carbon costs[29] in the early and mid-2010s (Ecofys, 2014[46]).

The High-Level Commission on Carbon Prices (2017[47]) proposed a price corridor of USD 40-80 per tonne for 2020, if countries want to decarbonise in line with the Paris Agreement and assuming that necessary complementary policies to carbon pricing are in place. Currently, 20% of the emissions base from fossil fuel energy use in Dutch industry is covered at or above EUR 40 per tonne and 7% are priced at or above EUR 80. Following the carbon levy trajectory, the future carbon price is expected to increase strongly.

Figure 5.9. Effective carbon rate on CO_2 emissions from fossil fuel energy use in Dutch industry, 2021

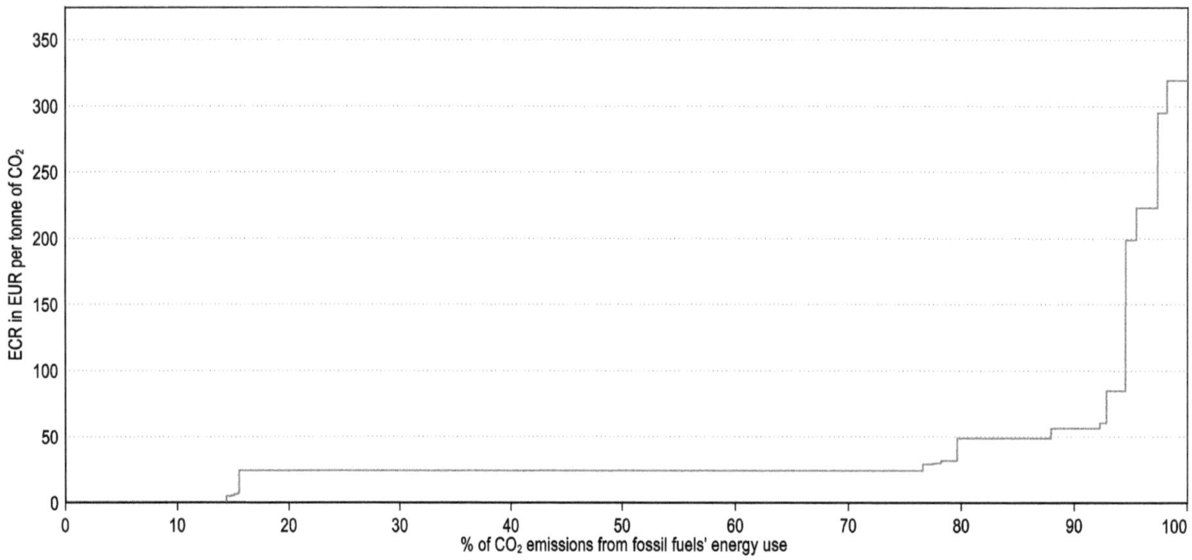

Note: The ECR includes energy tax on natural gas and ODE rates on natural gas applicable on 1 January 2021. The ETS permit price is the average price in 2020. Following the opportunity cost argument, the EU ETS price is added on emissions covered by the system even if an EU ETS allowance was freely allocated. The national component of the carbon levy is set to zero for 2021 because of the large amount of excess dispensation rights in 2021 that are not bankable, thereby losing their value for future trading periods.[30] Fossil fuel energy use data is for 2018 and adapted from IEA (2020[48]), World Energy Statistics and Balances.

A more detailed ECR profile for the main sub-sectors in the Dutch economy (chemicals, refineries, basic metals and food processing) is displayed in Figure 5.10. The profiles partition the CO_2 emissions base from fossil fuel energy use by energy users and fuels (horizontal axis). The vertical axis shows the estimated ECR in EUR per tonne of CO_2, identifying its different components: the combined rate of energy tax on natural gas ("fuel excise") and ODE on natural gas is depicted in blue and the ETS permit price in green. Due to the large amount of excess dispensation rights in 2021 that are not bankable, and will therefore be useless for future trading periods, the national component of the carbon levy is set to zero.

As previously discussed, some of the largest emitters are fully exempt from taxation, in particular energy users in the basic metals and refineries sector, or are taxed at the lowest available tax rates, such as the majority of natural gas emissions in the chemicals sectors, as they fall into the fourth consumption band with the lowest tax rate. Substantial taxation arises only for small and medium sized consumers of energy in the food processing sector.

Beyond taxation, the EU ETS broadens the carbon pricing base across all sectors. Although, free allocation of emissions allowances maintain the price level at the margin, they can weaken incentives to invest in less carbon-intensive technologies and bulky investments (Box 5.1). The shift towards a low- or zero-carbon economy requires abatement incentives beyond the margin that favour deep decarbonisation and technological switch. Freely allocating emission allowances based on product-specific benchmarks that often differs across carbon-intensive and low-carbon substitutes will affect economic rents and can make carbon-intensive investments relatively more attractive (Flues and Van Dender, 2017[18]). Depending on the allocation rules, free allocation can therefore weaken incentives for firms to invest in break-through low-carbon technologies and undermines the trading system's effectiveness to drive decarbonisation.

The individual industry profiles displayed in Figure 5.10 allow a differentiation between an ECR net of free permit allocation, the effective average carbon rate (EACR), and the standard effective marginal carbon rate (EMCR). Partitioning the price signal deriving from the EU ETS (green area) provides an estimate of how much of the EU ETS emissions in a sector are covered by an auctioned (dark green) or freely allocated emissions allowance (light green). This is different from the marginal price approach taken in Figure 5.9, which does not consider free allocation, but assigns permit price to the respective emissions base independently on whether allowances are freely allocated. The latter approach is rooted in the idea that freely allocated allowances retain CO_2 abatement incentives at the margin due to the opportunity cost (the allowance price) that they entail.

Accounting for free allocation significantly narrows the base of the ECR. More precisely, and as discussed in Section 5.1.3, the chemicals sector receives freely allocated allowances for 96%of emissions, the metallurgical sector 85% and refineries 73% (Table 5.14). This effectively drives a wedge between the marginal price emitters pay for an additional unit of emissions (EMCR) and the average price they pay for their entire emissions base (EACR).

The analysis of carbon pricing signals in 2021 allows drawing first policy recommendation (more details are provided in Section 9.1). The effective carbon rate is very heterogeneous both across and within sectors (Figure 5.10). For example, in the basic metals sector, a third of emissions are not priced at all and the rest priced at below EUR 30 per tonne. In the refinery sector, all emissions are priced below EUR 30 per tonne, whereas the food processing sector pays EUR 30 per tonne or more on 87% of its emissions. The chemicals sector stands in between and features important within-sector heterogeneity, with 63% of emissions priced below EUR 30 per tonne and 37% above EUR 30.

The carbon price also varies widely within sectors, yet for different reasons. In the basic metals and refinery sector, some emitters are simply fully exempt from taxation. In the chemicals sector, within-sector heterogeneity is driven by sector specific fuel use. Specifically, natural gas is subject to energy tax and ODE, while other fossil fuels are widely used too, but not taxed. In food processing, where natural gas constitutes the main fossil fuel consumed, variation arises from the size of energy users. The largest natural gas consumers pay the lowest available tax and ODE rates of the fourth consumption band. Substantial taxation arises only for small and medium sized consumers of energy.

A question arises on how these 2021 pictures may change with the phasing-in of the carbon levy base and the gradually increasing price. Future developments in industry structure, production processes and technology use and their effects on the CO_2 emissions in the Netherlands are challenging to predict.

Table 5.24 seeks to provide a static picture on ECRs, if the EUR 125 carbon levy applied in the current situation, but without taking potential changes in the emissions base into account. The table contrasts three ECR estimates: first, the marginal ECR in 2021 (ECR 2021) considering the EU ETS price signal independently whether allowances were freely allocated or not; second, the average ECR in 2021 (EACR 2021), i.e. net of free allocation; third, the average ECR assuming the 2030 levy rate (EUR 125 per tonne) and levy base applied on the current emissions base. The latter estimate assumes no behavioural adjustments to the emissions base, i.e. it does not consider technological shifts or efficiency improvements that industry may undertake by 2030. It, therefore, does not integrate the key policy objective (carbon abatement) of the Dutch carbon levy.

Figure 5.10. Effective carbon rates on CO_2 emissions from fossil fuel energy use in Dutch main industry subsectors, 2021

A. Basic Metals

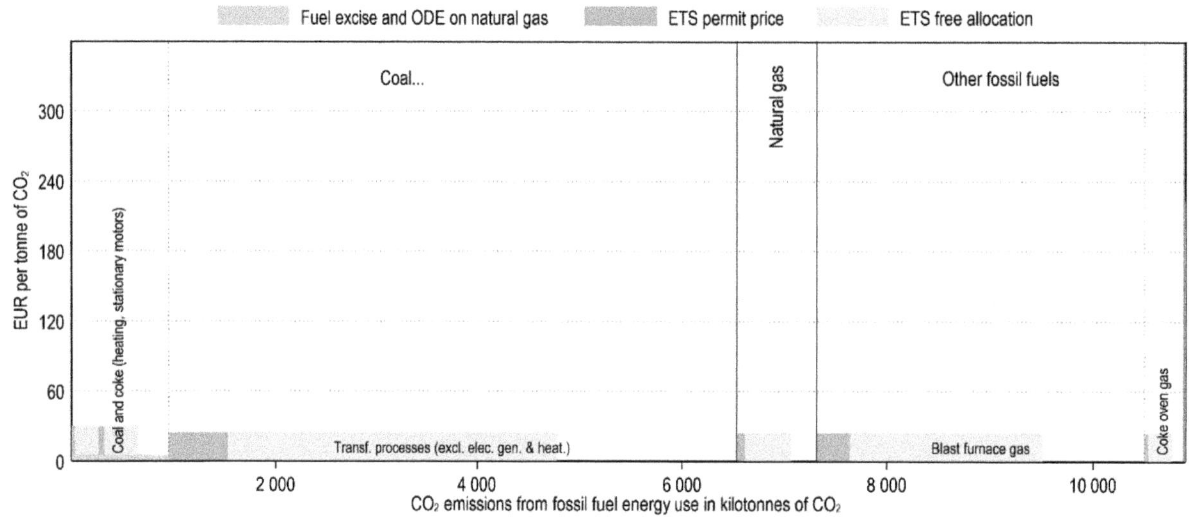

B. Chemicals

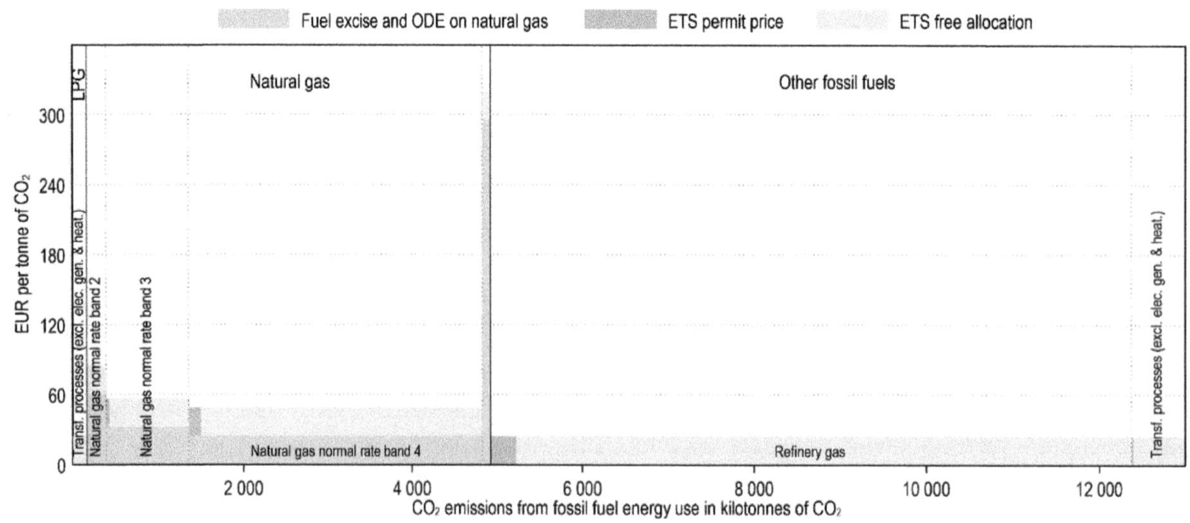

C. Food processing

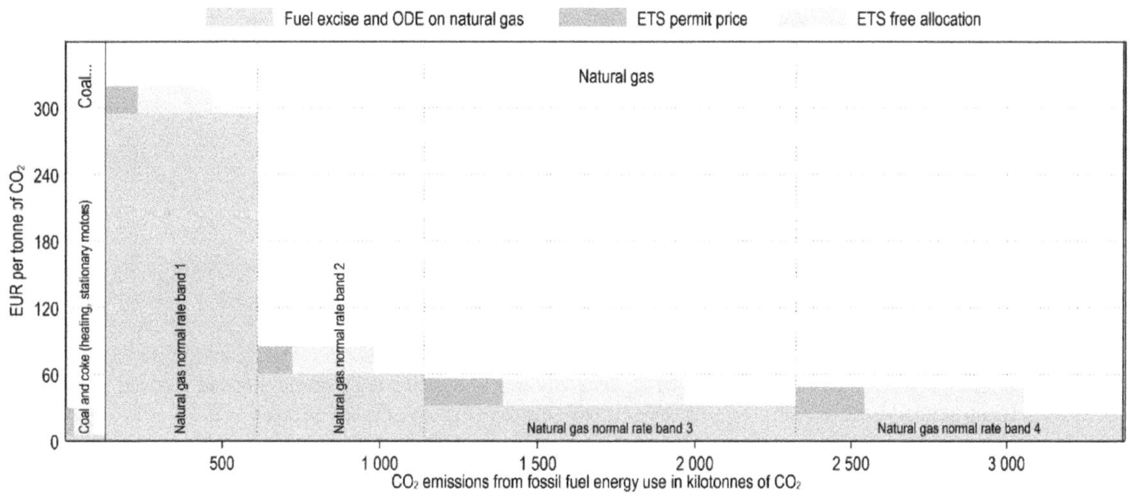

D. Refineries

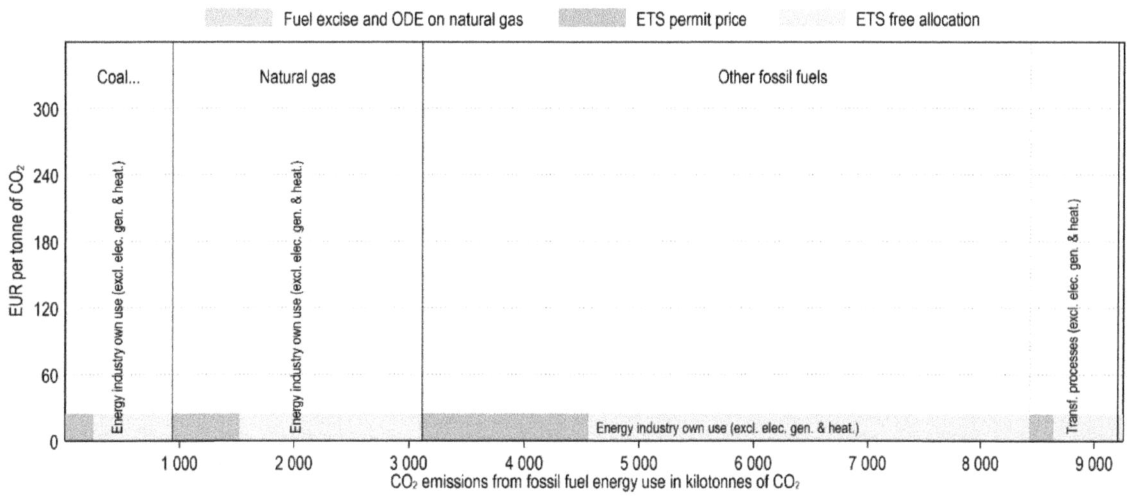

Note: The ECR includes energy tax on natural gas ("fuel excise") and ODE rates on natural gas applicable on 1 January 2021. The ETS permit price is the average price in 2020. The national component of the carbon levy is set to zero for 2021 because of the large amount of excess dispensation rights in 2021 that are not bankable, thereby losing their value for future trading periods. The methodology to estimate the overlap of taxes and ETS prices is explained in detail in OECD (2016[49]). ETS data from the Dutch emissions registry is matched to fossil fuel energy use data from IEA (2020[48]), World Energy Statistics and Balances. It is assumed that the EU ETS coverage distributes evenly across all fuels and users in each sub-sector.

The estimates confirm the uneven carbon pricing signal across sectors in 2021 due to generous tax exemptions and the regressive energy tax rates (first column). Taking free allocation of emissions allowances in the EU ETS into consideration (column 2) reveals even larger differences. In 2021, the EACR is estimated at EUR 76 per tonne on average for the food processing sector, against an average rate of EUR 13 per tonne in chemicals, and only EUR 7 and EUR 3 per tonne in refineries and in basic metals, respectively. Applied on the current emissions base, the carbon levy of EUR 125 per tonne would not close this sectoral gap, with EACRs estimated between EUR 24 in basic metals and EUR 92 in the food industry under such a scenario.

Table 5.24. Weighted average effective carbon rates in key sectors for 2021 and estimates for 2030

	Weighted average ECR (in EUR per tonne of CO_2)		
	ECR 2021	EACR 2021 (net of free allocation)	EACR levy-2030 (no behavioural adjustments)
Basic metals	17.51	3.30	23.98
Chemicals	36.64	13.26	50.61
Food	88.19	76.29	91.59
Refineries	24.35	6.57	41.62

Note: The energy data that is used to calculate the weighted averages is for 2018 and adapted from IEA (2020[48]), World Energy Statistics and Balances. ECR 2021 provides a summary of the marginal ECR in 2021, i.e. considering the EU ETS price signal independently whether allowances were freely allocated or not. EACR 2021 provides a summary of the ECR net of free allocation. EACR 2030 includes the carbon levy of EUR 125 per tonne and an ETS price at EUR 80 per tonne following price forecasts by BNEF (2020[50]). Free allocation of EU ETS emissions permits and levy dispensation rights in 2030 follow estimates by CE Delft (2021[27]). The 2030 scenario assumes no behavioural adjustments in the emissions base, i.e. no technological shifts no energy efficiency improvements or rebound effects compared to 2021.

5.8.2. Effective price signal on electricity use

The design of electricity taxation is also important for decarbonisation. Electricity taxes apply to an energy output (electricity) and are typically not distinguished by energy source. In this case, they make electricity more expensive even when it is produced from clean energy sources and fail to favour decarbonisation of the electricity mix. They also may discourage deep cuts in carbon emissions through electrification when electricity generation itself is decarbonised. Several instruments price electricity use in the Netherlands directly (e.g. electricity taxes, surcharge on electricity, indirect cost compensation). Carbon pricing instruments put a price on emissions of the input fuels used to generate electricity (e.g. EU ETS, carbon floor price for electricity). Fuels used as an input are typically exempt from energy tax and the surcharge.

As with energy taxes, the design of electricity pricing in the Netherlands raises equity concerns. Key industrial users of electricity do not pay the Dutch electricity tax and surcharge – or pay only little – either because electricity generation for own use is exempt or because large electricity consumers are subject to the lowest possible rate (Figure 5.11). This treatment favours concentrated, large electricity users at the expense of small industrial users as well as residential and commercial users.

Figure 5.11. Effective price signal on electricity use in main four industry sub-sectors, 2021

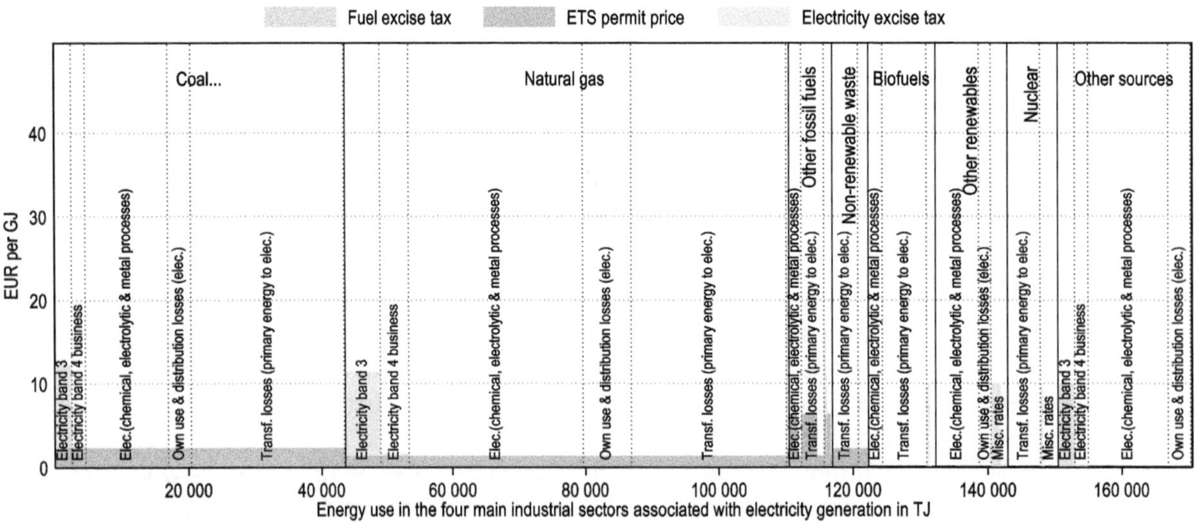

Note: Electricity tax includes the ODE on electricity use. Rates applicable on 1 January 2021. The ETS permit price is the average price in 2020. Fossil fuel energy use data is for 2018 and adapted from IEA (2020[48]), World Energy Statistics and Balances.

The current design of the Dutch electricity tax does not directly encourage power producers to shift to cleaner sources of energy and does not provide direct incentives for the decarbonisation of the power sector. The reason is that the electricity tax is not differentiated by energy source, but applies per unit of electricity used. Therefore, it increases the price on all energy sources used for electricity generation irrespective of their carbon content. In addition, another large part of the primary energy use associated with electricity generation is not subject to the electricity tax because it is lost in the conversion process – it never becomes electricity.

Electricity taxation still incentivises electricity savings in general. In liberalised power markets, fossil fuel-powered generators are frequently the marginal electricity producer. Energy savings induced by electricity taxes could thus indirectly decrease emissions.[31] Electricity taxes also have the advantage that they can be levied on electricity imported from abroad. (OECD, 2019[2])

Finally, electricity taxation may slow down electrification of industrial processes, which is often a good decarbonisation option provided electricity itself decarbonises. Contrasting the statutory energy tax rate for natural gas to the rate on electricity in GJ terms shows a bias in favour of using natural gas over electrifying industrial processes for all but the highest consumption band (Table 5.25). Everything else being equal, this favours the use of natural gas over electrification of industrial processes.

The total price differential between electricity and natural gas use is even more pronounced taking pre-tax prices into account, because the unit price for electricity (excluding taxes) exceeds the unit price of natural gas by EUR 12.5 EUR per GJ (Table 5.26). In 2020, pre-tax prices in Dutch industry are EUR 4.7 per GJ for natural gas and EUR 17.2 per GJ for electricity for the typical industrial producer.

However, it is not straightforward to compare the electricity and natural gas prices as reported in Table 5.26 as the GJ value of electricity and gas are not strictly comparable, mainly because they are affected by conversion efficiencies, amongst others. Upstream, the electricity price depends on the fuel- and technology-specific conversion efficiency to transform primary energy into electricity. For example, using solar or wind power has a high conversion efficiency (typically considered close to one), while the use of natural gas for producing electricity includes substantive losses bringing the conversion efficiency down to roughly 0.5. Everything else being equal, such a factor would translate into doubling the natural gas price displayed in the table that is needed to substitute for one GJ of electricity. Downstream, using natural gas as an input in some industrial processes may entail larger energy losses compared to using electricity. For example, substituting a gas boiler by an industrial heat pump used in low-temperature heat processes leads to fewer conversion losses. Such considerations are technology and process dependent and could lead to further reductions of the price differential between natural gas and electricity.

Table 5.25. Energy tax rates for natural gas and electricity in EUR per GJ, 2021

	Band 1	Band 2	Band 3	Band 4
Natural gas	13.31	2.50	0.91	0.49
Electricity	26.19	14.34	3.82	0.16

Note: Conversion follows the methodology set out in OECD (2019[2]) based on IEA *World Energy Statistics and Balances*.

Table 5.26. Pre-tax prices for natural gas and electricity in Dutch industry, Q2/2020

	Natural gas	Electricity
Unit price, excluding taxes [in EUR/GJ]	4.6944	17.222

Note: For natural gas, prices refer to the Eurostat consumption band I4 for industry (annual consumption: 100 000 – 1 000 000 GJ). For electricity, prices refer to the Eurostat consumption band ID for industry (annual consumption: 2-20 million kWh).
Source: Based on IEA *Energy Prices*.

5.8.3. Technology support

Figure 5.12 presents a back-of-the-envelope estimate of the amount of public funding available for the various stages. Where no specific budget exists (for example in the case of horizontal instruments), these estimates have to rely on specific assumptions on the share of funding channelled toward low-carbon technologies. These assumptions are detailed in Table 5.27.

First, within the RD&D phase, most of the policy instruments at the national level are focused on demonstration, rather than on research and development. In particular, the Netherlands strongly relies on European instruments to fund fundamental research. This allows benefiting from economies of scale by aligning research programs and co-operations at the European level and makes sense from an economic theory perspective (since knowledge externalities are larger at the EU level than at the domestic level). Nevertheless, it begs the question whether this strategy is sufficient to maintain technological leaders and sufficient absorptive capacity in the long term.

Moreover, within R&D, there is a clear financial focus on horizontal instruments, which cohabit with a myriad of targeted instruments with little individual funding. The advantage of horizontal instruments is their technological neutrality, but by construction, they benefit mostly technologies that are closest to the market. The ambitious 2050 objectives and the implied deployment of radically new technologies such as hydrogen might justify a stronger focus on targeted instruments for R&D.

The introduction of the SDE++ implies a novel focus on deployment compared with RD&D. This is generally a welcome development, in line with the overall objectives of the Climate Agreement, which rests on indicative public investment needs of EUR 500 million/year for RD&D and EUR 3 billion/year for deployment for the Netherlands as a whole (not only industry). However, within the deployment phase, there seems to be a focus on energy efficiency improvements through EIA (marginal approach) instead of technology shifts promoted through MIA/VAMIL, for example. Similarly, the set-up of the SDE++ scheme – which allocates subsidies to project applicants in decreasing order of subsidy requirement per tonne of CO_2 reduction, thus giving priority to least-cost options - makes the scheme less relevant to support technologies that are still at an earlier stage of development, such as hydrogen.

Deployment support is spread across many instruments, some of which have a very similar mechanism, e.g. the investment allowance schemes EIA, MIA and VAMIL. Streamlining could reduce fixed administrative costs, provide clarity and contribute to make it easier for industrial firms to price carbon emissions.

Finally, investments in infrastructure are a necessary condition to reach climate neutrality of industry in 2050. The use of sustainable energy and green techniques is highly dependent on the available infrastructure for electricity, hydrogen, CO_2 and heat networks. Important infrastructure is being constructed at the European level, such as the Porthos and Athos CO_2 transport networks and the North Sea Wind Power hub. At the national level, the Taskforce Infrastructure Climate Agreement Industry (TIKI) and the Multi-year Program Infrastructure Energy and Climate (MIEK) describe the infrastructure required for the energy transition and how bottlenecks can be solved. The six regional industry cluster plans also make infrastructure one of the most important conditions for accelerating the green transformation. As the construction of infrastructure takes time, more priority and speed is needed to ensure that the green transition is not delayed by infrastructure constraints. The Ministry of Economic Affairs and Climate has recently announced the creation of a national Infrastructure Programme for a Sustainable Industry (PIDI) which goes in this direction, but the resources associated with this Programme are not known yet.

Table 5.27. Estimated amounts and types of annual funding available by instrument

Programme name	Generic / specific	Annual funding available or spent on industry decarbonisation	Type	Author and type of evaluation conducted (descriptive or econometric)
		Fundamental research		
H2020	G	ca 70m/y for "energy" and "climate"	Grant	European Commission, (2017), descriptive
now	G	11m for "Energy transition and sustainability"	Grant	n.a.
		Research & Development		
EIC Accelerator	G	<1m/y for "energy" and "climate"	Grants and equity	n.a.
WBSO	G	~30m (300m/y for industry, assume 10% is low-carbon)	Tax credit	(Dialogic, APE and UNUMERIT, 2019[51]), Econometric
Innovation box	G	~30m (assuming similar proportion as for WBSO)	Tax credit	(Mohnen, Vankan and Verspagen, 2017[33]), Econometric
Nationaal Groeifonds	G	~100m (total budget 3.3bn/yr; assume 1/3 to R&D and 2/3 to infrastructure, 1/3 to climate, and 1/3 of this to industry)	Grant and/or equity	New scheme
MOOI	S	17m (+19m for renewables)	Grant	n.a.
IKIA/MMIPs	S	n.a.	Grant	New scheme
TKI/PPP	S	<10m (from Top Sector Energy review)	Grant	(Dialogic, 2016[52]), descriptive
MIT SME	S	<1m	Grant	(Technopolis, 2017[53]),econometric
TSE Industry	S	2.8m	Grant	n.a.
KIEM GoChem	S	2.6m	Grant	n.a.
		Demonstration		
EU Innovation Fund	G	~100m (assume 10% to NLD)	Grant	New scheme
InnovFin EDP	G	~3m (assume 10% to NLD)	Loans, guarantees, equity financing	n.a.
Top Sector Energy Studies Industry	S	8m	Grant	n.a.
DEI+	S	86.1m + 44m (CE)	Grant	(SEO and Dialogic, 2007[54])", econometric
HER+	S	30m	Grant	(SEO and Dialogic, 2007[54]), econometric
		Deployment		
SDE++	S	~300m (PBL: 3bn over 2020-30)	Grant	Evaluation SDE+: (CE Delft, 2016[38]), econometric
EIA	S	~75m (hyp: 1/2 x 147m budget 2020)	Tax credit	(CE Delft, 2018[39]), econometric
VEKI	S	28m	Grant	n.a.
MIA/VAMIL	S	~15m (hyp: 1/10 x [124+25] m budget 2020)	Tax credit	(CE Delft, 2018[44]), descriptive
KIA	G	~4m (hyp: 1/10 to industry x 1/10 to decarb x 379m budget 2019)	Tax credit	n.a.
Green project loan facility	S	~3m (hyp: 1/20 x 62m tax expense 2019)	Loan	n.a.
ISDE	S	~1m (hyp: 1/100 x 100m budget 2020)	Grant	(SEO, 2019[55]), econometric

Figure 5.12. Estimated amounts of annual funding available by stage (in EUR million)

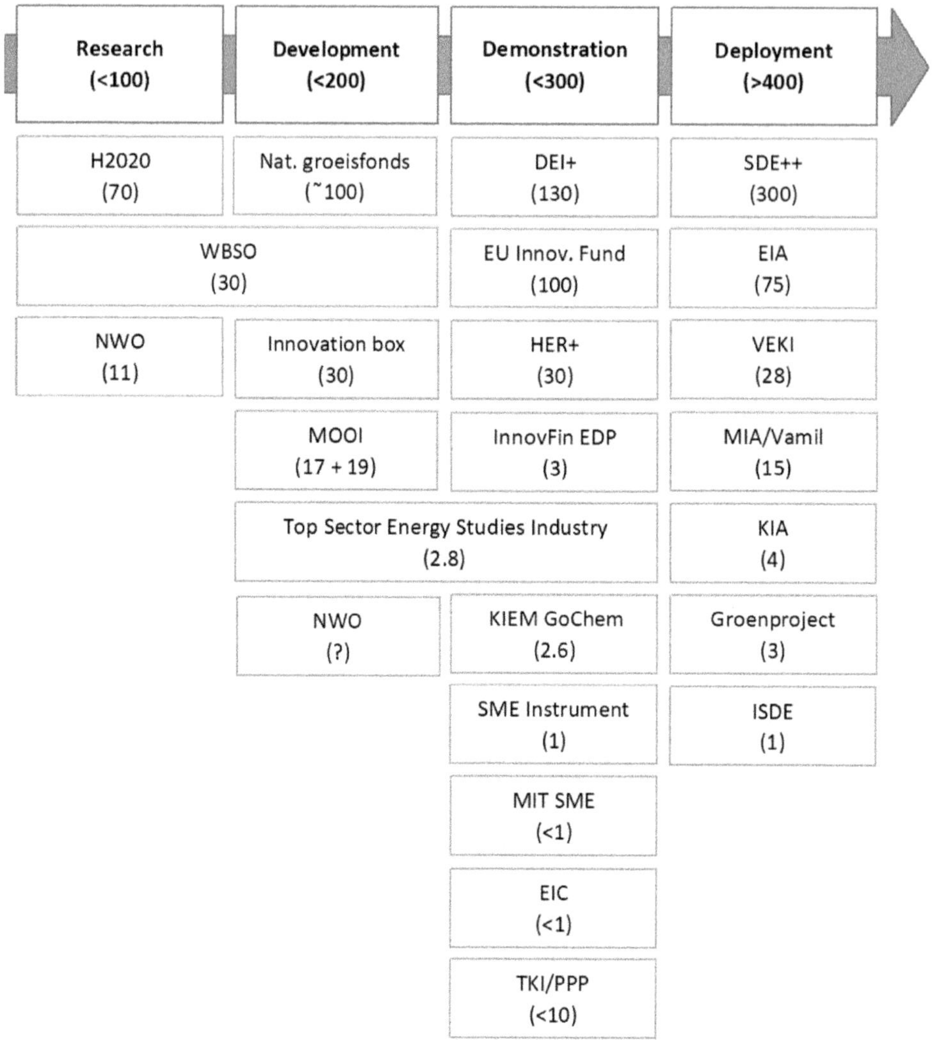

References

Belastingdienst (2020), *Tabellen tarieven milieubelastingen*, https://www.belastingdienst.nl/wps/wcm/connect/bldcontentnl/belastingdienst/zakelijk/overige_belastingen/belastingen_op_milieugrondslag/tarieven_milieubelastingen/tabellen_tarieven_milieubelastingen (accessed on 12 December 2020). [10]

Bloomberg NEF (2020), *EU Climate Goals Accelerate Eastern European Decarbonization*, https://assets.bbhub.io/professional/sites/24/BloombergNEF-Decarbonization-of-Eastern-Europe%E2%80%99s-Energy-Mix-Key-to-Higher-EU-Climate-Goals-Nov-2020.pdf. [50]

Brouwers, R., F. Schoubben and C. Van Hulle (2017), "The EU ETS and corporate environmental abatement", *Applied Economics Letters*, Vol. 24/5, pp. 334-337, https://doi.org/10.1080/13504851.2016.1189504. [19]

CBS (2020), *Overheid; ontvangen belastingen en wettelijke premies*, https://opendata.cbs.nl/#/CBS/nl/dataset/84120NED/table?ts=1605692052719 (accessed on 14 December 2020). [8]

CBS (2017), *Uitsplitsing verbruik elektriciteit en aardgas*, https://www.cbs.nl/nl-nl/maatwerk/2019/14/elektriciteit-en-aardgas-naar-energiebelastingschijf. [5]

CE Delft (2021), *Correspondance with CE Delft, February 2021*. [27]

CE Delft (2021), *Policy instruments stimulating the low carbon transition of Dutch Industry: an overview of existing policies in the field of climate and energy in the Netherlands*. [7]

CE Delft (2018), *Beleidsevaluatie Energie-investeringsaftrek 2012-2017*, https://www.ce.nl/publicaties/download/2558. [39]

CE Delft (2018), *Beleidsevaluatie Energie-investeringsaftrek 2012-2017*. [43]

CE Delft (2018), *Beleidsevaluatie MIA/Vamil*, https://www.ce.nl/publicaties/download/2555. [44]

CE Delft (2016), *Evaluatie van de SDE+ regeling*, https://www.cedelft.eu/en/publications/1957/review-of-the-dutch-sde-plus-renewable-energy-scheme. [38]

Dialogic (2016), *Tussenevaluatie TKI-toeslagregeling*. [52]

Dialogic, APE and UNUMERIT (2019), *Evaluatie WBSO 2011-2017*. [51]

Ecofys (2014), *Subsidies and costs of EU energy - Final Report*, https://ec.europa.eu/energy/sites/ener/files/documents/ECOFYS%202014%20Subsidies%20and%20costs%20of%20EU%20energy_11_Nov.pdf. [46]

Ecorys (2013), *Evaluatie Meerjarenafspraak Energie Efficiëntie 2008-2020*. [28]

Ecorys and Van Zutphen Economisch Advies (2012), *Evaluatie Energie Investeringsaftrek: Ex post evaluatie 2006-2011*, http://dx.doi.org/file:///C:/Users/Gonne_N/Downloads/blg-251649%20(1).pdf. [41]

EEX (2020), *EUA Primary Market Auction Report 2020*, https://www.eex.com/en/market-data/environmental-markets/eua-primary-auction-spot-download (accessed on 15 February 2021). [14]

European Commission (2020), *Auctioning*, https://ec.europa.eu/clima/policies/ets/auctioning_en (accessed on 14 December 2020). [13]

European Commission (2020), *Excise Duty Tables Part II Energy products and Electricity*, https://ec.europa.eu/taxation_customs/sites/taxation/files/resources/documents/taxation/excise_duties/energy_products/rates/excise_duties-part_ii_energy_products_en.pdf. [3]

European Commission (2020), *Market Stability Reserve*, https://ec.europa.eu/clima/policies/ets/reform_en (accessed on 14 December 2020). [15]

European Commission (2020), *Report on the functioning of the European carbon market*, https://eur-lex.europa.eu/legal-content/EN/TXT/PDF/?uri=CELEX:52019DC0557R(01)&from=EN. [22]

European Environment Agency (2020), *MMR article 17 auctioning*, http://cdr.eionet.europa.eu/nl/eu/mmr/art17_auctioning/envxwcnqg (accessed on 14 December 2020). [23]

Flues, F. and K. Van Dender (2020), "Carbon pricing design: Effectiveness, efficiency and feasibility: An investment perspective", *OECD Taxation Working Papers*, No. 48, OECD Publishing, Paris, https://doi.org/10.1787/91ad6a1e-en. [16]

Flues, F. and K. Van Dender (2017), "Permit allocation rules and investment incentives in emissions trading systems", *OECD Taxation Working Papers*, No. 33, OECD Publishing, Paris, https://dx.doi.org/10.1787/c3acf05e-en. [18]

Fowlie, M. and M. Reguant (2018), "Challenges in the Measurement of Leakage Risk", *AEA Papers and Proceedings*, Vol. 108, pp. 124-29, http://dx.doi.org/10.1257/PANDP.20181087. [4]

Government of the Netherlands (2019), *Climate Agreement*, National Climate Agreement, https://www.government.nl/documents/reports/2019/06/28/climate-agreement (accessed on 16 December 2020). [9]

High-Level Commission on Carbon Prices (2017), *Report of the High-Level Commission on Carbon Prices*, World Bank, Washington, D.C., https://static1.squarespace.com/static/54ff9c5ce4b0a53decccfb4c/t/59b7f2409f8dce5316811916/1505227332748/CarbonPricing_FullReport.pdf (accessed on 16 February 2018). [47]

IEA (2020), *Extended world energy balances*, https://doi.org/10.1787/data-00513-en (accessed on 14 December 2020). [48]

IEA (2011), *IEA Guide to Reporting Energy RD&D Budget/ Expenditure Statistics*, IEA, Paris, https://www.iea.org/reports/iea-guide-to-reporting-energy-rd-and-d-budget-expenditure-statistics (accessed on 22 December 2020). [35]

Kaufman, N. et al. (2020), "A near-term to net zero alternative to the social cost of carbon for setting carbon prices", *Nature Climate Change*, Vol. 10, pp. 1010-1014, https://www.nature.com/articles/s41558-020-0880-3. [45]

KPMG (2013), *Evaluatie Meerjaren afspraken energie efficiëntie MEE.* [29]

Lokshin, B. and P. Mohnen (2011), "How effective are level-based R&D tax credits? Evidence from the Netherlands", *Applied Economics*, Vol. 44/12, pp. 1527-1538, http://dx.doi.org/10.1080/00036846.2010.543083. [31]

Marten, M. and K. Van Dender (2019), "The use of revenues from carbon pricing", *OECD Taxation Working Papers*, No. 43, OECD Publishing, Paris, https://dx.doi.org/10.1787/fd193abd-en. [6]

Martin, R., M. Muûls and U. Wagner (2016), "The Impact of the European Union Emissions Trading Scheme on Regulated Firms: What Is the Evidence after Ten Years?", *Review of Environmental Economics and Policy*, Vol. 10/1, pp. 129-148, http://dx.doi.org/10.1093/reep/rev016. [20]

Ministry of Economic Affairs and Climate Policy (2021), *Correspondance with Dutch Ministry of Economic Affairs and Climate Policy, January 2021.* [12]

Mohnen, P., A. Vankan and B. Verspagen (2017), "Evaluating the innovation box tax policy instrument in the Netherlands, 2007–13", *Oxford Review of Economic Policy*, Vol. 33/1, pp. 141-156, http://dx.doi.org/10.1093/oxrep/grw038. [33]

OECD (2020), *Green budgeting and tax policy tools to support a green recovery*, OECD Publishing, Paris, http://www.oecd.org/coronavirus/policy-responses/green-budgeting-and-tax-policy-tools-to-support-a-green-recovery-bd02ea23/#contactinfo-d7e2280. [25]

OECD (2020), "The effects of R&D tax incentives and their role in the innovation policy mix: Findings from the OECD microBeRD project, 2016-19", *OECD Science, Technology and Industry Policy Papers*, No. 92, OECD Publishing, Paris, https://dx.doi.org/10.1787/65234003-en. [32]

OECD (2019), *Taxing Energy Use 2019: Using Taxes for Climate Action*, OECD Publishing, Paris, https://doi.org/10.1787/058ca239-en. [2]

OECD (2018), *Effective Carbon Rates 2018. Pricing Carbon Emissions Through Taxes and Emissions Trading*, OECD Publishing, Paris, https://doi.org/10.1787/9789264305304-en. [1]

OECD (2016), *Effective Carbon Rates: Pricing CO2 through Taxes and Emissions Trading Systems*, OECD Publishing, Paris, http://dx.doi.org/10.1787/9789264260115-en. [49]

OECD (2015), *Frascati Manual 2015: Guidelines for Collecting and Reporting Data on Research and Experimental Development*, The Measurement of Scientific, Technological and Innovation Activities, OECD Publishing, Paris, https://dx.doi.org/10.1787/9789264239012-en. [30]

OECD (2015), *Taxing Energy Use 2015: OECD and Selected Partner Economies*, OECD Publishing, Paris, https://dx.doi.org/10.1787/9789264232334-en. [56]

PBL (2020), *De energie-investeringsafrek: freeriding binnen de perken*, https://www.pbl.nl/sites/default/files/downloads/pbl-2020-de-energie-investeringsaftrek-binnen-de-perken-3772.pdf. [40]

PBL (2020), *Eindadvies basisbedragen SDE++ 2020*, Planbureau voor de Leefomgeving, Den Haag, https://www.pbl.nl/sites/default/files/downloads/pbl-2020-eindadvies-basisbedragen-sde-plus-plus-2020_3526_27-02-2020.pdf. [37]

Rijksoverheid (2020), *Vanaf 2021: wijzigingen tarieven energiebelastingen*, https://www.rijksoverheid.nl/onderwerpen/belastingplan/belastingwijzigingen-voor-ons-klimaat/energiebelasting-ode (accessed on 14 December 2020). [11]

Rijskoverheid (2020), *CO2-uitstoot Nederlandse deelnemers EU ETS, 2005-2018*, https://www.clo.nl/indicatoren/nl0584-ets-emissies-kooldioxide?ond=20883 (accessed on 14 December 2020). [17]

Rijskoverheid (2020), *Invoering CO2-heffing industrie vanaf 2021*, https://www.rijksoverheid.nl/onderwerpen/belastingplan/belastingwijzigingen-voor-ondernemers/co2-heffing (accessed on 14 December 2020). [26]

Ruijs, A. and H. Vollebergh (2013), "Lessons from 15 Years of Experience with the Dutch Tax Allowance for Energy Investments for Firms", *OECD Environment Working Papers*, No. 55, OECD Publishing, Paris, https://dx.doi.org/10.1787/5k47zw350q8v-en. [42]

RVO (2020), *Subsidieregeling Indirecte emissiekosten ETS*, https://www.rvo.nl/subsidie-en-financieringswijzer/indirecte-emissiekosten-ets (accessed on 14 December 2020). [21]

RVO (2020), *Topsector Energie Terugblik in cijfers 2012-2019*, https://www.topsectorenergie.nl/sites/default/files/uploads/Algemeen/RVO%20terugblik%20in%20cijfers.pdf (accessed on 2 September 2021). [34]

SEO (2019), *Evaluatie ISDE-KA*. [55]

SEO and Dialogic (2007), *Beleidsevaluatie Energie-innovatieregelingen*. [54]

Technopolis (2017), *Evaluatie MKB Innovatiestimuleringsregeling Topsectoren (MIT), 2013-2016*. [53]

Trinomics (2019), *Review SDE++ methodiek*, http://trinomics.eu/wp-content/uploads/2020/02/Review-SDE-Methodiek.pdf. [36]

Van Dender, K. and J. Teusch (2020), "Making environmental tax reform work", *La Revue des Juristes de Science Po*, Vol. 18, pp. 106-112, https://issuu.com/rjsp/docs/rjsp_18_-_le_droit_a__l_e_preu_ve_de_la_crise__col. [24]

Notes

[1] As long as VAT applies equally to a wide range of goods and services in an economy, it does not change relative prices between energy sources and other factors of production. Specifically, VAT does not make fossil fuels more expensive than other energy sources as long as it is applied uniformly. Only a concessionary VAT rate that applies to specific energy products would affect relative prices and should be considered when describing effective energy tax rates (OECD, 2015[56]). Because no concessionary VAT rates apply in the Netherlands, VAT is not covered in detail in this report.

[2] Natural gas used to produce electricity is exempt from the energy tax.

[3] Other EU countries also provide preferential treatment for large industrial users. For example, German industrial users that consume electricity above a certain threshold benefit from a reduced tax rate to counter potential negative effects on competitiveness. Different from the Dutch regressive rate on energy use, the preferential treatment of electricity consumption is reported in the German tax expenditure report.

[4] Because the large producer uses more energy, the nominal amount of tax paid will also be higher for the large as opposed to the small producer.

[5] While this argument holds directly for the energy tax on natural gas, its applicability for electricity is indirect, only for a given generation mix.

[6] Earmarked revenues are legal prescriptions that commit all or part of tax revenue to one or several specific spending items or to a spending programme.

[7] Note that these numbers do not take into account the change in ODE rates in 2020 and 2021, which increase rates in the third and fourth consumption band more proportionally.

[8] Exceptions to this rule during Phase 3 are Bulgaria, Cyprus, Czech Republic, Estonia, Hungary, Lithuania, Poland and Romania. During Phase 4 (2021-30) only Bulgaria, Hungary and Romania still transition to free allocation.

Note by Turkey

The information in this document with reference to "Cyprus" relates to the southern part of the Island. There is no single authority representing both Turkish and Greek Cypriot people on the Island. Turkey recognises the Turkish Republic of Northern Cyprus (TRNC). Until a lasting and equitable solution is found within the context of the United Nations, Turkey shall preserve its position concerning the "Cyprus issue".

Note by all the European Union Member States of the OECD and the European Union

The Republic of Cyprus is recognised by all members of the United Nations with the exception of Turkey. The information in this document relates to the area under the effective control of the Government of the Republic of Cyprus.

[9] Included are the following NACE categories: Manufacture of food products (NACE 1041, 1062 and 1081); manufacture of coke and refined petroleum products (all NACE 19); manufacture of chemicals and chemical products (NACE 2011-17 and 2060); manufacture of basic metals (NACE 2410-2420, 2431, 2442-2446 and 2451)

[10] These figures are based on prices at *General EUA auctions* at the European level between 1 January and 31 of December 2020.

[11] Effectively the MSR adjusts the cap by decreasing the amount of allowances that are distributed through auctions. Whether an adjustment takes place depends on the number of unused emission allowances in circulation at the end of each year. If this surplus exceeds a threshold of 833 million, the system automatically places a certain share of allowances in reserve and takes them off the market. When the number of allowances falls below another threshold, the reserve releases permits to the market. As of 2023, allowances in the reserve will be invalidated as long as the amount held in the reserve exceeds the number of allowance auctioned in the previous year (European Commission, 2020[15]).

[12] Figure provided by CE Delft, who "have allocated excess CO_2 content of waste gases in the iron and steel industry (above the emissions from natural gas) to the industrial sector in a way that is being explained in CE Delft (2016).

[13] Aluminium production (2742); mining of minerals for the chemical and fertiliser industry (1430); manufacture of other inorganic basic chemical products (2413); lead, zinc and tin production (2743); manufacture of leather clothing (1810); manufacture of basic iron and steel and of ferro-alloys and seamless steel pipes (2710, 272210); manufacture of paper and cardboard (2112); manufacture of fertilisers and nitrogen compounds (2415); copper production (2744); manufacture of other basic organic chemical products (2414); spinning cotton or cotton-like fibres (1711); manufacture of synthetic and artificial fibres (2470); iron ore mining (1310); some subsectors within the industry manufacture of plastics in primary forms (2416XXXX); Mechanical Pulp (21111400).

[14] Electricity generators are not covered by the levy. A separate minimum price on carbon emissions from electricity generation is currently being proposed for the electricity sector.

[15] The levy will start at EUR 12.30 per tonne of CO_2 raising to EUR 31.90 in 2030.

[16] Two main assumptions are part of the calculation: first, the emission reduction target will be achieved with a 75% probability; second, the carbon-abatement potential will be achieved with an 80% probability (i.e. 20% of the technologies in the ex-ante abatement curves drop out) – National Climate Agreement (Government of the Netherlands, 2019[9]).

[17] https://www.rvo.nl/sites/default/files/2020/11/resultatenbrochure-meerjarenafspraken-energie-efficientie-2019.pdf.

[18] The complete database of H2020 projects is available at https://cordis.europa.eu/.

[19] https://www.nwo.nl/en/researchprogrammes/kennis-en-innovatieconvenant-kic/mission-driven-calls-kic-2020-2023

[20] Note that there are other topics, such as "Advanced materials", "Future and emerging technologies" and "Advanced manufacturing and processing", which might include relevant projects for the industry's decarbonisation.

[21] The full list of projects supported by the SME Instrument and the EIC are available at https://sme.easme-web.eu/.

[22] https://www.tweedekamer.nl/kamerstukken/brieven_regering/detail?id=2017Z03803&did=2017D07791.

[23] https://www.rijksoverheid.nl/documenten/begrotingen/2019/09/17/bijlagen-miljoenennota-2020.

[24] https://www.rijksbegroting.nl/2019/kamerstukken,2018/9/18/kst248658_9.html.

[25] https://www.rvo.nl/sites/default/files/2020/08/Beleidsevaluatie Regeling groenprojecten 2010-2017.pdf.

[26] https://www.rvo.nl/sites/default/files/2020/07/Jaarcijfers Groen Beleggen 2019.pdf.

[27] https://www.pianoo.nl/en/public-procurement-in-the-netherlands/sustainable-public-procurement-spp

[28] Different from the usual practice in OECD Taxing Energy Use and Effective Carbon Rates publications (2018[1]; 2019[2]), the Dutch CO_2 emissions base used in the context of this project only covers emissions from the combustion of fossil fuels and excludes emissions from the combustion of non-renewable waste and biofuels. As usual, the indicator excludes emissions that are not related to energy use (such as process emissions) and carbon emissions embedded in fuels that are used as a feedstock.

[29] The carbon costs approach to carbon pricing estimates the damage to society that results from one tonne of CO_2 released into the atmosphere. Other approaches define benchmark carbon prices that are necessary to reach specific CO_2 emission reduction scenarios (e.g. Kaufman et al. (2020[45]) and High-Level Commission on Carbon Prices (2017[47])).

[30] Ultimately, depending on the allocation of dispensation rights, the national component of the carbon levy likely settles in a range between the rate set out through the price trajectory and a rate of EUR 0 per tonne. The former reflects the upper bound of the opportunity costs of holding a dispensation right. Generous allocation of dispensation rights will lower this rate. Indications are that it may yield an effective marginal price signal of zero in the early years of the levy.

[31] Note however that the Dutch power sector is additionally subject to the EU ETS, which may further decrease the effectiveness of electricity taxes when triggering net emission reductions.

6. Decarbonisation support in practice: case studies

This chapter presents the results of two case studies which illustrate the consequences of the current set of policy instruments for the financial viability of two representative decarbonisation projects identified as critical by the zero-emission scenario for the Dutch industry by 2050 (Chapter 3). The two projects are green hydrogen for ammonia production in the chemicals sector and CCS for hydrogen production by steam-methane reforming in the refinery sector.

The zero-emission scenario for the Dutch industry by 2050 described in Chapter 3 presents sector-specific technological pathways that would be compatible with full decarbonisation, while Chapter 5 presents a comprehensive analysis of the policy instruments currently in place to encourage the decarbonisation of the Dutch industry. In this chapter, two case studies are carried out in order to understand in practice the consequences of the current set of policy instruments for the financial viability of specific decarbonisation projects identified as critical in Chapter 3. Additional analysis of emerging technologies necessary for industry decarbonisation is carried out in Chapter 8.

The two selected case studies are: 1) green hydrogen for ammonia production in the chemicals sector; and 2) CCS for hydrogen production by steam-methane reforming (SMR) in the refinery sector. The chemicals and refineries sectors are the two largest CO_2-emitting sectors in the Dutch industry (Chapter 2). The case studies focus on hydrogen production, as this technology is expected to contribute the most to the low-carbon transition, accounting for more than 25% of emission reductions by 2050 (Chapter 3). It plays a significant role in the four sectors analysed in this report, but is of major importance in the chemical sector and for refineries. CCS represents more than 12% of the necessary emission reductions by 2050, and has applications in the chemical, metallurgical and refineries sectors because all three will remain partly reliant on fossil fuels in 2050 and, more generally, because it enables the production of blue hydrogen.

The two case studies also correspond to two different Technology Readiness Levels (TRL). Green hydrogen, based on electrolysis of water fuelled by renewable electricity, is an immature technology that still requires significant cost reductions, which could be brought about by research and development as well as through learning-by-doing and scale economies. Green hydrogen production also requires large amounts of renewable electricity, which is not yet available in the Netherlands. In comparison, blue hydrogen – a combination of CCS and steam-methane reforming (SMR) – is a fairly mature technology that can be deployed relatively soon and can enable the uptake of hydrogen as an energy carrier, but leads to direct abatement as well, by replacing current hydrogen production via grey steam-methane reforming.

The two projects are analysed from the perspective of a fictive firm that seeks to implement a carbon-reducing project and undertakes an assessment of its potential viability under the current policy landscape, which includes pricing mechanisms that discourage carbon emissions and also the various public subsidies that can potentially be requested. For each project, information is collected on the required amount of capital and the operational costs (under different energy price scenarios) and an assessment is made on the eligibility to various support mechanisms and the likelihood of obtaining the subsidies. The final objective is to assess whether the implementation of the projects is dependent on obtaining public subsidies.

6.1. Case Study 1: Green hydrogen in ammonia production

6.1.1. Introduction

Ammonia is an important feedstock for fertilisers and its production is currently the most energy-intensive process in this industry.[1] To produce ammonia (NH_3), nitrogen (N_2) and hydrogen (H_2) are required. The production of ammonia currently represents 43% of global hydrogen demand. Most of the remaining demand relates to oil refining into fuels and basic commodities, with 52% of global hydrogen demand (IEA, 2019[1]).

Currently, ammonia-producing plants use natural gas-based steam-methane reforming (SMR) for hydrogen production on site, a CO_2-emitting process because methane is used both for energy production and as feedstock. An option for sustainable ammonia production is to use electrolysis from renewable resources for hydrogen production. Electrolysis is the process by which electricity is used to split water into hydrogen and oxygen. This reaction takes place in a unit called an electrolyser. Electrolysers can range in size from small, appliance-size equipment that is well-suited for small-scale distributed hydrogen production, to large-scale, centralised production facilities that could be tied directly to renewable or other non-greenhouse-gas-emitting forms of electricity production.[2] If the electricity production is renewable, this process is called green hydrogen production.

According to Berenschot, the plausible technological pathway for ammonia production is based on a combination of green hydrogen and auto-thermal reforming with CCS (blue hydrogen, with an assumed carbon capture rate of 85%). A major determinant of the growth of green hydrogen is the amount of renewables in the Dutch energy mix. For ammonia production at sites that are connected to offshore wind farms, green hydrogen from electrolysis is a logical route. Electricity can then be used to produce the nitrogen with air separation units and to supply the compressors for the Haber-Bosch process. According to Berenschot, a total of 115 PJ of hydrogen will need to be produced on sites in 2050, which requires either 175 PJ of electricity supply for green hydrogen, or 115 PJ of natural gas and 30 PJ of electricity for blue hydrogen.

The Netherlands is the second largest hydrogen producer in Europe after Germany, producing an estimated volume of around 10 billion cubic metres per year.[3] According to *Fertiliser Netherlands* (Meststoffen Nederland), the Dutch ammonia market consists of four players: Yara (Sluiskil), OCI Nitrogen (Chemelot), Rosier (Sas van Gent) and ICL fertilisers (Amsterdam & Heerlen).[4] The sites in Amsterdam, Sas van Gent and Sluiskil are not land-locked and should soon have access to electricity from offshore wind. Therefore, these sites have the option to produce green hydrogen on site from electrolysis, because of the close proximity to offshore wind power.

Ørsted (the developer of the Borssele wind farm project) and Yara recently announced a plan to produce 75 000 tonnes of "green ammonia" per year at Yara's existing Sluiskil plant in the Netherlands. To realise this ambition, Yara intends to install a 100 MW electrolyser, which would be run using Ørsted's offshore wind energy (capacity 752 MW[5]). The final investment decision is expected in 2021-22, and production would begin in 2024-25.[6] This 100 MW electrolyser project will serve as the first case study.

The case study is potentially replicable to other sites in the Netherlands, provided that abundant renewable electricity supply is available and that a large electricity connection is established. For example, the electricity connection at OCI is currently limited to 12 MW[7] and the sites in Heerlen and Chemelot have less access to renewable electricity, requiring infrastructure adjustments to be made as a prerequisite for similar projects.

6.1.2. Case study characteristics

Yara Sluiskil produces around 5 million tonnes of fertiliser products per year. The three ammonia plants ('C', 'D' and 'E') use natural gas to produce ammonia and have a combined production capacity of approximately 1.8 million tonnes of NH_3 per year (Table 6.1) requiring about 0.22 million tonnes of hydrogen (Batool and Wetzels, 2019[2]).

Table 6.1. Overview of annual production and emissions of Yara ammonia plants

Yara	Estimated production capacity (kt/a)	CO_2 emissions 2017 (kt/a)
Ammonia plant C (1973)	449	793
Ammonia plant D (1984)	639	1 221
Ammonia plant E (1988)	731	1 128
Total	1 820	3 142

Note: Estimated production benchmark for year 2009
Source: PBL.

A 100 MW electrolyser can produce around 50 tonnes of hydrogen per day,[8] amounting to approximately 18 kt of hydrogen annually. With this production capacity of hydrogen, a back of the envelope calculation ($N_2 + 3\ H_2 \rightarrow 2\ NH_3$) shows that the potential ammonia production capacity is 100 kt annually.

How much carbon emissions would this project abate? According to PBL, Yara's ammonia plant C, the oldest and least efficient plant on the site, produces 449 kt of ammonia per year, leading to 793 kt of CO_2 emissions (Table 6.1). The substitution of 100 kt of production from plant C with green hydrogen would thus result in an abatement of (793*100/449=) 177 kt of CO_2, which should however be adjusted downward because some energy is used for pressurising. Similarly, the Ammonia Energy Association states that a 100 MW electrolyser would reduce Yara's CO_2 emissions by about 5%,[9] or 180 kt CO_2, considering the emissions of 3.6 million tonne CO_2 in 2017. Finally, Praxair, one of the world's largest hydrogen producers, reports that the carbon footprint for conventional (SMR) hydrogen production is 9.3 kg CO_2/kg H_2, leading to 167 kt (18*9.3) for our system.[10] Hence, we assume that with this project Yara can abate 160 – 180 kt CO_2 annually.

Although electrolysers are a mature technology, the significant scale of the hydrogen project of Yara is new. Three types of electrolysers exist: Alkaline Water Electrolysis (AWE), proton-exchange membrane cell (PEM) and solid oxide electrolysis cell (SOEC) (Grigoriev et al., 2020[3]). Of the AWE type, installations up to the MW scale are commercially available; of the PEM type, on the multi-MW scale; and of the last type, no installation is commercially available yet, only demonstration projects at lab scale (around 200 W). The AWE technology is the cheapest regarding CAPEX (EUR 700-800/kW), while the PEM has higher CAPEX (EUR 1 000-1 500/kW) but significant progress has been made over the past few years. For both the AWE and PEM, the OPEX is 2% of the CAPEX annually for a 20 MW installation, (Table 6.2).

Table 6.2. Expected costs and other technicalities of electrolyser types

Technology		Alkaline		PEM	
	Unit	2017	2025	2017	2025
Efficiency	kWh of electricity/kg of H_2	51	49	58	52
Efficiency (lower heating value)	%	65	68	57	64
Lifetime Stack	Operating hours	80 000	90 000	40 000	50 000
CAPEX – total system costs (incl. power supply and installation costs)	EUR/kW	750	480	1200	700
OPEX	% of initial CAPEX/year	2	2	2	2
CAPEX – stack replacement	EUR/kW	340	215	420	210
Typical output pressure	Bar	Atm.	15	30	60
System lifetime	Years	20		20	

Note: CAPEX and OPEX are based on a 20 MW system.
Source: Grigoriev et al. (2020[3]).

One hundred MW scale systems are under development. Large-scale implementation of electrolysis technologies still requires cost reductions; nonetheless, investments are being made towards the development of macroscale power-to-gas and breakthroughs in related fuel technologies facilitate cost reduction down to the target of EUR 500/kW. Indeed, OCI Nitrogen has estimated that a large-scale electrolysis pilot unit of 100 MW requires an investment of EUR 50 million.[11] Moreover, PBL uses EUR 525/kW for the electrolyser CAPEX (comparable with Grigoriev et al. (2020[3])) and estimates the OPEX to amount for 3% of the CAPEX (50% higher than Grigoriev et al. (2020[3])). The PBL estimates imply a CAPEX of EUR 52.5 million and an annual OPEX of EUR 1.5 million. This is in the same order of magnitude as Grigoriev et al. (2020[3])., therefore we assume CAPEX to be EUR 50-75 million, based on the PBL, OCI estimate and 2017 alkaline costs of Grigoriev et al. (2020[3]).

In the Netherlands, other hydrogen-related projects are currently being developed. Topsector Energie reports four other projects with a cost specification. In particular, a feasibility study for the HyNetherlands Eemshaven project (a 100 MW electrolyser) projects a CAPEX of EUR 50-100 million. Two other projects, H2ermes and H2.50, are in the phase of conducting a front end engineering design (FEED) study and estimate the CAPEX to be EUR 150 million and EUR 225-300 million for a 100 MW and 250 MW electrolyser project, respectively. The realisation of DJewels, a 20 MW electrolyser, specifies a EUR 16 million subsidy, but the total project costs are unknown.[12] Therefore, the order of magnitude of the costs are in line with the assumptions above. However, it is clear that the construction phase is really the last phase of the projects, which should include development costs and a possible FEED study. In this case study, a development study is assumed to amount to EUR 25-30 million, as calculated by the European Commission[13].

Finally, the lifetime of an electrolyser is estimated to be 80 000 hours, both by PBL and Grigoriev et al. (2020[3]). In a situation where the plant operates 24/7, it runs for 8 000 hours annually. Therefore, the installation depreciates in ten years (it is unknown whether there is residual value). It can reasonably be assumed that Yara would want to run the electrolyser full-time, as hydrogen supply is critical for the ammonia production supply chain. A situation where the installation acts as a balancing method of electricity supply would imply discontinuous hydrogen production. Then, either the ammonia production becomes discontinuous itself, or SMR hydrogen production should act as swing supply while emitting the corresponding greenhouse gases. The benefit of acting as a balancing method is cost reduction, because the electricity price is lower in times of 'over' supply. For the sake of simplicity, we assume that Yara favours a continuous production.

A summary of the ammonia production quantities, abated emissions, costs and electricity consumption is given in Table 6.3.

Table 6.3. Overview of case study characteristics

Case study characteristics	Quantity
Total annual production ammonia at Yara	1820 kt
Ammonia production of 100 MW electrolyser	100 kt
Emission abatement 100 MW electrolyser	160 - 180 kt CO2
CAPEX 100 MW electrolyser	50 - 75 EUR mln
OPEX 100 MW electrolyser	1.5 EUR mln/a
Development study	25-30 EUR mln
Lifetime 100 MW electrolyser	80.000 h (~ 10 year)
Electricity consumption 100 MW electrolyser	0.8 TWh/y
Natural gas savings 100 MW electrolyser	0.52 TWh/y
SMR OPEX savings	3 EUR mln/y

6.1.3. Policy instrument analysis

The construction of a 100 MW electrolyser can best be regarded as a pilot or demonstration project with a prior R&D component (FEED study). However, the SDE++ instrument – aimed at scaling up projects with the highest TRLs – also mentions green hydrogen in its call for tenders. Therefore, in this analysis all policy instruments will be considered, from R&D support to SDE++, in addition to the possible savings from the EU ETS, the Carbon Levy and energy taxes.

Research, Development and Demonstration Instruments

H2020 (Innovation Action, deadline 26 January 2021, single stage)

There is a special call from the European Commission to develop and demonstrate a 100 MW electrolyser.[14] The case study seems like an excellent example of a project that can respond to this call, as the operation in an industrial environment like a fertiliser production plant is mentioned explicitly. The EU proposes a contribution of EUR 25–30 million and support can be combined with other European or national financing instruments. In return for the funds, mandatory knowledge sharing is required, as is an evaluation of the project and its environmental impact. A list of expected technological impacts is presented, including reducing the electrolyser's CAPEX to EUR 480/kW. This is more ambitious than the estimates above, implying that a development study is required.

Innovation Action projects are typically assessed on two criteria: excellence and impact.[15] Because this is a special call, the excellence (technological impact) is already prescribed. Projects thriving for even higher efficiencies have higher chances of winning the subsidy, but this is not expected before 2025 based on Grigoriev et al. (2020[3]). Regarding the impact criterion, the electrolyser at the fertiliser plant has a direct impact on emissions, and could induce knowledge spillovers. To conclude, Yara's project is very likely eligible for the EUR 25-30 million subsidy, but it is unknown exactly how much competition there is for the grant.

WBSO

The WBSO is a tax credit on R&D expenditures, which are included in the first stages of the project. It consists of two parts, a fiscal deduction mechanism for R&D labour and prototype costs which do not have commercial value.[16] The fiscal deduction mechanism for labour costs amounts to 40% for the first EUR 350 000 and 16% above. The tax deduction is 100% for prototype costs. Yara is actively engaged in R&D activities[17], and could use their R&D personnel to work on the development study. If we assume that 80% of the development costs are labour costs and 20% prototype costs, EUR 8.2-9.8 million could be deducted, using the 16% rate.

MOOI (Mission-driven Research, Development and Innovation) under Topsector New Gas

As the name suggests, this policy instrument focuses on (industrial) research and development. The scheme excludes prototype/pilot activities, but includes development and FEED studies. Hence, the development part of the project is eligible. Moreover, green hydrogen and the development of a 100 MW electrolyser are explicitly mentioned as one of the missions[18] (MMIP 8), although it says "the road map pleads for green sustainable hydrogen but acknowledges that grey hydrogen in the short run and blue hydrogen in the middle run can help with its development". A total of EUR 17 million is available for industry, with a single project cap of EUR 4 million "for industrial research, experimental development or a feasibility study carried out by a consortium of at least three companies" and EUR 350 000 for 'other' project costs. The size of the project must be at least EUR 2 million and 50% of the development costs can be incurred.

Although the project is fully eligible (if it is developed by Yara together with at least two other companies), the cap of EUR 17 million shows that no more than four projects in the largest category can be supported. The ranking criteria are "meeting a mission", "quality of partnership/ consortium", "innovation level (with a system-level emphasis)", "success chance in Dutch market and society" and "quality of the project plan". If a project of the same type scores higher, the proposal will be rejected, even though it might score higher than other projects, to ensure a diversified subsidy portfolio. Therefore, whether or not the project could receive the subsidy depends on the degree of competition in the programme call.

Nationaal Groeifonds (development, infrastructure and innovation)

The funds concentrate on the growth of the national economy and creating public value and will allocate EUR 20 billion over five years.[19] Although an electrolyser technology can be applied across the fertiliser industry and across multiple sectors, potentially creating public value through knowledge spillovers, the project integrated into Yara's business, is an on-site innovation and does not imply direct growth of Dutch GDP. Examples of eligible projects that are regarded to create public value more directly are the Amsterdam metro line expansion and adaptations to the current gas network to create a hydrogen backbone.[20] Moreover, projects falling under other subsidy schemes are not eligible[21]. Therefore, this project is unlikely to be eligible to receive funds from the Nationale Groeifonds.

Demonstration Energy and Climate Innovation

The DEI+ supports pilot- and demonstration projects that contribute to cost-effective greenhouse gas abatement.[22] A project can be either a pilot or a demonstration project. Pilot or experimental development projects can apply for a direct subsidy of 25% and demonstration projects for 40% with a maximum of EUR 15 million, where the eligible amount is the additional costs of the climate-friendly investment in comparison with a similar non-climate friendly investment. The difference between a pilot project and a demonstration project is the practical application: while a pilot project focuses on testing, the aim of a demonstration project is to be commissioned and built. Both project types must have an experimental character and demonstrate the working of a new technology beyond lab conditions, such that the innovation can be brought to the market. Because this instrument is meant to develop and demonstrate technologies, projects should have a size no larger than strictly necessary, according to an expert interview from RVO. This categorisation leads to some ambiguity for this project, because part of the project, the development study, focuses on the development of a new technology, while the construction of a 100 MW electrolyser demonstrates this technology on a new scale. After consultation with the expert from RVO, it was concluded that only the development study for this project is eligible to the subsidy, because that part of the project focuses on innovation.

Three important grant criteria are: 'sufficient' abatement (cost-effectiveness), sufficient chance of success for the innovation in the Dutch market, and repetition potential. This project arguably scores less on the first criterion (although blue hydrogen projects are exempted), but well on the second and third. Nevertheless, the instrument works on a first come first serve basis, thus if the criteria are sufficiently fulfilled the subsidy should be granted.

Finally, among the categories of eligible project types for the DEI+, the category "flexibilisation of the electricity sector including hydrogen" explicitly mentions green hydrogen pilots where the resulting hydrogen may be used as feedstock for the industry. Hence, we assume that the project is eligible for a subsidy amounting to 25% of the costs of the development study, or EUR 6.25-7.5 million.

HER+

The explicit aim of the HER+ is to reduce future subsidy expenditures under the SDE++ scheme by investing in innovative projects that bring about cost-efficient emission reductions.[23] Hence, a leading criterion is that the future savings should outweigh the requested subsidy. HER+ is focused on demonstrating new technologies that are not yet close to the market, as opposed to DEI+. Still, the subsidy savings should be realised before 2030. The instrument works on a first come first served basis. Because the development of a large scale electrolyser does not reduce renewable electricity production costs, nor is in the list of 'regulation designation categories of sustainable energy production'[24], the project is likely not eligible. Furthermore, if green hydrogen would be eligible due to the (recent) inclusion of green hydrogen in the SDE++ scheme, and subsequent inclusion in the HER+, this project is unlikely to cause the potential future requested SDE++ subsidy to drop beyond the current cap of EUR 300/tCO_2. According to PBL, the current subsidy intensity for green hydrogen is EUR 1 064/t CO_2[25], and the project cannot be expected to reduce the costs by as much as EUR 765/t CO_2. Therefore, it is most likely not eligible to HER+.

Summary on RD&D instruments

Table 6.4 gives an overview of the RD&D policy instruments to which the electrolyser is eligible and the corresponding amount of the potential subsidy. All these instruments would subsidise the project's development study.

Table 6.4. Overview of RD&D subsidies to which the project's development study is eligible

Instrument	Amount Estimate
H2020 IA	EUR 25-30 mln
WBSO	EUR 8.2-9.8 mln
MOOI	EUR 4.35 mln
DEI+ (pilot)	EUR 6.25-7.5 mln

Deployment instruments

VEKI

VEKI is targeted at SMEs, hence Yara is not eligible.

Mia/Vamil

The project's technology must be on the *milieulijst*, which is not the case for the 100 MW electrolyser.

EIA

To be eligible the project must be on the *energielijst*. While power to hydrogen gas is on the list, installations for the purpose of feedstock production are excluded. Hence, the project is not eligible.

SDE++

The SDE++ is the largest Dutch policy instrument for deployment of low-carbon technologies and is similar to a contract-for-difference. The electrolyser in this case study is eligible, as hydrogen production by electrolysis is explicitly mentioned under the category "low CO_2 production".

However, the SDE++ is granted by tender. One of the criteria of subsidy for the SDE++ is the cost-effectiveness of CO_2 reductions. However, PBL estimates that hydrogen production by electrolysis requires a subsidy intensity of EUR 1 064/t CO_2, which is second to last in the cost-effectiveness ranking of various technologies for decarbonisation. Therefore, such a project will likely not be eligible for subsidy if the total requested subsidy of competing projects is larger than the allocated budget. This is acknowledged by the Minister of Economic Affairs and Climate in his letter to the parliament[26]. He writes: "From the broader perspective of the transition towards 2050, the development and timely start of hydrogen infrastructure and production scale-up is crucial to contribute to abatement after 2030" and "Although green hydrogen production is a relatively expensive option with respect to other techniques, I open this category to offer market parties the required perspective on the SDE++. Parties that run upfront – because of favourable conditions and/or other subsidies – can, in the meantime, be eligible for the SDE++ for the maximal subsidy amount of EUR 300/tCO_2. In that case the SDE++ covers part of the economic difference and other income (European or regional subsidy), lower costs (cheap installation of current) or a lower result covers the resulting amount." Furthermore, the Minister points to the hydrogen vision of the cabinet, published 30 March 2020.

In this vision, it is acknowledged that green hydrogen will not be able to compete in the SDE++, and hence "presents a new, temporary, instrument for exploitation support with the purpose of scaling up and reducing costs of green hydrogen production".[27] The government will allocate approximately EUR 35 million a year for this purpose by reallocating part of the existing funds for hydrogen pilots within the DEI+.

To conclude, green hydrogen projects are eligible for a support of EUR 300 per tonne of avoided CO_2, for 2 000 hours per year, but it remains ambiguous whether some of the SDE++ budget will be reserved for hydrogen projects. If this amount is not reserved, it is highly unlikely that a green hydrogen project will receive funds due to the low cost-effectiveness, until substantial cost reductions are achieved. The total eligible amount for this project would be EUR 12-13.5 million, based on the abatement of 160-180 kt CO_2 and taking into consideration that the subsidy is granted for a maximum of 2000 hours per year instead of 8000 hours.

Market-based instruments

ETS/Carbon Levy

Because the new Carbon Levy is coupled with the ETS, the two instruments are discussed together. The CO_2 levy is a baseline-and-credit system, where emissions above the baseline are taxed, and emissions below the baseline can be traded. The benchmark is set at the 2008 carbon efficiency and decreased by 0.2% per year to 2023 (i.e. the 2008 benchmark - 3% in 2023), the annual reduction factor starts at 1.2 and decreases by 5.7 percentage points per year until 2030. In 2021, the levy starts at EUR 30 /t CO_2, increases each year by EUR 10.56 /tCO_2 up to EUR 125 /tCO_2 in 2030. The ETS price of the previous year is subtracted from the levy. Yara is subjected to the tax and receives dispensation rights (1 DPR = 1 tonne of CO_2). Although the exact amount of dispensation rights (DPR) is unknown, it is given by the product of the activity level, the EU ETS benchmark and the reduction factor.

Using the (preliminary) EU ETS benchmark in 2008 (1.46 tCO_2/tNH_3),[28] accounting for the annual tightening, and assuming a constant production level of 1 820 t NH_3 (2009), the expected DPR for 2021-30 is given in column 2 of Table 6.5. EU ETS free allowances are granted based on the EU ETS benchmark and the plant's output. Since we assume that the plant will generate the same output with or without the electrolyser, the EU ETS free allowances are received in both cases and cancel out, so they do not have to be considered in this exercise.

Table 6.5. Effects of the carbon levy on the electrolyser project

Year	Reduction factor (CE Delft)	Expected DPR (kt CO_2)	Benchmark tCO_2/tNH_3 (2008)	Activity ammonia (2009) (kt NH_3)	CO_2 price (EUR/t CO_2)	Expected emission BAU (kt CO_2)	Expected penalty BAU (EUR)	Expected emissions 100 MW (kt CO_2)	Expected penalty 100 MW (EUR thsd)	Penalty Difference (EUR thsd)
2021	1.2	3 106	1.422	1 820	30.00	3 140	1 028	3 140	1 028	0
2022	1.14	2 944	1.419	1 820	40.56	3 140	7 934	3 140	7 934	0
2023	1.09	2 809	1.416*	1 820	51.12	3 140	16 897	3 140	16 897	0
2024	1.03	2 655	1.416	1 820	61.68	3 140	29 927	2 980	20 058	9 869
2025	0.97	2 500	1.416	1 820	72.24	3 140	46 222	2 980	34 664	11 558
2026	0.92	2 371	1.416	1 820	82.80	3 140	63 650	2 980	50 402	13 248
2027	0.86	2 217	1.416	1 820	93.36	3 140	86 205	2 980	71 268	14 938
2028	0.8	2 062	1.416	1 820	103.92	3 140	112 027	2 980	95 400	16 627
2029	0.74	1 907	1.416	1 820	114.48	3 140	141 115	2 980	122 798	18 317
2030	0.69	1 778	1.416	1 820	125.04	3 140	170 246	2 980	150 240	20 006

Note: where the 100 MW electrolyser is operational in 2024 and abates 160 kt CO_2. Note the BAU scenario is stationary, which is an unlikely representation of business activity, but useful for comparison with the case study, where, apart from the installation of a 100 MW electrolyser a stationary scenario is assumed. *New benchmark values will be established by the EU in 2021 and used from 2023 onwards.

When the carbon levy price is known, the expected carbon 'penalty' paid for the BAU scenario and for the '100 MW scenario', where Yara installs a 100 MW electrolyser which is fully operational in 2024, can be estimated. Both scenarios have to be considered as illustrative, as they are based on 2017 emissions by Yara. For the analysis of this case study however, the difference between the BAU and 100 MW scenario suffices. The aggregate amount of savings between 2020 and 2030 upon installing a 100 MW electrolyser with 160 kt CO_2 annual abatement is EUR 105 million (abstracting from discounting).

REB (Energy Tax) and ODE

The REB and ODE are the energy and electricity taxes, which Yara is subject to. According to Berenschot (2020[4]), the consumption factor of electricity to natural gas for hydrogen production is 175:115. A 100 MW electrolyser operating 8 000 h per year consumes 0.8 TWh/y and hence saves approximately 0.52 TWh/y (2.9 PJ/y) of natural gas, or 50 million Nm^3/y of natural gas.[29] An intensive analysis goes beyond the scope of this case study, therefore we take a constant electricity and natural gas price, based on a study of energy and electricity price scenarios for power to ammonia from CE Delft.[30] Two scenarios are described: a low price scenario and a high price scenario where the natural gas price is EUR 20/MWh and EUR 30/MWh and the electricity price is EUR 40/MWh and EUR 60/MWh, respectively. The tariffs for the REB+ODE are 2.36 eurocent/m^3 of gas (=0.23 eurocent/kWh) and 0.05 eurocent/kWh of electricity in 2022.[31] There is a significant reduction of 2.24 eurocent/kWh when exceeding 10 GWh annual consumption, but we assume Yara already exceeds 10 GWh annual consumption without the electrolyser. Four scenarios arise: a low and a high price scenario for both the BAU and 100 MW scenarios. Again, we only take into account the production of 100 kt ammonia. The annual energy expenditures including energy taxes are shown in Table 6.6. These calculations show that the additional electricity expenditures greatly exceed the OPEX of EUR 1-1.5 million as proposed by PBL and Grigoriev et al. (2020[3]). The additional annual operational expenditures in terms of feedstock for the 100 MW electrolyser is EUR 20.8-31.6 million depending on the price of electricity.

Two notes regarding the electricity expenditures need to be made. Firstly, through a contract with Ørsted, Yara might reduce the strike price to below the market price given the security of supply. Secondly, electricity expenditures might be reduced by not producing continuously, but 'flexibly'. Because the electricity price is expected to increase in volatility upon enlarging the renewable electricity share, the cost reduction might be significant, but would result in discontinuous production and a lower output.

Table 6.6. Annual energy expenditures for the production of 18 kt hydrogen as feedstock for the production of 100 kt of ammonia

	Annual energy consumption for 18 kt hydrogen production in TWh (gas, electricity, respectively)	Price (EUR/MWh)	Tax (EUR/MWh)	Total (EUR mln)
BAU – low energy price	0.52	20	2.3	11.6
BAU - high energy price	0.52	30	2.3	16.8
100 MW - low energy price	0.80	40	0.5	32.4
100 MW - high energy price	0.80	60	0.5	48.4

Summary on deployment and market-based instruments

Table 6.7 gives an overview of the deployment instruments to which the electrolyser is eligible (in effect, the SDE++) and the market-based instruments (EU ETS and carbon levy, energy taxes) which Yara is subject to, and the corresponding impacts on cash flows (potential subsidy, savings on carbon levy and additional energy-related expenditures).

Table 6.7. Impacts on cash flows from carbon levy, tax-inclusive energy costs and SDE++

Instrument	Impact on cash flows (EUR mln)	Description
ETS/Carbon Levy	105-118	Total savings up to 2030
Energy Bill and Taxes	20.8-31.6	Additional annual energy expenditures (including taxes)
SDE++	12-13.5	Annual subsidy

6.1.4. Cash flows, internal rate of return and project's viability

Figure 6.1 to Figure 6.3 show the combined result of the above analysis on green hydrogen's annual expected cash flows. Various scenarios are considered: high abatement (180 kt/year) vs low abatement (160 kt/year), and high versus low energy prices (as detailed in Table 6.6).

In each figure, various combinations of eligible subsidies are shown, with the solid black line corresponding to the most likely outcome. The four possible policy combinations include: no subsidy granted (bottom line), subsidies for RD&D granted (solid black line), SDE++ granted but no RD&D subsidies (dashed, light-blue) and all subsidies granted (RD&D and SDE++, top line).

Figure 6.1 presents a conservative scenario where abatement amounts to 160 kt CO_2 annually and energy prices are low. Without subsidies, the green hydrogen project is, not surprisingly, unviable despite the savings from the carbon levy. However, the main message from the figure is that current RD&D support programmes are insufficient to make the project financially attractive, even in the rather favourable case when all eligible subsidies (WBSO, MOOI and DEI+) would be granted. At the end of the period, the electrolyser becomes competitive with the BAU due to the CO_2 levy savings, but this is not enough to yield a return on the investment within this ten year period. Without support from the SDE++ (which we know is highly unlikely given the high costs associated with the project), the project never breaks even, but with the SDE++ granted (at EUR 300 per tonne of CO_2 avoided, for 2000 hours per year), it can do so before 2030.

Figure 6.1. Green hydrogen electrolyser cash flows (160 kt abatement, low energy prices)

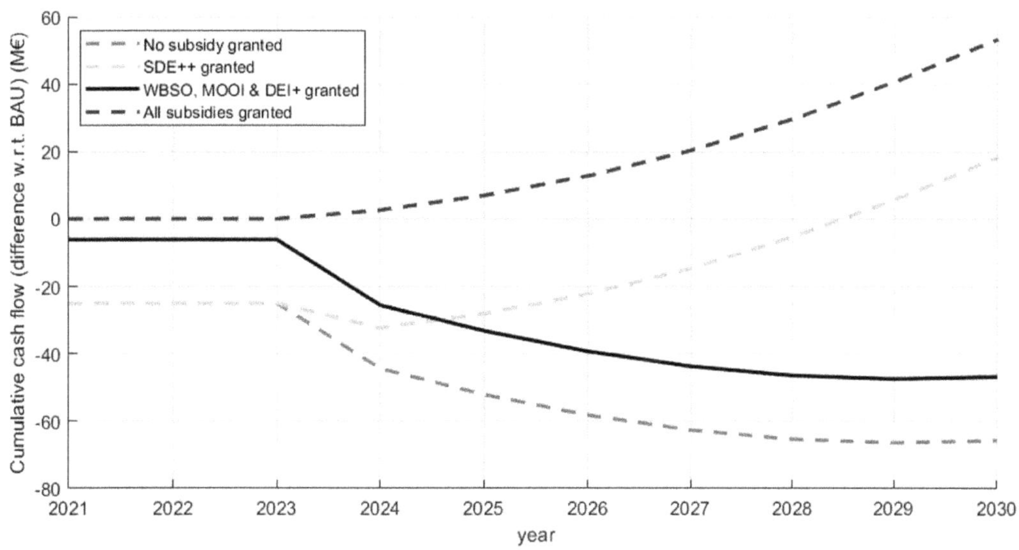

Note: the development cost is incurred in 2021 and the CAPEX in 2024.

As show in Figure 6.2, a more favourable high CO_2 abatement scenario (180kt per year instead of 160 kt) does not alter the conclusion substantially. The project becomes competitive with the BAU slightly earlier in terms of OPEX, but the additional benefits from the carbon levy savings are not high enough to make up for the initial investment costs.

Figure 6.2. Green hydrogen electrolyser cash flows (180 kt abatement, low energy prices)

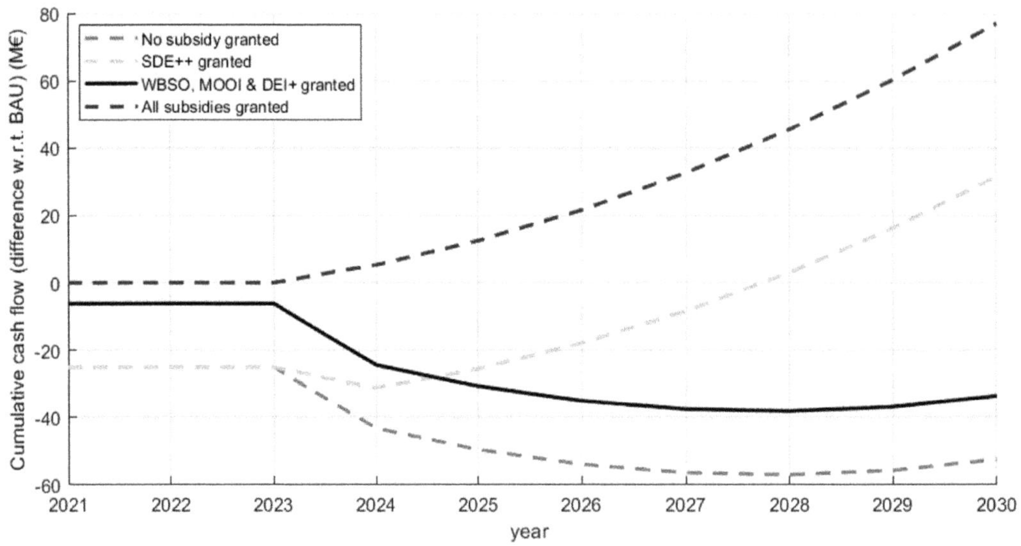

Note: The development cost is incurred in 2021 and the CAPEX in 2024.

Importantly, in the case of a high energy price scenario (with natural gas at EUR 30 /MWh and electricity price at EUR 60 /MWh), even with the SDE++ granted (at EUR 300 per tonne of CO_2 avoided, for 2 000 hours per year), the project is not financially viable until 2030 (Figure 6.3).

Figure 6.3. Green hydrogen electrolyser cash flows (160 kt abatement, high energy prices)

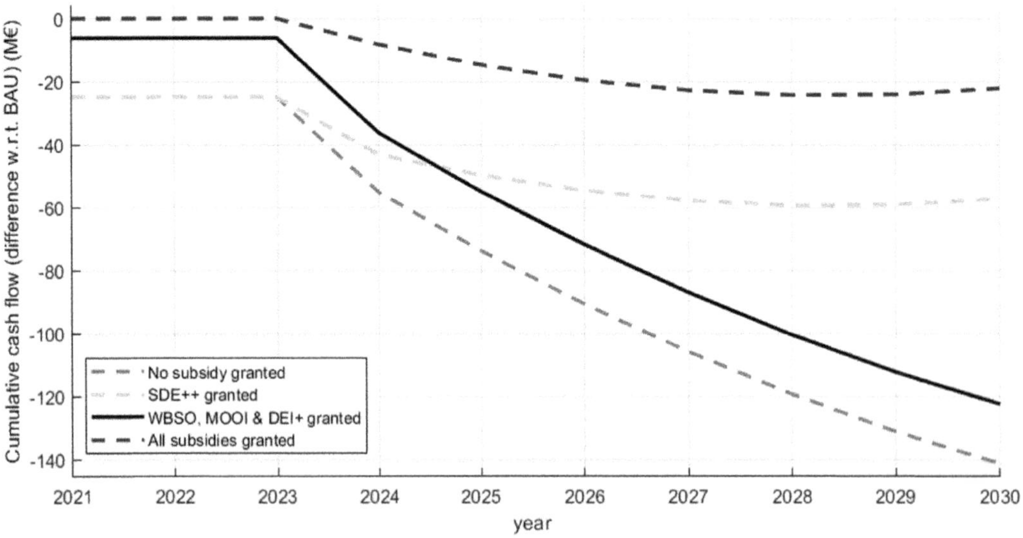

Note: The development cost is incurred in 2021 and the CAPEX in 2024.

6.1.5. Conclusion of Case Study 1

The analysis presented above has obvious limitations and is not designed for decision-making (this would require a more thorough modelling exercise taking into account future natural gas prices, electricity prices and feedstock contracts, etc). It has to be understood that it is illustrative of the most likely costs and benefits associated with a green hydrogen project. Nevertheless, it can be concluded that, while current policy instruments for green hydrogen should enable project developers to recoup some of the costs associated with research and development activities, they do not allow for deployment at scale. A low electricity price, abundant renewable electricity supply and an increased energy efficiency of electrolysers are drivers for the business case going forward, but at present, without the hypothetical support from the SDE++, green hydrogen projects are unlikely to be developed.

6.2. Case Study 2: Carbon capture and storage on steam methane reforming in refineries

6.2.1. Introduction

As presented in the first case study, steam methane reforming (SMR) is a CO_2-intensive process for producing hydrogen gas. In the refinery sector, hydrogen is an important feedstock used in several processes such as hydrocracking and hydrodesulphurisation. Currently, hydrogen production accounts for 21% of total CO_2 emissions in the refinery sector (2.3 Mt out of 10.7 Mt).[32] An option to produce the hydrogen more sustainably is to combine SMR with CCS. With this option, the existing SMR plants can be maintained, combined with carbon capture technology. The flue gas has a concentration of 24.2% CO_2, of which a 85% capture rate is assumed in Berenschot (2020[4]). Therefore, this option does not lead to zero emission, and in addition to this, the carbon capture technology requires electricity to run. Nevertheless, this process, referred to as "blue hydrogen" production, results in CO_2 abatement, and because of the maturity of the technology, currently at TRL 9[33], it can be implemented soon.

PBL and TNO[34] analysed different decarbonisation options for the refinery industry: 1) carbon capture; 2) fuel substitution; 3) feedstock substitution; and 4) process design. According to Berenschot (2020[4]), the vision of the petroleum industry is to apply CCS to steam methane reforming, the combination of these processes resulting in blue hydrogen. Another possibility for CCS would be to use it on centralised heat and power production, the main emission source in refineries.[35] However, the concentration of CO_2 in flue gases from these sources is insufficient to make CCS economically viable. Because electrification for CHP does not seem a viable option either, CHP could be decarbonised by replacing fossil fuel by hydrogen. Hence, the applications for hydrogen will be broader in the future, and production facilities and infrastructure, including blue hydrogen, need to be put in place.

The port of Rotterdam, where the majority of refineries in the Netherlands are located, developed a pathway towards zero emissions. This pathway consists of three consecutive steps, taking place between 2020 and 2025, between 2025 and 2030 and between 2030 and 2050. The three steps can be roughly described as: 1) energy efficiency and infrastructure; 2) change in processes; and 3) change in feedstock (Berenschot, 2020[4]). Therefore, up to 2 025 hydrogen infrastructures will be built, up to 2030 it will be reinforced to facilitate feedstock adaptations and be fully operational from 2030 onwards, at which point the Port of Rotterdam is assumed to benefit from abundant renewable electricity and to be equipped with large scale electrolysers. Either way, the demand for hydrogen gas will increase and lead to CO_2 abatement via two routes: direct abatement in hydrogen production and indirect abatement due to the switch to hydrogen as a feedstock.

Currently, there are six refineries located in the Netherlands, five of them being located in the port of Rotterdam: BP, Gunvor Petroleum Rotterdam, Vitol (Koch), EonMobil and Shell. Zeeland Refinery is located in Zeeland and is part of the Smart Delta Resources. The Port of Rotterdam is currently developing Porthos, a carbon transportation project. Of the five refineries, BP and Shell are part of the consortium of H-vision, the project aiming to have blue hydrogen available when Porthos is ready. These companies are also investigating green hydrogen options.

Among the refineries located in the Port of Rotterdam, Shell and Esso produce hydrogen via SMR. This technology accounts for about 35% of hydrogen production capacity (the two other technologies are gasification and naphtha reforming). Because Shell is part of the H-vision consortium and therefore will have access to Porthos and uses SMR, adapting a current SMR facility to a blue hydrogen facility producing 18 kt/year (comparable with the 100 MW electrolyser case study above) will be taken as the second case study.

6.2.2. Case Study Characteristics

Shells SMR facilities at the Port of Rotterdam have a nameplate capacity of 49 kt/y. These facilities cover multiple plants and therefore the integration level of these plants with capture technology is likely flexible. This enables the upgrade of part of the facility, with a capacity of 18 kt/y, towards a blue hydrogen facility. As we have seen in the first case study presented above, the associated CO_2 emissions of this activity are in the range of 160-180 kt of CO_2. Because carbon capture enables 85% abatement of these emissions, the resulting abatement is 135-150 kt CO_2 per year, while 25-30 kt of CO_2 is still released. With Shells total emissions level at its refinery being 4.25 Mt in 2016[36], this project abates about 3% of its emissions, with a potential to 8% if the entire capacity is adapted.

The carbon capture technology requires electricity. According to Berenschot (2020), the production of 115 PJ of hydrogen requires 115 PJ of natural gas and 30 PJ of electricity for blue hydrogen. Accordingly, the facility requires 0.52 TWh of natural gas and 0.14 TWh of electricity. It is unknown whether the natural gas demand rises upon installing capture technology, thus it is assumed that the natural gas consumption is unaltered and that the capture technology is entirely driven by electricity.

CCS on SMR is considered as a mature technology[37]. The flue gas typically has a concentration of 24.4% CO_2, a relatively high concentration making CCS on the system more economical than for lower concentration of flue gases. In the MIDDEN report, PBL published a breakdown of costs for CCS systems for flue gases with a concentration below 18% (Table 6.8) and a total costs estimate for blue hydrogen based on a report to be published (Table 6.9). Because the CAPEX of blue hydrogen is based on building a new SMR facility, as well as a CCS installation, in this case study the cost of a post-combustion capture system is used. With 135-150 kt of captured CO_2, the CAPEX for the capture technology is EUR 3.4-4.6 million. For the OPEX the values from (Cioli, Schure and van Dam, 2021[5]) are used, which include labour and maintenance costs, while excluding feedstock and energy costs and the cost of transport. For the installation under consideration this comes down to EUR 1.2-2.2 million per year.

Table 6.8. Costs of capture systems for different CO_2 concentrations

	Low CO2 concentration (5 %vol)	Medium CO2 concentration (8-10 %vol)	High CO2 concentration (10-18%vol)
CAPEX [EUR 2017/t CO2 captured]	45	31-39	28-31
Fixed OPEX40) [EUR 2017/ t CO2 captured/yr]	19	15-18	14-15
Steam consumption [GJ/ t CO2 captured]	2.5	2.5	2.5
Electricity consumed [kWh/ t CO2 captured]	183	149-185	162-166
CO2 avoided/CO2 captured	0.65	0.67	0.67

Source: (Oliveira and Schure, 2020[6])

Table 6.9. Costs of decarbonisation options for hydrogen production from PBL MIDDEN

Option	CAPEX	OPEX
Blue hydrogen production	90–145 EUR2017/t CO2 captured	10–15 EUR2017/t CO2 captured
Green hydrogen	3,193 EUR2017/t H2	159 EUR2017/t H2
H2 production via biomass	3,344 EUR2017/t H2	17 EUR2017/t H2
H2 production via thermal decomposition of methane	500–1,300 EUR2017/t H2	20–40 EUR2017/t H2

Source: (Oliveira and Schure, 2020[6])

In addition to the costs of the capture technology, the CO_2 needs to be transported and stored after capture. The exact business model of this value chain is not known yet, but the costs of this operation have to be covered. Although it is possible that (part of) the costs of transportation and/or storage will be subsidised directly by government funds. In this exercise we include them in the operational costs. In EBN and Gasunie (2017[7]), two firms in the Netherlands active in storage and transport in CCS projects, estimated the costs for transport and storage at EUR 9-11/t CO_2.[38] This estimate is far lower than the estimate from PBL, which stands at EUR 45/t CO_2. Because these estimates are so far apart, both are used separately in the analysis. Next to the transport and storage costs, the cost for the connection has to be paid by the emitter, which amounts to EUR 0.2-0.5 million per year. Hence, additional expenditures related to the transport and storage for this project amount to around EUR 1.4-2.2 million when assuming the Gasunie/EBN estimate, where the minimal abated emission level is multiplied by the lowest price and the maximal abated emission with the highest price. When using the PBL estimate, the transport and storage costs amount to EUR 6.3–6.8 million. CO_2 could be transported via lorries and ships, however the excellent connection with Porthos should make transportation via pipelines more economical.

An overview of the case study characteristics and costs is given in Table 6.10 below. Note that all the cost estimates are scaled by the amount of CO_2 captured.

Table 6.10. Overview of case study characteristics for a blue hydrogen project in the port of Rotterdam, where a novel CCS system is added to an existing SMR plant

Case study characteristic	Quantity
Total SMR hydrogen production Shell	49 kt/y
Blue hydrogen production capacity	18 kt/y
Emission abatement associated with CCS	135-150 kt CO2 /y
Unabated emissions	25-30 kt CO2 /y
Natural gas consumption SMR	0.52 TWh
Electricity consumption Capture Technology	0.14 TWh
CAPEX capture technology	EUR 3.8-4.6 mln
OPEX capture technology (excluding energy, transport and storage costs)	EUR 1.4-2.2 mln/y
OPEX SMR (excluding fuel costs)	EUR 3 mln/y
Transport and storage costs (including connection) using Gasunie/EBN estimate	EUR 1.4-2.2 mln
Transport and storage costs (including connection) using PBL estimate	EUR 6.3-6.8 mln/y

6.2.3. Policy instrument analysis

According to ECN and TNO, CCS technology for SMR is at TRL level 9[39]. Therefore, this technology does not require fundamental research, but rather needs to be deployed at an industrial scale. Of course, the deployment brings experience and this comes with potential cost-efficiency gains for future projects, which is an important criterion for some support schemes.

Research and Development Instruments

H2020

The H2020 grant is aimed to accelerate research. While there are calls available for CCS,[40] these are either concentrated on other sectors than the oil and gas industry, or focussed on developing parts of the technology, such as research on innovative nanocomposite membranes for capture processes. Because the case study considers the deployment of an existing technology, the project is not eligible for funds from H2020.

WBSO

The WBSO is a stimulus for R&D work, hence this project is not eligible.

MOOI (Mission-thrived Research, Development and Innovation)

This policy instrument focuses on (industrial) research and development. The scheme excludes prototype/pilot activities but includes FEED studies. Among the missions of this instrument is MMIP 6: closing industrial chains. This includes CCS[41], but due to the high TRL, this technology is covered under the DEI+ and SDE++. Also, CCS is not an innovation theme of the MOOI. Hence, this project (aside from a possible FEED study) is not eligible.

Nationaal Groeifonds (development, infrastructure and innovation)

The funds concentrate on the growth of the national economy and the creation of public value. EUR 20 billion will be injected into the Dutch economy over five years. While the infrastructure for CCS (such as CO_2 pipelines) might be part of the national growth fund, specific CCS projects are not eligible. Those are instead directed towards the SDE++ scheme in a letter dated October 2020 to parliament.[42]

Demonstration Instruments

EU Innovation fund (small scale projects, one-stage)

"Small scale projects" with capital costs between EUR 2.5 million and EUR 7.5 million are eligible for the innovation fund.[43] All sectors are included and the focus lies on CCUS, renewable energy, energy storage substitute products and cross-cutting projects. The total size of the instrument is EUR 100 million and beneficiaries can apply for a grant covering a maximum of 60% of the project costs, plus project development assistance. The project costs consider both CAPEX and OPEX,[44] the duration of which is based on the project planning, for this project it is limited to EUR 7.5 million, over 1 to 3.5 years. Although the project is eligible, special attention is given to "projects demonstrating highly innovative technologies, offering support tailored to market needs or complementing a large-scale call by targeting small-scale projects, thereby offering an opportunity in particular for small and medium-size companies". The evaluation criteria are: 1) the degree of innovation; 2) the project maturity and greenhouse gas avoidance potential; and 3) scalability and cost efficiency, with the scores for the first two criteria having a double weight compared to the last one. While the innovative character of this project is relatively low, the project scores relatively high on maturity, scalability and cost efficiency. The grant available for this project would be EUR 2-2.8 million for the CAPEX and EUR 0.7-1.3 million for the OPEX annually, with the sum maxed at EUR 4.5 million.

Demonstration Energy and Climate Innovation

The DEI+ supports pilot and demonstration projects that contribute to cost-effective greenhouse gas abatement.[45] A project can be either a pilot or a demonstration project. Pilot or experimental development projects can apply for a direct subsidy of 25% and demonstration projects for 40% with a maximum of EUR 15 million, where the eligible amount is the additional costs of the climate-friendly investment in comparison with a similar non-climate friendly investment. For CCS, only pilot projects are eligible. CCS pilot projects consider research and validation of innovations in capture technology, which are for example required for other processes than SMR, in other sectors, where TRL levels for carbon capture technologies are lower. Because the blue hydrogen project installs existing technology and does not validate an innovative technology, the project is not eligible for funds from the DEI+.

HER+

The explicit aim of the HER+ is to reduce future subsidy expenditures (SDE++), by investing in innovative projects that bring about cost-efficiency.[46] Hence, a leading criterion is that the future savings should outweigh the requested subsidy. The HER+ includes industrial and experimental research projects for CCS and blue hydrogen[47], but excludes CCS and blue hydrogen[48] demonstrations. Because this project aims to deploy an existing technology and does not contribute to CCS research directly, the project is not eligible for funds through the HER+.

Summary on RD&D and deployment instruments

Table 6.11 gives an overview of the RD&D policy instruments for which the electrolyser is eligible to the corresponding amount of the potential subsidy. The largest, but not very likely support instrument, is the EU Innovation Fund.

Table 6.11. Eligible subsidies from RD&D instruments

Instrument	Amount Estimate
MOOI	FEED study
EU Innovation fund	EUR 2-2.8 mln for CAPEX + EUR 0.7-1.3 mln/y OPEX with a max of EUR 4.5 mln
MIA	EUR 0.3-0.4 mln via tax deduction
EIA	EUR 0.4-0.5 mln via tax deduction

Deployment instruments

VEKI

This instrument targets SMEs, hence Shell is not eligible.

MIA/Vamil

The schemes allow for an investment deduction of 36% (MIA) or 75% (Vamil). The investment must be on the *milieulijst*, which is the case for CCS apparatus, but only for the MIA scheme[49]. The maximum amount for the asset is EUR 25 million. The asset of the case study is lower than this, which makes it possible to deduct EUR 1.4-1.7 million, leading to a net benefit of EUR 0.3-0.4 million considering a tax rate of 25%.[50]

EIA

To be eligible the project must be on the *energielijst*. CCS is on this list, in particular CO_2 cleaning apparatus, CO_2 compressors, transport pipes, and CO_2-buffer reservoirs. The project is therefore eligible. With this scheme, 45% of investment costs can be deducted from the fiscal profit. This instrument will have ambiguous effects however, as Shell did not legally pay taxes in 2016-18, because selective foreign losses can be deducted from Dutch profits.[51] [52] [53] If there are profit taxes to be paid which cannot be deducted from foreign losses, the rate for this tax is 15% for EUR 0-245 000 and 25% above EUR 245 000 in 2021 (the boundary is increased to EUR 395 000 in 2022).[54] Assuming the total profit would be higher than the EUR 245 000 or EUR 395 000 boundary, the potential of the instrument is to give a tax deduction of EUR 0.4-0.5 million.

SDE++

The SDE++ is the largest Dutch policy instrument and is similar to a contract-for-difference. CCS is eligible for this subsidy within the subcategory "new capture system on existing installation". The advised subsidy amount for this category is EUR 114.16/t CO_2 (across the four CCS categories, the average advised subsidy rate is EUR69/tCO_2). For the establishment of this amount, a rise in electricity expenditures of EUR 15/t CO_2 is taken into account and a transport cost of EUR 45/t CO_2 is taken into account, which is significantly higher than the cost estimate of Gasunie/EBN (EUR 9-11/t CO_2). With this subsidy rate, PBL estimates a break even period of nine to ten years, but this might be lower when taking into account CO_2 levy savings (although the calculations above are highly simplified) next to the savings from the ETS which PBL already takes into account.

The SDE++ grants subsidy to projects based on a cost-effectiveness criterion, for which the CCS category "new capture system on existing installation" is ranked 37th out of 95 and is the least cost-effective subcategory of CCS. This is still a fairly high position, considering for example that 12 different categories of wind on land are ranked higher (rank 1 to 36). To prevent crowding out projects in other categories, a 2.5 Mt/y cap on CO_2 emission reductions from CCS was introduced, corresponding to EUR 285.4 million annually. The requests for the SDE++ in 2020 (presented in Section 9.2) included seven CCS projects for a total subsidy requested (over the 15 years of each project) of EUR 2.135 billion and 2.35 million tonnes of CO_2 abated annually (implying a unit subsidy of EUR61/tCO_2). The total amount of annual emission reduction is lower than the 2.5 Mt cap, so in theory all projects could be granted a subsidy (especially since they have on average the lowest marginal abatement cost). This makes it very likely that the project analysed in this case study would receive the SDE++ subsidy. Depending on the exact amount of emissions abated, the total SDE++ subsidy would amount to EUR 13.7-17.1 million per year and can be granted for 15 years.

Market-based instruments

ETS/Carbon Levy

Because the new Carbon Levy is coupled with ETS, the two instruments are discussed together. The CO_2 levy is a baseline-and-credit system, where emissions above the baseline are taxed, and emissions below the baseline can be traded. The benchmark is set at the 2008 carbon efficiency and decreased by 0.2% per year to 2023 (i.e. the 2008 benchmark - 3% in 2023), the annual reduction factor starts at 1.2 and decreases by 5.7 percentage points per year until 2030. In 2021, the levy starts at EUR 30/t CO_2, increases each year by EUR 10.56/t up to EUR 125/t CO_2 in 2030. The ETS price of the previous year is subtracted from the levy. Shell is subjected to the tax and receives dispensation rights (1 DPR = 1 tonne of CO_2). Although the exact amount of DPR is unknown, it is given by the product of the activity level, the EU ETS benchmark and the reduction factor. EU ETS free allowances are granted based on the EU ETS benchmark and the plant's output. Since we assume that the plant will generate the same output with and without CCS, the EU ETS free allowances are received in both cases and cancel out, so they do not have to be considered in this exercise.

For the SMR technology, a benchmark in the form kg CO_2/kg H_2 is not available. For an isolated SMR system, the benchmark is ambiguous because the system is highly integrated at refinery sites, and the emission level depends on, for example, the use of export steam, the level of CO_2 recirculation and the hydrogen purity. Moreover, from a chemical perspective the best available technology (BAT) for SMRs is not about CO_2 concentration reduction, but about NOx and SOx reduction. Nevertheless, the best available techniques reference document[55] states that "for every tonne of hydrogen produced, some 10 tonnes of CO_2 are produced including the amount related to steam production". In addition, the EIGA report[56] states that "the process is chemically limited to emit at least one mole of CO_2 for every four moles of hydrogen produced", giving a mass ratio of 5.5, while the IEA GHG reports in 2017[57] that "modern hydrogen production facilities have achieved efficiency that could reduce CO_2 emissions to about 10% above the theoretical minimum". Finally, as mentioned already, an analysis of Praxair, one of the world's largest hydrogen producers, concluded that the CO_2/H_2 mass ratio is 9.3, considering a plant operating at 13% above the theoretical minimum.[58] Where the mass ratio of 5.5 considers only the chemistry, the 9.3 mass ratio includes heat for the reforming energy, combustion for steam and power for separation and compression, which explains the difference.

Because the abatement level for this innovation is not based on internal reports by Shell or a technology description, but on similar assumptions about the conversion ratio, it is important for the consistency of this analysis to even the emission level with the benchmark. That is, when we consider the emissions of a 100 MW SMR to be 140-180 kt CO_2, implicitly a conversion rate of 7.8-10 CO_2/H_2 is assumed. The average of 160 kt emissions corresponds to a conversion ratio of 8.9, which is taken as the benchmark in the numerical simulation exercise, and is in the same order of magnitude as the proposed conversion ratios above. In this way, the difference between the BAU and blue hydrogen (BH) case is consistent, but forces the assumption that Shell operates a modern SMR installation. For the BH scenario, it is assumed that the system is operational in 2024, this is consistent with case study 1 and consistent with the transport and storage infrastructure opening[59].

Table 6.12 presents the annual savings from the carbon levy based on the above assumptions. The aggregate saving on CO_2 expenditures up to 2030 is EUR 88 million for the average emission level assumption. For the low emission case (140 kt), and high emission case (180 kt) and corresponding benchmarks, the aggregate savings would amount to EUR 78 and EUR 98 million, respectively.

Table 6.12. Savings from the carbon levy for the SMR CCS project

Year	Reduction factor (CE Delft)	Expected DPR (kt CO_2)	Benchmark t CO_2/ t H_2	Activity hydrogen (kt/y)	CO_2 price (EUR/t)	Expected emission BAU (t/y)	Expected penalty (EUR thsd)	Expected emissions BH (kt/y)	Expected penalty (EUR thsd)	Penalty difference (EUR thsd)
2021	1.2	192	8.9	18	30	160	-967	160	-967	0
2022	1.14	183	8.9	18	40.56	160	-918	160	-918	0
2023	1.09	175	8.9	18	51.12	160	-747	160	-747	0
2024	1.03	165	8.9	18	61.68	160	-309	25	-8 636	8 327
2025	0.97	155	8.9	18	72.24	160	333	25	-9 420	9 752
2026	0.92	147	8.9	18	82.8	160	1 045	25	-10 133	11 178
2027	0.86	138	8.9	18	93.36	160	2 075	25	-10 528	12 604
2028	0.8	128	8.9	18	103.92	160	3 309	25	-10 720	14 029
2029	0.74	119	8.9	18	114.48	160	4 745	25	-10 709	15 455
2030	0.69	111	8.9	18	125.04	160	6 185	25	-10 696	16 880

Note: The table assumes that the carbon capture technology is operational in 2024 and abates 135 out of 160 kt CO_2.

REB (Energy Tax) and ODE

The REB and ODE are the energy and electricity taxes; which Shell is subject to. According to Berenschot (2020[4]), the additional use of electricity for blue hydrogen production is 30 PJ. For the blue hydrogen installation, the additional annual consumption is therefore 0.14 TWh electricity. Again, we assume a constant electricity price, based on a study of energy and electricity price scenarios for power to ammonia from CE Delft[60] and we use EUR 40/MWh and EUR 60 /MWh, for a low and high electricity price scenario, respectively. The tariffs for the REB+ODE are 2.36 eurocent/m^3 (=0.23 eurocent/kWh) and 0.05 eurocents/kWh in 2022.[61] There is a significant reduction of 2.24 eurocent/kWh when exceeding 10 GWh annual consumption, but we assume Shell already exceeds 10 GWh annual electricity consumption without the capture technology. The additional annual operational expenditures in terms of feedstock for the blue hydrogen system is thus EUR 5.7-8.5 million. As shown in Table 6.12, the additional feedstock expenditures are generally lower than the savings from the carbon levy expenditures.

Summary on deployment and market-based instruments

Table 6.13 gives an overview of the deployment instruments to which the electrolyser is eligible (in effect, the SDE++) and the market-based instruments (EU ETS and carbon levy, energy taxes) which the project is subject to, and the corresponding impacts on cash flows (potential subsidy, savings on carbon levy and additional energy-related expenditures).

Table 6.13. Impacts on cash flows from carbon levy, tax-inclusive energy costs and SDE++

Instrument	Monetary effect (EUR mln)	Type
ETS/Carbon Levy	88-98	Total savings up to 2030
Energy Bill and Taxes	5.7-8.5	Increased energy expenditures
SDE++	14.2-17.1	Annual subsidy

6.2.4. Cash flows, internal rate of return and project's viability

Figure 6.4 to Figure 6.6 show the combined result of the above analysis on green hydrogen's annual expected cash flows. Various scenarios are considered: high vs low energy prices, and PBL vs Gasunie-EBN CO_2 transport costs (as detailed in Table 6.10).

In each figure, various combinations of eligible subsidies are shown, with the solid black line corresponding to the most likely outcome. The three possible policy combinations include: no subsidy granted (bottom line), subsidies for RD&D and SDE++ granted (solid black line), and all subsidies granted (EU Innovation Fund, MIA & EIA and SDE++, top line).

Figure 6.4. Blue hydrogen project cash flows (low energy prices, PBL CO_2 transport costs)

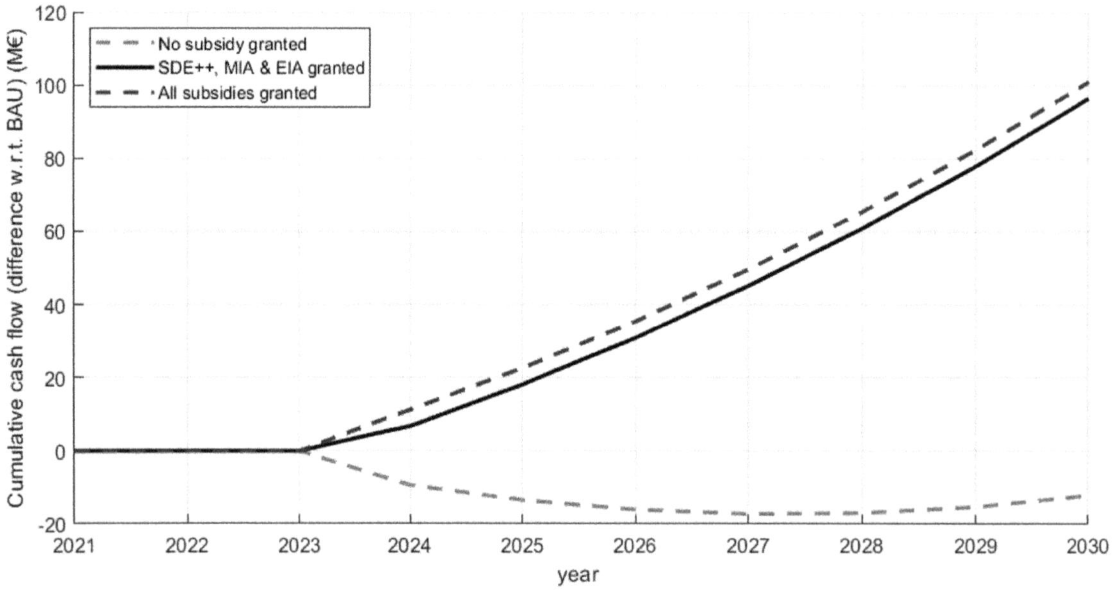

Note: The CAPEX is accounted for in 2024.An annual emission reduction of 135 Kt is assumed.

Figure 6.4 presents the conservative scenario where energy prices are low, the CO_2 transport costs are high (PBL estimate) and abatement amounts to 160 kt CO_2 annually. Without subsidies, the blue hydrogen project is unviable despite the savings from the carbon levy, but close to break even in 2030. However, the SDE++ makes the project highly attractive financially. Additional tax allowances or subsidy programmes (EU Innovation Fund, MIA & EIA) make an additional contribution, but are not critical if the SDE++ subsidy is granted, which is highly likely given the cost attractiveness of CCS projects compared to other eligible low-carbon projects. It is striking to observe that the SDE++ makes the CCS project a high return investment. This comes from the fact that savings from the carbon levy are not deducted from the SDE++ subsidy.

Figure 6.5. Blue hydrogen project cash flows (high energy prices, PBL CO_2 transport costs)

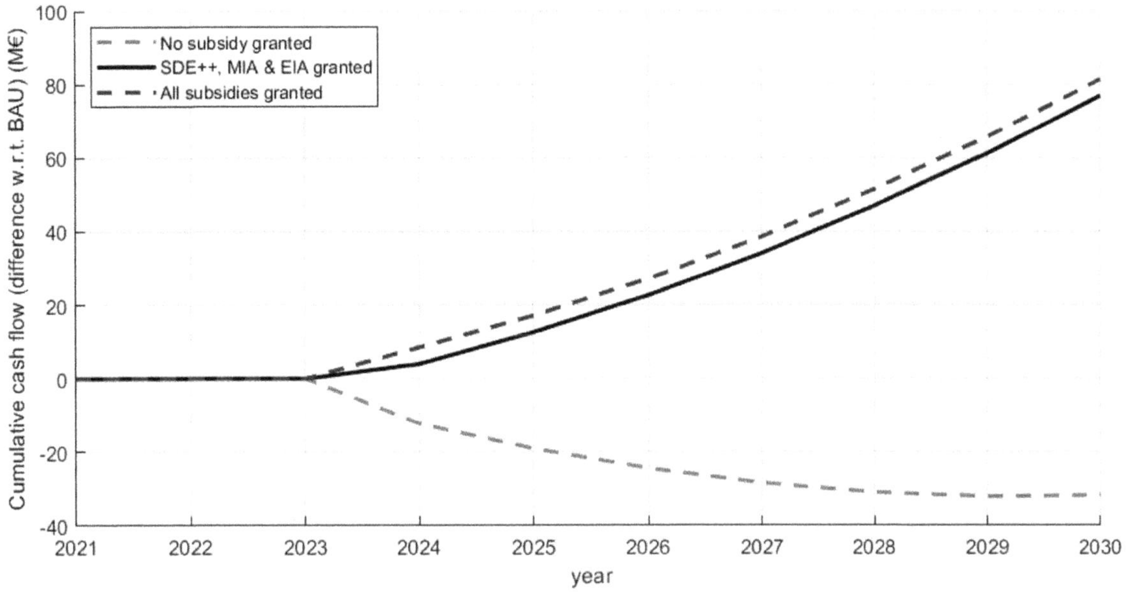

Note: The CAPEX is accounted for in 2024. An annual emission reduction of 135kt is assumed.

Figure 6.6. Blue hydrogen project cash flows (low energy prices, GasUnie-EBN CO_2 transport costs)

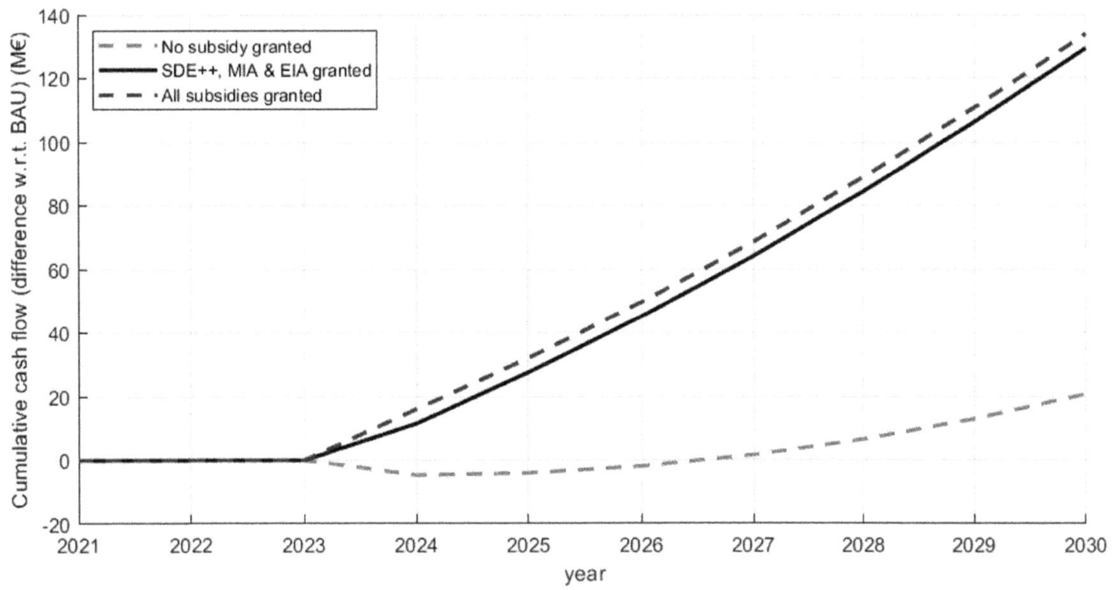

Note: The CAPEX is accounted for in 2024. An annual emission reduction of 135kt is assumed.

The conclusion holds if a high energy price scenario is considered (Figure 6.5). The higher relative electricity price implies additional costs, but the SDE++ subsidy is calibrated such that this does not make any difference to the overall viability of the project.

Finally, if CO_2 transport costs are lower than anticipated by PBL and closer to the Gasunie-EBN assumptions for the Porthos project, it is interesting to see that the blue hydrogen project is financially viable without support from the SDE++. The savings from the carbon levy allow the project to break even in 2027 (Figure 6.6).

6.2.5. Conclusion of Case Study 2

The analysis presented above has obvious limitations and is not designed for decision-making (this would require a more thorough modelling exercise accounting for future natural gas prices, electricity prices and feedstock contracts, etc). It has to be understood as illustrative of the most likely costs and benefits associated with a blue hydrogen project. However, the case study clearly demonstrates the attractiveness of blue hydrogen and CCS projects more generally given the current design of the SDE++. First, the relatively low costs per tonne of avoided CO_2 of CCS projects make such projects highly likely to receive subsidies from SDE++. Secondly, and more importantly, the savings from the carbon levy come in addition to the SDE++ subsidy, and make these projects doubly attractive. While savings from the EU ETS allowances are deducted ex post from the SDE++, this is not the case of carbon levy savings, which make a huge difference to the projects viability.

6.3. Conclusions from the case studies

In this chapter, two case studies are presented to put the current set of policy instruments in perspective and understand its implications for the financial viability of typical decarbonisation projects. The two case studies include green hydrogen for ammonia production in the chemicals sector (case study 1) and CCS for 'blue' hydrogen production by steam-methane reforming (SMR) in the refinery sector (case study 2). The chemicals and refineries sectors are the two largest CO_2-emitting sectors in the Dutch industry (Chapter 2). Together, hydrogen and CCS technologies would contribute to 37% of emission reductions by 2050 (Chapter 3).

Overall, the case studies confirm the major importance of the EU ETS and the two main instruments of the Dutch climate policy landscape recently introduced by the Climate Agreement: the carbon levy and the SDE++. Both instruments have large and rapid effects on the net annual cash flows associated with the two hypothetical projects. However, they have different implications.

6.3.1. Carbon levy

In the CCS case (blue hydrogen production), the avoided payments of ETS permits and carbon levy are such that they quickly compensate for the additional costs associated with the electricity consumption from the CCS device. In a rather favourable case – if energy prices remain low and transportation costs of CO_2 are lower than the current PBL estimates – the blue hydrogen project is even financially viable without additional support necessary. By contrast, in the green hydrogen case, the avoided payments of ETS permits and carbon levy are never sufficient to make the project viable and recoup the large initial investment. The carbon levy alone does not incentivise green hydrogen, but, with the current price trajectory, can quickly make the business case for CCS without other subsidies required.

6.3.2. SDE++

At present, the SDE++ appears critical for the viability of both projects, particularly in the green hydrogen case. While both projects are in theory eligible to the SDE++, the design of the SDE++, which favours projects with the lowest abatement cost, implies that the CCS project is very likely to obtain funding, provided the SDE++ ceiling on total abatement allowed through CCS is not reached, while the green hydrogen is very unlikely to receive the subsidy.

Moreover, the other key feature of the SDE++, which does not take into account savings from the carbon levy to determine the subsidy rate, implies that the CCS project gets somewhat "overcompensated" for its emission reductions. Since the CO_2 levy is not accounted for in the SDE++ scheme, the savings from the CO_2 levy are therefore a kind of "free lunch" when the SDE++ is granted. This may lead the SDE++ to incentivise the opening of new blue hydrogen production plants, resulting in higher absolute emissions (since not all emissions are captured) compared to installing capture technology on current installations or building electrolysers for green transition. It would make sense to at least partly account for carbon levy savings when determining the SDE++ subsidy rate, as savings from EU ETS allowances are already accounted for.

Strong support through climate innovation instruments (DEI+ and HER+) could help to bring about the necessary cost reductions in green hydrogen. However, further cost reductions can only be expected through scaling-up and learning-by-doing. In the absence of other available instruments to support the scaling up of green hydrogen, it could be possible to ensure that SDE++ does not only fund close-to-market technologies by allocating the tender across different TRLs in order to also support emerging technologies. At present, due to the cost-effectiveness criterion, technologies that should be scaled up to be able to allow for subsequent cost reductions are under the risk of being crowded out.

6.3.3. Electricity prices

Both the green hydrogen electrolyser and the CCS device consume large amounts of electricity. Therefore, for both projects, a low electricity price and abundant renewable electricity supply are important determinants of the business case. At present, both the pre-tax cost of electricity and the taxes on electricity consumption are higher in the Netherlands than the pre-tax cost of natural gas and the taxes on natural gas, respectively, for the same amount of energy consumed (i.e. per GJ).[62] Another implication of the case studies is thus that the current design of the electricity tax (which does not differ across energy sources used for generation) may discourage the electrification of the industry sector. With a strong carbon floor price in electricity, the elimination (or strong reduction) of the tax and ODE on electricity consumption may be envisaged. This would make the projects presented in the two case studies more viable, and make the SDE++ redundant for CCS projects, releasing funding for emerging technologies with lower TRLs, such as green hydrogen.

6.3.4. CO_2 transport costs

The CO_2 transportation and storage costs make a significant difference to the financial viability of the blue hydrogen project, which can become competitive with the current (grey) SMR process a few years after installation without the SDE++ subsidy, thanks to the carbon levy savings. Therefore, a final implication from the case studies is that infrastructure projects which help to lower the cost of CO_2 transportation and storage – such as the Porthos project – play a critical role and can contribute to reducing the future subsidies paid out of the SDE++ programme. The explicit aim of the HER+ is to reduce future subsidy expenditures through SDE++, but the programme excludes CCS and blue hydrogen demonstrations. Given the importance of CCS for short-term CO_2 emission reductions, and the large number of CCS projects submitted to the first round of SDE++ applications, making CO_2 transportation and storage projects eligible to HER+ could be envisaged. Otherwise, other programmes – potentially at European level through the Connecting Europe Facility (CEF) – could be necessary to support the deployment of a cost-effective CO_2 transportation and storage infrastructure.

References

Batool, M. and W. Wetzels (2019), *Decarbonisation options for the Dutch fertiliser industry*, PBL Publishers, https://www.pbl.nl/sites/default/files/downloads/pbl-2019-decarbonisation-options-for-the-dutch-fertiliser-industry_3657.pdf. [2]

Berenschot (2020), *Sustainable Transition of Dutch Industry: 2050 scenario's towards a zero emission industry in the Netherlands.* [4]

Cioli, M., K. Schure and D. van Dam (2021), *Decarbonisation options for the Dutch industrial gases production.* [5]

EBN and Gasunie (2017), *Transport en opslag van CO2 in Nederland*, https://www.ebn.nl/wp-content/uploads/2018/07/Studie-Transport-en-opslag-van-CO2-in-Nederland-EBN-en-Gasunie.pdf. [7]

Grigoriev, S. et al. (2020), "Current status, research trends, and challenges in water electrolysis science and technology", *International Journal of Hydrogen Energy*, Vol. 45/49, pp. 26036-26058, http://dx.doi.org/10.1016/j.ijhydene.2020.03.109. [3]

IEA (2019), *The Future of Hydrogen*, International Energy Agency, Paris, https://www.iea.org/reports/the-future-of-hydrogen. [1]

Oliveira, C. and K. Schure (2020), *Decarbonisation options for the Dutch refinery sector.* [6]

Notes

[1] https://www.pbl.nl/sites/default/files/downloads/pbl-2019-decarbonisation-options-for-the-dutch-fertiliser-industry_3657.pdf

[2] https://hydrogeneurope.eu/electrolysers.

[3] https://www.topsectorenergie.nl/sites/default/files/uploads/TKI%20Gas/publicaties/20180514%20Roadmap%20Hydrogen%20TKI%20Nieuw%20Gas%20May%202018.pdf.

[4] https://www.meststoffennederland.nl/getmedia/b677f87e-a46b-4193-8da6-d24d9be51d08/Productie-van-minerale-meststoffen-in-Nederland-sept-2015.aspx#:~:text=De%20ge%C3%AFnstalleerde%20ammoniak%2D%20capaciteit%20in,voor%20de%20productie%20van%20meststoffen.&text=De%20Nederlandse%20producenten%20hebben%20ongeveer,1%20ton%20NH3%20te%20produceren.

[5] https://orsted.com/en/media/newsroom/news/2020/11/448070886682487

[6] https://www.ammoniaenergy.org/articles/low-carbon-ammonia-in-nebraska-and-the-netherlands/ and www.smartdeltaresources.com

[7] https://www.pbl.nl/sites/default/files/downloads/pbl-2019-decarbonisation-options-for-the-dutch-fertiliser-industry_3657.pdf

[8] https://www.energy.gov/eere/fuelcells/fact-month-august-2018-global-electrolyzer-sales-reach-100-mw-year

[9] https://www.ammoniaenergy.org/articles/low-carbon-ammonia-in-nebraska-and-the-netherlands/

[10] https://www.forbes.com/sites/rrapier/2020/06/06/estimating-the-carbon-footprint-of-hydrogen-production/?sh=259db08124bd

[11] https://www.pbl.nl/sites/default/files/downloads/pbl-2019-decarbonisation-options-for-the-dutch-fertiliser-industry_3657.pdf

[12] Top Sector Energie: https://www.topsectorenergie.nl/sites/default/files/uploads/TKI%20Gas/publicaties/Overview%20Hydrogen%20projects%20in%20the%20Netherlands%20versie%201mei2020.pdf

[13] https://ec.europa.eu/info/funding-tenders/opportunities/portal/screen/opportunities/topic-details/lc-gd-2-2-2020

[14] https://ec.europa.eu/info/sites/info/files/research_and_innovation/green_deal/gdc_stakeholder_engagement_topic_02-2_electrolyser.pdf.

[15] https://ec.europa.eu/research/participants/data/ref/h2020/other/wp/2018-2020/annexes/h2020-wp1820-annex-h-esacrit_en.pdf.

[16] https://www.rvo.nl/sites/default/files/2020/10/Handleiding%20WBSO%202021.pdf.

[17] https://www.yara.nl/over-yara/yara-in-de-benelux/yara-sluiskil/over-yara-sluiskil/wat-we-doen/.

[18] https://zoek.officielebekendmakingen.nl/stcrt-2020-8625.html (MOOI regeling).

[19] https://www.rijksoverheid.nl/documenten/publicaties/2020/09/01/veelgestelde-vragen-over-het-nationaal-groeifonds.

[20] https://www.rijksoverheid.nl/documenten/kamerstukken/2020/10/16/kamerbrief-over-kabinetsreactie-op-advies-van-taskforce-infrastructuur-klimaatakkoord-industrie-tiki (p. 6).

[21] https://www.rijksoverheid.nl/onderwerpen/nationaal-groeifonds.

[22] https://www.rvo.nl/sites/default/files/2020/02/DEI-Handleiding-januari-2020-update.pdf.

[23] https://zoek.officielebekendmakingen.nl/stcrt-2020-32280.html#d17e1088.

[24] https://wetten.overheid.nl/BWBR0037669/2019-01-01.

[25] https://www.rijksoverheid.nl/documenten/kamerstukken/2020/02/17/kamerbrief-over-voortgang-verbrede-sde-en-eerste-openstelling-sde-2020.

[26] https://www.rijksoverheid.nl/documenten/kamerstukken/2020/02/17/kamerbrief-over-voortgang-verbrede-sde-en-eerste-openstelling-sde-2020.

[27] https://www.rijksoverheid.nl/documenten/kamerstukken/2020/03/30/kamerbrief-over-kabinetsvisie-waterstof.

[28] https://ec.europa.eu/clima/sites/clima/files/ets/allowances/docs/bm_study-chemicals_en.pdf, p. 38.

[29] https://www.convert-me.com/en/convert/energy/cmsgas/cmsgas-to-kwh.html?u=kwh&v=520%2C000.

[30] https://www.ce.nl/en/publications/1911/power-to-ammonia-energy-and-electricity-prices-scenarios-2020-2023-2030.

[31] https://www.rijksoverheid.nl/onderwerpen/belastingplan/belastingwijzigingen-voor-ons-klimaat/energiebelasting-ode.

[32] https://www.pbl.nl/sites/default/files/downloads/pbl-2020-decarbonisation-options-for-the-dutch-refinery-sector-3659_0.pdf.

[33] https://energy.nl/wp-content/uploads/2019/09/Steam-methane-reforming-SMR-for-hydrogen-production-with-carbon-capture-using-flue-gas-2.pdf.

[34] Oliveira and Schure (2020[6]).

[35] https://www.epa.gov/sites/production/files/2016-11/documents/refineries_2013_112516.pdf.

[36] https://www.pbl.nl/sites/default/files/downloads/pbl-2020-decarbonisation-options-for-the-dutch-refinery-sector-3659_0.pdf.

[37] https://energy.nl/wp-content/uploads/2019/09/Steam-methane-reforming-SMR-for-hydrogen-production-with-carbon-capture-using-flue-gas-2.pdf.

[38] https://www.ebn.nl/wp-content/uploads/2018/07/Studie-Transport-en-opslag-van-CO2-in-Nederland-EBN-en-Gasunie.pdf.

[39] https://energy.nl/wp-content/uploads/2019/09/Steam-methane-reforming-SMR-for-hydrogen-production-with-carbon-capture-using-flue-gas-2.pdf.

[40] https://ec.europa.eu/inea/en/horizon-2020/h2020-energy/projects-by-field/875.

[41] https://www.klimaatakkoord.nl/documenten/publicaties/2019/11/07/mmip6-sluiting-van-industriele-ketens.

[42] https://www.rijksoverheid.nl/documenten/kamerstukken/2020/10/16/kamerbrief-over-kabinetsreactie-op-advies-van-taskforce-infrastructuur-klimaatakkoord-industrie-tiki.

[43] https://ec.europa.eu/info/funding-tenders/opportunities/docs/2021-2027/innovfund/wp-call/call-fiche_innovfund-ssc-2020-single-stage_en.pdf.

[44] https://ec.europa.eu/inea/en/innovation-fund.

[45] https://www.rvo.nl/sites/default/files/2020/02/DEI-Handleiding-januari-2020-update.pdf.

[46] https://zoek.officielebekendmakingen.nl/stcrt-2020-32280.html.

[47]https://www.rvo.nl/subsidie-en-financieringswijzer/hernieuwbare-energietransitie/beoordelingscriteria-hernieuwbare-energietransitie.

[48] https://zoek.officielebekendmakingen.nl/stcrt-2020-32280.html#d17e1088.

[49] https://www.rvo.nl/subsidies-regelingen/milieulijst-en-energielijst/2021?search=carbon+capture&type=miavamil.

[50] https://www.pbl.nl/sites/default/files/downloads/pbl-2020-conceptadvies-sde-plus-plus-2021-ccs_4111.pdf.

[51] https://nos.nl/artikel/2301267-multinationals-als-shell-moeten-winstbelasting-gaan-betalen.html.

[52]https://nos.nl/artikel/2286805-waarom-betaalt-shell-hier-geen-winstbelasting-maar-in-het-buitenland-10-miljard.html.

[53] https://www.shell.nl/media/nieuwsberichten/2020/zes-vragen-over-shell-en-belastingafdracht.html.

[54]https://www.rijksoverheid.nl/onderwerpen/belastingplan/belastingwijzigingen-voor-ondernemers/vennootschapsbelasting#:~:text=Het%20lage%20tarief%20van%20de,verhoogd%20worden%20naar%20%E2%82%AC%20395.000.

[55] https://ec.europa.eu/jrc/en/publication/eur-scientific-and-technical-research-reports/best-available-techniques-bat-reference-document-refining-mineral-oil-and-gas-industrial.

[56] https://www.eiga.eu/index.php?eID=dumpFile&t=f&f=2567&token=77247387243829e86736fd6bf776964f1c9594c9.

[57] https://ieaghg.org/exco_docs/2017-TR3.pdf.

[58] https://www.forbes.com/sites/rrapier/2020/06/06/estimating-the-carbon-footprint-of-hydrogen-production/?sh=259db08124bd.

[59] https://www.porthosco2.nl/en/project/.

[60] https://www.ce.nl/en/publications/1911/power-to-ammonia-energy-and-electricity-prices-scenarios-2020-2023-2030 : CE Delft Power to Ammonia: Energy and electricity prices scenarios 2020, 2023, 2030.

[61] https://www.rijksoverheid.nl/onderwerpen/belastingplan/belastingwijzigingen-voor-ons-klimaat/energiebelasting-ode.

[62] It should be noted that the GJ value of gas and electricity are not strictly comparable.

7. Decarbonisation support: a comparison with Germany

This chapter reviews policy instruments aimed at reducing greenhouse gas emissions in German industry and compares the German and Dutch policy landscapes. The German policy mix focuses strongly on energy efficiency and on recycling. Compared with the Netherlands, the German government is more reluctant to develop biomass and CCS. Germany's innovation funding policies strongly focus on fundamental research and CAPEX support, while the Netherlands provide greater support to demonstration projects and deployment. As a consequence, high operational costs are still a major barrier for large-scale investments in Germany.

This chapter reviews policy instruments aimed at reducing greenhouse gas emissions in German industry and compares the German and Dutch policy landscapes. It offers fact sheets of relevant policies, an assessment of the policy mix and a comparison with the Netherlands. Emphasis is placed on the carbon intensive industry sectors in Germany, with a particular focus on policies supporting technology innovation and diffusion in the following fields: hydrogen (including blue and green hydrogen), electrification of industrial heat (and the corresponding development of renewable energy to attain zero net emissions), carbon capture and storage (CCS), bio-based materials, recycling of materials (notably metals and plastics).

7.1. Policy fact sheets

The fact sheets below review decarbonisation policies geared towards the industry sector. Other related and cross-cutting policies and targets upon which the industrial transition also depends indirectly are discussed in the next section. Examples are support regimes for renewable energies to decarbonise electricity supply, the building of necessary infrastructure like a hydrogen transport network or the availability of green hydrogen.

The 27 policies reviewed in this chapter are listed below:

- National and sectoral greenhouse gas (GHG) reduction targets
- Carbon and energy pricing
  1. EU emissions trading
  2. National emissions trading scheme - CO_2-price for transport and heating
  3. Energy taxes and exemptions ("Spitzenausgleich")
  4. Renewable energy surcharge (Erneuerbare-Energien-Gesetz [EEG]-Umlage) and compensation scheme ("Besondere Ausgleichsregelung")
- Technology development, demonstration and market introduction programmes aimed at industry decarbonisation
  5. National Decarbonisation Programme
  6. Programme CO_2 Avoidance and Use in Basic Industries
  7. National Hydrogen Strategy: Carbon Contract for Differences (CCfD) pilot
  8. National Hydrogen Strategy: Important Project of Common European Interest (IPCEI) "Hydrogen for industrial production"
  9. EU Emission Trading System (ETS) Innovation Fund: further development of the NER300 programme
- Research and innovation
  10. 7th Energy Research Programme
  11. FONA - Research for Sustainability
  12. Programme for Rational Use of Energy, Renewable Energies and Energy Saving (Programm für Rationelle Energieverwendung, Regenerative Energien und Energiesparen - progres.nrw) - Research
- Downstream: Material efficiency and circular economy
  13. Circular Economy Act, related acts and ordinances and current amendments
  14. German Resource Efficiency Programme ProgRess III
  15. Technology Transfer Programme Lightweight Construction (TTP LB)
  16. Funding directive and research concept "Ressourceneffiziente Kreislaufwirtschaft"

17. 5) EU Circular Economy Action Plan (EU)

- Energy efficiency

18. Federal support for energy efficiency in the economy - grant and loan
19. Energy audits in SMEs
20. The Kreditanstalt für Wiederaufbau (KfW) Energy Efficiency Programme: Low-interest loans for energy efficiency projects
21. Pilot programme "Einsparzähler" (savings meter)
22. Federal funding for energy efficiency in the economy - funding competition
23. Energy efficiency networks for businesses
24. Energy audit obligation for large companies (implementation of Article 8 EU Energy Efficiency Directive)
25. Minimum energy performance standards – EU Ecodesign Directive

- Other related policies

26. IN4climate.NRW
27. SME Initiative Energy system transformation and climate protection

7.1.1. Targets

The Climate Action Plan 2050,[1] adopted by the German Government in November 2016 affirms the target of the Paris Agreement to achieve CO_2-neutrality by mid-century, contains concrete actions to achieve the target and defines milestones for the year 2030 at a sectoral level. For the industry sector it sets a target of 49-51% GHG reduction compared to 1990. To achieve the sectoral target, substantial efforts on mitigation technologies are needed including large-scale investments in decarbonisation technologies, as presented in Figure 7.1. The targets were further strengthened through the climate protection law, which went into force in December 2019. It defines a (linear) path for emission reduction in all sectors towards the 2030 milestone and requires additional policy action, if the monitored emissions fall short of the minimum path in a certain year.

Figure 7.1. CO_2 emissions and reduction targets in Germany

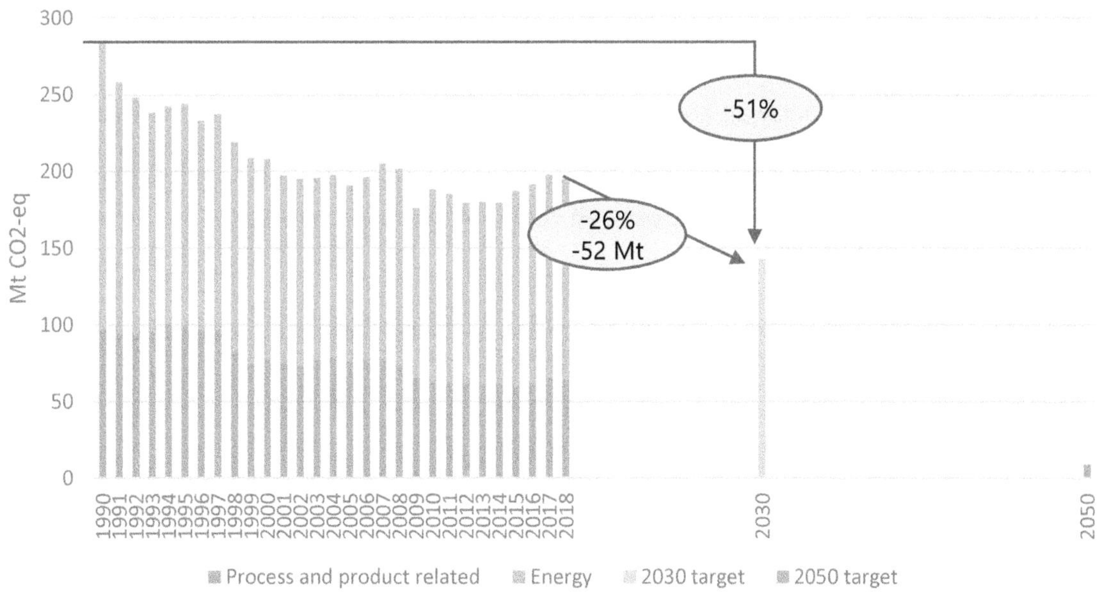

Source: Fraunhofer Institute.

7.1.2. Carbon and energy pricing

1) EU Emissions Trading Scheme (ETS)	
Description	The amendments to the Emissions Trading Directive for the fourth trading period 2021-30 came into force on 8 April 2018. The amended directive contains important innovations to strengthen EU emissions trading and its price signal. The total quantity of emission certificates auctioned and allocated free of charge will fall by 2.2% p.a. from 2021 (in relation to the reference value in 2010). With the market stability reserve (MSR), from 2019 to 2023, 24% instead of 12% of surplus certificates will be withdrawn from the market each year. From 2023, the maximum size of the market stability reserve is limited to the auction volume of the previous year. Surpluses exceeding this amount will be deleted from the MSR. In addition, member states have the option of reducing the number of certificates in circulation if fossil power plants are decommissioned as a result of additional national climate protection instruments. In Germany, about one quarter (124 Mt CO2) of the total emissions that fall under the EU ETS are from industry installations with refineries, chemicals, iron and steel and cement being emitting sectors. The ETS sets a CO_2-price for large emitters and an overall emissions cap and is, thus, a central element of the EU policy mix addressing the decarbonisation of industry. However, industrial companies in energy-intensive trade-exposed sectors receive a substantial number of emissions permits for free via the benchmarking procedure and electricity price compensation (EPC). Installations for production and heat generation receive partly free allocations, which falls from 80% of allocated certificates in 2013 to 30% in 2020, according to EU rules. However, to compensate for disadvantages in international competition, most industry installations receive nearly 100% free allocation, defined by a product-specific carbon leakage list published by the European Commission. The EPC intends to lower the burden on sectors in international competition by (partly) compensating the increase in electricity prices due to the ETS. The EPC is defined according to EU guidelines. However, CO2 costs for the purchase of one gigawatt-hour of electricity per year per installation are subtracted from the EPC. In 2018, the EPC in Germany amounted to EUR 219 million in total, with the largest share requested by the chemical industry. For 2019, substantially higher EPC cost occured (EUR 546 million) because of the higher emission price on the ETS.
Sources	https://www.dehst.de/SharedDocs/downloads/DE/spk/Auswertungsbericht_2018.pdf?__blob=publicationFile&v=3 https://www.dehst.de/SharedDocs/downloads/DE/spk/Auswertungsbericht_2019.pdf?__blob=publicationFile&v=4

Figure 7.2. Emissions in the EU Emissions Trading Scheme in Germany by sector in 2019

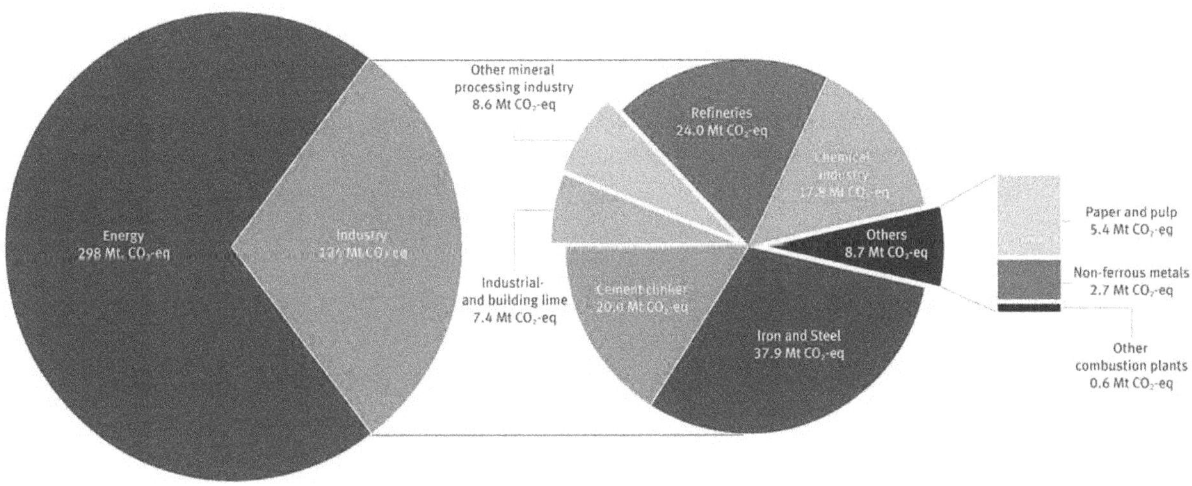

Source: German Emissions Trading Authority (DEHSt), German Environment Agency. https://www.dehst.de/EN/european-emissions-trading/understanding-emissions-trading/implementation/implementation_node.html

2) National Emissions Trading Scheme - CO2-price for transport and heating	
Description	In its climate protection programme 2030, the German government has advocated the introduction of CO2 pricing for the transport and heating sectors (non-ETS) from 2021 onwards. The Bundestag decided to introduce the CO2 pricing system as early as December 2019 by implementing the national emissions trading scheme (nETS). The nETS is an upstream system and covers emissions from the combustion of fossil fuels, in particular heating oil, liquid gas, natural gas, coal, petroleum and diesel. Until 2025, fuel or heat suppliers will need to buy certificates at a fixed price. From 2026 onwards, the system translates into cap and trade system with a predefined price corridor. This should create a reliable price path that enables private households and companies to anticipate and adapt to the development. The sectors affected by this law are mainly buildings, transport and industry. Industry installations that participate in the EU ETS are exempt from the nETS. Either the industry companies can apply for compensation or the upstream seller of fossil fuels can reduce its obligation to render emissions allowances by the respective amount sold to an EU ETS installation. Then, the total quantity of emissions under the scope of the nETS is resulting from EU ETS coverage and the overall emissions of the German industry sector and can be estimated as follows. In 2019, the total industry sector emissions (according to German sectoral garget definition) accounted for about 195 Mt CO2-equivalent. Of these, about 100 Mt CO2 fall under the scope of the EU ETS and thus are out of scope for the nETS. Therefore, less than 50% of all industry emissions fall under the nETS, probably substantially less, as these emissions include product-related F-gas emissions, which are also outside the nETS. Thus, a realistic estimate is that 20-40% of industry sector emissions fall exclusively under the nETS. The CO_2 price is set initially at EUR 25 per tonne in 2021 and will rise gradually to EUR 55 per tonne in 2025. For the year 2026, a price corridor of at least

	EUR 55 and at most EUR 65 per tonne applies. After that, the price will be determined by the market. The CO_2 prices in the EU ETS and the nETS are independent and will likely differ substantially, because mitigation measures in the non-ETS are expected to show higher marginal abatement costs. The basis for the nETS is the Fuel Emission Trading Act (Brennstoffemissionshandelsgesetz, BEHG).
CAPEX/OPEX	n.a.
Technology maturity	n.a.
Target group/sector/ technology	Upstream energy suppliers in entire non-ETS heating and transport sectors
Typical grant/project size	n.a.
Eligibility	n.a.
Budget available	n.a.
Evaluation	n.a.
Sources	https://www.dehst.de/SharedDocs/downloads/DE/nehs/nehs-hintergrundpapier.pdf?__blob=publicationFile&v=6. Fuel Emission Trading Act (BEHG)

3) Energy taxes and exemptions ("Spitzenausgleich")	
Description	With the law on the introduction of the ecological tax reform of 24 March 1999 and the corresponding follow-up laws, the taxation of various fossil fuels and electricity was increased to incentivise energy efficiency improvements. At the same time, the tax revenues were used to decrease non-wage labour costs. The Electricity Tax Act and the Energy Tax Act provide for differentiated tax rates according to energy sources. Some energy consumers are fully exempt from energy taxation, as are most of the large consumers from the heavy industry, as they receive exemptions for energy use in specifically defined energy-intensive processes and the tax reliefs discussed under the heading "Spitzenausgleich" below. Current discussions on reforming the energy taxes direct towards the high price of electricity, which is a major barrier for the diffusion of sector coupling technologies such as heat pumps. Lower taxes on electricity and EEG-levy (see below separate fact sheet 4), financed by higher taxes for fossil fuels according to their CO2-intensity is an option on the table.[2] **Energy tax reliefs ("Spitzenausgleich"):** Under the so-called "Spitzenausgleich", companies in the manufacturing sector receive reliefs on energy taxes. In 2013, the "Spitzenausgleich" was

	readjusted and continued beyond 2012 for another ten years. Accordingly, two conditions must be met by companies to receive tax discounts: ► The applying company must prove that it has introduced an energy management system in accordance with DIN EN ISO 50001 or an environmental management system in accordance with the Eco-Management and Audit Scheme (EMAS) that is operational as of end 2015. ► The energy intensity of manufacturing industry in Germany must decrease overall by a legally defined target value. This target valuc is 1.3% per year for the reference years 2013 to 2015 (application years 2015 to 2017) and 1.35% per year for the reference years from 2016 (application years 2018 to 2022). The new regulation of peak balancing is designed for a period of ten years.

4) The EEG-Levy and compensation scheme ("Besondere Ausgleichsregelung"))	
Description	In order to finance the support (feed-in-tariffs and permit) of renewable energy technologies for electricity generation a levy was introduced as a mark-up on the electricity tariff for all electricity consumers. In recent years, the mark-up reached up to EUR 0.06 per kWh for typical household consumers (large industry companies receive major discounts). A sharp increase in the EEG levy (renewable energy act) is expected for 2021. The main reason for this is the decline in economic output and the associated fall in the price of electricity at the stock exchange. In order to ensure greater reliability of the state electricity price components, a subsidy from federal budget funds is planned for the "gradual and reliable reduction" of the EEG levy, so that it will be EUR 0.065 per kWh in 2021 and EUR 0.06 per kWh in 2022. This measure will also be financed by government revenue from the new national emissions trading. After 2022, revenues from emissions trading will continue to be used to reduce the EEG levy. The necessary adjustments to the Renewable Energies Act have already been implemented in the amendment of 15 July 2020. The new EEG, which has also been amended, came into effect on 1 January 2021 ("EEG 2021") and will be notified in parallel as a subsidy. The high mark-up on the electricity price provides on the one side substantial incentives for energy-efficiency improvements, and, on the other side, is a strong barrier for electrification and sector coupling technologies (heat pumps, electric industrial furnaces, electric cars). Compensation scheme (BesAR) of the Renewable Energy Sources Act (EEG): Under BesAR, companies in electricity and trade-intensive industries with high electricity consumption are receiving discounts to the EEG levy. The aim of BesAR is, among other things, to protect the international competitiveness of the beneficiary companies. To receive discounts, companies have to apply and belong to electricity and trade-intensive industries. They must also prove that their electricity costs account for a high proportion of the gross value added. Furthermore, in order to qualify for the corresponding benefits, applicant companies' electricity consumption must exceed 1 GWh/y and have

	a certified energy or environmental management system. Companies with an annual electricity consumption of more than 5 GWh have to prove the operation of an energy or environmental management system (ISO 50001 or EMAS), companies with 1-5 GWh can also prove the operation of an alternative system for the improvement of energy efficiency in the sense of the Peak Energy Efficiency System Ordinance (SpaEfV). As a result, the compensation scheme has strongly contributed to the role-out of ISO 50001 energy management schemes in Germany.

7.1.3. Technology development, demonstration and market introduction programmes aiming at industry decarbonisation

5) National Decarbonisation Programme	
Description	The national Decarbonisation Programme is currently being implemented, as well as part of the Climate Protection Programme 2030. It is a support programme addressing technology development, demonstration and market uptake. The programme particularly aims for the reduction of process-related emissions in hard-to-abate sectors and thus addresses key production facilities in these sectors. For this purpose, projects in the area of emission-intensive industries with process-related emissions are supported via grants. The projects under scope range from application-oriented R&D and industrial-scale testing to the broad market introduction of mature or emerging technologies. The programme does not focus on a narrow definition of process-related emissions only, but also aims at reducing hard-to-abate emissions from fossil fuel combustion. The programme will provide grants to finance a share of the upfront costs of the investments in new plants, development of climate-neutral processes, switch from fossil to electricity-based fuels, innovative combinations of processes, development of climate-neutral product substitutes as well as bridge technologies. Applications are evaluated technically and economically. Current programme design focuses on capital expenditures only and does not foresee financing of operational costs. However, in order to add operational expenses (OPEX) support, it is possible to combine the grants with potential support from the EU Innovation Fund or the CCfD pilot from the German Hydrogen Strategy. In total, the programme aims to reduce annual GHG emissions in the industry sector by about 2.5 Mt eq CO_2 by the year 2030. The programme is overseen by the Ministry for the Environment (BMU) and the official funding directive was published on 16 December 2020 and went into force on 1 January 2021. In anticipation of this, the Environmental Innovation Programme (UIP) set up a funding window "Decarbonisation in Industry" for a transitional period until the new directive came into force to provide a basis for project proposals throughout 2020. The programme is implemented by the Competence Center Climate Protection in Energy-intensive Industries (KEI) based in Cottbus.

CAPEX/OPEX	Only Capital Expenditures (CAPEX) support (but combination with other programmes possible to add OPEX support).
Technology maturity	From applied research to demonstration and industrial-scale market introduction of emerging technologies (TRL 4-9).
Target group/sector/ technology	CO_2-intensive processes in the basic materials industry (steel, cement, chemicals, others).
Typical grant/project size	Up to now (January 2021), one project is selected for a grant: The Salzgitter AG received a EUR 5 million grant for the construction of a small scale demonstrator direct reduction ironmaking (DRI) plant that can flexibly use natural gas and hydrogen as fuel.
Eligibility	All companies located in Germany with process-related emissions that fall under the scope of the EU ETS.
Budget available	EUR 2 billion for 2020-24, thereafter EUR 0.5 billion per year is expected. The programme was announced in advance, so that companies could prepare proposals in time.
Evaluation	No evaluation available - programme started in 2021.
Sources	Directive for the support of research, development and investment-projects targeting greenhouse gas neutrality in the industry sector.[3] Press release BMU.[4] Temporary funding guidelines.[5]

6) CO_2 avoidance and use in basic industries	
Description	The focus of this programme, which is part of the Climate Protection Programme 2030, is the reduction of process-related GHG emissions in the basic materials industry. The main objective is to further develop central components of the process chain in the field of CO_2 capture, storage and utilisation (Carbon Capture and Storage - CCS and Carbon Capture and Utilisation - CCU) towards market maturity and thereby creating the necessary technical prerequisites for a permanent reduction of process-related greenhouse gas emissions. This involves the entire value chain covering CO_2 capture, transport and storage. The programme is administered by the German Ministry for Economics (BMWi). The related support directive is currently under development and not yet published.
CAPEX/OPEX	Focus on CAPEX (for CCS, OPEX support is also possible).

Technology maturity	Starting from TRL 5-6 with goal to achieve industrial-scale market introduction
Target group/sector/ technology	All sectors with process-related emissions, however, focus on cement, limestone and chemicals.
Typical grant/project size	Projects are expected to be very large, only a few projects will be financed (grant size probably >EUR 100 million per project).
Eligibility	n.a.
Budget available	~ EUR 0.5 billion total budget (2021-25), ~EUR 0.1 billion annually
Evaluation	n.a.
Sources	German climate protection programme 2030 Exchange with BMWi

7) National Hydrogen Strategy: Pilot programme Carbon Contracts for Difference	
Description	The National Hydrogen Strategy (NWS) of the Federal Government was adopted by the Federal Cabinet on 10 June 2020. For the consistent implementation and further development of the strategy, it is planned to create a flexible and result-oriented governance structure. The central point is the establishment of a National Hydrogen Council, which held its constituent meeting on 9 July 2020. While there is a strong commitment to hydrogen produced from renewable energy sources ("green hydrogen"), the NWS acknowledges the role of CO_2 neutral hydrogen produced within a European hydrogen market. As Germany is tightly connected to a European energy market, CO_2 neutral (blue/turquoise) hydrogen is likely to be used on an interim basis. However, it is stated that only green hydrogen is sustainable in the long-term. In the German government's economic stimulus package of 3 June 2020, it was decided to massively expand the promotion of hydrogen and fuel-cell technology. The economic stimulus package thus fully supports the measures defined in the NWS. A total of EUR 7 billion has been earmarked for national measures of which roughly EUR 2 billion are foreseen for the use of hydrogen to decarbonise industry. Several individual measures can be assigned to the industry sector. For example, the introduction of a pilot programme for CCfD is scheduled for 2021. Other measures, such as demand quota for climate-friendly raw materials, e.g. green steel, tendering models for the production of green hydrogen, which serves as an example for the decarbonisation of the steel and chemical industry, are also examined. An important instrument for the implementation of the NWS is the IPCEI Hydrogen. Here the German government plans to promote integrated projects along the entire hydrogen value chain and has offered co-ordination at

	EU level. Currently the German expression of interest procedure is being prepared, in which companies can submit appropriate proposals. A pilot programme for carbon contracts for difference (CCfD) is planned as part of the national hydrogen strategy published in June 2020. The programme is dedicated to the steel and chemical industries and has an allocation of around EUR 500 million of the national budget. Companies are to sign contracts with the government for low-carbon industrial production, and in return the government assures a fixed carbon price, a so-called strike price. As long as the ETS price is lower than the strike price, the difference will be covered by the Government. If the ETS price is higher than the strike price, then companies must pay back the difference between the two prices. Other cost components such as higher costs for different raw materials or higher CAPEX could be included in the design. CCfDs are designed to offset the higher operating costs of low-carbon production processes compared to the fossil fuel-based reference process. Thus, they address the operating costs, while the investment costs can be covered by other programmes, such as the National Decarbonisation Programme. CCfDs are to be selected through a tender. A first draft plan was published in April 2021 but issues such as conflicts with European state aid law or the determination of reference costs still need to be clarified..
CAPEX/OPEX	OPEX (CAPEX)
Technology maturity	All
Target group/sector/ technology	Steel and chemicals industry
Typical grant/project size	(not specified)
Eligibility	n.a.
Budget available	~EUR 0.5 billion in total until 2023
Evaluation	n.a.
Sources	National Hydrogen Strategy Deutscher Bundestag (2020): Antwort der Bundesregierung auf die Kleine Anfrage zu Pilotprogramm Carbon Contracts for Differences.[6]

8) National Hydrogen Strategy: IPCEI "Hydrogen in industrial production"	
Description	As part of the National Hydrogen Strategy a support programme to develop hydrogen technologies in the form of an IPCEI was agreed upon. The

	expression-of-interest procedure was published on 11 January 2021 and also covers the support of projects for hydrogen use in industry. While the entire IPCEI addresses all parts of the hydrogen value chain, the BMWi administers a part that particularly addresses the industrial application of hydrogen. For this part, about EUR 1.5 billion are expected to be available as funding for the period until 2026. This includes the use of hydrogen in industry as well as the development and production of fuel cell systems. Support is only given for the differential costs, i.e. the additional costs for a low-CO_2 process compared to the conventional CO_2-intensive process. Funding is for CAPEX, while OPEX can be funded in exceptional cases when the operation of the plant is needed for research purposes. IPCEI are transnational projects partly funded by governments to achieve European strategic objectives and improve its competitiveness. These projects are also expected to have a spill over effect on other countries, other companies and/or other sectors. Nine strategic fields have been identified, including hydrogen technologies and systems and low-carbon industry, as well as microelectronics and battery manufacturing.
CAPEX/OPEX	CAPEX (OPEX only for research projects)
Technology maturity	Starting from TRL 5-6 with goal to achieve industrial-scale market introduction
Target group/sector/ technology	Hydrogen use in all sectors, however, steel and chemicals are in the focus. Technologies to make industrial processes "hydrogen ready"
Typical grant/project size	Large scale projects (>EUR 10 million)
Eligibility	Particular requirements of IPCEI projects
Budget available	~ EUR 1.5 billion total for period 2021-26 (Only industry-sector funding)
Evaluation	n.a.
Sources	"Expression of interest for the planned support in the field of hydrogen technologies and systems" (Bekanntmachung des Interessenbekundungsverfahrens zur geplanten Förderung im Bereich Wasserstofftechnologien und -systeme)[7] BMWi (2020): Häufig gestellte Fragen zum "Important Project of Common European Interest (IPCEI)".[8] National Hydrogen Strategy

9) EU ETS Innovation Fund: further development of the NER300 programme	
Description	Within the framework of the European Emissions Trading Scheme, the innovation fund supports the commercial demonstration of innovative low-carbon technologies. It is a continuation of the former NER300 programme, but extends the funding scope by also including technologies addressing the reduction of GHG emissions in the energy-intensive industries. Additionally, it covers the following technologies similar to the NER300 programme: Carbon capture and utilisation (CCU), construction and operation of CCS, innovative renewable energy generation, energy storage. The Innovation Fund is part of the Emissions Trading System (EU-ETS) and is financed by revenues from the auctioning of CO_2 allowances. In the time period 2020 to 2030, a total of 450 million allowances will be used to finance the Innovation Fund. Currently, a resulting total budget of about EUR 10 billion is expected, however, it depends on the actual allowance price in the EU ETS. The first call of the EU Innovation Fund was published by the European Commission on 3 July 2020. This call for proposals addresses large projects with capital costs of >EUR 7.5 million. For large-scale projects funding is available for capital and operational costs. Small-scale projects will receive funding for capital costs only.
CAPEX/OPEX	CAPEX and OPEX (funding up to 60% of the additional capital and operational costs).
Technology maturity	TRL 6-9 ("commercial demonstration").
Target group/sector/ technology	Energy-intensive industries, CCS, CCU, renewable energies and energy storage.
Typical grant/project size	Large-scale projects: > EUR 7.5 million capital costs. Small-scale projects: < EUR 7.5 million capital costs.
Eligibility	n.a.
Budget available	~EUR 10 billion total until 2030 (EU wide, all technologies).
Evaluation	n.a.
Sources	https://ec.europa.eu/clima/policies/innovation-fund_en.

7.1.4. Research and innovation

10) 7th Energy Research Programme (7. Energieforschungsprogramm)	
Description	In 2018, the BMWi published the "7. Energieforschungsprogramm" (7th energy research programme) of the Federal Government under the heading

	"Innovationen für die Energiewende" (Innovations for the Energy Transition). The fundamental aim of the research programme is the technology and innovation transfer facilitating the energy transition. Besides institutional research funding and project funding in areas as energy generation, system integration as well as system-wide research topics, focus lies on the energy transitions in the consumption sectors. In total a budget of about EUR 6.4 billion is provided by the Federal Ministry for Economic Affairs and Energy, the Federal Ministry of Education and Research and the Federal Ministry of Food and Agriculture in the years 2018 to 2022. The major part - about EUR 4.2 billion - is assigned to the funding of projects. In the consumption sector comprising industry as well as trade, commerce and services the following research topics are supported: • energy-intensive basic materials industry (e.g. efficiency, electrification) • sector-specific measures (e.g. circular economy, efficiency) • cross-cutting topics (e.g. digitalisation, process heat).
CAPEX/OPEX	More details on the funding modalities are published in department-specific funding guidelines and funding announcements.
Technology maturity	TRL 1-9.
Target group/sector/ technology	SMEs, enterprises, higher education and research institutions.
Typical grant/project size	Depending on the individual funding guideline and funding announcement.
Eligibility	More details on the funding modalities are published in department-specific funding guidelines and announcements.
Budget available	EUR 4.2 billion in total for the years 2018 to 2022, about EUR 0.9 billion annually.
Evaluation	The energy research programme is evaluated in retrospect, thus the evaluation of the fifth version is currently available.
Sources	https://www.bmwi.de/Redaktion/DE/Artikel/Energie/Energieforschung/energieforschung-7-energieforschungsprogramm.html. https://www.bmwi.de/Redaktion/DE/Publikationen/Energie/7-energieforschungsprogramm-der-bundesregierung.pdf?__blob=publicationFile&v=14. https://www.bmwi.de/Redaktion/DE/Publikationen/Studien/evaluation-der-forschungsfoerderung-des-bundesumweltministeriums-im-rahmen-des-5-energieforschungsprogramms.pdf?__blob=publicationFile&v=3.

11) FONA: Research for sustainability	
Description	Based on the UN Sustainable Development Goals the Federal Ministry of Education and Research has developed a strategy for the "Forschung für Nachhaltigkeit" (FONA, research for sustainability) in 2005. The 4th Framework Programme (FONA4) will be effective from 2020 to 2024 and has a budget of EUR 4 billion in total. Research projects in the field of green hydrogen, circular economy, climate protection and bioeconomy are funded in specific funding guidelines and funding announcements. Besides a funding directive and research concept for resource-efficient circular economy (described in a separate policy fact sheet), individual projects and funding guidelines are of high relevance for the decarbonisation of the industrial sector. The funding guideline "Impulse für industrielle Ressourceneffizienz" (r+Impuls, impetus for industrial resource efficiency) is supported by the expiring FONA3. Between 2016 and 2021 26 joint projects are funded with EUR 22.3 million in the field of industrial resource efficiency. The funding is exclusively applicable from TRL 5 and thereby closing the gap between R&D projects and the broad market introduction. The funding guidelines "Epigenetik - Chancen für die Pflanzenforschung" (Epigenetics - opportunities for plant research) and "Zukunftstechnologien für die industrielle Bioökonomie" (future technologies for the industrial bioeconomy) are supported by FONA4. While the first one focuses on the food production, the second supports technologies in the field of bioeconomy in general. The funding volume is currently not published. The research project Carbon2Chem tests the capture and utilisation of CO_2-emissions (CCU) from metallurgical gases from the steel industry. The captured CO_2 will be used for the production of precursors for fuels, plastics or fertilisers. EUR 60 million was provided by the Federal Ministry of Education and Research as part of FONA3 during the first phase (2016-20) and about EUR 75 million will be provided in the second phase (2020-24). The funding guideline "Vermeidung von klimarelevanten Prozessemissionen in der Industrie" (Klim-Pro-Industrie, avoidance of climate-relevant process emissions in the industry) contributes to the implementation of the Klimaschutzplan 2050 (climate protection plan 2050), Hightech-Strategie 2025 (high-tech strategy 2025) and FONA3 are focussed on carbon direct avoidance, CCU and CCS. In total, up to EUR 80 million will be provided until 2025.
CAPEX/ OPEX	
Technology maturity	
Target group/sector/ technology	More details on the modalities are published in funding guidelines and funding announcements.
Typical grant/project size	
Eligibility	

Budget available	EUR 4 billion in total for the years 2020 to 2024.
Evaluation	The FONA Framework Programme is evaluated in retrospect, thus the evaluation of version 1 and 2 (2005-09 and 2020-14) is available.
Sources	https://www.bmbf.de/upload_filestore/pub/Forschung_fuer_Nachhaltigkeit.pdf. https://www.fona.de/de/ueber-fona/FONA-Strategie.php. https://www.isi.fraunhofer.de/content/dam/isi/dokumente/ccp/2020/BMBF_FONA_Evaluation_Abschlussbericht_2020.pdf. https://www.isi.fraunhofer.de/content/dam/isi/dokumente/ccp/2020/BMBF_FONA_Evaluation_Abschlussbericht_2020.pdf. https://www.fona.de/medien/pdf/Projektmappe_rplus_Impuls_2020_0.pdf. https://www.fona.de/de/massnahmen/foerdermassnahmen/epigenetik_biooekonomie.php. https://www.fona.de/de/massnahmen/foerdermassnahmen/zukunftstechnologien_biooekonomie.php. https://www.fona.de/de/massnahmen/foerdermassnahmen/carbon2chem.php. https://www.fona.de/de/vermeidung-von-klimarelevanten-prozessemissionen-in-der-industrie-.

12) Progress.nrw - Research	
Description	Progress.nrw - Research is a funding instrument established by the Ministry of Economic Affairs, Innovation, Digitalisation and Energy of the State of North Rhine-Westphalia as part of the "Energieforschungsoffensive.NRW". It supports the transition from basic to applied research on new products, processes or services in the field of energy system transformation and carbon-neutral industry.
CAPEX/OPEX	Purchase of research equipment (CAPEX) use of research equipment, personnel expenses, material expenses, travel expenses, overhead expenses (OPEX).
Technology maturity	Transition from basic to applied research (TRL 2-4).
Target group/sector/ technology	Higher education and research institutions.
Typical grant/project size	EUR 2 000 to EUR 70 000.
Eligibility	Non-economically viable projects with a duration up to six months.
Budget available	No information available.

Evaluation	No evaluation available.
Sources	https://progres-nrw-research.ptj.de/lw_resource/datapool/_items/item_95/Flyer_progresNRW.pdf. https://progres-nrw-research.ptj.de/lw_resource/datapool/_items/item_96/RL_progres_nrw_research.pdf.

7.1.5. Material efficiency and circularity

13) Circular Economy Act, related acts and ordinances and current amendments	
Description	The current version of the Circular Economy Act from 2012 and its October 2020 amendment constitute the legal framework for waste management in Germany and implements the EU Waste Framework Directive. The national regulation goes beyond the EU regulation by implementing a duty of care and by determining preferences for sustainable public procurement. Besides the definition of the terms waste and by-product, the determination of a waste hierarchy and the extended producer responsibility shapes the German waste management. In practise, the regulation introduces the separated collection of waste and recycling quotas. For specific product wastes (packaging, end-of-life vehicles, batteries, electrical devices, reclaim wood, waste oil etc.) additional acts and ordinances have been implemented in line with EU waste-specific directives. The new Packaging act from 2019 and the Commercial Waste Ordinance from 2017 are of particular importance. Both legislations are intended to further strengthen recycling. The Packaging Act introduces stricter quota requirements, monitoring and further developments, which will lead to increases in the recycling volumes of plastics and metals. Additionally, current amendments from November 2020 and January 2021 ban plastic bags by 2022 and define a minimum recycled share for PET bottles by 2025. Furthermore, a mandatory deposit for all non-refillable plastic bottles is implemented by 2022 and reusable options must be offered for to-go drinks by 2023. The new Commercial Waste Ordinance will have similar effects through requirements for stricter separate collection and the sorting and recycling of mixed commercial waste. Several studies show that this will save about 1 million t CO_2. This reduction is supported by waste prevention and resource conservation measures (e.g. increasing reuse), as described in the national Waste Prevention Programme (AVP) and the German Resource Efficiency Programme (ProgRess III). An overview of the recycling quotas in force as well as target values up to 2035 originating from the described legislation is given in Table 7.1.
CAPEX/OPEX	No financial support
Technology maturity	Not technology specific

Target group/sector/ technology	Waste management
Typical grant/project size	No financial support
Eligibility	Producers and owners of waste, operators of waste pretreatment and processing plants
Budget available	No financial support
Evaluation	No evaluation available for recycling measures
Sources	https://www.gesetze-im-internet.de/krwg/. https://www.verpackungsgesetz.com/ https://www.gesetze-im-internet.de/gewabfv_2017/BJNR089600017.html https://www.umweltbundesamt.de/themen/abfall-ressourcen/abfallwirtschaft/abfallrecht

Table 7.1. Recycling quotas in Germany

	Current	2022	2025	2030	2035
Residential waste	50%	n.a.	55%	60%	65%
Packaging	55%	n.a.	65%	70%	n.a.
Glass	80%	90%	n.a.	n.a.	n.a.
Paper	85%	90%	n.a.	n.a.	n.a.
Ferrous metals	80%	90%	n.a.	n.a.	n.a.
Aluminium	80%	90%	n.a.	n.a.	n.a.
Beverage cartons	75%	80%	n.a.	n.a.	n.a.
Other composite	55%	70%	n.a.	n.a.	n.a.
Commercial waste	30%	n.a.	n.a.	n.a.	n.a.

Source: Fraunhofer Institute

14) German Resource Efficiency Programme ProgRess III	
Description	The German Resource Efficiency Programme ProgRess III updates the previous ProgRess II from 2020 to 2023. The update is based on an evaluation of ProgRess II as well as current environmental policy challenges. Nevertheless, the objective of ProgRess II of doubling the raw material productivity from 1994 until 2020 is expected to be missed by a wide margin. In contrast to its predecessor, ProgRess III mentions the relevance of resource efficiency and digitalisation for achieving climate goals. The current ProgRess III includes 118 measures for improving resource efficiency in Germany. The measures cover the following areas: • resource protection in value chains and material cycles • cross-cutting instruments

	• resource protection at the international level • resource protection at the municipal and regional levels • resource protection in everyday life. For monitoring the impact of ProgRess II, a set of indicators is defined considering the total raw material productivity, the raw material consumption, the secondary raw material use and the material stock change. The German Resource Efficiency Programme and its current version ProgRess III are setting the framework for goals, ideas and approaches to protect natural resources. Hence diverse policy instruments addressing material efficiency and circular economy are based on this programme.
CAPEX/OPEX	The modalities depend on the respective policy design.
Technology maturity	
Target group/sector/ technology	
Typical grant/project size	
Eligibility	
Budget available	
Evaluation	Evaluation of ProgRess II included in ProgRess III.
Sources	https://www.bmu.de/fileadmin/Daten_BMU/Download_PDF/Ressourceneffizienz/progress_iii_programm_bf.pdf.

15) Technology Transfer Programme Lightweight Construction (TTP LB)	
Description	Based on the German Sustainability Strategy and the Industry Strategy 2030, the TTP LB focuses on lightweight construction for increasing growth and competitiveness as well as climate protection and sustainability. The Federal Ministry for Economic Affairs and Energy is providing around EUR 300 million in funding. Within the framework of the TTP LB, R&D projects relating to lightweight construction in five programme lines are funded. The first three programme lines have a thematic focus while the last two consider technology readiness (demonstration project or standardisation phase). The following three areas are considered, of which the last two are relevant for decarbonisation: • technology development to strengthen economy • new design techniques and materials

	• resource efficiency and substitution. The aim of the second programme line is to develop and promote material-related GHG reduction options. The measure is very broad and covers material efficiency, material substitution and product design with regard to new construction techniques. Between 2020 and 2024, the Energy and Climate Fund has earmarked funds of around EUR 0.15 billion, which will be continued in subsequent years. The third programme line is an accompanying anchoring of material efficiency issues and not a decidedly new measure. The measure builds on the approaches mentioned in the German Resource Efficiency Programme. The aim of increased resource efficiency and substitution is to anchor the principle of recycling in production processes and thus tap into previously untapped potential for reducing emissions. Priority target group are SMEs. From the first outline cut-off date of the TTP LB on 1 May 2020, 24 joint projects with more than 137 project participants will be launched promptly. This means that a total of EUR 49 million in funding will be drawn down over the next three years. The next cut-off date on 1 October 2020 is similarly well received.
CAPEX/OPEX	Research infrastructure (CAPEX)/ project-related costs (OPEX).
Technology maturity	R&D (TRL 3-8).
Target group/sector/ technology	Enterprises, higher education and research institutions, non-profit organisations, public institutions/ lightweight construction.
Typical grant/project size	EUR 2 million.
Eligibility	Projects with a duration up to three years, up to 50% funding for enterprises and up to 100% for higher education and research institutions.
Budget available	EUR 60 million in 2020 and EUR 70 million from 2021 onwards (financed via Energy and Climate Fund).
Evaluation	Based on ex ante evaluation which identified the economic and environmental relevance of lightweight construction.
Sources	https://www.bmwi.de/Redaktion/DE/Downloads/B/bekanntmachung-foerderung-ttp-lb.pdf?__blob=publicationFile&v=4. https://www.bmwi.de/Redaktion/DE/Artikel/Technologie/technologietransfer-programm-leichtbau.html. https://www.bmwi.de/Redaktion/DE/Publikationen/Studien/ex-ante-evaluation-technologietransfer-programm-leichtbau.pdf?__blob=publicationFile&v=6.

16) Funding directive and research concept "Ressourceneffiziente Kreislaufwirtschaft"

Description	Based on the second German Resource Efficiency Programme (ProgRess II) and funded by the Framework Programme for Research for Sustainability (FONA3) the Federal Ministry of Education and Research published the research concept "Ressourceneffiziente Kreislaufwirtschaft" (resource-efficient circular economy). The concept supports R&D in the field of resource efficiency considering eco-design, digitalisation, innovative product cycles and business models as well as specific relevant products (plastics, economically critical raw materials, mineral materials). Since 2017, three funding directives have been announced covering the following topics: • innovative product cycles (ReziProK, pub. 2017), • construction and mineral material cycles (ReMin, pub. 2018) and • plastics recycling technologies (KuRT, pub. 2020). The funding measure ReziProK started in 2019 with 25 joint projects and a transfer and networking platform hosted by the chemical industry association (DECHEMA). The funding periods ends in December 2022 and has a total budget of about EUR 30 million. The funding phase of ReMin started in February 2021. Consequently, information on the number of projects and budget is not yet available. Even though the measure KuRT was published subsequently, the funding phase started already in November 2020. Nevertheless, information about projects and budget are not available for KuRT either, even though the funding phase started in November 2020.
CAPEX/OPEX	Purchase of research equipment (CAPEX) personnel expenses, travel expenses, material expenses, subcontracts, services (OPEX).
Technology maturity	R&D (TRL 3-8).
Target group/sector/ technology	Enterprises, higher education and research institutions, non-profit organisations, public institutions.
Typical grant/project size	ReziProK: EUR 1.2 million.
Eligibility	Projects with a duration up to three or five years, up to 50% funding for enterprises and up to 100% for higher education and research institutions.
Budget available	EUR 150 million in total from 2018 to 2023.
Evaluation	No evaluation available.

Sources	https://www.bmbf.de/upload_filestore/pub/Ressourceneffiziente_Kreislaufwirtschaft.pdf. https://www.ptj.de/projektfoerderung/fona/produktkreislaeufe. https://www.ptj.de/projektfoerderung/fona/mineralische-stoffkreislaeufe. https://www.ptj.de/projektfoerderung/fona/kurt. https://www.bmbf.de/upload_filestore/pub/Bufi_2020_Hauptband.pdf. https://dechema.de/36_2019_d.html. https://www.fona.de/de/massnahmen/foerdermassnahmen/ressourceneffiziente-kreislaufwirtschaft-innovative-produktkreislaeufe.php. https://www.fona.de/de/massnahmen/foerdermassnahmen/ressourceneffiziente-kreislaufwirtschaft-bauen-und-mineralische-stoffkreislaufe.php. https://www.fona.de/de/massnahmen/foerdermassnahmen/recycling-kunststoffe.php.

17) Circular Economy Action Plan (EU)	
Description	As part of the European Green Deal the European Commission adopted the new Circular Economy Action Plan in March 2020 to enable sustainable economic growth. The plan includes 35 actions until 2022 in the fields of sustainable products, value chains, waste and crosscutting activities on regional, national and global level. Most of the proposed activities aim at the adaption of the legislative framework to foster the transformation to a circular economy. Additionally, a profound monitoring system (Circular Economy Monitoring Framework) is part of the proposed action plan. A first milestone was the proposal for modernisation of the EU legislation on batteries in November 2020. Further proposals in 2021/22 are intended to focus on waste management of electronic devices, end-of-life vehicles, packaging, plastics, textiles and construction materials. Additionally, legislation for sustainable design and lifetime extension shall be proposed. Especially relevant for the industry decarbonisation is the launch of an industrial symbiosis reporting and certification system by 2022. Nevertheless, circular economy is not a new topic at the EU level and has been implemented via an initial Circular Economy Action Plan in 2015. All 54 measures proposed in the plan have been adopted or are currently being implemented. Part of the efforts were the establishment of a Circular Economy Stakeholder Platform and the Circular Economy Package in 2018. Among others, the EU Strategy for Plastics in the Circular Economy was published in this course. At the EU level, the topics were additionally addressed by large funding budgets by Horizon 2020.
CAPEX/OPEX	No financial support.
Technology maturity	Not technology specific.

Target group/sector/ technology	EU member states.
Typical grant/project size	No financial support.
Eligibility	EU member states.
Budget available	No financial support.
Evaluation	Circular Economy Monitoring Framework.
Sources	https://eur-lex.europa.eu/legal-content/EN/TXT/?qid=1583933814386&uri=COM:2020:98:FIN. https://ec.europa.eu/environment/circular-economy/pdf/implementation_tracking_table.pdf. https://ec.europa.eu/environment/circular-economy/first_circular_economy_action_plan.html.

7.1.6. Energy efficiency

In the following, measures addressing energy efficiency improvement are briefly summarised to provide a complete overview. While some of the programmes also address topics beyond energy efficiency like renewable energies or material efficiency, the main focus of these programmes is clearly on energy efficiency.

18) Federal support for energy efficiency in the economy (grant and loan)

The programme represents a reorganisation of a number of previously individual support programmes. The programmes for the promotion of highly efficient cross-sectional technologies (e.g. electric motors), the Waste Heat Directive, the promotion of energy-efficient and climate-friendly production processes, the promotion of energy management systems and the promotion of renewable process heat in the Market Incentive Programme expired in December 2018 at the latest. They were relaunched as a joint promotion package with adapted promotion conditions and rates of support in January 2019. The programmes were bundled in the form of four modules and their application procedures were aligned. The aim of the restructuring is to offer an integrated energy efficiency support package for the industry, to reduce obstacles in the application process and to eliminate overlaps between programmes.

In the new funding programme "Federal funding for energy efficiency in the economy", funding is possible in four selectable and combinable modules:

- Module 1: Cross-cutting technologies (e.g. electric motors, pumps, fans)
- Module 2: Process heat from renewable energies
- Module 3: Reflective surfaces, sensor technology and energy management software
- Module 4: Energy-related optimisation of plants and processes.

The extent to which technologies and measures to increase material efficiency in Modules 1, 3 and 4 can also be promoted more intensively is being examined, provided that they demonstrably support the achievement of the relevant funding objectives. These activities also relate to the German Resource Efficiency Programme III (promoting material and energy-efficient production processes).

It is expected that the EUR 300 million budget for the programme set for 2020 will also apply to subsequent years.

19) Energy audits in SMEs

Small and medium-sized enterprises (SMEs) are offered the support of qualified energy consulting within the framework of the BMWi programme "Energy Consulting for SMEs" (Directive on the Promotion of Energy Consulting for SMEs of 11.10.2017, BAnz AT 07.11.2017 B1, [EBM)]). Qualified energy consultants identify potentials for energy saving and make concrete proposals for energy-efficiency measures for the respective company. The proposed measures can be used, for example, to create concepts for waste heat utilisation. The directive complies with the EU requirements for energy audits according to the EU Energy Efficiency Directive (2012/27/EU). The programme is administered by the Federal Office of Economics and Export Control (BAFA). The maximum funding amount per audit is EUR 6 000.

Identified energy-efficiency measures should also include material efficiency with the aim of saving energy in industrial processes. Corresponding training courses for auditors to identify material and resource efficiency measures are recognised. These activities also serve the implementation of measure 29 of the German Resource Efficiency Programme III, which aims, among other things, to improve the co-ordination of the content and structure of consulting services on material and energy efficiency and to avoid duplication of consulting services.

20) KfW Energy Efficiency Programme: Low-interest loans for energy efficiency projects

With the KfW Energy Efficiency Programme, the KfW grants low-interest loans to commercial enterprises for the implementation of energy efficiency measures. The programme promotes energy-efficient production facilities/processes including cross-sectional technologies with a relatively highest energy-saving potential. As the programme was further developed, both a new entry-level standard (10% savings) and a new premium standard (30% savings) were introduced. Thus, the funding intensity is aligned to the amount of energy savings, regardless of the size of the company. Projects with premium standard receive particularly favourable conditions. The improved funding conditions became effective in July 2015. By 2019, 219 commitments were made with a funding volume of EUR 974 million. The programme is financed from KfW's own funds.

21) Pilotprogramm "Einsparzähler" (Savings meter)

The pilot programme "Einsparzähler" aims to foster innovations in digitalisation to improve energy efficiency. Funding is available to companies that want to test and demonstrate innovative digital systems and related business models. The companies will receive funding of up to EUR 2 million. Within the pilot projects, energy consumption data must be metered precisely and assigned to individual devices or systems (groups). The current funding announcement "Pilotprogramm Einsparmeter" of the BMWi is dated 18 February 2019 (BAnz AT 21.02.2019). It is limited until 31 December 2022 and replaces the funding announcement "Pilotprogramme Einsparzähler" of 20 May 2016. BAFA is the granting authority. The pilot projects to date have achieved energy savings in the private household, commercial, trade, services, industry and transport sectors.

22) Federal funding for energy efficiency in the economy - funding competition

The programme promotes the implementation of energy efficiency projects in companies in a competitive process that is open to all actors, sectors and technologies with the objective to finance projects with the best cost/use-efficiency. The programme supports investment measures to optimise the energy efficiency of industrial and commercial plants and processes that contribute to increasing energy efficiency or reducing fossil energy consumption in companies, including measures for the provision of process heat from renewable energies and energy audits. This programme is a further development of the "Promotion of electricity savings within the framework of competitive tenders" programme introduced in 2016 with a budget of EUR 35 million for 2020.

23) Energy efficiency networks for businesses

Energy Efficiency Networks (EEN) are networks of companies that set common energy efficiency and CO_2 reduction targets and want to learn from each other. After a successful pilot phase of the EEN concept, the German government has decided in 2014 to implement EEN as a main pillar of the National Energy Efficiency Action Plan. Up to 500 new networks should be established by 2020. For this purpose, a voluntary agreement "Initiative Energy Efficiency Networks" on the introduction of EEN was signed in 2014 between the Federal Government (BMWi and BMU) and 22 business associations and organisations.. Based on the agreement extended in September 2020, 300-350 additional networks are to be created by 2025.

Companies participating in networks need to conduct an energy audit at company level and set a savings target at network level based on individual company targets. The networks are supported by a qualified energy consultant. The implemented measures are recorded in the context of an annual monitoring. As of 10 September 2020, 282 networks were established.

24) Energy audit obligation for large companies (implementation of Article 8 EU Energy Efficiency Directive)

"Large" companies are obliged to conduct energy audits as required by Article 8, Paragraph 4-7 of the EU Energy Efficiency Directive (2012/27/EU; EED). The energy audits should be carried out by qualified and/or accredited experts. The directive requires that the first energy audit be conducted by 5 December 2015 at the latest. In order to implement these requirements, the Energy Services Act (EDL-G) has been amended accordingly with effect from 22 April 2015. According to this, large companies (non-SMEs, i.e. companies that do not fall under the European Commission's definition of SMEs [<250 employees or turnover <EUR 50 million or annual balance sheet total < EUR 43 million]) are obliged to have carried out an energy audit according to DIN EN 16247-1 by 5 December 2015 and thereafter a further audit at least every four years. Companies that have an energy management system certified according to DIN EN ISO 50001 or an EMAS environmental management system are exempt from the obligation to conduct energy audits.

As part of the amendment in 2019, a threshold of 500 MWh total energy consumption was introduced. Below this threshold, a simplified energy audit can be carried out through a declaration of energy consumption and energy costs to the BAFA.

25) Minimum energy performance standards – EU Ecodesign Directive

All energy-related products are potentially covered by the EU Ecodesign Directive (2009/125), which sets general and specific requirements for 27 product groups, some of which are relevant for the industry (e.g. electric motors, industrial fans and ventilation units, water pumps or professional refrigerating appliances). Compliance is monitored through both physical and documentary checks as products are placed on the market.

Looking forward, the EU Ecodesign Directive includes opt-in material-related requirements regarding reparability, durability and recyclability but these have not been implemented to any significant extent.

7.1.7. Others

26) IN4climate.NRW	
Description	IN4climate.NRW is a platform for the sharing of knowledge, dialogue and collaboration between industry, science and politics for the decarbonisation of the industrial sector. Currently the platform consists of about 30 companies and associations from the following sectors: steel and metal, cement, glass, paper and construction materials as well as six research institutions and is supported by the Ministry of Economic Affairs, Innovation, Digitalisation and Energy of the State of North Rhine-Westphalia. Focussing on topics such as circular economy, hydrogen, carbon economy, heat or framework conditions, the platform strives to maintain the viability of North Rhine-Westphalia as industry location. For this purpose, the development of financial and technical strategies based on technology studies and innovation road maps as well as research projects is envisaged. In addition to the economic objective, the superordinate goal is the transition to a carbon-neutral industry. In 2019 and 2020 the platform released a hydrogen study as well as five papers discussing the issues of hydrogen, climate-friendly revitalisation of the economy, chemical plastics recycling, expansion of renewable energies and unavoidable GHG emissions. Furthermore, IN4climate.NRW carried out diverse events partly in co-operation with its scientific competence centre SCI4climate.NRW. This competence centre published, in addition, diverse reports and papers supporting the work of IN4climate.NRW.
CAPEX/OPEX	No financial support.
Technology maturity	Not defined (TRL 1-9).
Target group/sector/ technology	Industry (especially steel and metal, cement, glass, paper, construction materials).
Typical grant/project size	No financial support.
Eligibility	Industrial companies in North Rhine-Westphalia, relevant research institutions.
Budget available	No financial support.
Evaluation	No evaluation available.
Sources	https://www.in4climate.nrw/en/index/. https://www.wirtschaft.nrw/treibhausgasneutrale-industrie.

27) SME Initiative Energy system transformation and climate protection	
Description	The SME initiative is a joint project of BMWi, BMU, Deutscher Industrie- und Handelskammertag (DIHK) and ZdH. The first funding period expired on 31 December 2015. The second phase of the SME initiative was launched on 1 January 2016 and ran until 31 December 2018. Seven environmental centres of the crafts sector, which support regional development workshops in their districts, were included. In addition, around 10 000 company contacts were made throughout the federal Government to raise awareness of the topic of energy efficiency and 375 companies were visited directly. On 1 January 2019, a further period of the SME initiative was launched to continue the projects already started and to design new measures such as digitalisation, the development of a roadmap for SMEs and mobility-related topics. The measures are implemented on the basis of action plans co-ordinated with the environment centres and the ZdH, which are part of the approvals.

7.2. Assessment of the German policy mix

This section discusses the effectiveness of the overall policy mix to induce the low-carbon transition in the heavy industry in Germany, with a particular focus on the following technologies:

- hydrogen for process heating and feedstock (including blue and green hydrogen)
- electrification of process heating
- carbon capture and storage (CCS)
- bio-based materials
- recycling of materials (notably metals and plastics).

7.2.1. Decarbonisation technology developments

In recent years, the German policy mix has been extended by several instruments aiming at the development and large-scale market introduction of decarbonisation technologies in heavy industries. Five instruments can be particularly mentioned in this category (numbers refer to the list in the previous section and are used for the analysis):

- 5) National Decarbonisation Programme
- 6) Programme CO_2 Avoidance and Use in Basic Industries: Under preparation (effective 2 January 2021)
- 7) National Hydrogen Strategy: CCfD pilot
- 8) National Hydrogen Strategy: IPCEI "Hydrogen for industrial production"
- 9) EU ETS Innovation Fund: further development of the NER300 programme.

While all instruments aim at decarbonisation of heavy industry, they differ substantially in technology focus (Table 7.2). The *EU Innovation Fund* shows the broadest technology coverage and even includes switch to new low-carbon products. While the *Decarbonisation Programme* was first planned to only address process-related emissions, it was finally published with a broader technology scope. However, downstream activities like material efficiency or recycling are out of scope. The *Programme for CO_2 avoidance* was still under preparation and not finally published as of January 2021. It is currently intended to address

CCS/CCU as well as transport technologies. The *IPCEI for hydrogen* and the *CCfD Pilot* both aim at building large-scale industrial installations using hydrogen (green or blue) to replace fossil fuels. Overall, the programmes show a relatively complete technology coverage for the major decarbonisation options: hydrogen, electrification and CCS/CCU.

Table 7.2. Overview of technology scope of key technology development policies

2/dark green= high relevance; 1/light green = relevant; 0/white = out of scope

	TRL	Mitigation technologies						
Technology focus of policy		Hydrogen	Electrification	CCS/CCU	Bio-based materials	Circularity	Material efficiency	Energy efficiency
5) Decarbonisation Programme	4-9	2	2	1	1	0	0	0
6) CO_2 Avoidance and Use	8-9	0	0	2	0	0	0	0
7) Hydrogen CfDs	8-9	2	0	0	0	0	0	0
8) IPCEI Hydrogen	8-9	2	0	0	0	0	0	0
9) EU ETS Innovation Fund	6-9	2	2	2	2	2	2	0

Source: Fraunhofer Institute.

The three programmes *CO_2 Avoidance and Use, Hydrogen CCfDs and IPCEI for Hydrogen* mainly target large-scale industrial plants, while the *Decarbonisation Programme* and the *EU Innovation Fund* are also open for smaller demonstration projects.

The potential impact of these programmes can be estimated based on the available budget. This is summarised in Table 7.3 for the time horizon foreseen in the programmes' current planning. However, it is likely that the programmes continue beyond the currently planned time horizon, which will substantially increase the total budgets available until 2030.

The total budget of the programmes sums up to about EUR 5 billion, cumulated over the respective planned time horizon of the individual programmes, which ends between 2025 and 2030. The first programmes started to accept applications in 2020 (*EU Innovation Fund* and *Decarbonisation Programme)*. However, it is likely that most of the programmes will run longer than today's budget planning indicates. More specifically, a continuation of the programmes on the currently planned level towards 2030 would increase the total cumulated budget to EUR 12 billion.

From the total budget of about EUR 5 billion, about EUR 4 billion are directed exclusively towards CAPEX funding, EUR 550 million address OPEX (CCfDs) and EUR 800 million are more flexible (EU Innovation Fund). The total CAPEX funding seems a relevant amount, when compared to costs of industrial scale projects like a new DRI steel plant (EUR 0,4 billion invested for DRI+Electric Arc Furnace (EAF) plant of 1 Mt/y of crude steel production), a cement clinker kiln equipped with carbon capture (EUR 0.15 billion invested for 1 Mt/y clinker production). Thus, the estimated budgets are sufficient to support financing of several industrial-scale installations.

However, while the CAPEX funding seems substantial, the available funding for OPEX seems rather insufficient to close the gap between the traditional fossil-based processes and low-carbon production processes. Operational costs of low-carbon production processes can outweigh capital expenditures in these technologies within a few years, especially at low or exempted carbon prices, compromising the business case for low-carbon installations. In particular, hydrogen-based technologies show very high OPEX costs compared to fossil fuel alternatives. Assuming an emission quota price increase of about EUR 30 on average and hydrogen costs of EUR 150 per MWh, the OPEX cost gap is often several times higher than CAPEX costs for technologies like DRI steelmaking or the use of hydrogen for methanol/ethylene production. On the other side, assuming electricity costs of EUR 40 per MWh (today's tariff for very large electricity consumers) direct electrification options like electric glass melting might become cost-competitive without additional OPEX funding. CCS also requires comparably little OPEX funding.

Table 7.3. Estimate of planned budgets for the technology development programmes

Programme	CAPEX/OPEX?	2020	2021	2022	2023	2024	2025	> 2025	Total
5) Decarbonisation Programme	CAPEX	80	310	500	500	500			1 890
6) CO_2 Avoidance and Use	CAPEX	-	120	120	100	80	80		500
7) Hydrogen CfDs	OPEX		-	250	300				550
8) IPCEI Hydrogen	CAPEX	-	250	250	250	250	250	250	1 500
9) EU ETS Innovation Fund	CAPEX & OPEX	-	80	80	80	80	80	400	800
Total		80	760	1 200	1 230	910	410	650	5 240
CAPEX		80	680	870	850	830	330	250	3 890
OPEX		-	-	250	300	-	-	-	550
CAPEX & OPEX		-	80	80	80	80	80	400	800

Note: Budgets show only the share that is addressing industry decarbonisation, in case programmes also target other sectors such as energy. Estimates for the budget of the EU Innovation Fund based on the total projected available budget of ~EUR 10 billion in the EU, the population share of Germany and the assumption that 50% of the projects goes to the industry sector. For the IPCEI for Hydrogen, only the share going to the industry sector is taken into account.
Source: Fraunhofer Institute.

In summary, the recent introduction of specific programmes aimed at the development and industrial upscaling of key technology solutions for industry decarbonisation can be regarded as central milestones in establishing a policy mix for the transformation of the German industry sector towards GHG neutrality. The foreseen overall budgets are relevant and the technology scope covers the most important options. However, with the current regulatory frame (energy prices, hydrogen production costs and EU ETS), the budgets are most likely not sufficient to close the OPEX gap and make hydrogen-based technologies cost-competitive with today's fossil fuel-based technologies. Approaches to close this gap can include an ambitious minimum price path in the EU-ETS, higher budgets for CCfDs - if the instrument is working - or a supply-side approach that makes (green) hydrogen available at lower prices to industrial consumers. In addition, the creation of lead markets could generate higher product prices.

7.2.2. Material efficiency and circular economy

The relevance of material efficiency and the circular economy for achieving national and EU climate goals is well established.[9] In this context, increasing material efficiency is considered desirable to trigger the decarbonisation of the German industrial sector, although the implementation of material-based strategies does not necessarily mean a reduction in emissions due to, e.g. higher energy demand. Consequently, these strategies and the related policies need further assessment and evaluation against adequate targets, which lies beyond the scope of this report.

The German policy mix addressing material efficiency and circular economy is framed by the *German Resource Efficiency Programme ProgRess III* and comprises legislative as well as financing instruments. The implemented legislation in Germany is mostly a one-to-one implementation of the *EU Waste Framework Directive* and hence, the *EU Circular Economy Action Plan*. On a few aspects, the national legislation goes beyond the EU requirements. The financing instruments, with a total budget of EUR 490 million from 2018 to 2024, are mostly focussed on the funding of R&D projects in construction and plastics. An exception is the *r+Impuls funding guideline*, which helps bring technologies to the market.

Similar for decarbonisation technology support, the funding of CAPEX is more common during the implementation phase. In general, the effectiveness of these policies is questionable since the aim of the *German Resource Efficiency Programme Progress II* of doubling the resource productivity from 1994 to 2020 is expected to be missed. Nevertheless, recycling quotas defined by the relevant legislation have been achieved.

Figure 7.3. Comparison of recycling rates of residential waste, packaging and other waste

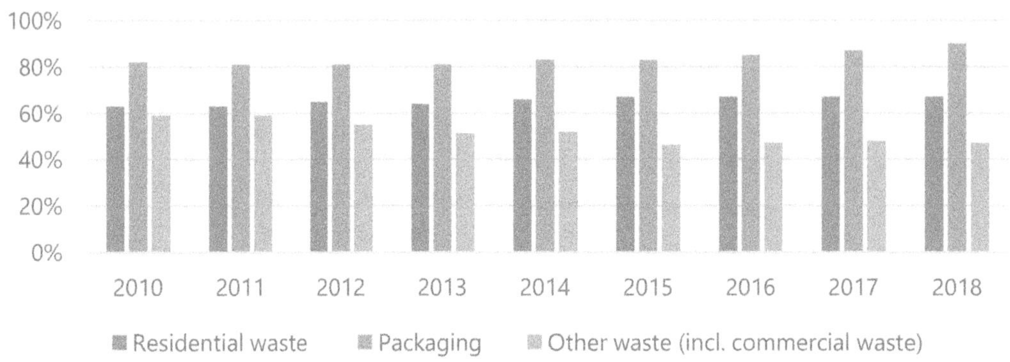

Note: Abfallbilanz - 2018 - Statistisches Bundesamt, http://www.destatis.de.
Source: Fraunhofer Institute

The Circular Economy Act defines recycling as the recovery of waste for the original or other purposes excluding energetic recovery, which therefore includes the preparation for recycling and the storage of waste. The calculation of recycling rates is obtained from an input-based method, which consists of comparing the input of the recycling processes with the total quantity of waste. In practice, the input that is actually recycled varies widely from 10% to 90%. In particular, incorrect sorting leads to the energetic recovery and disposal of the remaining quantities. The relevant waste types and the associated recycling rates are shown in Figure 7.3. While packaging stands out due to a high and increasing recycling rate, the rate for other waste has been decreasing since 2010.

The much-discussed plastic waste recycling rate is about 47% in 2017 and 2019.[10] Even though this information is used frequently, e.g. by the Parliament, the Environment Agency or the plastic packaging industry association,[11] its accuracy is questioned because the input-based calculation method does not consider losses during recycling. Additionally, exported waste is considered to be recycled even though the actual implementation is not tracked.[12] To overcome these challenges the recycled share of plastic processing is proposed as an indicator. This key figure compares plastic products from recycling with the total amount of processed plastics in Germany. Consequently, exported recycled plastics and quality losses during recycling are not considered. In Germany, recycled plastics are typically used in the construction sector, in agriculture and for the production of packaging. In 2017 the recycling share was about 12% and in 2019 about 14%. Historical data are not available for comparison.[13]

A similar approach calculating the share of secondary pre-materials is used for aluminium, copper and steel recycling as shown in Figure 7.4. The shares of secondary aluminium, copper and steel scrap are more or less constant over time. The highest share of recycled material is used for aluminium production.

Figure 7.4. Comparison of secondary pre-material share for aluminium, copper and steel

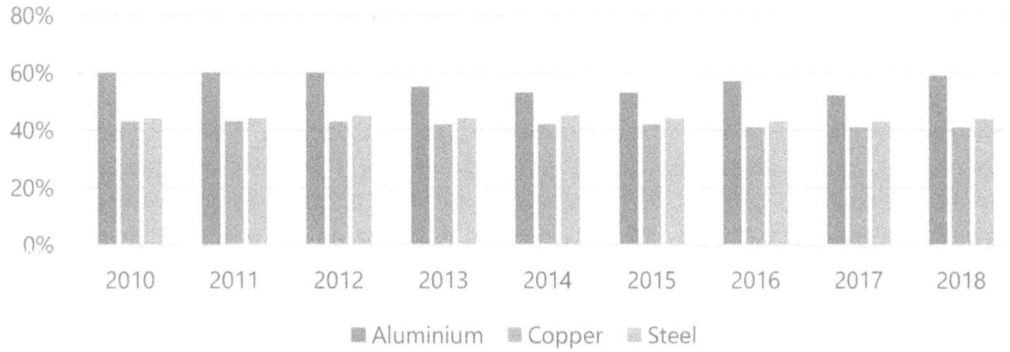

Note: For details see https://www.bgr.bund.de/DE/Themen/Min_rohstoffe/Produkte/produkte_node.html.
Source: Fraunhofer Institute.

The challenges of the input-based calculation method of recycling rates have been considered in the amendment of the EU Waste Framework Directive in 2018.[14] The new rules require an output-based calculation method, so that the output of the recycling plants is accounted for in the calculation. Hence the losses are taken into account. The required recycling quotas were lowered accordingly in the *Circular Economy Act*. Due to the newly introduced output-based calculation method the recycling rates shown in the preceding sections cannot be compared with the recycling quotas directly. A transfer of input-based recycling rates for residential waste in 2015 has shown, however, that the output-based recycling rates are significantly lower (input-based recycling rate for residential waste in 2015: 67%; output-based recycling rate for residential waste in 2015: 36-40%). In practice, a share depending on the specific waste type of the input material is used for energetic recovery.[15] Compared to the current legislation the quotas would consequently not be fulfilled. Nevertheless, the actual recycling rates for the relevant time period are not yet available. Hence, an assessment of the effectiveness of the policy mix from this perspective is currently not possible.

Recent Faunhofer-ISI work evaluates the ability of the policy mix to facilitate the circular economy innovation system in Germany (Gandenberger, 2021[1]). The conclusion is that ProgRess III does not enable the transformation from a linear to a circular economy for two reasons: non-existent markets for secondary products and insufficient financial resources for innovations. Therefore, ProgRess III would not achieve its objectives as framing for the circular economy. Recent amendments to the legislative framework and especially the Packaging Act, as well as further emerging technologies and innovations, are not considered in this evaluation. Two major approaches in this context are the chemical recycling of plastics and the transformation to a bioeconomy. In 2020 the National Bioeconomy Strategy was published by the German Government. The strategy includes general objectives and action fields focussing on the potential assessment and (inter-)national collaboration. The use of biogenic materials in industry is also mentioned, but limited by land availability.[16] The topic was additionally mentioned in *ProgRess III*, part of *FONA4* and to a smaller extent considered in funding guidelines. Nevertheless, the topic is less present in the societal and political discourse about industry decarbonisation - in contrast to chemical recycling of plastics.

The 2018 European Strategy for Plastics discusses chemical recycling as a promising option for the recycling of plastic waste. Chemical recycling summarises different technology options for the depolymerisation of plastic as preparation for recovery.[17] In accordance with the *EU Waste Framework Directive* and the national *Circular Economy Act,* chemical recycling contributes to the recycling quota achievement. In contrast, according to the German Packaging Act, chemical recycling is classified as recovery and not as recycling - just like the energetic recovery. Consequently, it can contribute to the recovery quota defined in the Packaging Act (90%) but not to the recycling quota (65%). Chemical recycling can thus substitute energetic use prospectively.

The Federal Ministry for the Environment, Nature Conservation and Nuclear Safety currently supports this legislative design. On the one hand, chemical recycling is perceived less ecologically reasonable due the high process energy demands. On the other hand, the incentives induced by the Packaging Act shall be ensured and risks avoided for extended sorting and recycling capacities. Thus chemical recycling is assessed exclusively as an alternative to the energetic recovery of contaminated plastic waste if economically and ecologically feasible.[18] A comparable position is taken by the Federal Environment Agency. However, it emphasises the need for further research to assess economic and ecologic advantages of chemical recycling.[19] Especially the liberal opposition party is challenging the position of the Federal Ministry for the Environment, Nature Conservation and Nuclear Safety and thereby the Federal Government against the backdrop of the intensification of the recycling quotas and technology openness.[20]

While environmental organisations such as the Nature and Biodiversity Conservation Union and Greenpeace support the current position of the Federal Government,[21] the national and the European chemical industry associations are pointing to barriers for technology development.[22] The legislative demands of the environmental organisations include the delimitation of chemical recycling to processes which again produce plastic and the inclusion of chemical recycling in the waste hierarchy between recycling and energetic recovery. On the contrary, the industry associations demand the full classification of chemical recycling as recycling. The development of this discourse will have an influence on the decarbonisation of the industry - even if the direction has not yet been determined.

In a nutshell, the German policy mix in the field of material efficiency and circular economy does not currently seem to have a strong impact on industry decarbonisation. In the evaluation of the innovation system for circular economy, Gandenberger (2021[1]) proposes dynamic standards for the use of secondary materials to create markets as well as product design standards enabling repair and recycling. He underlines the importance of accompanying measures to establish new business models.[23] Similar aspects have also been identified at the international level (IRP, 2020[2]). Particularly, steel and cement but also plastics, paper, glass and metals are relevant and should be targeted directly.[24] Technologies such as chemical recycling of plastics but also an increased share of secondary steel as well as an increased cement/concrete recycling are key solutions for the decarbonisation of the industry. Downgrading of materials should be avoided widely. Also the use of alternative or bio-based materials in the construction sector can have a significant impact. Additionally, an overall policy strategy focussing on decarbonisation via material efficiency and circular economy would benefit from co-ordinating the efforts on the national and the EU levels.

7.2.3. Overall assessment

An overall assessment of the policy mix and possible ways forward to make it more effective for decarbonisation are laid out below. Table 7.4 offers an overview of all policies in scope and their respective technology focus.

Traditionally, the policy mix to decarbonise the industry sector in Germany focused strongly on **energy efficiency** support policies like audit schemes or grants of efficiency improvement projects. These mostly addressed SMEs and lighter industries. A second major traditional pillar of the policy mix are regulations for **recycling** and the sorted collection of consumer waste. This resulted in high recycling rates for products like paper or glass. The main policy addressing **decarbonisation in the heavy industry** was for a long-time the EU ETS. **Energy taxes** and the EEG-levy are relevant mainly for small companies, while large energy consumers receive large tax exemptions.

GHG reduction targets have also evolved over the past decade. The Climate Action Plan 2050,[25] adopted by the German Government in November 2016 sets out concrete actions to achieve the target of the Paris

Agreement to achieve CO_2-neutrality by mid-century and defines milestones for the year 2030 at the sectoral level. For the industry sector it sets a target of 49-51% GHG reduction compared to 1990. To achieve the sectoral target, substantial efforts on mitigation technologies are needed, including large-scale investments in decarbonisation technologies. The targets were further strengthened through the climate protection law, which went into force in December 2019. It defines a (linear) path for emission reduction in all sector towards the 2030 milestone and requires additional policy action, if the monitored emissions fall short of the minimum path in a certain year. Overall, the sectoral target and the clear commitment to GHG neutrality by 2050 have facilitated activities to decarbonise industry from private, but also public actors, as it becomes obvious that the industry sector also needs to reduce emissions drastically to achieve the overall reduction target.

Two important milestones for the industrial transition were the publication of the Hydrogen Strategy (June 2020) and the Climate Action Programme 2030[26] (October 2019). Among others, they initiate several major **technology development programmes** (see policy fact sheets) providing investment support for the industrial-scale market-introduction of decarbonisation technologies in heavy industry sectors.

Despite this recent amendment, the policy mix is in several aspects not sufficient to put the industrial transition on track towards decarbonisation by 2050. These mainly relate to the fact that it does not provide a clear and robust perspective for the competitive operation of large-scale low-carbon plants in the medium term (towards 2025/2030). Here, policy initiatives could address the following issues:

- Technology development programmes currently focus on CAPEX support and lack **OPEX support**, which is particularly important for hydrogen-based technologies in the short and medium term. Expanding the pilot CCfD programme - if successful - can be a way forward. Alternatively, the supply of hydrogen at lower costs could also reduce this OPEX gap.
- **Lead markets for green products** that allow for a price-premium on products made from CO_2-neutral basic materials, like a car made from CO_2-neutral steel or a building from CO_2-neutral concrete, do not exist. Among others, public procurement could close this gap and induce niche markets.
- The EUA price in the ETS is too low to make key decarbonisation technologies like hydrogen, electrification or CCU/CCS cost-competitive and lacks a clear perspective that allows considering increasing CO_2-prices in cost-benefit assessments for new investments. A **minimum CO_2-price path** could solve both issues and provide a clear perspective for low-carbon investments towards cost-competitiveness.

Furthermore, the huge amounts of **CO_2-neutral energy carriers** required to operate CO_2-neutral industrial-scale plants (electricity, hydrogen, green gas) are not yet available. Even more, there is still a huge uncertainty by when and if such energy carriers will be sufficiently provided at a competitive price. For companies to make investments worth of several hundred million euros, the supply of such critical energy carriers needs to be ensured. This also includes the local availability of e.g. hydrogen and the needed **infrastructure** for generation/import and transport. For instance, investors in large-scale DRI-steel plants need to know if there will be access to a hydrogen network at a certain date in the future and if hydrogen is a strategic part of Germany's industry decarbonisation strategy. Thus, the industry policy mix also links to infrastructure planning.

In some sectors, **process emissions** cannot be mitigated by switching energy carriers or process routes. Cement and limestone production are the most prominent and relevant examples. Deep decarbonisation of these sectors most likely requires **CCS** or **CCU**. While the *Programme for CO_2 Avoidance and Use in Basic Industries* is currently being implemented, there is still a huge uncertainty for investors due to the public opposition towards CO_2 storage in Germany. Although this opposition was initially directed towards CCS for coal-fired power plants, it is not evident that the public opinion can distinguish CCS for process-related emissions. For CCU, a major challenge will be to find uses with a long-term storage - substantial R&D is still needed.

Another area where the current policy mix needs amendment to come on track towards industry decarbonisation is the entire field of **material efficiency and circular economy** along the industrial value chains down to the end-user sectors. CO_2-prices are not included in the prices of most end-consumer products. Consequently, CO_2 is not factored into investment decisions when for example materials are used to construct buildings or cars.

Circular Economy policies still show a rather traditional focus on the collection and recycling of waste. While some improvements were made (e.g. including stricter regulations on commercial waste), particularly materials with a very high emission intensity still show very low shares of secondary production routes. Circular economy policies can more effectively contribute to decarbonisation if amended in the following directions:

- Stronger focus on circularity of **plastics** products in order to close carbon cycles by including chemical recycling and avoid downgrading.
- Further replacing primary **steel** production by secondary production is a very effective decarbonisation measure, but would require improved collection of steel scrap and also use secondary steel for high-quality products, e.g. in the automobile industry.
- Development and use of alternative materials to decarbonise the construction sector and especially **concrete** production.

These goals require the creating of **markets for recycled products** and implementation of uniform product standards on the national and the European level.

Table 7.4. Overview of the German policy mix towards industry decarbonisation and respective technology focus

(2/dark green= high relevance; 1/light green = relevant; 0/white = out of scope)

Policy Instrument	Industry type		Mitigation technologies							TRL
	Heavy industry	Light industry	Hydrogen	Electrification	CCS / CCU	Bio-based materials	Circularity	Material efficiency	Energy efficiency	
Carbon and energy pricing										
1) EU emissions trading (EU)	2	0	1	1	1	0	0	0	1	-
2) National emissions trading	0	2	0	0	0	0	0	0	1	-
3) Energy taxes	0	1	0	0	0	0	0	0	1	-
3) Energy taxes: Exemptions and EMS	1	1	0	0	0	0	0	0	2	-
4) EEG-levy	0	1	0	0	0	0	0	0	1	-
4) ÈEG-levy: Exemptions and EMS	2	1	0	0	0	0	0	0	2	-
Technology development										
5) Decarbonisation Program	2	0	2	2	1	1	0	0	0	4-9
6) CO_2 Avoidance and Use	2	0	0	0	2	0	0	0	0	8-9
7) Hydrogen CfDs	2	0	2	0	0	0	0	0	0	8-9
8) IPCEI Hydrogen	2	0	2	0	0	0	0	0	0	8-9
9) EU ETS Innovation Fund (EU)	2	0	2	2	2	2	2	2	0	6-9

Research and innovation										
10) 7th Energy Research Program	1	1	1	1	1	1	1	1	2	All
11) FONA - Research for Sustainability	2	1	2	1	2	1	2	2	0	n/a
12) Progres.nrw - Research	1	0	1	1	1	1	1	1	0	2-4
Material efficiency and circular economy										
13) Circular Economy Act	2	2	0	0	0	1	2	1	0	-
14) ProgRess III	2	2	0	0	0	2	2	2	0	n/a
15) TTP LB - Lightweight Construction	2	2	0	0	0	0	2	2	0	3-8
16) Funding directive "Resource efficient CE"	2	2	0	0	0	1	2	2	0	3-8
17) EU Circular Economy Action Plan (EU)	2	2	0	0	0	1	2	2	0	n/a
Energy efficiency										
18) Federal support for energy efficiency	1	1	0	0	0	0	0	0	2	9
19) Energy audits in SMEs	0	2	0	0	0	0	0	1	2	9
20) Low-interest loans for energy efficiency	2	2	0	0	0	0	0	0	2	9
21) Pilot program "Einsparzähler"	2	2	0	0	0	0	0	0	2	9
22) Funding competition for energy efficiency	2	2	0	0	0	0	0	0	2	9
23) Energy efficiency networks	1	2	0	0	0	0	0	0	2	9
24) Energy audit obligation for LEs (EU)	2	1	0	0	0	0	0	0	2	9
25) Minimum energy performance standards (EU)	1	2	0	0	0	0	0	0	2	9
Other related policies										
26) IN4climate.NRW	2	0	2	2	2	0	0	0	0	
27) SME Initiative Energy transformation	0	2								

Source: Fraunhofer Institute.

7.3. Comparison with the Netherlands

7.3.1. Overall

Major differences are explained by structural differences in the industrial production between the two countries. Energy consumption by industrial sector is a useful indicator to illustrate such structural differences. Figure 7.5 compares the industrial energy demand of Germany with the Netherlands by 2019. The high relative importance of refineries and the chemical industry including feedstock use of energy carriers in the Netherlands stands out. While in Germany, the chemical and refineries industries are also important, energy demand is more equally spread across many sectors. The steel and cement production are highly important in Germany and disproportionately contribute to emissions due to their use of CO_2-intensive energy carriers and process-related emissions. SME-dominated sectors like transport equipment, machinery, food, paper and others show a high contribution to the overall energy demand in Germany.

Figure 7.5. Energy consumption in industry sectors in Germany and the Netherlands in 2019

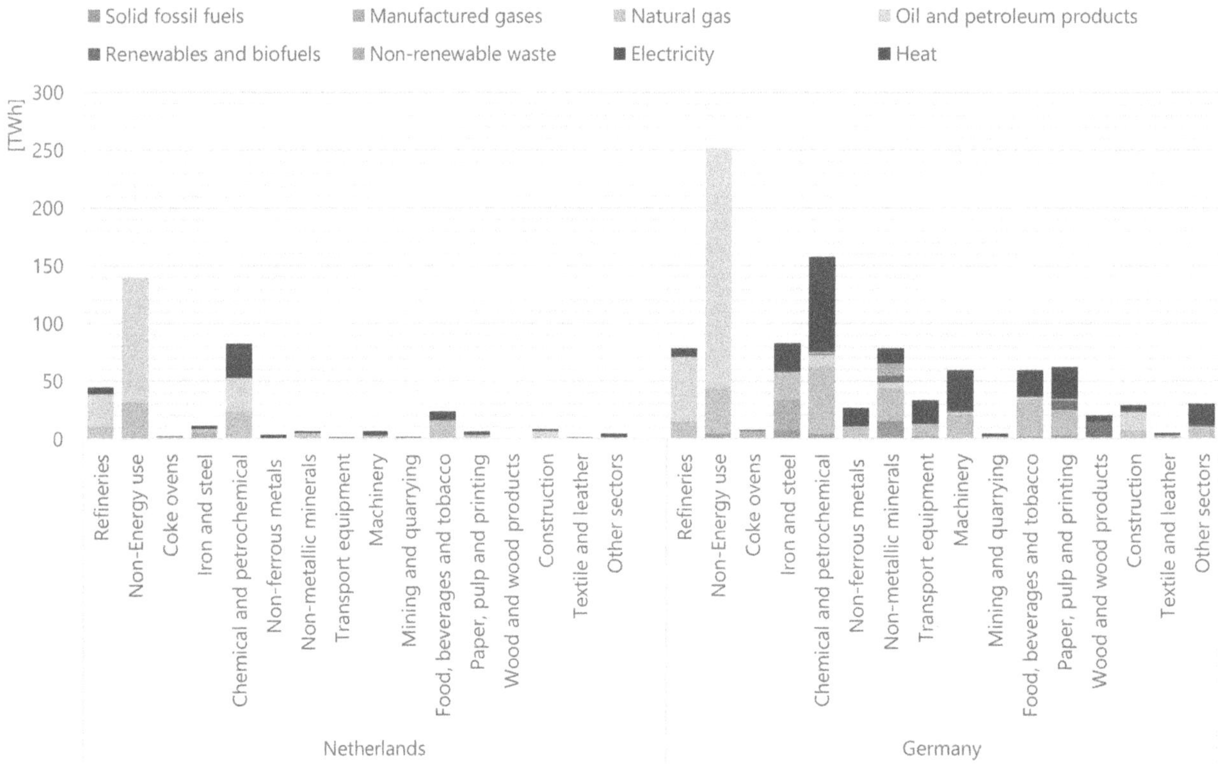

Source: Eurostat.

Major differences in the policy mix between the Netherlands and Germany include:

Sectoral focus

- The chemicals and refineries sectors play an important role in the Netherlands, which explains the important role of hydrogen and bio-based materials.
- The German policy mix has a broader sectoral focus and relies less on bio-based materials. It reflects a high importance of the primary steel production as a major expected buyer of green

hydrogen. Further SMEs are particularly addressed by several energy-efficiency policies, reflecting the strong SME basis in the German industry.

Infrastructure

- The built-up of hydrogen infrastructure is a central requirement for the large-scale roll-out of hydrogen based processes. Here, the current approach taken by Germany is mainly to finance hydrogen infrastructure on project basis (e.g. via IPCEIs). Currently, a strong public role in co-ordinating, planning and operating such infrastructure cannot be observed.

CCS

- In Germany, CCS (for power plants) has experienced strong public opposition and storage of CO_2 is even forbidden in several states. Still, the Government realises the need for CCS (or CCU) to decarbonise the large cement industry. Accordingly, an innovation funding programme with a total budget of about EUR 500 million (cumulated until 2025) for CCS and CCU is currently being prepared to support large-scale demonstration projects.

Electrification

- In Germany, electric process heating is part of CAPEX funding programmes. However, with the current EU ETS CO_2 price, it is not cost-effective, as abatement costs are in the order of magnitude of EUR 200 per tonne of CO_2 and above.

Hydrogen-based solutions: OPEX competitiveness gap

- In Germany, innovation funding policies strongly focus on CAPEX support and high operational costs are still a major barrier for large-scale investments. However, as part of the Hydrogen Strategy, a pilot programme for Carbon Contracts for Difference addressing green hydrogen use has been implemented. The foreseen budget, however, would need to be extended significantly if the entire industry should benefit.

Biomass and bio-based materials

- While the German Industry Association sees a very large role in biomass as a relatively low-cost energy carrier to decarbonise industrial process heating, the Government is more reluctant and the Ministry for the Environment even rather opposes the expansion of biomass use for process heating and other uses. Main arguments are low-costs and CO_2-neutrality on the one hand and on the other, scarcity and competition of biomass potentially needed in many sectors.

7.3.2. Material efficiency and circular economy

The differences and commonalities between the national decarbonisation policies of Germany and the Netherlands can also be identified for specific policy areas such as material efficiency and circular economy. In general, both countries are relying on the given EU framework for product standards. Similar to the Netherlands, Germany has implemented rules for sustainable public procurement by establishing an obligation to give preference to sustainable products. In contrast to these similar legislative instruments and hence similar weaknesses of the policy mix, the financing instruments vary to some extent. In the Netherlands, support is mostly provided via broader policy tools addressing multiple areas as shown in Table 7.5. Consequently, the three major aspects of the policy mix for the industry decarbonisation in the Netherlands identified in this report also apply to the policy tools relevant in the field of material efficiency and circular economy.

Firstly, the financial instruments at the national level in the Netherlands are focussing on demonstration projects rather than on fundamental research. In contrast, the policies in Germany have a stronger focus on R&D projects and fundamental research. Secondly, within R&D the policy tools in the Netherlands - and also in Germany, the policy instruments are mainly untargeted and thereby potentially ineffective on the deployment of radically new technologies. The third aspect considers the large number of R&D policy tools in the Netherlands, with little individual funding potentially leading to a high administrative burden but also a tailored funding. In contrast, the German policy tools comprise larger budgets and hence a lower administrative burden.

Table 7.5 Dutch Financing instruments in the field of material efficiency and circular economy

	Area	Type	Stage	Target group
Circular Economy Implementation Programme	Circular economy in biomass and food, plastics, manufacturing industry, construction and consumer good	Subsidy	Not defined	Industry
DEI+ CE	Reuse; recycling; bio-based raw materials	Subsidy	Pilot projects	Companies, knowledge institutions
Green project loan facility	Environment-friendly, circular economy and sustainable construction projects	Subsidised loan	Not defined	Companies
KIEM GoChem scheme	Sources and raw materials; processes and technology; molecules and materials; processing and application; chain and business models; recycling and upcycling	Subsidy	Innovations	SME, knowledge institutions
MIA/ Vamil	Circular economy and raw materials; CCU; bio-based economy; electrification; reduction of nitrogen and related emissions; greenhouse gas emission reductions	Tax allowance	Not defined	Companies
MOOI (mission-driven research, development and innovation)	CO_2-free electricity system; CO_2-free built environment; climate-neutral raw materials; circular products and processes	Subsidy	R&D leading to first market application	Companies
NWO funding instruments for the Knowledge and Innovation Covenant **(KIC)**	Climate and energy; Circular economy	Subsidy	Fundamental and practice-oriented research	PPP
TKI/ PPP allowance	Bio-based economy; chemistry; energy	Subsidy	Fundamental research, industrial research and experimental development	Companies, PPP
Top Sector Energy Studies Industry	Closure of industrial chains; CO_2-free industrial heating system; electrification; CCUS; other CO_2-reducing measures	Subsidy	Pilot and demonstration projects	Companies
TSE industry	Closure of industrial chains; CO_2-free industrial heating system; electrification; radically new processes	Subsidy	R&D leading to first market application	Companies
VEKI	Energy efficiency; recycling and reuse of waste; local infrastructure; other CO_2-reducing measures	Subsidy	Technology implementation after demonstration	Companies

Source: Fraunhofer Institute.

Besides these general aspects, the policy mix for circular economy and material efficiency are characterised by more specific differences and commonalities. The application of financial instruments in this field in Germany is usually implemented as subsidies while the Netherlands also includes tax allowances and subsidised loans for a more diverse policy design (Table 7.5). Also the target areas of the financial instruments vary. Even though both countries usually do not implement technology specific tools, the funding programmes in Germany are typically sector specific (construction or plastics). Besides the broader policy tools in the Netherlands without sector focus, the Circular economy Implementation

Programme presented in 2019 addressed five sectors in particular (biomass and food, plastics, manufacturing industry, construction and consumer good). Both countries provide measures targeting larger companies, SMEs and knowledge institutions, whereas the Germany policy mix for material efficiency and circular economy focuses more intensely on partnerships between knowledge institutions and companies.

The two emerging technologies described above – chemical recycling and bioeconomy – are promoted more specifically in the Netherlands than in Germany. Especially the bioeconomy is of high relevance for the refinery and the chemical sector in the Netherlands. For the same structural reason, chemical recycling of plastics is also part of the Dutch policy mix. A roadmap for the implementation of chemical recycling of plastics has been established in the Netherlands. Based on a comparable legislative policy mix, it seems that the Dutch financing policy mix enables more targeted actions in the field of material efficiency and circular economy. Nevertheless, both countries lack specific product design standards.

References

Gandenberger, C. (2021), "Innovationen für die Circular Economy - Aktueller Stand und Perspektiven: Ein Beitrag zur Weiterentwicklung der deutschen Umweltinnovationspolitik", *Umwelt, Innovation, Beschaftigung*, No. 2021/01, Fraunhofer-ISI, Karlsruhe. [1]

IRP (2020), *Resource Efficiency and Climate Change: Material Efficiency Strategies for a Low-Carbon Future. A Report of the International Resource Panel.*, United Nations Environment Programme, Nairobi, http://dx.doi.org/10.5281/zenodo.3542681. [2]

Notes

[1] Climate Action Plan 2050 – Principles and goals of the German government's climate policy (bmu.de).

[2] https://www.umweltbundesamt.de/publikationen/effiziente-ausgestaltung-der-integration and http://publica.fraunhofer.de/dokumente/N-599450.html.

[3] https://www.bundesanzeiger.de/pub/publication/sPdNMCSoJMQCRSvn4qr/content/sPdNMCSoJMQCRSvn4qr/BAnz%20AT%2015.01.2021%20B5.pdf?inline.

[4] https://www.bmu.de/themen/forschung-foerderung/foerderung/foerdermoeglichkeiten/details/31/.

[5] https://www.klimaschutz-industrie.de/fileadmin/user_upload/KEI_download_pdf/20200709_Hinweisblatt_Foerderprogramm_Foerderfenster.pdf.

[6] https://dipbt.bundestag.de/dip21/btd/19/236/1923624.pdf (2020-01-13).

[7] https://www.bmwi.de/Redaktion/DE/Downloads/I/ipcei-bekanntmachung-interessenbekundungsverfahren.pdf?__blob=publicationFile&v=16.

[8] Available at: https://www.bmwi.de/Redaktion/DE/FAQ/IPCEI/faq-ipcei.html (2020-01-13).

[9] For instance, increasing material efficiency in residential buildings and light duty vehicles constitutes is a key opportunity to achieve the aspirations of the Paris Agreement (IRP, 2020[2]).

[10] https://www.conversio-gmbh.com/res/Kurzfassung_Stoffstrombild_2017_190918.pdf and https://www.conversio-gmbh.com/res/Kurzfassung_Stoffstrombild_2019.pdf.

[11] http://dipbt.bundestag.de/doc/btd/19/046/1904634.pdf https://www.umweltbundesamt.de/daten/ressourcen-abfall/verwertung-entsorgung-ausgewaehlter-abfallarten/kunststoffabfaelle#kunststoffe-produktion-verwendung-und-verwertung and https://kunststoffverpackungen.de/wp-content/uploads/2020/11/IK-Jahresbericht-2020-online.pdf.

[12] https://www.gruene-bundestag.de/themen/umwelt/deutschland-ist-nicht-recyclingweltmeister, https://www.sueddeutsche.de/wirtschaft/plastik-dm-rossmann-recycling-1.4552045 and https://www.nabu.de/umwelt-und-ressourcen/abfall-und-recycling/26205.html.

[13] https://www.conversio-gmbh.com/res/Kurzfassung_Stoffstrombild_2017_190918.pdf.

[14] https://www.umweltbundesamt.de/indikator-recycling-von-siedlungsabfaellen#wie-ist-die-entwicklung-zu-bewerten.

[15] https://www.vivis.de/wp-content/uploads/EaA15/2018_EaA_059-078_Obermeier.

[16] Nationale Bioökonomiestrategie – Zusammenfassung (bmbf.de).

[17] Chemisches Recycling von gemischten Kunststoffabfällen als ergänzender Recyclingpfad zur Erhöhung der Recyclingquote | SpringerLink.

[18] 2020_EaA_065-070_Janz.pdf (vivis.de).

[19] Chemisches Recycling (umweltbundesamt.de).

[20] Drucksache 19/20175 (bundestag.de) Drucksache 19/21432 (bundestag.de).

[21] Chemisches Recycling von Kunststoffen - NABU Das Wegwerf-Prinzip | Greenpeace.

[22] VCI-Vorlage (bayerische-chemieverbaende.de).

[23] Innovationen für die Circular Economy - Aktueller Stand und Perspektiven: Ein Beitrag zur Weiterentwicklung der deutschen Umweltinnovationspolitik (umweltbundesamt.de).

[24] Resource Efficiency and Climate Change | Resource Panel.

[25] Climate Action Plan 2050 – Principles and goals of the German government's climate policy (bmu.de).

[26] Klimaschutzprogramm 2030 der Bundesregierung zur Umsetzung des Klimaschutzplans 2050.

8. Emerging technologies: cross-country experience

This chapter discusses policy options to accelerate the development and adoption of five technologies that are critical for the decarbonisation of Dutch industry: carbon capture, storage and utilisation (CCUS), electrification of heating, hydrogen, recycling of plastics and metals, and bio-based materials. It assesses their Technology Readiness Levels (TRL) and analyses the main challenges for their diffusion. A patent analysis provides empirical evidence on the performance of inventors based in the Netherlands with respect to these key technologies.

To reach net-zero by mid-century, Dutch industry will need to quickly deploy an array of emerging low-carbon technologies, as shown by Berenschot's modelling exercise. The objective of this chapter is to understand the current level of technological readiness of these various technologies, analyse the policy support that they benefit from in the Netherlands, and assess how other countries are advancing the development and adoption of these technologies in comparison to the Netherlands.

This chapter focuses on five technologies that the previous chapters have identified as critical for the decarbonisation of Dutch industry: CCUS, electrification of heating, hydrogen, recycling of plastics and metals, as well as bio-based materials. It is important to recognise that these technologies are not mutually exclusive. Even though this chapter is organised by technology, interventions in support of one technology could ultimately advance another.

Beyond the assessment of the Technology Readiness Levels (TRL) of the different techniques, this chapter analyses the main challenges for these technologies to thrive and the core policies needed to overcome them and accelerate the diffusion of these key technologies for the green transition. Some of the challenges relate to supply side problems, others to the demand side. Some technologies need more support for capital expenditures, others for operational expenses, while for some other support could come in the form of R&D subsidies, risk sharing or changes in the legal framework.

An important contribution of this chapter is the comparison of the Dutch strategies for the adoption of these emerging technologies with those of other countries, notably Germany. The aim is to show in which areas the Dutch policies differ from those in other countries, and what the Netherlands can potentially learn from these.

Of note, given the large amount of information in this chapter, key messages related to each technology are provided at the beginning of each section.

Finally, this chapter includes a patent analysis, the objective of which is to provide empirical evidence on the performance of inventors based in the Netherlands and how it stands with respect to these core technologies.

In Brief

CCUS and carbon capture and storage

The technological challenge of CCUS and carbon capture and storage (CCS) in industry, as compared to technologies like solar photovoltaics or wind, is that it is not a modular technology and needs to be tailored to each installation. The challenges to its deployment are not only technical. Industry faces performance risks, capital and operational risks, as well as political and legal risks. Overcoming these requires government involvement. Historically, the United States has been the biggest player with respect to CCUS – with the greatest number of existing installations. However, the United Kingdom is stepping up its ambition with respect to CCUS, as evident in Prime Minister Johnson's Ten Point Plan (announced at the end of November 2020). To date, the United Kingdom has the greatest number of planned or operating installations within Europe. Both of these countries have taken great lengths to work with industry to overcome capital and operational risks as well as political and legal risks through different instruments discussed above. The Netherlands provides funding to cover capital costs of CCUS. However, the discussion in Chapter 5 shows that for a blue hydrogen project in the port of Rotterdam, OPEX can mount to EUR 1.2-2.2 million per year which is substantial compared to the EUR 3.4-4.6 million CAPEX. Funding to cover operational costs has only recently become available in the Netherlands, when the Sustainable Energy Transition Incentive Scheme (SDE++) subsidy opened for CCUS and CCS in 2020. In addition, the legal framework is still largely undefined in the Dutch context, for example, the companies' liability with respect to the risk of leakage. These could make it challenging to deploy this technology in Dutch industry at a large scale in the future. Interest from business exists, as the data about applications for the SDE++ 2020 round shows. There seems to be a business case for CCS: seven applicants requested a total of EUR 2.1 billion subsidies for the capture and storage of 2.3 Mt CO_2.

Electrification of heating

Dutch industry has a large potential for the electrification of heating, which refers to an assortment of technologies depending on what the heat is being used for in a given industrial process (i.e. chemical conversion, melting, casting, baking, distilling, separating, drying or hot water). The technology readiness of the electrification of heating depends on the temperature that needs to be reached. The utility of electrifying heat for decarbonisation, however, requires access to low-carbon electricity. It therefore, requires a significant amount of clean electricity available for the Netherlands. The financial attractiveness of electrifying heat (and replacing a functional piece of equipment) rests heavily on the ongoing costs of energy to run the electrical equipment compared to conventional fuel equipment and the differences in fuel prices. The Netherlands offers incentives to cover the capital expenditures for investing in the deployment of these technologies, but it has not yet overcome one of the key barriers to electrification of heating, which is the relative price of fuels. Electricity (net of taxes and fees) is too expensive compared to fossil-based alternatives to make the electrification of heating viable for most technologies in most industries. In addition, the existing electricity tax and surcharge on electricity increase the price of electricity even further without differentiating the carbon content of the fuels used to produce electricity. This is also the case in other European countries, such as Germany. In order to deploy this technology, the relative price of electricity compared to other fuels would need to decrease in the future. While the carbon levy, and the exemption from energy tax on the use of self-produced electricity, are unlikely to be sufficient for most technologies in most sectors at the current time, the combination with SDE++ subsidies could make the business case for some electrification of low-temperature heating. This also follows from the SDE++ subsidy applications for electric boilers and heat pumps for low temperature heating by the paper and food processing industry.

Hydrogen

Hydrogen has a large potential in end-use sectors like industry. For hydrogen to be viable, there needs to be concerted efforts to develop infrastructure, standards (on the origin of hydrogen and its transport for instance), increased research and development on green production, transport and storage, along with international co-operation. The Netherlands Hydrogen Strategy elucidates similar goals and priorities to that of Germany and the European Union. All three hydrogen strategies set targets from now until 2030 for the installation of gigawatt (GW) for electrolysers, prioritise how to integrate hydrogen production with gas and the electricity grid, recognise the importance of standards (e.g. guarantees of origin), and the importance of international co-operation with neighbours in defining these standards and building infrastructure. The key difference between the three strategies is the explicit mention of carbon contracts for difference (CCfD) for hydrogen in the German and European Hydrogen Strategies. This could be because the Dutch carbon levy in combination with the SDE++ subsidy scheme acts in a similar way. However, the costs for green hydrogen per tonne of CO_2 emission reduction are high compared to competing technologies such as CCS or electrification of heating. As SDE++ subsidies are awarded to applicants who reduce CO_2 in the most cost-effective way, little or no SDE++ subsidy is expected to go to hydrogen. Given the high cost of producing hydrogen, it is unlikely that the carbon levy on its own will be sufficient to make green hydrogen profitable in the short term, which is confirmed in our case study on green hydrogen (Chapter 5). The case study shows that the cost for the construction of a demonstration plant and its subsequent operations are estimated to be EUR 70-75 million for CAPEX and EUR 22-31 million for OPEX. The case study shows that the combination of the carbon levy and the available subsidies through SDE++ are not enough to make green hydrogen cost-effective. To bridge this gap, the Netherlands does mention, in its hydrogen strategy, the desire to create a separate fund to help firms cover operational costs, which could have the same utility as CCfD in German and European contexts if designed appropriately.

The circular economy: recycling of plastics and metals

Recycling of plastics is essential to achieve a circular economy and reap the associated benefits for decarbonisation. Mechanical recycling of plastics is preferred to chemical recycling for environmental reasons. Where mechanical recycling is not possible, chemical recycling reaches better environmental outcomes to incineration of waste for heat or electricity production. Recycling of plastics is critical to the uptake of synthetic feedstock by the chemicals subsector, which is expected to rely heavily on advancements in chemical recycling. This is still a rather nascent technology, which is why further research and innovation is necessary to develop better and more cost-effective ways of chemical recycling. This could be a challenge given that the policy landscaping exercise of the Netherlands found that it is much more focused on deployment rather than on these initial stages. Other challenges are contradictory legislation at the EU-level with the Recycling Directive and the need to improve the traceability and accountability of recycled material, so that its use can be counted towards recycled content targets, e.g. through a mass-balance approach. Policy instruments such as taxes or subsidies should compensate for the price difference between cheaper fossil-based plastics and the more expensive recycled plastics. The main reason for the low uptake of recycled plastics is that there is no separate market for recycled plastics and virgin plastics are generally cheaper and of higher quality. Policies such as minimum recycled content standards, public procurement and public awareness campaigns are needed to create the required (separate) market for recycled plastics. Unlike plastics, the technological processes for the recycling of (major) metals is rather well established, but what remains a challenge for Dutch industry is access to scrap. More co-ordination at the EU level is needed to reclassify scrap and output of steel production, such as slag and fly ash, from 'waste' to 'product' in order to reduce the administrative burden for companies. This goes hand in hand with increasing possibilities to import scrap from other countries. While the collection and recycling rates for major metals are already high, the collection and recycling rates for minor metals are still low and therefore there is a great potential for improvement here.

Bio-based materials

The large refinery and chemical sectors in the Netherlands offer an enormous opportunity to accelerate the transition to a bio-based economy. Replacing fossil-based materials by bio-based materials, like bioplastics and biofuels, is technologically feasible, but the production of bio-based materials is generally still less cost-effective compared to their fossil counterparts. Additional steps by the Dutch government are therefore needed if the Netherlands wants to achieve its ambition to become one of the most important bio-based hubs in Europe. Subsidies for fossil fuels should be phased out and subsidies for bioenergy and biofuel should apply in the same way to bio-based materials and chemicals. This is necessary to create a level playing field and thus give the bioeconomy a fair chance to thrive. Risks to private sector investments in biofoundries should be reduced to scale up investments. Priority should be given to investments related to conversion technologies. The risk sharing can be achieved through public-private initiatives. One of the most important issues for the development of the bioeconomy is that the demand for bio-based products is lagging behind, which not only hinders investments in production, but also the necessary R&D in bio-based products. Therefore, policies should be implemented to increase demand, for example through quotas, mandates, standards, public procurement and public awareness campaigns.

8.1. Carbon capture utilisation and storage

Key messages

- The Dutch Climate Agreement foresees a significant role for CCS until 2030 and carbon capture utilisation and storage (CCUS) beyond.
- CCUS, however, is still a relatively immature technology with high costs of deployment. In addition, it is not a modular technology, and technological and performance risks, economic risks, and political and legal risks inhibit its greater deployment.
- The United States and the United Kingdom have sought to overcome barriers to CCS and CCUS deployment and share these risks with industry, e.g. by ensuring revenue streams and clearly defining liabilities for leakage.
- The Netherlands has only recently started to overcome these barriers, in particular by introducing a carbon levy and by opening SDE++ to CCS and CCUS in 2020. SDE++ provides funding to overcome the additional costs of reducing carbon emissions by covering part of the operational costs.
- Further improvements are possible by better defining responsibilities and liabilities, for example in the case of carbon leakage and for monitoring the storage sites.

CCUS is one of many technologies that can be used to decrease emissions from industry. Modelling by Berenschot suggests that it will feature prominently in the Dutch industrial transition to net-zero by 2050, particularly for refineries, chemicals, and iron and steel (Berenschot, 2020[1]). Likewise, the Dutch Government views CCS as critical to achieving its 2030 target in the Dutch Climate Agreement (Government of the Netherlands, 2019[2]). Yet, the Agreement emphasises, "CCS should not impede the structural development of alternative climate-neutral technologies or activities for carbon emission reduction" (Government of the Netherlands, 2019[2]). Beyond 2030, CCUS is envisaged, e.g. in the development of synthetic raw materials.

CCS and CCUS are not modular technologies and the scope of CCS and CCUS projects varies widely, as shown in Figure 8.2. For example, since 2004, the K12-B-project has stored a total of only 60 000 tonnes under the North Sea, while the Porthos[1] project is expected to store 2.5 Mt per year.[2] Although the size varies widely, larger CCS projects are generally more cost-effective due to economies of scale (Eccles and Pratson, 2014[3]). In 2020, seven CCS applicants applied for a total of EUR 2.1 billion subsidies from SDE++ for a requested capacity equal to 329 MW, which gives an idea of the size of CCS projects. For the Porthos project alone, approximately EUR 500 million in subsidies will come from the EU and more may come from SDE++. If the cost for Porthos is EUR 53 per tonne (Xodus Advisory, 2020[4]), this would imply that 2.5 Mt emission reduction would cost about EUR 130 million a year.

This section starts with a brief overview of technological readiness of these technologies in industry, followed by an analysis of the current costs associated with their deployment. It then presents the policies in place in the Netherlands to support CCUS, before reviewing instruments implemented in other countries, including tax incentives to facilitate capital investments, options for ensuring revenue streams for CCUS, and public funding incentives to facilitate upfront capital investments. It then overviews a number of other challenges facing CCUS, e.g. lack of clarity on liability for leakage and regulation that holds back the transportation of carbon.

8.1.1. Technological Readiness Levels of CCUS

To date, CCUS globally has mainly been deployed in natural gas processing and ammonia (i.e. capturing via chemical absorption) (IEA, 2020[5]; IEA, 2019[6]). Other large-scale industrial applications are less mature – e.g. for iron and steel as well as hydrogen. Figure 8.1 summarises the Technological Readiness Levels across the chain of CCUS. In terms of usage, CO_2 is typically used in urea production (for nitrogen-based fertilisers) and carbonated drinks. Either of which stores the CO_2 only briefly before releasing it later into the atmosphere. Other promising uses are opening, such as advancements in using CO_2 in building materials and synthetic feedstocks, which are in the demonstration and large prototype phases, respectively as shown on Figure 8.1 (IEA, 2020[5]).

Figure 8.1. Technological readiness across the CO_2 value chain

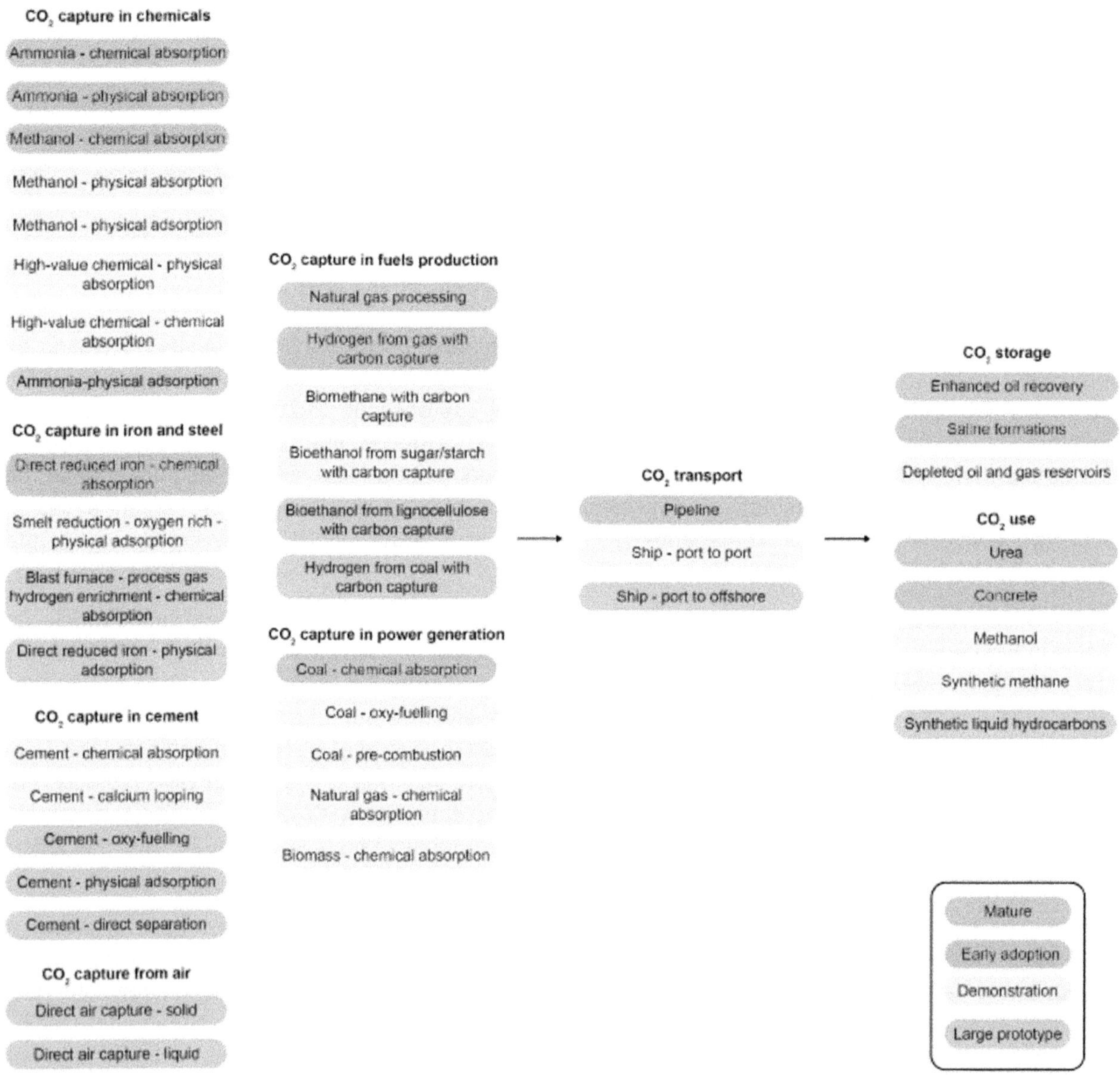

Source: IEA (2020[5]).

Enhanced oil recovery (EOR) has dominated CO_2 storage for the last five decades (IEA, 2020[5]). EOR is the extraction of crude oil from an oil field using the injection of carbon dioxide and water. EOR has provided a value on CO_2, roughly estimated at USD 15 per tonne of CO_2 in the United States, where the bulk of industrial CCUS projects are located (Friedmann, Ochu and Brown, 2020[7]; Beck, 2020[8]). Geological storage is starting to become a viable alternative, with five large-scale sites operating globally (Figure 8.1) (IEA, 2020[5]). Figure 8.2 summarises all industrial applications of CCUS by company, sector, and capacity as of 2020, according to the Global CCS Institute (Beck, 2020[8]).

Direct Air Capture (DAC) is more and more attractive since, in contrast to other CCS methods, it can be a modular technology. DAC technologies capture CO_2 directly from the atmosphere using chemicals (that either bind or stick to it), which can be stored and re-used (Global CCS Institute, 2019[9]). On the one hand, there is large-scale infrastructure for DAC using water that contains hydroxides that capture CO_2 from the air, but this requires temperatures above 800°C, which is typically provided with natural gas (Global CCS Institute, 2019[9]). On the other hand, DAC is a modular technology based on amine materials (which requires lower temperatures) that has the potential for future cost reductions through mass production (Global CCS Institute, 2019[9]).

Figure 8.2. Large-scale CCS projects by industry

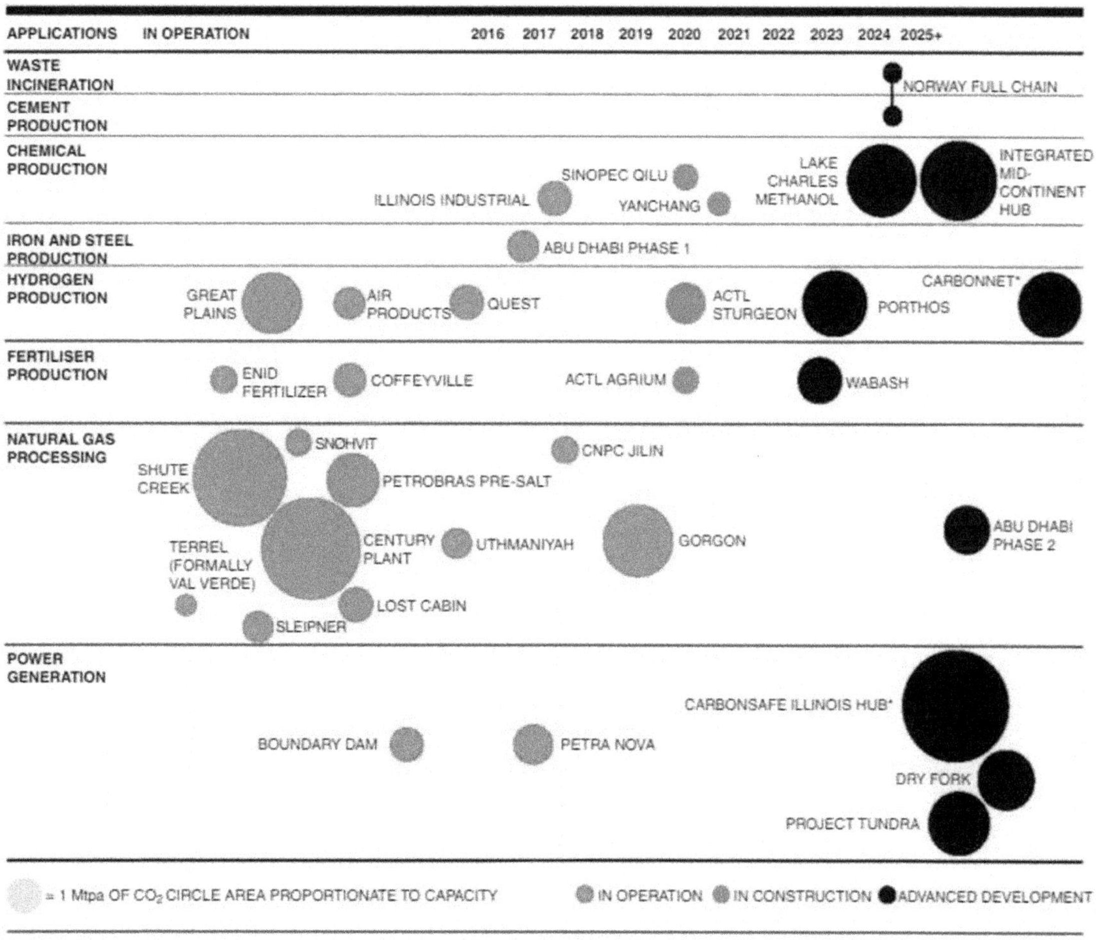

Source: Beck (2020[8]).

8.1.2. Costs of CCUS and regulatory risks

Costs remain a prohibitive factor for many industrial applications of CCUS. Capture, transport and storage, combined with a low valorisation of CO_2, make it a challenge to ensure a viable revenue stream (International Association of Oil and Gas Producers, 2020[10]).

Capture costs

Natural gas processing and ammonia production have the lowest costs (Table 8.1) – which is driven partly by the concentration of CO_2 from the point source and the capture technology (IEA, 2019[6]). On top of this, natural gas processing facilities have frequently used EOR storage, which places a value on CO_2 (making the projects economically viable). Iron and steel still has some of the highest costs (the range reflects the varying capture technologies) (IEA, 2019[6]).

Table 8.1. CCUS, capture cost ranges

Industry	CO_2 Concentration	Average capture cost (USD per tCO_2)
Natural gas processing	96 to 100%	15 to 25
Ammonia	98 to 100%	25 to 35
Ethylene oxide	98 to 100%	25 to 35
Hydrogen (Steam Methane Reforming)	30 to 100%	15 to 60
Iron and steel	21 to 27%	60 to 100

Note: Based on typical CCUS projects in the USA.
Source: IEA (2019[6]).

Transport costs

In Europe, reusing offshore oil and gas pipelines to transport CO_2 is estimated to be 1-10% of the cost of building a new CO_2 pipeline (International Association of Oil and Gas Producers, 2020[10]).Offshore CO_2 pipelines costs are estimated to be between EUR 2-29 per tonne of CO_2 in Europe (International Association of Oil and Gas Producers, 2020[10]). Transport costs by ships typically range from between EUR 10-20 per tonne of CO_2, which is preferable for small volumes over longer distances in Europe. The great uncertainty about the costs of CCS is reiterated by the PBL report on the SDE++ 2020 subsidy, in which the transport costs for Porthos are estimated at approximately EUR 45 per tonne of CO_2, but in which, it also states that previous estimates were only EUR 10 per tonne (EBN and Gasunie, 2017[11]) and EUR 30 per tonne in the PBL draft advice (PBL, 2020[12])..

Storage costs

The cost of CO_2 storage varies between locations, but in general, offshore deep saline aquifers have the highest costs in Europe and depleted oil and gas fields have the lowest costs because of pre-existing infrastructure that can be reused (Figure 8.3). However, the storage capacity in deep saline aquifers is much greater compared to onshore basins or offshore depleted oil and gas fields (International Association of Oil and Gas Producers, 2020[10]), which allows for better prospects for scaling-up and cost reduction (International Association of Oil and Gas Producers, 2020[10]). Economies of scale can be achieved for both transportation and storage costs, making larger CCS facilities more cost effective (Eccles and Pratson, 2014[3]). A cost of EUR 10-15 per tonne of CO_2 is also in line with the estimate of EUR 15 per tonne of CO_2 for Porthos (PBL, 2020[12]).

Figure 8.3. Storage costs in Europe per formation type

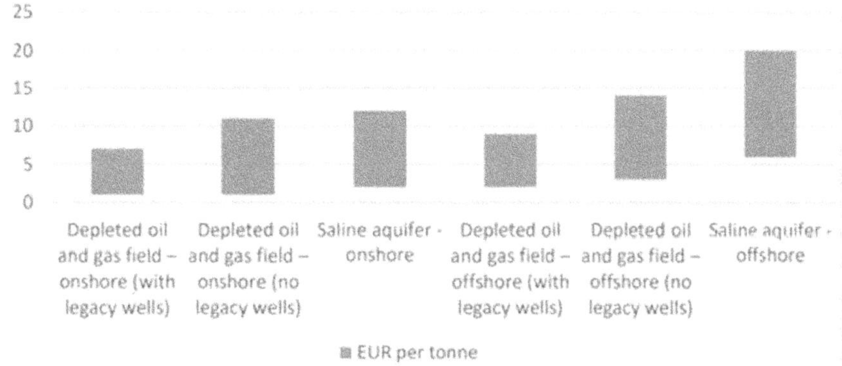

Source: International Association of Oil and Gas Producers (2020[10]).

Projected Costs for Porthos and other CCS projects

Porthos is the most advanced CCS project in the EU. Porthos stands for Port of Rotterdam CO_2 Transport Hub and Offshore Storage. For a period of 15 years, Porthos will store approximately 2.5 Mt CO_2 per year under the North Sea, supplied by Air Liquide, Air Products, ExxonMobil and Shell locations in Rotterdam. This corresponds to 10% of the total emissions produced by Rotterdam's industrial sector, making an important contribution to achieving the climate goals of the Netherlands.

Figure 8.4. Transport and Storage Tariffs of CCS projects

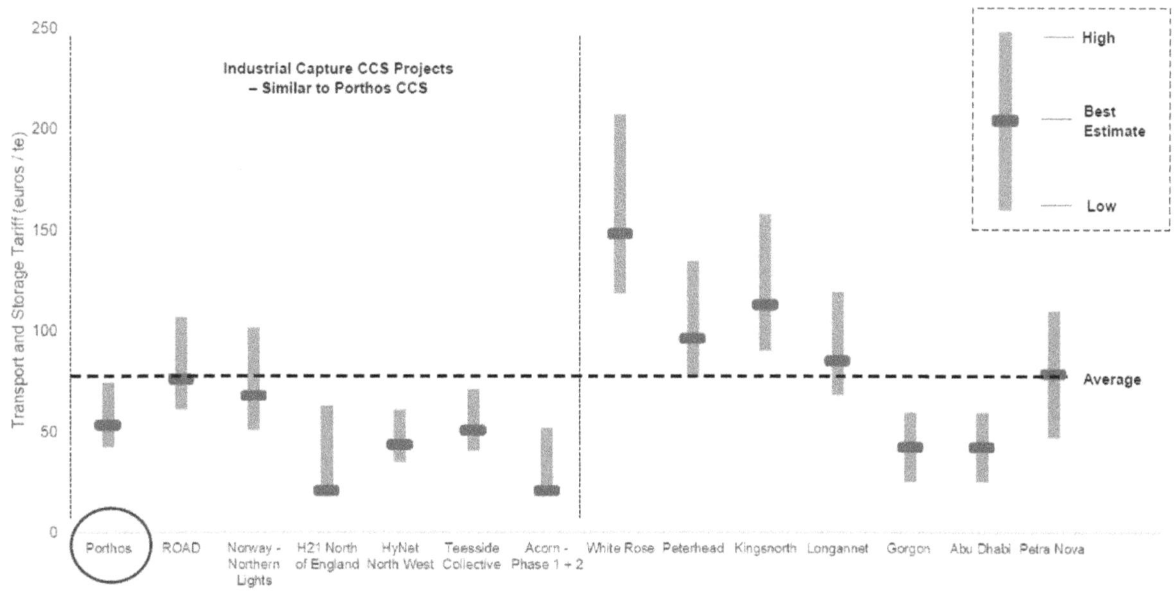

Source: Xodus Advisory (2020[4])

Xodus Advisory (2020[4]) estimate that a transport and storage tariff of EUR 53 per tonne would be enough to make the Porthos Transport and Storage project profitable. They calculate this tariff by comparing Porthos with other CCS projects yielding an average tariff of EUR 47 per tonne. However, this average is calculated based on a wide range of tariffs between EUR 20-100 per tonne for other projects, and by comparing different characteristics of CCS projects they arrive at EUR 53 per tonne for Porthos. Another approach, called the bottom-up analysis, is more like a cost-price approach recreating the Porthos design, and yields an average transport and storage tariff of EUR 51 per tonne with a range between EUR 45-60 per tonne. Both the figures from the Porthos project and the calculations for Porthos conducted by Xodus show that the share of the cost relating to CAPEX (EUR 24 per tonne) is about the same as the share of the cost relating to OPEX (EUR 22 per tonne).

Figure 8.4 shows the transport and storage tariffs of other CCS projects. It shows that Industrial CCS projects generally have lower transportation and storage costs compared to non-industrial CCS projects. On average, EUR 50 seems sufficient to cover the costs of CCS. Of the Industrial Capture CCS projects, the cost for Porthos appears to be average compared with the costs for the other Industrial Capture CCS projects.

Liabilities for CCS leakage

A continual hurdle for CCUS is the question of who can store what and where, the liability and the permanence of CO_2 storage, which challenges traditional risk and liability models. Modelling indicates that the risk of leakage rises throughout a project's first injection phase, then reduces substantially until the site is closed and the maximum storage potential is reached (however, a small risk does remain) (Havercroft, 2020[13]). To make CCS projects viable, regulators and policymakers must allocate responsibilities for CCS operations within a project's lifecycle. Tension can arise between regulators (who represent society's interests) and parties (who would like to invest and deploy the technology).

These questions remain unanswered for Dutch industry. The EU's CCS Directive on the Geological Storage of Carbon Dioxide created some harmonisation between EU Member States and started to answer these questions in June 2009. This Directive has been transposed into Dutch legislation in the Dutch Mining Act (Lako et al., 2011[14]). In September 2011, the Mining Act and subordinate legislation were amended in order to implement the CCS-Directive (2009/31/EC) and the OSPAR Decision 2007/2 (CMS, 2020[15]). This includes, among others, requirements in relation to the contents of the permit (application) and regulations pertaining to the transfer to the State of the responsibility for stored CO_2 after it has been established that this substance has been safely and permanently stored. However, the monitoring plan, the termination plan and the provision of financial security is supposed to be part of the CO_2 storage permit. The final decision on the permit application is taken by the Minister of Economic Affairs and Climate. The Dutch Climate Agreement states that it will address these outstanding issues related to monitoring and liability but has yet to do so.

The European Union amended the Environmentally Liability Directive, which enables national regulators to impose obligations on operators to undertake remedial or preventive measures, when damage has occurred or is threatened. Yet, this is still unclear in the Netherlands. A common element of many CCS-specific legal and regulatory frameworks is the inclusion of detailed requirements regarding site selection, monitoring and verification. Most regimes front-load requirements on operators (Havercroft, 2020[13]).

Transfer of stewardship remains an open question in the Netherlands. Operators also need assurance that storage operations are not liable in perpetuity. Some frameworks, therefore, transfer this liability to the state's relevant authority (e.g. Canada, United States, European Union). The EU instituted the European Commission Storage Directive to transfer liabilities, which many Member States have transferred directly into national legislation. However, those who want to foster the uptake of this technology have gone several steps further. For example, the United Kingdom's extensive transfer provisions encompass any potential civil claim or administrative liability arising from a leakage, *whether the leakage occurred before or after the transfer* (Havercroft, 2020[13]).

Regulation related to the transport of carbon

Two international agreements further hinder the deployment of the CCUS – i.e. the London Protocol and the ETS. The Dutch Government committed in the National Climate Agreement to try to amend these rules to ease the deployment of the technology for Dutch Industry (Government of the Netherlands, 2019[2]).

Article 6 of the London Protocol governs Parties' export of wastes for dumping in the marine environment (IEA, 2011[16]; Global CCS Institute, 2019[9]). An unintended consequence of this Protocol is that it effectively bans transboundary transportation of CO_2 for geological storage, i.e. parties interpret the legislation as prohibiting the export of CO_2 from a contracting party to other countries for injection into sub-seabed geological formations. The signatories to the London Protocol passed an amendment to resolve this issue in 2009; however, two thirds of the Protocol's contracting parties must ratify the amendment for it to come into force (Global CCS Institute, 2019[9]). So far, only Norway, United Kingdom, Netherlands, Finland, Estonia and Iran have done so (Global CCS Institute, 2019[9]).

The status of some forms of CO_2 transportation under European legislation also remains uncertain. Under the EU ETS, covered installations are not required to surrender emissions allowances for the CO_2 they have successfully captured for subsequent transportation by pipelines and geological storage, and they can benefit from the EU ETS carbon price by selling the corresponding allowances (Global CCS Institute, 2019[9]). The scope of the Directive, however, applies narrowly to CO_2 transport by pipelines and those installations that plan to transport CO_2 by other means, e.g. by ships or trucks, would still need to pay for these emissions (Global CCS Institute, 2019[9]).

Risk of CCS translating in more fossil fuel consumption

In addition to the technical costs and risks associated with the feasibility of CCS, there may also be unintended negative effects of CCS on fossil fuel consumption. The risk is that CCS is used as an excuse to avoid further reductions in fossil fuel consumption. Budinis et al. (2018[17]) shows that in a scenario without CCS, 26% of worldwide fossil fuel reserves would be consumed in 2050, against 37% consumed when CCS is available. This difference becomes even larger in 2100. If CCS is the most cost-effective way of reducing CO_2, it will become less attractive for companies to invest more in in the necessary R&D and use of other sustainable alternatives. This may slow down the development of sustainable alternatives such as renewable energy.

While CCS can reduce CO_2 emissions in heavy industry due to economies of scale, CCS could have unintended consequences for the decarbonisation of other sectors. If heavy industry can continue to use and process fossil fuels on a large scale, this would undoubtedly make fossil fuels cheaper elsewhere in the supply chain. As a result, lower emissions in industry risk to be partly offset in the future by increases in CO_2 emissions elsewhere in the supply chain.

Another problem with relying on CCS is that not 100% of CO_2 can be captured (as mentioned in relation to the different costs and varying concentration of CO_2 streams). Budinis et al. (2018[17]) show that these residual CO_2 emissions are the main factor limiting the long-term uptake, more than the costs of CCS.

The strategy of the Dutch government to limit the eligibility of CCS for the main subsidy scheme SDE++ to 2035 may strike the right balance between relying on CCS in the short-run, while maintaining the incentives for the development of sustainable alternatives required in the long-term.

8.1.3. Instruments to increase the uptake of CCS in the Netherlands

National policies

The greatest support for CCS and CCUS comes from **SDE++,** a subsidy for applying CO_2 reducing techniques (Chapter 5). This subsidy is intended for companies and organisations in sectors such as industry, mobility, electricity, agriculture and the built environment. The SDE++ builds on the former SDE+ scheme and extends the scope beyond technologies for sustainable energy production towards technologies that reduce CO_2 emissions such as CCS. In this way, the government wants to ensure that the zero-carbon transition in the Netherlands remains feasible and affordable. A total budget of EUR 5 billion is available in SDE++, of which a significant share is expected to go to CCS and/or CCUS. Indeed, in the first SDE++ call for tender, seven CCS projects were received, totalling around 2.3 million tonnes of captured CO_2 annually over 15 years, and requesting EUR 2.1 billion of total subsidies over the same period.

Since 2020, **Demonstration of Energy and Climate Innovation (DEI+)** subsidies are also open to support pilot and demonstration projects for CCS. The DEI+ transformed the DEI to become a vehicle for development of new and innovative technologies for CO_2-reduction from industry. However, the subsidy percentage depends on the type of project. For DEI+, the maximum budget is EUR 15 million per project.

In addition to support for CSS projects, EUR 10 million of public funding is also available for CCS-related R&D.

The **Dutch carbon levy**, which is discussed in detail in other chapters, is another way in which the Dutch government can make the use or storage of CO_2 more attractive compared to emitting CO_2 and paying a higher price for these emissions. Such a commitment to carbon pricing trajectories can render CCUS investments more viable. For example, the American Recovery and Reinvestment Act of 2009 provided USD 2 billion to develop CCS technologies for coal-fired power plants. Similarly, in 2009 the European Energy Programme for Recovery dedicated EUR 1 billion to co-finance CCS projects.

EU policies

As a member of the European Union, the Netherlands is also eligible for European funds, such as the EU's Innovation Fund and Horizon 2020. Since the Netherlands is a small open economy, it could be more efficient to invest in CCS, and particularly in the R&D component of CCS, at the EU level.

Innovation Fund (Replacement of NER 300)

The EU's Innovation Fund is the largest for financing CCUS in Europe at EUR 10 billion between 2020 and 2030. It finances innovative low-carbon technologies and processes in energy intensive industries, CCUS, renewable energy and energy storage projects. Innovation Fund grants can be combined with other funding sources; for example, with EU instruments like Horizon Europe or Connecting Europe Facility, with national programmes, or with private capital. Up to 40% of grant payments will be given in the project preparation phase, based on pre-defined milestones. The remaining 60%, linked to innovation, are based on verified emissions avoidance outcomes and can continue for up to ten years. The fund's simplicity, flexibility, increased synergies and streamlined governance are a result of lessons learned from its predecessor, the NER300 programme. The first call for proposals was made in 2020, with regular calls expected thereafter.

Horizon 2020

There are a few CCUS projects presently funded under H2020 (IEA, 2020[18]):

- LEILAC (Low Emissions Intensity Lime and Cement), which will pilot a breakthrough technology that has the potential to enable both Europe's cement and lime industries to reduce their emissions dramatically and cost-effectively. LEILAC is based on an innovative carbon capture and storage technology that enables capture of the process emissions in cement production. The EUR 21 million project has received EUR 12 million via the H2020 programme.
- STRATEGY CCUS, a three year programme (2019-22), which supports the development of low-carbon energy and industry in the Southern and Eastern regions of Europe. The programme aims

to identify potential CO_2 transport corridors in relation to industry clusters that can connect them with North Sea CCUS infrastructure is planned. The EU contribution for this project amounts to almost EUR 3 million.

- STEMM-CCS (Strategies for Environmental Monitoring of Marine Carbon Capture and Storage), a project that aims to address gaps in knowledge and capability needed for monitoring offshore carbon capture and storage sites. The EU contribution for this project amounts to over EUR 15 million.

8.1.4. Advancing the uptake of CCUS and CCS: an international comparison

Carbon capture and storage policies in Germany

Unlike the United States and the United Kingdom, which are covered in the next subsection, Germany is not much ahead of the Netherlands in terms of CCUS and CCS.

CCS (for power plants) has experienced strong public opposition and storage of CO_2 is even forbidden in several states. Still, the government realises the need for CCS (or CCU) to decarbonise the large cement industry. As explained in Chapter 6, an innovation funding programme for CCS and CCU is currently being prepared to support large-scale demonstration projects.

The main support for CCS and CCUS comes from a programme on CO_2 avoidance and use in basic industry, which is part of the Climate Protection Program 2030. The focus of this program is on the reduction of process-related greenhouse gas (GHG) emissions in the basic materials industry. The main objective is to further develop central components of the process chain in the field of CO_2 CCS and CCU towards market maturity and thus to create the necessary technical prerequisites for a permanent reduction of process-related greenhouse gas emissions. This involves the entire value chain covering CO_2 capture, transport and storage. This programme provides a total of EUR 500 million subsidies for CAPEX for the years 2021-25. Given the high cost of CCS, this is expected to cover only a few CCS projects.

For investments in R&D, the Hightech-Strategy 2025 and FONA 3 provide EUR 80 million in grants for research on carbon direct avoidance, CCU and CCS.

Compared to the Netherlands, CCS is not widely supported in Germany, but support for CCS is increasing. There are some subsidies to cover CAPEX for CCS, but there is hardly any support to cover OPEX for CCS in Germany as is the case in the Netherlands through SDE++.

Overcoming barriers to capital and operational costs via tax incentives in the United States

To date, the United States has the majority of CCUS installations globally, mainly for Enhanced Oil Recovery (IEA, 2019[6]). The United States has relied primarily on tax incentives to incentivise the use of CCUS, such as the 45Q tax credit (which can be combined with California's Low Carbon Fuel Standard) or accelerated depreciation rates targeted at CCUS projects; and a new incentive may apply within the next few years, such as Master Limited Partnerships. All of these help to create viable revenue streams for CCUS, helping industry to cover the capital and operational costs of CCUS. The Netherlands also offers a tax incentive under the energy investment allowance (EIA) tax, which is allows deductions from taxable income that relate to capital expenditures of specific investments. On average the effective allowance rate has varied over the years covering between 10-15% of capital expenditures (CE Delft, 2021[19]). This said, understanding how the corporate income tax framework works, as a whole, is crucial to understand any underlying technological biases that may exist. For example, with respect to electricity generation, current corporate income tax frameworks can create a technological bias away from generation technologies with high capital costs (Dressler, Hanappi and van Dender, 2018[20]).

The United States recently revised its 45Q Tax Credit (in the Budget Act of 2018), which offers *up to* USD 50 per tonne of CO_2 captured for CCUS operations brought online by 2026 (Krupnick and Bartlett, 2019[21]). This is a steep increase from the 2008 version that offered a maximum of USD 20 per tonne of CO_2 captured (Nagabhushan and Thompson, 2019[22]). The compensation depends on the type of storage: storage through EOR is between USD 10-35 per tonne of CO_2, while storage in saline reservoirs starts at USD 20 ramping up to USD 50 per tonne of CO_2 over ten years (Krupnick and Bartlett, 2019[21]). In its present formulation, the tax credit does not apply to carbon that is captured for re-use, e.g. for urea production or carbonated beverages, since this is not permanent storage (Krupnick and Bartlett, 2019[21]). Moreover, the latest revision eliminates any cap on credits (Nagabhushan and Thompson, 2019[22]). While the 45Q is administratively straightforward, and a fixed price incentivises the most efficient projects, the drawback of a fixed tax credit is the potential overcompensation of some emitters and failure to incentivise others (BEIS, 2018[23]). The Department of Business, Industry and Energy in the United Kingdom is investigating whether tax credits, similar to that of 45Q, could be used strategically to focus the development of CCUS infrastructure in strategic cluster locations to create efficient supply chains for CO_2 (BEIS, 2018[23]), and by consequence, minimise chain risks related to transportation and storage.

In addition, California modified its Low Carbon Fuel Standard (LCFS) on 1 January 2019 to include Direct Air Capture. What this means, in practice, is that any entity that captures and sequesters a tonne of CO_2 from the air can claim a tax credit (at an average price of USD 160 per tonne of CO_2) (Rathi, 2019[24]). In the LCFS, there is no specification of *where* the CO_2 is captured and stored. Therefore, oil and gas facilities with CCS, refineries with CCS, and other CCS projects (e.g. Ethanol with CCS) located anywhere can claim a credit, *if* the fuel is sold for transportation in California, whilst DAC located anywhere can claim the credit (Beck, 2020[8]). This combined with the 45Q means that a company can be compensated close to USD 200 per tonne of CO_2 for storage underground (Rathi, 2019[24]; Beck, 2020[8]). The largest DAC plant in the world is presently under construction in California and the company, Carbon Engineering, claims that this is only feasible because of the combined tax credits that make the project economically viable (Rathi, 2019[24]). States like Montana, Louisiana, Texas and North Dakota also provide tax incentives for CCS deployment, while others like Wyoming, are aiming to substantially progress CCS (Global CCS Institute, 2019[9]).

Accelerated depreciation rates specifically targeting CCUS infrastructure occurs under certain conditions in the United States, which lowers the net present value of taxes paid over the life of a project. In 1986, the US Government introduced the modified accelerated cost recovery system (MACRS), which is a depreciation method that allows tangible investment by firms to be recovered for tax purposes. This takes place over a specified time period through annual deductions for energy projects, in a very favourable five-year MACRS depreciation category (without this it would have depreciated over 20 years) (Friedmann, Ochu and Brown, 2020[7]). Presently, a carbon capture project that *earns the bulk of its revenue from the sale of captured CO_2,* is allowed to depreciate the carbon capture equipment over a five-year MACRS cost-recovery period by virtue of the CO_2 falling into Asset Class #28, "Manufacture of Chemicals and Allied Products," (Friedmann, Ochu and Brown, 2020[7]). An MACRS-like mechanism could be extended to CCUS that is permanently stored rather than sold. Beck (2020[8]) argues that this should be extended to all types of CCUS infrastructure to enable investment in CCUS.

Master Limited Partnerships (MLP) Tax Advantages is yet another option, which has been used to fund over USD 500 billion worth of American oil and gas pipelines as well as some coal-related infrastructure. This is presently under review by Congress in the United States to deepen investment in new energy technologies like CCUS (Financing Our Energy Future Act of 2019/2020) (Friedmann, Ochu and Brown, 2020[7]). An MLP is a pass-through entity for tax purposes, which means that taxable profits earned by a project are only taxed once — at the investor level. Otherwise, profits earned by a corporation that files under Subchapter "C" of the tax code may be taxed twice depending on their structure: first, at the level of the corporation via the corporate income tax, and second, at the shareholder level on dividends received (Friedmann, Ochu and Brown, 2020[7]).

There is further discussion on whether tax-exempt Private Activity Bonds (PAB) could be used to expand CCUS infrastructure in the United States, which is drawing on the success of creating solid waste, hazardous waste, and sewage facilities (Friedmann, Ochu and Brown, 2020[7]; Beck, 2020[8]). PAB lowers the costs of capital for projects by providing debt financing at interest rates that are more favourable, functioning like a public guarantee. Bonds are actually issued by the governmental body on behalf of the private party that will use the capital equipment when it is expected to benefit the public. However, *this private party is obligated to make the payments on the principal and interest*. Benefits of accessing tax-exempt bond market are lower interest rates and more favourable and flexible borrowing terms (Friedmann, Ochu and Brown, 2020[7]; Beck, 2020[8]).

Facilitating investment in CCUS in the United Kingdom

In Europe, the United Kingdom has the most CCUS projects, with six projects planned and existing (International Association of Oil and Gas Producers, 2020[10]). The United Kingdom, however, stepped up its commitment to CCUS even further, as part of its COVID-19 recovery package at the end of 2020. Prime Minister Johnson announced his Ten Point Plan (TPP) in late November 2020, doubling previously announced funding to CCUS in March 2020 (HM Government, 2020[25]). The new commitments under the TPP include: invest GBP 1 billion to support CCUS in four industrial clusters, creating "Super Places" (defined as hubs where renewable energy, CCUS and hydrogen congregate) in the North East, the Humber, North West, Scotland and Wales; establish CCUS in two industrial clusters by the mid-2020s (committing to an additional GBP 200 million); and aim for four of these sites to be completed by 2030 (if possible) (HM Government, 2020[25]). This step-up in ambition will help the United Kingdom meet its target to capture 10 $MtCO_2$ annually by 2030.

Ensuring revenue streams

As explained in Section 8.1.2, the costs of CCUS can still be prohibitively high and great uncertainty surrounds the valorisation of CO_2. The UK Department of Business, Energy and Industrial Strategy (BEIS) will release a plan in 2021 on how to guarantee a revenue stream for industry, which was affirmed in the Prime Minister's Ten Point Plan (HM Government, 2020[25]). This will build on prior work in the UK Government, *Industrial Carbon Capture Business Models*. One of the likely proposals is the creation of a Contracts-for-Difference.

A contract-for-differences (CfD) is a potential avenue for the deployment of the CCUS – presently, under consideration in the United Kingdom (BEIS, 2018[23]) as well as proposed by IDDRI[3] (Sartor and Bataille, 2019[26]). A CfD is between two parties, where the buyer guarantees a price (known as the "strike" price), in this case for CO_2 over a given period. The Buyer agrees to pay the difference between the Strike price and the market price of CO_2. The United Kingdom is drawing on its experience with CfDs in the power sector. An electricity generator receives a strike price from the government-owned Low Carbon Contracts Company – which pays the generator the difference between the strike price and the market price of electricity (BEIS, 2018[23]). The Low Carbon Contracts Company is a private limited company owned by the Secretary of State for Business, Energy and Industrial Strategy (BEIS), with the primary role to manage the CfDs as well as the Supplier Obligation Levy that funds CfD payments. Sartor and Bataille (2019[26]) estimate, for example, that for iron and steel with Steam Methane Reforming of Hydrogen with CCS the strike price would need to be around USD 50 per tonne of CO_2.

The CfD would provide the private sector with certainty about returns from capturing CO_2; the risks of bringing the project online will stay with the private sector. This makes incentives cost-effective, while preventing moral hazard. If the costs of capture are higher than expected, then the government could offer liability caps for unexpected OPEX and CAPEX.

CfD is not expected to be a necessary policy instrument in the Netherlands, as the revenue streams from SDE++ subsidies, lower amounts of paid carbon levy and the selling of dispensation rights are expected to already fully cover the cost of CCS.

RD&D in CCUS

Prime Minister Johnson committed GBP 1 billion to a CCUS Infrastructure Fund in his Ten Point Plan by 2025; the details of which will be released in 2021 (HM Government, 2020[25]). The Ten Point Plan states, "Our GBP 1 billion CCUS Infrastructure Fund will provide industry with the certainty required to deploy CCUS at pace and at scale". The ambition is to capture and store 10 Mt of CO_2 per year by facilitating the deployment of CCUS in four clusters by 2030. These clusters will be the starting point for a new carbon capture industry, which could support up to 50 000 jobs in the United Kingdom by 2030, including a sizeable potential to export their technologies. This commitment has come on top of already existing innovation programmes in the United Kingdom that seek to advance technologies for CCUS even further: CCUS Innovation Programme and the CCU Demonstration Programme.

Research: CCUS Innovation Programme (2018-21)

The UK CCUS Innovation Programme offers grant funding for projects that develop novel technology and processes to reduce the cost of deploying CCUS (BEIS, 2020[27]). The programme started in July 2018 and runs until the end of 2021. GBP 24 million has been allocated for feasibility studies, industrial research, experimental development projects, and infrastructure projects. Below is a list of projects funded under the scheme (as of 2020):

- **Negative CO_2 emissions from full scale BECCS utilising non-amine CCS chemistry**: C-Capture designs chemical processes for carbon dioxide removal. In collaboration with the Drax Group, carbon capture will progress its bioenergy and carbon capture and storage (BECCS) project at Drax Power Station in North Yorkshire in which CO_2 is captured in a plant producing power from biomass. The work includes: an extension of carbon capture's existing pilot facilities at Drax, plant performance and optimisation trials, a chemistry validation and testing programme, and process design development to move towards commercial scale deployment, including re-purposing the existing Drax infrastructure.
- **ACORN CCS – Front end engineering design (FEED) Programme:** Acorn is a full chain CCS project in north east Scotland. The goal of the project is to develop infrastructure and storage using the UK's built (offshore gas pipelines) and natural assets (at lowest cost). The CCUS funding is progressing the detailed engineering for this project towards a final investment decision in 2021.
- **Integration of CCUS technology to a 200 MW Open Cycle Gas Turbine TiGRE Project located in the UK Southern North Sea:** TiGRE™ projects under development by the TiGRE Group assess the feasibility of integrating conventional best-practice CCS technology into a real-life production facility.
- **Translational Energy Research Centre (PACT-2):** Funded by BEIS and the European Regional Development Fund, it establishes a scale of world class research infrastructure that supports the long-term competitiveness and international reputation of the United Kingdom in CCUS. The centre's state-of-the-art facilities will enable UK companies to develop, de-risk, and accelerate their innovations under realistic operating conditions. It will bridge the gap between fundamental research and pilot-scale demonstrations, whilst providing a training ground for the next generation of researchers.
- **HyNet Phase 1:** HyNet is an integrated blue Hydrogen / CCUS project to decarbonise the North West industrial cluster. Phase 1 of this ambitious but deliverable project is to develop the CCUS infrastructure to capture CO_2 emissions from industry and store them in the Liverpool Bay depleted gas fields.

- **Clean Gas Project & Tees Valley cluster Development Select Phase**: OGCI Climate Investments has entered a strategic partnership with BP, ENI, Equinor, Occidental Petroleum, Shell and Total to progress the Clean Gas Project, the United Kingdom's first commercial full-chain CCUS project in Teesside. This feasibility study is an important milestone to build the world's first commercial CCUS project for a gas-fired power plant. The Clean Gas Project will use natural gas to generate power, with CO_2 then captured and transported by pipeline for storage in a geological formation deep under the southern North Sea. The infrastructure created would enable industrial emitters in Teesside and elsewhere to capture and store CO_2 from their processes.
- **Allam-Fetvedt Cycle Power Plant for UK Deployment**: 8 Rivers Capital is conducting a feasibility study for the deployment of the Allam-Fetvedt power cycle. The Allam-Fetvedt Cycle or Allam Cycle is a process for converting gaseous fuels into thermal energy, while capturing the generated carbon dioxide and water. This technology achieves highly efficient and low cost electricity generation with zero emissions through use of a novel supercritical carbon dioxide as the primary process fluid. This technology has been successfully demonstrated at 50 MW scale in La Porte, Texas, and is now being commercialised by NET Power LLC, with 8 Rivers leading development of full-scale commercial projects.

Deployment: CCU Demonstration Innovation Programme (Phase 3)

This programme was designed to encourage industrial sites to capture carbon dioxide which could then be used in industrial applications. The goal of the programme is to demonstrate CCU at a number of key industrial sites in the United Kingdom; to demonstrate and accelerate cost reductions of about 20-45% in carbon capture technology, or about GBP 10-20 per MWh; to encourage a project pipeline of follow-on CCU projects that will help less mature, but more novel technology to be demonstrated at scale; to improve understanding of the cost and performance of carbon capture technology and to de-risk the capture technology (BEIS, 2019[28])

The programme is now in Phase 3: Funding for construction and demonstration. Phase 3 offered GBP 14 million grant funding for a number of construction and demonstration projects. The projects provide: learning opportunities about the best way to configure plants and crucial operational data and experience on performance and degradation of the plants. The funding for projects is up to 24 months; all of which finished before 31 March 2021 (BEIS, 2019[28]).

Phase 2 called for FEED studies for five projects for GBP 5 million (BEIS, 2019[28]). The studies produced cost estimates for the construction and operation of demonstration CCU at the host site. The costs estimates were expected to be within an accuracy of 15% to allow the BEIS Developer to make a final investment decision. The funding for this phase was 6 to 9 months and completed by November 2019.

Phase 1 focused on an initial scoping study for an engineering supplier to work on BEIS' behalf with potential host sites, carbon dioxide users and technology suppliers to produce site-specific cost estimates for deploying CCU at UK industrial sites.

8.1.5. The policies needed to further encourage CCUS

The technological challenge of CCUS in industry, as compared to technologies like solar photovoltaics or wind, is that it is not a modular technology. With a modular technology, investors are more flexible and can more easily reduce costs via learning-by-doing, as well as easily replicate. Chemical absorption (for capture), for example, needs to be tailored and designed for each company. Nevertheless, if more companies use CCUS at the global level, then the costs may go down, and there are still significant cost reductions to be reaped.

However, it is not only technical challenges that hold back CCUS deployment. Greater de-risking may help companies that presently face a number of risks (BEIS, 2018[29]; IEA, 2019[6]; Global CCS Institute, 2019[9]):

- **Technology and performance risks**: those associated with the integration of capture technology into existing facilities (e.g. a temporary shutdown of operations), challenge of space restrictions of existing sites, or performance (e.g. lower capture rates than expected).
- **Economic and market risks**: capital and operational costs, uncertainties about markets for lower-carbon materials through CCS, competitiveness, and valorisation of CO_2.
- **Political and legal risks:** associated with policy, regulation, as well as liabilities.
- **Cross-chain risks**: associated with the integration and co-ordination across parts of the CCUS chain – e.g. transportation and storage.

Overcoming these requires government involvement to bring regulatory clarity, share the ownership of these risks and financially contribute in order to create some revenue certainty and incentivise investments.

The Netherlands has dedicated innovation funding to overcome the technological barriers in CCUS. DEI+ subsidy supports pilot and demonstration projects for cost-effective CO_2 reductions in 2030. CATO is the Dutch national R&D programme for CO_2 capture, transport and storage in which nearly 40 partners co-operate. However, the economic, legal risks and cross-chain risks remain:

- The primary funding mechanism for CCS/CCUS in the Netherlands is the SDE++ Scheme, but the restrictions for the use of the scheme for CCS causes great uncertainty for industry (Government of the Netherlands, 2019[2]). SDE++ can only be used at sites for CCS where there is no demonstrably cost-effective alternative available at the time of the application (which will be determined each year based on independent advice) (Government of the Netherlands, 2019[2]). In addition, there is a cap on the level of emission reductions via CCS that SDE++ scheme will fund: in total, a maximum of 7.2 Mt CO_2 by 2030 will be funded. Lastly, after 2035, no CCS applications will be funded under SDE++, which underlines the temporary nature of this subsidy to encourage cost savings and the development of alternatives (Government of the Netherlands, 2019[2]).
- Under the Climate Agreement, Dutch industry can only store CO_2 under the sea. In other words, no onshore storage is permitted, which is common practice in other European countries (Government of the Netherlands, 2019[2]). For example, five federal states in Germany ban storage of CO_2, which is why the large potential for CO_2 in Northern Germany is untapped (due largely to public opposition). Similar bans exist in Austria, Croatia, Czech Republic, Latvia, Slovenia, Sweden, the United Kingdom, and Norway (International Association of Oil and Gas Producers, 2020[10]). The Dutch Climate Agreement leaves scope for storage of CO_2 in other countries (that are part of the EU ETS), but this would require, on the one hand, changes to international agreements to enable the transportation of CO_2 (e.g. London Protocol), and on the other, a willing counterpart. For the time being at least, the only two options for Dutch industry are to store the CO_2 in the North Sea or to use it.
- The legal framework for CCUS in the Netherlands could be improved. The specific monitoring requirements per storage site have yet to be identified. In principle, the government will embed the statutory periods of liability and responsibility into the storage permit, but this is yet to be determined (Government of the Netherlands, 2019[2]).

8.2. Electrification of heating

Key messages

- There is a large potential for the electrification of industrial heating in the Netherlands of approximately 177 PJ (Chapter 3).
- The financial attractiveness of electrifying heat (and replacing a functional piece of equipment) rests heavily on the energy costs of running the electrical equipment compared to conventional fuel equipment, which depends on differences in fuel prices including taxation.
- So far, the relative fuel prices between electricity and others, e.g. natural gas, have not incentivised industry to electrify heat in the Netherlands like in many other European countries.
- The Netherlands has a number of incentives in place to bring down capital costs of new equipment, but the relative fuel price disadvantage needs to be resolved in order to address the issue of operational costs.
- The numerous SDE++ subsidy applications for electric boilers and heat pumps indicates that the carbon levy in combination with the SDE++ subsidies start to make the business case for the electrification of heating.
- Higher temperature heat pumps need further innovation for applications in industry, and the Netherlands appears to be at the forefront of research and innovation in this respect, with TNO's Heat Pump Programme for 2020 to 2025.

Electrification of heating will play a key role in transitioning Dutch industry to net-zero, particularly for the food and chemicals sectors (according to Berenschot projections). Electrification is the process through which heating that is currently powered by solid, liquid, or gaseous fossil fuels (e.g. natural gas or fuel oil) is instead powered by electricity (Deason et al., 2018[30]). "Electrification of heating", therefore, refers to an assortment of technologies depending on what the heat is being used for in a given industrial process – i.e. chemical conversion, melting, casting, baking, distilling, separating, drying or hot water.

The rest of this section outlines the technological readiness of these different technologies, the business case for electrifying heat, summarises various initiatives to further electrify heat in industry and ends with a discussion of a few other barriers that make it challenging to electrify heat.

8.2.1. Technological readiness of various technologies to electrify heat

Different strategies for the electrification of heat

There are two distinct strategies for electrifying heat in Dutch industry, whose potential varies based on the electrification technology, the energy system, and the industrial production process: 1) flexible electrification; and 2) baseload electrification (Den Ouden et al., 2017[31]).

Flexible electrification can be ramped up and down and could even switch between electricity and another mode (for example, to accommodate fluctuations in the renewable electricity supply). Flexible electrification is promising in industries that use batch processes, especially if the process is relatively OPEX- rather than CAPEX-intensive and there is some overcapacity. This allows to run production processes when the costs of electricity are low, which is when renewable electricity is available.

Baseload is relatively constant and not easily adjustable to accommodate large fluctuations in a future electricity system. Baseload electrification becomes attractive when the electrification technologies offer co-benefits compared to a reference technology, for example a higher efficiency in generating heat (high

Coefficient of Performance), environmental benefits through lower emissions, higher selectivity or otherwise lower production costs or induced product/process (quality) improvements.

A number of technologies exist to electrify the uses of heat outlined above, which can be broadly classified as Power to Heat, Power to Chemicals, Power for Separation, and Power for Sterilisation. Table 8.2 lists these specific technologies.

Table 8.2. Electrification technologies by use

	Technologies	Category
Process heat – steam and hot water, thermal oil	Heat pumps Electric boiler/ electrode boiler Steam recompression/vapour recompression	Power to heat Power to pressure
Process heat – baking, melting and casting	Induction furnace Microwave heating Electric melting Electric arc furnace Plasma heating/plasma recycling Infrared heating	Power to heat
Drying	Infrared drying Impulse drying Impingement drying Microwave drying Vapour recompression Heat pumps with low temperature drying	Power to heat
Distilling and separation	Mechanical Vapour Recompression Filtration Mechanical techniques e.g. centrifugation	Power to heat Power for separation
Sterilisation and pasteurisation	Infrared sterilisation UV Microwave pasteurisation and sterilisation Microwave blanching of vegetables Heat pumps HP sterilisation	Power to heat Power for sterilisation
Direct process input: electrolysis/ electrochemical conversion	Electro synthesis Electro catalysis Plasma chemistry	Power to chemicals Power to specialities

Source: Den Ouden et al. (2017[31]).

Den Ouden et al. (2017[31]) discuss the potential applications of these technologies in the Netherlands (Figure 8.5). Power-to-Heat technologies can be applied for a number of uses. High temperature heat pumps, in particular, appear to be a highly promising technology for electrification in the Dutch context, however, technological readiness is a limiting factor. In contrast, Mechanical Vapour Recompression (MVR) and Steam Recompression are already available although CAPEX support is needed for MVR and heat pumps. Electric boilers are commercially available, but these can be unviable in the current Dutch context due to grid connection costs, capacity tariffs, and relatively high power prices. Power for Separation likely has only limited potential and is mainly focused on the food industry. In this context, there are interesting, current initiatives in the Netherlands to develop existing technologies (ultra filtration, nano filtration, reverse osmoses). Power-to-hydrogen is both relevant in core processes (for instance in producing ammonia) and in utility processes. For Power to Chemicals, flexible production of chlorine seems most promising. This does not lead to an increase of electrification, but rather to a more flexible power consumption (demand side management). Power-to-Hydrogen and Power-to-Chemicals will be discussed in greater detail in forthcoming sections.

Figure 8.5. Timescale for technologies in the Netherlands

	Short term 0-5 years	Medium term 5-10 years	Long term 10-30 years
Breakthrough of electrification categories & promising technologies	High potential: Power to Heat • Steam recompression / Mechanical Vapour Recompression (baseload) • Electric boilers (flex) • Electromagnetic radiation (baseload / flex) • HT heat pumps (baseload / flex) → Limited potential: Power for Mechanical Drive • Replacement of steam drive by electric drive (baseload) High potential: Power to Chemicals • Electrolysis for chemical production, i.e. chlorine / ammonia (DSM)* (flex)	Limited potential: Power for Separation • Ultra filtration/Nano filtration/Reversed osmosis (baseload)	High potential: Power to Hydrogen • Electrolysis (flex) Limited potential: Power to Gas • Electro synthesis (baseload/flex)

Source: Den Ouden et al. (2017[31]).

Main barriers to electrification of heating

As a rule of thumb, the fuel costs over the lifetime of a piece of equipment, e.g. industrial boiler, are typically ten times the initial capital investment (Roelofsen et al., 2020[32]). Therefore, the financial attractiveness of electrifying heat (and replacing a functional piece of equipment) rests heavily on the ongoing costs of energy to run the electrical equipment compared to conventional fuel equipment and the differences in fuel prices (Roelofsen et al., 2020[32]; Deason et al., 2018[30]). The *biggest* barriers to electrification of heating are typically economic, not technical. These include:

- **Fuel and other operational costs**: Where commercially available electric and non-electric alternatives exist for a given end use, relative fuel prices often explain adoption decisions.
- **Capital costs of fuel switching**: Generally, in order to electrify, direct fuel equipment needs to be replaced with electrically powered alternatives. The relative upfront costs vary, and if the switch occurs before the end of useful life of the existing direct fuel equipment, this effectively raises the costs per unit of output.
- **Heterogeneity of industrial sectors**: Each industry sub-sector and product has its own process heating requirements and product specifications that require specific designs and performance requirements for electrified processing (Chapter 3, the 2050 scenario).
- **Risk aversion**: Electric equipment and appliances are not identical to their fuel counterparts, which means industry may avoid them even if it is financially viable. For example, the speed of heat provision is often slower (e.g. heat pumps). Therefore, electrification may introduce financial and operational risks for firms. The impact of this is even more pronounced in low margin, commodity type industries like food processing. To limit this risk, natural gas boilers can be used with biogas or hydrogen.
- **Electricity delivery infrastructure:** Extensive changes in large industrial facilities could require distribution system upgrades and in the long run, transmission system upgrades.
- **Heating temperatures are low:** Using electricity for heating becomes less efficient for higher temperatures.

Electrification is most viable in processes, therefore, "with relatively low energy costs; where the degree of process complexity and process integration is more limited and extensive process re-engineering would not be required; where combined heat and power is not used; and where process heating temperatures are lower," (Deason et al., 2018[30]).

Another potential barrier could be electricity storage, as the production of batteries must increase from 320 GWh of batteries per year worldwide to 1 000 GWh in 2025 (IEA, 2020[33]). Fortunately, battery production has become much cheaper over the past decade, therefore, scaling up the production and use of batteries should not be a problem if investments are made on time. However, building a large-scale battery factory can take two to five years, suggesting investments are needed now.

Research and development on heat pumps for industry

Of the potential technologies for Power-to-Heat, heat pumps are the least technologically ready, especially for high temperatures. Currently, the development of heat pumps for the process industry is driven by scattered national initiatives targeted towards local industry sectors, some of which are taking place in the Netherlands. The main motivation for these development projects is typically focused towards saving operational costs, which result from the energy savings. In Europe, the low priority of industrial heat pumps on the research agenda means that only a limited number of projects containing heat pump developments have been undertaken in recent years.

The following projects have received support from national governments:

- SkaleUp (SINTEF): Heat pump solution for combined process cooling (0°C to 4°C) and process heating (90°C to 110°C) with a combined coefficient of performance of 2.8, resulting in the reduction of CO_2 emissions to near-zero.
- LowCapex and FUSE (TNO, Netherlands): Demonstration of heat pump technology on an industrial scale (2 MW), producing process steam at temperatures between 120°C to 150°C from waste heat at 60°C to 90°C with efficiencies above 50% of the theoretical maximum. The heat pumps developed within these projects have the potential to reduce emissions between 20% and 35% compared to the reference scenario.
- Efficiency in Industrial Processes (Swiss Competence Center for Energy Research [SCCER]): The goal is to create energy efficient technologies and components which can be applied in many different processes such as steam and heat generation and applied to numerous industries, allowing for energy savings between 20-50% with respect to common technologies.
- SuPrHeat (DTI/DTU): Development and demonstration of three pilot scale (500 kW) high temperature heat pump technologies based on natural refrigerants, for supplying process heat up to 200°C. The project also develops methods for heat pump integration in existing plants and new process equipment for dairies, slaughterhouses, breweries and other industry sectors.
- SteamHP (Steam-based heat pump systems [DTI]): Development, demonstration and long-term testing of a highly efficient evaporator using a turbo-compressor, which is based on an automobile turbo-charger.

Other projects have been supported by the European Union:

- BAMBOO (AIT): Development and demonstration of a heat pump steam generator for low pressure steam up to 150°C.
- DryFiciency (AIT): Demonstration and integration of three high temperature heat pump technologies in the production plants of starch, brick and waste treatment processes. The heat pump technology can produce heat at temperatures up to 160°C, reducing CO_2 emissions by up to 75%.
- CHESTER (TECNALIA): Assessment of the possibility of storing low price electricity as heat at a high temperature with a heat pump, and then producing electricity at the highest price periods, by employing the stored heat to produce electricity by means of an Organic Rankine Cycle (ORC)

generator. The CHESTER high temperature heat pump must reach temperatures around 140°C in order to charge the phase change material of the thermal energy store, which stores heat at 133°C.

8.2.2. Electrification of heating in the Netherlands

The potential to electrify heat in the Netherlands

The potential to electrify heat in Dutch industrial processes is vast. Table 8.3 breaks down the heat demand in Dutch industry by use, which adds up to more than 400 PJ of heat. However, not all of these can be electrified, for example because required temperatures are too high. Also, significant energy saving is expected to take place before 2050. As shown by estimates in Chapter 3, about 177 PJ of fossil fuel can be replaced by electrification in the four most emitting sectors. Table 8.3 shows how the currently used 400 PJ of heat is distributed across different industries and used for different purposes. Approximately 185 PJ of energy is used for chemical conversion, melting, casting and baking, of which 42 PJ is for melting, casting and baking (Den Ouden et al., 2017[31]). Nearly 150 PJ for distilling and separating, 60 PJ for distilling and separation, along with the approximately 20 PJ for hot water (Den Ouden et al., 2017[31]).

In practice, the potential and the appeal of electrification depends on the plant. The appeal of electrifying heat in a plant wanes if it already uses integrated industrial processes – e.g. use of waste heat generated from fuel combustion or own-use fuel combustion (Box 8.1).

Table 8.3. Dutch industry heat demand by use

In PJ, Estimates for 2017

	Total energy demand	Total heat demand	Breakdown of heat demand by use			
			Chemical conversion, melting, casting, baking	Distilling, separation	Drying	Hot water
Chemicals	279	240	>110	85	>15	
Refining	132	111	n.a.	65		
Base metal ferrous	40	30	30			
Base metal non-ferrous	11.3	3	3			
Metal products	21	12	12			
Food and beverage	85	55	7	2.5	26	16
Pulp and paper, board	23	18	2		4	1
Textile	3.7	3			3	
Construction materials	24	19	19			
Other	53	12				

Source: Den Ouden et al. (2017[31]).

The value of electrifying heat for decarbonisation, however, relies on access to low-carbon electricity. Whether or not this is available for Dutch industry in the future remains to be seen. The projections for electricity production from renewable sources in the Netherlands would not meet industrial heat demand in 2030, for example, if all heat-related processes that are technically possible were electrified (Den Ouden et al., 2017[31]). In other words, electricity production from renewable sources should reach about 375 PJ in 2030 in the Netherlands given present commitments in the 2030 Climate Agreement (Berenschot, 2020[34]), whilst the technical potential for electrifying heat is 400 PJ in the industry sector. This, of course, overlooks the needs of other sectors like transport or buildings. Alternatives for the Netherlands would be to import renewable electricity, slow down the electrification of heating, or rely on a diverse portfolio of carbon-neutral technologies for heat production (including hydrogen, biomass and electrification).

Box 8.1. Lack of appeal of electrifying heat with integrated industrial processes

The refineries and chemicals subsectors may be less likely to electrify heat than foundries or the food processing industry if the facilities already use **integrated industrial processes** – namely, the use of waste heat generated from fuel combustion or own-use fuel consumption. Chemicals and refineries often have fully developed combined heat and power systems (Table 8.4). Electrically powered heating would *not* generate nearly as much as waste heat at the current stage. Further, the oil refining industry has extensive "own-use" fuel consumption where by-products of the oil refining process (e.g. refinery or still gases obtained during the distillation of crude oil) are used as fuel in upstream or downstream processes. Attempting to electrify these processes would complicate the design and increase the energy cost over and above a sector that does not have this type of extensive process integration and own-use energy consumption.

Table 8.4. Industrial subsector breakdown of onsite fuel consumption for heating

	Boiler system	Combined Heat Power (CHP)	Process heating	Facility Heat, Ventilation and Air-conditioning (HVAC)
	Percentage on-site fuel consumption			
Iron and steel mills			87%	4.1%
Food and beverages	25%	40.3%	24.9%	4.2%
Chemical manufacturing	16.8%	43%	32%	1.3%
Refineries (Petroleum and coal products manufacturing)	11.4%	22.0%	57.9%	0.4%

Note: Data are based on the United States. Please note that the percentage of on-site fuel consumption is based on a literature review by Deason et al., (2018[30]). It should be treated as an estimate.
Source: Deason et al. (2018[30]).

Policies to accelerate the electrification of heat in the Netherlands

The Netherlands offers incentives to cover the capital investments necessary to deploy these technologies, but this does not overcome one of the key barriers to electrification of heating, which is the relative prices of energy carriers. Carbon pricing instruments discussed in Chapter 5 may reduce the relative price disadvantage of electricity compared to fossil fuels, under the assumption that electricity decarbonises. However, the current design of the electricity tax and the surcharge on electricity use risks slowing down electrification of industrial processes by increasing the relative price of electricity (Section 5.8.2). In addition, the SDE++ (Stimulering Duurzame Energieproductie) provides significant support for electrification through a subsidy to cover the additional operational costs of CO_2-reducing techniques (Chapter 5). A total of EUR 5 billion is available in SDE++ of which a significant part is expected to go to electric boilers and heat pumps. In the first SDE++ tender in 2020, 27 electric boiler projects applied for a subsidy of EUR 618 million for a capacity of 563 MW, and 38 heat pump projects request a subsidy of EUR 240 million subsidy for a capacity of 192 MW.

On top of this, the capital investments of these technologies "could" qualify for tax allowances and grants under the following schemes:

- EIA (*Energie-InvesteringsAftrek):* Tax allowance for energy-saving investments, which allows deducting up to 45% of eligible investment expenditures from taxable income in addition to the standard depreciation allowance. In past years, the EIA tax rebate lies between 10-15%. Qualifying investments must be in assets new to the firm, amount to at least EUR 2,500 and up to EUR 2.4 million per year, and be part of RVO's energy list (Energielijst).

- VEKI (*Versnelde Klimaatinvesteringen Industrie):* VEKI is an investment subsidy of minimum EUR 125 000 of which the rate depends on the underlying asset.
- MIA (*Milieu-InvesteringsAftrek* - environmental investment deduction): Tax allowance for environmentally-friendly investments, which allows deducting a fraction of the investment expenditures from taxable income. It comes on top of the standard depreciation allowance.
- Vamil is a one-off accelerated depreciation of 75% of the investment expenditures that is targeted specifically to environmental investments.
- ISDE (InvesteringsSubsidie Duurzame Energie) is a subsidy available to firms and business owners for the purchase and installation of heat pumps or solar water heaters (cannot be used with EIA).
- TNO Agenda on Heat Pumps for 2020-25 (Netherlands).

8.2.3. Electrification policies in Germany

National Decarbonisation program

An important German programme for the electrification of heat is the National Decarbonisation program.

The National Decarbonisation Program addresses technology development, demonstration and market uptake. The program particularly aims for the reduction of process-related emissions in hard-to-abate sectors and thus addresses key production facilities in these sectors. For this purpose, Chapter 6 projects in the area of emission-intensive industries with process-related emissions, are supported via grants of total EUR 2 billion for 2020-24 and probably EUR 0.5 billion a year afterwards.

The projects under scope range from application-oriented R&D and industrial-scale testing to the broad market introduction of mature or emerging technologies. The program will provide grants to finance a share of the upfront costs of the investments in new plants, development of climate-neutral processes, switch from fossil to electricity-based fuels, innovative combinations of processes, development of climate-neutral product substitutes as well as bridge technologies. Applications are evaluated technically and economically. Current program design focuses on capital expenditures only and does not foresee financing of operational costs.

8.2.4. Making the business case for the electrification of heating in the Netherlands

The missing business case for electrification of heat

The decision to invest in a given technology to electrify heat is generally assessed by the trade-off between the capital expenditure (investment) needed to purchase and install the technology versus the reduced operational costs (including energy or carbon costs) resulting from the investment. According to TNO, a simple payback period is commonly used to assess this trade-off, and the payback period demanded by industry is typically in the range of one to two years, although this can be extended to the range of two to five years under certain circumstances. This short payback period contrasts with other investments, where returns of about 10% per year are considered sufficient, and questions the idea whether energy savings are really considered as a priority by industry. A plausible explanation for this relatively short payback period for electrification could be that heavy industry is reluctant to take technological risks. The optimised large-scale processes often run continuously and failure in production could be disastrous (ECN, 2015[35]).

The relatively high price of electricity compared to alternative fuels - often three to four times higher than that of natural gas over the last decade in the Netherlands - has likely acted as a disincentive to electrify heat. The ratio of electricity to gas prices in European countries for small scale industrial end-users, which varies from less than 2 in the case of Norway, Finland and Sweden to over 4 in the case of Belgium, the United Kingdom, Italy and Germany, can be a significant barrier to electrification of heating uptake in some countries (de Boer et al., 2020[36]).

Even though, emissions in the industry sector are subject to fuel-specific energy taxes, a surcharge on natural gas and the EU emissions trading system (ETS) (which are included, for example, in the figure above), these may not have tipped the balance in favour of electrifying. This may be partly due to compensation of indirect costs for ETS and exemptions from paying the fuel tax and surcharge. Electricity taxation and the surcharge on electricity use are policy instruments in place that may further slowdown electrification by raising their costs as discussed more in detail in Section 5.8.2.

Will the carbon levy and SDE++ make the business case for the electrification of heating?

While the carbon levy makes a better business case for the electrification of heating, the taxation of energy is not done in the most efficient way, as discussed in the section on energy taxation in Chapter 5. Table 8.5 and Table 8.6 show again the gas and electricity prices and energy tax rates in Dutch industry in EUR per gigajoule (GJ), which were already presented in Section 5.8.2 on the effective price on electricity use (Chapter 5). Table 8.5 shows that the unit price per GJ is almost four times as high for electricity compared to natural gas. Table 8.6 shows that energy taxes are only exacerbating this price difference as electricity is taxed at substantially higher rates for all bands, except for the highest (band 4).

While the carbon levy will reduce the price differential between gas and electricity, the question remains whether this will be sufficient to make the business case for the electrification of heating. Table 8.5 shows that the unit price for electricity (excluding taxes) is approximately EUR 12.5 per GJ higher than the unit price of natural gas. Table 8.6 shows that energy tax rates are likely to increase this price difference substantially in the lower consumption bands. A relatively low electricity tax rate applies to the most energy-intensive consumers in consumption band 4.[4]

Table 8.5. Gas and electricity prices net of tax in Dutch industry, Q2/2020

	Natural gas	Electricity
Unit price, excluding taxes [in EUR/GJ]	4.69	17.22

Note: For natural gas, prices refer to the Eurostat consumption band I4 for industry (annual consumption: 100 000-1 000 000 GJ). For electricity, prices refer to the Eurostat consumption band ID for industry (annual consumption: 2 000-20 000 MWh).
Source: Based on IEA *Energy Prices*.

Table 8.6. Energy tax rates in EUR per GJ for natural gas and electricity in 2021

	Band 1	Band 2	Band 3	Band 4
Natural gas	13.31	2.50	0.91	0.49
Electricity	26.19	14.34	3.82	0.16

In 2020, pre-tax prices in Dutch industry are EUR 4.7 per GJ for natural gas and EUR 17.2 per GJ for electricity for the typical industrial producer. The carbon levy of EUR 125 per tonne of CO_2 applying to the entire emissions base would translate into a EUR 7 rate per GJ for natural gas, thereby reducing the differential to some extent. This increase of EUR 7 per GJ constitutes an upper bound estimate, as it is based on the assumption that everyone would pay the same levy in 2030 and that no dispensation rights would be distributed. While the policy chapter shows that only about half of the users are expected to pay the carbon levy and that half of them receive dispensation rights, i.e. pollution permits under the levy, for free (Chapter 5).

A caveat for this comparison of electricity and gas is that a GJ of energy from electricity is not the same as a GJ of energy from gas, as there are different upstream and downstream conversion efficiencies that may narrow the price differential in favour of electricity, as explained in Section 5.8.2 of Chapter 5 The carbon levy may therefore close the necessary price difference for the electrification of some technologies in some industries, like low temperature heating through electric boilers and heat pumps in the food and paper industry that pay relatively high energy taxes compared to the heavy industry. It is unlikely that the carbon levy alone is sufficient to make the business case for the electrification of high temperature heating in the chemical, refineries and metal industries. (More details on electricity pricing and the carbon levy are described in the section analysing the policy package and the Dutch effective carbon rate and electricity price signal (Chapter 5).

In addition to the carbon levy, SDE++ subsidies may narrow the price differential between natural gas and electricity. The relatively large number of SDE++ subsidy applications for electric boilers (27) and heat pump projects (38) may be an indication that technology support can bridge the gap for low temperature heating in some industries, especially the paper industry and food processing industry. The subsidy requests for electric boilers amount to EUR 618 million for a total capacity of 563 MW and the applications for heat pump projects relate to another EUR 240 million for a capacity of 192MW. However, under the current policies, there does not seem to be a business case yet for breakthrough technologies that could be developed and deployed for high-temperature heating in the chemical, metallurgical and refineries sectors. It is uncertain, when and if their costs will come down, to take advantage of the policy package combining technology support, carbon levy and the tax exemption for auto-generated electricity.

8.3. Hydrogen

Key messages

- Hydrogen is a promising technology with great potential to decarbonise not only industry, but transport, buildings, and power. However, technological maturity along the hydrogen value chain varies.
- The Netherlands Hydrogen Strategy elucidates similar goals and priorities to that of Germany and the European Union. All three hydrogen strategies set targets from now until 2030 for the installation of GW for electrolysers, prioritise how to integrate hydrogen production with gas and electricity grid, recognise the importance of standards (e.g. guarantees of origin), and the importance of international co-operation with neighbours in defining these standards, building infrastructure, and so on.
- The key difference between the three strategies is the explicit mentioning of Contracts for Difference for hydrogen in the German and European Hydrogen Strategies in order to help industry cover operating costs. It remains to be seen if such a mechanism would be needed in addition to the existing toolkit in the Netherlands, because alternative instruments like the carbon levy, SDE++ and the Hydrogen Strategy provide support in this respect.
- The costs for green hydrogen per tonne of CO_2 emission reduction are, however, high compared to other technologies that compete for the SDE++ subsidy. Therefore, and due to the design of SDE++, it is unlikely that much of the subsidy will be awarded to the production of green hydrogen. It is also unlikely that the carbon levy alone is sufficient for the necessary increase in investments in the development and use of green hydrogen. Reserving part of SDE++ subsidies for green hydrogen may be a possible solution.

- Fully realising the potential of hydrogen requires a high-level commitment from government and dedicated attention to mitigate risks, strategic R&D and demonstration, work to harmonise standards and remove barriers, and above all, policies to stimulate demand.
- International standardisation will be crucial in this value chain, including guarantees of origin, hydrogen purity, the design of liquefaction/conversion and regasification/reconversion facilities, for equipment specifications and for blending hydrogen into the gas grid.
- Research and demonstration support should focus on CCUS, underground storage of hydrogen, higher-risk demonstration projects for localised grid conversions, carriers for shipping and the scale-up of liquefaction and regasification facilities.
- Future demand for hydrogen, the supply of renewable energy to produce hydrogen and the infrastructure for hydrogen transportation must be ensured by the Dutch government before companies are prepared to make significant investments that are required for the production of (green) hydrogen.

Hydrogen is already being used in each of the sectors of interest – refining, chemicals (i.e. ammonia and methanol), and metallurgy (i.e. iron and steel) - as an input into industrial processes. Either to purify oil in refineries (i.e. remove sulphur), as a feedstock in ammonia and methanol production, or to remove oxygen from iron ore to create iron. Virtually all of the existing industrial uses of hydrogen today are supplied using fossil fuels (IEA, 2019[37]),[5] which is known colloquially as grey hydrogen. Two existing low-carbon alternatives are blue and green hydrogen. The former still produces hydrogen from natural gas but removes carbon emissions via CCUS (Figure 8.1), while the latter breaks down water into dihydrogen and dioxygen using renewable energy and thereby does not emit CO_2 through fossil fuel use (IEA, 2020[5]).

The first section starts with the Technological Readiness Levels of these technologies across the hydrogen value chain. The second section explains the Netherlands Hydrogen Strategy and the third section then overviews and compares the policies of other countries in five key areas: high-level commitment, mitigating risks, strategic R&D and demonstration, harmonised standards and removal of barriers, and creating demand. The section concludes with policy recommendations to accelerate the development and use of hydrogen in the industrial sector.

8.3.1. Technological Readiness Levels of Hydrogen

Technological Readiness across the hydrogen value chain

The hydrogen value chain involves varying states of technological maturity. Figure 8.6 classifies technologies into production (left-hand column), infrastructure (middle column) and usage by sector (right-hand column). The rest of this section reviews the technological readiness of relevant technologies for decarbonising Dutch industry by 2050.

Low-carbon hydrogen production (left-side of Figure 8.6) lists technologies that produce hydrogen from water via electrolysis or fossil fuels with CCUS (IEA, 2020[5]). Electrolysis (colloquially known as "green hydrogen") is in its "early stages of adoption" (IEA, 2020[5]). This encompasses three technologies - alkaline electrolysis, proton exchange membrane (PEM), solid oxide electrolysis cells (SOEC) – which differ in maturity (IEA, 2019[37]). The production of hydrogen through Alkaline electrolysis is a mature technology (Technology Readiness level [TRL] of 9) that has been used since the 1920s and was replaced in the 1970s, with grey hydrogen – natural gas and steam methane reforming (the most common technique for producing hydrogen today) (IEA, 2019[37]). PEM is less mature than Alkaline electrolysis, with a TRL of 8 (demonstration), but was first used in the 1970s and produces *compressed* hydrogen, making it amenable to decentralised production and storage. A key drawback for PEM is the need for expensive materials to acts as catalysts and membranes (IEA, 2019[37]). The least developed of the techniques is SOEC, which uses steam as a heat source to break down the water into hydrogen and oxygen. The disadvantage of this technology is that it requires high temperatures that are more difficult to obtain in a sustainable way and, therefore, typically receives less attention than the other two techniques (IEA, 2019[37]). In principle, these technologies could be modular unlike CCUS – easing its diffusion and uptake by industry. However, this is all still in development but ideas are already emerging, for example, for PEM (Wirkert et al., 2020[38]).

Figure 8.6 shows that blue hydrogen, i.e. natural gas reforming with CCUS and coal gasification with CCUS, is already in “early adoption” phase and a large prototype exists for the latter (TRL 5) (IEA, 2020[5]). Methane splitting (Figure 8.6) is a misfit and not usually labelled blue – as of yet. This technique has existed since the 1990s and produces hydrogen from natural gas, combined with methane as the feedstock and electricity as the energy source – which ultimately, produces hydrogen and solid carbon (the latter of which can be used in rubber, for example) (IEA, 2020[5]). One relevant feature of methane splitting is that it uses *significantly less* electricity than any of the electrolysis techniques – on average, about three times less (and there is presently a large prototype of this technology being used at a chemicals plant) (IEA, 2020[5]).

Figure 8.6. Technological readiness levels across the hydrogen value chain

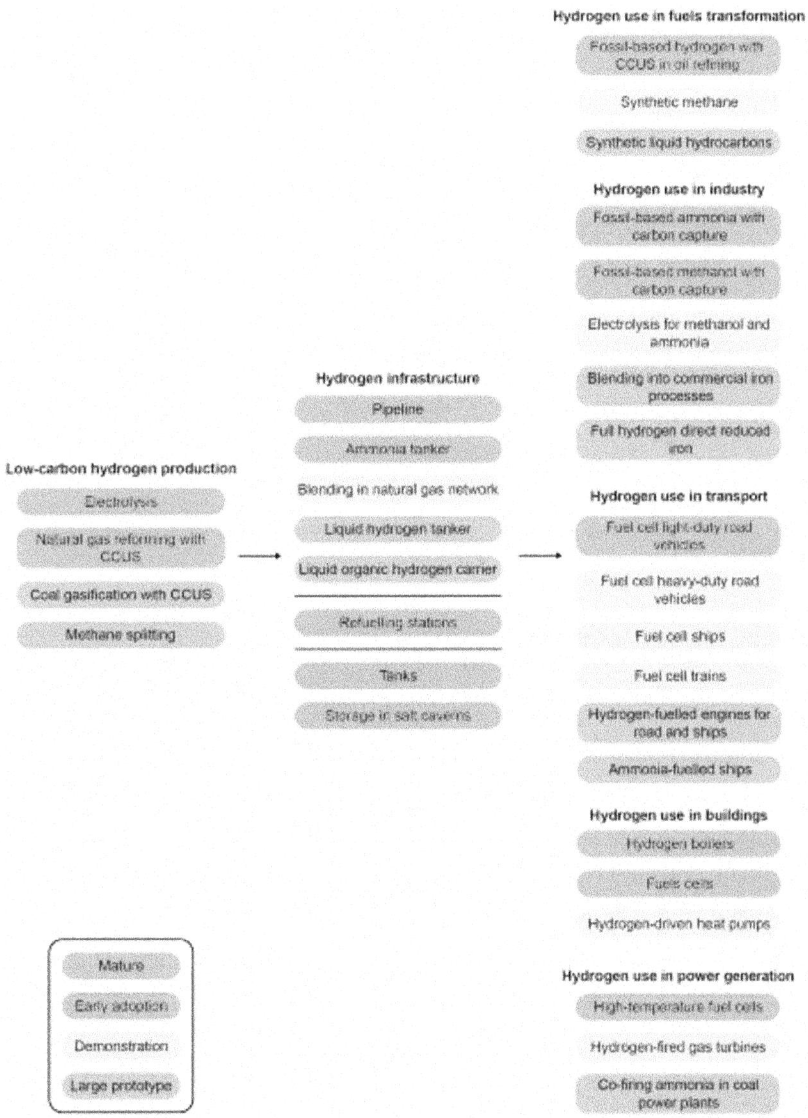

Source: IEA (2020[5]).

The costs of these different production techniques range considerably in 2030 – and the IEA estimates that at least, in the short term, blue hydrogen will be cheapest at approximately USD 2.50 per kgH_2 (IEA, 2019[37]). Hydrogen produced via electrolysis with grid electricity is by far the most expensive option over the next decade at around USD 5 per kgH_2 – if there was a surplus of electricity, perhaps it could become cheap enough. For electrolysis, a dedicated supply of renewable energy is often needed (to ensure that it is low-carbon hydrogen). This is root to the speculation that green hydrogen production will shift to parts of the globe with ample and cheap renewable electricity – i.e. Morocco or Australia.

On-site production of Hydrogen

Hydrogen can be produced on-site by refineries, chemicals or steel plants or it could be supplied to them. Dutch plants will likely produce some of their blue hydrogen (and maybe green) on-site in 2050. Table 8.7 lists a few plants in the sectors of interest that are already doing this. For plants producing green hydrogen, the amount of renewable capacity needed is included where possible. Nearly all plants using blue hydrogen use the captured CO_2 for EOR, with the exception of Air Liquide selling CO_2, meaning that the captured CO_2 is eventually released into the atmosphere. One ammonia plant in Australia plans to use geological storage.

Table 8.7. On-site production for blue or green hydrogen by relevant industries

	Hydrogen	Project	Status	Capacity	Technology
Refineries	Blue	Product's Port Arthur project (Texas, USA)	Completed demonstration phase	Plans to use the CO_2 for EOR	
		Air Liquide's Port Jerome (France)	Operational	Sells CO_2 to the beverage industry	
		Hokkaido Refinery (Japan)	Pilot		
	Green	WESTKUESTE 100 (Heide, Germany)	Under construction, could be operational by 2030	3 kt of H_2 annually	Alkaline electrolysers
		REFHYNE (Rhineland, Germany)	Under construction, to be completed in second half of 2020	1.3 kt of H_2 annually	PEM Technology
Chemicals	Blue	Three ammonia-based fertiliser plants (USA)	Operational	150ktH_2 annually 2MtCO_2 annually (used in EOR)	
		2 ammonia-based fertiliser plants (USA) 1 ammonia-based fertiliser plants (CAN) 1 ammonia-based fertiliser plants (CHN)	Planned, to be operational by 2022	All plan to use EOR	
		1 ammonia-based fertiliser plants (AUS)	To be operational by 2025	No EOR, only geological storage	
	Green	1 ammonia-based fertiliser (NOR)	Prototype by 2022	5 MW to decarbonise 1% of the plant's output	Alkaline electrolysers
		1 ammonia-based fertiliser at the Kapuni plant (NZE)	Project completion date 2021	16 MW to decarbonise 2% of the plant's output	
Steel	Green	HYBRIT: 1 plant in SSAB site in Luleå, Sweden	Planned for construction in 2021, Goal is to have fossil fuel free steel by 2035		Alkaline electrolysis

Source: IEA (2019[37]).

Box 8.2. On-site production of hydrogen through public private partnerships

Current status of blue hydrogen

- **Air Product's Port Authority** project in Texas (demonstration phase) – Operating since 2013 (1 Mt of CO_2 per year, Source: Steam Methane Reformers, Capture type: vacuum swing adsorption technology, Storage: EOR in West Hasting's and Oyster Bayou oil fields in Texas)

In February 2009, the American Recovery and Reinvestment Act (AARA) designated USD 3.4 billion for CCS programs. This funding was broken down into three major sources, one of which was USD 1.52 billion for a competitive bidding for industrial CCS projects. Three demonstration projects were selected (a total of 6.5 million tonnes of CO_2 per year), one of which was Air Product's Port Authority in Texas. The US Department of Energy (DOE) awarded the Port Arthur project USD 900 000 from the American Recovery and Reinvestment Act (ARRA) in October 2009. The project also received an additional USD 253 million from the ARRA as part of the DOE's CCS Program's Phase 2 in June 2010. USD 368 million in private funding matched this money. In June 2016, Air Products announced that it had successfully captured more than 3 million $MtCO_2$ at Port Arthur after three and half years of operation.

The 1 $MtCO_2$ per year, dried and purified to 97% purity of CO_2 at the Port Arthur facility. The CO_2 is then delivered, via a 12-mile connector pipeline, to Denbury's Green Pipeline (Texas). The CO_2 is then piped 101-150 km before injection for EOR in Denbury's onshore operations. The CO_2 then aids in recovering 1.6-3.1 million additional barrels annually of domestic oil.

- **Air Liquide's Port Jerome** project in France already captures and sells CO_2 (Operating since 2015, Source: Steam Methane Reformers, Capture Type: Pressure Swing Absorption, Sold not stored).

In 2002, the ExxonMobil group signed a long-term contract with Air Liquide for the supply of around 50 000 Nm^3 per hour of hydrogen for its Esso refinery in Port-Jérôme. Several key features were demonstrated: the integration of the CRYOCAP™ (hydrogen) H_2 unit within the existing H_2 production plant, the increase of H_2 production flow, the operation of the cold box near the triple point, and the production of liquid food grade CO_2 (300 TPD – Temperature Programme Desorption), which is then used by the beverage industry – e.g. sparkling beverages (13 tonne per hour of liquid CO_2 at food grade quality). Air Liquide received funding from ADEME for CRYOCAP™ at Port-Jérôme (Dubettier, 2010[39]).

- **Hokkaido Refinery** in (Tomakomai) Japan (Operating since 2016, Capture Technology: Activated Amine/Pressure Swing Absorption, Stored: Offshore geological storage)

Tomakomai started capture from its pilot plant in March 2016. Tomakomai plans to capture at least 100 000 tonnes of CO_2 per year for three years. The CO_2 will be stored in offshore geological units (Tanaka et al., 2014[40]). About JPY 34 billion (USD 300 million) had been set aside for the project by the Ministry of Economy, Trade and Industry for the four years through the end of this month to build the project site.

A portion of the PSA (Pressure Swing Adsorption) offgas containing approximately 52% CO_2 generated by a hydrogen production unit in the Idemitsu Kosan Co., Ltd. Hokkaido Refinery is transported by a 1.4 km pipeline to the adjacent capture facilities, where CO_2 is captured. The CO_2 is compressed and stored 3-4 km offshore in two sub-seabed reservoirs at different depths.

The project will continue monitoring other efforts, including observing very small oscillations in the areas surrounding the reservoir point, surveying marine environments and checking behaviours of injected CO_2, e.g. displacement and spreading. The project will conduct a demonstration test for carbon recycling, e.g. methanol synthesis, effectively taking advantage of the facilities for the CCS

Demonstration Project, and advance establishing a base for demonstration of CCS and carbon recycling in Tomakomai City.

Current status green hydrogen 2020

- **Shell's Rheinland refinery** (Germany) announced a 10 MW electrolyser project for 2020

The project is funded by the European Commission's Fuel Cells and Hydrogen Joint Undertaking and will install and operate the world's largest hydrogen electrolyser the Shell Rheinland Refinery in Wesseling, Germany. The plant will be operated by Shell and manufactured by ITM Power. The electrolyser has a peak capacity of 10 megawatts (MW) and will be able to produce approximately 1 300 tonnes of hydrogen per year. This decarbonised hydrogen can be fully integrated into refinery processes including the desulphurisation of conventional fuels. The project will use the hydrogen produced for processing and upgrading products at the Wesseling refinery site, and testing the PEM technology at the largest scale achieved to date. The REFHYNE project began in January 2018 and will run for five years to December 2022.

The total investment is EUR 16 million, of which the European Fuel Cell Hydrogen Joint Undertaking contributes EUR 10 million. EUR 6 million will be contributed by the REFHYNE consortium with Shell, ITM Power, SINTEF, thinkstep and Element Energy.

- **Heide** (Germany) announced a 30 MW electrolyser project (alkaline electrolysers) to replace its purchase of 3kt H_2 per year (currently under construction and could be up and running by 2030)

The partners involved in the Heide refinery project, known as WESTKUESTE 100, received approval for EUR 30 million in funding from the German Ministry of Economic Affairs. They are providing EUR 59 million making at total investment of EUR 89 million. The plant will pass electricity from wind turbines through water to extract carbon-free hydrogen that will be used by the Heide refinery to replace fossil fuel-based hydrogen.

The ten partners in the project include the German sections of French utility EDF and cement maker Holcim, gas pipeline operator Open Grid Europe (OGE), Danish wind company Orsted, the Heide refinery, the Heide town's municipal utility, local utility network Thuega and Thyssenkrupp Industrial Solutions. Eight of the partners are companies, which are working with the Heide region's public sector development agency and the Westkueste University of Applied Sciences.

The Alkaline Electrolysers will split water into hydrogen and oxygen. The hydrogen will be used by the gas plant and the oxygen will be sold to the cement plant (for use as oxyfuel), with the waste heat being sold to the district heating system. Some of the green hydrogen will also be used to make synthetic methanol, which could then be refined into carbon neutral kerosene (i.e. aviation fuel).

The Heide refinery happens to have huge salt caverns on its land where up to 10 million tonnes of hydrogen can be stored, as well as a dedicated bidirectional hydrogen pipeline to a Linde grey-hydrogen facility 30 km away — so large amounts of green hydrogen could eventually be stored and transported via a pipeline for use elsewhere, including injection into the natural-gas grid.

- **BP, Nouryon and the Port Rotterdam** assessing the feasibility of 250MW electrolyser project for the BP refinery in Rotterdam

The parties have signed a memorandum of understanding to study the feasibility of a 250 MW water electrolysis facility to produce up to 45 000 tonnes of green hydrogen yearly using renewable energy. Nouryon would build and operate the facility based on its leadership position in sustainable electrochemistry. The Port of Rotterdam would facilitate local infrastructure and investigate options for further development of a green hydrogen hub in the area. The partners intend to take a final investment decision on the project in 2022. In March, BP established a USD 100 million fund for projects. The study will also take into account a possible connection to the heat grid and oxygen pipelines.

- **Uniper and the Port of Rotterdam** are investigating the possibilities for large-scale production of green hydrogen on the Maasvlakte.

The ambition is to realise a hydrogen plant with a capacity of 100 MW on the Uniper site by 2025 and eventually expand that capacity to 500 MW. The feasibility study will be completed this summer. Following the recent successful pre-qualification for the EU IPCEI (Important Projects of Common European Interest) program, the conceptual design and technical dimensions of the hydrogen plant will be under investigation in the coming months.

While this project is about green hydrogen, Box 8.3 gives more information about the production of blue hydrogen in Rotterdam.

- **Ørsted and Yara** want to develop a green ammonia project in the Netherlands aiming at replacing fossil hydrogen with green hydrogen.

Ørsted, the world's leading developer of offshore wind energy, and Yara, the world's leading fertiliser manufacturer, have joined forces to develop a ground-breaking project to replace fossil hydrogen with renewable hydrogen in ammonia production with the potential to reduce CO_2 emissions with more than 100 000 tonnes per year. The renewable hydrogen would generate around 75 000 tonnes of green ammonia per year. If the necessary public co-financing is guaranteed and the appropriate regulatory framework is in place, the project could be operational in 2024/2025.

Hydrogen transport

The alternative to on-site production of hydrogen is to purchase from suppliers, yet this requires infrastructure (IEA, 2020[5]). A key challenge to transport hydrogen is its low density, which makes transport very costly today. Natural gas tends to be liquefied or compressed for transport, but for hydrogen this is not easily done. Liquefying is possible, but the process consumes about 25% of the hydrogen as compared to gas, which only consumes 10% (IEA, 2019[37]). Even when compressed hydrogen is very expensive to transport over long distances because its density will still represent only 15% of the density of gasoline (IEA, 2019[37]). Hydrogen can be transported via dedicated pipelines (similar to natural gas). Today, approximately 5 000 km of hydrogen pipelines exist (compared to the 3 million km of natural gas pipelines) (IEA, 2019[37]). These tend to be found in dense industrialised clusters since it lowers costs, such as in the Rotterdam industrial cluster in the Netherlands. Existing high pressure natural gas transmission lines could be used (if no longer used for natural gas) with slight upgrades, but their suitability needs to be assessed on a case-by-case basis. Also, hydrogen can be blended with natural gas and can then be used by conventional end users of natural gas to generate power and heat. A certain amount of hydrogen can be blended into existing natural gas pipelines (around 2-10% in Europe), which is currently the cheapest option for transport over distances of less than 1 500 km (IEA, 2019[37]).

For long distance transport (more than 1 500 km), the most cost effective option is to store the hydrogen in other larger molecules – either ammonia or liquid organic hydrogen carrier (IEA, 2019[37]). However, such molecules cannot be consumed as final products so the hydrogen will need to be liberated as a final step before consumption. There are experiments with marine tankers, which are either in early adoption or large prototype, respectively (IEA, 2020[5]). The other option is that ammonia can be transported by pipelines, which could be cheaper to build than new pipelines for pure hydrogen.

Box 8.3. H-Vision: Potential for blue hydrogen in Rotterdam (research)

The H-Vision feasibility study investigated the potential for blue hydrogen (Box 8.2) in Rotterdam. The captured CO_2 will be stored either in the depleted gas fields in the North Sea or used for basic chemicals, such as methanol. The H-Vision project includes parties from Rotterdam Region - Deltalinqs, Air Liquide, BP, Gasunie, the Port of Rotterdam Authority, Power Plant Rotterdam, Shell, Uniper, Royal Vopak and ExxonMobil, supported by province of Zuid-Holland and City of Rotterdam, and benefited from funding under DEI+). The hope is that Rotterdam will become the "seed of the new hydrogen economy."

In 2019, a feasibility study found that blue hydrogen would enable local industry of Rotterdam to reduce its emissions significantly before 2030. Estimate savings would increase from 2.2 $MtCO_2$ in 2026 up to 4.3 $MtCO_2$ in 2031. Adopting blue hydrogen as an energy carrier would lead to emission reduction of 16% of total CO_2 emissions of Rotterdam's industrial sector in 2018 (26.4 $MtCO_2$). The goal H-vision to build an annual production capacity of over 700 kt – equivalent to some 3200 MW, which would enable Rotterdam's industrial sector to produce at least 20% of its required heat and power using blue hydrogen. Constructing these installations would require an investment of approximately EUR 1.3 billion. If the technical and infrastructure adaptions required by industrial users is included, estimated investment would be around EUR 2 billion.

H-Vision is now in a phase of conferring with government and other partners about risk hedging, financial support, and regulations.

Source: https://www.deltalinqs.nl/h-vision-en and https://www.portofrotterdam.com/en/news-and-press-releases/h-vision-kicks-off-the-hydrogen-economy-in-rotterdam

8.3.2. Netherlands hydrogen strategy

Research priorities

Basic research takes place in the Electrochemical Conversion & Materials programme, which connects strong knowledge positions in the Netherlands in the fields of chemistry, energy and high-tech manufacturing. Applied research takes place in the Top Sector Energy, as part of the various multi-year mission-driven innovation programmes (MMIPs).

Link hydrogen to offshore wind energy. TNO studies the advantages and disadvantages of linking hydrogen production to offshore wind energy via integrated tenders. There is the possibility for the eventual tendering of a specific amount of electrolysis capacity at landing sites for offshore wind energy. It is the first place in the world where an offshore hydrogen factory is being built, which is expected to reduce the cost of green hydrogen enormously as the transport of hydrogen from offshore wind parks is much cheaper than the transport of electricity from offshore wind parks.

Support schemes

The two main schemes to support the development of green hydrogen is DEI+ and SDE++. The Government plans to implement a new, temporary support scheme for operational costs related to scaling up and cost reduction processes for green hydrogen as mentioned in the Dutch Climate Agreement.

The Dutch plan on using mission-driven research, development and innovation (MOOI) Tenders for applied research and development of hydrogen production. In addition, the DEI+ can subsidise 25% of the eligible costs, and potentially up to 45% under certain conditions. This subsidy is up to a maximum of EUR 15 million per project.

Scaling up will be supported through the Climate Budget funds available for temporary operating cost support as of 2021 (approximately EUR 35 million per year, by rearranging part of the existing funds for hydrogen pilot projects in DEI+).

Through the SDE++, approximately 2 000 load hours are eligible for subsidy, which will result in a subsidy intensity of maximum of EUR 300 per tonne of CO_2; blue hydrogen can apply via the CCS category.

In addition to these direct support schemes, the carbon levy will support closing the price differential between using hydrogen compared to cheaper fossil fuels. However, at the current stage and given the design of SDE++, it is unlikely that the combination of carbon levy with SDE++ will be enough to make green hydrogen production a competitive choice for industry in order for them to step in and start producing at a large scale (Chapter 5).

The Netherlands is still exploring the different possibilities to finance the transition to green hydrogen, as it is aware that the current support for green hydrogen is not yet sufficient to achieve its ambitions (EZK, 2020[41]). Several options for financing the transition to green hydrogen include the European funds and instruments, such as the Recovery and Resilience Facility (RRF), the Just Transition Fund (JTF) and the European Innovation Fund. Also the National Growth Fund gives possible opportunities to finance hydrogen programmes.

8.3.3. Comparison between Dutch, German and EU Hydrogen Strategies

Key elements of European, German and Dutch Hydrogen Strategies

To accelerate the innovation and deployment in hydrogen, several countries have created hydrogen strategies: China, France, Germany, Italy, Japan, Netherlands, Norway, Korea, United Kingdom, and the United States. In addition to subnational governments, e.g. Leeds (UK), London (UK), Northern England (UK), and California, as well as supranational governments like the European Union. Table 8.8 compares the key features of the European Union, German and Dutch hydrogen strategies in terms of targets, key instruments for industry, infrastructure priorities, standards, and international co-operation (Government of the Netherlands, 2020[42]; Federal Ministry for Economic Affairs and Energy, 2020[43]; European Commission, 2020[44]). The three strategies also outline innovation programmes (e.g. basic and applied research, allocated funding mechanisms), however, these will be discussed in detail in the next section. All three hydrogen strategies set targets from now until 2030 for the installation of GW for electrolysers, prioritise how to integrate hydrogen production with the gas and electricity grid, recognise the importance of standards (e.g. guarantees of origin), and the importance of international co-operation with neighbours in defining these standards, building infrastructure, and so on. Each of these is discussed in turn.

As can be seen in Table 8.8, the Dutch's commitment to renewables for electrolysers is comparable to Germany. Germany plans to build 5 GW for electrolysers and the Netherlands 2-4 GW. Neither country specifies a production target.

The Hydrogen Strategies of all three countries nominate or create task forces to discern how to best use the existing gas grid for transportation infrastructure. This is by far the cheapest option at present, since it can avoid significant capital costs. However, hydrogen volumes of more than 2% may result in cracks of steel pipes, may affect the durability and integrity of transmission pipelines. Different countries allow for different levels of blended gas – some as high as 10% (i.e. Germany), whilst the Netherlands only allows 2% blending. However, for blending to happen, it would be considerably easier if these regulations were harmonised across European borders. The reason for different regulations is due to some of the challenges of blending. First, blending hydrogen into the gas grid can reduce the energy content of the delivered gas so end users would need greater gas volumes, so industrial sectors that rely on the carbon contained in natural gas could ultimately use more natural gas. In addition, hydrogen could have an adverse impact on the operation of equipment designed to accommodate only a narrow range of gas structure (could affect the quality of some industrial processes). In addition, the upper limit for hydrogen blending in the grid depends on the equipment connected to it. If these differences persist, hydrogen blended into gas may actually be rejected by other Member States. This could impact the uptake by industry if they need to purchase hydrogen by suppliers.

All strategies also discuss the importance of establishing standards, in particular guarantees of origin (GO). The EU has a pilot scheme, CertifyHY that differentiates between low-carbon or green hydrogen. This could help develop technologies if the scheme is more widely applied. A GO essentially labels the origin of a product and provides information to customers on the source of their products. It operates as a tracking system ensuring the quality of hydrogen. The proposed premium hydrogen GO system, similar to the existing green electricity GO scheme, decouples the green attribute from the physical flow of the product and makes premium hydrogen available EU-wide, regardless of where the specific molecule is ultimately consumed.

Table 8.8. Key elements of European, German and Dutch Hydrogen Strategies

	Europe	Germany	Netherlands
Targets	**2024** • At least 6 GW of renewable hydrogen electrolysers • Production of 1 million tonnes of clean hydrogen **2030** • 40 GW renewable hydrogen electrolysers in Europe • Production of 10 million tonnes of renewable hydrogen in the EU • 40 GW of electrolysers in Europe's neighbourhood with export to Europe	**2030** 5 GW of renewable hydrogen electrolysers **2040** 10 GW of renewable hydrogen electrolysers	**2025** 500 MW of renewable hydrogen electrolysers **2030** 2-4 GW of renewable hydrogen electrolysers
Highlighted Instruments	**Carbon Contracts for Difference** in order to bridge the cost gap - in particular to support the production of low carbon and circular steel, and basic chemicals.	• A new pilot programme entitled Carbon Contracts for Difference, which mostly targets the steel and chemical industries with their process-related emissions. • Rewards for industry for switching from conventional fossil-fuel based technologies and avoiding using CO2 in industries relying on base substances'. • The fund for 'Decarbonising the industrial sector' and the programmes for 'hydrogen use in industrial production' (2020-24) • A demand quota for climate-friendly base substances, e.g. green steel, is being considered. • Efficient use of electricity from renewables, to create greater scope for the production of green hydrogen and exempt electricity used for the production of green hydrogen from taxes, levies, and surcharges.	• Carbon levy • SDE++ subsidy • MOOI Tenders for applied research and development of hydrogen production • DEI+ subsidy
Infrastructure priorities	**Gas Grid** Up to 2030: Review of Trans-European Networks for Energy to review the internal gas market legislation to ensure compatibility with pure hydrogen and cross-border operation rules. Elements of the existing gas infrastructure will be repurposed for the cross-border transport of hydrogen.	**Gas grid** Compile report to use existing structures (dedicated hydrogen infrastructure as well as parts of the natural gas infrastructure that can be adjusted and back-fitted to make it H_2-ready), starting with the supplier to the end consumer. **Electricity grid** • Efforts to better link up the electricity, heat, and gas infrastructure will continue. The aim is to shape the planning, financing, and the regulatory framework in a way that makes it possible to co-ordinate these different parts of the infrastructure.	**Gas grid** Government will review whether and under what conditions part of the gas grid can be used for the distribution of hydrogen (with the aim of developing of North-Western Europe hydrogen market). Gradually increase blending obligation from 2% to 10-20%. **Electricity grid** • Gasunie and TenneT develop and co-ordinate hydrogen and electricity grid

	General: Ten-Year Network Development Plans (TYNDPs) (2021) taking into account also the planning of a network of fuelling stations.	• New business and co-operation models for operators of electrolysers and for the grid and gas network operators (principle of regulatory unbundling)	• Government will co-ordinate the precise locations of electrolysers (Main Energy Infrastructure Programme) The Netherlands sets a target to realise the "Hydrogen Backbone" in Europe – which would be a mix of newly constructed hydrogen pipelines and the conversion of existing natural gas pipelines throughout Europe reaching from Spain to Sweden. The goal is to create an initial 6 800 km pipeline network by 2030, connecting hydrogen valleys. The infrastructure would then further expand by 2035 and stretch into all directions by 2040 with a length almost 23 000 km.
Standards	• Establish common low-carbon threshold/standard for hydrogen production installations (full lifecycle GHG) • Comprehensive terminology and European-wide criteria for the certification of renewable and low-carbon hydrogen • Establish Guarantees of Origin between low-carbon and green hydrogen	• To ensure that a market can develop which contributes to the energy transition and to decarbonisation, as well as boosting export opportunities for German and European companies, there is a need for reliable sustainability standards and for a sophisticated quality infrastructure, proof (of origin) for electricity from renewable energy and for green hydrogen and its downstream products. • Advocacy for an international harmonisation of standards for mobility applications for hydrogen and fuel-cell-based systems (e.g. refuelling standards, hydrogen quality, official calibration, hydrogen-powered car type approval, licencing for ships etc.).	• Guarantees of Origin system is required, Vertogas (Certifies green gas) will be designated to develop this system • Hydrogen Safety Innovation Programme – implemented as PPPs – to adequately address any issues
International co-operation	• Strengthen EU leadership in international fora for technical standards, regulations and definitions on hydrogen. • Develop the hydrogen mission within the next mandate of Mission Innovation (MI2). • Promote co-operation with Southern and Eastern Neighbourhood partners and Energy Community countries, notably Ukraine on renewable electricity and hydrogen. • Set out a co-operation process on renewable hydrogen with the African Union in the framework of the Africa-Europe Green Energy Initiative. • Develop a benchmark for euro-denominated transactions by 2021.	• One option is the creation of a new IPCEI for the field of hydrogen technologies and systems as a joint project with other Member States. The focus here should be on the entire value and use chain for hydrogen (generation, transport, distribution, use). To this end, the Federal Government is proactively approaching the European Commission and EU Member States in order to attract support for such a project (ongoing process). • The establishment of a European hydrogen company to promote and develop joint international production capacities and infrastructure is being explored and will be progressed if there is sufficient European backing. • Strengthening the existing international activities, particularly in the context of the energy partnerships and of multilateral co-operation, such as that of the International Partnership for Hydrogen and Fuel Cells in the Economy (IPHE), the International Renewable Energy Agency (IRENA) and the International Energy Agency (IEA), and we will make use of them to progress the supra-regional aspects of hydrogen. • Pilot projects in partner countries of Germany, not least as part of German development co-operation involving German firms, are to show whether and how green hydrogen and its downstream products can be produced and marketed there on a sustainable and competitive basis.	• Direct contact with European Commission at every conceivable level • Pentalateral Forum (Benelux, Germany, France, Austria and Switzerland) – develop standards, market incentives, regulations • Consultations with North Sea countries, North Sea Wind Power Hub Project • Feasibility study – on Dutch/Germany offshore wind energy and the benefits for scaling up green hydrogen, which would then be made available through Dutch gas pipelines (HY3 project) • IPCEI – Netherlands will be focusing on green hydrogen

Source: Dutch, German and EU Hydrogen strategies.

Research priorities

Germany hydrogen strategy

The National Hydrogen Strategy (NWS) of the German Federal Government is supported by the German government's economic stimulus package, in which it massively expands the promotion of hydrogen and fuel cell technology. A total of roughly EUR 2 billion is foreseen for the use of hydrogen to decarbonise industry. This includes the development of a new pilot program for Carbon Contracts for Difference (CCfD) and the examination of demand quota for climate-friendly raw materials (e.g. green steel) and tendering models for the production of green hydrogen to de-carbonise the steel and chemical industry. An important instrument for the implementation of the NWS is IPCEI Hydrogen in which the German government wants to promote integrated projects along the entire hydrogen value chain and offers co-ordination at EU level.

New cross-ministry research campaign entitled 'hydrogen technologies 2030' will see a strategic bundling together of research activities into hydrogen-related enabling technologies. (Implementation began in Q2 2020). Key elements of the research campaign include:

- Regulatory sandboxes for the energy transition so as bring up Power-to-X technologies[6] that are close to market to an industrial scale and accelerate the process of innovation transfer.
- Large-scale research projects entitled 'hydrogen in the steel and chemical industries' that pave the way for climate neutrality.
- Projects in the transport sector that will use research, development and innovation to further bring down the cost of hydrogen technologies.
- Feasibility studies and atlases of potential to help pinpoint economically suitable global location for a future, green hydrogen industry. This work will take into account future developments of energy needs and of the natural resources available in the various countries.
- International networks and Research and Engineering (R&E) co-operation to prepare new markets for German technology exports.
- The establishment of a new research network on hydrogen technologies to foster networking and an open dialogue between business and science that can inform public funding policy.

European Union Hydrogen Strategy

- Larger size cost-effective electrolysers in a range of gigawatts (a call for 100 MW electrolysers launched in 2020).
- Infrastructure needs further development to distribute, store, and dispense large volumes of hydrogen and repurposing of existing gas infrastructure.
- Large-scale end-use applications (notably in industry).
- Improved and harmonised (safety) standards, assessing the environmental impacts of hydrogen technologies of large scale electrolysers.

Funding Mechanisms

- Clean Hydrogen Partnership – support research, development and demonstration of technologies.
- ETS Innovation Fund – EUR 10 billion between 2020 and 2030.
- Launch of a call for pilot action on interregional innovation under cohesion policy on Hydrogen Technologies in carbon-intensive regions (2020).

Support to help industry cover operational costs in the Netherlands and in Germany

The key difference between the Netherlands, the German and EU hydrogen strategies is that CCfDs are only mentioned in the German and EU strategies. Neither strategy specifies the detail of this mechanism in great length, but both Germany and the European Union mention CCfDs as a way to help cover the operational costs of hydrogen and to catalyse its deployment.

CCfDs are contracts that companies can sign with the government for low-carbon industrial production, and in return the government assures a fixed carbon price, a so-called strike price. As long as the carbon price is lower than the strike price, the difference will be paid to the company by the government. If the carbon price is higher than the strike price, companies must pay back the difference between the two prices. CCfDs are designed to offset the higher operating costs of low-carbon production processes compared to the fossil fuel-based reference process. In the German hydrogen strategy, a pilot program for CCfDs is planned for the steel and chemical industries. CCfDs are selected through tenders. However, this and other issues such as conflicts with European state aid law or the determination of reference costs are still under investigation.

While CCfD policies are well suited to cover the price difference between hydrogen and fossil fuels, the budgets of EUR 250 million in 2022 and EUR 300 million in 2023 are likely not enough to close the OPEX gap to make hydrogen-based technologies cost-competitive with today's fossil fuel-based technologies.

It is possible that the Netherlands does not need a CCfD instrument because of the ambitious carbon levy and the SDE++ subsidies which could be used to close the OPEX gap for hydrogen. However, it is unclear when the carbon levy and SDE++ would actually cover the costs of the hydrogen technology. The carbon levy is not expected to bite in the coming years and the expected allocation of SDE++ to hydrogen is limited per design of the scheme, as it is not one of the most cost-effective ways of reducing emissions. It is not a good sign that of the applications for SDE++ in 2020, only EUR 2 million was requested for hydrogen production for a capacity of only 2 MW. The Netherlands mentions in their hydrogen strategy the desire to create a fund to help firms cover operational costs, which could have the same utility as CCfDs in the German and European contexts if designed appropriately.

Hydrogen targets in other countries

Table 8.9 lists other national commitments (outside of the EU, Germany and the Netherlands) that relate to hydrogen, excluding targets related to fuel cell technology (Hydrogen Policy Database – G20 Japan). The usage of hydrogen in transport is different to that of industry. Fuel cell technologies – whether for buses, trains, planes, ships, or even vehicles – combine hydrogen and oxygen to create electricity and work similar to a conventional battery, except that instead of metals as the reactants it uses gases (i.e. hydrogen provides the electrons). Fuel cell technology, in itself, is not immediately relevant to industry since hydrogen is an input into industrial processes, rather than a means to electricity. Therefore, fuel cell targets – e.g. France's target for 200 hydrogen fuel cell buses by 2023 - are excluded from Table 8.9. Some of the targets in Table 8.9 relate to bringing down the costs of decarbonised hydrogen – i.e. Japan, Korea, California (USA), and Shandong (CHN) – with no bifurcation of green and blue (Hydrogen Policy Database – G20 Japan). Korea and the Netherlands also specify targets for the transmission and distribution of hydrogen – both aim to create pipelines, whilst Korea also set targets for storage of hydrogen.

Table 8.9. Targets related to the uptake of hydrogen by industry

	Target
France	10% of decarbonised H_2 (ca. 90 000 tonnes) used in the industry by 2023 and 20-40% by 2028
Italy	The Government's plan to help boost production of green hydrogen, as stated in the draft document, is to introduce about 5 GW of electrolysing capacity to extract the gas from water over the 2021-30 period.
Japan	Procure 300 000 tonnes of hydrogen/year by 2030. Reduce the cost of hydrogen to USD 3 per kg by 2030 and USD 2 per kg in 2050. Subsidy for R&D, demonstration (national government initiative)
Korea	Establish overseas production base to stabilise hydrogen production, import with demand. By 2040, the annual supply of hydrogen will reach 5 260 000 tonnes, and the price per kg will reach KRW 3 000. Transmission and distribution targets: • Improve efficiency by diversifying storage methods such as high pressure gas, liquid, and solid • Relax regulations on storage of high-pressure gas, and develop liquefaction and liquid-storage technology with excellent safety and economic efficiency. • Use of tube trailer, pipeline. Use Lightweight high-pressure gaseous hydrogen tube trailers and reduce transport costs, and build a long-term hydrogen pipeline that connects the entire country.
California (USA)	Cost Target: USD 4 per kg (produced, delivered, dispensed) ultimately, USD 7 per kg by 2025, to supply early markets
Shandong (CHN)	By 2028, the province's H_2 energy industry output value will strive to exceed CNY 50 billion (USD 7.22 billion).

Source: Hydrogen Policy Database – G20 Japan.

8.3.4. Policies to accelerate the development and use of hydrogen in industry

Hydrogen value chains - from its production, transmission, distribution and storage - are complicated and full of risks. Investors face co-ordination difficulties across the value chain, rapidly changing technological costs and development (of hydrogen and its competitors), in addition to fluctuating regulations when crossing borders. IEA (2019[37]) pinpoints near-term opportunities to start to unravel this complexity in coastal industrial clusters ("as gateways to lower-cost and lower-carbon hydrogen hubs"), existing gas infrastructure (to scale up supply), and the creation of first shipping routes (to kick start international hydrogen trade). Moreover, as hydrogen is a technology featuring large network externalities, standardisation will be key in ensuring complementarity with other policy instruments (Vollebergh and van der Werf, 2014[45]). Fully realising this potential requires a high-level commitment from government and dedicated attention to mitigate risks, strategic R&D and demonstration, work to harmonise standards and remove barriers, and above all – policies to stimulate demand.

Working to harmonise standards and remove barriers will have to be done in close co-operation with other countries, the Netherlands will not be able to resolve these issues alone. International standardisation will be crucial in this value chain, including guarantees of origin, hydrogen purity, the design of liquefaction/conversion and regasification/reconversion facilities, and for equipment specifications. There are a number of risks associated with blending into the gas grid – legal differences between European member states on what amount of hydrogen can be transported in pipelines, ambiguities surrounding third-party access (hydrogen suppliers) to natural gas pipelines, and how to regulate returns for systems operators. As hydrogen in the gas grid, whether blended or 100% hydrogen, will be used in people's homes, ensuring safety is of paramount importance. Public safety concerns or adverse events could seriously impair the speed of deployment or prevent it altogether. Standards will also be important for new appliances and equipment. A key barrier to be addressed is the current low level of blending permitted in many jurisdictions, especially where cross-border pipelines exist.

For R&D, The IEA's Hydrogen Strategy points to the following as being the top research priorities for the immediate future:

- First major applications of CCUS technologies in a given region and large-scale integrated electrolyser demonstrations can help ensure that some of the resulting knowledge is widely shared to accelerate subsequent adoption.
- R&D for underground storage of hydrogen in depleted oil and gas fields and aquifers is likely to be necessary to prove their suitability for use with hydrogen.

- Higher-risk demonstration projects for localised grid conversions are also likely to need public support.
- Uncertainty remains about the most effective type of carrier for shipping hydrogen, with much scope for thorough investigation of the options and improvement of efficiency and capital costs.
- Liquefaction efficiency, boil-off management, scalability and the efficiency of the cooling cycle require improvement. Strategic demonstration projects could target the scale-up of liquefaction and regasification facilities for hydrogen directly or in the form of ammonia.

Finally, the huge amounts of carbon-neutral energy carriers required to produce green hydrogen are not yet available. Important uncertainty exists on when and if such energy carriers will be sufficiently provided at a competitive price. For companies to make investments worth several hundred million euros, the supply of such renewable energy carriers need to be ensured. This also includes the local availability of hydrogen infrastructure for generation/import and transport. Investors in hydrogen applications need to know if there will be access to a hydrogen network at a certain date in the future and if hydrogen is a strategic part of the Netherlands industry decarbonisation strategy. Thus, increase in the development and deployment of hydrogen also links to infrastructure planning.

8.4. The circular economy: Recycling of plastics and metals

Key messages

- For plastics, the technological readiness level for mechanical recycling is high, but chemical recycling of plastics is still very much under development.
- For the recycling of major metals, the technological readiness level is high, but much more improvement is possible for the recycling of minor metals.
- From an environmental point of view, mechanical recycling of plastics is preferred to chemical recycling, but where mechanical recycling is not possible, chemical recycling is preferred to incineration of waste for heat or electricity production.
- In line with the EU Circular Economy Action Plan, the Netherlands has an ambitious circular economy agenda to reduce raw materials consumption by 50% by 2030 and to have a circular economy by 2050.
- The main reason for the low uptake of recycled plastics is that there is no separate market for recycled plastics and virgin plastics are cheaper and often of higher quality. Policies such as minimum recycled content standards, public procurement and public awareness campaigns are needed to create the required market for recycled plastics.
- More investment in R&D is needed to develop better and more cost-effective ways of chemical recycling and the recycling of minor metals.
- For metals, by-products of steel production, such as slag and fly ash, have to be carefully relabelled from 'waste' to 'product' in order to reduce the administrative burdens associated with purchasing scrap for companies. This requires more co-ordination at the EU level. This goes hand in hand with increasing possibilities for import of scrap from other countries.
- Trade policies can help increase recycling of metals by enabling economies of scale, harmonising legal frameworks and by addressing the problem of exports to countries with inadequate recycling facilities.
- For the recycling of metals, the main constraint is the supply of scrap, while for the recycling of plastics the main constraint is on the demand side.

As the circular economy is a very broad concept, we limit ourselves in the rest of the chapter to the role of three of the core materials for industrial production: recycling of plastics and metals in this section, and bio-based materials in the next section.

8.4.1. Technological Readiness Levels across the recycling value chain of plastics

Plastics have different polymer types and different origins (fossil-fuel based, bio-based, as well as CO and CO_2-based, as summarised in Table 8.10), with greater demand in different sectors for different polymers. The steps to recycling these plastics involve: plastic stream preparation, sorting and separation, plastic waste preparation, and finally, recycling – either via mechanical or chemical technologies. The rest of this subsection summarises the key challenges to perform these activities, the relevant polymers, the key technologies to overcome these challenges, and the state of the technology.

Plastic stream preparation

Plastic waste contains solid and liquid contaminants that result from their specific use and history, which can significantly affect the quality of the recycling output and are not easily removable. For example, it is difficult to remove inks – i.e. very costly and energy intensive. As a result, plastic waste with printed inks are often recycled "as is" and used in lower value products such as plastic shopping bags.

Table 8.10. Challenges in plastic stream preparation and technological options

Challenge	Technology	Polymers	2020
Removal of contaminants from plastic articles	Solvating fluid treatment during continuous extrusion to treat flowable polymer masses	All	Pilot/Demonstration
	Use of sensors	PE-LD, PE-LLD, PE-HD, PE-MD	Pilot/Demonstration
Removal of ink	De-inking	PE-LD, PE-HD, PP, PET, PVC	Pilot/Demonstration
Removal of odour	Supercritical fluid extraction	PP, PE-LD, PE-LLD, PE-HD, PE-MD, PVC, PET, PUR, PS, PS-E	Pilot/Demonstration
	Friendly oxidants water-based treatments	PP, PE-LD, PE-LLD, PE-HD, PE-MD, PVC, PET, PUR, PS, PS-E	Pilot/Demonstration

Source: Suschem (2020[46]).

Sorting and separation

Table 8.11 shows the main challenges in sorting and separation of plastics and the main technological options to deal with them. The composition of waste varies from a stream composed solely of bottles (e.g. PET) to streams containing additional trays, pots and films, with a wide range of different polymers. Moreover, rigid plastics are often multi-layered, and therefore, difficult to separate. Bottles can be covered in PVC sleeve labels, or PET grade materials that need to be separated from bottles and trays. Furthermore, applications polymers are often mixed with other materials (e.g. wood, metals, oil, etc.) and can contain legacy additives and also organic additives (e.g. dyes) for which sorting and separation is difficult. In order to recycle these streams efficiently, polymer articles need to be sorted by their constituent materials to minimise waste and ensure a high quality end product. The two main routes currently employed, namely wet and dry sorting, need further technological development and cost reduction to be deployed widely.

Table 8.11. Challenges in sorting/separation and technological options

Sorting	Challenge	Technology	Polymers	Short-term investment needs
Wet	Separation of light or similar plastics	Hydro-cyclone	All	Demonstration/ industrial/first of a kind
		Floatation	All	Demonstration/ industrial/first of a kind
		Polymer tracing	All	Pilot/ demonstration
		Magnetic Density Sorting (MDS)	PP, PE-LD, PE-LLD, PE-HD, PE-MD, PVC, PET, PUR, PS, PS-E	Pilot/demonstration
	Sorting waste while reducing environment impact of consumables	Closed loop process to eliminate contaminants	PP, PE-LD, PE-LLD, PE-HD, PE-MD, PVC, PET, PUR, PS, PS-EI	Pilot/demonstration
Dry	Recovery of black polymers	RAMAN spectroscopy	ABS, PP, PC, PS, PE-HD, PA, PVC, PET	Pilot/demonstration
		XRF, XRT	ABS/HIPS, PP, PC, PS, PE-HD, PA, PMMA, PVC, PET	Demonstration/First of a kind
		Laser Induced Breakdown Spectroscopy (LIBS)	ABS/HIPS, PP, PC, PS, PE-HD, PA, PMMA, PVC, PET	Pilot/demonstration
		Mid-infrared spectroscopy	POs, PVC	Pilot/demonstration
	Sorting of packaging articles	Optical sorting (Near Infrared Technology – NIR, Visible sorting - VIS)	All	Research/Pilot
	Increase recovery of plastics from the construction sector	Optical sorting (NIR, VIS)	All	Research/Pilot
	Identifying additives of very high concern in older (legacy) plastic applications)	LIBS	All	Research
		Laser sorting	All	Pilot/Demonstration
	Heterogeneity of waste streams	Combination of NIR, VIS, and Mid-infrared thermography (MIR-T)	All	Pilot
		Artificial intelligence algorithms	All	Pilot/Demonstration
		Tera Hz	PHA	Research/Pilot

Source: Suschem (2020[46]).

Plastic waste preparation

Table 8.12 shows the main challenges of waste preparation and the technological options. The separation of the various polymers in a stack is often difficult and must be done manually most of the time.

Table 8.12. Challenges for waste preparation and technological options

Challenge	Technology	Polymers	Short-term investment needs
Separation of polymer layers	Integrated solution of grinding machinery with thermal and chemical, and magnetic separation	PU/PE	Research/Pilot
Delamination	Delamination with supercritical CO_2	All	Research/Pilot

Source: Suschem (2020[46]).

Recycling technology: mechanical and chemical

Mechanical

Mechanical recycling aims to recover plastic waste via mechanical processes (i.e. grinding, washing, separating, drying, re-granulating and compounding). In these processes, polymers stay intact, which enables the re-use of polymers in the same or similar products — effectively creating a closed loop. It currently represents the most common form of plastic recycling due to its cheap and simple nature. However, such processes cannot remove additives (e.g. dyes), impurities (e.g. dust), or other organic contaminants meaning the results tends to be impure and low-quality. Another limitation is that some quality is lost with each cycle and is typically limited to five cycles. For this reason, recycled plastics are often mixed with virgin plastics, and are still partly based on fossil fuels.

Advanced mechanical recycling techniques could be enhanced by developing:

- Stable reagents for high temperature processing by means of twin screw extruders/compounding to permit the re-introduction in the value chain of cross-linked polymers that cannot be reprocessed, under normal conditions.
- New mechanical methods to break the chemical bonds by using twin screw extruders with the combination of high shear and high energy sources (radiation).
- New mixers based on extensional flow (specific reactor) to improve dispersion and distribution quality for a wide range of viscosity ratios and avoiding thermal degradation.
- Fibre functionalisation and reactive compatibilisation extrusion.
- Reactive extrusion process to improve adhesion between the recycled fibre and polymer matrix (compatibilisation).

Chemical recycling of plastics

Chemical recycling requires a lot of energy, which has to be renewable to achieve the climate ambitions. As for mechanical recycling, chemical recycling can close the cycle, but the cycle is bigger with chemical recycling because polymers are broken down to produce synthetic feedstock before they are re-processed into polymers again by the chemical industry.

Pyrolysis is a process to chemically decompose organic materials at elevated temperatures in the absence of oxygen. Conventional pyrolysis is called **thermal cracking** which is used to recycle mixed plastics, such as multi-layer plastic packaging, that cannot be recycled mechanically. The process is performed at moderate to high temperatures between 300°C and 700°C and without oxygen. The main problems are the complexity of the reactions and the large amount of energy required in the process. Pyrolysis has a low tolerance for PVC in the raw material, as the chlorinate compounds can then be formed in the pyrolysis oil which make it difficult to use. The products from waste plastics thermal cracking are gas, char and liquid oil. Pyrolysis oil is the most valuable product form of thermal cracking as it can be used for many applications, e.g. in petroleum blends or for the production of new plastics.

This section reviews the technological readiness levels for chemical recycling of heterogeneous plastic waste streams (Figure 8.7, for an overview of these technologies, and Table 8.13 for a summary), and therefore, concentrates on cracking and gasification. This subsection reviews the seven technologies in dark blue that relate to heterogeneous waste and assesses these on process temperature, sensitivity to feedstock contamination and level of polymer breakdown. In general, higher temperatures can more comprehensively breakdown polymers, which can lead to a higher purity in the processed material and a greater portfolio of products that can be regenerated. The lower the process temperature of a technology, the greater sensitivity of the technology to the quality of the waste, which often requires more advanced separation before chemical recycling. Of course, the sensitivity of different technologies to the quality of waste stream, in turn, impacts the needed logistics to separate (and costs).

Figure 8.7. Chemical recycling technologies

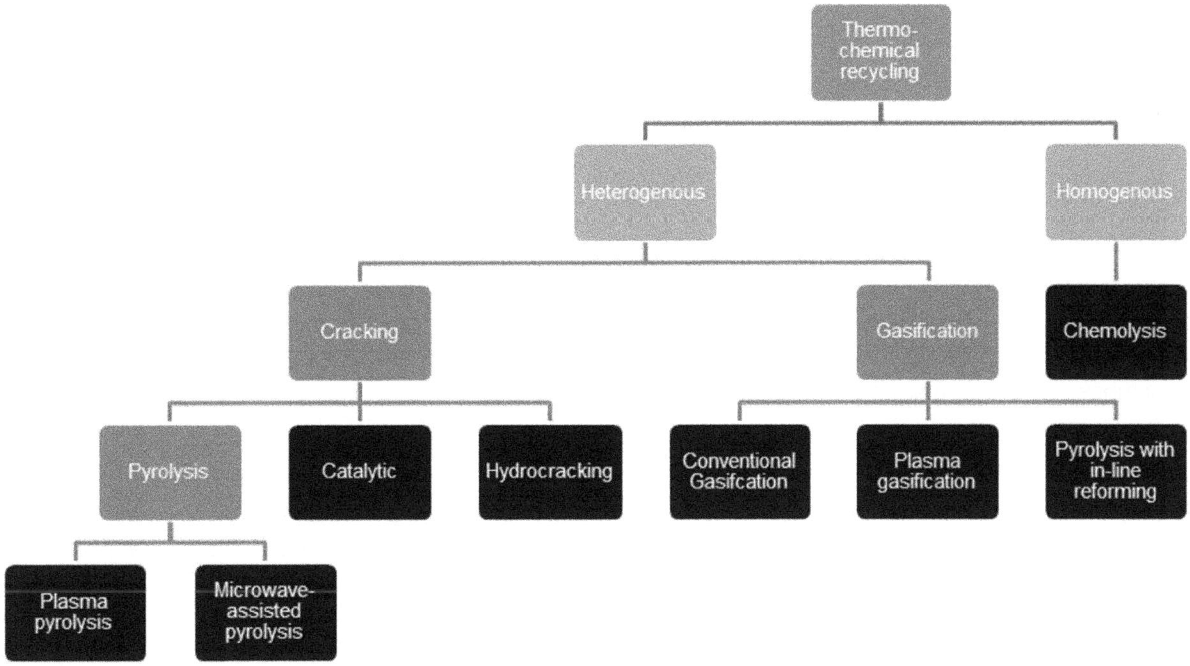

Source: Adapted from Solis and Silveira (2020[47]).

Figure 8.7 gives a summary of TRLs of chemical recycling technologies. Two promising technologies include: plasma pyrolysis and micro-wave assisted pyrolysis.

Plasma pyrolysis is promising for gaseous fuels, chemical production, and suitable for electricity generation in turbines or in hydrogen. It transforms plastic waste into syngas (by integrating conventional pyrolysis with the thermochemical properties of plasma). The syngas is composed of CO, H_2, and small amounts of higher hydrocarbons. These process temperatures can be very high from 1730°C to 9730°C and are very fast, typically lasting between 0.01-0.05 seconds (depending on temperature and waste). The advantage of this technology is the production of gas with less toxic compounds (than other methods) since the temperature is high enough to decompose them. Thermal plasma technology is well-established in metallurgy, material synthesis, and destruction of hazardous waste. Plasma pyrolysis of waste plastics has only been investigated at the laboratory scale, since several technological challenges remain before the technology can be deployed at scale.

Microwave-assisted pyrolysis mixes waste plastics with a highly microwave-absorbent dielectric material (i.e. a substance that is a poor conductor of electricity, but an efficient supporter of electrostatic field). The heat absorbed from microwaves is transferred to the plastics by conduction. This process allows for very high temperatures and is very efficient at converting electrical energy into heat. It offers more control over the process than conventional pyrolysis techniques. Plastics have poor dielectric strength, however, and when mixed with an absorbent, the heating efficiency may vary and it may be difficult to use these efficiently at industrial scale. So far, this has only been studied at laboratory and pilot scales.

Catalytic cracking adds a catalyst to the pyrolysis process to reduce the process temperature, which saves energy and reduces costs. Catalytic decomposition of polymers follows the same reaction stems as hydrocarbon catalytic cracking used in refineries, even the catalysts are similar. With a catalyst, the temperature can be lowered to 300-350°C, rather than 450°C for conventional pyrolysis. Moreover, it has a higher oil yield than conventional cracking for most plastics, ranging from 86-92%. Most of the work on this has been performed with pure polymers since this process can be impacted by contaminants present in plastic waste streams. There are several commercial catalytic cracking processes at industrial scale. One of world's largest catalytic cracking projects was Sapporo Plastics Recycling which, together with Toshiba, co-owned the world's largest waste plastic liquefaction facility in Japan. The facility converted 15 000 tonnes of mixed waste plastic into light oil, which was used as feedstock for new plastic products, medium fuel oil equivalent to diesel and heavy oil used for electricity generation. However, Sapporo Plastic Recycling withdrew from the business in 2010 due to financial problems.

Hydrocracking adds hydrogen to the cracking process (which results in higher product quality). The process has a temperature range of 375-500°C and occurs at elevated hydrogen pressures. The waste plastic first goes through a lower temperature pyrolysis, which leads to plastic liquefaction, which is then sent over to the catalyst bed. The catalyst is important in the hydrocracking process since it reduces the temperature and increases the oil yield and quality. The biggest obstacle in implementing this technology is the cost of hydrogen. Hydrocracking of waste plastic feedstock is only available at a pilot scale. Several challenges remain to make it commercially viable.

Conventional gasification of waste plastics leads to a mixture of hydrocarbons and syngas, which can then be used to produce energy, energy carriers such as hydrogen as well as chemicals from syngas. It usually occurs at temperatures between 700-1 200°C depending on the gasifying agent – i.e. air, steam or plasma. The agent, in turn, determines the composition of the syngas produced and possible applications. Two undesirable products – tar and char – can result from the process, the actual amounts depend on the plastic waste characteristics. An operational full-scale plant is owned by Enerkem, and located in Edmonton, Canada. It converts 100 000 tonnes of dried and post-sorted plastic waste annually into 38 million litres of biofuels: methanol, then ethanol and ethylene. The company is part of a consortium planning a waste-to-chemicals plant in Rotterdam, which will have capacity to convert up to 360 000 tonnes of non-recyclable waste plastics and other mixed wastes into 220 000 tonnes (270 million litres) of methanol. This is more than the total annual waste from 700 000 households and reduces CO_2 emissions by approximately 300 000 tonnes, compared to incineration.

Table 8.13. Summary table of technology readiness levels (TRLs) of chemical recycling technologies

Technology	Scale of operation	Temperature (in process)	Sensitivity to feedstock quality	Polymer breakdown	TRL
Conventional pyrolysis	Commercial	300 to 700	High	Moderate	9
Plasma pyrolysis	Laboratory	1 800 to 10 000	Low	Very detailed	4
Microwave assisted	Laboratory	Up to 1 000	Medium	Detailed	4
Catalytic cracking	Commercial	450 to 550	High	Moderate	9
Hydrocracking	Pilot	375 to 500	High	Detailed	7
Conventional gasification	Commercial	700 to 1 200	Medium	Detailed	9
Plasma gasification	Commercial (hazardous waste)	1 200 to 15 000	Low	Very detailed	8
Pyrolysis with in-line reforming	Pilot	500 to 900	Medium	Detailed	4

Source: Solis and Silveira (2020[47]).

Plasma gasification is a process where plasma is used to pass an electric current through the gas. The process temperature is very high, up to 15 000°C. However, it has a high tolerance to low quality feedstock. It results in a higher quality gas with lower level of tars. Yet, these have a very high electricity requirement compared to, for example, a plasma gasification plant with around 1 200-2 500 MJ per tonne of waste. Some of the first commercial applications of plasma gasification are located in Japan - a waste-to-energy (WTE) plant owned by Westinghouse Plasma Corporation and Hitachi Metals located in Eco Valley and a WTE plant owned by Hitachi Metals located between cities of Mihama and Mikata. Other operating plants exist in China and India, however, there are none in Europe. There were plans to construct two plants in the United Kingdom (in Tess Valley), but these fell through when the project became economically unfeasible.

Pyrolysis with in-line reforming is carried out in two connected in-line reactors for pyrolysis and reforming steps. The interest in this lies in high hydrogen production from the process and the gas is free of tars. The process temperature varies between 500-900°C depending on the feedstock, reactor configuration and bed material. This is currently only at laboratory scale.

8.4.2. Technological Readiness Levels of recycling of Metals

For the recycling of metals, it is essential to facilitate the uptake of scrap in the metallurgical sector for the production of steel and aluminium. Foundries in the metallurgical sector use mechanical recycling technologies. The present recycling rates for metals varies substantially in the European Union:

- The use of recycled metals saves a lot of energy compared to the production of metals from raw materials. For the recycling of aluminium only 5% of the original energy consumption is used, as aluminium retains energy from its primary production.
- Over 90% End-of-Life (EoL) stainless steel is currently collected and recycled into new products. 70% of the steel produced to-date, however, is still in use (European Recycling Industries' Confederation, 2020[48]).
- Of the total amount of aluminium scrap generated in the EU at EoL (i.e. 4 338 thousand tonnes of aluminium), about 2,986 thousand tonnes of aluminium were collected and recycled, resulting in an EoL recycling rate of 69% (European Recycling Industries' Confederation, 2020[48]).
- With respect to metals, the obstacle is one of access more than technological (as noted in the industry consultations). Mechanical recycling is sufficient for recycling of metals. Metals do not lose quality when melted and recycled, which means that they are infinitely recyclable in principle. Therefore, the key policies needed to incentivise the uptake of scrap are those that facilitate access. In addition to increased collection rates of discarded products, improved design for recycling (e.g. to not use different layers of different metals) and the enhanced deployment of modern recycling methodology can help to create a closed-loop metal material system (Reck and Graedel, 2012[49]).

8.4.3. Recycling in the Netherlands

Recycling of plastics will likely play a role in the decarbonisation of the chemicals subsector, for instance through the use of synthetic feedstock (e.g. pyrolysis oil) as a replacement to fossil fuels, which will use chemical recycling technologies. The present recycling rates for plastics varies substantially in the European Union.

Of all plastic waste collected in Europe, 31% was recycled in 2018, with the remainder either incinerated or landfilled (Hesselink and Van Durren, 2019[50]; Plastics Europe, 2019[51]). For plastic packaging specifically, the recycling percentage for collected waste is a bit higher at 41% (Hesselink and Van Durren, 2019[50]; Plastics Europe, 2019[51]).

Figure 8.8 shows that recycling rates for packaging waste reported by the European Environmental Agency are relatively high for the Netherlands and already meet the EU target for recycling 75% of packaging waste by 2030. However, this share also includes non-plastic materials like wood, metal, paper and glass. According to Eurostat, this is estimated to be around 50% for plastics in 2017.

According to the transition agenda for plastics, 250-300 Kt plastics were recycled in the Netherlands in 2018, while 2 000 Kt was produced. More than five times as much plastic (1 313 Kt) is used for incineration plants to produce heat and electricity. The ambition is to reduce the amount that is incinerated by 44% by 2030. This must be achieved through better separation of plastics and better sorting machines.

Figure 8.8. Packaging waste recycling share in percentage of generated packaging waste

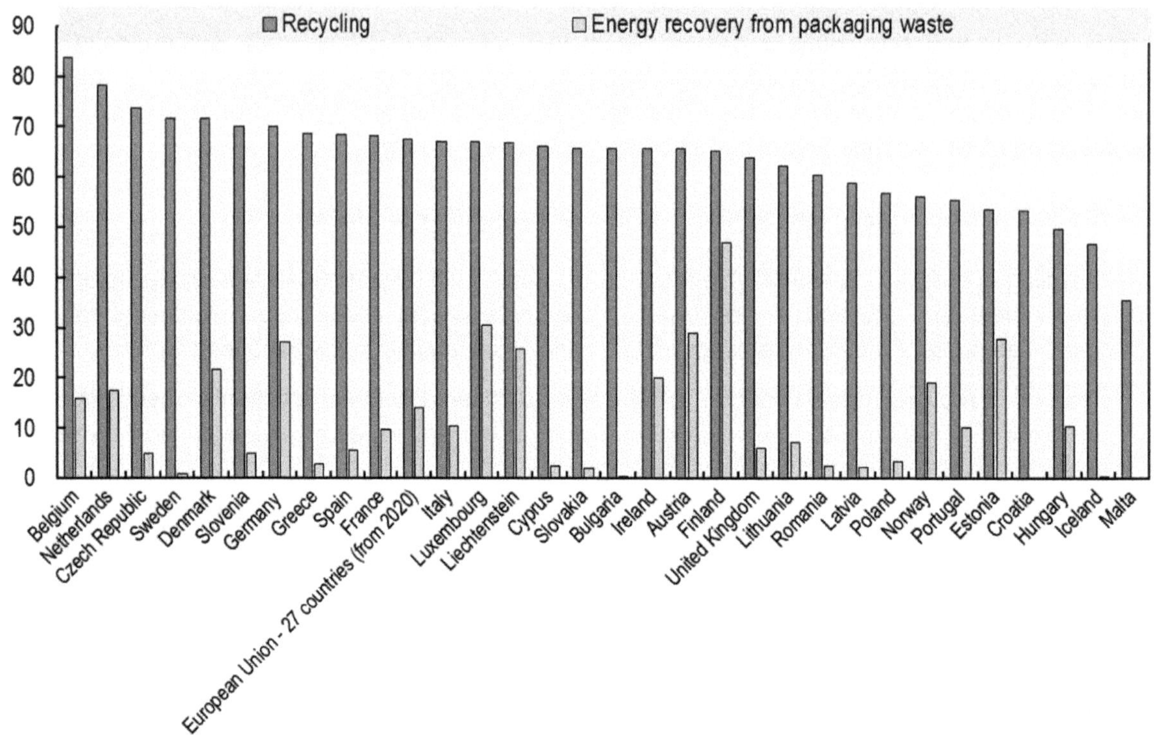

Source: Packaging waste by waste operation and waste flow provided by Eurostat, 2017.

There is a push by countries worldwide to ameliorate these recycling rates in order to catalyse the shift from a linear to circular economy. A thorough review of these agendas is beyond the scope of this section. Instead, this chapter focuses on two distinct challenges for the chemicals and metallurgical sector, respectively.

Synthetic feedstocks from plastics is still far from reality. Open questions remain across the plastics value chain that need to be resolved. We have now briefly overviewed the outstanding challenges to recycling plastics for each step in the value chain, presented the key technologies to overcome these barriers, as well as the state of the technology as of 2020, and provided a deep-dive into chemical recycling. The next section reviews how the Netherlands and other countries are advancing chemical recycling compared to the Netherlands and how to enable the policy environment for chemical recycling.

Dutch strategy for a circular economy by 2050

The circular economy is an economy that aims to eliminate waste and to create a closed system, to minimise resource use, waste production, pollution and carbon emissions. This is achieved through reusing, sharing, repairing, refurbishing, remanufacturing and recycling. The ambition of the Dutch government is to reduce raw materials consumption by 50% in 2030 and to have a circular economy run entirely on reusable materials by 2050. However, this still has to be operationalised, as the base year for this 50% has not yet been defined and it is also unclear whether the reduction is measured in kilos or another unit (PBL, 2019[52]).

The Dutch government formulated three objectives to reach a circular economy. First of all, existing production processes have to make more efficient use of raw materials, so that fewer raw materials are needed. Second, when raw materials are needed, sustainably produced, renewable and widely available raw materials, such as biomass, are used as much as possible. Third, new production methods and circular products need to be developed.

The Netherlands follows a timeline for the transition to a circular economy in 2050. This timeline begins with the Government-wide programme for a Circular Dutch Economy by 2050 that was adopted in 2016 (Ministry of Infrastructure and the Environment and Ministry of Economic Affairs, 2016[53]). This programme describes what needs to be done to use raw materials, products and services more intelligently and efficiently.

In 2017 the Raw Materials Agreement was signed by 180 parties from both government and industry. This agreement sets out what needs to be done to ensure that the Dutch economy can run on renewable resources. Partners in this agreement commit themselves to jointly draw up five transition agendas in 2018 for sectors and value chains that have a high environmental impact but are also economically important to the Netherlands. These five transition agendas are for the following sectors: biomass and food, plastics, manufacturing industry, construction and consumer goods.

Biomass is used for animal feed, chemicals, biofuels and energy. Biomass can make many sectors greener and reduce CO_2 emissions. A more extensive overview of the importance of biomass is provided in the next section on bio-based materials.

With the Plastic Pact, government, industry and environmental organisations are fighting against plastic waste. In 2050, plastics need to have a low carbon footprint, be made from recycled or renewable bio-based materials and will no longer be incinerated.

The manufacturing industry processes materials, such as metals, into new products. These processes are often harmful to the environment. A circular design for high-quality sustainable reuse of materials is required. Three important points in the transition agenda for the manufacturing include: 1) Material efficiency, optimising life cycle products and closing raw material chain at the end-of-life; 2) recycling technology to close cycles, optimising not only on quantity but also on quality with the ambition to have no net outflow of critical raw materials; 3) facilitate circular business models: transition from product sales to service models.

The construction sector accounts for 50% of the raw material consumption in the Netherlands. Much waste is demolition waste. In order to organise our living environment in a sustainable way, an acceleration of innovations (circular and modular construction) within the construction sector is necessary.

Consumer goods must be reused to avoid unnecessary waste.

In 2019, the Dutch government presented the Circular Economy implementation programme, which translates the five transition agendas into concrete actions and projects between 2019 and 2023. Examples from this implementation program include: the production of bioasphalt from natural adhesives from trees, the use of components in mattresses that can be easily separated and reused, the reduction of plastic waste through the Plastic Pact, and a circular Central Government Real Estate Agency.

In addition to the Dutch Circular Economy programmes, the European Commission also has a Circular Economy Action Plan, in which 35 actions are formulated for the implementation of the circular economy. With this action plan the EU wants to lead global efforts on the circular economy by introducing legislative and non-legislative measures targeting areas where action at the EU level brings added value. This action plan makes sustainable products the norm in the EU and focuses on the sectors that use most resources and where the potential for circularity is thus the highest, which are electronics and ICT, batteries and vehicles, packaging, plastics, textiles, construction and buildings, food, water and nutrients. Consumers and public buyers are empowered and circularity must work for people regions and cities.

A new Dutch National Platform for chemical recycling should promote knowledge exchange and co-ordinate chemical recycling initiatives. The platform will also identify areas of innovation, so that (development) programs are designed to cover blind spots. The platform was created at the request of the

Top Sector Chemistry and the Dutch ministries of Infrastructure and Water Management and Economic Affairs and Climate (EZK). Chemical recycling is one of the most important subjects in the Dutch Plastics Transition Agenda and is part of the innovation agendas in the context of the Climate and Resources Agreement.

The funding for innovation and demonstration for the circular economy amounted to approximately EUR 180 million in 2018, with the largest budgets coming from DEI+ Circular Economy (EUR 44 million), the EU Horizon 2020 (EUR 43 million to the Netherlands), WBSO (EUR 35.6 million), Top Sector policies (EUR 26.9 million), LIFE (EUR 12 million) and PPS bonus (public-private partnership bonus) (EUR 11.3 million) (RVO, 2020[54]). This is in addition to other budgets for the circular economy, such as the region-envelopes (EUR 90 million in 2019) and national climate envelopes (EUR 22.5 million in 2019), consisting of EUR 10 million for encouraging the recycling of plastics and consumer goods, EUR 5 million for recycling of asphalt, and steel, and EUR 7.5 million for climate neutral procurement. Finally, MIA and Vamil are responsible for another EUR 45 million subsidy for the circular economy in 2019. Hundreds of millions in total are thus targeted at the circular economy (Ministry of Infrastructure and the Environment and Ministry of Economic Affairs, 2019[55]).

Chemical recycling in the Netherlands and climate change impact

Three types of plastic waste streams seem most interesting for chemical recycling: left-overs from mechanical recycling, difficult to recycle mono-streams such as PET trays and expanded polystyrene (EPS) from construction, and mixed plastics. In the Netherlands, this amounts to 230 kton of plastics in 2020. In 2030 this will amount to 260-340 kton a year.

A first analysis of the climate impact of various waste processing techniques, based on life cycle assessment (LCA), shows that chemical recycling is having a climate impact between 0 and -0.5 tCO_2-eq/tonne of inputs (CE Delft, 2019[56]). This is in between the impact of approximately -2.3 tonnes CO_2-eq/tonne input for mechanical recycling and the 1.5 tonnes CO_2-eq/tonne for incineration where production of heat (e.g. for buildings) and electricity has already been taken into account (CE Delft, 2019[56]).

By 2030, 10% of all plastics used in the Netherlands will be chemically recycled according to the Dutch circular economy transition agenda.

A roadmap for chemical recycling of plastics in 2030 has been developed by the employers' organisation VNO-NCW together with the Rebelgroup (VNO NCW and Rebelgroup, 2020[57]). It contains three pillars: the potential of chemical recycling for the Netherlands in 2030, the sourcing of plastics for chemical recycling and support for circular economy policy.

Ambitions from industry show that a strong upscaling of chemical recycling is needed. Shell wants to use 1 Mt of plastic waste a year as feedstock in its production process, Dow 100 Kt a year, Nestle wants to reduce the use of virgin plastics in its packaging by one third and use 100% recycled or reusable packaging by 2025.

The Industry roadmap starts with 50 Kt of recycling capacity in 2020 and scales up to 500 Kt in 2025 and 1-1.5 Mt in 2030. From 2025 onwards, large scale projects should follow the pilot phase. The ambition is to have at least one or two large-scale plants producing 200-400 Kt recycled plastics in 2030. To realise this, it is important to have large-scale investments in sorting capacity and enough supply of used plastics.

Table 8.14 displays an overview of the volume of plastic waste streams that could be used as inputs for chemical recycling in the Netherlands in 2020 and 2030. For 2030, conservative and optimistic scenarios are created, based on assumptions regarding for example the growth in plastics consumption and post-consumer sorting efficiency. In addition, the optimistic scenario assumes that a part of the plastics discarded in Belgium, Germany and the United Kingdom are imported to the Netherlands. The table shows that by 2030, the Netherlands is estimated to produce a plastic waste volume of around 260 to 330 Kt per year that could be treated in chemical recycling technologies.

Table 8.14. Volume of waste

	2020	2030		
		Conservative	Optimistic	
			Netherlands	Imports
Recycling losses	97	107	161	558
PET trays	32	36	40	0
Mixed plastics (DKR-250)	101	112	126	583
Bromine-containing EPS	7	8	9	0
Total	237	263	336	1 141

Note: EPS stands for Expanded PolyStyrene, which is a white foam plastic produced form solid polystyrene beads.
Source: CE Delft (2020[58]).

8.4.4. Some of the countries at the forefront of the circular economy

Regulatory measures in Germany

Germany has a Circular Economy Act since 2021, which is the legal framework for waste management and implements one-to-one the EU Waste Framework Directive. Besides defining waste and by-products, Germany is known for using hierarchy within waste management. Separated collection of waste and recycling quotas are important in Germany.

The German Resource Efficiency Program ProgRess III mentions the relevance of resource efficiency for achieving climate goals and the relevance of digitisation for resource efficiency in particular. The ProgRess III includes 118 measures to improve resource efficiency in Germany. The measures concern: protection of resources in value chains and material cycles, transversal instruments, protection of resources at the international level, national, municipal and regional level and protection of resources in everyday life. ProgRess II is monitored through a set of indicators taking into account total raw material productivity, raw material consumption, secondary raw material use and material stock change. The German Resource Efficiency Program and its current version ProgRess III provide the framework for goals, ideas and approaches to protect natural resources. That is why various policy instruments are based on this program in the field of material efficiency and circular economy.

The German Packaging Act introduces stricter quota requirements and describes how to monitor and further develop recycling of plastics and metals. Plastic bags are banned from 2022 onwards and there is an amendment under discussion on a minimum recycled content for disposable bottles to increase demand for recycled plastics.

The German Commercial Waste Ordinance will impose stricter requirements for separation, sorting and recycling of mixed commercial waste. This will save about 1 million tonnes of CO_2 equivalent. This reduction is supported by waste prevention and resource conservation measures as described in the national Waste Prevention Programme and the German Resource Efficiency Programme. Table 8.15 gives an overview of the ambitious German recycling quotas as well as targets up to 2035.

In addition to recycling, Germany funds the Technology Transfer Programme Lightweight Construction (TTP LB) with a total EUR 300 million. This programme follows from the German Sustainability Strategy and the Industry Strategy 2030. Part of this project is about new design techniques and materials and another part about resource efficiency and substitution.

Table 8.15. Overview of German recycling quotas

	Current	2022	2025	2030	2035
Residential waste	50%	n.a.	55%	60%	65%
Packaging	55%	n.a.	65%	70%	n.a.
Glass	80%	90%	n.a.	n.a.	n.a.
Paper	85%	90%	n.a.	n.a.	n.a.
Ferrous metals	80%	90%	n.a.	n.a.	n.a.
Aluminium	80%	90%	n.a.	n.a.	n.a.
Beverage cartons	75%	80%	n.a.	n.a.	n.a.
Other composite	55%	70%	n.a.	n.a.	n.a.
Commercial waste	30%	n.a.	n.a.	n.a.	n.a.

Source: Fraunhofer ISI (2021).

As in the Netherlands, Germany generally does not implement technology specific tools, but the funding programmes in Germany are typically sector specific (construction or plastics), which is not the case in the Netherlands. Both countries offer measures targeting larger companies, SMEs and knowledge institutions, whereas the Germany policy mix is more focussed on PPP .The emerging technologies chemical recycling and bioeconomy are addressed more specifically in the Netherlands than in Germany. The bioeconomy in particular is of great importance to the refinery and chemical sectors in the Netherlands. For the same structural reason, chemical recycling of plastics is also part of the Dutch policy mix. In the Netherlands, a roadmap for the implementation of chemical recycling of plastics, including quotas, has been established. Based on a comparable legislative policy mix, it seems that the Dutch funding policy mix allows for more targeted actions in the field of material efficiency and the circular economy than Germany. Nevertheless, both countries lack specific product design standards.

R&D support in Germany and other countries

Another important angle through which Germany supports the circular economy is through speeding up the technological possibilities through investments in R&D. The FONA (Forschung für Nachhaltigkeit) research for sustainability includes the “Ressourceneffiziente Kreislaufwirtschaft” (resource-efficient circular economy) which covers the following topics: innovative product cycles, construction and mineral material cycles and plastic recycling technologies. Projects up to five years can get 50% funding for enterprises and up to 100% for higher education and research institutions. The budget available for 2018-23 is EUR 150 million.

Another stream of funding in Germany comes from the "Impulse für industrielle Ressourceneffizienz" (r+Impuls, impetus for industrial resource efficiency), which is supported by the expiring FONA3. Between 2016 and 2021, 26 joint projects are funded with EUR 22.3 million in the field of industrial resource efficiency. The funding only applies to TRL 5-9 and thereby closes the gap between R&D projects and introduction on the market.

Besides important transitions at the EU level, for example in Germany and overall in the European Union through Horizon 2020 funding, also the United States and the United Kingdom have ambitious plans for the transition to a circular economy.

UK Research and Innovation (UKRI) Industrial Strategy Challenge Fund is investing GBP 20 million in four chemical recycling plants. The four projects receiving funding are: ReNew ELP’s Catalytic Hydrothermal Reactor (Cat-HTR™) plant, Recycling Technologies’ chemical recycling plant, Poseidon Plastics’ hard-to-recycle PET chemical recycling plant, a collaboration between Veolia, Unilever, Charpak Ltd and HSSMI to develop the United Kingdom’s first dual PET bottle and tray recycling facility.

The DOE announced over USD 27 million in funding for 12 projects that will support the development of advanced plastics recycling technologies and new plastics that are recyclable-by-design. As part of DOE's Plastics Innovation Challenge, these projects will also help improve existing recycling processes that break plastics into chemical building blocks, which can then be used to make new products.

8.4.5. Addressing the main risks and bottlenecks for the recycling of plastics and metals

Enabling policy environment for recycling of plastics

For plastics, the main reason why the recycling rate is still much too low is that no separate market for recycled plastics exists, as primary and recycled plastics are treated as substitutes (OECD, 2018[59]). This causes the price of recycled plastics to be disconnected from the costs producing them and ultimately be driven by highly fluctuating oil prices. In addition, the average recycled plastics producer is about ten times as small as the average primary plastics producer, making the sector more vulnerable for market shocks such as the recent collapse in oil prices.

In the absence of a separate market, industry prefers to use virgin plastics, as making plastics from oil is very cost efficient, and therefore still easier and cheaper compared to producing recycled plastics, especially if the full environmental costs are not reflected in market prices. Recycled plastics are relatively expensive because of the technological barriers for sorting of plastics and chemical recycling as explained above. Policy interventions to create a market for recycled plastics include (OECD, 2020[60]):

- Setting statutory targets for recycling to drive supply of material, increase economies of scale, reduce costs and increase resilience.
- Using Extended Producer Responsibility (EPR) regulation to drive supply of material and increase economies of scale, reduce costs and increase resilience. Under EPR, a producer's responsibility extends throughout a product's lifespan, from production to the post-consumer stage – in other words producers must collect and recycle packaging after use.
- Green public procurement to create a market for greener products.
- Raising public awareness to create demand for plastics recycling, reduce contamination and to reduce dumping in the environment.
- Regulatory instruments such as recycling targets, product standards, recycled content requirements, lifetime warranties, bans and restrictions and deposit-refund systems.
- Market instruments, such as taxes, subsidies and tradable permit schemes, e.g. virgin material taxes or landfill taxes, cap-and-trade schemes for waste management. The full price difference should be captured by either taxes on virgin plastics or subsidies for recycled plastics.

Chemical recycling

In addition to the policies described to create a separate market for recycled plastics, more is needed if the Netherlands wants to exploit the potential of chemical recycling. Dutch waste policies view chemical recycling as low-value recycling, and therefore Extended Producer Responsibility systems for packaging do not regard chemical recycling as recycling. However, environmental analyses show that chemical recycling can still make a non-negligible contribution to emission reduction (CE Delft, 2019[56]), albeit much less than mechanical recycling. To give chemical recycling technologies the push needed to become commercialised, a level playing field with mechanical recycling could help. This is important for waste treatment policies and permits, for monitoring and reporting of recycling figures and also for producer responsibility schemes which support recycling (CE Delft, 2019[56]).

For chemical recycling the main challenge is the unavailability and inconsistent quality of feedstock, and again the before mentioned inefficient and thereby costly sorting, non-existing markets and unclear regulations for plastic waste management (Qureshi et al., 2020[61]). Solutions include:

- Tight co-operation between feedstock providers and converters to secure steady quantity and quality of feedstock.
- Advanced pre-treatment as basis for cost-effective recycling, classification of pyrolysis liquid as a product instead of waste.
- REACH (Registration, Evaluation, Authorisation and Restriction of Chemicals) registration should be carried out to standardise the liquid oil as product.

Another issue is the traceability and accountability of recycled material, so that its use can be counted towards recycled content targets. Mass-balance can be introduced to create a workable set of rules to ensure the attribution of recycled feedstock into new products, such as naphtha, syngas, oil or monomers. Mass balance can enable a credible and transparent traceability between feedstock input and product output, and along the value chain to the producer of a final article. The European Chemical Industry Council recommends: the adoption of a mass balance approach in the tracing of chemically recycled plastics; Transparent certification by an independent party at each step of the value chain and the development of a standard which includes clear and credible rules on feedstock qualification, mass balance calculation and the use of appropriate product claims.

Chemical recycling installations become more economical with a larger scale. A common European policy on chemical recycling could make import and export for efficient chemical recycling easier. This requires the following policies at the **European level**:

- Ensure a level playing field with mechanical recycling of plastic waste. Chemical recycling falls under the recycling definition in EU Directive 2008/98/EC, except when it leads to reprocessed products in fuel. Therefore, there could be a trade-off between achieving recycling targets and chemical recycling.
- Develop a clear and harmonised recycling-rate and recycled-content rule throughout the EU, building on the common recycling definition in the EU Directive 2008/98/EC.
- Public sector co-funding to accelerate R&D partnerships and address the higher risk areas (e.g. bridging the valley of death, co-ordinating innovation across the whole value chain).
- Ensure an open single market for plastic waste. This can be achieved with a “fit for purpose” and harmonised approach for the shipment of plastic waste for use in recycling facilities within Europe, and potentially also imported into Europe to help other regions in the creation of low carbon circular economy for plastics.

  Create legal acceptance of a mass balance approach for chemical recycling based on a recognised standard and transparency when implementing or amending legislation. A mass balance approach refers to a set of rules on how to allocate the recycled content to different products to be able to claim and market the content as recycled. This is a crucial precondition for creating a separate market for recycled plastics.

Policies to increase the recycling rates of metals

Increase the availability of scrap

An important distinction for the recycling of metals is between major metals, such as aluminium and steel, and minor metals such as magnesium, ruthenium and lithium. For major metals, collection and recycling rates are already high and therefore the potential for further increases is limited. For minor metals collection and recycling, rates are low and therefore a large potential for improvement exists.

Major metals

If the world wants to decrease primary production, then scrap needs to be available for secondary material production. Aluminium can be recycled infinitely and re-melted. Scrap steel can be re-used in electric arc furnaces, in principle, if there is scrap steel without qualitative and quantitative losses. Either of which produces less emissions than primary production.

The availability of scrap is thus the main constraint to the increase in recycled metals. Availability mainly limited because 70% of the steel produced to-date is still in use due to the sustainable nature of steel (European Recycling Industries' Confederation, 2020[48]).

Another reason why the availability is under further pressure is that much scrap is exported to lucrative markets outside the EU (European Aluminium and Aluminium Center Belgium, 2016[62]). However, from a global recycling perspective this may be optimal if developing countries are specialised in low quality steel.

The Netherlands should strive for greater availability of scrap for industry. This calls for innovations in the collection and sorting of scrap, so that every piece of metal is saved. Waste should always be pre-treated to prevent recyclable metal products from ending up as waste.

Policies that can help to increase the supply of scrap include better sorting, pre-treatment of waste, legal reclassification of scrap from 'waste' to 'products', harmonisation of different national regulations at the EU level, a reduction in exported scrap and legislation facilitating the import of scrap.

Minor metals

Many of the 60 metals analysed by UNEP (2011[63]) have a very low end-of-life recycling rate: only eighteen of these metals are above 50% and many of them even below 1%. Reasons for these low recycling rates of minor metals are low efficiency in collection and treatment of most metal-containing discarded products, limitations in recycling processes, and because primary material is often relatively abundant and therefore relatively cheap compared to recycling (UNEP, 2011[63]).

Define waste to facilitate the trade and usage of scrap

First, the demarcation between scrap, waste, and end-of life products changes by country; forcing any exporter of scrap to comply with multiple regulations for the same piece of material, all of which adds costs and impedes trade. For example, member states' interpretations of the waste framework directive in the EU (2008/98/EC) and the end-of-waste criteria (Commission Regulation 333/2011) differ. The outputs from steel production, such as slag and fly ash, are labelled as "product" or "waste" from one region to the next, which results in a situation where the same material must comply with both product and waste legislation.

Classification, restricts what can be done with the material, e.g. whether and where it can be further processed or used leading to further administrative burdens and costs (Technopolis, 2016[64]). Material, which is classified "end-of-waste", is usually more expensive because of the administrative processes involved, and a material can only obtain end of-waste status when the producer possesses the necessary certifications, which do necessarily correspond with any existing standards in the industry. For example, the end-of-waste regulation in the European Union was aimed to increase the recycling of scrap steel, but it was largely unsuccessful. In all but one member state, steel scrap is still classified as a waste, which inhibits its use in secondary production, inadvertently fostering the use of primary materials (Technopolis, 2016[64]). While the waste status is there for environmental and health protection, its limitations on recycling may increase environmental harm. There is still no consensus among EU member states on the criteria and definitions for waste regulations that could lift this waste status.

Harmonisation of terminology is a first step to understanding what the potential uptake of scrap could be within the European Union, but also internationally. A convention, similar to the Basel Conventions for hazardous waste is needed, which can be used to set harmonised standards by the International Standards

Organisation for these kinds of materials. Clarifying this terminological ambiguity is a first step to facilitating its use in production.

Despite this definitional quandary, trade in waste already exists, but import and export bans also exist. These bans partly stem from health and safety, in addition to protecting domestic industry. As of 2018, China no longer imports 24 types of waste and since then 32 other materials have been added to the list – including plastics and some types of scrap metal, such as high-grade copper and aluminium. The rationale for this is partly from the health consequences of the informal recycling sector on humans and the surrounding environment. The traded volumes reached an enormous magnitude, along with efforts to minimise the cost of disposing waste, which led to the increasing use of landfills and incinerators rather than more advance recycling methods. The burning of uncategorised waste also produced toxins contaminating the environment and harming human health.

Trade policies can help increase recycling of metals not only by harmonising legal frameworks but also by enabling economies of scale, and by addressing the problem of exports to countries with inadequate recycling facilities (de Sa and Korinek, 2021[65])

European legislation is needed to further allow and stimulate the import of scrap to increase the recycled share in metal production.

8.5. Bio-based materials

Key messages

- The production of various bio-based materials, like bioplastics and biofuels, is technologically feasible, but generally still less cost-effective and in some cases of lower quality than their fossil counterparts.
- Most emission reductions can be achieved through the use of biofuels in the refinery and petrochemical industry. However, this could require great amounts of land use, raising concerns about unintended negative effects on the environment, such as illegal logging. Therefore, biomass should primarily be used to produce bio-based materials for which no renewable alternatives exist, instead of using biomass to produce energy.
- The large refinery and chemical sectors that are clustered in the Netherlands offers an enormous opportunity to accelerate the transition to a bio-based economy.
- The Dutch government closely monitors developments in the bioeconomy and tries to support them through numerous policy measures. However, additional steps are needed to speed up the process and achieve its ambition to become one of the most important bio-based hubs in Europe.
- Subsidies for fossil fuels should be phased out and subsidies for bioenergy and biofuel should apply in the same way to biomaterials and biochemicals. This is necessary to get a level playing field and thus a fair chance for the bioeconomy to thrive.
- Risks to private sector investments in biofoundries should be reduced to scale up investments. Biofoundries are facilities that provide an integrated infrastructure to enable the rapid design, construction, and testing of genetically reprogrammed organisms for biotechnology applications and research. Biofoundries are biotech infrastructure independent of manufacturing, i.e. biorefineries. Biofoundries can help make the bioeconomy more profitable by creating a bioecosystem of industrial symbiosis. Priority should be given to investments related to conversion technologies. Reducing risks to increase private investments can be achieved through public-private initiatives.

- One of the most important issues for the development of the bioeconomy is that the demand for bio-based products is lagging behind, which not only hinders investments in production, but also the necessary R&D in bio-based materials. For this reason, policies should be implemented to increase demand, for example through quotas, mandates, regulatory standards, public procurement or public awareness campaigns.

The European Commission defines the bioeconomy as using renewable biological resources from land and sea, like crops, forests, fish, animals and micro-organisms to produce food, materials and energy. The aim of a bio-based economy is both to meet climate objectives and to become less dependent on fossil fuels and other scarce raw materials.

There are important synergies between the bioeconomy and the circular economy described in Section 8.4. The circular economy is about sustainable use, reuse and recycling of products, while the bioeconomy tries to reach the same climate objectives through using renewable bio-based materials.

The synergies between the bioeconomy and the circular economy also follow from including 'biomass and food' action points in the Dutch transition agenda for the circular economy (Ministry of Infrastructure and the Environment and Ministry of Economic Affairs, 2016[53]). Other commitments to the bioeconomy are about the mobilisation of biomass, innovation, support and the development of market demand for bio-based products (Ministry of Economic Affairs and Climate Policy, 2018[66]).

In 2016, the Netherlands counted around 1 200 companies that are active in the bio-based economy, with an estimated turnover of EUR 21 billion, which is rather average at the European level (Ministry of Economic Affairs and Climate Policy, 2018[66]).

While the Netherlands was one of the first countries with a bioeconomy strategy (Ministry of Economic Affairs, 2015[67]), it is now time for additional steps to bring the bioeconomy to the next level. The Netherlands has a very good starting position for the transition to a bioeconomy, thanks to its well-developed agriculture, refinery and chemical sectors. The refinery and chemical sector require workers with similar skills and knowhow as the bioeconomy, therefore an enormous unutilised potential could be tapped into to accelerate the transition to a bioeconomy. The only disadvantage for the Netherlands is that it has little biomass, but biomass can be imported and the available biomass that is currently used for energy generation must first be used for bio-based materials for which there is no CO_2-neutral alternative.

8.5.1. Technological readiness levels (TRL) of bio-based materials

Figure 8.9 shows that most promising bio-based materials still have a relatively low TRL 5 or 6, but that 22% of the bio-based materials studied by Fabbri et al. (2018[68]) already reach a TRL of 7 or 8. This shows that the bioeconomy is still a concept that is under development and that more is expected for the future.

Most bio-based materials relate to platform chemicals, plastics, biofuels and bioenergy. Biofuels and bioenergy have a relatively low added value per tonne of biomass, but because the vast majority of biomass is used for this, they still have the greatest economic and environmental impact.

The rest of this section will focus on bioplastics and biofuels. Other forms of bioenergy, like the use of biomass for electricity production, is beyond the scope of this report and many studies on bioenergy are already available.

Figure 8.9. TRLS Distribution for 20 of the most promising bio-based materials

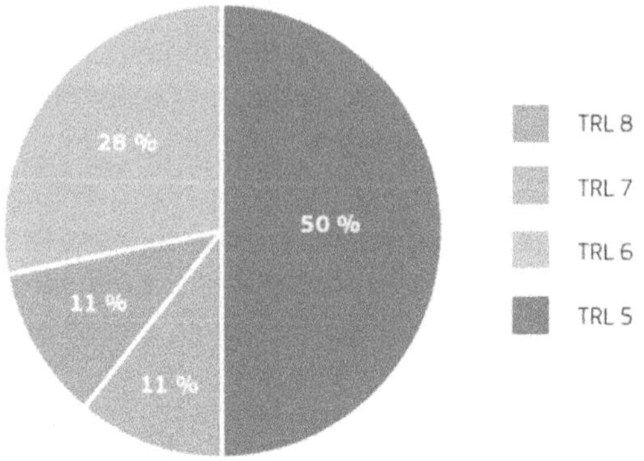

Source: Fabbri et al. (2018[68]).

Bioplastics

Bioplastics are plastic materials produced from biomass, usually in the form of sugar derivatives, including starch, cellulose and lactic acid. Biodegradable plastics are plastics that can be decomposed by the action of living organism into water, carbon dioxide and biomass. Bioplastics are not necessary biodegradable and biodegradable plastics are not necessarily bio-based.

The production of bioplastics is technologically feasible but generally still more expensive than fossil-fuel based plastics. Therefore, bioplastics account for only less than 1% of all plastics manufactured worldwide (Rujnić-Sokele and Pilipović, 2017[69]). Moreover, when replacing plastics, there is a risk of using arable land that can no longer be used for food production, unless waste industrial gases are used as feedstock. Biodegradable plastics designed to be compostable are often sent to landfills due to a lack of proper composting or waste disposal facilities.

However, to reach a climate neutral economy, fossil-fuel based products should be replaced by sustainable alternatives, meaning that the share of bioplastics is expected to sharply increase in the future, which requires more R&D to increase the quality and cost-effectiveness of bioplastics.

Bioplastics are expected to become a more attractive alternative for fossil-based plastics if in the future it can be made from biomass flows with limited other uses. Bioplastics are currently made from carbohydrates such as corn or sugarcane. In the future, fermentation technologies are expected to enable the utilisation of lingo-cellulosic feedstock sources, for example non-food crops, waste industrial gases, domestic waste, forestry and agricultural residue materials, that have limited other uses. However, these types of bioplastics are still under development. Some of the new bioplastics hold great promise for commercial deployment within the next 5-10 years (Fabbri et al., 2018[68]).

Fabbri et al. (2018[68]) provide an overview of the 20 most promising bio-based materials and their TRL levels. Bio-based innovations relate to plastics in more than half of these 20 materials. Different types of plastics, like thermosets and thermoplastic materials, are being developed. Innovation can take place in the synthesis of completely new polymers (e.g. limonene-based engineering polymers: polyurethanes, polycarbonates, polyamides) or in drop-in substitutes from renewable resources (e.g. biophenolic resins). Polyhydroxalkanoates (PHAs) are being investigated for biodegradable substitutes for polymers as high-density polyethylene, PP and others. PHAs can be obtained through a purely biotechnological route using carbon-rich biomass, including agricultural waste or solid municipal waste and urban wastewater. The development of these PHAs based on renewable oils and fats and urban waste (OFMSW and UWW) is at TRL 6-7, while bioplastics based on sugars are already at TRL 9.

About half of the current bioplastics are not biodegradable (Rahman and Bhoi, 2021[70]). The polymers of some bioplastics, e.g. drop-ins such as PE and PET, have identical molecules as the polymers from fossil-fuel based plastics and both can therefore be recycled together. In contrast, it is more difficult, if not impossible, to recycle plastics when they are mixed with biodegradable plastics. Waste consisting of Bio-PE and bio-PP can also serve as feedstock for gasoline and diesel production. Bio-PET, bio-PA and PLA can be a potential feedstock for the gasification process (Rahman and Bhoi, 2021[70]).

Biofuels

A biofuel is a fuel that is produced from biomass and is usually used for transportation, but can also be used for energy generation and to provide heat, for example in the chemical sector. The two main types of biofuel are bioethanol and biodiesel.

Bioethanol is an alcohol made by fermentation, usually from carbohydrates produced in sugar or starch crops such as corn, sugar cane or sweet sorghum. Cellulosic biomass, from non-food sources such as trees and grasses, is also being developed as a raw material for ethanol production. Ethanol can be used in its pure form as a vehicle fuel (E100), but it is most commonly used as a gasoline additive to increase octane rating and improve vehicle emissions. Bioethanol is widely used in the United States and Brazil.

Biodiesel is produced from oils or fats through transesterification and is the most common biofuel in Europe. It can be used as a fuel for vehicles in its pure form (B100), but it is most commonly used as a diesel additive to reduce particulate matter, carbon monoxide and hydrocarbon content in diesel vehicles.

Technologies for the production of biodiesel and hydro treated vegetable oil (HVO) from animal fats and waste oil are technically mature and account for 8% of all biofuel production in 2018 (IEA, 2020[71]). Production of new advanced biofuels from other technologies is still limited and progress is needed to improve technology readiness levels. These technologies in development are important to make use of more commonly available raw materials which have other limited uses (for example agricultural residues and municipal waste).

The investment landscape for advanced biofuels is challenging, with only a small proportion of announced projects under construction.

8.5.2. Bioeconomy strategy in the Netherlands

The chemical and plastics industry use fossil fuels for the production of a wide range of products (including plastics, coatings, adhesives, detergents) and also use fossil fuels as energy source in their production processes. This fossil fuel based material needs to be replaced as much as possible by bio-based materials to achieve a climate neutral industrial sector.

The government programme "Netherlands circular in 2050" mentions 'biomass and food' as one of their top priorities (Ministry of Infrastructure and the Environment and Ministry of Economic Affairs, 2016[53]). Three strategic targets within this top priority are:

- The optimal use of biomass through the closing of cycles. Part of this is using biomass as efficiently as possible through cascading, preventing waste and efficient combustion.
- Reducing and replacing fossil fuels by sustainably produced biomass.
- Development and implementation of new ways of production and consumption.

These strategic goals translate into the operational objectives of replacing fossil resources by biomass and to also base chemical production on biomass (called 'green chemistry'). Examples are support for biochemical factories and biorefineries for advanced bio-based fuels, chemicals and resources. The Vision Biomass 2030 formulates the ambition to reduce fossil resources by 70% in 2030.

In addition to the circular economy agenda, the Dutch government has also adopted a strategic vision for the use of biomass in 2030 (Ministry of Economic Affairs, 2015[67]). The strategic vision also states that the use of biomass plays an important role to replace fossil fuels by renewables and therefore reduce GHG emissions.

A number of actions are taken to meet the operational objectives. Ecological and social sustainability criteria are used for the sustainable production of biomass. Agricultural and forestry areas can be used more efficiently for biomass generation and more can be done to reduce losses in the biomass chain. For the origin of biomass, it is important that it does not have an unintended effect of increasing emissions elsewhere, e.g. by illegal logging.

Better cascading should take place, meaning that biomass should be used for products that create the most economic value over multiple lifetimes and that energy generation should be the last option only after all higher-value products and services have been exhausted (Keegan et al., 2013[72]). Cascading crosses sectors and applications, which requires measures to stimulate cross-sectoral co-operation.

The Netherlands recognises that in the long term it is important to use biomass primarily for applications where there are (hardly any) alternative cost effective sustainable sources. This concerns high temperature heat for industry, biofuels for aviation and shipping, and raw materials for chemicals and materials. The Dutch government argues that in the short and medium term, there are subsidies and investments in bioenergy to increase the supply of sustainable woody biomass flows. However, it is questionable whether this is the best possible strategy, since similar subsidies for bio-based materials can have a greater impact (OECD, 2018[73]).

The Dutch government expects that the demand for biomass for energy, biofuels, chemicals and materials will be between 432-570 PJ in 2030 (Ministry of Economic Affairs, 2015[67]). It expects that there will be enough supply of biomass to meet the demand, but this depends on the condition that the supply of biomass will increase and be used more efficiently and that additional biomass can be imported.

To support the bioeconomy, the Dutch government uses the following instruments: smart market incentives, stimulating legislation and regulations, innovation, the government as network partner and greening through trade and investments (Ministry of Economic Affairs, 2015[67]).

These instruments are used to: 1) increase the supply of sustainable biomass; 2) encourage the demand for sustainable biomass; 3) increase sustainability of production and use of biomass; 4) use all applications of biomass including materials; 5) focus on innovation and earnings capacity (Ministry of Economic Affairs, 2015[67]).

- The supply of biomass will increase by making better use of residual flows, increase productivity in agriculture and forestry at a European and global scale, produce blue biomass in the North Sea, use degraded land for biomass production and use European agriculture subsidies to support the transition to the bioeconomy.
- Demand for biomass will be increased by promoting product policies at the European level aimed at the phasing out of harmful substances if there is a good bio-based alternative, stimulating bio-based and biodegradable products in applications where products are left behind in nature or when bio-based products score better on sustainability and health than their current alternatives.
- The increase of sustainability of production and use of biomass is reached by developing a sustainable framework for all raw materials, push for the development of a harmonised European sustainability system, and promote cross-sectoral co-operation and cascading.
- To stimulate the use of all applications of biomass including materials, the Netherlands pursues policy integration at the EU level on renewable energy, climate and materials, with a focus on one parameter, CO_2 reduction.

- The focus on innovation and the earnings capacity is achieved by stimulating investments in new production capacity for advanced biofuels, chemicals and materials. The Top consortium for Knowledge and Innovation Biobased Economy (TKI-BBE) is strengthening research and innovations for the long term, such as on refineries of wood and agro residual streams.

The Netherlands wants to transform the Dutch "oil hub of North-West Europe" into the 'green energy-hydrogen and plastic recycling hub' of Europe, linked to a climate neutral industry. The refinery sector, together with the chemical sector, invest in renewable separation technology and new techniques for biotic raw materials (bio-based feedstock) (Ministry of Economic Affairs and Climate, 2020[74]). The application of bio-based resources is already taking place on a commercial scale for the production of biofuels. In addition, commercially feasible production of bio-based plastics would be possible in the Netherlands, but the bottleneck is often the demand side and European source policy is required to increase demand (Ministry of Economic Affairs and Climate, 2020[74]).

Another ambition is to have at least one or two installations on a commercial scale for each major GHG reducing technique (CCU, chemical recycling, electrification and bio-based resources). The government wants to realise these flagship-projects to build national experience to attract multinationals. Rotterdam is developing as one of the most important European bio-based clusters, including Neste's biofuel refinery. In this refinery, they produce renewable biofuels from algae, among other things, in addition to traditional biofuels from waste.

There are a number of policies used to support the transition to a bioeconomy. The TKI Biobased Economy aims to have both the energy and chemical sector replace fossil resources with biomass, and focuses on the development of bio-based innovation throughout the entire biomass value chain, according to the principle of cascading. TKI biobased consists of four programme lines: thermal conversion, chemical catalytic conversion, microbiological conversion and solar capturing and biomass production.

Other policies aimed at the circular economy also apply to bio-based materials. For example, the Mission Oriented Innovation Programme 6 (MMIP 6) is about the closing of industrial cycles and also includes the bioeconomy. The same is true for MOOI subsidies, DEI+ and DEI+ Circular Economy, the MIA and Vamil tax credits and the Green project loan facility. These instruments are explained in more detail in Chapter 5 on the current policy package.

8.5.3. Bioeconomy strategies in other countries.

Germany

Although the Association of German Industry believes that biomass plays an important role as a relatively cheap energy carrier for decarbonising the heating of industrial processes, the government is more cautious and the Ministry of Environment is even against expanding the use of biomass for process heating due to significant competition with other sectors and other applications (Fraunhofer ISI report).

The fourth FONA Research for Sustainability Framework Programme (FONA4) is effective from 2020 to 2024 and has a total budget of EUR 4 billion. It provides grants for a wide range of research projects in the fields of green hydrogen, circular economy, climate protection and the bioeconomy in specific funding guidelines and funding announcements. As part of this FONA4 programme, the funding guidelines "Epigenetik - Chancen für die Pflanzenforschung" (Epigenetics - opportunities for plant research) and "Zukunftstechnologien für die industrielle Bioökonomie" (future technologies for the industrial bioeconomy) are supported. While the first one focuses on food production, the second supports bioeconomy technologies in general. The funding amount is currently not published.

The bioeconomy is addressed more specifically in the Netherlands than in Germany, which may be related to its high relevance for the refinery and the chemical sector in the Netherlands. The German policy mix has a broader sectoral focus and is less dependent on bio-based materials. This is also consistent with finding a relatively large number of patents related to the bioeconomy in the Netherlands, while Germany is underperforming in this area, (Figure 8.12, Figure 8.14).

United Kingdom

The United Kingdom has an ambitious bioeconomy strategy for 2030 (Department for Business, Energy and Industrial Strategy, 2018[75]). The United Kingdom wants to boost their productivity by using their world class bioscience base to: 1) create new forms of clean energy; 2) produce smarter and cheaper materials such as bioplastics; 3) reduce plastic waste and pollution by developing environmentally sustainable biodegradable plastics; 4) provide sustainable healthy affordable and nutritious food; 5) increase sustainability of agriculture and forestry and use microbes instead of chemicals to create medicines and cosmetics (Department for Business, Energy and Industrial Strategy, 2018[75]).

The United Kingdom takes the lead on the transformation to sustainable plastics by investing GBP 60 million through the Industrial Strategy Challenge Fund to make plastics more sustainable, efficient and productive. An additional GBP 20 million is invested in the Plastics Research Innovation Fund, GBP 25 million in the Commonwealth Marine Plastic Research and Innovation Framework and GBP 20 million for research and development into new, smarter more sustainable packaging and boosting recycling.

The bioeconomy strategy for the United Kingdom relies on four main strategic goals: 1) capitalising on world-class research, development and innovation base to grow the bioeconomy; 2) maximising productivity and potential from existing UK bioeconomy assets; 3) delivering real, measurable benefits for the UK economy; 4) creating the right societal and market conditions to allow innovative bio-based products and services to thrive.

The UK Plastics Pact sets out the ambition for all plastics to be reusable, recyclable or compostable by 2050. This should be achieved through a strong innovation-based supply chain.

The Synthetic Biology Leadership Council (SBLC) is installed to set out the details on delivering the strategic actions required to support the development of technology platforms such as synthetic biology and industrial biotechnology; and to provide a regulatory framework to support the bioeconomy.

Global biofoundries alliance

Biofoundries are fundamental for the development of cheaper high-quality bio-based materials. Biofoundries provide an integrated infrastructure that makes it possible to rapidly design, build and test genetically reprogrammed organisms for research and biotechnology. Most biofoundries are in the United Kingdom and United States, with some in China and South Korea, but no biofoundry exists in the Netherlands yet. The Global Biofoundry Alliance (GBA) has recently been established to co-ordinate activities around the world.

The objectives of the GBA are: 1) to develop, promote, and support non-commercial biofoundries established around the world; 2) to intensify collaboration and communication among biofoundries; 3) to collectively develop responses to technological, operational, and other types of common challenges; 4) to enhance visibility, impact and sustainability of non-commercial biofoundries; 5) to explore globally relevant and societally impactful grand challenge collaborative projects (Global Biofoundries Alliance, 2021[76]).

8.5.4. Advancing the uptake of bio-based materials

Level playing field with fossil fuels, but also with biofuels and bio-energy

The Dutch government provides 13 individual subsidies for fossil fuels for a total amount of EUR 4.483 billion government revenue per year (IEA, 2020[77]). Most of these subsidies are related to tax exemptions for international flights and maritime transport. This huge number of fossil fuel subsidies is many times the amount of subsidies for the bio economy. The bioeconomy lacks significant subsidies which prevents scaling up for the more efficient production of bio-based products.

Even without fossil fuel subsidies it is already hard to compete with the fossil fuel industry, given that refineries and the petrochemical industries are very old and large, and therefore already very efficiently organised with perfectly aligned value chains. The bioeconomy is still a very new and upcoming industry and therefore it has not yet reached the most efficient scale, nor perfectly aligned value chains in which each component of biomass is used where it has the highest value added. The removal of fossil fuel subsidies is a necessary but probably not a sufficient condition to give the bioeconomy a fair chance to reach similar levels of efficiency (OECD, 2017[78]).

Competition is not only unfair with fossil fuels, but there is also no level playing field for the input of biomass, between bio-based materials and biochemicals on the one hand, which are hardly supported, and the much more subsidised biofuels and bioenergy (OECD, 2018[73]) on the other hand. Scaling up the bioeconomy requires a holistic approach to understand the complex interactions of value chains in the societal carbon cycle. First of all, to ensure that different components of biomass are used in the most economical and environmental friendly way. Second, because only subsidising bioenergy and biofuels, but not biomaterials, is expected to have a negative impact on the amount of biomass available for the production of bio-based materials and chemicals. This may unintentionally undermine the development of the bioeconomy. Therefore, some have called for the Renewable Energy Directive (RED) to be transformed into a Renewable Energy and Materials Directive (REMD) (Nova Institute, 2014[79]). Bio-based materials use, such as bioethanol and biomethane, could be accounted for in the renewable quota the same way as it counts for the energy use of the same building block, e.g. fuel. A third risk is that subsidies to bioenergy and biofuels can lead to unintended consequences elsewhere in the world, such as illegal logging.

Derisking private sector investments

Large uncertainty exists about the economic returns of biofoundries and biorefineries. Often, bio-based materials do exist, but the production is more expensive than their fossil fuel counterparts. Therefore, additional investments are required to further develop the quality of bio-based alternatives in biofoundries and to help upscale the bio-based materials production to a more economically efficient level.

Systemic business risks exist as suppliers of bio-based materials are dependent on the uptake of bio-based materials further down in the value chain. This means that a holistic approach is needed to reduce risks caused by dependencies between different parts of the value chain (Marvik and Philp, 2020[80]).

Public private initiatives, and other forms of risk sharing such as government venture capital, may help to reduce these risks and increase private investments in bioeconomy. Involvement in public-private partnerships would also give the Dutch government instruments to give a bit more direction to the development of the bioeconomy.

Given the importance of focusing on the development of new materials that are of higher quality and more cost-effective, the focus should be on supporting biofoundries, the place where innovation in the field of bio-based materials is currently taking place. Biofoundries provide integrated experimental and computational infrastructure for designing building and testing of bio-based materials (Kitney et al., 2019[81]). Within these biofoundries, one of the things that should be further invested in are **conversion technologies**, as feedstock is often bio-based, but conversion technologies are often still chemistry based. Engineering biology may provide the breakthrough to cost-effective lignocellulose conversion in bioprocessing. In addition, support should be given to cross-disciplinary research and education to embed computer-aided biology.

Technical barriers for commercialisation of biotechnology can partly be solved by setting standards for reproducibility and reliability (Kitney et al., 2019[81]). Given that small changes in cellular or environmental context are important for bio-based materials, small changes may underpin learning from earlier iterations.

While the construction of bio-based materials is often a formulaic exercise in engineering, it is much more difficult to create an ecosystem of stakeholders, from feedstock owners and producers to customers for bio-based products, to end-of-life recycling (Philp and Winickoff, 2019[82]). The main problem is to get commercially viable value chains. A large industrial refinery and chemical sector in the Netherlands has the potential to exploit this local agglomeration effects. Policies can help to co-ordinate between different stakeholders in the value chain.

Increasing demand through standards, public procurement and awareness campaigns.

As much of the uncertainty for investors comes down to uncertainty about future demand for bio-based products, commitment of the government to the bioeconomy is important. This subsection explains how the increase in demand for bio-based materials can help solve this problem of uncertainty and how policies can increase demand for the bioeconomy.

The risk is being locked into a vicious circle, in which the lack of demand for more expensive bio-based products prevents investments in better and cheaper bio-based materials. Reducing uncertainty, by setting ambitious expectations on future demand, could therefore break this vicious circle, by stimulating investments. These investments are expected to speed up the development of high quality bio-based alternatives for fossil fuels based products. A second mechanism is that the increase in demand will help to scale up, which makes it possible to gain economies of scale, and to have for example more efficient cascading in which many different components of biomass are used where it has the highest value added. Also a bigger market makes producers less dependent on a few suppliers or customers.

There are numerous ways by which the Dutch government could increase demand for bio-based products, for example through standards, public procurement, certification and public awareness campaigns (OECD, 2018[59]).

Regulatory standards can help to increase demand. The transition to a bio-based chemical and plastics industry can be achieved through quotas for renewable plastics and standards for life-cycle assessments (LCA) of products. An example where standards helped was when in China single-use plastics had to become biodegradable, which was a huge push for industry to invest more in higher quality biodegradable plastics (Swift, 2019[83]). Similar standards could be set at the Dutch or European level. Standards can sometimes relate to the composition of materials for products, for example that a certain share of a fuels are required to be bio-based. The same can be done for bio-based plastics that are not biodegradable as they can be recycled together with fossil-based plastics, but this is harder in the case of biodegradable plastics as these cannot be recycled together with non-biodegradable plastics. If the government wants to push for biodegradable products, then it could set a standard that some products, e.g. single-use plastics, have to be biodegradable.

In addition, public procurement could help to have enough demand for industry to scale up to a more efficient level of production. The public and semi-public sectors are large in the Netherlands, meaning that public procurement could make a big difference for the demand of bio-based products, such as bio-based food packaging in canteens, office equipment, furniture, construction, etc (InnProBio, 2017[84]). The public sector could also commit for multiple years of procurement, reducing uncertainty and stimulating investments in cheaper products to increase profits of the bioindustry. The Netherlands could learn from the BioPreferred Program of the United States Department of Agriculture (United States Department of Agriculture, 2021[85]).

Also certification, as is done for fair trade or FSC wood, could also help to increase demand for bio-based products. Without certification it is almost impossible to get a market for bio-based products as differentiation is needed to distinguish from their often cheaper fossil fuel based counterparts. In addition, public awareness campaigns can help customers to buy more bio-based products. For public awareness campaigns, however, it may be desirable for the government to also control or monitor certification to ensure that these campaigns contribute to the climate goals.

8.6. Dutch innovation in emerging technologies: insights from patent data

In order to provide empirical insights into the Dutch industry's innovation efforts on emerging technologies for the low-carbon transition, a patent data analysis was conducted based on the OECD's STI MicroData Lab infrastructure. The use of patent data as a measure of innovative activity is widespread, particularly in the field of climate change mitigation technologies for which the European Patent Office has developed a dedicated classification scheme (referred to as the Y02/Y04S tagging scheme) to identify relevant inventions in global patent databases such as PATSTAT.

Although patents do not provide a measure of all innovation, they provide a wealth of information on both the nature of the invention and the applicant – including the location of innovation activity, allowing for interesting cross-country comparisons. More importantly, patent data can be disaggregated into highly specific technological areas. Finally, patent data provide information about not only the countries where new technologies are developed but also where they are used.

Before describing the indicators used in this section, we briefly review how the patent system works. When a firm or an inventor from a particular country discovers a new technology, they must decide where to market this invention and how to protect the associated intellectual property. A patent in a given country grants the applicant the exclusive right to commercially exploit the invention in that country. Accordingly, firms patent their inventions in a country if they plan to market the invention in that particular country. Patenting is costly, in terms of both the costs of preparing the application and the administrative costs and fees associated with the approval procedure. Thus, inventors are unlikely to be willing to incur the cost of patent protection in a country unless they expect there to be a market for the technology concerned. The set of patents protecting the same invention across several countries is called a patent family.

The data used for this section comes from the PATSTAT database, maintained by the European Patent Office. PATSTAT is unique in that it covers more than eighty patent offices worldwide and contains over a hundred million patent documents. It is updated biannually. Patent documents are categorised using both the international patent classification (IPC) and the Co-operative Patent Classification (CPC).

Patent applications related to the five emerging low-carbon technologies discussed in this section were identified using IPC and CPC codes. PATSTAT includes the country of residence of the inventors of those technologies for which patent protection is sought (independent of the country in which the applications are actually filed). This information is used to measure a country's innovation performance.

A well-known limitation of patent data is that the value of individual patents is heterogeneous, making cross-country comparisons of innovative activity based on simple patent counts problematic. In this analysis, international patent filings through the Patent Co-operation Treaty (PCT) are used as the main measure of innovation. It has been shown that only patents of a certain value are transferred internationally. Thus, PCT patents provide a quality threshold that make cross-country comparisons more robust. In addition, PCT patents are available with a shorter lag than other measures of patent quality, such as patent citations. With this, we are able to observe patent activity until 2018. To observe trends in patent filings over time, we focus on the last 15 years of available data, covering the period 2004-18.

Over the period 2004-18, 33 648 PCT patents were filed globally in the five low-carbon technologies combined: bio-based materials, CCUS, electrification of industrial heating processes, hydrogen and recycling of plastics and metals. This represents 1.2% of all PCT patent filings in all technologies. However, this share has decreased over time, from 1.4% in 2004 to less than 1% in 2018.

Of these 33,648 low-carbon patents, 555 were filed by inventors located in the Netherlands. Therefore, Dutch inventors are responsible for 1.65% of global patent filings in the five low-carbon technologies under consideration. This is slightly less than the proportion of Dutch patents across all technology fields, which stands at 1.87%. On average, therefore, Dutch inventors do not appear specialised in these emerging low-carbon technologies, as their performance simply reflects the Netherlands' general contribution to global innovation efforts in all technologies.

Figure 8.10 shows the trends in low-carbon patenting activity, for the five selected technologies combined, by Dutch inventors and inventors worldwide. There has been a considerable increase in innovation efforts directed at the five low-carbon technologies in the Netherlands between 2004 and 2010: the proportion of patents covering these five technologies in total patenting activity of the Netherlands tripled, 0.5-1.5%. Interestingly, this period corresponded to a significant increase in public support for RD&D in low-carbon technologies, in particular toward CCUS and hydrogen.[7] Since then, Dutch efforts have been closely following the global average, decreasing regularly until 2018. In 2018, it represented around 1% of total Dutch patenting activity, exactly on par with the global average, suggesting that Dutch inventors are not particularly specialised in low-carbon innovation. The slowdown in low-carbon innovation activity has been observed more generally (including in other areas such as renewable energy) and has been partly attributed to the decrease in global oil prices, which makes low-carbon and energy-saving innovation less profitable.

Figure 8.10. Patents for the five low-carbon technologies as a share of total patents in all technologies

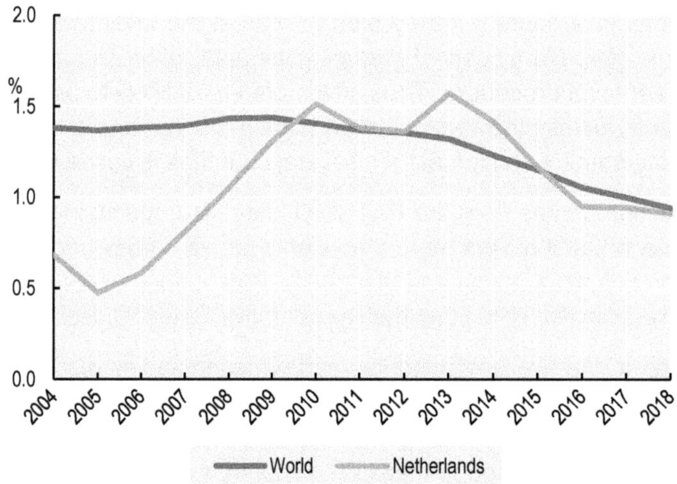

Note: Data refers to patents invented in the five selected low-carbon technologies. Statistics are based on two years moving average.
Source: OECD, STI Micro-data Lab: Intellectual Property Database, http://oe.cd/ipstats, January 2021.

Looking at individual categories, most of Dutch low-carbon innovation efforts are directed at hydrogen technologies (48 PCT patents in the 2014-18 period), closely followed by CCUS (46 patents) and bio-based materials (also 46). Recycling of plastics and metals is slightly below (37 patents over that period) while patents related to electrification of production processes appears extremely marginal (2 patents). The relatively low number of patents related to electrification is also observed for the rest of the world, albeit to a lesser extent than in the Netherlands. A plausible reason for this relatively low number of patents for electrification is that this technology is more mature and that therefore less frontier innovation is taking place. Figure 8.11 shows the evolution of Dutch inventors' patent filings between the periods 2004-08 and 2014-18. The largest increases can be found in the CCUS and bio-based materials categories. In comparison, hydrogen and recycling have remained fairly constant. Technologies related to electrification of production processes have remained marginal throughout the period.

The finding of a sharp increase in the number of patents for bio-based materials is in line with the increased technological readiness and policy focus on bioplastics and other bio-based materials, as described in Section 8.5. The increase in patents for CCUS technologies can plausibly be explained by an increased likelihood that these technologies will be needed in the fight against climate change. Section 8.1 describes an increasing policy focus on CCS in the rest of the world, most prominently in the United States and the United Kingdom. Another plausible explanation may be related to the first carbon storage operation that was installed in the Netherlands in 2004, which may have triggered more research into this technology.

Figure 8.11. Patents filed by Dutch inventors, by technology

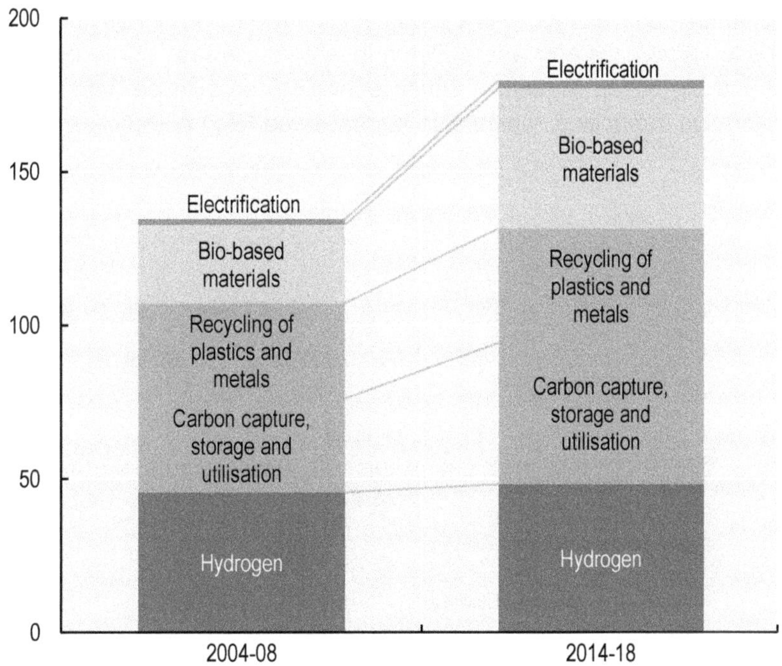

Note: Data refers to patents invented in the Netherlands for selected low-carbon technologies. Patent counts are based on the filing date.
Source: Source: OECD, STI Micro-data Lab: Intellectual Property Database, http://oe.cd/ipstats, January 2021.

Figure 8.12 shows the Relative Technological Advantage (RTA) of Dutch inventors for the five emerging low-carbon technologies in the two periods (2004-08 and 2014-18), based on PCT patents (the last line corresponds to the five technologies combined). The RTA is defined as the share of global patents in each technology filed *by Dutch inventors* divided by the share of patents in the same technology filed by inventors *from all countries*. Therefore, an RTA of one corresponds to a situation where the performance of Dutch inventors is exactly equal to the world's average effort toward this technology (this is actually the case for low-carbon technologies in the 2014-18 period, where the bar lies exactly on the vertical line). An RTA above one indicates relative specialisation in the technology (i.e. the Dutch output is higher than the world's average output); an RTA below one indicates under-specialisation in the area.

As shown in Figure 8.12, the CCUS and bio-based materials categories, which have seen the largest increases over the recent period, also correspond to the areas where Dutch inventors appear most specialised. In bio-based materials in particular, the share of Dutch innovation efforts going into this field is more than three times that of the world average in the most recent period (2014-18). In CCUS, Dutch inventors are twice as specialised as the average world's inventor. Specialisation in bio-based materials has markedly increased over the last fifteen years, while specialisation in CCUS was already similar fifteen years ago. This is in line with the TRL levels and policy attention to these technologies described in Section 8.5 for bio-based, and to a somewhat lower extent also in Section 8.1 on CCUS. In the other three technological fields – namely hydrogen, electrification of industrial heating processes and recycling of plastics and metals – Dutch inventors appear under-specialised. The increase in the combined RTA for the five technologies (last line) is entirely driven by recent efforts toward bio-based materials.

These results confirm findings in Sections 8.2, 8.3 and 8.4; that more policy efforts are needed to achieve the climate goals for the Dutch industry. In addition to higher R&D subsidies, a business case must be made for electrification of heat, hydrogen and recycling. This can be done, for example, by changing the (future) relative prices of electricity, hydrogen and recycling relative to their fossil fuel counterparts.

For a small country like the Netherlands, and given that research into emerging technologies like hydrogen typically entails large fixed costs, specialising in all of these emerging low-carbon technologies with a view to promote national champions in all these new technological areas is less obvious. A sensible strategy therefore seems to be to focus on areas where Dutch inventors possess some comparative advantage, which include CCUS and bio-based materials. Other technologies could be "imported" from abroad, but adoption requires absorptive capacities, which also necessitates R&D activity – although not targeted at frontier research.

Figure 8.12. Relative Technological Advantage (RTA) of Dutch inventors by technology

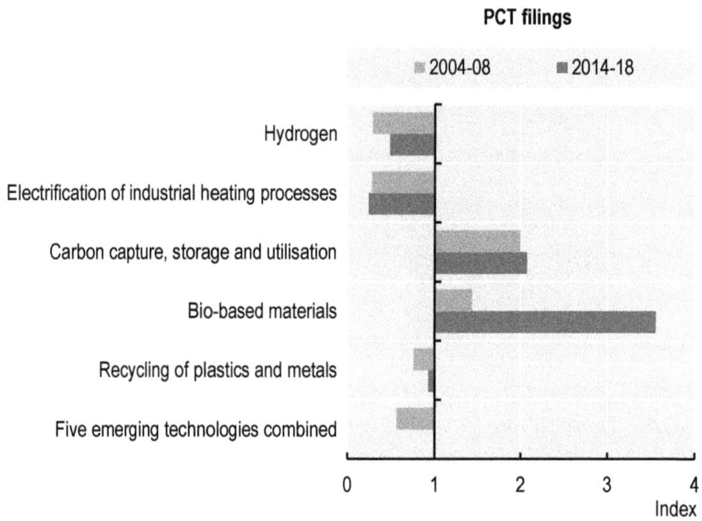

Note: Data refers to patent invented in the Netherlands for selected low-carbon technologies. Patent counts are based on the filing date under the Patent Co-operation Treaty (PCT).
Source: OECD, STI Micro-data Lab: Intellectual Property Database, http://oe.cd/ipstats, January 2021.

The average absence of specialisation of the Netherlands in the five technologies of interest can be compared to the RTA of other countries. This is done in Figure 8.13. Many countries appear more specialised than Dutch inventors in these emerging low-carbon technologies, and many have also become more specialised over the last 15 years. It is important to keep in mind that RTA only reflects *relative* performance, not absolute number of patents. Yet, it is interesting to observe that some countries such as Saudi Arabia, Chile or Australia have disproportionately high numbers of patents in these areas compared to their overall innovation performance. In short, the data suggests that Dutch inventors have not taken a head start in the global innovation race in emerging low-carbon technologies.

Figure 8.14 reproduces Figure 8.12 for Germany and shows the Relative Technological Advantage (RTA) of German inventors for the five emerging low-carbon technologies in the two periods (2004-08 and 2014-18). On average across the five technologies, inventors operating in Germany appear slightly more specialised in low-carbon innovation than the Netherlands, but the difference is not large. What is striking from Figure 8.14 is the strong specialisation of German inventors in both hydrogen and electrification of heating processes – two technologies where inventors based in the Netherlands relatively under-perform. Moreover, this specialisation is recent and was not the case fifteen years ago.

Figure 8.13. Relative Technological Advantage (RTA) of the Netherlands compared to other countries for the five selected low-carbon technologies

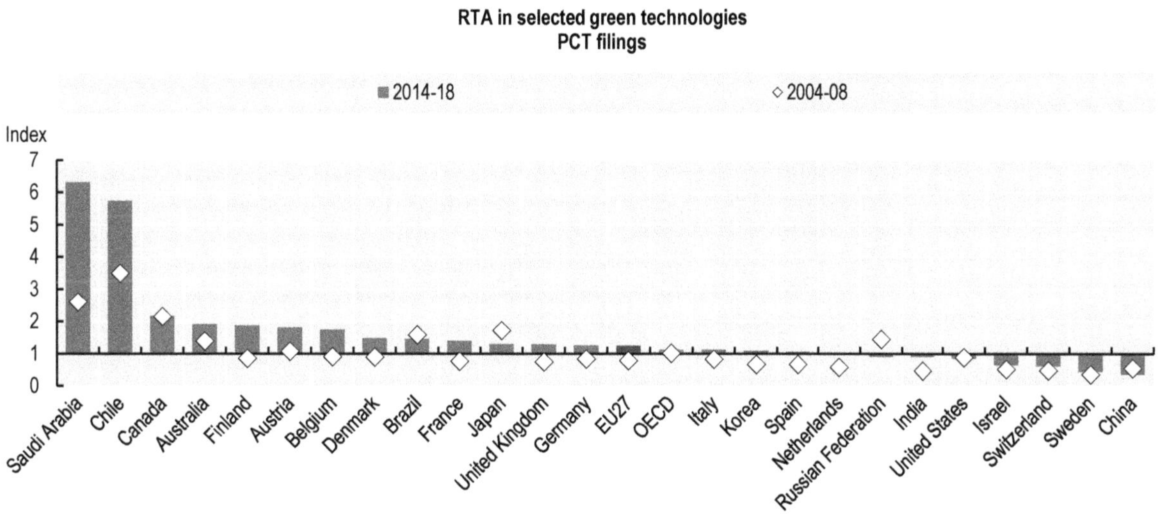

Note: Data refers to patent applications filed under the Patent Co-operation Treaty (PCT) in selected low-carbon technologies. Patent counts are based on the filing date and the inventor's country, using fractional counts. Only countries featuring more than 50 low-carbon technology patents over the period 2014-18 are included.
Source: OECD, STI Micro-data Lab: Intellectual Property Database, http://oe.cd/ipstats, January 2021.

Figure 8.14. Relative Technological Advantage (RTA) of German inventors by technology

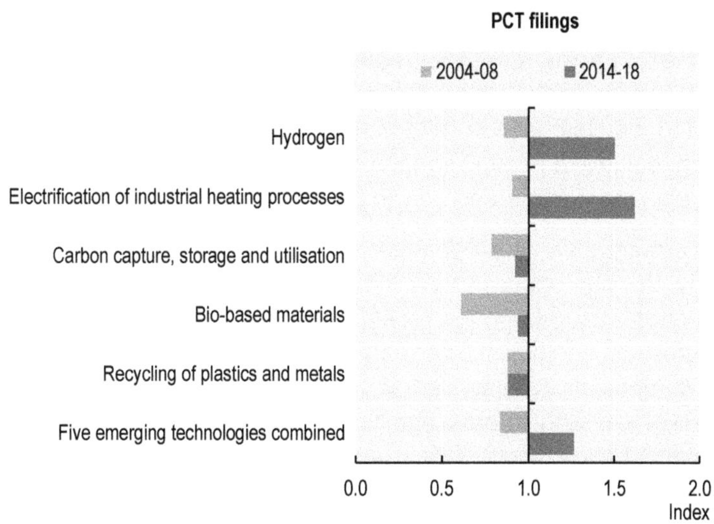

Note: Data refers to patent invented in Germany for selected low-carbon technologies. Patent counts are based on the filing date under the Patent Co-operation Treaty (PCT).
Source: OECD, STI Micro-data Lab: Intellectual Property Database, http://oe.cd/ipstats, January 2021.

As mentioned above, patents include information not only on the country in which the invention was developed (the indicator that was at the centre of the analysis until now) but also on countries or regions (for multinational patent offices) where intellectual property protection is sought. Figure 8.15 presents the main foreign patent offices in which inventions developed in the Netherlands seek patent protection. These correspond to the expected markets for Dutch inventions. In the figure, the bars refer to low-carbon technologies, while the diamonds refer to all technologies.

Figure 8.15. Top 10 foreign markets for inventions made in the Netherlands, 2010-18

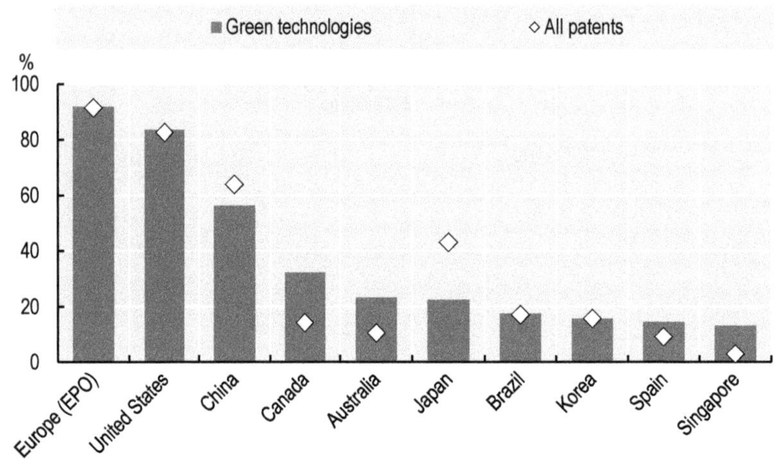

Note: Data refers to IP5 patent families invented in the Netherlands, by IP offices in which family members were filed.
Source: OECD, STI Micro-data Lab: Intellectual Property Database, http://oe.cd/ipstats, January 2021.

The main destination patent offices for Dutch inventors are the European Patent Office (EPO) and the United States patent office, with respectively 90% and 80% of low-carbon inventions being applied for in these offices. These rates exactly correspond to the rate observed for all technologies. In contrast, China and Japan do not appear as attractive markets for low-carbon technologies relative to others, while Canada and Australia see a much higher rate of "technology export" in low-carbon technologies than in other innovations developed by Dutch inventors. A plausible explanation for this is that Canada and Australia appear to specialise themselves in low-carbon technologies, as shown in Figure 8.13.

Conversely, is the Netherlands an attractive market for foreign inventors in emerging low-carbon technologies? Figure 8.16 addresses this question by showing the share of patents granted by the EPO that are then transferred to the Netherlands (and hence, protected in the country). The EPO is the main entry point of foreign technologies in most European countries (contrary to the Dutch patent office, which mostly targets domestic applicants interested only in the local market).

Figure 8.16 shows that around 23% of all patents granted by the EPO are ultimately transferred and protected in the Netherlands. The share is very similar at 22% for emerging low-carbon technologies, implying that the Netherlands was not – in the recent period until 2018 – seen as a particularly attractive market by inventors for these technologies. There are, however, marked differences across technologies. Fifty percent of bio-based materials patents filed at the EPO and 40% of CCUS patents are validated in the Netherlands, and 30% of recycling patents, against only 20% of patents related to electrification of heat processes and, perhaps most surprisingly, 13% of patents in hydrogen-related technologies. Combined with the absence of specialisation of Dutch inventors in hydrogen patents, this signals that the country was not seen – at least until recently – as an attractive market for hydrogen technology. The knowledge and technology base in the country, therefore, is currently poor, and the number of available technologies ready to be deployed might similarly be low. Given the critical importance of hydrogen for the decarbonisation of the Dutch industry, and the recent political focus on this technology, this observation has important policy implications: both domestic innovation and international transfer of foreign technologies are currently weak and could be in need of policy support.

Figure 8.16. Share of European Patent Office patents validated in the Netherlands

As a share of patents granted at the European Patent Office

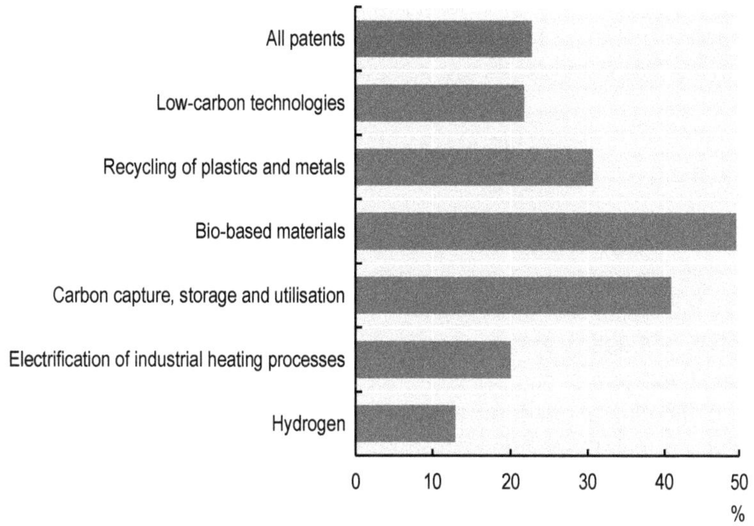

Note: Data refers to EPO patent grants protecting selected green technologies, and validated in the Netherlands, by date of grant.
Source: OECD, STI Micro-data Lab: Intellectual Property Database, http://oe.cd/ipstats, January 2021.

Figure 8.17. European Patent Office patents in low-carbon technologies validated in the Netherlands, 2014-18

Top 20 inventor countries

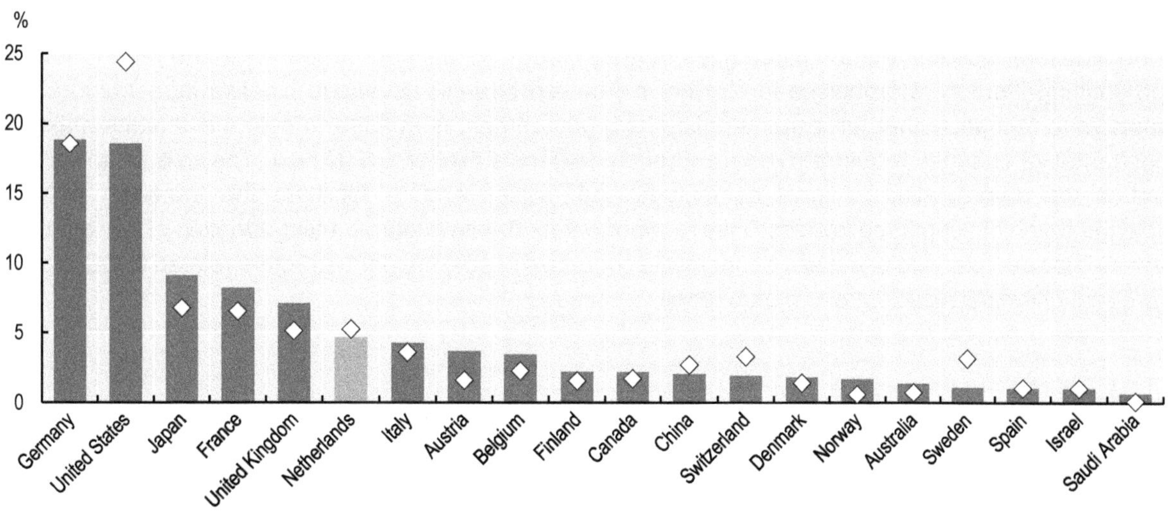

Note: The blue bars refer to EPO patent grants protecting emerging low-carbon technologies, and validated in the Netherlands, by date of grant and inventors' country, using fractional counts. The diamonds represent the rate for all patents.
Source: OECD, STI Micro-data Lab: Intellectual Property Database, http://oe.cd/ipstats, January 2021.

Where are low-carbon technologies protected in the Netherlands currently coming from? Figure 8.17 shows the proportion of EPO patents validated in the Netherlands by inventor country. The main supplier of foreign low-carbon technologies in the Netherlands is Germany, followed by the United States, Japan, France and the United Kingdom. This is a reflection of the general innovative capacity of these countries, but there are some differences with the rate observed for all patents (represented by a diamond). For example, low-carbon patents from the United States are less likely to be validated in the Netherlands than the average US invention filed at the EPO. The opposite is true for inventions coming from Japan, France and the United Kingdom.

There are also some specificities in particular technologies. For example, Norway is an important importer of CCUS inventions into the Netherlands, as are Austria and Belgium for recycling technologies.

8.7. Cross-technology policy lessons

Considering the cross-technology perspective, we can conclude that the carbon levy and the SDE++ subsidies are crucial policy instruments for the development and deployment of the key emerging technologies for Dutch industry's decarbonisation. In particular they support the business case for CCUS/CCS, electrification of heating and hydrogen. While the carbon levy and SDE++ are expected to make up for the cost disadvantage arising through operational expenses for most technologies related to CCUS/CCS and the electrification of low-temperature heating. However, if the Netherlands wants to realise its green hydrogen ambitions with these two instruments only, it will be challenging since these operational costs of hydrogen are not covered. Given that the development and deployment of the main emerging technologies are so dependent on the carbon levy and on SDE++, it is important to further strengthen these two core instruments. For SDE++, a policy consideration would be to reserve part of the SDE++ budget for green hydrogen to push for the necessary investments to make green hydrogen more cost-effective in the future. For the carbon levy to remain a credible instrument, it is important that the carbon levy takes effect in the future and that uncertainty about possible abolition is reduced. While the carbon levy can also help to accelerate the transition to a circular economy, for the recycling of plastics and metals and for the bioeconomy, additional policies are necessary to increase the demand for recycled products and biobased materials. Standards for minimum recycled content and public procurement can boost the demand for recycled materials and bio-based products.

One risk of a very different nature, from the policy side, is that insufficient account is taken of the importance of the industrial clusters and the differences between them. As pointed out earlier in the report, much of high-emitting industry is organised in clusters connected through advanced pipeline infrastructure. It is important to recognise that tailor-made policy from government is needed to help the clusters make the transformative changes required (Climate Friendly Materials Platform, 2021[86]). The role for the cluster level is the co-ordination of local companies and utilities and to facilitate the transition with the implementation of supporting policies. This is important for the development and adoption of key emerging technologies, for example because of important economies of scale for infrastructure related to CCS, green hydrogen, chemical recycling and biofoundries.

References

Beck, L. (2020), "Carbon capture and storage in the USA: the role of US innovation leadership in climate-technology commercialization", *Clean Energy*, Vol. 4/1, pp. 2-11, http://10.1093/ce/zkz031 (accessed on 11 September 2020). [8]

BEIS (2020), *CCUS Innovation Programme: selected projects*, BEIS, https://www.gov.uk/government/publications/call-for-ccus-innovation/ccus-innovation-programme-selected-projects (accessed on 16 December 2020). [27]

BEIS (2019), *Carbon Capture and Utilisation Demonstration (CCUD) innovation programme - GOV.UK*, Funding Programmes, https://www.gov.uk/government/publications/carbon-capture-and-utilisation-demonstration-ccud-innovation-programme (accessed on 16 December 2020). [28]

BEIS (2018), *Department of Business, Industrial and Energy Strategy*, https://www.gov.uk/government/organisations/department-for-business-energy-and-industrial-strategy (accessed on 11 December 2018). [29]

BEIS (2018), *Industrial Carbon Capture Business Models*. [23]

Berenschot (2020), *Klimaatneutraal in 2050: vier scenario's*, https://www.berenschot.nl/nieuws/2020-april-nederland-klimaatneutraal-in-2050 (accessed on 26 May 2021). [34]

Berenschot (2020), *Sustainable Transition of Dutch Industry: 2050 scenario's towards a zero emission industry in the Netherlands*. [1]

Budinis, S. et al. (2018), "An assessment of CCS costs, barriers and potential", *Energy Strategy Reviews*, Vol. 22, pp. 61-81, http://dx.doi.org/10.1016/j.esr.2018.08.003. [17]

CE Delft (2021), *Policy instruments stimulating the low carbon transition of Dutch Industry: an overview of existing policies in the field of climate and energy in the Netherlands*. [19]

CE Delft (2020), *Exploration chemical recycling: What is the potential contribution of chemical recycling to Dutch climate policy*, https://www.cedelft.eu/en/publications/download/2832. [58]

CE Delft (2019), *Verkenning chemische recycling update 2019: Hoe groot zijn - en worden - de kansen voor klimaatbeleid*. [56]

Climate Friendly Materials Platform (2021), *Transforming industrial clusters to implement the European Green Deal*. [86]

CMS (2020), *Implementation of the CCS Directive into the Dutch mining legislation (CO2-storage)*, CMS Law. Tax, https://cms.law/en/nld/publication/implementation-of-the-ccs-directive-into-the-dutch-mining-legislation-co2-storage (accessed on 16 December 2020). [15]

de Boer, R. et al. (2020), *Strengthening Industrial Heat Pump Innovation Decarbonizing Industrial Heat*, TNO, http://publications.tno.nl/publication/34636827/LyEUaZ/TNO-2020-heatpump.pdf (accessed on 7 May 2021). [36]

de Sa, P. and J. Korinek (2021), "Resource efficiency, the circular economy, sustainable materials management and trade in metals and minerals", *OECD Trade Policy Papers*, No. 245, OECD Publishing, Paris, https://dx.doi.org/10.1787/69abc1bd-en. [65]

Deason, J. et al. (2018), *Electrification of buildings and industry in the United States Drivers, barriers, prospects, and policy approaches*, Berkeley Lab, https://ipu.msu.edu/wp-content/uploads/2018/04/LBNL-Electrification-of-Buildings-2018.pdf (accessed on 8 December 2020). [30]

Den Ouden, B. et al. (2017), *Electrification in the Dutch process industry In-depth study of promising transition pathways and innovation opportunities for electrification in the Dutch process industry*, Berenschot, CE Delft, Industry Energy Experts, Energy Matters, https://blueterra.nl/wp-content/uploads/2018/03/Electrification-in-the-Dutch-process-industry-final-report.pdf (accessed on 9 December 2020). [31]

Department for Business, Energy and Industrial Strategy (2018), *Growing the Bioeconomy, Improving lives and strengthening our economy: A national bioeconomy strategy to 2030.* [75]

Dressler, L., T. Hanappi and K. van Dender (2018), "Unintended technology-bias in corporate income taxation: The case of electricity generation in the low-carbon transition", *OECD Taxation Working Papers*, No. 37, OECD Publishing, Paris, https://dx.doi.org/10.1787/9f4a34ff-en. [20]

Dubettier, R. (2010), *Démonstrateur pré-industriel de production d'hydrogène bas*, https://www.ademe.fr/sites/default/files/assets/documents/cryocaph2.pdf. [39]

EBN and Gasunie (2017), *Transport en opslag van CO2 in Nederland*, https://www.ebn.nl/wp-content/uploads/2018/07/Studie-Transport-en-opslag-van-CO2-in-Nederland-EBN-en-Gasunie.pdf. [11]

Eccles, J. and L. Pratson (2014), "A "carbonshed" assessment of small- vs. large-scale CCS deployment in the continental US", *Applied Energy*, Vol. 113, pp. 352-361, http://dx.doi.org/10.1016/j.apenergy.2013.07.002. [3]

ECN (2015), *Doorbreek de lock-in van het energiebeleid voor de zware industrie.* [35]

European Aluminium and Aluminium Center Belgium (2016), *Aluminium Recyclen: De weg naar een duurzame economie.* [62]

European Commission (2020), *A hydrogen strategy for a climate-neutral Europe*, European Commission, Brussels. [44]

European Recycling Industries' Confederation (2020), *Metal Recycling Factsheet*, European Recycling Industries' Confederation. [48]

EZK (2020), *Kamerbrief over voortgang beleidsagenda kabinetsvisie waterstof*, https://www.rijksoverheid.nl/onderwerpen/duurzame-energie/documenten/kamerstukken/2020/12/15/kamerbrief-over-voortgang-beleidsagenda-kabinetsvisie-waterstof. [41]

Fabbri et al. (2018), *Top emerging bio-based products, their properties and industrial applications.*, Ecologic Institute, Berlin. [68]

Federal Ministry for Economic Affairs and Energy (2020), *The National Hydrogen Strategy (Nationale Wattersoft Strategie)*, The Federal Government of Germany. [43]

Friedmann, S., E. Ochu and J. Brown (2020), *Capturing investment: Policy design to finance CCUS projects in the US Power Sector*, Center on Global Energy Policy (Columbia University), http://www.sipa.columbia.edu (accessed on 10 September 2020). [7]

Global Biofoundries Alliance (2021), *The overall objectives of GBA*, https://biofoundries.org/. [76]

Global CCS Institute (2019), *Global Status of CCS 2019: Targeting climate change*, Global CCS Institute. [9]

Government of the Netherlands (2020), *Government Strategy on Hydrogen*, Government of the Netherlands. [42]

Government of the Netherlands (2019), *Climate Agreement*, National Climate Agreement, https://www.government.nl/documents/reports/2019/06/28/climate-agreement (accessed on 16 December 2020). [2]

Havercroft, I. (2020), *Lessons and perceptions: Adopting a commercial approach to CCS liability*, The Global CCS Institute, https://www.globalccsinstitute.com/wp-content/uploads/2020/04/Thought-Leadership-Liability-Study_FINAL_Digital.pdf (accessed on 11 September 2020). [13]

Hesselink, T. and E. Van Durren (2019), *The plastic recycling opportunity: An industry ready for consolidation*, https://assets.kpmg/content/dam/kpmg/xx/pdf/2019/10/the-plastic-recycling-opportunity.pdf (accessed on 16 December 2020). [50]

HM Government (2020), *The Ten Point Plan for a Green Industrial Revolution*, HM Government. [25]

IEA (2021), “RD&D Budget”, *IEA Energy Technology RD&D Statistics* (database), https://dx.doi.org/10.1787/data-00488-en (accessed on 9 March 2021). [87]

IEA (2020), *Batteries and hydrogen technology: keys for a clean energy future*, https://www.iea.org/articles/batteries-and-hydrogen-technology-keys-for-a-clean-energy-future. [33]

IEA (2020), *Energy Technology Perspectives 2020 - Special Report on Clean Energy Innovation*, OECD Publishing, Paris, https://dx.doi.org/10.1787/ab43a9a5-en. [5]

IEA (2020), *Horizon 2020 funding for carbon capture, utilisation and storage*, https://www.iea.org/policies/11694-horizon-2020-funding-for-carbon-capture-utilisation-and-storage (accessed on 16 December 2020). [18]

IEA (2020), *The Netherlands’ Effort to Phase Out and Rationalise its Fossil-Fuel Subsidies*, https://www.iea.org/reports/the-netherlands-effort-to-phase-out-and-rationalise-its-fossil-fuel-subsidies. [77]

IEA (2020), *Transport Biofuels*, https://www.iea.org/reports/transport-biofuels. [71]

IEA (2019), *The Future of Hydrogen: Seizing today’s opportunities*, OECD Publishing. [37]

IEA (2019), *Transforming Industry through CCUS*, OECD/IEA, Paris. [6]

IEA (2011), *Carbon Capture and Storage and the London Protocol*, OECD/IEA, https://webstore.iea.org/download/direct/569 (accessed on 11 September 2020). [16]

InnProBio (2017), *Handboek Bio-Based Inkopen*, https://www.biobasedconsultancy.com/uploads/files/InnProBio_handbook-NL_download.pdf. [84]

International Association of Oil and Gas Producers (2020), *The potential for CCS and CCU in Europe*, https://ec.europa.eu/info/sites/default/files/iogp_-_report_-_ccs_ccu.pdf (accessed on 16 December 2020). [10]

Keegan, D. et al. (2013), "Cascading use: a systematic approach to biomass beyond the energy sector", *Biofuels, Bioproducts and Biorefining*, Vol. 7/2, pp. 193-206, http://dx.doi.org/10.1002/bbb.1351. [72]

Kitney, R. et al. (2019), "Enabling the Advanced Bioeconomy through Public Policy Supporting Biofoundries and Engineering Biology", *Trends in Biotechnology*, Vol. 37/9, pp. 917-920, http://dx.doi.org/10.1016/j.tibtech.2019.03.017. [81]

Krupnick, A. and J. Bartlett (2019), *Subsidizing Carbon Capture Utilization and Storage: Issues with 45Q*, Resources for the Future. [21]

Lako, P. et al. (2011), *Issues concerning the implementation of the CCS Directive in the Netherlands*, Elsevier Ltd, http://dx.doi.org/10.1016/j.egypro.2011.02.533. [14]

Marvik, O. and J. Philp (2020), "The systemic challenge of the bioeconomy", *EMBO reports*, Vol. 21/10, http://dx.doi.org/10.15252/embr.202051478. [80]

Ministry of Economic Affairs (2015), *Biomassa 2030: Strategische visie voor de inzet van biomassa op weg naar 2030.* [67]

Ministry of Economic Affairs and Climate (2020), *Visie verduurzaming basisindustrie 2050.* [74]

Ministry of Economic Affairs and Climate Policy (2018), *The position of the bioeconomy in the Netherlands.* [66]

Ministry of Infrastructure and the Environment and Ministry of Economic Affairs (2019), *Uitvoeringsprogramma Circulaire Economie 2019-2023.* [55]

Ministry of Infrastructure and the Environment and Ministry of Economic Affairs (2016), *Nederland circulair in 2050: Rijksbreed programma Circulaire Economie.* [53]

Nagabhushan, D. and J. Thompson (2019), *Carbon Capture & Storage in The United States Power Sector*, Clean Air Task Force, https://www.catf.us/wp-content/uploads/2019/02/CATF_CCS_United_States_Power_Sector.pdf (accessed on 10 September 2020). [22]

Nova Institute (2014), *Proposals for a Reform of the Renewable Energy Directive to a Renewable Energy and Materials Directive (REMD).* [79]

OECD (2020), "Improving resource efficiency and the circularity of economies for a greener world", *OECD Environment Policy Papers*, No. 20, OECD Publishing, Paris, https://dx.doi.org/10.1787/1b38a38f-en. [60]

OECD (2018), "Enabling bio-based materials policy", in *Meeting Policy Challenges for a Sustainable Bioeconomy*, OECD Publishing, Paris, https://dx.doi.org/10.1787/9789264292345-12-en. [73]

OECD (2018), *Improving Markets for Recycled Plastics: Trends, Prospects and Policy Responses*, OECD Publishing, Paris, https://dx.doi.org/10.1787/9789264301016-en. [59]

OECD (2017), *The Next Production Revolution: Implications for Governments and Business*, OECD Publishing, Paris, https://dx.doi.org/10.1787/9789264271036-en. [78]

PBL (2020), *Eindadvies basisbedragen SDE++ 2020*, Planbureau voor de Leefomgeving, Den Haag, https://www.pbl.nl/sites/default/files/downloads/pbl-2020-eindadvies-basisbedragen-sde-plus-plus-2020_3526_27-02-2020.pdf. [12]

PBL (2019), *Doelstelling circulaire economie 2030*, https://www.pbl.nl/sites/default/files/downloads/pbl-2019-policy-brief-doelstelling-circulaire-economie-2030-3551.pdf. [52]

Philp, J. and D. Winickoff (2019), "Innovation ecosystems in the bioeconomy", *OECD Science, Technology and Industry Policy Papers*, No. 76, OECD Publishing, Paris, https://dx.doi.org/10.1787/e2e3d8a1-en. [82]

Plastics Europe (2019), *Plastics-the Facts 2019 An analysis of European plastics production, demand and waste data*, Plastics Europe. [51]

Qureshi, M. et al. (2020), "Pyrolysis of plastic waste: Opportunities and challenges", *Journal of Analytical and Applied Pyrolysis*, Vol. 152, p. 104804, http://dx.doi.org/10.1016/j.jaap.2020.104804. [61]

Rahman, M. and P. Bhoi (2021), "An overview of non-biodegradable bioplastics", *Journal of Cleaner Production*, Vol. 294, p. 126218, http://dx.doi.org/10.1016/j.jclepro.2021.126218. [70]

Rathi, A. (2019), *The story behind the world's first large direct air capture plant*, Quartz, https://qz.com/1638096/the-story-behind-the-worlds-first-large-direct-air-capture-plant/ (accessed on 11 September 2020). [24]

Reck, B. and T. Graedel (2012), "Challenges in Metal Recycling", *Science*, Vol. 337/6095, pp. 690-695, http://dx.doi.org/10.1126/science.1217501. [49]

Roelofsen, O. et al. (2020), *Plugging in: What electrification can do for industry | McKinsey*, McKinsey, https://www.mckinsey.com/industries/electric-power-and-natural-gas/our-insights/plugging-in-what-electrification-can-do-for-industry (accessed on 8 December 2020). [32]

Rujnić-Sokele, M. and A. Pilipović (2017), "Challenges and opportunities of biodegradable plastics: A mini review", *Waste Management & Research: The Journal for a Sustainable Circular Economy*, Vol. 35/2, pp. 132-140, http://dx.doi.org/10.1177/0734242x16683272. [69]

RVO (2020), *Monitoring Transitie naar een Circulaire Economie*. [54]

Sartor, O. and C. Bataille (2019), *Decarbonising basic materials in Europe: How Carbon Contracts-for-Difference could help bring breakthrough technologies to market*. [26]

Solis, M. and S. Silveira (2020), *Technologies for chemical recycling of household plastics – A technical review and TRL assessment*, Elsevier Ltd, http://dx.doi.org/10.1016/j.wasman.2020.01.038. [47]

Suschem (2020), *Sustainable Plastics Strategy*, European Technology Platform for Sustainable Chemistry, http://file:///C:/Users/ANDERSON_B/Downloads/Suschem_Sustainable_Plastics_Brochure-18.12.2020.pdf (accessed on 7 May 2021). [46]

Swift, R. (2019), *Chinese plastics makers are switching to biodegradable materials as Beijing stresses on pollution-free economic progress*, https://www.scmp.com/business/china-business/article/3002888/chinese-plastics-makers-are-switching-biodegradable. [83]

Tanaka, Y. et al. (2014), "Tomakomai CCS Demonstration Project in Japan, 2014 Update", *Energy Procedia*, Vol. 63, pp. 6111-6119, http://dx.doi.org/10.1016/j.egypro.2014.11.643. [40]

Technopolis (2016), *Regulatory barriers for the Circular Economy*, Technopolis, https://www.technopolis-group.com/wp-content/uploads/2017/03/2288-160713-Regulary-barriers-for-the-circular-economy_accepted_HIres.pdf. [64]

UNEP (2011), *Recycling Rates of Metals: A Status Report.* [63]

United States Department of Agriculture (2021), *BioPreferred Program*, https://doi.org/10.15252/embr.202051478. [85]

VNO NCW and Rebelgroup (2020), *Roadmap chemische recycling kunststof 2030 Nederland.* [57]

Vollebergh, H. and E. van der Werf (2014), "The Role of Standards in Eco-innovation: Lessons for Policymakers", *Review of Environmental Economics and Policy*, Vol. 8/2, https://doi.org/10.1093/reep/reu004. [45]

Wirkert, F. et al. (2020), "A modular design approach for PEM electrolyser systems with homogeneous operation conditions and highly efficient heat management", *International Journal of Hydrogen Energy*, Vol. 45/2, pp. 1226-1235, http://dx.doi.org/10.1016/j.ijhydene.2019.03.185. [38]

Xodus Advisory (2020), *Porthos CCS - Transport and Storate (T&S) Tariff Review.* [4]

Notes

[1] Porthos stands for Port of Rotterdam CO_2 Transport Hub and Offshore Storage.

[2] In this project, the CO2 is separated from the production stream prior to gas transport to shore. The CO2 is then injected into the same reservoir from which its gas originated.

[3] Institut du Développement Durable et des Relations Internationales.

[4] Also, electricity tax applies to electricity supplied via a connection to the energy grid only, leaving electricity production for own use ("auto-generation") untaxed. Electricity auto-generation from renewable energy sources is also exempt from taxation.

[5] Often this involves steam methane reforming of natural gas. Asia still produces a large proportion of hydrogen from coal (e.g. ammonia and methanol producers).

[6] Power-to-X technologies are energy conversion technologies that can be used to store power surpluses from renewable energy sources.

[7] Average annual public RD&D support to CCUS and hydrogen was respectively EUR 15.5 million and EUR 4 million over 2004-10, against EUR 1.8 million and EUR 1.9 million over 2011-18. There was no public funding for either technology before 2004 (IEA, 2021[87]).

9. Competitiveness and sectoral change in Dutch industry's low-carbon transition

This chapter simulates the potential economic and social impacts of input costs increases implied by the low-carbon transition on the competitiveness of the Dutch industry, based on a static model describing the industrial structure of the Netherlands and its interactions with the rest of the world through international trade and value chains. It shows that, while the aggregate economic impact of carbon pricing in the Netherlands is likely to be small, energy-intensive and trade-exposed sectors such as iron and steel can be significantly affected if they do not shift toward low-carbon technologies. Support to technology adoption and co-ordination at the European level can attenuate competitiveness effects.

As evident from the previous chapters, the transition to a more sustainable manufacturing sector entails additional costs, in terms of investment, feedstock, energy or taxes. These costs weigh on competitiveness and can affect the industrial structure, especially in a small open economy like the Netherlands. They may also cause carbon leakage, jeopardise the national efforts and undermine public support for climate policy.

At the same time, the green transition can contribute to building a new comparative advantage. Carbon pricing and other climate policies can send the right incentives to ensure Dutch industry remains competitive in the long run. It is important to send the right incentives to ensure the transformation of the industrial sector and allow the Netherlands to thrive in a future net-zero carbon economy, instead of creating stranded assets. In addition, R&D, demonstration and deployment subsidies are meant to reduce the costs of new installations and processes, in terms of capital and operational expenditures (notably energy and feedstock costs, for instance through material and energy efficiency gains).

Moreover, the relationship between climate policy and competitiveness crucially depends on the efforts of trade partners to simultaneously decarbonise their manufacturing sector. For the Netherlands, this is particularly important at the European level, but also at the global level.

Sectoral factors are of primary importance in shaping this relationship, as manufacturing activities are heterogeneous in terms of carbon-intensity, exposure to international competition or availability of low-carbon alternatives (Chapter 2).

Mitigating the adverse impact of carbon pricing on competitiveness can rely on exemptions to energy-intensive trade-exposed sectors, support to adopt low-carbon technologies or co-ordination with trade partners. The Netherlands historically chose the first option, but the second option is now being implemented (Chapter 5).

The objective of this chapter is to simulate the economic and social impacts of the low-carbon transition using a static model describing the industrial structure of the Netherlands and its interactions with the rest of the world through international trade and value chains. This model takes into account the different factors that mediate the relationship between climate policy and competitiveness at a granular sectoral level: carbon-intensity and energy use, degree of trade openness, level of competition with foreign substitutes, ability to switch to less carbon-intensive production modes …

This chapter shows that, consistent with ex post evaluations of the European Emissions Trading System (ETS), the aggregate economic impact of carbon pricing in the Netherlands is likely to be small. Although a significant concern from a microeconomic and human impact perspective, the number of jobs at stake remain limited. This calls for keeping the strong carbon price signal delivered through the carbon levy trajectory in place and to implement accompanying measures to ensure that affected workers can thrive in the labour market (e.g. re-skilling of displaced workers and other active labour market policies, Chapter 9).

Despite small aggregate effects, some sectors, in particular energy-intensive, trade-exposed sectors producing standardised goods subject to an intense competition on worldwide markets such as iron and steel, can be significantly affected under the assumption that they do not shift technologies. This chapter also shows that complementing the carbon price signal with support to low-carbon technology adoption and co-ordination at the European level can attenuate concerns over the short-run competitiveness of those sectors and substitute to sectoral exemptions.

9.1. Modelling the impact of low-carbon policies on the competitiveness of the Dutch economy

The effects of the low-carbon transition on the Dutch economy are simulated thanks to an augmented input-output (IO) model (Box 9.1 presents a more detailed description of the model). It is designed to reflect the current input-output structure of the economy in three regions (the Netherlands, the rest of the European Economic Area – EEA – and the rest of the world) at a granular sectoral level (39 sectors).

The IO modelling has the advantage of providing results at a detailed sectoral level, allowing to measure the impact of shocks on the structure of the economy and accounting for inter-sectoral linkages.

The standard IO approach however suffers from important limitations, in particular the absence of economic behaviour and cost optimisation. To overcome the latter, this chapter relies on an augmented IO model, which incorporates some important margins of adjustment relevant for the low-carbon transition of the Dutch economy. First, it models the substitution between energy and other factors of production, for instance allowing sectors that face a higher energy price to reduce their energy intensity, but at the expense of higher capital or labour costs. Second, demand is reacting to price changes, allowing to measure the impact of competitiveness changes on the economic activity in different regions. This analysis can be carried out for the energy-intensive sectors that are directly confronted with the transition, but also for the upstream or downstream sectors that are affected by changes in demand or in prices.

Although the model incorporates a general equilibrium dimension (domestic revenues affect domestic demand), it is not a fully-fledged Computable General Equilibrium (CGE) model. In particular, there is no price channel, which is usually key in CGE models to limit the impact of demand shocks and bring back the model to the equilibrium determined by the supply side. In such models, countries cannot run trade surplus or deficits for a long period as real exchange rates (through wages or nominal exchange rates) adjust to bring back the trade balance close to equilibrium.

Moreover, and very importantly, the augmented IO model corresponds to a comparative statics approach. It does not feature dynamics or any notion of time. For instance, investment is not modelled, which precludes simulating the dynamic effect of carbon pricing, deployment or R&D subsidies. This requires the modelling of endogenous productivity growth and spillovers, which are seldom found even in larger CGE models. The results of the model should therefore not be interpreted as the results of more stringent climate policy. Rather it shows what sectors will need specific attention when transitioning to a low- or net-zero carbon economy.

Compared to more complex CGE models, the augmented IO approach allows for a more granular sectoral approach while keeping a high degree of transparency, so that users and readers can easily understand the factors driving the results.

Box 9.1. An augmented input-output model to assess the impact of the green transition on the Dutch economy

Structure of the model

Figure 9.1 presents the functioning of the model, which is based on the OECD Inter-Country Input-Output (ICIO) Tables (OECD, 2018[11]) . It can be divided into three main building blocks:

The Input-Output price model. Following a shock affecting some of the prices, the model simulates the impact of the shock on the prices of all the products using input-output linkages and substitution between energetic inputs and other factors of production.

- For instance, if the shock corresponds to a tax on the Dutch natural gas sector, the price model will compute the impact on the price of products using Dutch natural gas as an input (e.g. refineries in the Netherlands or abroad). Beyond this first order effect, the model provides price effects taking into account all the input-output linkages (e.g. chemical products using refined petroleum products, food products using chemicals…) by using a Leontief inverse matrix.

- This block also models the substitution between energetic and non-energetic inputs. Faced with an increase in energy prices, firms may want to reduce their costs by lowering their energy intensity, at the expense of higher labour costs and capital expenditures. The sectoral elasticities of substitution are taken from Hebbink et al. (2018[2]), estimated for the Netherlands on the period 1978-2015, and applied in the model to the three regions.

<u>The final demand block</u>. This block simulates the impact of price changes on the final demand addressed to producers in each region.

- Final demand is broken down into exports and domestic final demand (final consumption, investment, changes in inventories) and sectoral price elasticities of demand are applied. The price elasticity of exports is generally higher than the one for domestic final demand since competition is fiercer in international markets, and foreign consumers usually do not have a strong preference over the origin of products once they are imported. The sectoral price elasticities for exports and domestic final demand are taken from Hebbink et al. (2018[2]), relying on an extensive review of the empirical literature.
- Imports of goods are indirectly affected by these elasticities as they correspond to exports from one of the two other geographical regions.

<u>The Input-Output quantity model</u>. This block simulates the impact of changes in final demand on the production of each sector in each region.

- Using the input-output tables, the model simulates the impact of changes in final demand on the demand for intermediate inputs. As for the price model, in order to take into account all the linkages, the Leontief inverse matrix is used. This allows obtaining the effect on value-added, production or employment at the sectoral level.
- The model also features a feedback loop between this block and the final demand block to take into account the 'income effect'. This feedback loop is estimated by first considering the changes in household's income resulting from changes in economic activity, which by its turn has an impact on household's consumption. This impact on consumption is measured by considering the use of household's income elasticities at the product level, based on the Global Trade Analysis Project (GTAP) model (Hertel and van der Mensbrugghe, 2016[3]). The resulting change in consumption is then used in the Leontief model to estimate its impact on the economy.

Figure 9.1. Overview of the input-output model

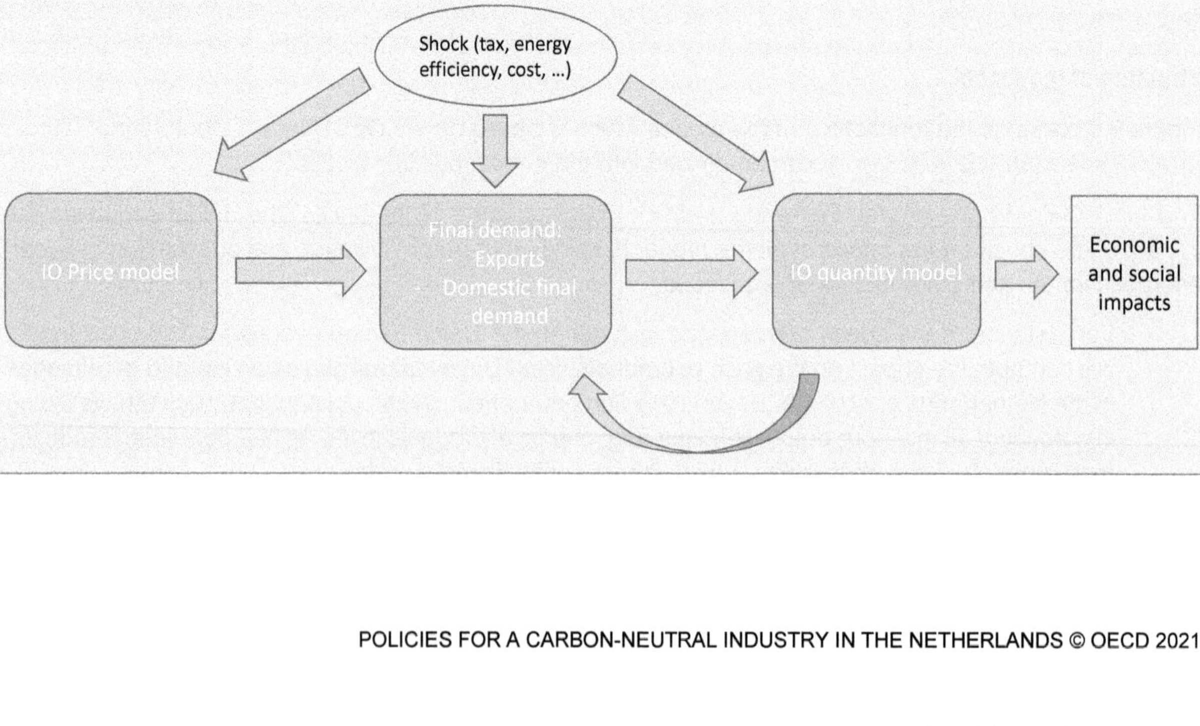

Starting from an initial situation (data for 2015), the model is designed to simulate the effect of various types of shocks (carbon pricing and subsidies, energy efficiency gains, etc.). Shocks can affect the three regions and enter the model through three gateways:

- They can affect prices (e.g. a price on carbon emissions).
- They can affect final demand (e.g. revenues from a carbon price can be consumed either by the government or by households and firms after a transfer through tax cuts or subsidies).
- They can affect intermediate consumption through the IO quantity model (e.g. energy efficiency gains in the manufacturing sector).

Scenarios simulated using the augmented IO model

Several scenarios are simulated using the model to provide a plausible narrative on the potential short-run sectoral effects of the low-carbon transition. In these scenarios, proceeds of carbon pricing are assumed to increase proportionally the final demand from a given region, without affecting the structure of the final demand by product or by origin of the products.

The first set of scenarios is designed to understand what sectors will need specific attention when transitioning to a low-carbon economy and some measures to limit this impact:

- Scenario A: Uniform tax increase of EUR 50 per tonne of CO_2 on all the CO_2 emissions in the Netherlands.
- Scenario B: Uniform tax increase of EUR 50 per tonne of CO_2 on all the CO_2 emissions in the European Economic Area.
- Scenario C: Uniform tax increase of EUR 50 per tonne of CO_2 on all the CO_2 emissions in the European Economic Area and a similar tax on the carbon content of imported carbon-intensive goods from the rest of the world. It is implemented on the products that are usually considered for a Border Carbon Adjustment (non-metallic mineral products – including cement, refined products, chemicals and metals – ferrous and non-ferrous). The emission intensity of imports used to calculate the tax is the one for the rest of the world.

The second set of scenarios is designed to illustrate policy options in the Netherlands:

- Scenario D: Carbon levy of EUR 125 per tonne, without SDE ++ nor technical change. Scenario D simulates the effect of a carbon levy at its 2030 rate on the four manufacturing sectors that are responsible for the vast majority of the emissions (food processing sector, refineries, chemical sector, metallurgical sector – both 'iron and steel' and 'non-ferrous metals'). The scenario implicitly assumes that firms do not adjust their production processes but keep the same technology and the same emissions-intensity of output. This scenario is meant to illustrate a worst-case in which firms do not undertake any investment to reduce their emissions and are not supported by innovation and deployment subsidies. The additional costs for Dutch firms are obtained by assuming that the ETS price reaches EUR 80 per tonne of CO_2. Preferential treatment via free allocation of pollution permits is included. The share of free allowances for the ETS and dispensation rights for the carbon levy follow estimates by CE Delft (2021[4]).
- Scenario E: A flat effective average carbon tax rate. This scenario assumes that regressive rates and exemptions in the energy tax and surcharge are removed, to reach an effective average carbon price of EUR 30 per tonne of CO_2 (including fuel taxes, ODE on natural gas, the carbon levy and the EU ETS price). This flat rate is also applied to the same four manufacturing sectors that are responsible for the vast majority of emissions, except food processing, for which the effective average carbon rate is already above EUR 30 (**Table 5.24**).

Several studies have already investigated the impact of the low-carbon transition on the short-run competitiveness of the Dutch economy. Hebbink et al. (2018[2]) use the same augmented IO approach, although the models and scenarios differ. PwC (2020[5]) instead relies on case studies on the "big 12" firms to assess the impact of the carbon levy, the energy tax and the surcharge reforms on their earnings before interest, taxes, depreciation, and amortisation (EBITDA) and the attractiveness of investing in the Netherlands. Vollebergh et al. (2019[6]) analyse the economic impact of several CO_2 pricing options using the recursive dynamic general equilibrium Worldscan, developed by the Centraal Planbureau (CPB). Finally, CPB and PBL (2019[7]) compare the results obtained from the three above-mentioned studies.

A few results of these studies stand out:

- The competitiveness impact of emission pricing is limited at the aggregate economy level but may be significant for some sectors (Hebbink et al., 2018[2]; CPB and PBL, 2019[7]).
- The competitiveness impact is significantly smaller when emission pricing is implemented at the European level, and not only in the Netherlands (Hebbink et al., 2018[2]) under the assumption that no additional technology support is granted.
- The use of carbon pricing revenue dramatically affects the impact of the simulations (Hebbink et al., 2018[2]; Vollebergh et al., 2019[6]).
- The results are sensitive to several assumptions, notably the substitutability between domestic and foreign goods, the time horizon on which these elasticities are estimated, in particular whether these take into account location decisions in the long run (PwC, 2020[5]; CPB and PBL, 2019[7]).

This study is closest in spirit to Hebbink et al. (2018[2]) and Vollebergh et al. (2019[6]). It complements their findings by implementing new carbon pricing scenarios and using a different model. While Vollebergh et al. (2019[6]) use a CGE model, the augmented IO approach used in this chapter is simpler, although it integrates additional economic behaviours compared to Hebbink et al. (2018[2]).

This sensitivity of the results to the price elasticity of demand also applies to the model used in this chapter. For this reason, elasticities were selected to lie in the middle of available estimates and be treated in a conservative way (Hebbink et al., 2018[2]; Imbs and Méjean, 2010[8]). A doubling of price elasticities roughly leads to a doubling of sectoral effects.

9.2. Short-run competitiveness concerns require flanking policies in some sectors, but macroeconomic effects are small

9.2.1. Even under a worst-case scenario, the adverse impacts of carbon pricing are limited to a small number of sectors

This subsection provides the simulated impact of the carbon levy at its 2030 rate (EUR 125 per tonne of CO_2) on the four manufacturing sectors that are responsible for the vast majority of the emissions (food processing, refineries, chemical sector and metallurgy (Box 9.1, Scenario D).

Similar to most models the augmented IO model is unable to simulate the impact of the price signal on the uptake of new low-carbon technologies, on energy efficiency improvement, and the impact of technology support measures. The emissions base in the model remains the same. Therefore the results of this simulation do not necessarily reflect the effects of a more stringent climate policy in the Netherlands. Rather they point to the sectors that are particularly affected by the low-carbon transition and may need specific attention. The simulation is meant as a thought experiment to better understand the mechanisms at play and represent an unlikely worst-case scenario in which emissions remain at their initial level and affected industries are not supported through subsidies. The next subsections shed light on how support schemes such as Sustainable Energy Transition Incentive Scheme (SDE++) and co-ordination at the European level can drastically reduce the effects.

This scenario corresponds to an increase in the average effective carbon price, reaching a level of EUR 25-40 per tonne of CO_2 depending on the sector (Table 5.24). These numbers are much lower than implementing a marginal price of EUR 125 per tonne of CO_2 (Table 5.17) because a significant share of the emissions in these sectors benefit from free allowances in the EU ETS and free dispensation rights for the carbon levy (Tabme 5.19).

Even without technology support and emission reduction, increasing the price to EUR 125 per tonne now would be mild on the Dutch economy (Figure 9.2, -0.1% on total value added). As the carbon levy mainly weighs on manufacturing sectors, the impact on the value added of these sectors would be higher (-0.9%), although not major. In contrast, the impact on services sectors would be nil. On the one hand, domestic services are affected by higher prices of domestic manufacturing goods used as inputs, although this effect is mitigated by the possibility of substitution by imports. On the other hand, as they represent a high share of final demand, they benefit from the redistribution of the carbon levy revenues[1].

The impact is however very heterogeneous across manufacturing subsectors. Iron and steel is by far the most affected sector, with a decrease of -7.2% in value add. The effect is also significant in the coke and refined products sector and the chemical sector (respectively -2.2% and -3.9%), whereas the impact on the non-ferrous metal sector is lower (-1.1%).

The size of the effect mainly depends on four sectoral factors:

- The emission intensity, which impacts the amount of the carbon price and the extent to which it will weigh on the production costs.[2]
- The price elasticity of demand, which governs the response of the domestic and foreign demand to price hikes.
- The degree of openness to trade, which tends to increase the sensitivity of demand to price changes. The price elasticity of exports being usually higher than the one of domestic demand, the more export-oriented the sector, the higher the response of total demand to price changes.
- The substitution between energy and other factors of production, which allows firms to smoothen the impact of the carbon levy by substituting away from energy.

In addition to these four factors, sectors are differently affected through their input-output linkages, i.e. they suffer from price increases of their emission-intensive inputs and from reduced demand if they supply downstream emission-intensive sectors.

Iron and steel is the most affected sector in these simulations as it cumulates a current high emission intensity, a high elasticity of demand and significant openness to trade (i.e. the sector produces standardised goods which are intensively traded).

Figure 9.2. Estimated impact of two carbon pricing scenarios on the value-added of selected sectors in the Netherlands (in percentage)

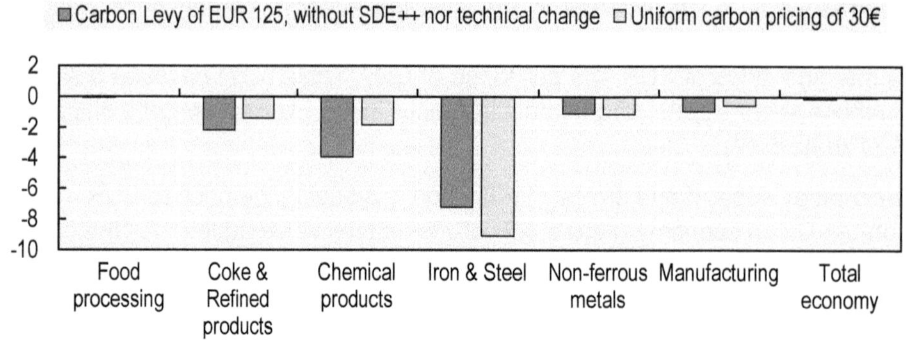

Note: The first scenario assumes a current carbon price of EUR 125 per tonne, no technology support through SDE++ and no technological change (i.e. the emissions base remains the same as in the BAU. See Scenario D, Box 9.1. Value-added in the coke & refined products sector is reduced by -2.2%.
Source: Calculations based on the augmented IO model described in Box 9.1.

The impact in terms of employment would also be limited (-0.03%, representing 2 500 workers in the total economy, Figure 9.3). Employment losses are concentrated in manufacturing (-3 700 workers), while the employment slightly increases in the rest of the economy. Within the manufacturing sectors, most of the employment losses are found in the chemical sector (-1 700 workers) and the iron and steel sector (-1 000 workers). While the relative impact is the highest in the iron and steel sector, this sector only represents a small share of employment (1.8% of jobs in the manufacturing sector).

Figure 9.3. Estimated impact of two carbon pricing scenarios on the total employment of selected sectors in the Netherlands (in thousand workers)

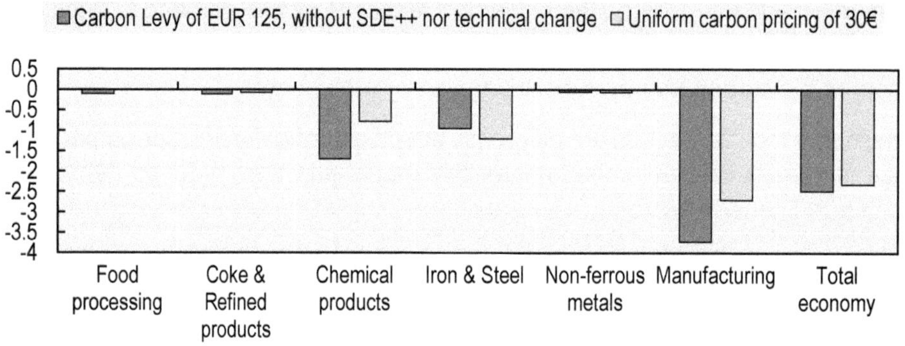

Note: The first scenario assumes a current carbon price of EUR 125 per tonne, no technology support through SDE++ and no technological change (i.e. the emissions base remains the same as in the BAU). See Scenario D, Box 9.1. Employment in the chemical sector is reduced by 1 700 persons.
Source: Calculations based on the augmented IO model described in Box 9.1.

Figure 9.2 and Figure 9.3 also display the impact of another scenario in which an average effective carbon price of EUR 30 per tonne of CO_2 is applied to the same four subsectors of the industry (Box 9.1, Scenario E,) The impact of this scenario for the total economy and the manufacturing sector (respectively -0.1% and -0.6%) is comparable to the carbon levy scenario. However, the impact on some sectors, in particular "iron and steel" and "non-ferrous metals", is significantly higher. This effect is driven by the removal of significant preferential treatment (i.e. these sectors disproportionately benefit from tax exemptions and free permit allocation in the current situation). The *average* carbon price amounts to

EUR 3.3 per tonne of CO_2 in BAU for the basic metals sector[3], compared to for example EUR 76.3 tonne CO_2 in the food processing sector. For more details of the tax and ETS treatment of these sectors (Chapter 5).

This scenario is meant to represent the impact of reducing the exemptions benefitting energy-intensive sectors, and is complementary to the previous one. While the carbon levy scenario principally affects the *marginal* price of carbon, this second scenario mainly focuses on the *average* price by removing exemptions. Playing both on the marginal and average prices would increase the effectiveness of the carbon price signal while improving its fairness, although the impact on competitiveness could be higher in the absence of accompanying measures.

9.2.2. Combining carbon pricing with technology support can limit potential adverse impacts in affected sectors.

In the previous subsection, the proceeds of the carbon pricing are supposed to be spent according to the share of each product in the Dutch final demand. This is however not in the spirit of the Climate Agreement,[4] according to which carbon levy proceeds should be used to finance the greening of the industry (Chapter 5).

Channelling these revenues back to the sectors paying the carbon tax is likely to significantly reduce the impact on their competitiveness. If the proceeds were returned to the sectors contributing to the levy to exactly match the payments, the competitiveness impact would be nil according to the augmented IO model, as their additional costs are completely offset by subsidies.

In practice, these sectors are likely to invest these revenues to reduce emissions, particularly if benefits from abatement payments are explicitly conditioned on green investments as in the SDE++ scheme. In that case, although costs are temporarily higher in the short run and may affect competitiveness, these investments are meant to offset the higher carbon price and could allow competitiveness gains in the medium run.

Figure 9.4. Estimated sectoral energy efficiency gains required to offset the effect of carbon pricing on competitiveness (in percentage)

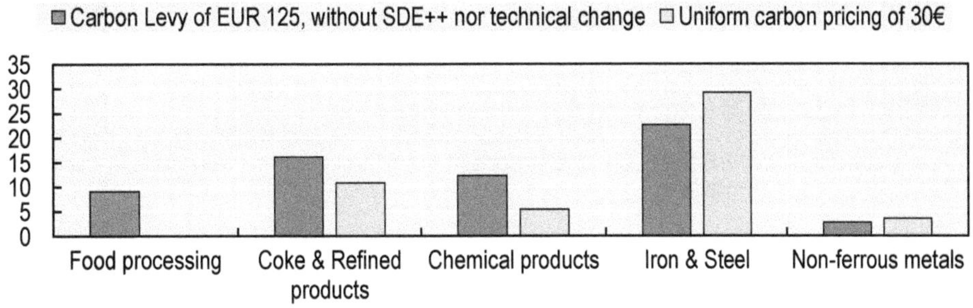

Note: In the first scenario (carbon levy as of 2030, without SDE++ nor technical change – Box 9.1, Scenario D), energy efficiency gains of 12% are required in the chemical sector to offset the competitiveness impact of carbon pricing.
Source: Calculations based on the augmented IO model described in Box 9.1.

Figure 9.4 displays the sectoral efficiency gains that would be needed to completely offset the effect of carbon pricing on competitiveness. These efficiency gains are illustrative of the efforts required by the manufacturing industries to recover their competitiveness, but do not constitute an energy efficiency gain target since industries have other alternatives to reduce their emissions, such as switching to carbon-free energy sources (biomass, blue or green hydrogen, renewable electricity) and carbon capture and storage (CCS). For the carbon levy scenario, these efficiency gains range from 3% in the non-ferrous metal sector to 23% for iron and steel. Despite a roughly similar increase in the average carbon price, the required energy efficiency gains are higher for sectors using emission-intensive energy (e.g. coal in the iron and steel sector compared to electricity in the non-ferrous metal sector). For comparison purposes, emissions are supposed to be reduced by around 38%[5] in the industry between 2017 and 2030 under the Climate Agreement.

9.2.3. European co-ordination in carbon pricing can also significantly reduce the adverse impact on competitiveness

Implementing carbon pricing at the European level would significantly reduce the negative competitiveness effect on the affected sectors. Figure 9.5 compares the impact of carbon pricing, if implemented at the Dutch or European level. It shows that the average competitiveness effect in manufacturing is more than halved (-59%) when carbon pricing is implemented at the European level. This effect is heterogeneous across sectors, depending on two factors. First, it is affected by the respective importance of intra-European and extra-European trade for Dutch firms. Second, it depends on the emission intensity of Dutch firms compared to their European counterparts. If Dutch firms emit less than their European competitors, carbon pricing at the EU level gives them a comparative advantage. The reduction of the competitiveness effect is the smallest in the chemical sector (-42%), while it is almost fully offset in the food-processing sector (-97%).

Figure 9.5. Carbon pricing at the European level and BCA mechanisms significantly reduce the estimated impact on competitiveness

Reduction of competitiveness effects (measured in terms of value-added loss), compared to unilateral carbon pricing

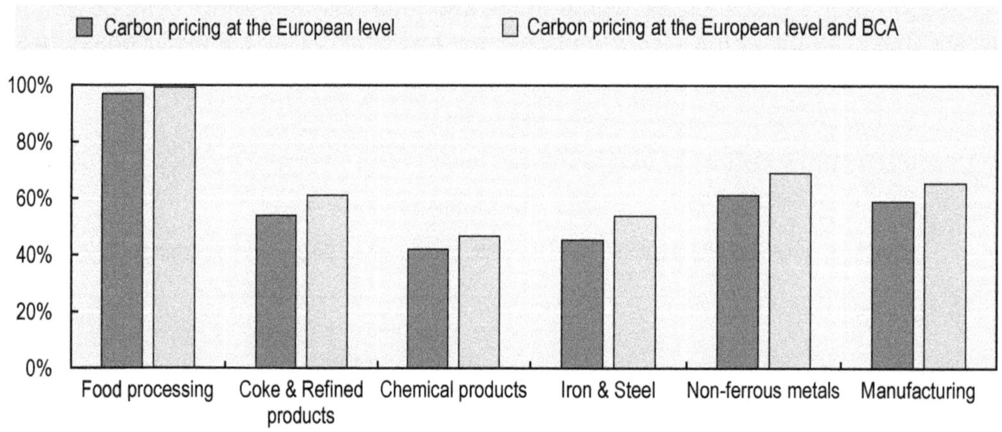

Note: When a carbon price increase is implemented at the European level (Box 9.1, Scenario B), the negative competitiveness effect on the Dutch manufacturing sector is reduced by 59% compared to a unilateral carbon price (Box 9.1, Scenario A,). If the European carbon price increase is supplemented by a BCA (Box 9.1, Scenario C), the negative competitiveness effect on the Dutch manufacturing sector is reduced by 65% compared to a unilateral carbon price (Box 9.1, Scenario A)
Source: Calculations based on the augmented IO model (Box 9.1).

On top of carbon pricing at the European level, the hypothesis of levelling the playing field between European producers, subject to carbon pricing and extra-European producers through a border carbon adjustment (BCA) is often considered by policy makers and academia, even if this option raises unresolved practical and legal questions (OECD, 2020[9]). Figure 9.5 confirms that implementing a BCA at the European level on five products (food processing, refined products, chemicals and metals – ferrous and non-ferrous) would further limit the competitiveness effect on Dutch producers, in particular for the iron and steel and non-ferrous metals sectors. However, the additional impact would remain modest as the BCA implemented in these simulations only benefits the competitiveness of European producers in the European market, but not in foreign markets. If coupled with an export-based rebate (offsetting carbon pricing for exported products), the impact would be significantly greater (Fischer and Fox, 2012[10]; Branger and Quirion, 2014[11]), but the rebate could reduce the incentives to decarbonise the domestic production.

References

Branger, F. and P. Quirion (2014), "Would border carbon adjustments prevent carbon leakage and heavy industry competitiveness losses? Insights from a meta-analysis of recent economic studies", *Ecological Economics*, Vol. 99, pp. 29-39, http://dx.doi.org/10.1016/j.ecolecon.2013.12.010. [11]

CE Delft (2021), *Correspondance with CE Delft, February 2021.* [4]

CPB and PBL (2019), *Expert-workshop CO2-heffing en verplaatsing.* [7]

Fischer, C. and A. Fox (2012), "Comparing policies to combat emissions leakage: Border carbon adjustments versus rebates", *Journal of Environmental Economics and Management*, Vol. 64/2, pp. 199-216, http://dx.doi.org/10.1016/j.jeem.2012.01.005. [10]

Hebbink, G. et al. (2018), *The price of transition: An analysis of the economic implications of carbon taxing.* [2]

Hertel, T. and D. van der Mensbrugghe (2016), *Behavioral Parameters*, Purdue University, https://www.gtap.agecon.purdue.edu/resources/res_display.asp?RecordID=5138. [3]

Imbs, J. and I. Méjean (2010), *Trade Elasticitie: A Final Report for the European Commission*, http://dx.doi.org/10.2765/46193. [8]

OECD (2020), *Climate policy leadership in an interconnected world: What role for border carbon adjustments?*, OECD Publishing, Paris, https://doi.org/10.1787/8008e7f4-en. [9]

OECD (2018), *Inter-Country Input-Output Database.* [1]

PwC (2020), *Speelveldtoets 2020.* [5]

Vollebergh, H. et al. (2019), *Economische effecten van CO2-beprijzing: varianten vergeleken.* [6]

Notes

[1] See below a discussion on an alternative use of tax revenues.

[2] The emission intensity in the current model does not change, i.e. it is assumed that no technological improvements are made thanks to the carbon levy and SDE++.

[3] It consists in the 'iron and steel' and 'non-ferrous metals' subsectors. Average effective carbon rates are however not available at that level of disaggregation.

[4] "Any revenue generated by the carbon levy will be channelled back into making industry greener. This will be achieved through a generic subsidy scheme, which will be linked to an already existing subsidy scheme".

[5] Emissions in the industry are 58 Mt eq CO_2 in 2017. The Climate Agreement plans an additional reduction of emissions of 14.3 Mt eq CO_2, on top of the 7.7 Mt eq CO_2 reduction already included in the National Energy Outlook 2017.

10. Policies for decarbonising Dutch industry

This chapter proposes overall policy recommendations for achieving industry decarbonisation based on the analyses presented in Chapters 2 to 9. The recommendations concern the three main areas for policy action: carbon pricing, technology support, and complementary policies and framework conditions.

The current Dutch policy mix for industry decarbonisation combines an ambitious carbon pricing policy with extensive and targeted technology support in a bottom-up cluster-based strategy. Combining carbon prices with technological-specific support forms the basis of an effective and cost-efficient policy package. On one hand, well-designed carbon pricing makes a technology-neutral case for low-carbon investments and consumption choices. On the other hand, support schemes for low-carbon technology development and deployment, such as the Sustainable Energy Transition Incentive Scheme (SDE++) subsidy or the energy investment allowance (EIA) tax allowance, encourage the adoption of emerging low-carbon technologies that may achieve significant cost-efficient emission reductions in the long run. Carbon pricing and technology support are not substitutes but mutually reinforcing policy instruments, as strong future carbon prices help create demand for new low-carbon technologies developed with the help of technology-specific support. Complementary policies aimed at providing adequate infrastructure and framework conditions preserving business dynamism are necessary to ensure the success of such decarbonisation strategy.

Consolidating elements from the analyses in Chapters 2 to 9, this chapter develops overall policy recommendations for achieving industry decarbonisation. The recommendations concern the three main areas for policy action: carbon pricing, technology support, and complementary policies and framework conditions.

10.1. Carbon pricing – a cornerstone of the Dutch climate policy package

Carbon pricing is an effective and low-cost means of achieving carbon abatement. While most likely not in itself sufficient to deliver the degree of abatement required to reach the Dutch climate objectives, carbon pricing is an essential part of the solution. Carbon pricing makes polluters pay for the damage their emissions cause to society. Increasingly, carbon prices are set at levels to help societies reach their abatement targets. By raising the user cost of carbon-intensive assets, well-designed carbon pricing provides a technology-neutral case for low-carbon investment and consumption choices. Strong carbon pricing in the future increases the benefit of carbon-neutral technologies, making them worthwhile even in the absence of significant additional support. Carbon pricing can also support public finances by augmenting tax revenues.

The design of electricity taxation matters for decarbonisation too. Electricity taxes apply to an energy output (electricity) and are typically not distinguished by energy source, therefore, they typically do not send a carbon pricing signal and are discussed separately below. If they apply per output and independently of the energy source, they make electricity more expensive even when it is produced from clean energy sources and fail to favour decarbonisation of the electricity mix. They also may discourage deep cuts in carbon emissions through electrification of production processes when electricity generation itself is decarbonised.

In 2021, the Netherlands implemented a new carbon levy in industry that sets out an ambitious price trajectory until 2030, providing a clear signal to invest in long-term low-carbon assets and infrastructure. The carbon levy comes on top of several other existing instruments that effectively put a price on Dutch carbon emissions: the EU ETS, energy tax on natural gas[1] (fuel excise) and a sustainable energy surcharge (Opslag Duurzame Energie [ODE]) on natural gas[2]. However, concerns over competition that domestic energy users may face from firms in countries with less ambitious carbon pricing and energy taxation policies have led the authorities to grant extensive preferential treatment to energy-intensive users, such as tax exemptions, regressive tax rates, and freely allocated emission allowances. Such preferential tax treatment reduces the abatement incentive from carbon pricing. Although free allocation of pollution permits preserves the price signal at the margin, they can counteract incentives to shift towards low-carbon technologies (Box 5.1 in Section 5.1.3). Beyond preferential treatment through carbon pricing instruments, energy-intensive trade-exposed sectors receive significant financial support.

As a result, the overall carbon pricing signal on fossil fuel use in the Netherlands, measured in terms of the OECD Effective Carbon Rate (Box 5.5 in Section 5.8.1), is heterogeneous across the key industry sectors. Figure 10.1 provides a summary measure, indicating to what extent emissions from fossil fuel energy use are priced at different carbon pricing intervals, taking energy tax on natural gas, ODE rates on natural gas and the ETS permit price into account.[3] The carbon pricing analysis focuses on CO_2 emissions from fossil fuel-based energy use, thereby excluding emissions from using fossil fuels as feedstock.

Figure 10.1. Proportion of CO_2 emissions from fossil fuel energy use in industry at different marginal price intervals in 2021

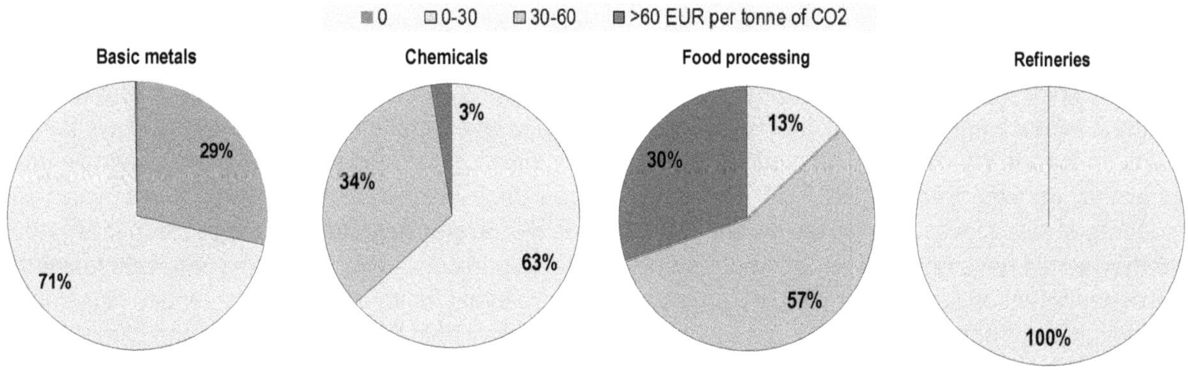

Note: Figures are based on OECD Taxing Energy Use and Effective Carbon Rates methodology (2018[1]; 2019[2]). They include price signals from energy tax and ODE on natural gas (net of exemptions) and the EU ETS permit prices (independently of whether an allowance was allocated for free or not, following the opportunity cost argument). Please refer to Figure 5.10 in Section 5.8 for a more detailed explanation. CO_2 emissions in each sector are calculated based fossil fuel energy use data adapted from IEA (2020[3]), World Energy Statistics and Balances.

The analysis below offers three key policy insights on carbon pricing for the Dutch industry. First, the newly implemented carbon levy for industry sends a strong medium-term signal to encourage significant decarbonisation. Keeping the carbon levy trajectory in place – and potentially expanding it to the period of 2050 – will be critical. The level of the carbon levy in 2030 is determined as the price consistent with the 2030 abatement objective given an estimated *ex-ante* abatement cost curve. Second, the effective carbon-pricing signal, which derives from the carbon levy, EU ETS, energy tax on natural gas and the ODE on natural gas, applies unevenly across industrial users, fuels, production-processes and consumption levels, putting at risk the efficiency and effectiveness of carbon pricing in the Netherlands. This uneven price signal also entails horizontal equity concerns across sectors and energy users. Third, the current design of the Dutch electricity tax and ODE on electricity use does not directly encourage power producers to shift to cleaner sources of energy and, therefore, does not provide direct incentives for the decarbonisation of the power sector. Fourth, provisions aiming at preserving trade-exposed sectors from potential competitiveness losses are pervasive with potentially strong negative effects on the Dutch decarbonisation efforts: shielding carbon-intensive production from carbon pricing can harm the long-run competitiveness of the Dutch economy, leading to stranded assets and stranded jobs in a Paris Agreement-compatible, net-zero carbon world. It can make the decarbonisation of Dutch industry more expensive than needed. Substantive amounts of deployment and other subsidies are distributed to energy-intensive industries largely attenuating competitiveness concerns. This support should be reassessed in the light of the policy developments in Europe and abroad, with the view of phasing out inefficient carbon pricing exemptions and strengthening the policy ambition of carbon pricing across all users. The next sections discuss these insights and associated policy recommendations in more detail.

Recommendation 1 – Maintain the carbon levy trajectory to provide a strong medium-term signal and encourage significant decarbonisation

Maintain the carbon levy trajectory – and potentially expand it to the period of 2050 – to provide a strong medium-term signal to encourage significant decarbonisation

10.1.1. The carbon levy trajectory sends a medium-term signal to encourage significant decarbonisation. The carbon levy's success will depend crucially on not compromising on this design feature in the future.

The newly introduced national carbon levy acts as a complement to the EU ETS and aims at setting a minimum price trajectory on Dutch emissions covered by the system. The carbon levy is supposed to provide insurance against the risk that EU ETS prices drop to levels that threaten investment in low-carbon assets. In theory, effective minimum prices lowers risk for investors beyond the volatile and uncertain price signal that derives from the EU ETS. Excessive carbon price volatility limits emission reductions and discourages clean investment to the extent that it causes risk-averse investors to forego clean investment that they would have undertaken with more stable prices. In particular, volatile carbon prices increase the cost of capital linked to an investment, which is particularly relevant for investments that require high capital expenditures upfront. Stable carbon prices in turn limit the increase in the cost of capital and can convince risk-averse investors that clean investment provides reliable returns in the future and is worthwhile (Flues and Van Dender, 2020[4]).

Setting a pre-defined price trajectory is an important feature of the national carbon levy (Table 10.1). Committing today to future price increases can create strong incentives, particularly for investments in long-lived assets and infrastructure – which are typical in the industry sector. It will also reduce economic and competitiveness disruptions that may be driven by high prices in those sectors where costs to implement decarbonisation technologies are high in the short-run but relatively lower in the long run (e.g. some sectors may be able to switch to a new zero-carbon technology in the longer run, but cutting emissions may be difficult as long as the existing technology remains in use). Phasing-in the levy base over time (Table 10.2) further attenuates short-run competitiveness concerns. Carbon price trajectories can also increase acceptance of the policy through transparency and by leaving room for adjustments (e.g. technological shifts or efficiency measures) to avoid paying the higher future price.

Table 10.1. Statutory price trajectory of carbon levy in 2021

	2021	2022	2023	2024	2025	2026	2027	2028	2029	2030
Levy rate (in EUR per tonne of CO_2)	30	40.56	51.12	61.68	72.24	82.8	93.36	103.92	114.48	125.04

Note: Calculation based on legislative proposal "Wetsvoorstel Wet CO_2-heffing industrie", Art. 71p.

One important success factor of the carbon levy in driving emission reductions is the government's ability to commit to rising prices in the future. As changes to the governing coalition may lead to a revision of the price trajectory, or a removal of the levy in the extreme case, it does not provide a perfect commitment device. The recent general elections provide uncertainty in this respect. Wide-ranging agreement across the political spectrum on future prices can help increase the credibility of price expectations. Having developed the carbon levy and price trajectory through ongoing conversations with stakeholders in the context of the Climate Agreement may increase and have widened the acceptability of the instrument by the relevant parties.

These positive features of the carbon levy, however, may not play out their full potential. In particular, the generous (over)allocation of dispensation rights to carbon-intensive sectors[4] largely erodes the carbon pricing signal, particularly in the early years of the levy (Table 10.2). The small market size may hamper the efficient allocation of dispensation rights as only little trade may occur, and most likely only within the industry clusters. Also, indexing the allocation of dispensation rights on the current production volume does not encourage energy-intensive users to reduce emissions by producing less. In addition, the complex design of the carbon levy increases the administrative and compliance burden for liable firms.

Table 10.2. Estimated proportion of emissions paying the levy in key sub-sectors

	2021	2022	2023	2024	2025	2026	2027	2028	2029	2030
Chemical industry	5%	10%	14%	19%	24%	27%	32%	37%	42%	46%
Food	0%	2%	6%	11%	16%	21%	26%	31%	36%	40%
Metallurgical industry	1%	6%	10%	15%	20%	24%	29%	34%	39%	43%
Refineries	10%	14%	18%	23%	27%	31%	35%	40%	44%	48%

Note: The estimation assumes benchmark values follow the draft revisions to the EU ETS benchmarks published in December 2020. No behavioural adjustments in the emissions base, i.e. no technological shifts, no energy efficiency improvements or rebound effects compared to 2021 are assumed.
Source: CE Delft (2021[5])

10.1.2. Importance of carbon levy for promoting emerging technologies

The carbon levy trajectory is critical to the further development and deployment of the new emerging technologies discussed in Chapter 7. The main reason why industry is not yet investing extensively in these technologies is their cost compared to the carbon-intensive alternatives currently in use. The carbon levy helps to bridge price differentials between substitute processes that differ in the carbon-intensity and thereby encourage investments in these key emerging technologies.

If low-carbon technologies become profitable, the carbon price will not only stimulate their uptake, but also provide an incentive for the industry to invest in R&D. These investments in R&D in turn lead to better and more cost-effective green technologies needed to achieve the climate ambitions. Since investments in R&D only yield a return in the future, it is important that the carbon levy is guaranteed to take effect in the future, as uncertainty about future profitability of using green technologies will decrease investments in R&D today.

The business case for both CCUS/ carbon capture and storage (CCS) and the electrification of heating are highly dependent on the carbon levy trajectory. For hydrogen, the carbon levy is not sufficient to tip the break even point in the industrial sector, but without the carbon levy trajectory in place, the production of green hydrogen would be even less profitable. Also for the circular economy, the carbon levy helps to create a level playing field for recycling and bio-based materials with fossil fuels based products.

Recommendation 2 – Gradually eliminate energy tax and ODE exemptions, as well as regressive rates, to strengthen the efficiency, effectiveness and fairness of the carbon pricing signal

Gradually eliminate tax exemptions and ensure that remaining preferential treatment is aligned with trade-exposure of a specific industrial sector, not only its energy intensity

Different policy instruments are in place that put an effective price on Dutch carbon emissions: the carbon levy, the EU ETS, energy tax on natural gas and the ODE on natural gas. While carbon pricing is an explicit *policy intent* of the first two instruments, it is a *policy effect* of the latter two instruments. The central policy objective of the Dutch energy tax and the ODE is to fund the general budget and the SDE++ subsidies.

A parallel across all four effective carbon pricing instruments is that they grant extensive preferential treatment to energy-intensive industry users, in particular the chemicals, refineries and basic metals sector. Dispensation rights and pollution permits are allocated freely under the carbon levy and the EU ETS and generous exemptions are granted under the energy tax and ODE on top of their regressive rate structure. These instruments and preferential treatment yield a very heterogeneous carbon rate net of free allocation across energy users within industry. Figure 10.2 provides a detailed overview on how taxes and emission trading prices apply to all fossil fuel energy use in the specific sectors. Free allocation of permits reduces average carbon prices significantly in the basic metals, chemicals and refineries sector. Food processing is subject to relatively high energy taxes because of their nearly exclusive use of natural gas as an energy source and some energy use falling in the relatively highly taxed first consumption bin. Sectoral average effective carbon rates in 2021 are estimated at EUR 76 per tonne for the food processing sector, against an average rate of EUR 13 per tonne in chemicals, EUR 3 per tonne in basic metals and EUR 7 per tonne in refineries. More details on the figure can be found in Sections 5.1 and 5.8.

Figure 10.2. Effective carbon rates on CO_2 emissions from fossil fuel energy use in Dutch main industry subsectors, 2021

A. Basic Metals

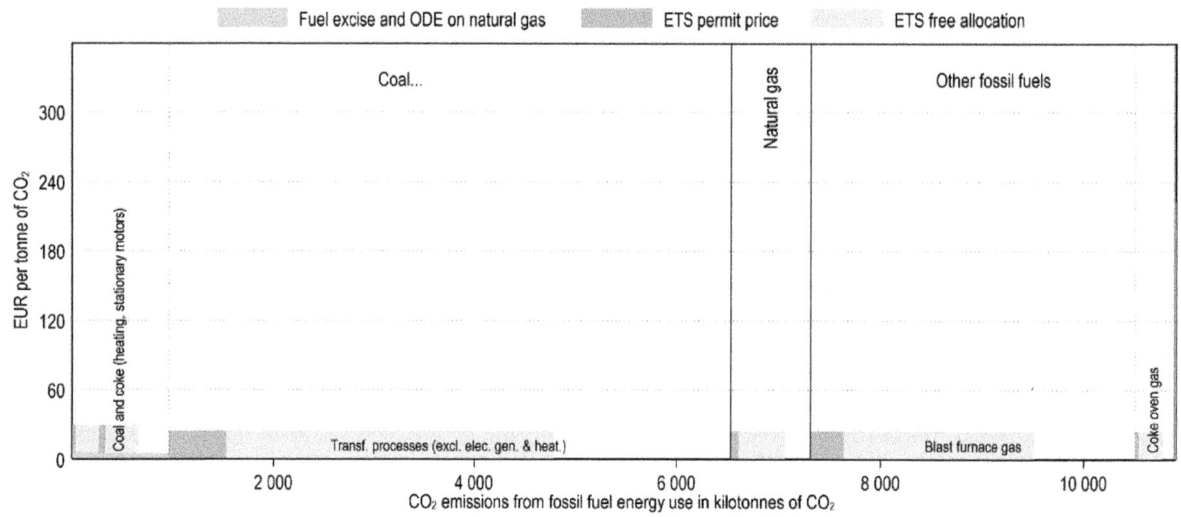

B. Chemicals

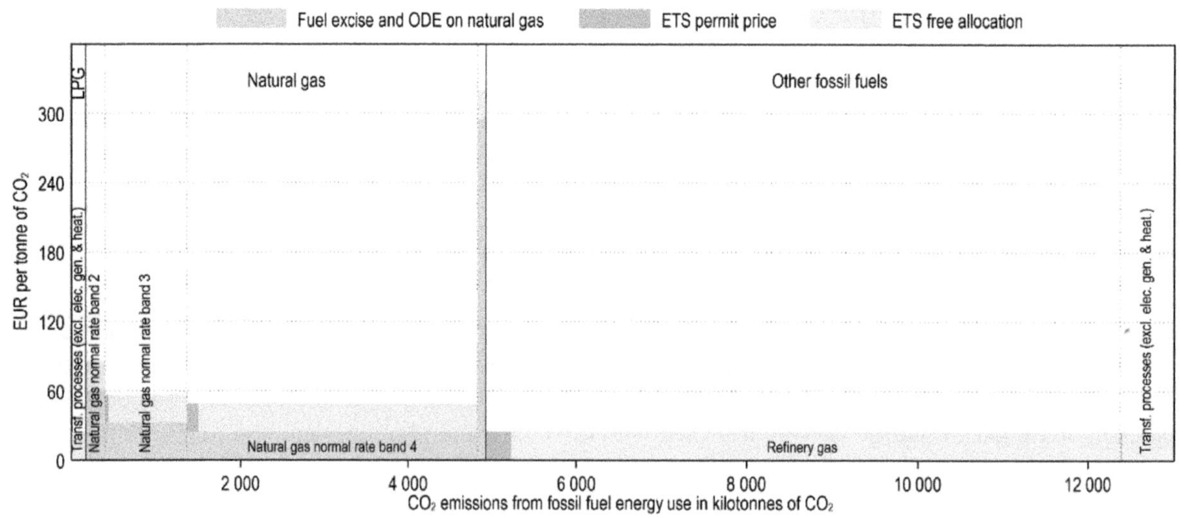

C. Food processing

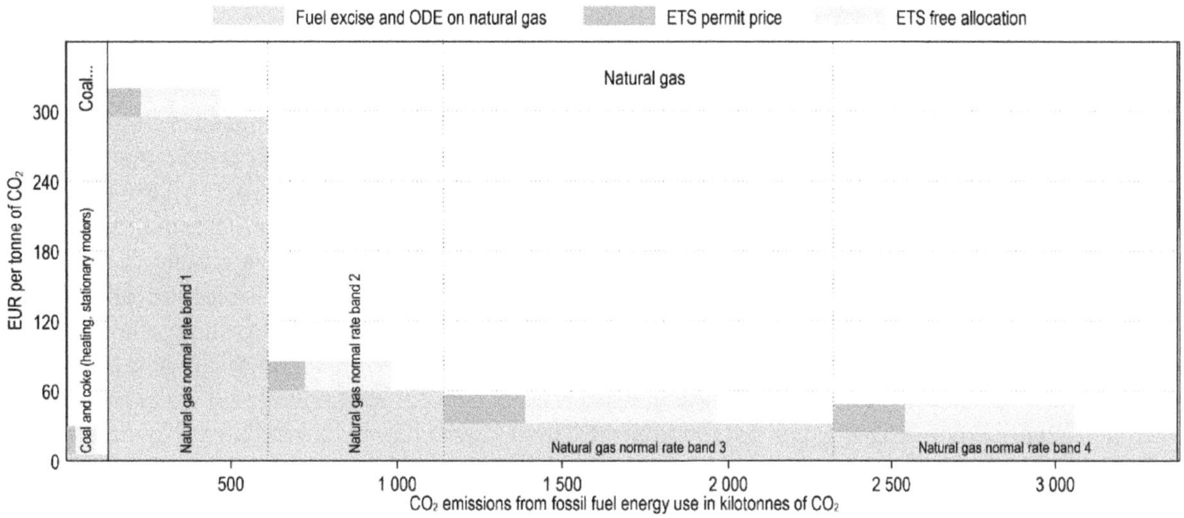

D. Refineries

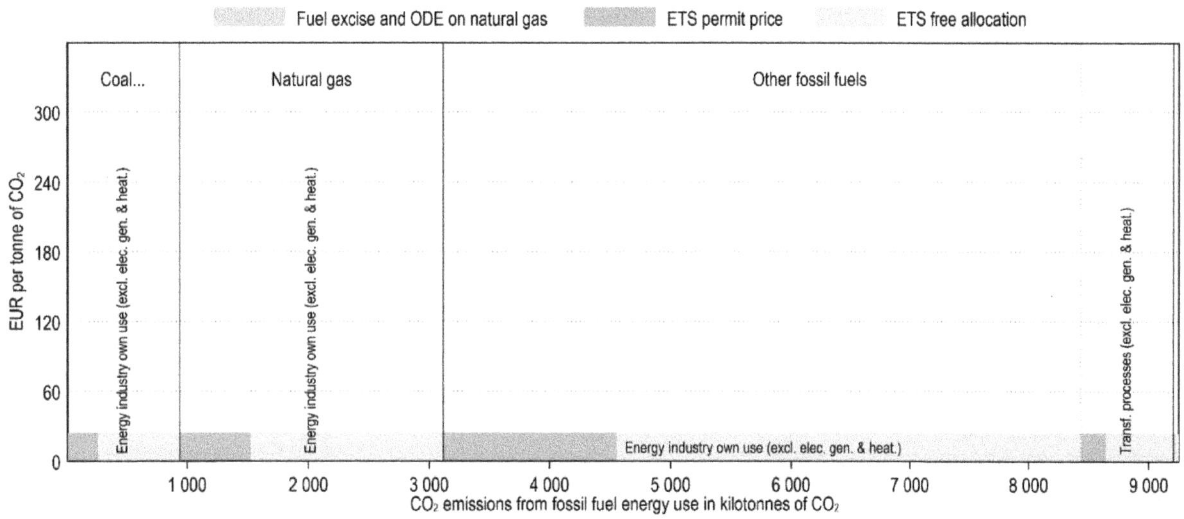

Note: Please refer to Sections 5.1 and 5.8 for a more detailed discussion. The effective carbon rate (ECR) includes energy tax on natural gas ("fuel excise") and ODE rates on natural gas applicable on 1 January 2021. The ETS permit price is the average price in 2020. The national component of the carbon levy is set to zero for 2021 because of the large amount of excess dispensation rights in 2021 that are not bankable, thereby losing their value for future trading periods. The methodology to estimate the overlap of taxes and ETS prices is explained in detail in OECD (2016[6]). ETS data from the Dutch emissions registry is matched to fossil fuel energy use data from IEA (2020[3]), World Energy Statistics and Balances. It is assumed that the EU ETS coverage distributes evenly across all fuels and users in each sub-sector.

The Dutch climate policy package provides significant support to the deployment of low-carbon technologies in energy-intensive trade-exposed sectors, which cushions competitiveness concerns and can be considered as duplicating the generous carbon pricing exemptions and regressive rates. To avoid duplicating policy efforts and driving down abatement incentives, the gradual phase-out of inefficient exemptions could be envisaged without compromising on industries' long run competitiveness. Additional advances at the EU level may further limit competitiveness concerns (see below).

10.1.3. Gradually eliminating energy tax and ODE exemptions could strengthen the efficiency and effectiveness of the carbon pricing signal in the Netherlands and will generate additional revenues

In the Netherlands, most energy-intensive industry is exempt from paying energy tax and ODE on natural gas. If energy-intensive users are not fully exempt, they are subject to the lowest possible rates given the regressive rate structure of both instruments. More precisely, we estimate that 78% of industrial emissions from fossil fuel energy are exempt from paying energy tax or ODE on natural gas, while 12.5% fall into the bands with the lowest possible rate (bands 3 and 4). Energy tax exemptions for industrial users are a widespread practice within Europe and the rest of the world. Their main objective relates to supporting specific production and addressing competitiveness concerns for certain trade-exposed and energy-intensive industries. However, the regressive rate structure in the Netherlands provides relief to energy users on the sole criteria of energy-intensity and size, with no differentiation based on the actual exposure of a sector to international competition. Similarly, fossil fuels of high carbon content (e.g. coal) are exposed to a much lower carbon pricing signal per tonne of CO_2 than lower carbon content fuels (e.g. natural gas).

From a decarbonisation perspective, this preferential treatment of energy-intensive users adds inefficiency to the overall carbon-pricing signal and entails horizontal equity concerns. As price-induced decarbonisation incentives are not evenly distributed, abatement efforts may not arise where they are cheapest. These policy choices risk increasing the total costs of decarbonising the Dutch industry sector. In addition, while minimal price signals reach the energy-intensive users, the less concentrated industries (e.g. companies in the food processing sector) and small energy users in other sectors pay a relatively high energy tax and surcharge per tonne of carbon.

Equity and political economy challenges are further exacerbated as energy-intensive industry is effectively exempt from financing low-carbon technology support via the ODE-SDE++ linkage, the ODE surcharge is supposed to finance the SDE++ subsidies for specific technologies. The generous exemptions and low ODE rates in the third and fourth consumption bands limit the contribution of energy-intensive industrial users to the ODE-SDE++ redistribution mechanism (Table 10.3). If the framework for providing exemptions is not reformed in the future, small industrial energy consumers risk contributing highly to the expanded SDE++ budget, while potentially having little opportunity for claiming SDE++ subsidies, which are directed mainly at technologies for energy-intensive industry.

Exempting emissions from energy tax and the ODE on natural gas also reduce the effectiveness of carbon pricing via two channels. First, there is no incentive to cut emissions in the sectors that are exempt from the energy tax and surcharge, meaning that at a given carbon price some relatively cheap abatement opportunities are likely foregone. Second, there is an incentive to shift emissions from the emission base that is covered by a price to the emission base that is not covered. For example, as the coal tax is lower (both in CO_2 and gigajoule [GJ] terms) than the lowest rate band of the energy tax on natural gas, there is an incentive for emitters to reduce gas consumption and increase the use of coal.

A standard tax policy advice that applies in this context calls for broadening tax bases, that is removing exemptions, refunds and preferential rates. A future review of the energy tax and ODE on natural gas could aim to rationalise the design of the tax, establish a uniform rate across users and fuels (including coal and liquid fuels) based on their carbon content and remove exemptions. A carbon price that covers all fuels at equal rates expressed per tonne of CO_2 will alter prices more effectively for high-carbon fuels than for low-carbon fuels. This means, for example, the price of coal will increase more than that of natural gas, encouraging energy users to substitute coal with natural gas. Potential positive and negative side-effects on other environmental outcomes and fuel use related externalities could be discussed in that context.

Phasing-out inefficient and unequal tax and surcharge exemptions is facilitated through the generous low-carbon technology-specific support for energy-intensive users and even more so if European trade partners act accordingly. In the context of the ongoing discussions on the EU Green Deal, a revision of the Energy Tax Directive provides room for such an approach.

Table 10.3. Energy tax and ODE payments on natural gas use (2017) and energy base (2016)

	Energy tax payments on natural gas use (in mio EUR)	ODE payments on natural gas use (in mio EUR)	Energy base (natural gas) (in mio m³)
Industry total	221.6	36.48	5 896.1
Contribution by subsector (in %)			
Food, drinks and tobacco	36.3%	37.5%	24.3%
Textile and leather	4.0%	3.5%	1.4%
Wood, paper and graphic industry	7.6%	7.6%	4.0%
Petroleum industry	3.2%	3.8%	8.7%
Chemical and pharma industry	18.5%	22.3%	34.3%
Building materials	0.5%	0.7%	9.7%
Basic metals	0.0%	0.0%	6.8%
Machinery (incl. transport means)	18.9%	15.3%	7.3%
Other industry and repair	10.9%	9.3%	3.6%

Note: Small differences in the sectoral definitions across energy and ODE payments and the energy base may remain.
Source: CE Delft (2021[7]) and CBS (2017[8]).

10.1.4. The current free allocation of EU ETS permits may reduce the incentive of business to invest in break-through production-processes that are necessary for decarbonising the sector

The EU ETS adds an additional price signal to industry emissions beyond energy taxes and ODE. It covers a large part of those emissions that benefit from a full tax exemption (Figure 5.9), thereby providing a market-based incentive for emissions abatement beyond the forgone signal from taxation. There is also some overlap between emissions paying the ETS price, energy tax and ODE (e.g. in the food processing sector, Figure 10.2). The overlap of instruments (ETS, energy tax on natural gas, ODE on natural gas) increases the effective price signal for the given emissions base.

The ETS provides an incentive to reduce emissions at the margin. However, the current mechanism of free allocation of EU ETS allowances limits the decarbonisation incentives for Dutch industry. For example, according to CE Delft, the Dutch chemicals, refinery and basic metal sectors have received free allowances in 2019 that amount to approximately 96%, 73% and 85% of their emissions base – acting similarly to an output subsidy. Poorly designed free allocation rules can weaken incentives for firms to invest in break-through low-carbon technologies and undermine the trading system's effectiveness to drive decarbonisation (Box 5.1).

10.1.5. The short-term risk for a 'waterbed effect' in the EU ETS is uncertain, but likely limited thanks to the design of the market stability reserve (MSR)

The effects of the interaction between the national carbon levy and the EU ETS is complex (Flues and Van Dender, 2020[4]; Perino, Ritz and van Benthem, 2020[9]). There is some limited risk that the combination of implementing the national carbon levy in the presence of the EU ETS leads to no 'additional' emission reduction. Because the EU's overall emissions cap is set at the EU level, additional emission reductions that are taking place in the Netherlands may be offset by emission increases in other parts of the EU, the so-called 'waterbed effect'.

However, the current design of the newly established MSR would lead to some invalidation of emissions allowances following the carbon levy, in particular if cleaner products or cleaner production processes of existing products would substitute the Dutch production. Substitution towards cleaner products or production processes likely increases the amount of unused allowances in circulation at the end of each year. This puts pressure on the allowance price but would also increase the number of allowances placed in the reserve. As described in Chapter 5, if more allowances accumulate in the reserve than are auctioned in the previous year, the surplus of allowances will be invalidated keeping in check the waterbed effect. Because the amount of auctioned allowances decreases every year, all else being equal, additional allowances placed in the reserve in the future are likely to be eventually invalidated. The ultimate effect will depend on whether and when the change in production and additional carbon abatement leads to an accumulation of allowances in the MSR (in which case the carbon levy likely has an "additional" effect on emission reductions) or to a contemporary shift of emissions towards dirty producers in other European countries (in which case there may be a waterbed effect).

Independently of the MSR, the combination of the national carbon levy with the EU ETS introduces inefficiencies in the structure of decarbonisation incentives across the EU, when high cost abatement in the Netherlands that is triggered by the levy replaces cheaper abatement in other EU member states in the short term.

Recommendation 3 – Engage in a thorough review of electricity taxation to support the country's need to electrify industrial processes, without burdening small industrial, residential and commercial consumers

With a strong carbon floor price in place, the elimination of the energy tax and the ODE on electricity use – or a strong reduction towards a low and uniform price per GJ across consumption bins – may be envisaged.

To avoid conflicts between environmental and fiscal objectives, the phasing-down of energy tax and ODE on electricity use could be co-ordinated with the removal of energy tax exemptions on natural gas and the phasing-in of an effective carbon floor price in electricity to generate additional revenue.

Eventually, as the energy system is approaching full decarbonisation, electricity taxes could be reintroduced if so desired.

10.1.6. Engaging in a thorough review of electricity taxation to support the country's need to electrify industrial processes without burdening residential and commercial users

The current design of the Dutch energy tax and ODE on electricity consumption does not directly encourage power producers to shift to cleaner sources of energy, and does not provide direct incentives for the decarbonisation of the power sector. The reason is that the electricity tax is not differentiated by energy source but applies per unit of electricity used. Therefore, it increases the price on all energy sources used for electricity generation irrespective of their carbon content. Electricity taxation still incentivises electricity savings in general.

Pricing the fossil fuel inputs to electricity generation, e.g. via the Dutch carbon floor price in electricity and the EU ETS, specifically applied to fossil fuels, would make them more expensive relative to non-fossil energy sources. Given that the energy tax and ODE on natural gas and direct carbon pricing mechanisms are directly levied on the energy product, they also provide direct incentives to increase power plant efficiency – unlike electricity taxes (OECD, 2019[2]).

Another major concern is that the Dutch energy tax and ODE on electricity consumption discourages the electrification of the industry sector, because taxing electricity use makes switching to electricity less profitable for end users, everything else being equal. This can compromise the decarbonisation efforts under the assumption that the electricity mix is green, or at least greener than the alternative. For example, the tax rate in GJ terms is much higher for electricity than for gas use in all but the highest consumption band (Table 10.4). This favours the use of natural gas over electrification of industrial processes, everything else being equal.

The total price differential between electricity and natural gas use becomes more pronounced taking pre-tax prices into account (Table 10.5). In 2020, pre-tax prices in Dutch industry are EUR 4.7 per GJ for natural gas and EUR 17.2 per GJ for electricity for the typical industrial producer. A carbon levy rate of EUR 125 per tonne applying to the entire emissions base translates into a EUR 7 rate per GJ of natural gas, thereby reducing the differential to some extent.

However, it is not straightforward to compare the electricity and natural gas prices as reported in Table 10.5, as the GJ value of electricity and gas are not strictly comparable, mainly because they are affected by conversion efficiencies, amongst others. Upstream, the electricity price depends on the fuel- and technology-specific conversion efficiency to transform primary energy into electricity. For example, using solar or wind power has a high conversion efficiency (typically considered close to one), while the use of natural gas for producing electricity includes substantive losses bringing the conversion efficiency down to roughly 0.5. Such a factor would translate into doubling the natural gas price displayed in the table that is needed to substitute for one GJ of electricity, everything else being equal. Downstream, using natural gas as an input in some industrial processes may entail larger energy losses compared to using electricity. For example, substituting a gas boiler by an industrial heat pump used in low-temperature heat processes leads to fewer conversion losses. Such considerations are technology and process dependent and could lead to further reductions of the price differential between natural gas and electricity.

Table 10.4. Energy tax rates for natural gas and electricity in EUR per GJ, 2021

	Band 1	Band 2	Band 3	Band 4
Natural gas	13.31	2.50	0.91	0.49
Electricity	26.19	14.34	3.82	0.16

Note: Conversion follows the methodology set out in (OECD, 2019[2]) based on IEA *World Energy Statistics and Balances*.

Table 10.5. Pre-tax prices for natural gas and electricity in Dutch industry, Q2/2020

	Natural gas	Electricity
Unit price, excluding taxes [in EUR/GJ]	4.69	17.22

Note: For natural gas, prices refer to the Eurostat consumption band I4 for industry (annual consumption: 0.1-1 PJ). For electricity, prices refer to the Eurostat consumption band ID for industry (annual consumption: 2-20 TWh).
Source: Based on IEA *Energy Prices*.

The design of electricity taxation also raises equity concerns. Currently, key industrial users of electricity do not pay the full Dutch energy tax and surcharge on electricity consumption, either because users are exempt from the tax (for example, electricity generation for own use is exempt) or, for the large electricity users, because they are subject to the lowest possible rate (Table 5.3 and Table 5.9). This treatment favours concentrated, large consumers at the expense of small industrial users and the residential and commercial sector that face the high rate of the lowest band for all consumption (Table 10.6).

Table 10.6. Energy tax and ODE payments on electricity consumption (2017) and energy base (2016)

	Energy tax payments on electricity use (in mio EUR)	ODE payments on electricity use (in mio EUR)	Energy base (electricity) (in mio kWh)
Industry total	186.7	36.48	31 930.7
Contribution by subsector (in %)			
Food, drinks and tobacco	31.4%	33.7%	18.3%
Textile and leather	4.4%	3.1%	1.1%
Wood, paper and graphic industry	11.9%	10.9%	6.9%
Petroleum industry	0.5%	0.6%	2.3%
Chemical and pharma industry	11.9%	14.1%	34.2%
Building materials	3.2%	4.1%	3.9%
Basic metals	0.0%	0.0%	15.1%
Machinery (incl. transport means)	16.9%	17.4%	11.2%
Other industry and repair	19.9%	16.0%	6.9%

Note: Small differences in the sectoral definitions across energy tax and ODE payments and the energy base may remain.
Source: CE Delft (2021[7]) and CBS (2017[8]).

The new carbon price for Dutch power generation puts a floor price on emissions from electricity generation in the EU ETS and is a welcome development as it raises the carbon price on input fuels equally across electricity users and fuels. Rather than increasing the price of electricity for all types of generation, including zero-carbon energy, it provides incentives to shift towards decarbonised electricity. With a strong carbon floor price in place, the elimination of the energy tax and the ODE on electricity users – or a strong reduction towards a low and uniform price per GJ across consumption bins – may be envisaged. It should be noted though that the current rate of the carbon floor price falls well below the EU ETS permit price and therefore currently does not affect the price signal.

The United Kingdom has introduced a Carbon Price Support (CPS) in 2013 at GBP 9 per tonne of CO_2 for emissions in the electricity sector that increased over time reaching GBP 18 in April 2015. Different to the Dutch floor price, the UK CPS was charged on top of the EU ETS permit prices and increased over time. Emissions from the electricity sector decreased by 58% from 2012, before the CPS was introduced, to 2016. The decrease in emissions was explained by a sharp drop in the use of coal for the generation of electricity. Coal use fell by 78% in the same period. It was partly replaced by natural gas, which is about half as emission intensive as coal per unit of energy, and partly by zero-carbon renewables. The British experience shows how fast emissions can decline if carbon prices are at levels high enough to encourage a switch to cleaner fuels (OECD, 2018[1]).

To avoid conflicts between environmental and fiscal objectives, the phasing-down of electricity tax and surcharge could be co-ordinated with the phasing-in of an effective carbon floor price in electricity and the removal of energy tax exemptions and preferential rates to generate additional revenue. Revenues from the energy tax and surcharge on electricity contribute substantially to the general budget and the SDE++. The carbon floor price in electricity and additional revenue from removal of tax expenditures may replace existing electricity taxes and ODE in such a way that overall revenues remain constant. At the beginning, the gradual erosion of the carbon price base would be mitigated by increasing the floor price over time. Eventually, as the energy system is approaching full decarbonisation, electricity taxes could be reintroduced if desired (OECD, 2019[2]).

Recommendation 4 – Re-evaluate provisions aimed at preserving the short run competitiveness of trade-exposed energy-intensive sectors in light of policy developments in the Netherlands and beyond

The Dutch government providing extensive support for key technologies in trade-exposed sectors, likely limits disruptions to competitiveness substantially.

With the EU and more and more non-EU countries committing to carbon neutrality by the second half of the century, competitiveness concerns are likely to fade away rapidly.

Mechanisms to preserve remaining competitiveness concerns should be chosen based on their ability to maintain decarbonisation incentives, instead of decreasing climate policy ambition as tax exemptions and free allocations do.

A variety of measures exists to address concerns over competition that domestic energy users may face from firms located in countries with less ambitious carbon pricing policies. Competitiveness provisions in the Dutch policy toolkit are pervasive. Each carbon pricing mechanism includes a specific provision in that respect. Most recently, the carbon levy phases-in the carbon price and emissions base and provides generous free allocation of dispensation rights in an attempt to give industry enough time to adapt and invest in the necessary low-carbon technologies. The combination of these carbon pricing design features with multiple support instruments for key technologies, most notably the generous technology-specific abatement payment for industrial users (SDE++), likely reduces short-run competitiveness concerns substantially. In addition, with the EU and more and more non-EU countries committing to carbon neutrality by the second half of the century, competitiveness concerns are likely to fade away rapidly.

10.1.7. To avoid conflicts with the Dutch decarbonisation objective, mechanisms should be chosen based on their ability to address remaining competitiveness concerns while maintaining incentives to decarbonise and invest in low-carbon assets and infrastructure

In case international competitiveness remains a concern in the future, alternative mechanisms to generous tax exemptions, regressive rates and free allocation for energy-intensive industry are worth discussing. The current tools are not optimal from a decarbonisation perspective as they erode the carbon-pricing signal. Alternative measures exist that address competitiveness concerns of energy-intensive and trade-exposed sectors, while keeping carbon prices at levels that provide incentives to reduce energy use and shift to low-carbon investment. Such measures can help level the playing field of climate policies by elevating them to the higher level of ambition, instead of decreasing the ambition as exemptions and free allocations do.

Alternative measures can be implemented at different levels of governance, e.g. nationally, at EU level, or internationally. Such national and EU-wide approaches include border carbon adjustments (BCA), carbon consumption charges and abatement payments. The necessity and suitability of such measures in the Dutch context requires a discussion of their design features and implementation. All measures entail advantages and have their limitations. It seems important to start a discussion on these measures at the national and international level.

The European Commission has proposed to implement a European Green Deal that should transform the EU into a modern, resource-efficient and competitive economy with no net GHG emissions by 2050, an economic growth model that is both decoupled from resource use and leaves no-one behind. The Green Deal also aims at proposing a revision of the EU's climate and energy legislation by June 2021, including several pieces that are relevant in this respect. Proposals to revise the European Energy Tax Directive, and the EU ETS directive may further align carbon pricing and energy taxation efforts across EU Member States. The implementation of a potential carbon border adjustment mechanism would directly reduce competitiveness concerns from firms situated outside the EU countries. Several mechanisms for a European carbon border adjustment mechanism are currently being discussed and it remains to be seen whether a mechanism emerges eventually and, if so, what specific design features it entails.

A BCA can be defined as "a measure applied to traded products that seeks to make their prices in destination markets reflect the costs they would have incurred had they been regulated under the destination market's greenhouse gas emission regime" (Cosbey, 2012[10]). The design and implementation of BCAs are challenging, involving trade-offs between effectiveness and feasibility and they need to be designed carefully, taking into account countries' commitment under the multilateral trading system. OECD (2020[11]) provides an overview of different policy instruments that can limit carbon leakage, with a particular focus on BCAs, and offers a technical review of the literature and of the legal specificities around BCA as well as of alternative instruments to BCAs. These include measures that are the result of an internationally co-ordinated effort (e.g. international sectoral agreements of the type of CORSIA in international aviation) and unilateral instruments, such as excise taxes on domestic consumption of specific carbon-intensive goods and abatement payments (as in the Dutch SDE++).

Excise taxes on domestic consumption of certain carbon-intensive material, such as steel, cement or aluminium, (sometimes called carbon consumption charges) represents a policy approach that the Netherlands may envisage in addition to carbon pricing to reply to both policy challenges unilaterally: competitiveness concerns and decarbonisation. Excise tax rates could be based on the average carbon content of the goods or alternatively on the EU ETS product benchmarks. A simple implementation of excise taxes would only price the average emissions or benchmark emissions of goods. Excise taxes would then not create incentives to switch to a cleaner production method of given carbon-intensive goods, such as steel or aluminium. From a decarbonisation perspective, such taxes would therefore need to be complemented by additional incentives, including carbon prices (OECD, 2020[11]). Competitiveness concerns from higher carbon prices would be reduced by passing them on in the value chain, where carbon costs are less important.[5] Carbon consumption charges could also strengthen the incentives to efficiently use, reuse and recycle such materials.

Compared to BCAs, the implementation of excise taxes involves much less administrative complexity. The Netherlands already have experience with differentiating taxes by CO_2 emissions and other environmental criteria, as they levy vehicle registration taxes that differentiate by CO_2 emissions of the car and the benchmarks used in the context of the carbon levy may be used. Compared to abatement payments such as the Dutch SDE++, excise taxes generate additional revenue. Abatement payments, on the contrary, require that sufficient funds are available as well as an efficient design for the allocation of payments, which can be costly. Additional administrative costs arise due to the potential complexity of the scheme.

A broader tax shift in the Netherlands can also, to some extent, attenuate international competitiveness concerns. A tax shift implies that revenues generated through more ambitious carbon pricing provides a rationale for reducing taxes derived from other sources, such as income, profits and employment. For example, in British Columbia parts of the revenues from the carbon tax contribute to lowering corporate income tax rates (Murray and Rivers, 2015[12]). Such a shift could provide business with the full incentive to reduce emissions through a higher carbon price, while keeping their total tax contribution in check. However, it would entail a potentially significant redistribution across sectors, benefiting in particular the service sector, which represent a large share of the economic activity but have a low carbon-intensity.

10.2. A strong support for low-carbon technology deployment

By complementing carbon pricing with strong support for technology deployment, the Netherlands seeks to achieve two policy goals: decarbonising its industrial sector and becoming a world leader in emerging low-carbon technologies. Support intends to bridge the remaining profitability gap of key low-carbon technologies with existing carbon-intensive technologies –a task that the current carbon price alone is unable to achieve – in order to create the necessary business case for their deployment, including CCS, the electrification of heating processes and hydrogen.

The Dutch support policy for low-carbon technology focuses on the cost-efficient deployment of a number of both emerging (e.g. blue hydrogen) and radically new (e.g. green hydrogen) technologies through several subsidy programs, with the new SDE++ being the spearhead. At earlier stages of technology readiness (R&D and demonstration), most policy instruments at the national level focus on demonstration. For R&D, the Netherlands mostly rely on horizontal support and EU funding (Chapter 5). Overall, the support for technology deployment available to Dutch industry is relatively important. While Germany – a much larger economy – plans on a budget of about EUR 5 billion for technology deployment support over the period 2020-30, the part of the SDE++ devoted to the industry amounts to EUR 3 billion alone in the same period (Chapter 6).

Taken together, the analyses of zero-emission scenarios (Chapter 3), of the current policy package (Chapter 5) and of emerging low-carbon technologies (Chapter 7) point to several issues deserving particular attention with a view to the 2050 horizon. First, support chiefly promotes close-to-market technologies, possibly crowding out support for breakthrough technologies required for the net-zero emission economy in favour of bridge technologies. Second, a funding gap seems to exist for large-scale demonstration projects, possibly creating a "valley of death" for breakthrough entrepreneurs and firms. Finally, the myriad of available support instruments, particularly at the demonstration stage, may imply relatively large administration costs and create access barriers for young and small firms.

Recommendation 5 – Ensure greater support for technologies that are still far from the market, as part of a more balanced approach to technology support across levels of technology maturity

Maintain strong and predictable support for low-carbon technology diffusion as the necessary complement to carbon pricing in order to provide investors with the necessary long-term investment incentives and bridge the current cost handicap of key decarbonisation technologies

Leverage either the EU ETS Innovation Fund, the EU Important Project of Common European Interest (IPCEI) or the Dutch National Growth Fund to close the funding gap for large-scale demonstration projects and help breakthrough innovators escape the "valley of death" of clean tech venturing.

10.2.1. Complementing carbon pricing with technology support makes a business case for key decarbonisation technologies and preserves cost-competitiveness

Two key advantages arise from the Dutch decarbonisation strategy consisting in complementing predictable carbon pricing signals at levels compatible with the zero-net emission objective by 2050 with strong support for low-carbon technology deployment. First, it places the Dutch industry on a faster decarbonisation path, as it makes up for the suboptimal level of private investments in technological innovation arising from knowledge externalities, which carbon taxation alone cannot achieve (Chapter 4). Second, it preserves the cost-competitiveness of industrial firms by returning in subsidies what was collected through the surcharge, thereby safeguarding Dutch industrial firms' edges on international markets and ensuring industry buy-in.

In particular, combining technology support via the SDE++ abatement payment with a strong carbon price trajectory can provide strong incentives for the deployment of the key emerging technologies for decarbonising the Dutch industry, specifically to make the business case for CCS, the electrification of heating and, in the near future, hydrogen. The subsidy is expected to cover the operational expenses for most technologies related to CCS and some technologies related to the electrification of heating.

The successful deployment of these key emerging technologies heavily depends on both a predictable and increasing carbon price and strong technology support. The analysis in Chapter 3 on zero-emission scenarios makes the case for maintaining and strengthening these two pillars, where adequate. Specifically, targeting part of the technology support to bridge the cost handicap gap of green hydrogen seems necessary (see below on the SDE++). Simultaneously, the carbon levy needs to "bite" relatively fast and uncertainty about its implementation should be minimised.

In line with best practices, spending should be monitored carefully, as well as the risk of windfall profits to investors for activities they would have undertaken even in the absence of support.

10.2.2. The balance of the technology support package tilts towards short-run cost-efficiency

Most technology support from the Dutch government focuses on deployment (and demonstration to a lesser extent), with the SDE++ scheme as a spearhead. Apart from the SDE++, deployment focuses on incremental energy efficiency with the EIA scheme more than on technology shifts with the MIA (*Milieu-Investerings Aftrek* - environmental investment deduction)/VAMIL (Figure 10.3). By contrast, R&D is mostly funded at the European level, while national support is mostly horizontal, with instruments such as WBSO or the Innovation box. Such balance of the technology support package can make sense in principle: deployment is urgent, while horizontal support ensures technological neutrality and the existence of large cross-country knowledge spillovers from R&D imply that funding at the supra-national level is desirable.

However, such strategy raises several issues pointing to the potential conflict between short-term and long-term cost-effectiveness. First, horizontal measures disproportionately benefit technologies that are closest to the market by design. Yet, the ambitious 2050 objectives and the implied need for radically new technologies might justify a stronger focus on targeted instruments at the R&D stage. Targeting technologies that are further away from market but critical for the long-term decarbonisation objective, such as green hydrogen, could provide incentives that are more compatible with long-run cost-efficiency. Additional R&D support would also be justified in light of the strong focus of the SDE++ scheme on least-cost options (see below).

The strategy also seemingly favours technological absorption over innovation. This makes sense for the Dutch economy, which enjoys a sufficient absorptive capacity given its large stock of human capital, pre-existing infrastructure and availability of financing capital, both private and public. It does, however, risk to be insufficient to induce leadership in low-carbon technologies and maintain the Netherlands position as an industrial leader in the transition to the net-zero emission economy.

The current package's apparent funding gap for large-scale demonstration projects also contributes to tilting technology towards short-run cost-efficiency. Leveraging either the EU ETS Innovation Fund, the EU IPCEI or the Dutch National Growth Fund and/or re-balance the innovation policy package to close the funding gap for large-scale demonstration projects would help breakthrough innovators escape the "valley of death" of clean tech venturing (Section 10.3).

Figure 10.3. Tilting towards deployment

Estimated amounts of annual public funding available for technology support, by stage (EUR million)

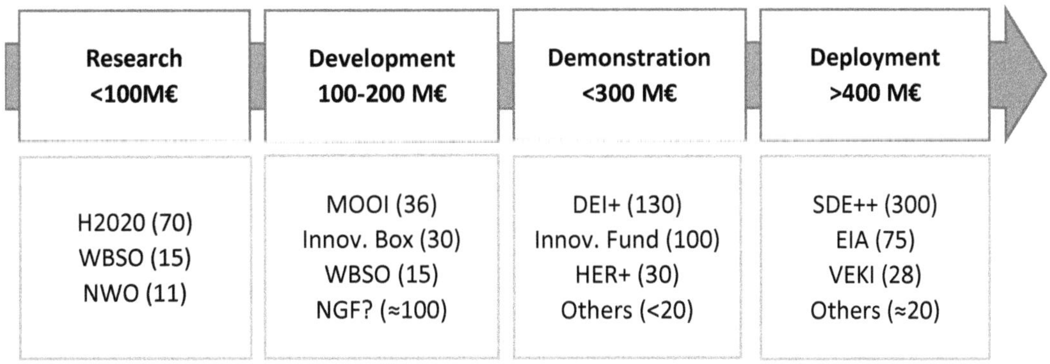

Note: See Chapter 5 for details. The maximum budgeted expense on SDE++ subsidy for CO_2 reduction in industry increases from EUR 50 mln in 2022 to EUR 550 mln in 2030 for a total of EUR 2.675 bln over the 2022-30 period, or about EUR 300 mln per year on average. Whether these amounts are structural remains subject to uncertainty due to current discussions regarding ODE reforms and the need to fund more expensive abatement in other sectors in the long run.

Recommendation 6 – Consider changes in the design of the SDE++, in particular holding different tenders by technology or production process, and at least partially accounting for the savings from the carbon levy

Ensure that SDE++ does not only fund close-to-market technologies by allocating the tender across different TRLs in order to also support breakthrough technologies

Take the carbon levy into account when calculating the subsidy to avoid over-subsidizing technologies close to breaking even.

10.2.3. The technology deployment package favours close-to-the-market technologies, possibly crowding out funding for needed breakthrough technologies

The Dutch government implements three major schemes to support the deployment of low-carbon technologies – SDE++, VEKI and MIA/Vamil –, with an estimated yearly budget in the long run of about EUR 350 million for the industry sector. By far the more important is the SDE++, which essentially subsidises the revenue shortfall of low-carbon technologies to make up for the difference with current carbon-intensive technologies. The other schemes, the VEKI grant and the MIA/Vamil tax allowances, subsidise capital expenses for low carbon technologies and their budget is expected to be significantly lower (Chapter 5). Another deployment scheme with substantial funding, the EIA focuses on marginal energy efficiency improvement rather than on new low-carbon technologies.

In principle, the SDE++ allocates subsidies on a pure cost-efficiency basis as all subsidy requests are pooled in one single tender. This tends to favour close-to-the-market technologies, for which the revenue shortfall with respect to business as usual technologies is small. Preliminary analysis of SDE++ subsidy applications confirms this built-in characteristic. A large share of the total amount of requested subsidies in categories that are potentially relevant for industrial applications concern CCS, a technology with TRL 7, i.e. system prototype demonstration in operational environment. By contrast, a negligible share of applications concerns green hydrogen, a breakthrough technology with lower TRL (Table 10.7). The data also partly reveals the private sector's marginal carbon abatement costs, pointing to large disparities across technologies (Figure 10.4). The technology-specific average subsidy per tCO_2 abated requested by the private sector does not necessarily align with the subsidy intensity defined by PBL.

Reforming the design of the SDE++ to re-balance the tender allocation across TRLs instead of solely favouring low-cost options would contribute to promoting investment in breakthrough low-carbon technologies. Put differently, the SDE++ currently trades off the promotion of less mature technologies for short-term cost efficiency, thereby potentially compromising long-term cost efficiency. Ensuring that support is distributed more evenly across the TRL scale (e.g. through exploiting synergies between DEI and SDE++) would contribute to avoiding budget gaps and overcoming the "valley of death". The cap on CCS will partially achieve such redistribution across TRL but only in the future when the cap is binding. The four successive application windows could be exploited for the purpose of ensuring that part of the tender goes to higher-cost breakthrough technologies. In that case, it should be made explicit and assessed against this objective.

Figure 10.4. CCS might crowd out less mature technologies from the SDE++

SDE++ subsidy demand curve in first tender

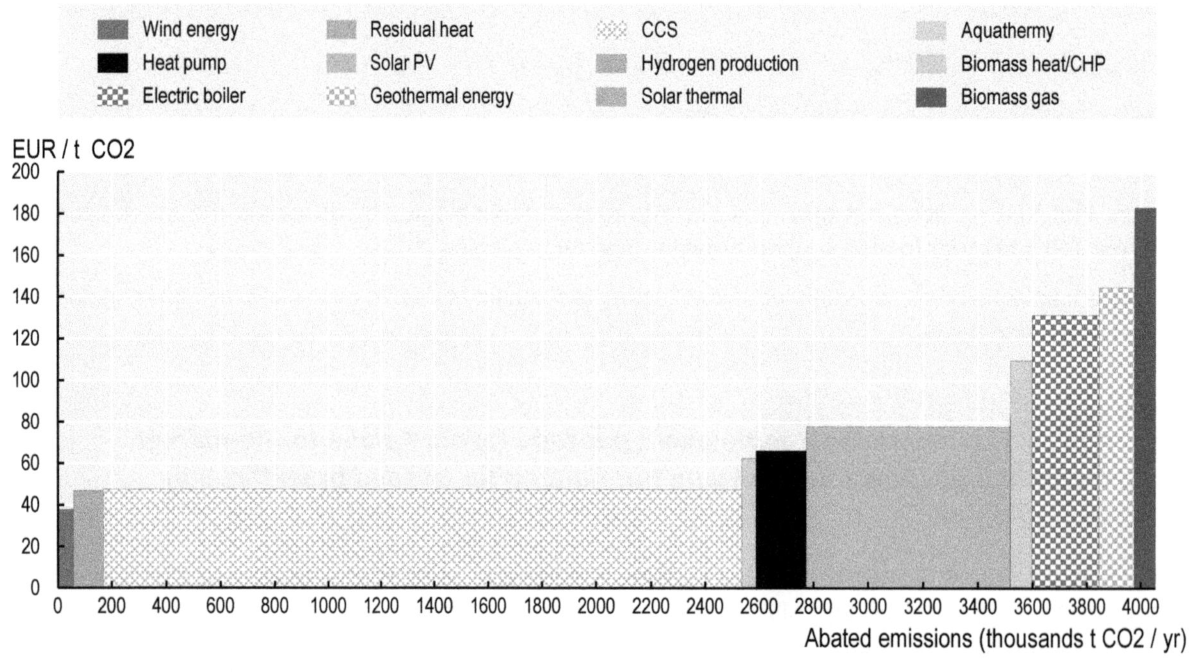

Note: Areas represent the expected subsidy payment based on RVO's long-term prices; actual payout will depend on market prices and RVO's decision. Category CCS includes "blue hydrogen"; category hydrogen production is "green hydrogen". Amount tendered to hydrogen production and solar thermal is barely visible. Average subsidy per tonne CO_2 at the technology category level and cumulated abated emissions calculated based on RVO data.
Source: Based on RVO data.

Table 10.7. The tilt towards short-run cost efficiency

SDE++ 2020 tender application data

Category	Number of applications	Requested budget (EUR mln)
Solar PV	3 989	2 360
CO_2 capture and storage	*7*	*2 135*
Electric boiler	*27*	*618*
Geothermal energy	6	355
Heat pump	*38*	*240*
Biomass gas	8	215
Biomass heat and CHP	5	139
Waste heat	*5*	*137*
Wind energy	16	100
Aquathermy	4	96
Hydrogen production	*1*	2
Solar thermal	6	1
Total	4 112	6 398
of which relevant to industry	*78*	*3 132*

Note: Italic indicates main relevant technologies for the industry.
Source: Rijksdienst voor Ondernemend Nederland (RVO).

10.2.4. The SDE++ tends to over-subsidise bridge technologies but stays short of making breakthrough technologies profitable

Two case studies of low-carbon alternative to business-as-usual production of hydrogen illustrate the built-in bias of the SDE++ scheme in favour of high-TRL technologies (Chapter 5). On one hand, the blue hydrogen alternative (adjunction of CCS on the standard steam-methane reforming) is a mature technology with the potential to bridge several chemical and refinery activities to the low-carbon economy. On the other hand, the green hydrogen technology alternative (renewable electricity-based electrolysis) lies at a lower TRL and requires further scale-up and greater cost reductions.

These two cases illustrate the interplay of the carbon levy and the SDE++ by contrasting the cumulative net cash flows associated with the two projects as analysed in Chapter 5 conditional on a conservative scenario of low energy prices and average carbon transportation costs (Figure 10.5). The solid lines on the chart correspond to a scenario where no subsidy is received, while the dashed lines show the cumulative cash flows when SDE++ support is granted. All scenarios take the savings from the carbon levy into account, with assumed dispensation rights based on EU benchmarks and counterfactual (BAU) projects' emission intensity. For the blue hydrogen project (black line on the chart), the cost savings on the carbon levy partially make up for the additional cost of CCS and the SDE++ subsidy is large enough to make the project immediately profitable. Under somewhat more favourable energy and/or carbon transportation prices, the blue hydrogen project would not even need the subsidy to break even. By contrast, the cost savings on the carbon levy are largely insufficient to make up for the cost of the investment in the case of the green hydrogen project (blue line on the chart) and the SDE++ subsidy fails to make up for the revenue shortfall.[6]

Besides vindicating the Climate Agreement's limit on the subsidisation of CCS and making the case for targeting part of the SDE++ subsidies for green hydrogen, the elements above raise the question of the sufficiency of the SDE++ to incentivise industry investment in breakthrough technology. A 100MW electrolyser capable of decarbonising feedstock for roughly 1-2% of the Dutch ammonia production costs EUR 50 million to build alone. The abatement subsidy required to make up for such large initial investment is very large and the available SDE++ budget may not be sufficient (about EUR 300 million per year on average until 2030 in total for all technologies [Chapter 5). Here too, resorting to the EU IPCEI or the Dutch

National Growth Fund could offer a way forward. Alternatively, making green hydrogen projects capital expenditures eligible under the DEI scheme would create synergies with the funding of the operational expenses under the SDE++.

Figure 10.5. CCS requires less support than green hydrogen

Cumulative net cash flows, with and without SDE++ support

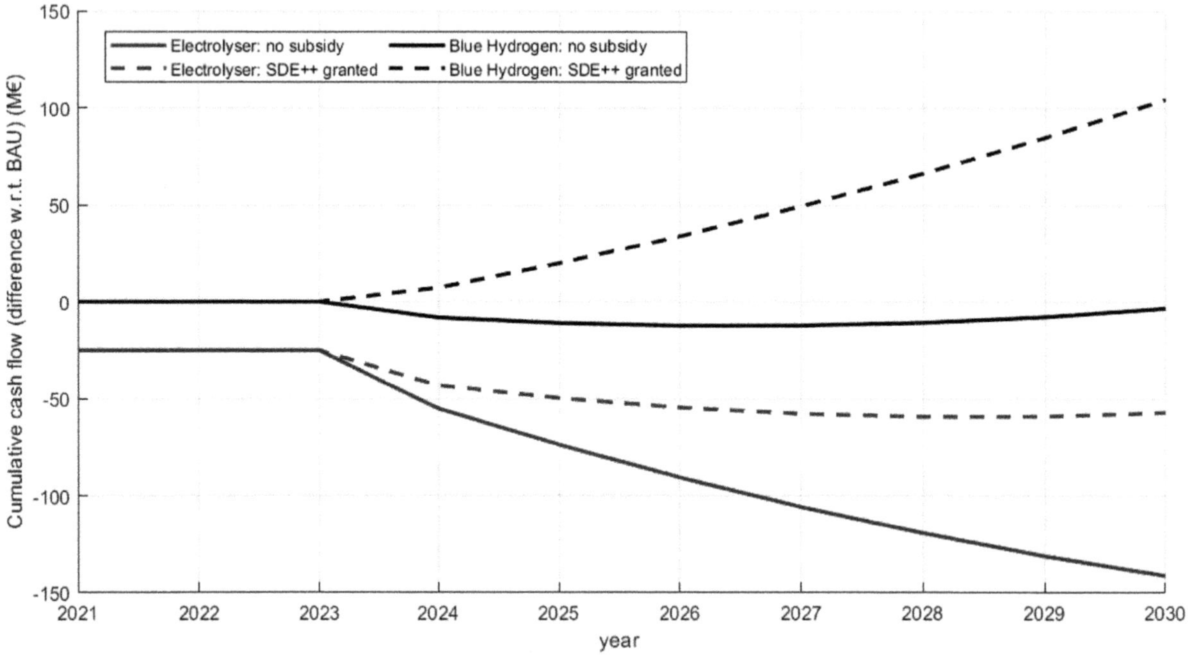

Note: Net cash flows calculated by differencing out the business-as-usual (carbon-intensive) alternative. Scenario of high electricity prices and average carbon transportation costs, taken as the mean of the PBL estimate and the Gasunie/EBN estimate. Feasibility study cost incurred in 2021. Capital investment incurred in 2024. Savings from the carbon levy account for dispensation rights based on EU benchmarks and counterfactual (BAU) projects' emission intensity. See Chapter 5 for details on hypotheses, methodology, subsidy schemes considered and detailed discussion of the results.

Recommendation 7 – Ensure adequate support at all RD&D stages in areas where Dutch inventors have (or potentially have) a comparative advantage, including CCUS and biomaterials, to enable technological leadership, and boost absorptive capacity in the others

Aim at technological leadership in areas of strong technological advantage, such as CCS and bio-based materials.

Boost absorptive capacities in the other technological areas, both through R&D activity and adequate framework conditions.

10.2.5. The Dutch industry has high leadership potential in selected technologies such as CCS and bio-based materials but needs to build enough absorptive capacity for other technologies

Over the past 15 years, Dutch inventors have had a strong relative technological advantage in such key bridge technologies as carbon capture, storage and utilisation (CCUS) (Figure 10.6). Moreover, specialisation in bio-based materials has markedly increased over the last fifteen years.

Figure 10.6. The Netherlands' high leadership potential in CCS and bio-based materials

Relative technological advantage

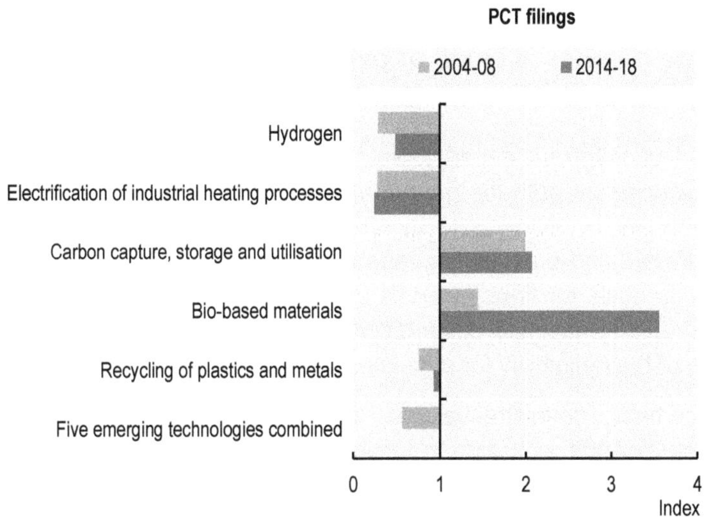

Note: Index computed as the ratio of the share of patents filed for the selected technology by inventors located in the Netherlands to the share of patents in the same technology filed by inventors located in the rest of the world.
Source: Calculations based on STI Micro-data Lab: Intellectual Property Database, http://oe.cd/ipstats, January 2021.

As R&D activity is mostly funded at the supra-national (EU) level and includes fixed costs, public support to such technological specialisation makes sense in the case of the Netherlands, a relatively small country with pre-existing infrastructure amenable to CCUS. The Netherlands has the potential to aim at leadership in a few low-carbon technologies and absorb the rest. In that context, ensuring support for the other area of specialisation, bio-based material, would be a good step in promoting technological leadership in longer-term decarbonisation solutions.

A key enabler regarding specialisation in selected technologies regards the absorptive capacity of the Dutch industry. The availability of human capital, such as green skills and know-how, is a necessary condition for technology diffusion (see below).

Recommendation 8 – Streamline the innovation support package, particularly at the demonstration stage, in order to improve administration cost efficiency and reduce transaction costs for young firms and SMEs

Assess available innovation support instruments and streamline where necessary in order to improve administration cost efficiency and reduce the cost to access these schemes for young firms and SMEs.

10.2.6. The large number of small or overlapping programs create administrative costs for the government, and transaction and compliance costs for business

The Dutch policy support package for decarbonisation includes a relatively large number of schemes, which may create inefficiencies on both the government and firms' side. First, the multiplication of fixed implementation, allocation and monitoring costs are unnecessary for the government. Second, the existence of so many different and potentially overlapping programmes creates complexity and leads to information and transaction costs for firms in terms of searching for the best instrument and application costs. These information and transaction costs disproportionately affect young firms and SMEs, which might not even be aware of their eligibility for subsidies.

Streamlining could reduce fixed administrative costs, provide clarity and contribute to making it easier for industrial firms to implement carbon emission reduction projects. For example, there exist many targeted R&D instruments with little individual funding. When it comes to deployment, support is spread across many instruments, some of which have a very similar mechanism. Moreover, the SDE++ sometimes overlaps with MIA and EIA, even though these two schemes are meant for installing mature technologies.

10.3. The key role of complementary policies and framework conditions

The industry decarbonisation strategy combining carbon pricing and technology support is not implemented in a vacuum: its success will depend on whether the business environment is conducive to the shift towards a low-carbon economy. This section highlights requirements regarding infrastructure, the level playing field, the provision of green skills and the availability of venture capital.

Recommendation 9 – Update the regulatory framework for decarbonisation technologies (particularly CCS) and ensure standardisation (especially for hydrogen and recycling), if possible at the European level

Create and update the regulatory and legal framework for decarbonisation technologies to reduce risk of investing.

In particular, define liabilities for CCS and build international regulatory standards for hydrogen and recycling technologies.

10.3.1. Uncertainty, outdated regulatory frameworks and lack of standardisation are barriers to investment in low-carbon technology

Reducing regulatory uncertainty is an important and cost-effective way to promote the necessary investments in industry decarbonisation technologies. In particular, defining liabilities related to carbon leaks is key to enable investors to price the risk of CCS project accurately and potentially make CCS risks insurable.

Regulatory standards are another way to promote investments in low-carbon technologies by improving transparency and avoiding unnecessary frictions across countries. At the EU level, they can help to ensure the inter-operability and transparency of low carbon technologies across countries, thereby increasing the size of the market and the incentives to develop new solutions. The importance of standardisation is perhaps most obvious for hydrogen, as it promotes complementarity with other instruments in the presence of network externalities. Key items include international standardisation on guarantees of origin (e.g. blue or green) but also on hydrogen purity, the design of liquefaction/conversion and regasification/reconversion facilities, for equipment specifications and for blending hydrogen into the gas grid.

Regulatory standards are also important for the definitions and regulations of waste and scrap, as the absence of clear and harmonised regulations hamper the development of recycling. For example, the labelling of steel production by-products as "waste" makes it difficult to trade, especially across borders, and creates shortages. Relabelling by-products of steel production at the European level (e.g. slag and fly ash) from 'waste' to 'product', with all due care to reduce pollution hazard, would reduce the administrative burden associated with purchasing scrap for companies and increase imports opportunities.

Recommendation 10 – Encourage the creation of markets for the circular and bio-based economy in order to address Scope 3 emissions by setting minimum content standards for recycled plastics and bio-based products, and re-labelling by-products of steel production from "waste" to "product" to ease scrap purchase

Introduce minimum content standards and use public procurement to create separate circular economy markets for recycled plastics and bio-based products.

Remove fossil fuel subsidies and align subsidies across different uses of biomass.

Increase R&D to further develop chemical recycling and the recycling of minor metals.

Review the definition and labelling of waste and scrap, with all due care to avoid pollution hazard, to reduce administrative burden and promote the development of recycling.

A carbon-neutral society implies the existence of a thriving circular economy. Recycling of plastics and metals and the use of bio-based products are important pillars for realising this circular economy, and their technological readiness levels and main policy challenges are discussed in detail in the circular economy and bio-based materials sections in Chapter 7.

The main problem for the circular economy is that there is no separate market for recycled and bio-based products and that fossil fuel based plastics are cheaper (OECD, 2018[13]). Additional policies are therefore required to create these separate markets, in particular for synthetic and bio-based feedstock. Demand-pull policies such as minimum content standards and public procurement can help to create these markets.

While such policy effort would be ideally implemented at the EU level, national minimum content standards and public procurement could already give a necessary boost to the recycling and bio-based industry.

Moreover, the existence of fossil fuel subsidies constitutes a barrier to the development of the circular economy. Removing fossil fuel subsidies is necessary for achieving the level playing field needed to give recycled and bio-based materials a fair chance.

A level playing field should also be created by applying subsidies for bioenergy and biofuel in the same way to biomaterials and biochemicals, as more biomass should flow to the latter (OECD, 2018[14]). Not only because the added value for bio-based materials and chemicals is higher, but even more importantly because the massive use of biomass for energy production raises concerns about unintended negative effects, such as illegal logging elsewhere in the world. Therefore, biomass should primarily be used to produce bio-based materials and chemicals for which no carbon-free alternative exists.

For the recycling of plastics, mechanical recycling of plastics is preferred to chemical recycling from an environmental point of view, but chemical recycling is still preferred to the incineration of waste for heat or energy production. Since possibilities for further increasing the use of mechanical recycling are limited, R&D support to further develop both mechanical and chemical recycling is required. Recycling rates for minor metals that are still low should also be improved.

For the bioeconomy, it is important that policies reduce risks to private sector investments in biofoundries. Biofoundries are facilities that enable the rapid design, construction and testing of biotechnology applications and research. Biofoundries can increase returns and therefore stimulate the bioeconomy by creating an ecosystem of industrial symbiosis. Within these biofoundries, priority should be given to conversion technologies, as feedstock is often bio-based, but conversion technologies are often still chemistry based (Kitney et al., 2019[15]).

Recommendation 11 – Provide visibility on the infrastructure programmes related to the transportation of hydrogen, electricity, heat and captured carbon, and clarify the role of the National Growth Fund in funding the low-carbon industrial infrastructure

Make the MIEK process operational.

Prop up the Infrastructure Programme for a Sustainable Industry (PIDI) in its role of stakeholder co-ordination and decision-making body, and make it operational as soon as possible, in order to promote the development of the infrastructure necessary to the diffusion of key low-carbon technologies, in particular for the transportation of hydrogen, electricity, heat and captured carbon.

Develop a clear and predictable methodology to select infrastructure programs.

Clarify the role of the National Growth Fund in funding the low carbon industrial infrastructure.

Promote co-ordination beyond industrial sectors and with neighbouring countries.

10.3.2. The uptake of low-carbon technology requires urgent infrastructure investments and hinges on the supply of large quantities of renewable energy

Infrastructure needs are extremely important for the decarbonisation of the Dutch industry, as it appears clearly from the scenario analysis in Chapter 3. In particular, the transition to a low-carbon industry requires infrastructure regarding the heat network, hydrogen production and distribution, and carbon transportation (potentially using the existing gas pipeline infrastructure). Moreover, industry decarbonisation hinges on the supply of large quantities of sustainable electricity, which creates further infrastructure needs regarding the electricity grid and renewable energy capacities.

Infrastructure is a necessary condition for the uptake of most low-carbon technologies in the industry. Decarbonisation requires the delivery of complementary low-carbon infrastructure projects in a range of technologies. These infrastructure needs were established by the Taskforce Infrastructure Climate Agreement Industry (TIKI) and the Multi-year Program Infrastructure Energy and Climate (MIEK). The six regional industry cluster plans also consider infrastructure one of the most important enablers of the transition toward a carbon-neutral industry.

The Dutch government envisages a model where grid operators finance and manage the energy transportation infrastructure – either electricity, heat, hydrogen or captured carbon – while firms pay user fees, which can be subsidised by the relevant instruments (e.g. cost of carbon transport in SDE++). The Porthos project illustrates this model. Porthos is building a transportation network for the CO_2 captured by firms in the Rotterdam cluster to be stored in depleted gas and oil fields beneath the North Sea. The infrastructure is joint venture between the Port of Rotterdam Authority, Gasunie and EBN, and benefits from substantial funding from the EU's Connecting Europe Facility (CEF) fund. CO_2-capturing firms will pay a fee for transport and storage. To bridge the current difference between the current level of carbon pricing and the fee-inclusive cost of CCS, firms can apply for an abatement subsidy within the SDE++ scheme (see above).The timing of infrastructure rollout is a key challenge for achieving the zero-net emission economy in 2050. On one hand, infrastructure building is a typically long process. On the other, industrial firms need immediate clarity on the availability of new energy sources in order to undertake investments in low-carbon technologies. Therefore, prioritisation is needed to ensure that the green transition is not delayed by infrastructure constraints.

The Ministry of Economic Affairs and Climate has recently announced the creation of a national Infrastructure Programme for a Sustainable Industry (PIDI). PIDI is a co-ordination body emanating from the Ministry and tasked with speeding up decision-making concerning the national energy infrastructure (hydrogen, carbon dioxide, electricity, heat, gas, circular economy) required for decarbonising the industry. Stakeholders include the clusters, the national and provincial governments, industrial firms and infrastructure companies. PIDI acts as the safe house for data on infrastructure investment projects and has decision-making power regarding the allocation of infrastructure projects based on feasibility studies.

The creation of PIDI is a step in the right direction. In view of the infrastructure needs implied in the scenario analysis, accelerated action at the national, regional and local levels seems pressing for the timely rollout of energy infrastructure. The National Growth Fund may contribute to financing infrastructure projects following PIDI's recommendations. Therefore, making PIDI operational should be a priority so that investments can take place. The Netherlands can leverage its experience gained from water infrastructure investments under the Delta Programme, which informs the OECD's best practice for developing robust project pipelines for low-carbon infrastructure, in particular regarding its combination of a long-term perspective, an iterative decision-making cycle and a dedicated fund to guide and implement investments (OECD, 2018[16]).

Further, infrastructure investment and management pose two key challenges, which should be carefully addressed. First, dynamic cost efficiency should be considered, in particular the risk of following too many technology routes that may prove unnecessary or even mutually exclusive, at great cost to public finance. Second, pricing the use of this monopoly infrastructure should be designed to take into account the pricing of externalities such as the integration of more renewables into the grid or demand schedule pricing allowing for intermittencies.

10.3.3. Co-ordination with other infrastructure programmes is key, both beyond industry and in neighbouring countries

PIDI makes infrastructure decisions on the grid operators side. However, co-ordination is necessary with the supply side of the system. In the Netherlands, wind energy from the North Sea is expected to be one of the main drivers of the energy transition. Therefore, it is crucial that PIDI collaborates with the Exploration of Landing Wind at Sea (VAWOZ) programme. Linking demand and supply, the Energy Main Structure (PEH) programme is tasked with designing the energy structure for the 2030 and 2050 horizons.

Given the interconnectedness in the region, infrastructure programs should be designed in close co-operation with neighbouring countries, in particular Germany and Belgium. The Porthos project, which will build and operate a CO_2 transport network between the port of Rotterdam, the port of Antwerp, the North Sea Port and depleted gas and oil fields beneath the North Sea is an example of such cross-country infrastructure planning with significant financing by the Connecting Europe Facility (CEF) of the European Commission. The Athos project, which is less advanced, is planning to transport CO_2 from the Amsterdam region to the North Sea.

Several levels of governance matter regarding the provision of infrastructure in relation with clusters (van der Reijden et al., 2021[17]). With their own industrial structure and historic legacies, clusters are well-placed for co-ordinating local firms and energy suppliers. Clusters are also key stakeholders for the implementation of policies that support the transition. By contrast, co-ordination between national clusters and between clusters and the rest of the economy lies at the national level, while the overall co-ordination of the industrial transition and cross-country linkages between clusters is better left to the EU level. This includes financing the low-carbon transition or regulatory interventions to facilitate the transition.

Recommendation 12 – Foster competition within and between clusters, ensuring a level playing field for young firms and SMEs, and an adequate supply of green skills

Ensure a level playing field for young firms and SMEs to benefit from the bottom-up, cluster-based decarbonisation support strategies in order to enable the emergence of innovative clean tech start-ups.

Ensure the necessary supply of green skills through re-skilling and up-skilling of displaced workers from emission-intensive industries.

10.3.4. Promoting business dynamism within and between clusters will ensure that innovation can flourish while taking advantage of scale economies

The reliance on infrastructure for achieving decarbonisation is a consequence of the geographic structure of the Dutch industry around highly integrated clusters. This cluster structure contributes to the cost efficiency of decarbonisation as it promotes the internalisation of scale economies and knowledge spillovers, e.g. the efficient provision of energy carriers and the exploitation of synergies. However, it may also contribute to locking in sectoral and geographical allocation of resources at the expense of efficiency-enhancing dynamism, therefore coming at a cost in terms of flexibility and adaptability in the longer run – potentially a major issue at the 2050 horizon, given the uncertainty regarding the technologies that will eventually emerge in the low-carbon transition.

Figure 10.7. Relatively low business dynamism

A. Product market regulation indicators

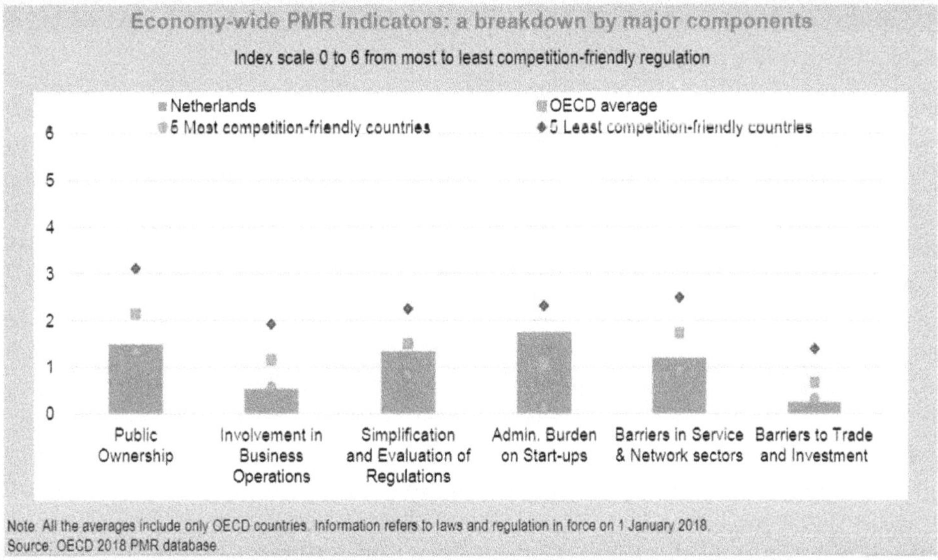

B. Job reallocation rate among incumbent firms

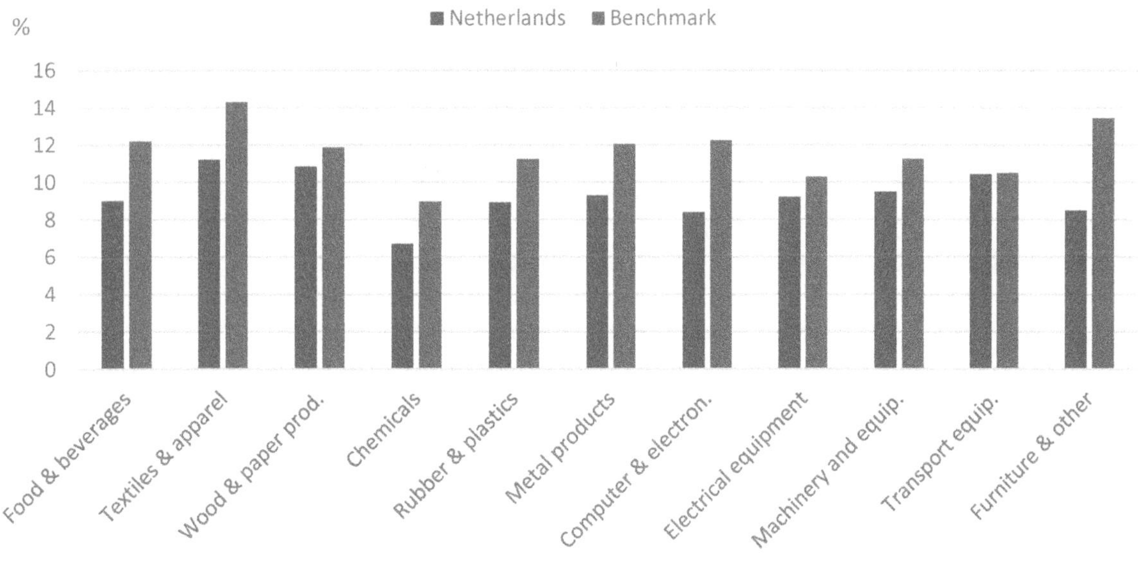

Note: Panel B, churning rates of incumbents defined as the sum of the job creation rates and job destruction rates of incumbent firms, reported by SNA A38 as averages over the period of 2012-15. Benchmark countries include Austria, Belgium, Brazil, Canada, Costa Rica, Finland, France, Hungary, Italy, Japan, Portugal, the Netherlands, New Zealand, Norway, Spain, Sweden and Turkey.
Source: OECD Indicators of Product Market Regulation: Netherlands, https://www.oecd.org/economy/reform/indicators-of-product-market-regulation/# (Panel A); OECD calculations based on DynEmp3 Database (August 2019, Panel B).

The Dutch clusters typically harbour a few large players that considerably contribute to international competitiveness. However, young firms and start-ups are also key to foster innovation and enable the emergence of the next generation of technological leaders. Therefore, maintaining a sufficient level of competition is key to minimise the downsides of the cluster structure. First, competition should be sufficient *inside* the clusters, so that new firms can effectively enter into these structures, compete and eventually challenge large incumbents. Enabling the reallocation of production factors can have an indirect positive effect on both challengers' and incumbents' incentives to innovate. Second, resource reallocation should be enabled *between* the clusters and the rest of the country, so as to allow and foster the emergence of alternative decarbonisation options that do not rely on large infrastructure and can be implemented for scattered industries when relevant.

Moreover, ensuring that the cost of carbon emissions and the level of support is the same across sectors and across small and large firms is equally important to avoid favouring large firms that are already in clusters and locking in the current industry structure at a time where the low-carbon transition requires significant reallocation of capital and labour resources. In that respect, the pervasive energy tax and surcharge exemptions enjoyed by incumbent energy-intensive industries contribute to shielding them from the potential competition of innovative green entrants. Such detrimental impact on business dynamism is another rationale for phasing them out (see above). Overall, firms in the Netherlands enjoy among the most accommodative regulatory conditions for doing business in the OECD (Figure 10.7, Panel A). However, the administrative burden on start-ups and the cost for starting a business remain comparatively high (OECD, 2019[18]). Such barriers typically increase the cost of entrepreneurship; hence they reduce market entry and weaken innovation incentives. Indeed, entry rates in Dutch manufacturing industries are lower than in other countries (OECD, 2019[19]) Moreover, relatively low job reallocation rates across incumbent firms in Dutch manufacturing industries including metallurgy, food processing and chemical industry suggest a lack of business dynamism compared to other OECD countries (Figure 10.7, Panel B). Enhancing business dynamism through facilitating entry and labour reallocation would contribute to enabling innovative clean tech companies to emerge.

10.3.5. Adequate green skills supply is a necessary condition for industrial firms to invest in decarbonisation and absorb new technologies

Decarbonisation and the transition to the net-zero emission economy will affect both labour supply and demand in the industry. On the one hand, skilled installation and maintenance workers are already in short supply in the industry (Climate Agreement, 2019) and will be increasingly demanded in the low-carbon economy, given the massive necessary capital investments. For example, it is expected that the Netherlands will need 10 000 bioeconomy experts by 2026 (Biomass Research Wageningen, 2016[20]). On the other hand, decarbonisation will bring about large labour reallocation of economic activity. For example, the capacity of refineries is projected to decrease by (at least) 40% between 2020 and 2050 (Chapter 3).

Workers with the skills to navigate changes in products and processes due to climate change and to environmental requirements and regulations are a key complement to technological supply-push policies. Adequate green skills supply is particularly important for firms engaging in low-carbon technology deployment and scale-up, and likely to promote investment. More generally, it contributes to the overall absorptive capability of the Dutch industry, which is a necessary condition for reaping the benefits of supra-national (mostly European) R&D and translate it into local deployment.

Re-skilling and up-skilling displaced workers with green skills through active labour market policies and adult training is immediately necessary to both address social concern and contribute to reducing skill shortages in the future low-carbon industries. Cross-sector training programmes can ease labour market transitions from surplus to shortage sectors. Timely and transparent information on sectoral labour markets can help workers to anticipate future labour needs and policy makers to monitor and accompany the changes. With a view to the longer run, education programmes need to incorporate new material and competences in curricula, so that the next cohort of workers can cope with the low carbon transition in the workplace. This implies re-training teachers so they can teach the new curricula.

In the Netherlands, the Social and Economic Council (SER) co-ordinates labour market and training matters, facilitates the development of sectoral training and labour market agendas and liaises with relevant institutions to ensure information dissemination on labour market policies and training. In that capacity, there is a guaranteed insight into the general and sector-specific progress on the agreements of the Climate Agreement. Special SER committees are tasked with identifying the threat and opportunities posed to employment by the low-carbon industrial transition. In its 2018 *Energy Transition and Employment* advisory report, the SER points to the necessary support to displaced workers, with a focus on lifelong learning, in close co-operation with the Top Sectors, as well as other platforms of public and private stakeholders aiming at addressing technological skill mismatch (the Technology Pact) and strengthening the green knowledge system in the Netherlands (the GroenPact).

The Top Sectors are also key stakeholders regarding the provision of green skills. Through their Human Capital Roadmap 2020-23, the top sectors aim at promoting better quality, equality and accessibility of education, including the acquisition of skills that are relevant for the low-carbon transition. They mostly act as facilitators and foster co-operation between all relevant stakeholders for the provision of skills.

The climate agreement contains provisions regarding the development of a sectoral agenda for skills in the industry, building on the 2018-22 implementation agenda for smart industry and the Chemicals and High-Tech Systems and Materials Top Sectors. It also points to the necessity of proactive labour market policy with sufficient training facilities at the regional level, with a special focus on the regions in which the five industrial clusters are located. Given the large structural transformation arising from the low-carbon transition, transforming this ambitious agenda into concrete policy steps is urgent.

Recommendation 13 – Ensure sufficient funding for green start-ups, in particular through venture capital

Monitor the venture capital (VC) investment and needs of green tech start-ups in order to assess whether INVEST-NL contributes to promoting industry decarbonisation by complementing the bottom-up, cluster-based approach.

10.3.6. Venture capital complements government technology support and help escape the "valley of death"

Venture capital is instrumental in creating markets and scale-up for the most market-ready technologies, by providing finance and imposing private capital market discipline. VC is a key complement to government support for technology, as it helps entrepreneurs through the "valley of death" by financing pilots and demonstrations of innovative ideas and prospective technologies, which are often the output of government-funded R&D (Stefano Breschi et al., 2019[21]). VC is also important for small companies to move beyond an initial niche market. Moreover, VC contributes to knowledge transfer across venture capitalists' portfolios (Bottazzi, Da Rin and Hellmann, 2008[22]). Data on VC deals suggest that private investors anticipate growing market opportunities in low-carbon technologies, driven by expectations of more stringent environmental policies (IEA, 2020[23]).

In the Netherlands, total VC investments amount to 0.064% of gross domestic product (GDP) in 2019, on a par with the OECD median (Figure 10.8, Panel A). However, when looking at different investment stages, the Netherlands performs less well regarding early stage VC investments (Figure 10.8, Panel B). The government is very involved in providing VC, a common trend in other European countries. About half of VC invested in the Netherlands was related to a government entity as of 2015, either directly with the government as "general partners" managing the VC fund or as a "limited partner" behaving like a passive investor (Alperovych, Quas and Standaert, 2018[24]). The Dutch government is targeting high-potential SMEs and supports tech initiatives. Examples include the Dutch Venture Initiative II, a EUR 200 million venture and growth capital fund-of-funds that invests in sectors such as ICT or clean or medical tech; and the EUR 100 million Dutch Growth Co-Investment Programme, which targets the second equity gap that start-ups face when they intend to grow (OECD, 2019[25]).

Figure 10.8. VC market in the Netherlands

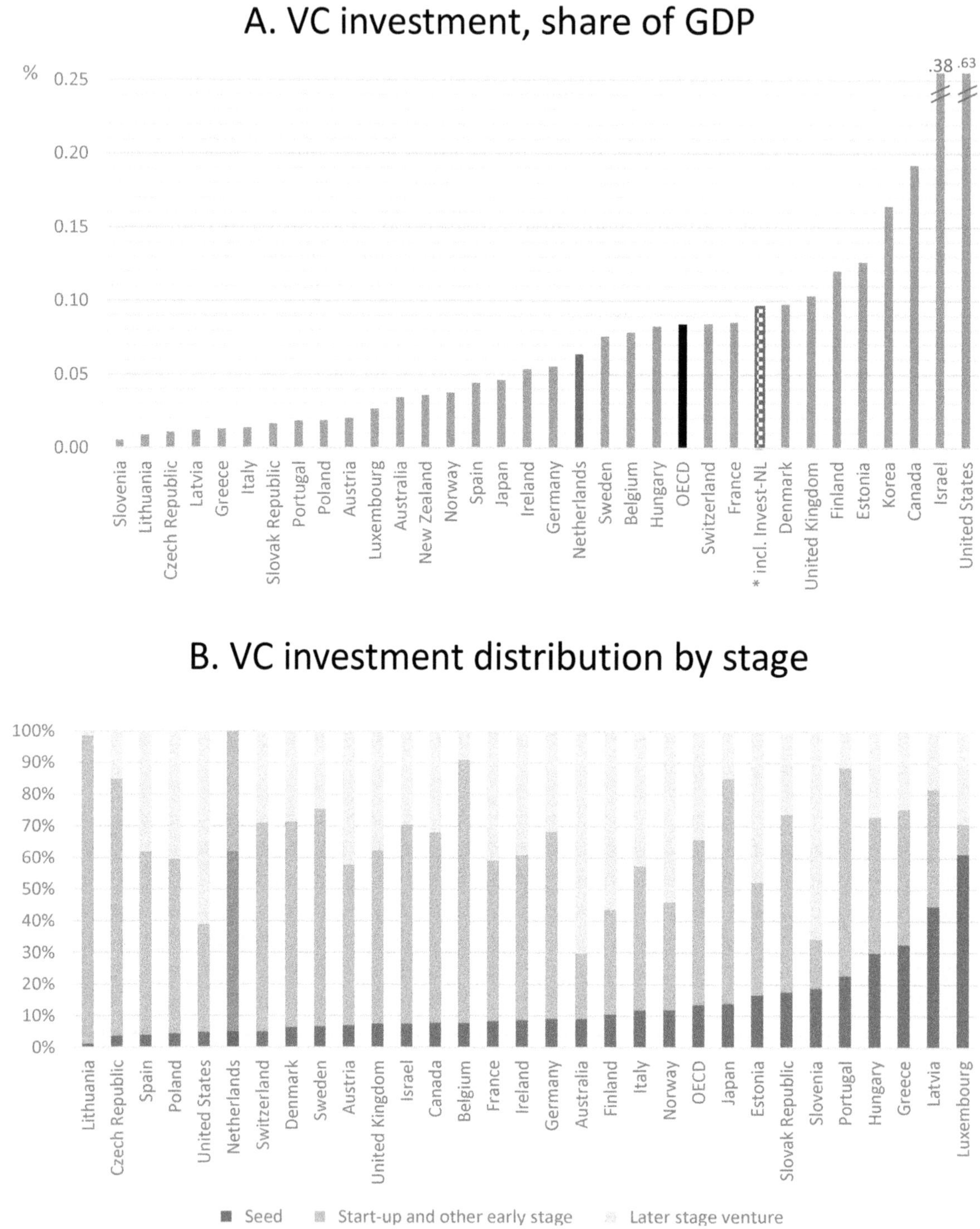

Note: VC investment is the sum of early stage (including pre-seed, seed, start-up and other early stage) and later stage VC. Given the absence of harmonised definitions across venture capital associations and other data providers, original data have been re-aggregated to fit the OECD classification of VC by stages. Data from 2019 or latest year available.
Source: OECD Entrepreneurship Financing Database

10.3.7. Invest-NL will be key in bringing low-carbon innovation to the market and its assessment should be a priority

A relatively large share of VC investments focus on sustainable energy technologies in the Netherlands. Data on VC deals in Europe suggest that over the period 2016-20, a yearly average of about 10% of total VC investments in the Netherlands concern "affordable and clean energy" technology firms, leading most other European countries (Figure 10.9). The share of these technologies in the total yearly value of VC deals was relatively stable in the Netherlands over the considered period, reflecting a long-standing interest in sustainable energy production. At the global level however, that share has fallen from around 10% to around 5% since 2012 as VC capital funded other technology areas such as biotechnology and information technology (IEA, 2020[23]). In the clean technology area, energy storage, hydrogen, CCUS, smart grid and bioenergy saw the most growth (IEA, 2020[23]).

Figure 10.9. VC investments in sustainable energy technologies

Average yearly share of total VC investment, 2016-20 or available years

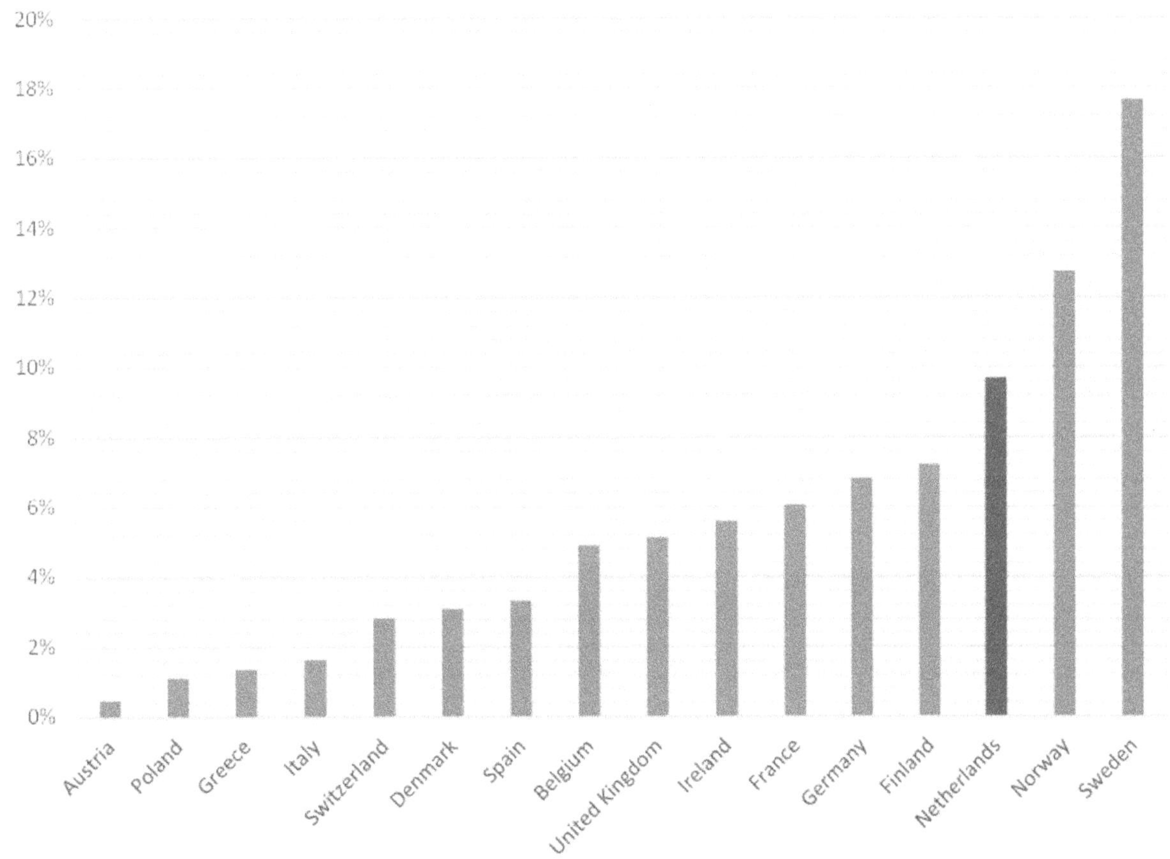

Note: VC investment in sustainable energy technologies in a given country defined as the value of all VC deals classified as "affordable and clean energy" by the data provider. Total VC investment is the total value of VC deals taking place in that country.
Source: OECD calculations based on DealRoom data

The launch of Invest-NL is expected to radically alter the Dutch VC landscape, in particular for low-carbon technologies. Announced in 2017 and launched in January 2020, this government-owned national investment fund has a mandate to finance the energy transition through both equity financing and loans, with a focus on electrification and energy, circularity, agrifood and the built environment, and the scale-up of innovative high-growth firms in industrial technologies.[7] It works as a revolving fund with EUR 1.7 billion capital, amounting to a ~EUR 242 million investment capacity per year assuming seven year investment horizon, that is, ~.032% GDP, implying a 50% increase in Dutch VC market volume (0.064% of GDP in 2019).

By launching Invest-NL, the Dutch government signals that VC will be key in funding the transition to the net-zero emission economy and provides the necessary strike force for complementing its technology support policies. VC will bring capital market discipline within the bottom-up, cluster-based overall decarbonisation strategy. Against this background, both VC investments and the needs of green tech start-ups should be monitored in order to assess to what extent Invest-NL contributes to promoting industry decarbonisation.

References

Alperovych, Y., A. Quas and T. Standaert (2018), "Direct and indirect government venture capital investments in Europe", *Economics Bulletin*, Vol. 28/2, http://www.accessecon.com/Pubs/EB/2018/Volume38/EB-18-V38-I2-P117.pdf. [24]

Biomass Research Wageningen (2016), *The Biobased Economy and the Bioeconomy in the Netherlands*. [20]

Bottazzi, L., M. Da Rin and T. Hellmann (2008), "Who are the active investors?. Evidence from venture capital", *Journal of Financial Economics*, Vol. 89/3, pp. 488-512, http://dx.doi.org/10.1016/j.jfineco.2007.09.003. [22]

CBS (2017), *Uitsplitsing verbruik elektriciteit en aardgas*, https://www.cbs.nl/nl-nl/maatwerk/2019/14/elektriciteit-en-aardgas-naar-energiebelastingschijf. [8]

CE Delft (2021), *Correspondance with CE Delft, February 2021*. [5]

CE Delft (2021), *Policy instruments stimulating the low carbon transition of Dutch Industry: an overview of existing policies in the field of climate and energy in the Netherlands*. [7]

Cosbey, A. (2012), *A Guide for the Concerned: Guidance on the elaboration and implementation of*, International Institute for Sustainable Development, https://www.iisd.org/library/guide-concerned-guidance-elaboration-and-implementation-border-carbonadjustment. [10]

Flues, F. and K. Van Dender (2020), "Carbon pricing design: Effectiveness, efficiency and feasibility: An investment perspective", *OECD Taxation Working Papers*, No. 48, OECD Publishing, Paris, https://doi.org/10.1787/91ad6a1e-en. [4]

IEA (2020), *Energy Technology Perspectives 2020 - Special Report on Clean Energy Innovation*, OECD Publishing, Paris, https://dx.doi.org/10.1787/ab43a9a5-en. [23]

IEA (2020), *Extended world energy balances*, https://doi.org/10.1787/data-00513-en (accessed on 14 December 2020). [3]

Kitney, R. et al. (2019), "Enabling the Advanced Bioeconomy through Public Policy Supporting Biofoundries and Engineering Biology", *Trends in Biotechnology*, Vol. 37/9, pp. 917-920, http://dx.doi.org/10.1016/j.tibtech.2019.03.017. [15]

Murray, B. and N. Rivers (2015), "British Columbia's revenue-neutral carbon tax: A review of the latest "grand experiment" in environmental policy", *Energy Policy*, Vol. 86, pp. 674-683, https://doi.org/10.1016/j.enpol.2015.08.011. [12]

Neuhoff, K. et al. (2016), *Inclusion of Consumption of carbon intensive materials in emissions trading*, Climate Strategies, https://climatestrategies.org/wp-content/uploads/2016/10/CS-Inclusion-of-Consumption-Report.pdf. [26]

OECD (2020), *Climate policy leadership in an interconnected world: What role for border carbon adjustments?*, OECD Publishing, Paris, https://doi.org/10.1787/8008e7f4-en. [11]

OECD (2019), *Netherlands: Business dynamism*, https://www.oecd.org/sti/ind/oecd-business-dynamics-insights-netherlands.pdf. [19]

OECD (2019), *OECD SME and Entrepreneurship Outlook 2019*, OECD Publishing, Paris, https://doi.org/10.1787/34907e9c-en. [25]

OECD (2019), *SME and Entrepreneurship Outlook 2019: The Netherlands*, OECD Publishing, Paris, https://doi.org/10.1787/10e63d8e-en. [18]

OECD (2019), *Taxing Energy Use 2019: Using Taxes for Climate Action*, OECD Publishing, Paris, https://doi.org/10.1787/058ca239-en. [2]

OECD (2018), *Developing Robust Project Pipelines for Low-Carbon Infrastructure*, OECD Publishing, Paris, https://doi.org/10.1787/9789264307827-en. [16]

OECD (2018), *Effective Carbon Rates 2018. Pricing Carbon Emissions Through Taxes and Emissions Trading*, OECD Publishing, Paris, https://doi.org/10.1787/9789264305304-en. [1]

OECD (2018), "Enabling bio-based materials policy", in *Meeting Policy Challenges for a Sustainable Bioeconomy*, OECD Publishing, Paris, https://dx.doi.org/10.1787/9789264292345-12-en. [14]

OECD (2018), *Improving Markets for Recycled Plastics: Trends, Prospects and Policy Responses*, OECD Publishing, Paris, https://dx.doi.org/10.1787/9789264301016-en. [13]

OECD (2016), *Effective Carbon Rates: Pricing CO2 through Taxes and Emissions Trading Systems*, OECD Publishing, Paris, http://dx.doi.org/10.1787/9789264260115-en. [6]

Perino, G., R. Ritz and A. van Benthem (2020), "Overlapping Climate Policies", *Cambridge Working Papers in Economics*, No. 20111, http://www.econ.cam.ac.uk/research-files/repec/cam/pdf/cwpe20111.pdf. [9]

Stefano Breschi, J. et al. (2019), "Public research and innovative entrepreneurship: Preliminary cross-country evidence from micro data", *OECD Science, Technology and Industry Policy Papers*, No. 64, OECD Publishing, Paris. [21]

van der Reijden, R. et al. (2021), *Transforming industrial clusters to implement the European Green Deal*, Climate Strategies, https://climatestrategies.org/wp-content/uploads/2021/01/CFM-Industrial-Clusters-briefing_FINAL.pdf. [17]

Notes

[1] The terms *energy tax on natural gas* and *fuel excise* are used interchangeably in the text.

[2] The terms *ODE* and *surcharge* are used interchangeably in the text.

[3] In the analysis the national component of the carbon levy is set to zero for 2021 because of the large amount of excess dispensation rights in 2021 that are not bankable, thereby losing their value for future trading periods.

[4] Dispensation rights are, to some extent, the levy's analogue to free allocation and are attributed yearly following EU ETS benchmarks. Installations have to pay the levy on their annual emissions that are not covered by a dispensation right. The amount of dispensation rights that is distributed decreases over time, i.e. the levy base phases in over time.

[5] Neuhoff et al. (2016[26]) propose to combine an ETS that allocates permits for free based product benchmarks with excise taxes on carbon intensive products, where the excise taxes rate is derived from the product benchmark. The idea is that permit prices provide a marginal incentive to improve the carbon efficiency of existing products and that the excise taxes encourage the consumption of more carbon efficient goods.

[6] If the SDE++ subsidy is granted at all. This is not the most likely outcome, given the cost-efficiency allocation criterion (see chapter 5 and Figure 10.4).

[7] The aim of Invest-NL is to "contribute to the financing and realisation of societal transition tasks carried out by companies and to facilitate access to corporate financing, in cases where the market does not sufficiently provide these provisions" (Section 3 of the Invest-NL Foundation Act, adopted by both houses of parliament in 2019). In line with parliamentary decision and in agreement with the Ministry of Economic Affairs and Climate Policy, financing the energy transition was set as Invest-NL's priority, with a focus on scale-ups (www.invest-nl.nl).

www.ingramcontent.com/pod-product-compliance
Ingram Content Group UK Ltd.
Pitfield, Milton Keynes, MK11 3LW, UK
UKHW051457290926
15471UKWH00008B/1247

9 789264 608368